Collins
Complete
Woodworker's
Manual

Albert Jackson & David Day

Collins
Complete
Woodworker's
Manual

Albert Jackson & David Day

TED SMART

This edition produced for The Book People Ltd, Hall Wood Avenue, Haydock, St Helens WA11 9UL

Collins Complete Woodworker's Manual
was originally conceived, edited and designed by Jackson Day Jennings trading as Inklink.

For this edition:
Authors
Albert Jackson
David Day

Designer
Elizabeth Standley

Editor
Peter Leek

Illustrators
Robin Harris
David Day
John Pinder
Albert Jackson

Studio photography
Colin Bowling
Neil Waving
Paul Chave

Proofreader and indexer
Mary Morton

General consultants/contributors
Simon Gilham
Mark Ramuz

Specialist consultants
Fred Spalding – machine tools
Les Reed – veneering and marquetry
John Perkins – routers
Ronnie Rustin – wood finishes

Wood samples and examples of wood finishing prepared by
David Day

Joint-making
Bill Brooker

Chapter-title panels
Des Ryan

Woodcarving examples
Marcus Cornish
David Day

For a complete list of suppliers and technical support, see page 8.

For HarperCollins
Angela Newton – Senior managing editor
Alastair Laing – Editor
Luke Griffin – Design
Chris Gurney – Production

This revised edition published in 2005 by Collins, an imprint of HarperCollinsPublishers 77–85 Fulham Palace Road London W6 8JB
Previous edition published in 1996

Copyright © 2005
HarperCollinsPublishers

The CIP catalogue record for this book is available from the British Library

ISBN 0-00-773619-3

Colour origination by
Saxon Photolitho, Norfolk

Printed and bound by
Rotolito, Italy

PLEASE NOTE
Great care has been taken to ensure that the information contained in **Collins Complete Woodworker's Manual** is accurate. However, a book of this nature cannot replace specialist advice in appropriate cases and therefore no responsibility can be accepted by the publishers or by the authors for any loss or damage caused by reliance upon the accuracy of such information. If you live outside Britain, your local conditions may mean that some of this information is not appropriate; if in doubt, you should always consult a specialist.

Designer/makers
Alison Frazer 79CR; 324TR
Andy Murch 79BR
Anthony Jackson 79BL
Ashley Cartwright 73BL
Chris Auger 74TR
Daniel Hughes 79TR
David Pye 75C
Dawn Keylock 78TL
Derek Pearce 78BL
Des Ryan 74B; 75B
Gordon Russell 76TR
Hugh Scriven 75TL
Ian Norbury 297; 303T
Jane Cleal 72BL, BC
John Hunnex 77BR; 330L
Julian Rendall 75TR
Mike Scott 77T
Nicholas Dyson 77BL
Nick Neenan 78BR
Paul Mathews 323
Raymond Winkler 77CR
Richard La Trobe-Bateman 72BR
Richard Shrives 76BR
Richard Williams 79TL
Robert Kay 78TC
Robert Williams 71B
Rod Wales 75BR; 76TR, BL
Roderick Willis 74TL
Stewart Linford 71T; 330R
Wendy Maruyama 77CL

Photographers
Neil Waving took the photographs for this book with the following exceptions:

Ben Jennings 283; 308; 310; 313R; 314TL; 316; 318; 325; 326TR; 331C
Colin Bowling 68; 128L; 133TL; 140TL; 149B; 154; 155BR; 157UC, BL; 158C; 159TR; 162B; 166; 167; 168B; 170; 171R; 183T; 185B
Paul Chave 172L; 173CL, C, TR; 174; 175; 176; 177; 180; 306; 314B; 324BL

Picture sources
The authors and producers also wish to acknowledge the following companies and individuals who supplied photographs for reproduction.

A. F. Suter & Co. Ltd 317TL
Albert Jackson 158L; 159BR; 160TL
Argos Ltd 155TL; 159BL
Ashley Cartwright 73
Axminster Power Tool Centre 108L; 150L; 152TR; 162L; 168T; 184; 186L; 190BR; 195; 196L; 217BR; 219
Buckinghamshire Chilterns University College 72BL, CL; 74TL; 75TR; 76TL, BL, BR; 77CR; 78TL, TR, BR; 79; 276TR; 323; 324 TR
Clarke International 327
Cuprinol Ltd 320R; 321B
David Day 320L
DeWalt 163BR; 194; 211
Freud Tooling (UK) Ltd 196C
Gavin Jordan 17T
Georg Ott Werkzeug-und Maschinen Fabrik GmbH & Co. 234T
Hugh Scriven 75TL; 313TL
Jim Lee (Southeastern Lumber Manufacturing Association) 57
John Hunnex 77BR; 330L
John Perkins 181
Malaysian Timber Company 29
Nicholas Dyson 77BL
Pearl Dot Ltd 41B
Record Power Ltd 189BR; 202C; 216

Richard La Trobe-Bateman 72BR
Robert Bosch Ltd 185UC, CR
Rod Wales 76TR
Ryobi 189T; 200; 201; 202BL; 203TR; 209
Schauman Wood Oy 56
Shona Wood 321TR
Simon Hannelius 64
SIP Industrial Products Ltd 188; 211BR; 212; 218
Stuart Linford Furniture 330R
The Woodworker 74TR
Theo Bergstrom 71T
Trend Machinery and Cutting Tools Ltd 182
Triton Manufacturing & Design Co. Pty 165
Wagner Europe 13BR
Wendy Maruyama (Cary Okazaki Studios) 77CL

Key to credits
L = Left
R = Right
T = Top
TL = Top left
TC = Top centre
TR = Top right
C = Centre
UC = Upper centre
CL = Centre Left
CR = Centre right
B = Bottom
BL = Bottom left
BC = Bottom centre
BR = Bottom right

INTRODUCTION

All of us rely on structures and objects made from wood.
Our homes and workplaces are partially, if not entirely,
constructed from timber; most of us have wooden
furniture; our children play with toys made from wood;
and, both as children and adults, wood supplies our
recreational needs in the form of sports equipment or
games boards and pieces. In short, wood is so
commonplace we invariably take it for granted.

By shaping wood with blades and cutters, woodworkers
gain a unique insight into its special qualities. For them,
wood is anything but ordinary. It has lasting appeal, being
both warm and pleasing to the touch, and offering a wealth
of colour and texture that is a delight to the eye. Indeed,
the nature of wood is such that it imparts a uniqueness to
every workpiece – something that cannot be said of
precious metals.

Woodworkers around the world are acutely aware that
certain woods are now a diminishing resource. Responsible
action must therefore be taken to preserve what remains of
the world's rainforests and to replant native hardwood
trees that are becoming rarer year by year. If future
generations of woodworkers are to inherit the same
privileges we enjoy today, it is imperative that we take
steps to protect and replace the sources of this precious
raw material and that we actively support individuals and
agencies dedicated to that end.

CONTENTS

ACKNOWLEDGMENTS

The authors are indebted to the companies listed below who supplied samples of their products for artist's reference and photography:

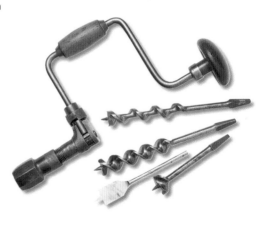

Wood samples
Annandale Timber &
Moulding Co. Pty Ltd
Art Veneer Co. Ltd
Avon Plywood Ltd
C. F. Anderson & Son Ltd
Desfab
E. Jones & Son
Egger (UK) Ltd
F. R. Shadbolt & Sons Ltd
Highland Forest Products plc
John Boddy Timber Ltd
Ravensbourne College of Design
and Communication
Seaboard International Ltd

Handtools
Alec Tiranti Ltd
Art Veneer Co. Ltd
Axminster Power Tool Centre
Burton McCall Ltd
E. C. Emmerich
Garrett Wade Co. Ltd
George Higgins Ltd
John Boddy Timber Ltd
Record Marples Ltd
Skarsten Manufacturing Co. Ltd

Power tools
Axminster Power Tool Centre
DeWalt
Makita (UK) Ltd
Robert Bosch Ltd
Ryobi

Machine tools
Coronet Tool Co.
Hegner Ltd
Robert Sorby Ltd
Tyme Machines Ltd
Warren Machine Tools Ltd

Benches and accessories
Emmerich (Berlon) Ltd

Wood finishes
A. F. Suter & Co. Ltd
Clarke International

CSM Trade Supplies
E. Parsons & Sons
English Abrasives & Chemicals Ltd
Foxell & James Ltd
Graco Ltd
John Myland Ltd
Langlow Products Division (Palace
Chemicals Ltd)
Liberon
Ronseal Ltd
Rustins Ltd
Wm. Zinsser & Co. Inc.

Fixings and fittings
European Industrial Services Ltd
John Myland Ltd
Laserfix Ltd
Woodfit Ltd

The authors and publishers also wish to thank the following companies and organizations for their help in the preparation of this book:

Advanced Machinery Imports Ltd
Alec Tiranti Ltd
American Hardwood Export
Council
American Plywood Association
Australian Particleboard Research
Institute
Blount UK Ltd
Carl Zeiss Jena Ltd
Ciba-Geigy Plastics
Clico (Sheffield) Tooling Ltd
Council of Forest Industries
of Canada
Craft Supplies
Department of the Environment
Dunlop Adhesives
English Nature
Ensign Accessories Ltd
Evode Ltd
Felder Woodworking Machines
Finnish Forest Industries
Federation
Finnish Plywood International

Fitchett & Woolacott
Forest Products Laboratory
Forests Forever
Friends of the Earth
Furniture Industry Research
Association
Ian and Betty Norbury
John Boddy Timber Ltd
Karl Danzer Furnierwerke
Lathams Ltd
Leigh Industries (UK) Ltd
Louisiana-Pacific Corporation
Malaysian Timber Council
Milland Fine Timber Ltd
Oxford Forest Institute
P & J Dust Extraction Ltd
Plywood Association of Australia
Practical Woodworking
Royal Botanic Gardens, Kew
Ryobi Ltd
Schauman Wood Oy
Stuart Batty
Theodor Nagel (GmbH & Co.)
Timber Development Association
(NSW) Ltd
Timber Research and
Development Association
Timber Trade Federation
Union Veneers plc.
Woodworking Machinery Pty Ltd

CHAPTER ONE

WOOD THE RAW MATERIAL

Even the most experienced woodworkers can rarely identify every species of timber, and the rest of us are generally able to recognize only the more commonly used woods. But choosing the right wood for a project requires far more than the ability to recognize its colour, figure, grain pattern and texture. An appreciation of the wood's working characteristics and potential uses not only helps prevent problems but can also make the work more pleasurable.

In addition, a modern woodworker needs to be familiar with the various veneers and man-made boards that can be used as a substitute for solid wood, or which may be preferable because they are better for the job in hand.

It is important to ensure that woods come from well-managed sources and to be aware of which species are at risk. Informed choices can then be made, and steps taken to help ensure continued supplies.

THE ORIGINS OF WOOD

Trees, whether growing in forests or standing alone, not only help control our climate but also provide habitats for a vast number of plants and living creatures. Tree derivatives range from natural foodstuffs through to extracts used in manufacturing products such as resins, rubber and pharmaceuticals. When cut down and converted into wood, trees provide an infinitely adaptable and universally useful material.

Leaf-bearing branches
Leaves produce nutrients to feed the tree by photosynthesis.

Trunk
The trunk supports the branches and is the main source of useful wood.

Angiosperms –
broadleaved trees

Gymnosperms –
needle-leaved trees

Root system
Roots anchor the tree and absorb moisture and minerals from the soil.

WHAT MAKES A TREE?

Botanically trees belong to the Spermatophyta (seed-bearing plants), which are subdivided into Gymnospermae and Angiospermae. The needle-leaved coniferous trees known as softwoods are gymnosperms, while the broadleaved trees (both deciduous and evergreen) known as hardwoods are angiosperms. All trees are perennials, which means they continue their growth for at least three years.

The trunk or bole carries a crown of leaf-bearing branches. A root system both anchors the tree in the ground and absorbs water and minerals to sustain it. The outer layer of the trunk carries sap from the roots to the leaves.

Nutrients and photosynthesis

Trees take in carbon dioxide from the air through pores in the leaves called stomata, and evaporation from the leaves draws the sap through minute cells (see right). When the green pigment present in leaves absorbs energy from sunlight, organic compounds are made from carbon dioxide and water. This reaction, called photosynthesis, produces the nutrients on which a tree lives and at the same time gives off oxygen into the atmosphere. The nutrient produced by the leaves is dispersed down through the tree to the growing parts and is also stored by particular cells.

It is often said that wood 'breathes' and needs to be nourished as part of its maintenance, but once a tree is felled it dies. Any subsequent swelling or shrinking is simply a reaction of the wood to its environment, as it absorbs and exudes moisture in a similar way to a sponge. Wood finishes such as waxes and oils enhance and protect the surface and to some extent help stabilize movement – but they do not 'feed' the wood.

Cellular structure

A mass of cellulose tubular cells bond together with an organic chemical called lignin to form the structure of the wood. These cells provide support for the tree, circulation of sap and food storage. They vary in size, shape and distribution, but are generally long and thin and run longitudinally with the main axis of the tree's trunk or branches. Their orientation produces characteristics relating to the direction of grain, and the way the size and distribution of cells varies between different species produces the character of wood textures, from fine to coarse.

Identifying wood

Examining the cells enables you to identify timber as a softwood or hardwood. The simple cell structure of softwoods is composed mainly of tracheid cells, which provide initial sap conduction and physical support. They form regular radiating rows and make up the main body of the tree.

Hardwoods have fewer tracheids than softwoods. Instead, they have vessels or pores that conduct sap and fibres that give support to the tree.

HOW TREES GROW

A thin layer of living cells between the bark and the wood, called the cambium layer, subdivides every year to form new wood on the inner side and phloem or bast on the outside.

As the inner girth of the tree increases, the old bark splits and new bark is formed by the bast. Cambial cells are weak and thin-walled; in the growing season, when they are moisture-laden, the bark can be easily peeled. In winter months, the cells stiffen and bind the bark firmly. The new wood cells on the inside develop into two specialized types: living cells which store food for the tree, and non-living cells which conduct sap up the tree and provide support for it. Together, they make up the sapwood layer.

Each year, a new ring of sapwood is built up on the outside of the previous year's growth. At the same time, the old sapwood nearest to the centre is no longer used to conduct water and is chemically converted into the heartwood that forms the structural spine of the tree. The area of heartwood increases annually, while the sapwood remains around the same thickness during the tree's life.

Ray cells
Ray cells, also called medullary rays, radiate from the centre of the tree. They carry and store nutrients horizontally through the sapwood, in the same way as the cells that follow the axis of the trunk. Although the flat vertical bands formed by ray cells can hardly be detected in softwoods, in some hardwoods – such as oak, particularly when quarter-sawn – the ray cells are plainly visible.

Sapwood
Sapwood can usually be recognized by its lighter colour, which contrasts with the darker heartwood. However, this difference is less distinct in light-coloured woods, particularly softwoods. Because sapwood cells are relatively thin-walled and porous, they tend to give up moisture quickly and therefore shrink more than the denser heartwood. Conversely, because it is porous, sapwood can readily absorb stains and preservatives.

For the woodworker, sapwood is inferior to heartwood. Furniture makers usually cut it to waste. It is not very resistant to fungal decay, and the carbohydrates stored in some cells are liable to insect attack.

Heartwood
The dead sapwood cells that form the heartwood have no further part in the tree's growth, and can become blocked with organic material. Hardwoods with blocked cells (white oak, for instance) are impervious and so are well suited to tasks such as cooperage, whereas woods that have open heartwood cells (such as red oak) are relatively porous.

The chemical substances that cause the dead cell walls to change colour – sometimes deeply in the case of hardwoods – are called extractives. They also provide some resistance to insect and fungal attack.

Annual rings
The distinct banding made by earlywood and latewood corresponds to one season's growth and enables the age of a felled tree, and the climatic conditions through which it has grown, to be determined. Wide annual rings indicate good growing conditions and narrow ones poor or drought conditions, but, to an expert, the study of a tree's annual rings can reveal its history in much greater detail.

Earlywood
Because earlywood (also called springwood) is laid down in spring, at the early part of the growing season, it is the more rapid part of the annual-growth ring. In softwood, thin-walled tracheid cells form the bulk of the earlywood and facilitate the rapid conduction of sap. In hardwood, open tube-like vessels perform the same function. Earlywood can usually be recognized as the wider band of paler-coloured wood in each growth ring.

Earlywood and latewood

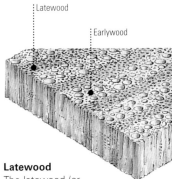

Latewood

Earlywood

Latewood
The latewood (or summerwood) grows more slowly, in the summertime, and produces thicker-walled cells. Their slower growth creates harder and usually darker wood, which is less suitable for conducting sap but provides support for the tree.

Cambium layer
The thin layer of living cell tissue that forms the new wood and bark.

Sapwood
The new wood, the cells of which conduct or store nutrients.

Heartwood
The mature wood that forms the tree's spine.

Pith
The central core of the tree. This can be weak and often suffers from fungal and insect attack.

Annual-growth ring
The layer of wood formed in one growing period, made up of large earlywood and small latewood cells.

Ray cells
Radiating sheets of cells that conduct nutrients horizontally (these are also called 'medullary rays').

Phloem or bast
The inner bark tissue that conducts synthesized food.

Bark
The outer protective layer of dead cells. The term can also include the living inner tissue.

CONVERTING WOOD

Although it can take many years for a tree to grow to a commercially viable size, modern forestry methods can cut down, top and debark a straight-growing tree, such as pine, in a matter of minutes. In addition, the laborious task of sawing logs into boards or beams by hand in a saw-pit has been superseded: today milling is a highly mechanized process, where logs are converted into sawn timber by computer-controlled bandsaws or circular saws.

MILLING TIMBER

Most usable commercial wood comes from the trunk of the tree. Although larger limbs can be cut into logs, asymmetric growth rings in branches or slanted trunks usually produce 'reaction wood', which is unstable and warps and splits easily.

In softwoods the annual-ring growth is mainly on the underside of the branch and produces 'compression wood'; in hardwoods, the growth is mainly on the upper side and is called 'tension wood'.

Good-quality felled trees are cut into logs or butts and transported to local sawmills for conversion into rough-sawn timber. Top-quality hardwood logs with large even boles fetch high prices and are usually converted into veneer. Tree trimmings and subgrade wood are generally used for manufactured boards and paper products.

Planes of reference

The terms refer to the direction of the cut in relation to the annual-growth rings.

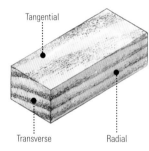

Tangential

Transverse

Radial

Types of cut
1 *Plain-sawn*
2 *Rift-sawn*
3 *Quarter-sawn*

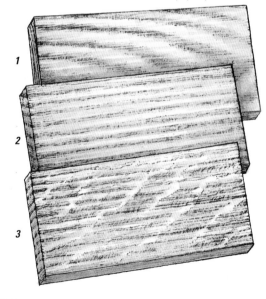

Types of cut

The main cuts produced by modern machine methods are 'plain-sawn' and 'quarter-sawn'. Plain-sawn boards are cut at a tangent to the annual-growth rings, to display a decorative and distinctive elliptical figure. Quarter-sawing reveals a straight figure that is sometimes, in hardwoods such as oak, crossed with a ribbon-like 'flake' figure.

Different terms are used for boards within the two categories. Plain-sawn timber is also known as flat-sawn, flat-grain or slash-sawn timber. Quarter-sawn timber includes rift-sawn, comb-grain, edge-grain and vertical-grain.

Plain-sawn boards in Britain and elsewhere in Europe have growth rings meeting the face of the board at an angle of less than 45 degrees. In quarter-sawn boards, the angle of growth rings to the face of the board is greater than 45 degrees.

Plain-sawn boards in North America have growth rings meeting the face at an angle of less than 30 degrees. Boards where the rings meet at an angle between 30 and 60 degrees are called rift-sawn; these boards display straight figure with some ray-cell patterning and are sometimes referred to as comb grain.

True quarter-sawn boards are cut radially, with the annual rings perpendicular to the board's face, but in practice boards with the rings at an angle of not less than 60 degrees are classified as quarter-sawn.

Converting a log

The stability and figure of wood are determined by the relationship of the plane of the sawcut to the annual-growth rings. The most economical method of converting a log is to cut it 'through and through' (**1**). In this process, parallel cuts are made through the length of the log to produce plain-sawn, rift-sawn and a few quarter-sawn boards.

Plain-sawn logs (**2**) are partly cut through and through, producing a mixture of plain-sawn and rift-sawn boards.

There are a number of ways to cut a log so that it produces quarter-sawn boards. The ideal method is to cut each board parallel with the rays, like the radiating spokes of a wheel, but this is wasteful of timber and is not used commercially. The usual method is to cut the log into quarters and convert each quadrant into boards (**3**). Commercial quarter-sawing first cuts the log into thick sections and then into quartered boards (**4**).

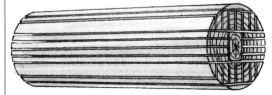

1 *Through and through*

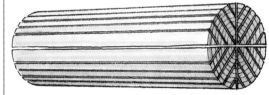

2 *Plain-sawn*

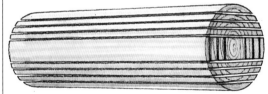

3 *Conventional quarter-sawn*

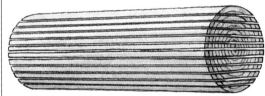

4 *Commercial quarter-sawn*

DRYING WOOD

'Seasoning' (drying) green newly felled wood involves removing the free water and much of the bound moisture from the cell walls in order to stabilize the wood. This process changes the wood's properties, increasing its density, stiffness and strength.

In newly felled wood, the cell walls are saturated and the cell cavities hold free water. As the wood dries, the free water evaporates from the cavities until moisture remains only within the cell walls. Although this fibre-saturation point varies according to the species, it occurs at about 30 per cent moisture content (by weight).

Shrinkage begins when the moisture is lost from the cell walls. When the moisture content is in balance with the relative humidity of its surroundings – known as the equilibrium moisture content (EMC) – the wood stops losing water and stabilizes.

To avoid stresses and ensure that the EMC is at the appropriate level to prevent uneven swelling and shrinkage, seasoning must be carried out properly.

Air-drying
In this traditional method, stacks of wood are stored in ventilated sheds or in the open and the wood is dried by natural airflow through the stack. The boards are evenly stacked on 25mm (1in) square spacer battens called 'stickers', spaced 450mm (1ft 6in) apart. For hardwoods, it takes approximately a year to dry each 25mm (1in) thickness; for softwoods, it takes about half that time.

Air-drying reduces the moisture content to about 14 to 16 per cent, depending on the ambient humidity. For interior use, the wood should then be dried in a kiln or, where possible, restacked and left to dry naturally in the environment in which it is to be used.

Kiln-drying
Wood intended for interior use needs a moisture content of about 8 to 10 per cent, sometimes lower. The advantage of kiln-drying is that it takes only days or weeks to reduce the moisture content of wood to below air-dry levels; some woodworkers, however, prefer to work air-dried wood. Kiln-drying changes the colour of some woods – beech, for example, takes on a pink shade.

The 'stickered' stacks of boards are loaded onto trolleys and rolled into the kiln, where a carefully controlled mixture of hot air and steam is pumped through the piled wood and the humidity is gradually reduced to a specified moisture content. Wood dried to below air-dry levels will try to take up moisture if left exposed – which is why kiln-dried wood is best stored in the environment where it will be used.

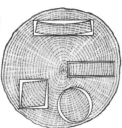

Air-drying at home
Constuct an even stack of 'stickered' boards for air to pass through.

Weights · Stickers · Cover · Boards · Cross bearers · Supports

Shrinkage movement
Sections of wood distort differently, depending on growth-ring orientation.

> ### Checking moisture content
> The moisture content of wood is given as a percentage of its oven-dry weight. This is calculated by comparing the original weight of a sample block of newly felled wood (preferably taken from the middle of the board rather than the ends, which may be drier) with the weight of the same sample after it has been fully dried in an oven. To find the lost weight, subtract the dry weight from the original weight. The following formula is used to calculate the moisture-content percentage:
>
> $$\frac{\text{WEIGHT OF WATER LOST FROM SAMPLE}}{\text{OVEN-DRY WEIGHT OF SAMPLE}} \times 100$$

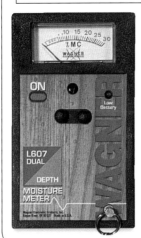

Moisture meters
A moisture meter is a convenient tool for checking moisture content. The meter measures the electrical resistance of the moist wood and provides an instant reading of the moisture-content percentage. Insert the tool's electrodes into the wood at various points along the board to check the average level, as not all parts of the board dry at the same rate.

> ### Stability
> Because wood shrinks as it dries, the shape of a board can change or 'move' as shrinkage takes place. In general, wood shrinks roughly twice as much along the line of the annual rings as it does across them. Tangentially cut plain-sawn boards shrink more in their width, whereas quarter-sawn boards shrink only slightly in width and very little in thickness.
>
> Shrinkage can also cause boards to distort. The concentric growth rings of a tangentially cut plain-sawn board run approximately edge to edge and have different lengths; the longer outer rings shrink more than the inner rings, so the board tends to 'cup' (bend across its width). Square sections of wood may become parallelogram-shaped, and round sections can become oval.
>
> Because the growth rings of a quartered board run from face to face and are virtually the same length, less distortion takes place. This stability makes quartered boards the first choice for flooring and furniture-making.

Commercial air-drying
Sawn boards are dried by natural airflow through the stack.

SELECTING WOOD

Timber suppliers usually stock the softwoods most commonly used for carpentry and joinery – spruce, fir and pine. They are generally sold as dimension stock or dressed stock, the trade terms for sawn or surface-planed sections cut to standard sizes. One or more faces may be surfaced.

Most hardwoods are sold as boards of random width and length, although some species can be bought as dimension stock. Dimension timber is sold in 300mm or 1ft units. Check which system of measurement your supplier uses, as the metric unit is about 5mm (⅛in) shorter than an imperial foot. Whichever system you use, always allow extra length for waste and selection. When working out your timber requirements, remember that planing removes at least 3mm (³/₁₆in) from each face of the wood, making the actual width and thickness less than the nominal (sawn) size quoted by the merchant. The length, however, is always as quoted.

Checking for defects

If wood is not dried carefully, stresses can spoil its appearance and make it difficult to work. Insufficient drying can cause warping and splitting. Check the surface for faults, such as splits, knots and uneven grain. Look along the length to test for twisting or bowing. Look for evidence of insect attack or traces of fungal growth, and for water stains.

Grading wood

Softwoods are graded for evenness of grain and the amount of allowable defects, such as knots. For general woodworking, the 'appearance' and 'non-stress' grades are probably the most useful. Stress-graded softwoods are rated for structural use where strength is important. The trade term 'clear timber' is used for knot-free or defect-free wood, but is not usually available from suppliers unless specified.

Hardwoods are graded by the area of defect-free wood – the greater the area, the higher the grade. The most suitable grades for general woodworking are 'firsts' and FAS ('firsts and seconds').

Although specialist firms supply wood by mail order, personal selection is the best option. Take a block plane with you when buying timber, so you can expose a small area of wood to check colour and grain.

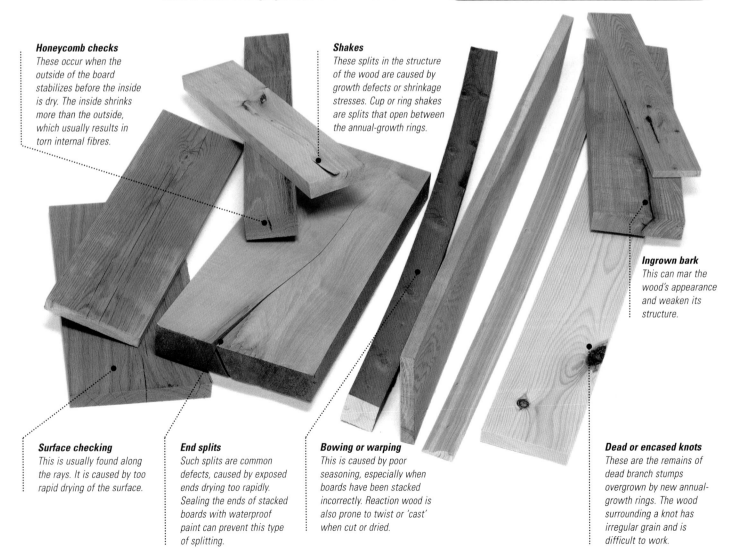

Honeycomb checks
These occur when the outside of the board stabilizes before the inside is dry. The inside shrinks more than the outside, which usually results in torn internal fibres.

Shakes
These splits in the structure of the wood are caused by growth defects or shrinkage stresses. Cup or ring shakes are splits that open between the annual-growth rings.

Ingrown bark
This can mar the wood's appearance and weaken its structure.

Surface checking
This is usually found along the rays. It is caused by too rapid drying of the surface.

End splits
Such splits are common defects, caused by exposed ends drying too rapidly. Sealing the ends of stacked boards with waterproof paint can prevent this type of splitting.

Bowing or warping
This is caused by poor seasoning, especially when boards have been stacked incorrectly. Reaction wood is also prone to twist or 'cast' when cut or dried.

Dead or encased knots
These are the remains of dead branch stumps overgrown by new annual-growth rings. The wood surrounding a knot has irregular grain and is difficult to work.

PROPERTIES OF WOOD

In many woodworking projects, the grain pattern, colour and texture are the most important factors when deciding which woods to work. Although equally important, the strength and working characteristics are often a secondary consideration – and when using veneer, the appearance is all.

Working wood is a constant process of discovery and learning. Each piece is unique: every section of wood taken from the same tree, even from the same board, will be different and a challenge to the woodworker's skills. You can only gain a full understanding of wood's properties by working it and experiencing the way it behaves.

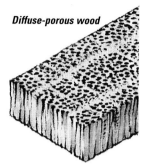

Diffuse-porous wood

Grain

The mass of the wood's cell structure constitutes the grain of the wood, which follows the main axis of the tree's trunk. The disposition and degree of orientation of the longitudinal cells create different types of grain.

Trees with straight and even growth produce straight-grained wood. When cells deviate from the main axis of the tree, they produce cross-grained wood. Spiral grain comes from trees that twist as they grow; when this spiral growth veers from one angle to another, each change taking place over a few annual-growth rings, the result is interlocked grain. Wavy grain – which has short even waves – and irregular curly grain occur in trees with an undulating cell structure.

Wild grain is created when the cells change direction throughout the wood; irregular-grained woods of this kind can be difficult to work.

Random and undulating grain make various patterns, depending on the angle to the surface of the wood and the light reflectivity of the cell structure. Boards with these configurations are particularly valued for veneer.

Figure

The term 'grain' is also used to describe the appearance of wood; however, what is really being referred to is a combination of natural features collectively known as the figure. These features include the difference in growth between the earlywood and latewood, the way colour is distributed, the density, concentricity or eccentricity of the annual-growth rings, the effect of disease or damage, and how the wood has been converted.

When tree trunks are cut tangentially, the plain-sawn boards display a U-shaped pattern. When the trunk is cut radially or quarter-sawn, the series of parallel lines usually produces a less distinctive pattern.

The fork where the main stem of the tree and a branch meet provides curl (or crotch) figure that is sought-after for veneer. Burr wood, an abnormal growth on the side of a tree caused by injury, is also used for veneer. It is popular among woodturners – as is the random-grain figure of stumpwood, from the base of the trunk or roots.

Texture

Texture refers to the relative size of the wood's cells. Fine-textured woods have small closely spaced cells, while coarse-textured woods have relatively large cells. Texture also denotes the distribution of the cells in relation to the annual-growth rings. A wood where the difference between earlywood and latewood is marked has an uneven texture; one with only slight contrast in the growth rings is even-textured.

Coarse-textured woods, such as oak or ash, tend to have finer cells and are also lighter and softer when they are slow-grown. Fast-grown trees usually produce a more distinctive figure and harder, stronger, heavier wood.

The difference in texture between earlywood and latewood is important to the woodworker, as the lighter-weight earlywood is easier to cut than the denser latewood. If tool-cutting edges are kept sharp, this should minimize problems; but latewood can be left proud of the earlywood when finished with a power sander. Woods that have even-textured growth rings are generally the easiest to work and finish.

Durability

Durability refers to a wood's performance when it is in contact with soil. Perishable wood is rated at less than 5 years, very durable at 25 years or more. The durability of a species can vary according to the level of exposure and climatic conditions.

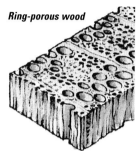

Ring-porous wood

Hardwood porosity

The distribution of hardwood cells can have a marked effect on wood texture. 'Ring-porous' hardwoods, such as oak or ash, have clearly defined rings of large vessels in the earlywood, and dense fibres and cell tissue in the latewood. This makes them more difficult to finish than 'diffuse-porous' woods, such as beech, where the vessels and fibres are relatively evenly distributed. Although woods like mahogany can be diffuse-porous, their larger cells often make them more coarse-textured.

WORKING WOOD

- Planing 'with the grain' means planing with the fibres of the wood parallel to or sloping away from the direction of the cutting action – resulting in a smooth trouble-free cut.

- Planing 'against the grain' means planing with the fibres sloping towards the direction of the cutting action – which produces a rough cut.

- Sawing 'with the grain' means cutting in the same direction as the fibres.

- Sawing or planing 'across the grain' means sawing or planing more or less at right angles to the grain of the wood.

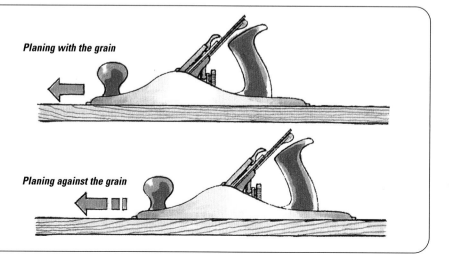

Planing with the grain

Planing against the grain

CONSERVATION OF TREES

Trees play a vital part in regulating our environment, and the products derived from them feature prominently in all our lives. Increasing ecological awareness has highlighted the plight of forests endangered by overcutting and pollution and the importance of developing more sustainable energy sources and controlling carbon-dioxide emissions and other pollutants.

Environmental threats

Carbon dioxide, a by-product of burning fossil fuels, makes up part of the Earth's atmosphere. Living trees absorb this gas, which helps maintain the natural balance of the atmosphere. However, the level of carbon dioxide is rising faster than can be naturally absorbed – leading to the 'greenhouse effect', whereby carbon dioxide and other gases trap the Earth's radiated heat, causing global warming.

In the southern hemisphere, logging and the deliberate burning of Amazonian rainforests to clear land for large-scale farming and cattle ranching not only reduce the stock of virgin forest but also contribute to the greenhouse effect. Polluted air from industries in the northern hemisphere produces acid rain that is killing entire forests.

Growing concerns

Depending on who you speak to, the survival of tropical hardwoods and even some South American softwoods is either in crisis and at the point of collapse or is being responsibly managed. The reality is somewhere in between.

Environmental groups have drawn the world's attention to the mass defoliation of tropical forests. However, a complete ban on imported tropical hardwoods, as some propose, would damage the timber trade and deprive developing countries of revenue. In addition, more trees are destroyed by local burning than by logging or by felling for export. Multinational mining and dam-construction projects also contribute to the problem, as does the pulping industry, by stripping mixed virgin forest for monoculture reforestation.

CITES REGULATIONS

At the time of writing, the only international conservation regulations to be implemented are those evolved by CITES (the Convention on International Trade in Endangered Species of Wild Flora and Fauna). The CITES regulations have three graded appendices. Every two years all species listed in the three appendices are reviewed and additions and deletions made.

• Appendix I lists species threatened with extinction. All commercial imports, exports and sales of these species are prohibited, including seeds and manufactured products (both new and antique).

• Appendix II lists species that may become threatened if trade in them is not controlled and monitored. Any export of these species must be accompanied by an Export Certificate issued by a government authority of the exporting country, after investigation showing that the specimen was legally obtained and that export would not be detrimental to the survival of the species. Importers must obtain a CITES Import Certificate.

• Appendix III lists species noted by any country to which they are indigenous as threatened or at risk. Listing in Appendix III provides the country with a measure of control over the amount exported. Importers must have a CITES Import Certificate.

Gas build-up
Carbon dioxide and CFCs in the atmosphere prevent heat radiating into space.

Radiated heat
Some low-frequency radiated heat escapes, but the rest is trapped by gases in the atmosphere, contributing to global warming.

Radiation from the sun
Light and heat from the sun pass through the atmosphere to the Earth's surface.

The greenhouse effect

The timber trade

Trees are a renewable resource, and responsible programmes could ensure a continued supply of tropical hardwoods. There is increasing pressure on timber producers, suppliers and users to trade in and make use of only those woods that come from certifiable managed sources.

Organizations such as the Forest Stewardship Council and Forests Forever include timber traders and suppliers among their ranks and aim to increase wood users' responsibility for, and knowledge about, their material. Both of these groups are in the process of devising methods of certifying tropical, temperate and boreal woods according to the way they are grown and managed by foresters and timber companies.

USING ALTERNATIVES

For the woodworker, CITES regulations mean that, in future, certain exotic timbers will be found only among old stock or as reclaimed timber. It is therefore worth considering the use of alternative timbers and those produced in temperate zones. Timber suppliers will advise you about alternative woods and on the availability of tropical hardwoods from reputable sources, and so help you to 'act locally, think globally'.

Temperate hardwoods

Timbers of the temperate forests of North America and Europe are already produced by sustainable methods. In the United States, the Multiple-Use Sustained-Yield Act requires that trees harvested from Federal land do not exceed the annual growth. It recognizes that public forests also provide wildlife habitats and control watershed and soil erosion, as well as being used for recreational purposes. A 30-year policy of continual regeneration has produced around 50 per cent more hardwood than has been used in the same time.

Most commercial hardwoods are from either second-cut, third-cut or fourth-cut forests that are managed on a rotational basis. The remaining virgin forests are now protected, and no old-growth timber can be felled.

*Endangered species
A supplier of recycled timber may be your only source of species such as Brazilian rosewood (Dalbergia nigra), which is listed under CITES Appendix I and is therefore no longer commercially available.*

Recycled timber

To help sustain the supply of new wood, many woodworkers are turning to architectural salvage yards as alternative sources of useful timber. Seasoned softwoods and hardwoods are available in the form of recycled floorboards, beams and joists, and there's often a variety of wood panelling and mouldings to choose from. In some cases, these yards have become the only reliable suppliers of certain species of wood and timber in sizes that are difficult to obtain from elsewhere. Storing this number of disparate components can be difficult. Add to that the labour of denailing and resawing to usable sizes, and you can see why the cost of recycled timber is usually comparable with prices asked for new wood.

Second-hand wardrobes and cabinets can be dismantled with care and the wood reused for other projects. You should always check frames and panels for signs of insect infestation or mould growth before buying this type of furniture.

As a service to other woodworkers, find out whether you can deposit your own usable waste wood in a designated area at your local waste-disposal site.

SOFTWOODS OF THE WORLD

Softwood timber comes from coniferous (cone-bearing) trees belonging to the botanical group Gymnospermae – plants that have exposed seeds. It is this scientific grouping, rather than their physical properties, that determines which trees are classed as softwoods. When converted into boards, softwoods can be identified by their relatively light colours, ranging from pale yellow to reddish brown. Other characteristic features are the grain pattern created by the change in colour and density of the earlywood and latewood.

Softwood-producing regions of the world

The majority of the world's commercial softwoods come from countries in the northern hemisphere. These range from the Arctic and subarctic regions of Europe and North America down to the southeastern United States.

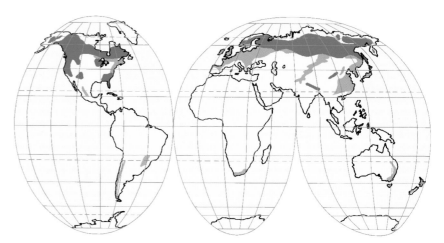

Distribution of softwoods

- Coniferous forest
- Mixed forest (coniferous and deciduous broadleaved trees)

Cultivated softwoods

Grafting, crossbreeding and carefully controlled pollination are just some of the methods used today to produce fast-growing trees. Softwoods are cheaper than hardwoods and are used in building construction, joinery and the manufacture of paper and fibreboard.

BOTANICAL CLASSIFICATION

The softwood samples on the following pages are listed alphabetically by the botanical classification of each genus and species. These are given in small type below the heading, which is the main commercial name. Other local or commercial names appear at the beginning of the text.

Colour changes

It is the nature of wood to be as varied in its colour as in its figure and texture. Furthermore, the colour alters in time, becoming lighter or darker. However, the most dramatic changes occur when a finish is applied – even a clear finish enriches and slightly darkens natural colours. With the description of each species, you will find a square photograph showing what the wood looks like before and after the application of a clear finish.

Softwood seedling

Cone-bearing trees

Although cone-bearing trees are mostly depicted as having a tall, pointed outline, this is not true of all conifers. Most are evergreens, with narrow, needle-shape leaves.

Buying softwood boards

Local sawmills will sell you whole home-grown timber boards. These can come complete with bark and waney edge (the uncut edge of the board). In contrast, imported boards are usually supplied debarked or square-edged.

Yellow cedar   Larch   Hoop pine   Parana pine

Waney edge

18

SILVER FIR

Abies alba

Other names: Whitewood.
Sources: Southern Europe, Central Europe.
Characteristics of the tree: A straight, thin tree, growing to about 40m (130ft) in height and 1m (3ft 3in) in diameter, losing its lower branches in the process.
Characteristics of the wood: The almost colourless pale-cream wood bears a resemblance to Norway spruce (Picea abies), with straight grain and a fine texture. However, it is prone to knots and is not durable; for exterior uses, a preservative treatment is required.
Common uses: Building construction, joinery, plywood, boxes, poles.
Workability: It can be worked easily, using sharp handtools and machine tools to produce a very smooth finish. It glues well.
Finishing: It takes stains, paints and varnishes readily.
Average dried weight: 480kg/m³ (30lb/ft³).

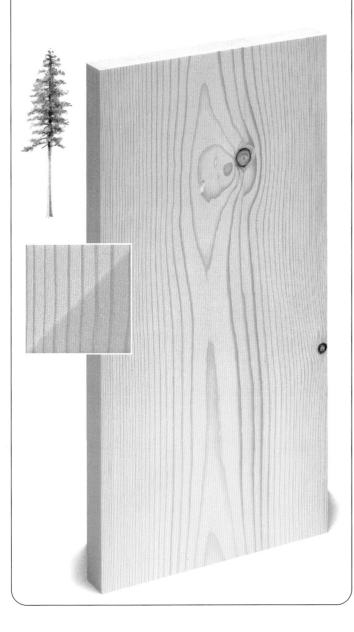

QUEENSLAND KAURI

Agathis spp.

Other names: North Queensland kauri, South Queensland kauri.
Sources: Australia.
Characteristics of the tree: Although it can grow to more than 45m (150ft) high and 1.5m (5ft) in diameter, overcutting has led to a scarcity of larger trees; medium-size ones are the most common.
Characteristics of the wood: The straight-grained wood is not durable and varies in colour from pale cream-brown to pinkish brown, with a fine, even texture and lustrous surface.
Common uses: Joinery, furniture.
Workability: It can be worked readily and brought to a fine, smooth finish using handtools and machine tools. It glues well.
Finishing: It accepts stains and paints well, and can be polished to an excellent finish.
Average dried weight: 480kg/m³ (30lb/ft³).

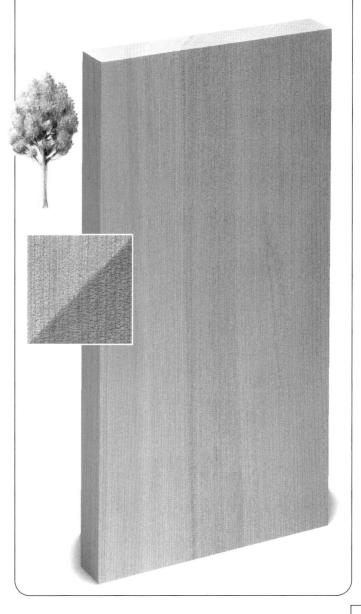

PARANA PINE

Araucaria angustifolia

Other names: Brazilian pine (USA).
Sources: Brazil, Argentina, Paraguay.
Characteristics of the tree: It can reach about 36m (120ft) in height, with a flat crown of foliage at its top. The long, straight trunk can be up to 1m (3ft 3in) in diameter.
Characteristics of the wood: The mostly knot-free wood has barely perceptible growth rings, an even texture and straight grain. It is not durable, and must be well-seasoned to avoid large boards buckling. The core of the heartwood is dark brown, often flecked with streaks of bright red, while the rest is light brown.
Common uses: Joinery, furniture, plywood, turnery.
Workability: It is an easy wood to work and bring to a smooth finish with handtools and machine tools. It glues well.
Finishing: It accepts paints, stains and polishes well.
Average dried weight: 530kg/m³ (33lb/ft³).

HOOP PINE

Araucaria cunninghamii

Other names: Queensland pine.
Sources: Australia, Papua New Guinea.
Characteristics of the tree: This tall, elegant tree, with tufts of foliage at the tips of thin branches, is not a true pine. The average height is about 30m (100ft); the trunk diameter is about 1m (3ft 3in).
Characteristics of the wood: The versatile wood is not durable; it has straight grain and a fine texture. The heartwood is yellow-brown in colour, while the wide sapwood is light brown.
Common uses: Building construction, joinery, furniture, turnery, pattern-making, plywood.
Workability: If the cutting edges of handtools and machine tools are kept sharp to avoid tearing grain around fine knots, the wood can be worked easily. It glues well.
Finishing: It accepts paints and stains well, and can be polished to an attractive finish.
Average dried weight: 560kg/m³ (35lb/ft³).

CEDAR OF LEBANON

Cedrus libani

Other names: True cedar.

Sources: Middle East.

Characteristics of the tree: Parkland-grown examples of this tree have large low-growing branches and a distinctive broad crown of foliage. It can reach a height of about 40m (130ft) and a diameter of about 1.5m (5ft).

Characteristics of the wood: The aromatic wood is soft and durable, though brittle, with straight grain that is often clearly marked by the contrast between earlywood and latewood. The heartwood has a medium-fine texture and is light brown in colour.

Common uses: Building construction, joinery, interior and exterior furniture.

Workability: Although it can be worked easily with handtools and machine tools and sands well, knots can be difficult to work.

Finishing: It accepts paints and stains well, and can be polished to a very fine finish.

Average dried weight: 560kg/m³ (35lb/ft³).

YELLOW CEDAR

Chamaecyparis nootkatensis

Other names: Alaska yellow cedar, Pacific coast yellow cedar.

Sources: Pacific coast of North America.

Characteristics of the tree: This elegant conical-shaped tree grows slowly to 30m (100ft) in height and about 1m (3ft 3in) in diameter.

Characteristics of the wood: The durable pale-yellow wood has straight grain and an even texture. When dry, it is stiff, stable, relatively light and very strong. It wears well and is resistant to decay.

Common uses: Furniture, veneers and high-class joinery (doors, windows, flooring, decorative panelling and mouldings), boatbuilding, oars and paddles.

Workability: It can be cut to fine tolerances and glues well.

Finishing: It accepts paints and stains well, and can be polished to a fine finish.

Average dried weight: 500kg/m³ (31lb/ft³).

RIMU

Dacrydium cupressinum

Other names: Red pine.

Sources: New Zealand.

Characteristics of the tree: This tall straight-growing tree can reach 36m (120ft) in height. It has a long, clean trunk that can be as large as 2.5m (8ft) in diameter.

Characteristics of the wood: The moderately durable wood has straight grain and a fine even texture, with pale-yellow sapwood that darkens to a reddish-brown heartwood. The colour of the somewhat indistinct figure, with patches and streaks of brown and yellow blending together, lightens and fades on exposure to light.

Common uses: Interior furniture, decorative veneer, turnery, panelling, plywood.

Workability: It can be worked well with handtools and machine tools. It can be planed to a fine texture and brought to a smooth finish. It glues well.

Finishing: It can be stained satisfactorily, and finished well with paints or polishes.

Average dried weight: 530kg/m³ (33lb/ft³).

LARCH

Larix decidua

Other names: None.

Sources: Europe, particularly mountainous areas.

Characteristics of the tree: One of the toughest softwoods, larch sheds its needles in winter. It grows to about 45m (150ft) in height, with a straight cylindrical trunk about 1m (3ft 3in) in diameter.

Characteristics of the wood: The resinous wood is straight-grained and uniformly textured; it is relatively durable in outside use. The sapwood is narrow and light-coloured, the heartwood orange-red. Hard knots may loosen after the seasoning process and can blunt cutting edges.

Common uses: Boat planking, pit props, joinery (including staircases, flooring, and door and window frames), posts, fencing.

Workability: The wood can be worked relatively easily with handtools and machine tools; it sands well, although hard latewood grain may be left proud of the surface.

Finishing: It can be painted and varnished satisfactorily.

Average dried weight: 590kg/m³ (37lb/ft³).

NORWAY SPRUCE

Picea abies

Other names: European whitewood, European spruce, whitewood.
Sources: Europe.
Characteristics of the tree: This important timber-producing tree has an average height of 36m (120ft) but can grow to 60m (200ft) in favourable conditions. Young trees provide the source of the traditional Christmas tree.
Characteristics of the wood: The non-durable, lustrous wood is straight-grained and even-textured, with almost-white sapwood and pale yellow-brown heartwood. The strength properties are similar to the European redwood (Pinus sylvestris), but with less prominent annual-growth rings.
Common uses: Interior building construction, flooring, boxes, plywood. Slow-grown wood is used for piano soundboards and the bellies of violins and guitars.
Workability: It can be worked easily with handtools and machine tools, and cuts cleanly. It glues well.
Finishing: It accepts stains well, and can be finished satisfactorily with paints and varnishes.
Average dried weight: 450kg/m³ (28lb/ft³).

SITKA SPRUCE

Picea sitchensis

Other names: Silver spruce.
Sources: Canada, USA, UK.
Characteristics of the tree: This widely cultivated tree can reach a height of 87m (290ft), with a buttressed trunk of up to 5m (16ft) in diameter, although most fast-grown trees are smaller.
Characteristics of the wood: The non-durable wood is usually straight-grained and even-textured, with cream-white sapwood and slightly pink heartwood. It can be steam-bent and is relatively light and strong, with good elasticity.
Common uses: Building construction, interior joinery, aircraft and gliders, boatbuilding, musical instruments, plywood.
Workability: It can be worked easily with handtools and machine tools, but cutting edges must be kept sharp to avoid tearing bands of earlywood. It glues well.
Finishing: It stains well, and can be finished satisfactorily with paints and varnishes.
Average dried weight: 450kg/m³ (28lb/ft³).

SUGAR PINE

Pinus lambertiana

Other names: Californian sugar pine.

Sources: USA.

Characteristics of the tree: It typically reaches about 45m (150ft) in height and 1m (3ft 3in) in diameter.

Characteristics of the wood: The even-grained wood is moderately soft, with a medium texture. It is not durable. The sapwood is white, and the heartwood a pale-brown to reddish-brown colour.

Common uses: Light building construction, joinery.

Workability: Because of its softness, cutting edges must be kept sharp to avoid tearing the wood; otherwise, it can be worked well with handtools and machine tools. It glues well.

Finishing: It can be brought to a satisfactory finish with stains, paints, varnishes and polishes.

Average dried weight: 420kg/m³ (26lb/ft³).

WESTERN
WHITE PINE

Pinus monticola

Other names: Idaho white pine.

Sources: USA, Canada.

Characteristics of the tree: The average height is 37m (125ft), with a straight trunk about 1m (3ft 3in) in diameter.

Characteristics of the wood: The wood has straight grain and an even texture, with fine resin-duct lines. It is not durable. Both earlywood and latewood are pale yellow to reddish brown in colour. In many respects it is similar to yellow pine (Pinus strobus), but it is tougher and shrinks slightly more.

Common uses: Building construction, joinery (including doors, windows and moulded skirting boards), boatbuilding, built-in furniture, pattern-making, plywood.

Workability: It is easily worked with handtools and machine tools, and glues well.

Finishing: It accepts paints and varnishes well, and can be polished to a good finish.

Average dried weight: 450kg/m³ (28lb/ft³).

PONDEROSA PINE

Pinus ponderosa

Other names: British Columbian soft pine (Canada); Western yellow pine, Californian white pine (USA).

Sources: USA, Canada.

Characteristics of the tree: This tree can reach 70m (230ft) in height; a typical straight trunk is about 750mm (2ft 6in) in diameter. It has an open conical-shape crown.

Characteristics of the wood: The non-durable wood can be knotty and has resin ducts showing up as fine dark lines on board surfaces. The wide pale-yellow sapwood is soft and even-textured. The heart-wood is resinous, heavier, and a deep-yellow to reddish-brown colour.

Common uses: Sapwood for pattern-making, doors, furniture, turnery. Heartwood for joinery and building construction.

Workability: Both sapwood and heartwood can be worked well with handtools and machine tools, but knots can cause problems when planing. It glues well.

Finishing: It takes paints and varnishes satisfactorily, but resinous wood needs a sealer before finishing.

Average dried weight: 480kg/m³ (30lb/ft³).

YELLOW PINE

Pinus strobus

Other names: Quebec pine, Weymouth pine (UK); Eastern white pine, Northern white pine (USA).

Sources: USA, Canada.

Characteristics of the tree: It grows to about 30m (100ft) in height and up to 1m (3ft 3in) in diameter.

Characteristics of the wood: Although the wood is soft, weak and not durable, it is stable. It has straight grain, a fine even texture, fine resin-duct marks, and inconspicuous annual-growth rings. The colour varies from pale yellow to pale brown.

Common uses: High-class joinery, light building construction, furniture, engineering, pattern-making, carving.

Workability: It can be worked easily with handtools and machine tools, providing they are kept sharp. It glues well.

Finishing: It accepts stains, paints and varnishes, and polishes well.

Average dried weight: 420kg/m³ (26lb/ft³).

EUROPEAN
REDWOOD

Pinus sylvestris

Other names: Scots pine, Scandinavian redwood, Russian redwood.

Sources: Europe, Northern Asia.

Characteristics of the tree: It grows to up to 30m (100ft) in height and 1m (3ft 3in) in diameter. It is conical in shape when young, but becomes flat-topped when mature.

Characteristics of the wood: Although the resinous wood is stable and strong, it is not durable unless treated. The sapwood is a light white-yellow colour, and the heartwood varies from yellow-brown to reddish brown; there is a distinct figure, with light earlywood and reddish latewood. The light colouring mellows with time.

Common uses: Building construction, interior joinery, turnery, plywood. Selected knot-free timber is used for furniture.

Workability: Although knots and resin can cause problems, the wood works well with handtools and machine tools. It glues well.

Finishing: It stains satisfactorily, but resin and latewood can prove resistant. It accepts paints and varnishes well, and can be polished to a good finish.

Average dried weight: 510kg/m³ (32lb/ft³).

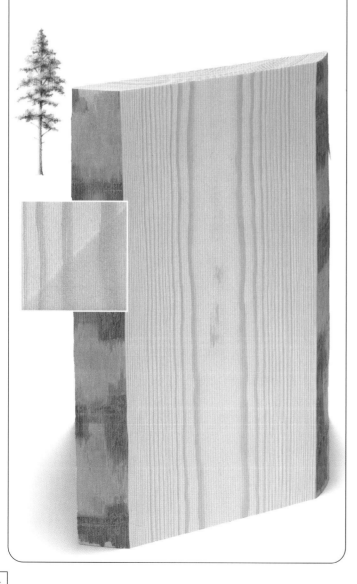

DOUGLAS FIR

Pseudotsuga menziesii

Other names: British Columbian pine, Oregon pine.

Sources: Canada, Western USA, UK.

Characteristics of the tree: The average height is about 60m (200ft), but some trees reach 90m (300ft). Trunks of forest-grown trees can be up to 2m (6ft 6in) in diameter, and are free of branches for much of their height.

Characteristics of the wood: The straight-grained reddish-brown wood is moderately durable, with distinctive earlywood and latewood grain. It produces large sizes of knot-free timber.

Common uses: Joinery, plywood, building construction.

Workability: It works well with handtools and machine tools that have sharp cutting edges, and glues satisfactorily. It can be finished smooth, but latewood may be left proud of the surface after sanding.

Finishing: Latewood can be resistant to stains; earlywood takes them relatively well. Both accept paints and varnishes satisfactorily.

Average dried weight: 510kg/m³ (32lb/ft³).

SEQUOIA

Sequoia sempervirens

Other names: Californian redwood.

Sources: USA.

Characteristics of the tree: This magnificent straight tree grows to about 100m (300ft) in height. The buttressed trunk with short drooping branches can exceed 4.5m (15ft) in diameter; even the distinctive red-fissured bark can be more than 300mm (1ft) thick.

Characteristics of the wood: Despite being relatively soft, the straight-grained reddish-brown wood is durable and suitable for exterior use. The texture can vary from fine and even to quite coarse, and there is a marked contrast between earlywood and latewood.

Common uses: Exterior cladding and shingles, interior joinery, coffins, fence posts.

Workability: So long as cutting edges are kept sharp to prevent break-out along the cut, it can be worked well with handtools and machine tools. It glues well.

Finishing: It sands and accepts paints and polishes well.

Average dried weight: 420kg/m³ (26lb/ft³).

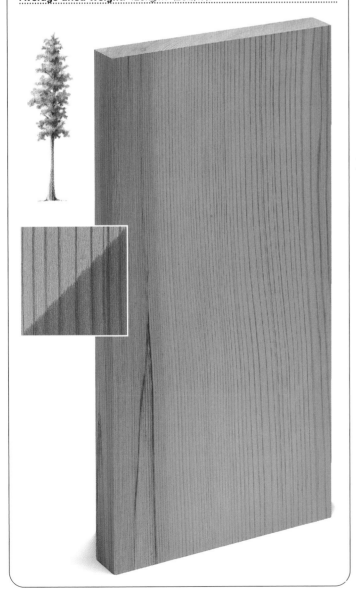

YEW

Taxus baccata

Other names: Common yew, European yew.

Sources: Europe, Asia Minor, North Africa, Myanmar, Himalayas.

Characteristics of the tree: The yew is the longest-living European tree (one specimen in Austria is over 3,500 years old). It grows to an average height of 15m (50ft), with dense evergreen foliage and a short trunk of up to 6.1m (20ft) in diameter, deeply fluted where intergrown shoots produce an irregular form.

Characteristics of the wood: The wood is hard, tough and durable, with a decorative growth pattern, orange-red heartwood and a distinct light-coloured sapwood – which often appears in irregularly shaped boards, along with holes, small knots and bark inclusions. It is a good wood for steam-bending.

Common uses: Furniture, carving, interior joinery, veneer. It is particularly good for turning.

Workability: Straight-grained wood can be machined and hand-worked to a smooth finish, but irregular-grained wood can tear and be difficult to work. Its oily nature means care must be taken with gluing.

Finishing: It accepts stains satisfactorily, and can be polished to an excellent finish.

Average dried weight: 670kg/m³ (42lb/ft³).

WESTERN RED CEDAR

Thuja plicata

Other names: Giant arbor vitae (USA); red cedar (Canada); British Columbian red cedar (UK).

Sources: USA, Canada, UK, New Zealand.

Characteristics of the tree: This large, conically shaped, densely foliated tree reaches a height of up to 75m (250ft) and a diameter of up to 2.5m (8ft).

Characteristics of the wood: Although relatively soft and brittle, the non-resinous aromatic wood is durable; after long exposure to weathering, its reddish-brown colour fades to silver-grey. It has straight grain and a coarse texture.

Common uses: Shingles, exterior boarding, construction, furniture, cladding and decking, interior panelling.

Workability: It is easily worked with handtools and machine tools, and glues well.

Finishing: It accepts paints and varnishes well, and can be brought to a good finish.

Average dried weight: 370kg/m³ (23lb/ft³).

WESTERN HEMLOCK

Tsuga heterophylla

Other names: Pacific hemlock, British Columbian hemlock.

Sources: USA, Canada, UK.

Characteristics of the tree: This tall, straight, elegant tree with a distinctive drooping top can reach 60m (200ft) in height and 2m (6ft 6in) in diameter. It produces large pieces of timber.

Characteristics of the wood: The even-textured straight-grained wood is not durable and must be treated before exterior use. Pale brown and semi-lustrous, it is knot-free and non-resinous, with relatively distinctive growth rings.

Common uses: Joinery, plywood, building construction (where it is often used in place of Douglas fir).

Workability: It can be worked easily with handtools and machine tools, and glues well.

Finishing: Accepts stains, paints, polishes and varnishes well.

Average dried weight: 500kg/m³ (31lb/ft³).

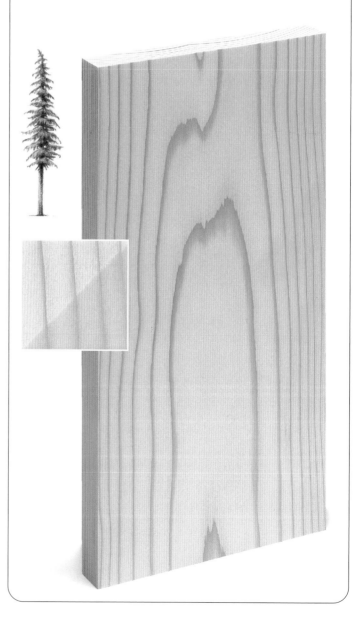

HARDWOODS OF THE WORLD

Hardwood trees belong to the botanical group Angiospermae – flowering broadleaved plants.
Although it is this scientific grouping that determines which trees are classed as hardwoods, it is true
that most hardwoods are harder than softwood timbers. The greatest exception to this rule is balsa:
the tree belongs to the botanical hardwood group, yet it has the softest timber commercially available
from either group.
*   Most broadleaved trees grown in temperate zones are deciduous, losing their leaves in winter;*
some, however, have developed into evergreens. Broadleaved trees grown in tropical forests are
mainly evergreen.

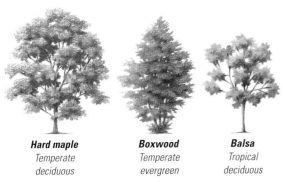

Hard maple
Temperate
deciduous

Boxwood
Temperate
evergreen

Balsa
Tropical
deciduous

Harvesting hardwoods
Of the thousands of species of hardwood trees found throughout the world, only a few hundred are harvested for commercial use. Because hardwoods are generally more durable than softwoods and have a wider range of colour, texture and figure, they are sought-after and expensive. Highly prized, and increasingly rarer, exotic woods are often converted into veneer to satisfy demand.

Regenerating hardwood forests
Young trees are planted and tended in the natural environment of a tropical forest, to maintain hardwood stocks for future generations.

Hardwood-producing regions of the world
Climate is the primary factor in determining where species grow. For the most part, deciduous broadleaved trees grow in the temperate northern hemisphere whereas broadleaved evergreens are found in the southern hemisphere and tropical regions.

Distribution of hardwoods
■ *Evergreen broadleaved forest*
  Deciduous broadleaved forest
  Mixed broadleaved forest (evergreen and deciduous)
■ *Mixed forest (coniferous and deciduous broadleaved trees)*

Endangered species
Overproduction and a lack of international regulatory cooperation have led to a severe shortage of many tropical hardwoods. In the following pages, those species marked with a felled-tree symbol are most at risk; check with suppliers that their woods come from certified sources. Some species may be available only as recycled timber.

BOTANICAL CLASSIFICATION

The hardwood samples on the following pages are listed alphabetically by the botanical classification of each genus and species. These are given in small type below the heading, which is the main commercial name. Other local or commercial names appear at the beginning of the text.

Colour changes
Wood is as varied in its colour as in its figure and texture. Furthermore, the colour alters in time, becoming lighter or darker. However, the most dramatic changes occur when a finish is applied – even a clear finish enriches and slightly darkens natural colours. With the description of each species, you will find a square photograph showing what the wood looks like before and after the application of a clear finish.

EUROPEAN SYCAMORE

Acer pseudoplatanus

Other names: Plane (Scotland); sycamore plane, great maple (UK).

Sources: Europe, Western Asia.

Characteristics of the tree: A medium-size tree, it reaches a height of 30m (100ft) and has a diameter of 1.5m (5ft).

Characteristics of the wood: The lustrous white to yellowish-white wood is not durable and is unsuitable for exterior use, but it is good for steam-bending. It has a fine even texture. Although it is generally straight-grained, wavy grain produces the fiddleback figure prized for violin backs.

Common uses: Turnery, furniture, flooring, veneer, kitchen utensils.

Workability: It can be worked well with handtools and machine tools, though care needs to be taken with wavy-grained wood. It glues well.

Finishing: It stains well, and polishes to a fine finish.

Average dried weight: 630kg/m³ (39lb/ft³).

SOFT MAPLE

Acer rubrum

Other names: Red maple (USA, Canada).

Sources: USA, Canada.

Characteristics of the tree: This medium-size tree can reach 23m (75ft) in height and 750mm (2ft 6in) in diameter.

Characteristics of the wood: The light creamy-brown wood is straight-grained, with a lustrous surface and fine texture. It is not durable and not as strong as hard maple (Acer saccharum), but it is good for steam-bending.

Common uses: Furniture and interior joinery, musical instruments, flooring, turnery, plywood, veneer.

Workability: The wood works readily with handtools and machine tools, and can be glued satisfactorily.

Finishing: It accepts stains well, and can be polished to a fine finish.

Average dried weight: 630kg/m³ (39lb/ft³).

HARD MAPLE

Acer saccharum

Other names: Rock maple, sugar maple.

Sources: Canada, USA.

Characteristics of the tree: It can grow to a height of about 27m (90ft) and reach a diameter of 750mm (2ft 6in).

Characteristics of the wood: The heavy wood is hard-wearing but not durable, with straight grain and fine texture. The heartwood is a light reddish brown, while the light sapwood is often selected for its whiteness.

Common uses: Furniture, turnery, musical instruments, flooring, veneer, butcher's blocks.

Workability: The wood is difficult to work with handtools or machine tools, particularly if it is irregularly grained. It glues well.

Finishing: It accepts stains, and can be polished satisfactorily.

Average dried weight: 740kg/m³ (46lb/ft³).

WESTERN RED ALDER

Alnus rubra

Other names: Oregon alder.

Sources: Pacific coast of North America.

Characteristics of the tree: This smallish tree grows to a height of about 15m (50ft), with a diameter of 300 to 500mm (1ft to 1ft 8in).

Characteristics of the wood: The straight-grained even-textured wood is soft and not particularly strong. It is not durable, but can be treated with preservative. The colour ranges from pale yellow to reddish brown, with a subtle figure.

Common uses: Furniture, turnery, carving, decorative veneer, plywood, toy-making.

Workability: It can be worked well with handtools and machine tools, if cutting edges are kept sharp. It glues well.

Finishing: It accepts stains well, and can be painted or polished to a fine finish.

Average dried weight: 530kg/m³ (33lb/ft³).

GONÇALO ALVES

Astronium fraxinifolium

Other names: Zebrawood (UK); tigerwood (USA).
Sources: Brazil.
Characteristics of the tree: The average height is 30m (100ft), but some trees reach 45m (150ft). The diameter is about 1m (3ft 3in).
Characteristics of the wood: The medium-textured wood is hard and very durable, with hard and soft layers of material; its reddish-brown colour is streaked with dark brown and is similar to rosewood. The grain is irregular and interlocked.
Common uses: Fine furniture, decorative woodware, turnery (for which it is particularly good), veneer.
Workability: It is a difficult wood to work by hand, and cutting edges of both handtools and machine tools must be kept sharp. It has a natural lustre and glues well.
Finishing: It can be polished to a fine finish.
Average dried weight: 950kg/m³ (59lb/ft³).

YELLOW BIRCH

Betula alleghaniensis

Other names: Hard birch, betula wood (Canada); Canadian yellow birch, Quebec birch, American birch (UK).
Sources: Canada, USA.
Characteristics of the tree: The largest North American birch usually reaches about 20m (65ft) in height, with a straight, slightly tapering, trunk about 750mm (2ft 6in) in diameter.
Characteristics of the wood: The non-durable wood is usually straight-grained. It has a fine even texture and is good for steam-bending. The light yellow sapwood is permeable; and the reddish-brown heartwood, with distinctive darker growth rings, is resistant to treatment with preservatives.
Common uses: Joinery, flooring, furniture, turnery, high-grade decorative plywood.
Workability: It can be worked reasonably well with handtools, and well with machine tools. It glues well.
Finishing: It accepts stains well, and can be polished to a fine finish.
Average dried weight: 710kg/m³ (44lb/ft³).

PAPER BIRCH

Betula papyrifera

Other names: American birch (UK); white birch (Canada).
Sources: USA, Canada.
Characteristics of the tree: The average height of this relatively small tree is about 18m (60ft). The straight, clear, cylindrical trunk is about 300mm (1ft) in diameter.
Characteristics of the wood: The wood is fairly hard, has straight grain and a fine even texture, and is moderately good for steam-bending. It is not durable. The sapwood is creamy white; and the heartwood, which is relatively resistant to treatment with preservatives, is pale brown.
Common uses: Turnery, domestic woodware and utensils, crates, plywood, veneer.
Workability: It can be worked reasonably well with handtools and machine tools, and glues well.
Finishing: It accepts stains well, and can be polished to a fine finish.
Average dried weight: 640kg/m³ (40lb/ft³).

BOXWOOD

Buxus sempervirens

Other names: European, Turkish, Iranian boxwood, according to origin.
Sources: Southern Europe, Western Asia, Asia Minor.
Characteristics of the tree: This small shrub-like tree reaches a height of up to 9m (30ft). The short lengths or billets produced are usually up to 1m (3ft 3in) long, with a diameter of up to 200mm (8in).
Characteristics of the wood: The wood is hard, tough, heavy and dense, with a fine even texture and straight or irregular grain. When first cut it is pale yellow, but the colour mellows on exposure to light and air. The heartwood is durable, and the permeable sapwood can be treated with preservative. It has good steam-bending properties.
Common uses: Tool handles, engraving blocks, musical-instrument parts, rulers, inlay, turnery, carving.
Workability: Although it is a hard wood to work, sharp tools cut it very cleanly. It glues readily.
Finishing: It accepts stains well, and polishes to a fine finish.
Average dried weight: 930kg/m³ (58lb/ft³).

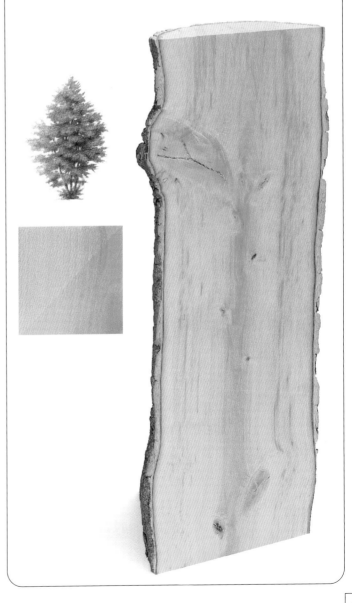

SILKY OAK

Cardwellia sublimis

Other names: Bull oak, Australian silky oak (UK); Northern silky oak (Australia).

Sources: Australia.

Characteristics of the tree: It reaches a height of about 36m (120ft) and has a straight trunk, up to 1.2m (4ft) in diameter.

Characteristics of the wood: The coarse even-textured wood is reddish brown in colour, with straight grain and large rays. It is moderately durable for exterior use; and is good for steam-bending, despite its moderate strength. Although a similar colour to American red oak (Quercus rubra), it is not a true oak.

Common uses: Building construction, interior joinery, furniture, flooring, veneer.

Workability: It works well with handtools and machine tools. Care must be taken not to tear the ray cells when planing. It glues well.

Finishing: The wood accepts stains well and can be polished to a satisfactory finish.

Average dried weight: 550kg/m³ (34lb/ft³).

PECAN/HICKORY

Carya illinoensis

Other names: Sweet pecan.

Sources: USA.

Characteristics of the tree: This tree, which bears edible nuts, can reach a height of 30m (100ft) and a diameter of 1m (3ft 3in).

Characteristics of the wood: When cut, pecan and hickory look so similar that suppliers often mix the two. The dense, tough, coarse-textured wood is similar in appearance to ash (Fraxinus spp.), with white sapwood and reddish-brown heartwood. It is shock-resistant but not durable, and is excellent for steam-bending. The grain, although usually straight, can be irregular or wavy. The growth rings are porous.

Common uses: Chairs and bentwood furniture, sports equipment, striking-tool handles, drumsticks.

Workability: If the tree has been grown fast, the dense wood will quickly dull cutting edges of handtools and machine tools, making it difficult to work. It glues satisfactorily.

Finishing: It can be stained and polished well, despite its porosity.

Average dried weight: 750kg/m³ (46lb/ft³).

SWEET CHESTNUT

Castanea sativa

Other names: Spanish chestnut, European chestnut.

Sources: Europe, Asia Minor.

Characteristics of the tree: This largish tree, which bears edible nuts, can reach a height of more than 30m (100ft) and produces a straight trunk about 1.8m (6ft) in diameter and 6m (20ft) long.

Characteristics of the wood: The durable coarse-textured wood is yellow-brown in colour and has straight or spiral grain. When plain-sawn, the colour and texture resemble oak (Quercus spp.). Like oak and American chestnut (Castanea dentata), the wood can corrode ferrous metals and become stained in contact with them.

Common uses: Furniture, turnery, coffins, poles, stakes.

Workability: It is easy to work with handtools and machine tools, and the coarse texture can be brought to a smooth finish. It glues well.

Finishing: It accepts stains well, and can be varnished and polished to an excellent finish.

Average dried weight: 560kg/m³ (35lb/ft³).

BLACKBEAN

Castanospermum australe

Other names: Moreton Bay bean, Moreton Bay chestnut, beantree.

Sources: Eastern Australia.

Characteristics of the tree: This tall tree is found in moist forest regions from New South Wales to Queensland. It can reach about 40m (130ft) in height and 1m (3ft 3in) in diameter.

Characteristics of the wood: The hard, heavy wood is rich brown streaked with grey-brown. Generally straight-grained, although interlocking grain is not uncommon, it has a rather coarse texture and an attractive figure. The heartwood is durable and resistant to treatment with preservatives.

Common uses: Furniture, turnery, joinery, carving, decorative veneers.

Workability: Softer patches of this hard wood can crumble if cutting edges are not kept sharp, so it is not particularly easy to work with handtools or machine tools. In general, it glues reasonably well.

Finishing: It accepts stains well, and can be polished to a fine finish.

Average dried weight: 720kg/m³ (45lb/ft³).

SATINWOOD

Chloroxylon swietenia

Other names: East Indian satinwood.

Sources: Central and Southern India, Sri Lanka.

Characteristics of the tree: This smallish tree reaches about 15m (50ft) in height, with a straight trunk about 300mm (1ft) in diameter.

Characteristics of the wood: The lustrous, durable wood is light yellow to golden brown in colour, with a fine even texture and inter-locked grain that produces a striped figure. It is heavy, hard and strong.

Common uses: Interior joinery, furniture, veneer, inlay, turnery.

Workability: It is a moderately difficult wood to work with handtools or machine tools, and to glue.

Finishing: If care is taken, it can be brought to a smooth surface and polished to a fine finish.

Average dried weight: 990kg/m³ (61lb/ft³).

KINGWOOD

Dalbergia cearensis

Other names: Violet wood, violetta (USA); bois violet (France); violete (Brazil).

Sources: South America.

Characteristics of the tree: This small tree, botanically related to rosewood, produces short logs or billets of wood up to 2.5m (8ft) long; with the white sapwood removed, the diameter of the billets is between 75 and 200mm (3 and 8in).

Characteristics of the wood: This fine even-textured and durable wood is usually straight-grained. The dark, lustrous heartwood has a variegated figure, striped violet-brown, black and golden-yellow.

Common uses: Turnery, inlay, marquetry.

Workability: If cutting edges are kept sharp, it is an easy wood to work. It glues satisfactorily.

Finishing: It can be burnished to a fine finish, and can be polished well with wax.

Average dried weight: 1200kg/m³ (75lb/ft³).

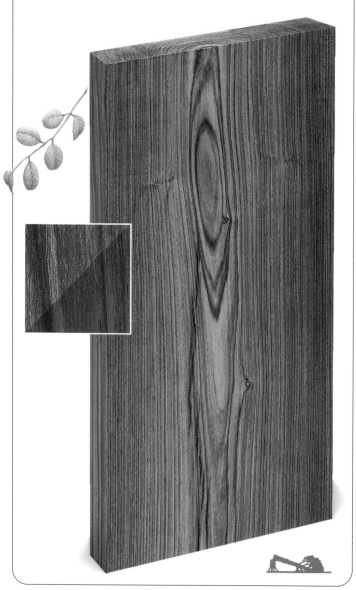

SONOKELING
ROSEWOOD

Dalbergia latifolia

Other names: Indian rosewood.

Sources: Indonesia

Characteristics of the tree: This tree can reach 24m (80ft) in height, with a straight, clear, cylindrical trunk up to 1.5m (5ft) in diameter.

Characteristics of the wood: The durable wood, which is hard and heavy, has a moderately coarse uniform texture. The colour is a golden to purple brown, streaked with black or dark purple. Narrow bands of interlocked grain produce a subtle ribbon figure.

Common uses: Furniture, musical instruments, turnery, veneer.

Workability: It is moderately difficult to work using handtools, but machines well. It glues satisfactorily.

Finishing: Although the grain requires filling in order to achieve a high polish, it can be finished well with wax.

Average dried weight: 870kg/m³ (54lb/ft³).

COCOBOLO

Dalbergia retusa

Other names: Granadillo (Mexico).

Sources: West coast of Central America.

Characteristics of the tree: A medium-size tree, reaching a height of 30m (100ft), with a fluted trunk up to 1m (3ft 3in) in diameter.

Characteristics of the wood: The durable, irregular-grained wood is hard and heavy, with a uniform medium-fine texture. The heartwood has a variegated colour, ranging from purple-red to yellow, with black markings; on exposure, the colour turns to a deep orange-red.

Common uses: Turnery, brush backs, cutlery handles, veneer.

Workability: Although hard, it can be worked readily with handtools and machine tools, as long as the cutting edges are kept sharp. The oily nature of the wood means it can be machined to a fine, smooth surface. It is difficult to glue.

Finishing: It can be stained and polished to a fine finish.

Average dried weight: 1100kg/m³ (68lb/ft³).

EBONY

Diospyros ebenum

Other names: Tendo, tuki, ebans.
Sources: Sri Lanka, India.
Characteristics of the tree: This tree grows up to 30m (100ft) in height, with a straight trunk about 4.5m (15ft) in length and 750mm (2ft 6in) in diameter.
Characteristics of the wood: The hard, heavy, dense wood can have straight, irregular or wavy grain and has a fine even texture. The durable, lustrous heartwood is the familiar dark brown to black colour, whereas the sapwood is non-durable and is yellowish white.
Common uses: Turnery, musical instruments, inlay.
Workability: Other than on a lathe, it is a difficult wood to work, because it tends to chip cutting edges and dulls them quickly. It does not glue well.
Finishing: It can be polished to an excellent finish.
Average dried weight: 1190kg/m³ (74lb/ft³).

JELUTONG

Dyera costulata

Other names: Jelutong bukit, jelutong paya (Sarawak).
Sources: Southeast Asia.
Characteristics of the tree: This large tree can reach a height of 60m (200ft), with a long straight trunk as much as 27m (90ft) high and 2.5m (8ft) in diameter.
Characteristics of the wood: The soft straight-grained wood has a lustrous fine even texture and a plainish figure; it is not durable. There are usually latex ducts. Both the sapwood and heartwood are a creamy pale-brown colour.
Common uses: Interior joinery, pattern-making, matches, plywood.
Workability: It can be worked easily and brought to a smooth finish with handtools and machine tools, and is easy to carve. It glues well.
Finishing: It accepts stains and varnishes well, and can be polished to a fine finish.
Average dried weight: 470kg/m³ (29lb/ft³).

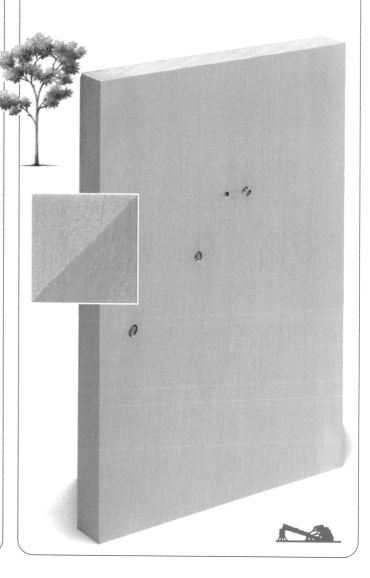

QUEENSLAND WALNUT

Endiandra palmerstonii

Other names: Australian walnut, walnut bean, oriental wood.

Sources: Australia.

Characteristics of the tree: This tall tree can reach a height of 42m (140ft). The long buttressed trunk is about 1.5m (5ft) in diameter.

Characteristics of the wood: Although the non-durable wood looks similar to that of the European walnut (Juglans regia), it is not a true walnut. The colour can vary from light to dark brown, streaked with pink and dark grey; the interlocked wavy grain produces an attractive figure. The ray cells often contain silica.

Common uses: Furniture, interior joinery, shop fittings, flooring, decorative veneer.

Workability: It is a difficult wood to work with handtools or machine tools, due to its dulling effect on cutting edges, but it can be brought to a smooth natural finish and glues satisfactorily.

Finishing: It polishes to a fine finish.

Average dried weight: 690kg/m³ (43lb/ft³).

UTILE

Etandrophragma utile

Other names: Sipo (Ivory Coast); assié (Cameroon).

Sources: Africa.

Characteristics of the tree: It is a tall tree, about 45m (150ft) in height, with a straight cylindrical trunk about 2m (6ft 6in) in diameter.

Characteristics of the wood: This moderately strong, durable wood with a medium texture is pinkish brown when freshly cut, deepening with exposure to reddish brown. The interlocked grain produces a ribbon-stripe figure when quarter-sawn.

Common uses: Interior and exterior joinery, boatbuilding, furniture, flooring, plywood, veneer.

Workability: If care is taken not to tear the ribbon-stripe figure when planing, the wood can be worked well with handtools and machine tools. It glues well.

Finishing: It accepts stains and polishes well.

Average dried weight: 660kg/m³ (41lb/ft³).

JARRAH

Eucalyptus marginata

Other names: None.
Sources: Western Australia.
Characteristics of the tree: This tall tree can reach a height of 45m (150ft), with a long, clear trunk about 1.5m (5ft) in diameter.
Characteristics of the wood: The very durable wood is strong, hard and heavy, with an even medium-coarse texture. The narrow sapwood is a yellowish-white colour; the heartwood, light to dark red when first cut, deepens to red-brown. The grain is usually straight, but can be wavy or interlocking; the figure displays fine brown decorative flecks (caused by the fungus Fistulina hepatica) and occasional gum veins.
Common uses: Building and marine construction, exterior and interior joinery, furniture, turnery, decorative veneers.
Workability: Although moderately difficult to work, with either handtools or machine tools, it is good for turning. It glues well.
Finishing: It polishes very well, particularly with an oil finish.
Average dried weight: 820kg/m³ (51lb/ft³).

AMERICAN BEECH

Fagus grandifolia

Other names: None.
Sources: Canada, USA.
Characteristics of the tree: This relatively small tree reaches an average height of 15m (50ft), with a trunk about 500mm (1ft 8in) in diameter.
Characteristics of the wood: Slightly coarser and heavier than European beech (Fagus sylvatica), the straight-grained wood has similar strength and good steam-bending properties. It is light brown to reddish brown in colour, with a fine even texture. Although it is perishable on exposure to moisture, it can be treated successfully with preservative.
Common uses: Cabinet-making, interior joinery, turnery, bentwood furniture.
Workability: It can be worked well with handtools and machine tools, though it has a propensity to scorch on crosscutting and drilling. It glues well.
Finishing: It accepts stain well, and can be polished to a fine finish.
Average dried weight: 740kg/m³ (46lb/ft³).

EUROPEAN BEECH

Fagus sylvatica

Other names: English, French, Danish beech etc., according to origin.
Sources: Europe.
Characteristics of the tree: This large tree can reach a height of 45m (150ft), with a clear straight trunk about 1.2m (4ft) in diameter.
Characteristics of the wood: Whitish brown when first cut, the fine even-textured straight-grained wood deepens to yellowish brown on exposure; 'steamed beech', which has been steamed as part of the seasoning process, is a reddish brown. It is a strong wood, excellent for steam-bending, and when seasoned is tougher than oak. Although perishable, it can be treated with preservative.
Common uses: Interior joinery, cabinet-making, turnery, bentwood furniture, plywood, veneer.
Workability: It works readily with handtools and machine tools, but ease of working depends on the quality and seasoning. It glues well.
Finishing: It accepts stains well, and can be polished to a fine finish.
Average dried weight: 720kg/m³ (45lb/ft³).

AMERICAN WHITE ASH

Fraxinus americana

Other names: Canadian ash (UK); white ash (USA).
Sources: Canada, USA.
Characteristics of the tree: Grows to about 18m (60ft) in height, with a trunk about 750mm (2ft 6in) in diameter.
Characteristics of the wood: The strong shock-resistant wood is ring-porous, with a distinct figure. It has coarse generally straight grain, with almost-white sapwood and pale-brown heartwood. Although non-durable, treatment with preservative allows exterior use. It is a good wood for steam-bending.
Common uses: Joinery, boatbuilding, sports equipment, tool handles, plywood, veneer.
Workability: It works well with handtools and machine tools, and can be brought to a fine surface finish. It glues well.
Finishing: It accepts stains well and is often finished in black; it can be polished to a fine finish.
Average dried weight: 670kg/m³ (42lb/ft³).

EUROPEAN ASH

Fraxinus excelsior

Other names: English, French, Polish ash etc., according to origin.
Sources: Europe.
Characteristics of the tree: A medium-size to large tree, it has an average height of 30m (100ft), with a trunk 500mm to 1.5m (1ft 8in to 5ft) in diameter.
Characteristics of the wood: This tough coarse-textured straight-grained wood is flexible, relatively split-resistant and shock-resistant, and excellent for steam-bending. The wood is perishable, and only suitable for exterior use when it has been treated with preservative. Both sapwood and heartwood are normally whitish to pale brown. 'Olive ash' is produced from logs with dark-stained heartwood; pale, strong 'sports ash' is in high demand.
Common uses: Sports equipment and tool handles, cabinet-making, bentwood furniture, boatbuilding, vehicle bodies, ladder rungs, laminated work, plywood, decorative veneer.
Workability: It can be worked well with handtools and machine tools, and can be brought to a fine surface finish. It glues well.
Finishing: It accepts stains well, and can be polished to a fine finish.
Average dried weight: 710kg/m³ (44lb/ft³).

RAMIN

Gonystylus macrophyllum

Other names: Melawis (Malaysia); ramin telur (Sarawak).
Sources: Southeast Asia.
Characteristics of the tree: It reaches a height of about 24m (80ft) and has a long, straight trunk about 600mm (2ft) in diameter.
Characteristics of the wood: The moderately fine even-textured wood is usually straight-grained, but sometimes the grain is slightly interlocked. Both sapwood and heartwood are a pale cream-brown colour. The wood is perishable, and not suited to exterior use.
Common uses: Interior joinery, flooring, furniture, toy-making, turnery, carving, veneer.
Workability: It can be worked reasonably well with both handtools and machine tools, but care must be taken to keep cutting edges sharp. It glues well.
Finishing: It accepts stains, paints and varnishes well, and can be polished to a satisfactory finish.
Average dried weight: 670kg/m³ (41lb/ft³).

LIGNUM VITAE

Guaiacum officinale

Other names: Ironwood (USA); bois de gaiac (France); guayacan (Spain); pala santo, guayacan negro (Cuba).

Sources: West Indies, tropical America.

Characteristics of the tree: This small, slow-growing tree attains a height of 9m (30ft), with a diameter of about 500mm (1ft 8in). The wood is sold in short billets.

Characteristics of the wood: The fine uniform-textured wood with closely interlocked grain is one of the hardest and heaviest commercial timbers. Very durable and resinous, with an oily feel, it is much in demand for its hardness and self-lubricating properties. The narrow sapwood is cream-coloured, the heartwood dark greenish brown to black.

Common uses: Bearings and pulleys, mallets, turnery.

Workability: It is very difficult to saw and work with handtools or machine tools, but can be brought to a fine finish on a lathe. An oil solvent must be used for it to glue well.

Finishing: It can be burnished to a fine natural finish.

Average dried weight: 1250kg/m³ (78lb/ft³).

Lignum vitae is listed in Appendix III in CITES.

BUBINGA

Guibourtia demeusei

Other names: African rosewood; kevazingo (Gabon); essingang (Cameroon).

Sources: Cameroon, Gabon, Zaire.

Characteristics of the tree: It grows to about 30m (100ft) in height, with a long straight trunk about 1m (3ft 3in) in diameter.

Characteristics of the wood: The hard, heavy wood has a moderately coarse even texture. Although not resilient, it is reasonably strong and durable. The grain can be straight or interlocked and irregular; the heartwood is red-brown, with red and purple veining.

Common uses: Furniture, woodware, turnery, decorative veneer (known as kevazingo when rotary cut).

Workability: Although it can be worked well with handtools and machined to a fine finish, cutting edges must be kept sharp. Gum pockets in the wood can cause problems when gluing.

Finishing: It accepts stains well, and can be polished to a fine finish.

Average dried weight: 880kg/m³ (55lb/ft³).

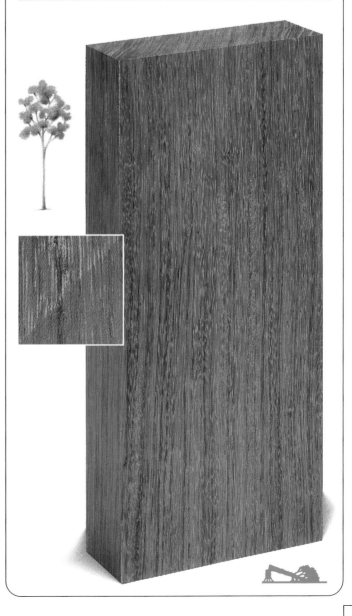

BRAZILWOOD

Guilandina echinata

Other names: Pernambuco wood, bahia wood, para wood.
Sources: Brazil.
Characteristics of the tree: This small to medium-size tree produces short billets or lengths up to 200mm (8in) in diameter.
Characteristics of the wood: The heavy, hard wood is tough, resilient and very durable, with generally straight grain and a fine even texture. The sapwood is pale, in contrast to the heartwood, which is a bright, lustrous orange-red that turns to a rich red-brown on exposure.
Common uses: Dyewood, violin bows, exterior joinery, parquet flooring, turnery, gun stocks, veneer.
Workability: It can be worked reasonably well with handtools and machine tools, as long as cutting edges are kept sharp. It glues well.
Finishing: The surface can be polished to an exceptionally fine finish.
Average dried weight: 1280kg/m³ (80lb/ft³).

BUTTERNUT

Juglans cinerea

Other names: White walnut.
Sources: Canada, USA.
Characteristics of the tree: This is a relatively small tree, reaching a height of about 15m (50ft), with a trunk up to 750mm (2ft 6in) in diameter.
Characteristics of the wood: The coarse-textured straight-grained wood is relatively soft and weak, and is not durable. The figure resembles that of black American walnut (Juglans nigra), but the medium-brown to dark-brown heartwood is lighter in colour.
Common uses: Furniture, interior joinery, carving, veneer, boxes, crates.
Workability: If cutting edges are kept sharp, it can be worked easily with handtools and machine tools. It glues well.
Finishing: It accepts stains well, and can be polished to a fine finish.
Average dried weight: 450kg/m³ (28lb/ft³).

AMERICAN
BLACK WALNUT

Juglans nigra

Other names: American walnut.

Sources: USA, Canada.

Characteristics of the tree: It grows to a height of about 30m (100ft), with a trunk about 1.5m (5ft) in diameter.

Characteristics of the wood: The tough moderately durable wood has an even but coarse texture; the grain is usually straight, but can be wavy. Light-coloured sapwood contrasts with rich, dark purplish brown heartwood. It is a good wood for steam-bending.

Common uses: Furniture, musical instruments, interior joinery, gun stocks, turnery, carving, plywood, veneer.

Workability: It can be worked well with handtools and machine tools. It glues well.

Finishing: It can be polished to a fine finish.

Average dried weight: 660kg/m³ (41lb/ft³).

EUROPEAN WALNUT

Juglans regia

Other names: English, French, Italian walnut etc., according to origin.

Sources: Europe, Asia Minor, Southwest Asia

Characteristics of the tree: This nut-bearing tree reaches a height of about 30m (100ft). The average trunk diameter is 1m (3ft 3in).

Characteristics of the wood: The moderately durable wood has a rather coarse texture, with straight to wavy grain. It is typically grey-brown with darker streaks, although this can vary according to origin. The wood is reasonably tough, and good for steam-bending. Italian walnut is considered to have the best colour and figure.

Common uses: Furniture, interior joinery, gun stocks, turnery, carving, veneer.

Workability: It can be worked well with handtools and machine tools, and glues satisfactorily.

Finishing: It can be polished to a fine finish.

Average dried weight: 670kg/m³ (42lb/ft³).

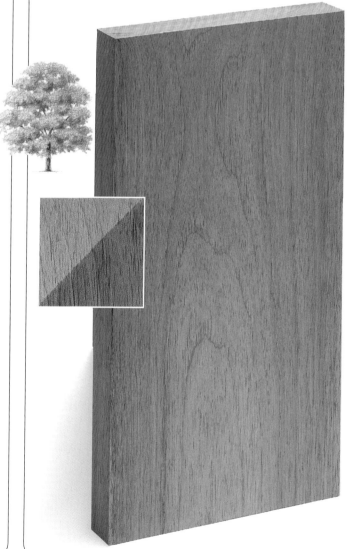

TULIPWOOD

Liriodendron tulipifera

Other names: Canary whitewood (UK); yellow poplar, American poplar (USA).

Sources: Eastern USA, Canada.

Characteristics of the tree: It reaches a height of about 37m (125ft), and has an average diameter of 2m (6ft 6in).

Characteristics of the wood: The fine-textured straight-grained wood is quite soft and lightweight. It is not durable, and should not be used in contact with the ground. The narrow sapwood is white; the heartwood ranges from pale olive-green to brown, streaked with blue.

Common uses: Light construction, interior joinery, toy-making, furniture, carving, plywood, veneer.

Workability: It can be worked easily with handtools and machine tools, and glues well.

Finishing: It accepts stains, paint and varnish well, and can be polished to a good finish.

Average dried weight: 510kg/m³ (31lb/ft³).

BALSA

Ochroma lagopus

Other names: Guano (Puerto Rico, Honduras); topa (Peru); lanero (Cuba); tami (Bolivia); polak (Belize, Nicaragua).

Sources: South America, Central America, West Indies.

Characteristics of the tree: This fast-growing tree reaches a height of about 21m (70ft) in six to seven years, with a diameter of about 600mm (2ft); the growth rate then declines. It reaches maturity in 12 to 15 years.

Characteristics of the wood: The lustrous open-textured straight-grained wood is the lightest commercial hardwood. It is graded on its density, fast-grown wood being lighter in weight than the denser, harder wood produced by older, slower-growing trees. The colour is pale beige to pinkish.

Common uses: Insulation, buoyancy aids, model-making, packaging for delicate items.

Workability: If cutting edges are kept sharp to avoid crumbling or tearing, it can be worked and sanded easily with handtools and machine tools. It glues well.

Finishing: It can be stained, painted and polished satisfactorily.

Average dried weight: 160kg/m³ (10lb/ft³).

PURPLEHEART

Peltogyne spp.

Other names: Amaranth (USA); pau roxo, amarante (Brazil); purplehart (Surinam); saka, koroboreli, sakavalli (Guyana).

Sources: Central America, South America.

Characteristics of the tree: This tall tree can reach a height of 50m (165ft), with a long, straight trunk about 1m (3ft 3in) in diameter.

Characteristics of the wood: The wood is durable, strong and resilient. It has a uniform fine to medium texture; the grain is usually straight, but can be irregular. When first cut, the wood is a purple colour – which in time darkens, through oxidation, to rich brown.

Common uses: Building construction, boatbuilding, furniture, turnery, flooring, veneer.

Workability: It can be worked well, although cutting edges must be kept sharp, as dull edges bring gummy resin to the surface. It is a good wood for turning, and glues well.

Finishing: It accepts stains well and can be wax-polished – but polishes with a methylated-spirit (alcohol) base may affect the colour.

Average dried weight: 880kg/m³ (55lb/ft³).

AFRORMOSIA

Pericopsis elata

Other names: Assemela (Ivory Coast, France); kokrodua (Ghana, Ivory Coast); ayin, egbi (Nigeria).

Sources: West Africa.

Characteristics of the tree: A relatively tall, long-trunked tree, it reaches a height of about 45m (150ft), with a diameter of about 1m (3ft 3in).

Characteristics of the wood: The yellow-brown heartwood of this durable wood darkens to the colour of teak (Tectona grandis). However, the straight to interlocked grain has a finer texture than teak, and the wood is stronger and less oily. In moist conditions, it may react with ferrous metals and develop black stains.

Common uses: Veneer, interior and exterior joinery and furniture, building construction, boatbuilding.

Workability: If care is taken with interlocked grain, it saws well and can be planed smooth. It glues well.

Finishing: It can be polished to a fine finish.

Average dried weight: 710kg/m³ (44lb/ft³).

Afrormosia is listed in Appendix II in CITES.

EUROPEAN PLANE

Platanus acerifolia

Other names: London, English, French plane etc., according to origin.
Sources: Europe.
Characteristics of the tree: Easily identified by its flaking mottled bark, this tree is often found in cities because of its tolerance of pollution. It grows to a height of about 30m (100ft), and produces a trunk about 1m (3ft 3in) in diameter.
Characteristics of the wood: The straight-grained fine to medium-textured wood is perishable and not suitable for exterior use. The light reddish-brown heartwood has distinct darker rays; when quarter-sawn, these produce a fleck figure known as 'lacewood'. Similar to, but darker than, American sycamore, it is a good wood for steam-bending.
Common uses: Joinery, furniture, turnery, veneer.
Workability: It can be worked well with handtools and machine tools, and glues well.
Finishing: It accepts stains and polishes satisfactorily.
Average dried weight: 640kg/m³ (40lb/ft³).

AMERICAN SYCAMORE

Platanus occidentalis

Other names: Buttonwood (USA); American plane (UK).
Sources: USA.
Characteristics of the tree: This large tree can grow to 53m (175ft) in height and 6m (20ft) in diameter.
Characteristics of the wood: The fine even-textured pale-brown wood is perishable and not suitable for exterior use. It is usually straight-grained, and distinct darker rays produce lacewood when quarter-sawn. Botanically it is a plane tree, but the wood is lighter in weight than European plane (see left).
Common uses: Joinery, doors, furniture, panelling, veneer.
Workability: The wood works well with handtools and power tools, and glues well. When planing, keep cutters sharp.
Finishing: It accepts stains and polishes satisfactorily.
Average dried weight: 560kg/m³ (35lb/ft³).

AMERICAN
BLACK CHERRY

Prunus serotina

Other names: Cabinet cherry (Canada).
Sources: Canada, USA.
Characteristics of the tree: This medium-size tree reaches a height of 21m (70ft), with a trunk about 500mm (1ft 8in) in diameter.
Characteristics of the wood: The durable wood has straight grain and a fine texture; it is hard and moderately strong, and can be steam-bent. The narrow sapwood is a pinkish colour, while the heartwood is reddish-brown to deep red, with brown flecks and some gum pockets.
Common uses: Furniture, pattern-making, joinery, turnery, musical instruments, tobacco pipes, veneers.
Workability: It can be worked well with handtools and machine tools, and glues well.
Finishing: It accepts stains well, and can be polished to a fine finish.
Average dried weight: 580kg/m³ (36lb/ft³).

AFRICAN PADAUK

Pterocarpus soyauxii

Other names: Camwood, barwood.
Sources: West Africa.
Characteristics of the tree: It grows to a height of 30m (100ft). The diameter of the trunk above the buttresses can reach 1m (3ft 3in).
Characteristics of the wood: The hard, heavy wood has straight to interlocked grain and a moderately coarse texture. The pale-beige sapwood can be 200mm (8in) thick; the very durable heartwood is rich red to purple-brown, streaked with red.
Common uses: Interior joinery, furniture, flooring, turnery, handles. Also used as a dyewood.
Workability: It can be worked well with handtools, and machined to a fine finish. It glues well.
Finishing: It can be polished to a fine finish.
Average dried weight: 710kg/m³ (44lb/ft³).

AMERICAN
WHITE OAK

Quercus alba

Other names: White oak (USA).

Sources: USA, Canada.

Characteristics of the tree: In good growing conditions, it can reach a height of 30m (100ft) and a diameter of about 1m (3ft 3in).

Characteristics of the wood: The straight-grained wood is similar in appearance to European oak (Quercus robur), but it is more varied in colour, ranging from pale yellow-brown to pale brown, sometimes with a pinkish tint. The texture is medium-coarse to coarse, depending on growing conditions. The wood has good steam-bending properties, and is reasonably durable for exterior use.

Common uses: Building construction, interior joinery, furniture, flooring, plywood, veneer.

Workability: It can be readily worked with handtools and machine tools, and glues satisfactorily.

Finishing: It accepts stains well, and can be polished to a good finish.

Average dried weight: 770kg/m³ (48lb/ft³).

JAPANESE OAK

Quercus mongolica

Other names: Ohnara.

Sources: Japan.

Characteristics of the tree: It grows to a height of about 30m (100ft). The straight trunk reaches a diameter of about 1m (3ft 3in).

Characteristics of the wood: The coarse texture of this straight-grained wood is milder than that of the European and American white oaks due to its slower, more even rate of growth. The colour is a light yellowish brown throughout. It is a good wood for steam-bending, and is generally knot-free. The heartwood is moderately durable for exterior use.

Common uses: Interior and exterior joinery, boatbuilding, furniture, panelling, flooring, veneer.

Workability: Compared to other white oaks, it is easy to work well with handtools and machine tools. It glues well.

Finishing: It accepts stains, and can be polished very well.

Average dried weight: 670kg/m³ (41lb/ft³).

EUROPEAN OAK

Quercus robur/Q. petraea

Other names: French, Polish oak etc., according to origin.

Sources: Europe, Asia Minor, North Africa.

Characteristics of the tree: It can grow to above 30m (100ft) in height, with a trunk up to 2m (6ft 6in) in diameter.

Characteristics of the wood: The coarse-textured wood has straight grain, distinct growth rings, and broad rays that show an attractive figure when quarter-sawn. The sapwood is much paler than the pale yellowish-brown of the heartwood. A tough, durable wood that is good for steam-bending, it is acidic and causes metals to corrode. Oaks grown in Central Europe tend to be lighter and less strong than those from Western Europe.

Common uses: Joinery and external woodwork, furniture, flooring, boatbuilding, carving, veneer.

Workability: If sharp cutting edges are maintained, it can be worked readily with handtools and machine tools. It glues well.

Finishing: Liming, staining and fuming are all possible, and it can be polished to a good finish.

Average dried weight: 720kg/m³ (45lb/ft³).

AMERICAN RED OAK

Quercus rubra

Other names: Northern red oak.

Sources: Canada, USA.

Characteristics of the tree: Depending on the growing conditions, it can reach a height of 21m (70ft) and a diameter of 1m (3ft 3in).

Characteristics of the wood: The non-durable wood has straight grain and a coarse texture, though this can vary according to the rate of growth – northern wood is not as coarse as the faster-grown wood from the southern states. Its pale yellowish-brown colour is similar to that of the white oaks, but with a pinkish-red hue. It is good for steam-bending.

Common uses: Interior joinery and flooring, furniture, plywood, decorative veneer.

Workability: It can be worked readily with handtools and machine tools, and glues satisfactorily.

Finishing: It accepts stains well, and can be polished to a good finish.

Average dried weight: 790kg/m³ (49lb/ft³).

RED LAUAN

Shorea negrosensis

Other names: None.
Sources: Philippines.
Characteristics of the tree: This large tree can reach a height of 50m (165ft), with a long, straight trunk, about 2m (6ft 6in) in diameter, above the buttresses.
Characteristics of the wood: The wood is moderately durable, with interlocked grain and a relatively coarse texture. An attractive ribbon-grain figure is shown on quarter-sawn boards. The sapwood is a light creamy colour, while the heartwood is medium to dark red.
Common uses: Interior joinery, furniture, boatbuilding, veneer, boxes.
Workability: It can be worked easily with handtools and machine tools, but care must be taken not to tear the surface of the wood when planing. It glues well.
Finishing: It accepts stains well, and can be varnished and polished to a good finish.
Average dried weight: 630kg/m³ (39lb/ft³).

BRAZILIAN MAHOGANY

Swietenia macrophylla

Other names: Honduran, Costa Rican, Peruvian mahogany etc.
Sources: Central America, Southern America.
Characteristics of the tree: This large tree can grow to 45m (150ft) in height, and reach about 2m (6ft 6in) in diameter above the heavy trunk buttresses.
Characteristics of the wood: The naturally durable wood has a medium texture, with grain that may be either straight and even or interlocked. The white-yellow sapwood contrasts with the heartwood, which is reddish brown to deep red.
Common uses: Interior panelling, joinery, boat planking, furniture, pianos, carving, decorative veneer.
Workability: It can be worked well with handtools and machine tools, so long as cutting edges are kept sharp. It glues well.
Finishing: It accepts stains very well, and can be polished to a fine finish when the grain is filled.
Average dried weight: 560kg/m³ (35lb/ft³).

Brazilian mahogany is listed in Appendix III in CITES.

TEAK

Tectona grandis

Other names: Kyun, sagwan, teku, teka.

Sources: Southern Asia, Southeast Asia, Africa, Caribbean.

Characteristics of the tree: It can reach 45m (150ft) in height, with a long, straight trunk about 1.5m (5ft) in diameter. The trunk may be fluted and buttressed.

Characteristics of the wood: The strong, very durable wood has a coarse uneven texture with an oily feel. The grain may be straight or wavy. 'Burma' teak (from Myanmar) is a uniform golden brown, while other areas produce a darker, more marked wood. It is a moderately good wood for steam-bending.

Common uses: Interior and exterior joinery, boatbuilding, turnery, exterior furniture, plywood, veneer.

Workability: It can be worked well with handtools and machine tools, but quickly dulls cutting edges. Newly prepared surfaces glue well.

Finishing: It accepts stains, varnishes and polishes, and can be finished well with oil.

Average dried weight: 640kg/m³ (40lb/ft³).

BASSWOOD

Tilia americana

Other names: American lime.

Sources: USA, Canada.

Characteristics of the tree: This medium-size tree averages a height of 20m (65ft) and a diameter of 600mm (2ft). The straight trunk is often free of branches for much of its length.

Characteristics of the wood: The straight-grained wood has a fine even texture. It is not durable, and is lighter in weight than the related European lime (Tilia vulgaris). The soft, weak wood is cream-white when first cut, turning pale brown on exposure, with little contrast between latewood and earlywood.

Common uses: Carving, turnery, joinery, pattern-making, piano keys, drawing boards, plywood.

Workability: It can be easily and cleanly worked with handtools and machine tools, and can be brought to a fine surface finish. It glues well.

Finishing: It accepts stains well, and can be polished to a fine finish.

Average dried weight: 416kg/m³ (26lb/ft³).

LIME

Tilia vulgaris

Other names: Linden (Germany).
Sources: Europe.
Characteristics of the tree: It can reach a height of more than 30m (100ft), with a clear trunk about 1.2m (4ft) in diameter.
Characteristics of the wood: The straight-grained wood has a fine uniform texture. Although soft, it is strong and resists splitting, making it particularly good for carving and turning. It is perishable, but can be treated with preservative. The overall colour is white to pale yellow, darkening to light brown with exposure. The sapwood and heartwood are not distinct.
Common uses: Carving, turnery, toy-making, broom handles, hat blocks, harps, piano soundboards and keys.
Workability: It is an easy wood to work with handtools and machine tools, as long as cutting edges are kept sharp. It glues well.
Finishing: It accepts stains well, and can be polished to a fine finish.
Average dried weight: 560kg/m³ (35lb/ft³).

OBECHE

Triplochiton scleroxylon

Other names: Ayous (Cameroon); wawa (Ghana); obechi, arere (Nigeria); samba, wawa (Ivory Coast).
Sources: West Africa.
Characteristics of the tree: This large tree can grow to more than 45m (150ft) in height, with a trunk about 1.5m (5ft) in diameter above heavy buttresses.
Characteristics of the wood: The fine even-textured wood is lightweight and not durable. The grain may be straight or interlocked. There is little contrast between the sapwood and heartwood, both of which are cream-white to pale yellow in colour.
Common uses: Interior joinery, furniture, drawer linings, plywood, model-making.
Workability: If cutting edges are kept sharp, the soft wood is easy to work with handtools and machine tools. It glues well.
Finishes: It accepts stains, and polishes well.
Average dried weight: 390kg/m³ (24lb/ft³).

AMERICAN ELM

Ulmus americana

Other names: Water elm, swamp elm, soft elm (USA); orhamwood (Canada).

Sources: Canada, USA.

Characteristics of the tree: This medium to large tree usually reaches a height of 27m (90ft), with a trunk 500mm (1ft 8in) in diameter; but good growing conditions can produce larger trees.

Characteristics of the wood: The coarse-textured wood is not durable. It is strong – tougher than the European elms – and, like them, good for steam-bending. The grain is usually straight, but can be interlocked. The heartwood is a pale reddish brown.

Common uses: Boatbuilding, agricultural implements, cooperage, furniture, veneer.

Workability: Sharp cutting edges enable it to be readily worked with handtools and machine tools. It glues satisfactorily.

Finishing: It accepts stains, and polishes satisfactorily.

Average dried weight: 580kg/m³ (36lb/ft³).

DUTCH AND ENGLISH ELM

Ulmus hollandica/U. procera

Other names: English elm: Red elm. Dutch elm: Cork bark elm.

Sources: Europe.

Characteristics of the tree: This relatively large tree can reach 45m (150ft) in height and up to 2.5m (8ft) in diameter. However, elms are usually cut when they reach a diameter of about 1m (3ft 3in).

Characteristics of the wood: The coarse-textured wood has beige-brown heartwood and distinct irregular growth rings, with an attractive figure when plain-sawn. It is not durable. The Dutch elm is tougher than the English, with more-even growth and straighter grain, making it better for steam-bending. Dutch elm disease has led to short supplies of the wood.

Common uses: Cabinet-making, Windsor-chair seats and backs, boat-building, turnery, veneer.

Workability: Wood with irregular grain can be difficult to work (especially when planing), but it can be brought to a smooth surface finish. It glues well.

Finishing: It accepts stains and polishes well, and is particularly suited to a wax finish.

Average dried weight: 560kg/m³ (35lb/ft³).

WOOD VENEERS

Veneers are very thin sheets or 'leaves' of wood that are cut from a log for constructional or decorative purposes. Whether selected for their natural colour and figure or worked into formal patterns, veneers bring a unique quality to furniture and woodware. With the widespread use of stable man-made boards for groundwork and the development of modern adhesives, today's veneered products are superior to solid wood for certain applications.

VENEER PRODUCTION

Highly sophisticated production techniques are used to satisfy the growing demand for veneer. Every stage in the manufacture of veneer requires specialist knowledge.

Choosing logs

The process starts with the log buyer, who must have the skill and experience to assess the condition and commercial viability for veneer within a log, basing this solely on an external examination. By looking at the end of the log, the buyer has to determine the quality of the wood, the potential figure of the veneer, the colour, and the ratio of sapwood to heartwood. Other factors – such as the presence and extent of staining and weaknesses or defects in the form of shakes, ingrown bark, excessive knots or resin ducts – will also affect the value or suitability of the log and must be taken into consideration.

Much of this information will be revealed by the first cut through the length of the log – but the log must be purchased before this first cut can be made.

Treating logs

Before they are converted into veneer, logs are softened, either by immersion in hot water or by being steamed. Depending on the cutting method, the log may be treated whole or it may first be cut into flitches by a huge bandsaw.

The time taken for this softening is controlled by the type and hardness of the wood and the thickness of the veneer to be cut. The process can take days or weeks.

Some pale woods, such as maple and sycamore, are not pretreated because the softening process would discolour the veneer.

Cutting veneer

Another skilled production expert is the veneer cutter, who decides the best way to convert the log so that it will provide the maximum number of high-quality leaves.

Most veneer logs are cut from the main stem of the tree between the root butt and the first branch. The bark is removed and the log is checked for foreign matter, such as nails or wire.

As soon as decorative veneers are cut, they are taken from the slicer and stacked in sequence. This stack, or set, then passes through a machine-drying process before being graded.

Although most species are clipped on a guillotine to trim them to regular shapes and sizes, others, such as yew or burr veneer, are kept as when cut from the log.

Grading decorative veneer

Veneers are inspected for natural or milling defects, thickness, colour and type of figure, then graded and priced according to their size and quality. The veneers from a log may vary in value: the better or wider ones, graded as

Veneer production
It is possible to produce continuous sheets of peeled-and-dried veneer.

face quality, have a higher value than the narrower or poorer backing quality (also known as balancing veneer). The veneers are kept in multiples of four for matching purposes and bound into bundles of 16, 24, 28 or 32 leaves. The bundles are then stacked in the order they were sliced from the log, and stored in a cool warehouse, ready for sale.

CUTTING METHODS

The three basic methods for cutting veneer are saw cutting, rotary cutting and flat slicing. There are also variations on rotary cutting and flat slicing.

Saw cutting

Until the development of veneer-slicing machines, all veneers were cut using saws: first by hand, then later with powered circular saws. The veneers thus cut were relatively thick, around 3mm ($^1/_{16}$in).

Sawn veneers are still produced, using huge circular saws, but only for very hard woods such as lignum vitae and irregular-grained timber such as curls, or where sawing is the most economical method (despite generally being a wasteful process). These veneers are approximately 1mm ($^1/_{25}$in) thick.

A workshop bandsaw or table saw is sometimes used to produce strips of veneer for laminating purposes, particularly if this is likely to be more economical or will provide better matched material than is commercially available.

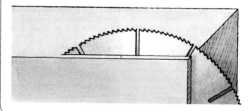

Rotary cutting

Although mostly used for making constructional veneers from softwood and some hardwoods, the rotary-cutting method is also used to produce decorative veneers such as bird's-eye maple.

A complete log is mounted on a huge lathe, which peels off a continuous sheet of veneer. The log is rotated against a

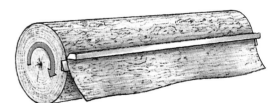

pressure bar and knife that run the full length of the machine; the knife is set just below the bar and forward of it by the thickness of the veneer. The settings of the bar and knife are critical if checks (cracks) are to be prevented. The knife automatically advances by the thickness of the veneer for each revolution of the log.

Veneer produced in this way can be identified by a distinctive watery patterned figure where the continuous tangential cut has sliced through the growth rings.

Rotary cutting is particularly suitable for the manufacture of man-made boards, as the veneer can be cut to any width.

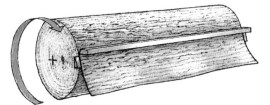

Off-centre cutting
By offsetting a log in the lathe chucks to produce an eccentric cutting action, a rotary lathe can be used to produce wide decorative veneers with sapwood on each edge. This results in a figure something like that of typical flat-sliced crown-cut veneers.

Half-round cutting
A mounting called a 'stay-log' can be positioned between the lathe centres to hold a full or half-round log. Veneers cut on a stay-log are sliced at a shallower angle than those taken from an eccentrically mounted log but are not so wide. The figure produced is close to that of flat-sliced crown-cut veneer.

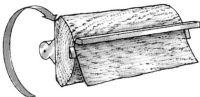

Back cutting
For back cutting, half-round logs are mounted on a stay-log with the heartwood facing outwards. This method is used for cutting decoratively figured butts and curls.

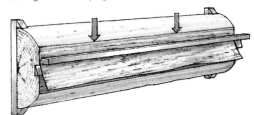

Flat slicing
The flat-slicing method produces decorative hardwood veneers. First, the log is cut in half through its length, and the grain assessed for figure. It may then be further cut into flitches, according to the type of figure required. The character of the figure depends on the way the log is cut

and mounted for slicing. The width of flat-sliced veneer is determined by the size of the flitch.

A half log or quartered flitch is mounted on a vertically sliding frame. A pressure bar and knife are set horizontally in front of the wood, removing a slice of veneer with every downstroke of the frame. Depending on the type of machine, either the knife or the flitch is advanced by the required thickness after each cut.

A flat-sliced half-round log produces the crown-cut veneers commonly used in cabinet work; these have the same figure as tangentially cut flat-sawn boards.

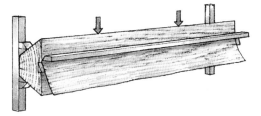

Quarter-cut slicing
Woods that display striking and attractive figure when radially cut are converted into quarter-cut or near-quarter-cut flitches. These are mounted so that the rays of the wood follow the direction of the cut as far as possible, to produce the maximum number of radially cut veneers.

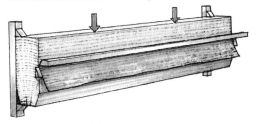

Tangential flat slicing
Quartered flitches can also be mounted to produce tangentially cut flat-sliced veneers. Although these are not as wide as crown-cut veneers cut from half-round logs, they can display attractive figure.

Sliced veneers
The scale of commercial veneer production is huge. Here, veneers sliced from the log are drawn away from the machine by conveyer belts.

OPEN AND CLOSED FACES

The back face of the veneer is called the open face, and the other the closed face. Where possible, try to lay veneer with the open face down, as the slightly coarser surface does not finish quite so well.

Identifying the face
You can identify the faces by flexing the veneer, along the grain. It will bend more when the open face is convex.

Knife checks
Veneer-slicing machines cut like giant planes; it is vital that the shaving is produced to fine tolerances and with a clean cut. The quality of the cut is controlled by the pressure bar and knife setting.

Fine cracks known as knife checks can occur on the back or open face of the veneer, particularly when it has been cut by the rotary method.

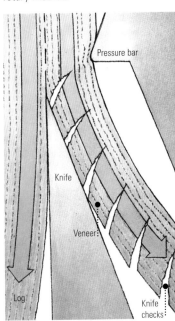

57

TYPES OF VENEER

Veneer figure derives both from the wood's natural features and from where and how it is cut. The description can refer to the method of cutting, such as 'crown-cut'; or to the part of the tree from which the veneer comes, as in 'burr' veneer. Most decorative sliced veneer is about 0.6mm ($\frac{1}{42}$in) thick. 'Construction veneer', 1.5 to 6mm ($\frac{1}{16}$ to $\frac{1}{4}$in) thick, is also produced.

Buying veneer

Each veneer is unique and is unlikely to be matched from other bundles, so a generous allowance for wastage should be made when the area needed for a project is calculated.

Leaves are traditionally priced by the square foot, although the thickness may be given in metric measurements. Some merchants supply pre-cut lengths at a set price per piece.

For matching purposes, veneers are almost always kept in the order they were sliced from the log, so leaves and bundles are taken from the top of the stack. Suppliers do not normally pull out selected leaves, as doing so reduces the value of the veneer flitch.

Mail-order veneer

Full veneers supplied by mail order are usually rolled for despatch. Smaller pieces, such as burrs or curls, may be flat-packed; if they are sent with a package of rolled veneer, they may be dampened to allow them to bend without breaking.

A rolled package should be opened carefully, to prevent it springing open and damaging the fragile veneer inside. End splits, particularly on light-coloured woods, must be repaired promptly with gummed paper tape, to prevent dirt getting into the split.

Veneer that is still curled after being unpacked can be either dampened with steam from a kettle or passed through a tray of water, and then pressed flat between sheets of chipboard. Damp veneer left between boards may develop mildew.

Because wood is light-sensitive and can lighten or darken (according to species), veneers should be stored flat and protected from dust and strong light.

Inspecting veneer

Veneer should be inspected thoroughly for faults such as rough or open grain, splits or knife checks, knife marks from a chipped blade, worm holes, and hard inclusions in the pores.

Crotch or fork
Distinctive curl veneers come from this part of the tree.

Trunk
Depending on the tree and the method of cutting, a variety of veneer patterns can be cut from the trunk.

Abnormal growth
Leaves of wild-grain veneer are cut from a burr.

Stump of butt
Highly figured veneer is cut from the tree stump.

BURR OR BURL VENEER

Burrs or burls are abnormal growths on tree trunks. The fragile veneers cut from them display an attractive pattern of tightly packed bud formations that appear as rings and dots. Burr veneer is highly prized for furniture, turnery and woodware, and is therefore relatively expensive. It is supplied in irregular shapes in various sizes, from 150mm to 1m (6in to 3ft 3in) long and from 100 to 450mm (4in to 1ft 6in) wide.

Top to bottom:
Elm burr; thuja burr; ash burr

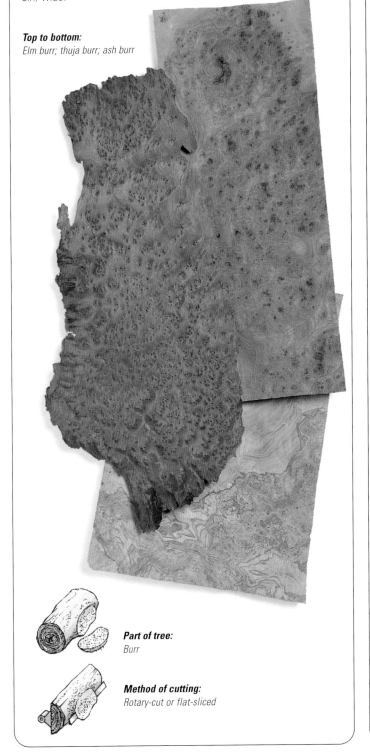

Part of tree:
Burr

Method of cutting:
Rotary-cut or flat-sliced

BUTT VENEER

Butt veneers are cut from butts (stumps). Half-round cutting on a rotary lathe produces highly figured veneers caused by distorted grain. These are fragile veneers, and may have holes where small pieces have become detached. To repair very small holes, matching filler can be applied after the veneer is laid.

Top to bottom:
American walnut burry-butt veneer; ash butt veneer; American walnut butt veneer

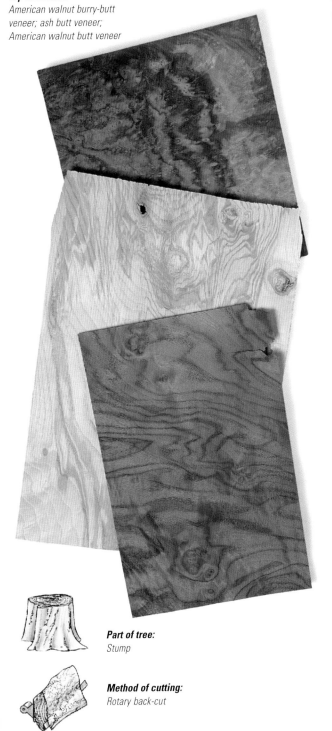

Part of tree:
Stump

Method of cutting:
Rotary back-cut

CROWN-CUT VENEER

Tangentially cut flat-sliced veneers are known as 'crown-cut'. They have an attractive figure of bold sweeping curves and ovals along the centre of the leaf, with striped grain nearer the edges. Crown-cut veneers are produced in lengths of 2.4m (8ft) or more; and in widths ranging from about 225 to 600mm (9in to 2ft), depending on the species used. They are used for furniture-making and interior wall panelling.

Left to right:
Crown-cut kingwood; crown-cut rosewood; crown-cut ash; crown-cut American walnut

Part of tree:
Trunk

Method of cutting:
Flat-sliced

CURLY-FIGURED VENEER

Wavy-grained woods produce curly-figured veneers with bands of light and dark grain running across the width of the leaf. 'Fiddleback' sycamore and ripple ash are typical examples; the former gets its name from its use in making violin backs. Curly-figured veneer is employed to give a distinctive horizontal decorative effect – for instance, on cabinet doors and panels.

Left to right:
Fiddleback sycamore; ripple ash

Part of tree:
Trunk

Method of cutting:
Flat-sliced

CURL VENEER

When the 'crotch' or fork of a tree, where the trunk divides, is cut perpendicularly, an attractive 'curl figure' is revealed. The distorted diverging grain of the wood produces a lustrous upward-sweeping plume pattern known as 'feather figure', often used on panelled cabinet doors. Curl veneer is available in lengths from 300mm to 1m (1ft to 3ft 3in) and widths from 200 to 450mm (8in to 1ft 6in).

Top to bottom:
Mahogany curl; European walnut curl

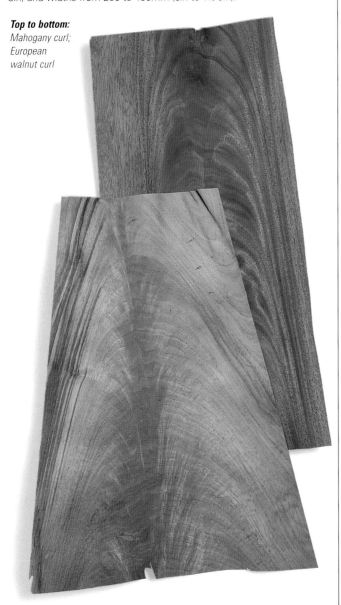

Part of tree:
Crotch

Method of cutting:
Rotary back-cut

FREAK-FIGURED VENEER

Veneers displaying various unusual patterns are rotary-cut from hardwood logs with irregular growth. Bird's-eye maple and masur birch are well-known examples of such freak-figured veneers. The distinctive brown marks of masur birch are caused by woodboring larvae that attack the cambium layer of the growing tree. Woods with irregular grain also produce veneers with 'blistered' and 'quilted' figures.

Left to right:
Quilted makoré; masur birch; bird's-eye maple; quilted willow

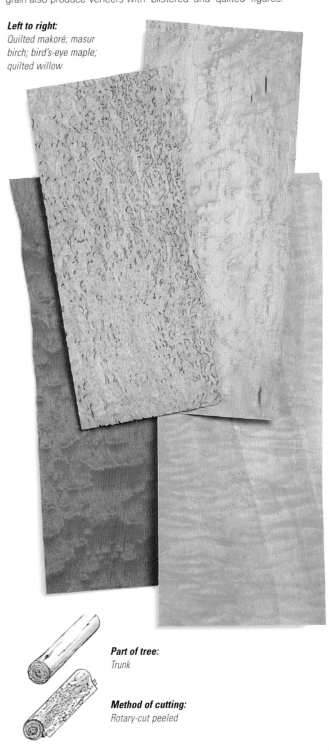

Part of tree:
Trunk

Method of cutting:
Rotary-cut peeled

RAY-FIGURED VENEER

When quarter-cut, woods that have a pronounced ray-cell structure, such as oak and plane, display striking figure. Quarter-cut plane veneer, with speckled or fine wavy-grain figure, is known as lacewood. Distinctive wide ray cells in oak produce 'ray-fleck' or 'splash' figure, long in demand for furniture-making and panelling. Ray-figured veneer is available in lengths of up to 2.4m (8ft) and in widths of 150 to 350mm (6in to 1ft 2in), depending on the species used.

Left to right:
Quarter-cut silky oak; quarter-cut lacewood; quarter-cut ray-fleck oak

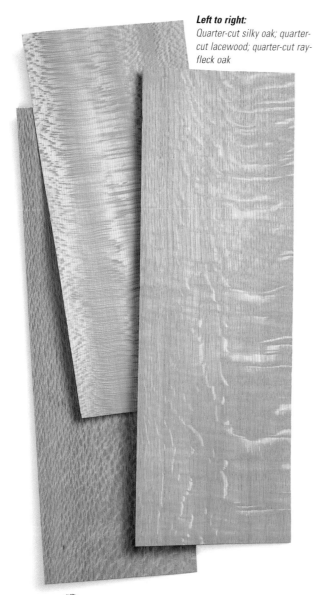

Part of tree:
Trunk

Method of cutting:
Quarter-cut flat-sliced

STRIPED OR RIBBON VENEER

Where the radial cut is taken across the width of the growth rings, quarter-cut veneers usually display a striped or 'ribbon' figure. Striped quarter-cut veneers are produced in lengths of 2.4m (8ft) or more, and widths of 150 to 225mm (6 to 9in). On woods that grow with interlocked reverse-spiral grain, the stripes appear to change from light to dark, depending on the degree of reflectivity of the cells (end-on cells absorb light) and the angle from which they are viewed.

Left to right:
Strip-figured zebrano; ribbon-figured sapele; ribbon-figured ayan

Part of tree:
Trunk

Method of cutting:
Quarter-cut flat-sliced

COLOURED VENEER

Specialist veneer suppliers sell artificially coloured veneers made from light-coloured woods such as sycamore and poplar. 'Harewood' is sycamore that has been treated chemically, turning it silver-grey to dark grey. Other colours are produced by pressure-treating dyed veneers to achieve maximum penetration of the dye.

Clockwise from top left:
Turquoise-dyed veneer; blue-dyed veneer; chemically coloured harewood; green-dyed veneer

Method of colouring:
Harewood (sycamore) is immersed in a ferrous-sulphate solution. Commercially dyed woods are processed in an autoclave.

RECONSTRUCTED VENEER

Spectacular effects of colour, grain and pattern can be achieved using a computerized process that involves scanning, dyeing, high-pressure gluing and pressing veneer into a solid block, and then reslicing it into conventional and decorative-veneer patterns. Single leaves, which are produced up to 700mm (2ft 4in) wide and 2500 to 3400mm (8ft 4in to 11ft 4in) long, range from 0.3 to 3mm (1/84 to 1/8in) thick.

Top to bottom:
Geometric-stripe pattern; tessellated geometric pattern; freak-figured pattern; crown-cut pattern

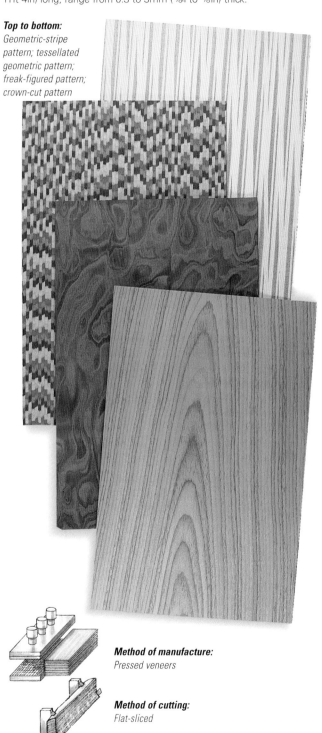

Method of manufacture:
Pressed veneers

Method of cutting:
Flat-sliced

MAN-MADE BOARDS

Man-made boards have become popular among wood users of almost every kind, from the construction industry to the home woodworker, mostly for building work and furniture-making. A wide range of manufactured boards is available, which can be roughly divided into three basic types, each with its own subdivisions: laminated boards (plywood), particle boards, and fibreboards.

PLYWOOD

Plywood is made from thin laminated sheets of wood called construction veneers, laminates or plies. In order to counter the natural movement of the wood, plywood is constructed with the fibres or grain of alternate plies set at right angles to one another, thus producing a stable warp-resisting board. The greatest strength of a panel is usually parallel to the face grain.

Plywood construction

Most plywood is made with an odd number of plies (three or more) to give a balanced construction. The number varies according to the thickness of the plies and the finished board.

The surface veneers of a typical plywood board are known as face plies. Where the quality of one ply is better than the other, the better ply is designated the face and the other the back. The quality of the face plies is usually specified by a letter code (see below left), indicating the grade. The plies that are immediately beneath and laid perpendicular to the face plies are known as cross-plies. The name given to the centre ply or plies is the core.

Birch destined for plywood

Standard sizes

Plywood is available in a wide range of sizes. The thickness of most commercially available plywood ranges from 3mm (1/8in) to 30mm (1 3/16in).

A typical board is 1.22m (4ft) wide, but boards 1.52m (5ft) wide are also available. The most common length is 2.44m (8ft). Boards up to 3.66m (12ft) long can be purchased, too.

The grain of the face ply usually, but not always, follows the longest dimension of the board. It runs parallel to the first dimension quoted by the manufacturer, so a 1.22 x 2.44m (4 x 8ft) board will have the grain running across the width.

Interior plywood (INT)

These plywoods are used for non-structural interior applications. They are generally produced with an appearance-grade face ply and poorer-quality ply for the back. They are manufactured with light-coloured urea-formaldehyde adhesive. Most are suitable for use in dry conditions – for instance, for furniture or wall panelling. The modified adhesive used in some boards affords them some moisture resistance, enabling them to be used in areas of high humidity.

Exterior plywood (EXT)

Depending on the quality of the adhesive, EXT-grade plywoods can be used for exposed or semi-exposed conditions, where structural performance is not required. Boards suitable for fully exposed conditions are bonded with dark-coloured phenol-formaldehyde (phenolic) adhesive. Plywoods produced using melamine urea-formaldehyde adhesive are classed as semi-durable.

Marine plywood

Marine plywood is a high-quality face-graded structural plywood, constructed from selected plies within a limited range of mahogany-type woods. It has no 'voids', or gaps, and is bonded with a durable phenolic-resin adhesive. It is primarily produced for marine use, and can be used for interior fitments where water or steam may be present.

Structural plywood

Structural or engineering-grade plywood is produced for applications where strength and durability are the prime considerations. It is bonded with phenolic adhesive. A lower-quality appearance-grade face ply is used, and boards may not have been sanded.

APPEARANCE GRADING

Plywood producers use a coding system to grade the appearance of face plies. The letters do not refer to structural performance. Typical grades assigned to softwood boards are A, B, C, C plugged, and D.

The A grade is the best quality, being smooth-cut and virtually defect-free; the D grade is the poorest, and has the maximum amount of permitted defects, such as knots, holes, splits and discoloration. A-A grade plywood has two good faces, while a board classified as B-C has poorer-grade outer plies, with B grade used for the face and C grade for the back.

Decorative plywoods are faced with selected matched veneers and are referred to by the wood species of the face veneer.

1 Trademark of the grading authority
In this case, the American Plywood Association.

2 Panel grade
Identifies the grades of the face and back veneers.

3 Species group number
Group 1 is the strongest species.

4 Exposure classification
Indicates bond durability.

5 Mill number
Code number of the producing mill.

6 Product Standard number
Indicates board meets U.S. Product Standard.

APA **1**
A-C **2** GROUP **3** 1
EXTERIOR **4**
000 **5**
6 PS 1-83

Stamp applied to back face

A-B · G-1 · EXT-APA · 000 · PS1-83

Stamp applied to edge

Grading stamps

Boards with A-grade or B-grade veneer on one side only usually have the grade stamped on the back. Those where A or B grade veneers are used for both faces are normally stamped on the edge.

TYPES OF PLYWOOD

Plywood boards are manufactured in many parts of the world, and the species of wood used depends on the area of origin. Performance and suitability are affected by the species of wood, type of bond and grade of veneer.

Plywood timbers

Softwood boards are commonly made from Douglas fir or species of pine, while hardwood veneers are mostly made from light-coloured temperate woods such as birch, beech and basswood. Red-coloured plywoods are made from tropical woods such as lauan, meranti and gaboon.

The face veneers and core may be made from the same species throughout, or may be constructed from different species.

Applications

Different types of plywood are manufactured for such diverse applications as aircraft and marine construction, agricultural installations, building work, panelling, musical instruments, furniture and toys.

Flexible plywood

You can buy plywood sheets made from three plies, all with the grain running in the same direction. This allows the boards to be bent easily into relatively tight curves. Flexible plywood is manufactured in 5, 6 and 8mm (^{3}/16, ^{1}/4 and ^{3}/8in) thicknesses, and several sheets can be laminated together to form a structure of any required thickness.

Flexible plywood is ideal for making simple curved components that are very strong and comparatively light in weight.

Decorative plywood
This is faced with selected rotary, flat-sliced or quarter-cut matched veneers, usually from hardwoods such as ash, birch, beech, cherry, mahogany or oak, sanded ready for polishing. A balancing veneer of lesser quality is applied to the back of the board. Decorative plywood is mainly used for panelling.

Three-ply board
The face veneers are bonded to a single core veneer. The thickness of each veneer may be the same; or the core may be thicker to improve the balance of construction. The latter type is sometimes called balanced or solid-core plywood. Composite laminated boards, with the core made from reconstituted wood, are used in the building industry.

Drawerside plywood
The exception to the cross-ply construction method, this has the grain of all the plies running in the same direction. It is made of hardwood to a nominal thickness of 12mm (^{1}/2in) and is used for making drawer sides, in place of solid wood.

Multi-ply
This has a core consisting of an odd number of plies. The thickness of each ply may be the same; or the cross-plies may be thicker, which helps give the board equal stiffness in its length and width. Multi-ply is much used in making veneered furniture.

Six-ply
This board has two thick-cut core plies bonded together, with their grain running in the same direction. The core is sandwiched between pairs of thinner plies. A four-ply board (not shown) has similar core plies, with a single face ply on each side. Both types are stiffer in one direction, and are used mainly for structural work.

BLOCKBOARD AND LAMINBOARD

Blockboard is a form of plywood, by virtue of having a laminated construction. Where it differs from conventional plywood is in having its core constructed from strips of softwood cut approximately square in section; these are edge-butted but not glued. The core is faced with one or two layers of ply on each side.

Laminboard is similar to blockboard, but the core is constructed with narrow strips of softwood, each about 5mm ($^3/_{16}$in) thick; these are usually glued together.

Laminboard

Because the core is less likely to 'telegraph' or show through, this is superior to blockboard for veneer work. It is also more expensive. Boards of three-ply and five-ply construction are produced. With the latter, each pair of thin outer plies may run perpendicular to the core; alternatively, the face ply only may run in line with the core strips.

Blockboard

This stiff material is suitable for furniture applications, particularly shelving and worktops. It makes a good substrate for veneer work, although the core strips can telegraph. It is made in similar panel sizes to plywood, with thicknesses ranging from 12 to 25mm ($^1/_2$ to 1in). You can also buy boards of three-ply construction up to 44mm (1$^3/_4$in) thick.

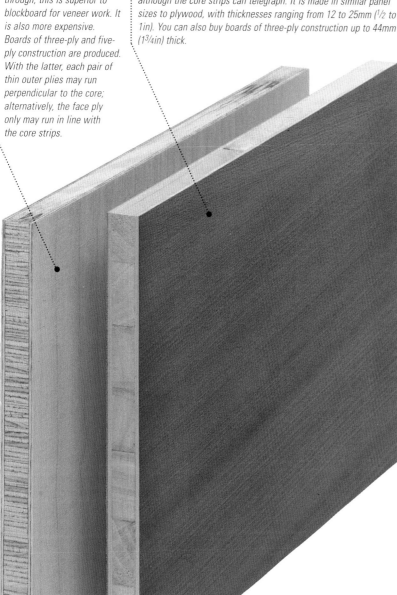

PARTICLE BOARDS

These are made from small chips or flakes of wood bonded together under pressure; softwoods are generally used, although a proportion of hardwoods may be included. Various types of boards are produced – according to the shape and size of the particles, their distribution through the thickness of the board, and the type of adhesive used to bind them together.

Types of particle board

Particle boards are stable and uniformly consistent. Those constructed with fine particles have featureless surfaces and are highly suited as groundwork for home veneering. Decorative boards, preveneered with wood, paper foil or plastic laminates, are also available. Most particle boards are relatively brittle and have a much lower tensile strength than plywood boards.

Chipboard

The types of particle board most used by woodworkers are those of interior quality, commonly known as chipboard. Like other wood products, interior-grade chipboard is adversely affected by excess moisture – the board swells in its thickness and does not return to shape on drying. However, moisture-resistant types, suitable for flooring or wet conditions, are also available and are used extensively in the building-construction trade.

STORING BOARDS

To save space, store man-made boards on edge. A rack will keep the edges clear of the floor and support the boards evenly at a slight angle. To prevent a thin board bending, support it by placing a thicker board behind it.

Single-layer chipboard
Made from a mat of evenly distributed similar-size particles, this type of chipboard has a relatively coarse surface suitable for wood veneer or plastic laminate, but not for finishing with paint.

Three-layer chipboard
This board has a coarse-particle core sandwiched between two outer layers of fine high-density particles. The high proportion of resin in the outer layers produces a smooth surface that is suitable for most finishes.

Graded-density chipboard
This type of chipboard is a blend of coarse and very fine particles. Unlike three-layer chipboard, there is a gradual transition from the coarse interior through to the fine surface.

Decorative chipboard
These boards are faced with selected wood veneers, plastic laminates or thin melamine foil. Veneered boards are sanded for polishing; laminated boards are supplied ready-finished. Some plastic-laminate boards for worktops are made with finished profiled edges. Matching edging strips are available for both melamine-faced and wood-veneer boards.

Oriented-strand board
This is a three-layer material made with long strands of softwood. The strands in each layer are laid in a particular direction, and each layer is laid perpendicular to the next in the same manner as plywood.

Flakeboard or waferboard
This type of board incorporates large shavings of wood laid horizontally, overlapping one another. Flakeboard has greater tensile strength than standard chipboard. Although made for utilitarian applications, it can be used as a wallboard when finished with a clear varnish. It can also be stained.

FIBREBOARDS

Fibreboards are made from wood that has been broken down to its basic fibre elements and reconstituted to make a stable homogeneous material. The density of the boards depends on the pressure applied and the type of adhesive used in the manufacturing process.

Hardboards

Hardboard is a high-density fibreboard produced from wet fibres pressed at high pressure and temperature. The natural resins in the fibres are used to bond them together.

Standard hardboard has one smooth and one textured face. It is made in a range of thicknesses, most commonly from 3 to 6mm (1/8 to 1/4in), and in a wide range of panel sizes. An inexpensive material, it is often used for drawer bottoms and cabinet backs.

Duo-faced hardboard is made from the same material as standard board, but has two smooth faces.

Decorative hardboard is available as perforated, moulded or lacquered boards. The perforated types are used for screens, most others for wall panelling.

Oil-tempered hardboard is impregnated with resin and oil to produce a strong abrasion-resistant material that is also water-resistant.

Medium-density fibreboard (MDF)

Medium-density fibreboard is made by combining fine wood fibres with resins. The mix is compacted in a heated press and the end product has a smooth uniform texture. MDF can be cut, planed and moulded with ease, and the surface will take stains, paints or varnishes. Generally, thicknesses range from 3 to 30mm (1/8 to 1 1/8in).

Standard MDF is ideal for interior cabinetwork, such as fitted bedroom units. Moisture-resistant boards are more suitable for the conditions found in kitchens or bathrooms. Ready-coloured MDF can be used to make children's furniture and toys. For radiator covers and screens, pierced MDF panels are sold in a range of modern and traditional designs. Specialist panel suppliers stock bendable MDF, which is grooved on one side to allow the board to be formed into curved and S-shaped components.

Hardboards

1 Oil-tempered
2 Standard
3 Lacquered
4 Perforated

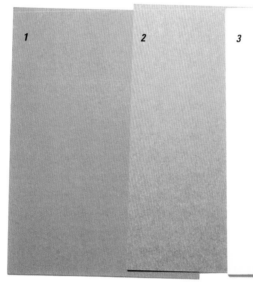
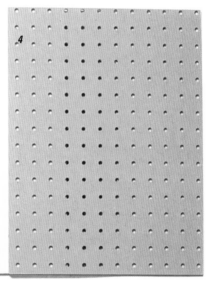

Medium-density fibreboards (MDF)

5 Bendable
6 Standard
7 Ready-coloured
8 Perforated
9 Veneered

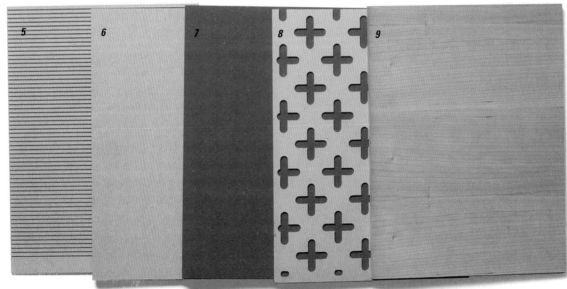

CHAPTER TWO

DESIGNING IN WOOD

Designing in three dimensions requires the ability, before you embark on making an object, to visualize how it will eventually look. The design process is never easy, and if you are working with unfamiliar forms or materials it becomes even more complex than usual. Indeed, you may find it is often necessary to construct a series of prototypes in order to evaluate each design decision and to make sure the object you are designing will function satisfactorily. However, even if you are a beginner, you can draw on the experience and expertise accumulated by generations of craftsmen-designers. This chapter looks at the questions a designer needs to consider, including structure, safety and intended use, as well as aesthetic and decorative considerations. Also included are sketches illustrating the basic principles of chair, table and storage-unit construction, which you can use as a source of ideas and as a guide to the various practical aspects of furniture design, such as choice of joints and order of assembly.

THE DESIGN PROCESS

New forms or concepts are rarely dreamed up out of thin air. In the past, furniture construction gradually evolved as woodworkers learned to deal with the way solid timber changes shape and size in response to levels of humidity. Techniques were modified to keep pace with changes in technology, and the appearance of furniture was influenced by contemporary taste. But the rate of change was slow. The majority of woodworkers were artisans, rather than designers in the modern sense. They would continue to make familiar objects, using the same tools, methods and materials as their forefathers. The most fashionable workshops might produce innovative designs, but only for clients wealthy enough to pay what we today call development costs. These innovations had to be tried and tested before they became part of the average tradesman's repertoire.

A modern-day woodworker could do a lot worse than follow this example in order to acquire the basic skills of designing in wood. There's no desire to stifle originality or to discourage woodworkers from developing their creative talents, but it would be perverse to ignore the wealth of common experience simply to avoid copying what's been done previously. Before attempting to break new ground, a designer needs to understand how his or her chosen material behaves and how the finished item is to function, and should try to avoid visual gimmickry.

FUNCTION

Much is said about designing for function, but to understand what that means one has to examine the concept from several angles. A solid block of wood can function as a stool, but a well-designed stool is something else. A bar stool supports a seated human being and so does a milking stool – yet they have completely different functions and, consequently, different dimensions. Should a stool be light enough to be portable – or should it, in a public building, be bolted to the ground to prevent it being toppled, perhaps blocking a fire-escape route? Should a stool be adjustable in height? Should it fold for storage? And will it tip easily when someone shifts their weight?

A designer has to pose questions of this nature in order to define how an object is to function, then provide a design solution based on real requirements, as opposed to preconceptions. But even then, the solution will almost certainly to some extent be a compromise. An elegant solution is one that comes close to answering all the questions – it will seldom, if ever, be perfect.

Designing for people

In order to be functional, most items of woodwork have to relate in some way to the human body. As a species we differ widely in size, shape and weight – so when designing a chair for an individual, you need to take careful measurements of that person's anatomy before you can be sure the chair will be comfortable. However, anthropometry and ergonomics – the statistical sciences concerned with the comparative study of the human body and how it relates to its environment – provide designers with the optimum dimensions for furniture and work stations that suit people of average height and build. Most people are reasonably comfortable using furniture based on these dimensions, but if you are making something for a specific group of people, such as children or the elderly, you may have to create custom-built artefacts tailored to their needs. Specific anthropometric data is given where appropriate throughout this chapter.

Adaptability

Designing something to be adaptable increases its usefulness. Bunk beds that convert to two full-size beds – especially welcome in a family with growing children – are a good example of built-in adaptability. An ergonomic typist's chair is designed to be comfortable for people of any stature; and a draw-leaf table is an example of compactness coupled with flexibility. For storage, adjustable shelves are more useful than fixed ones; and simple drawers, sliding trays or baskets may give a greater degree of versatility than rigid compartments.

Structural requirements

Nothing functions well or lasts long unless it is properly constructed. A table that rocks when you are cutting your steak is annoying; a desk top that vibrates while you're typing is distracting; and a chair that collapses is positively dangerous. A wooden structure can support considerable weight without noticeable distortion, providing it is designed to counteract the stresses and strains of normal use.

The leg frame of a traditional stick chair illustrates the principle perfectly. The four legs are plugged into the underside of a solid seat. Horizontal stretcher rails not only prevent the legs bending under load, but also stop them sliding apart. The angles at which the components meet are such that they reinforce one another against shifting forces, mainly because a straight pull is never exerted on any of the joints. And if the chair is tipped onto its splayed back legs, they are ideally placed to support the additional weight at that angle. The structure is, in fact, superbly suited to its intended purpose.

The average human
The American designer Henry Dreyfuss pioneered the study of anthropometrics. His book Designing for People provides us with detailed dimensions of the average male and female.

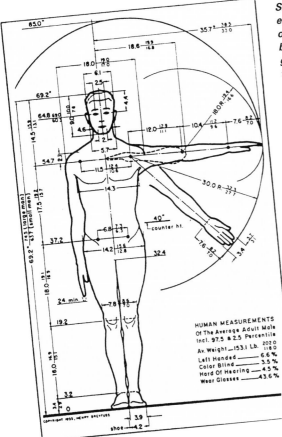

HUMAN MEASUREMENTS
Of The Average Adult Male
Incl. 97.5 & 2.5 Percentile
Av. Weight 153.1 Lb.
Left Handed — 6.6%
Color Blind — 3.5%
Hard Of Hearing — 4.5%
Wear Glasses — 43.6%

An overloaded shelf will sag and may eventually break because of the combination of compression and tension. But if you cut off a 50mm (2in) strip, turn it through 90 degrees and glue it to the underside of the shelf, it will be able to support more weight without bending – by turning the strip on edge you have constructed an effective beam. The rails supporting a table top or chair seat perform a similar function.

The load on a beam is transferred to whatever is supporting it at each end – the legs of a table or chair, for example. The joints between the rails and legs must be capable of resisting shear forces (the downward pressure of the load being opposed by the rigid supports). Shear forces are increased considerably when sideways pressure is applied to a structure, exerting leverage on the joints. A strong dowel joint or the tongue of a mortise-and-tenon is able to cope with this leverage, especially if the rail is deep enough to provide decent shoulders for the joints and if glued corner blocks are used to reinforce the structure on the inside of the rails.

The joints of a cabinet or a box are especially vulnerable to sideways pressure, which causes the frame to 'rack', forming a parallelogram. However, a rigid back panel, vertical pilasters or corner plates will prevent movement in the joints and create a rigid structure. A built-in plinth or shelf-support rails will achieve the same purpose, while metal-strip cross-bracing prevents racking by tying opposite diagonal corners together.

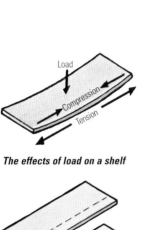

The effects of load on a shelf

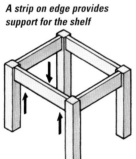

A strip on edge provides support for the shelf

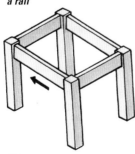

Legs oppose the load on a rail

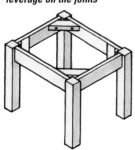

Sideways pressure exerts leverage on the joints

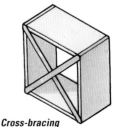

Strong joints and corner blocks hold the frame rigid

The traditional stick chair
The underframe components are ideally placed to counteract the stresses and strains imposed by normal use.

The near-perfect back rest
An ergonomic back rest can be both beautiful and comfortable.

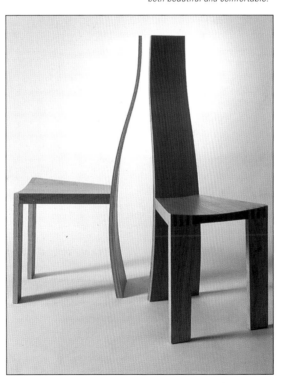

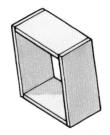

An unsupported box will collapse

Making a box rigid
To create a rigid structure the joints of a box or cabinet must be reinforced using one of the following methods.

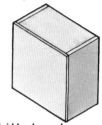

Rigid back panel

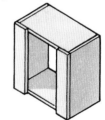

Vertical pilasters

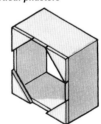

Corner plates

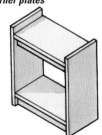

Plinth and shelf rails

Cross-bracing

DESIGNING FOR SAFETY

If it is possible to misuse something, you can be sure someone will eventually do so. People often stand on even the flimsiest of chairs, or use stretcher rails as a ladder to reach the top shelf of a bookcase. Tipping a dining chair onto its back legs is another common abuse. Even though a chair is not built for such purposes, you should take them into consideration as part of the design process in order to minimize the risk of accidents.

The effects of leverage

People often sit on tables. Providing the rails and joints are strong enough, the table rarely suffers anything more than scuffs and scratches caused by back-pocket studs or buttons. But if the top is cantilevered – like a fall flap on a bureau, for example – the leverage created at the hinges is considerable, even when someone merely rests their weight on the flap. Suspending the flap from folding metal stays alleviates the risk of tearing out the hinges, or you can use lopers (rails that slide out from the bureau) to support the flap from below. Both methods move the effective pivot point forward, away from the hinge line towards the front of the flap, thus reducing the leverage.

If the door of a sideboard or kitchen unit is allowed to swing towards a tier of drawers next to it, it is only a matter of time before the corner of a drawer that has not been pushed home acts as a fulcrum to pull the door off its hinges. If you cannot alter the position of the door or drawers, use stays to stop the door opening further than 90 degrees.

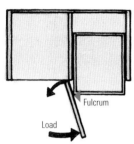

The effect of leverage
Levering a door against a drawer can pull it off its hinges.

Oak bureau
Pull-out lopers housed in the underframe (below) support a leather-lined fall flap (centre).

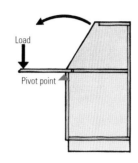

An unsupported flap strains the hinges

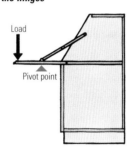

Folding stays reduce leverage

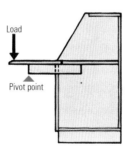

Lopers have a similar effect

Stability

A piece of furniture may be stable under normal circumstances, but ask yourself whether it can be easily toppled. A dining chair will be stable provided its centre of gravity remains within the area defined by the four points where the legs meet the floor (**1**); but if leaning against the back rest moves the centre of gravity outside that area (**2**), the chair becomes unstable and will topple. For this reason, the back legs of a chair are often made to slope (**3**), so that it will remain safely balanced even when tipped slightly backwards (**4**).

A chest of drawers can become dangerously unstable if all the drawers are open at the same time. However, a short cabinet with a wide base has a relatively low centre of gravity and will maintain its equilibrium unless it is toppled deliberately. A taller cabinet may have to be screwed to the wall or floor. Similarly, large heavy doors that would cause a freestanding wardrobe or broom cupboard to topple are usually made to slide, instead of being hinged.

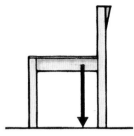

1 *Stable chair*

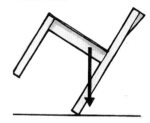

2 *Unstable chair*

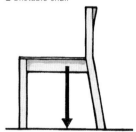

3 *Sloping back legs widen a chair base*

4 *Centre of gravity acts within the base area*

Splayed-leg chair
The wide base of this robust armchair prevents it being toppled accidentally.

Avoiding hazardous details

Even small details can cause serious injuries. Think twice about leaving sharp edges or corners, especially if they are at a level where children may fall against them. Glass table tops are especially dangerous in this respect. A round top is relatively safe providing that all the sharp edges are removed by polishing, but it is advisable to enclose a rectangular glass top within a rebated frame.

Sharp edges are even worse if they close with a scissor action. Trapping your fingers between a heavy inset lid and the side of a box is painful, to say the least; but the consequences of a similar accident with a folding chair collapsing under your weight can be far more serious.

A swivelling desk chair with arms constitutes a less obvious risk. There should be sufficient clearance for your knuckles between the underside of the desk top and the chair arms if you are to avoid an unpleasant surprise as you swivel the chair in order to stand up.

Sharp projecting handles can tear clothing, even though they may not cause actual physical harm – so choose smooth rounded knobs and handgrips or fit flush or drop handles.

Safe detailing

Integral drawer handles can be a safe yet striking feature.

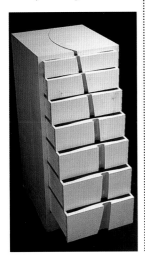

Most factors relating to function and safety are applicable no matter what material you are using – but when working with wood you have to take into consideration the fact that timber continues to absorb and exude moisture according to the humidity of its surroundings, regardless of when it was cut from the tree. If you take a 100-year-old chest of drawers from an unheated room and stand it next to a radiator, it will still dry out; and if you return it to its original environment, it will absorb moisture from the air. The problem for the woodworker is the dimensional changes that accompany these exchanges of moisture: wood shrinks as it loses water and expands when it takes it up. If this movement is restricted, the wood splits or warps. Allowing for such movement to occur without detriment to the work is another aspect of the designer's activity.

Fixings that allow for movement

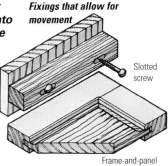

Slotted screw

Frame-and-panel construction

Allowing for movement

The differential movement that occurs even within a single piece of timber often causes problems.

Owing to the grain structure of wood, a solid board will shrink or expand to a greater extent across its width than along its length (**1**). If you make a box from four pieces of similar wood and join them at the corners so that all four pieces have their grain running in the same direction, they will move together by exactly the same amount and no damage or distortion will occur (**2**).

If you attach other components rigidly with their grain running contrary to the wood grain of the box's sides, they restrict the natural movement across the box until the resulting stresses are relieved by splits opening along the grain (**3**). The solution is to devise a way of attaching components with fixings such as slotted screws that allow for an element of movement.

A common safeguard against movement in thin solid-wood panels is to locate them in grooved components – they should never be glued in place. This is the principle employed in traditional frame-and-panel construction.

1 Shrinkage is greater across the grain

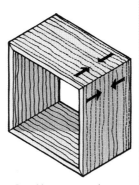

2 Box sides move together

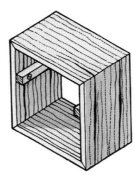

3 Cross battens restrict movement until splits relieve the stresses.

Disguising the effects of movement

An experienced designer uses some form of visual distraction whenever he or she anticipates that movement in the timber will affect the detailing of a workpiece. An inset drawer front may fit like a glove when it leaves the bench, but an unsightly gap can open up all round after only a few months. A narrow moulding attached to or cut around the edges of the drawer front or surrounding frame is enough to disguise the gap (**1**).

Alternatively, you can make a feature of a gap from the outset, knowing that it is going to occur in any case. For example, the movement between the components of tongue-and-groove panelling is imperceptible due to the strong linear pattern created deliberately by the open joints (**2**).

The edge of a table top planed flush with the underframe may look beautifully crisp at first, but the effect is spoiled as soon as the top shrinks (**3**). A rebate cut in the top or rail creates a strong shadow-line so the movement is indiscernible (**4**). Alternatively, let the top overhang the rail (**5**) or mould and set back the edge from the face of the rail (**6**).

Avoiding the problem

Selecting stable man-made boards for table tops or cabinet construction avoids the problem of shrinkage that occurs in solid-timber.

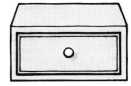

1 Disguising a gap

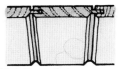

2 A deliberate feature

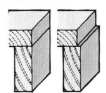

3 Shrinkage spoils the effect of a flush top

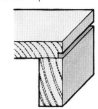

4 Rebated table top

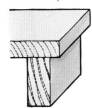

5 Overhanging top

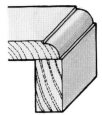

6 Set-back table top

DESIGNING FOR APPEARANCE

It might seem reasonable to assume that the appearance of a piece you are designing should be largely determined by selection of optimum dimensions and by features or mechanical devices that will make the end product function as well as possible. Indeed, the overused maxim 'Form follows function' is based on that premise, but in reality this is too simplistic a view. Designers often go to great lengths in order to get something to look its best. They will tinker with its proportions, take time to select the piece of wood that will enhance its appearance and incorporate mouldings, carvings, inlays or shaped components, all to increase its visual appeal. In short, the appearance of a piece of work may be just as important as its function, but it is virtually impossible to be objective about the aesthetic merits of any design. The only solution is to develop your own sense of what is pleasing and what is most likely to be acceptable.

1 Padauk box
A simple design that features distinctive square-knuckle hinges cut from solid wood.

2 Hexagonal boxes
These are machined from solid Indian rosewood with burr-veneered lids.

3 Dominoes
African-blackwood dominoes inlaid with sycamore 'spots'.

4 One-piece box
A small decorative box cut from yew.

Reversible chair
A chair that can be turned upside down provides the opportunity for a change of colour or upholstery.

Traditional oak tool cabinet
A beautifully proportioned tool cabinet that seems almost too good for the workshop.

Suitability

How is it we can appreciate the quality of a simple undecorated Windsor chair yet find a fine Sheraton-style dining chair just as appealing? They could hardly be more different in appearance. One possible reason is the way we envisage them in totally different settings – in the rooms for which they were originally designed. Stick or Windsor chairs would look incongruous beside a highly polished table in an elegantly decorated dining room, whilst a Sheraton-style chair would look equally out of place in a cottage kitchen. Swap them around, and each fits naturally into its intended environment.

It is necessary to anticipate how and where an object is to be used and then design it accordingly, selecting the appropriate timbers, shapes, proportions and finish to achieve the desired result. Although some people have a talent for combining furniture and fittings of all styles and periods, it is easier if you reflect the style and decor of the intended location. This doesn't mean you have to reproduce period furniture: if you use similar materials and detail, your design will at least be in harmony with its surroundings .

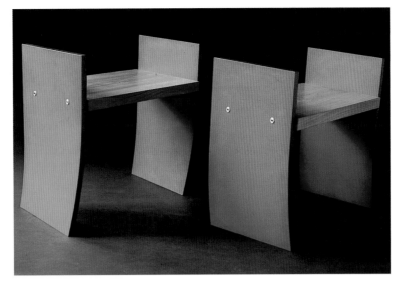

Laminated stools (above left)
A matching pair of stools designed to catch the eye from any angle.

Ash dining chair (above)
Selecting a flexible wood suited to steam-bending was the key to this sophisticated styling.

Carved wooden bowls (left)
Cut and carved from solid cherry, rosewood and walnut, these bowls are decorated with precise fluting.

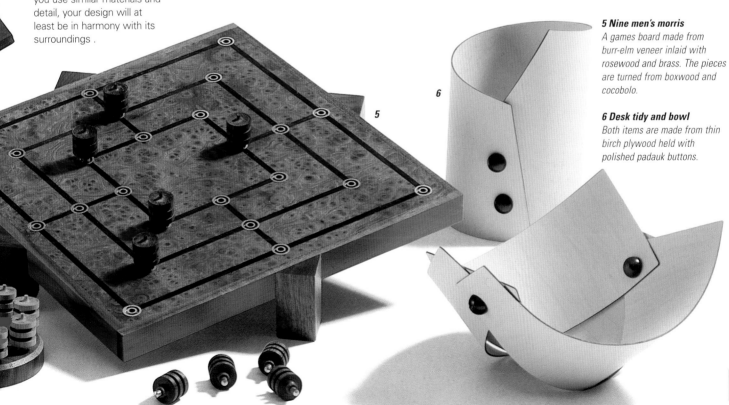

5 Nine men's morris
A games board made from burr-elm veneer inlaid with rosewood and brass. The pieces are turned from boxwood and cocobolo.

6 Desk tidy and bowl
Both items are made from thin birch plywood held with polished padauk buttons.

5

6

75

London-plane cheval mirror
A stylish full-length pivoting mirror is surrounded by pigeonhole storage compartments.

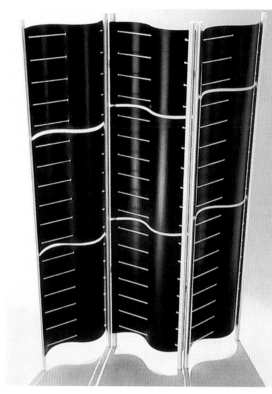

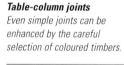

Table-column joints
Even simple joints can be enhanced by the careful selection of coloured timbers.

Decorative detailing
Padauk-veneer inserts interrupt the line of a laminated cherry lipping.

Refined simplicity
This ash tripod table reflects the classic tradition of elegant drawing-room furniture – a style that has been adapted successfully for centuries.

Folding screen *(above)*
Constructed largely from bent-plywood panels, this folding screen is an attractive combination of black lacquer, ash and stainless steel.

Riven-oak chair *(below)*
A perfect combination of material, manufacturing process and form.

Including decoration

Mouldings are often used to disguise the effects of shrinkage, and carving can be used to texture a surface that would otherwise have to be finished immaculately. In the days when all wood-work was produced by hand this was a common ploy; but now that machines are available to alleviate the chore of planing and sanding flat surfaces, designers tend to employ decoration purely for richness of effect. Exotic veneers, for example, are used exclusively for their decorative qualities, as are marquetry, parquetry and wood or metal inlays.

With imagination, you can exploit virtually any aspect of woodworking for visual impact. Indeed, skilled craftsmen sometimes design pieces specifically to focus attention on exquisitely made joints – deliberately creating features for fellow woodworkers to admire.

Aiming for simplicity

If there is no designated location for a piece you are making, it is often best to aim for simplicity so it will look right in virtually any setting. But don't be misled into thinking this is an easy option. Professional designers spend years honing their skills in order to achieve the subtlety required to reduce a piece of work to its bare essentials and to arrive at precise proportions upon which the aesthetic qualities of the design will stand or fall. Moreover, making a simple workpiece requires craftsmanship of a high standard — since, when there is not the slightest embellishment to distract the eye, defects such as a less-than-perfect finish, imprecise joints or clumsy detailing become noticeable at a glance.

Colour and texture

Selecting the right timber may be all that is needed to upgrade a mundane workpiece, but combining wood with other materials provides further opportunities to delight the eye. The cool smooth texture of glass or marble can make a pleasing contrast to a rich grain pattern, and the gleam of polished brass fittings or inlay may add to the appeal of a dark-coloured timber.

The choice of surface finish can transform the appearance of a piece significantly. Stains and clear finishes enhance any timber's depth of colour, and then there is the difference between the reflective qualities of a matt polish and a gloss varnish. There are also endless possibilities for the application of pure colour in the form of sprayed or brushed paint.

Creating optical illusions

If you are not satisfied with the exact proportions of a piece or want to make it appear lighter or heavier than it really is, you can use detailing to create the desired effect.

Adding a deep lipping to a shelf or the edge of a panel suggests solidity and mass without significantly increasing its weight. Conversely, applying a linear moulding or inlay to a deep rail has a slimming effect.

You can lend elegance to a thick table top by cutting wide shallow bevels on the underside so that a thin edge only is visible all round. Tapering the legs of a table will make it look taller and lighter, and a deep curve cut in the underside of a plinth rail gives a lift to a heavy-looking sideboard or chest of drawers.

Even the texture and tone of the wood used for a piece can affect the way we perceive it. A large expanse of dark wood may dominate a room, whereas a paler tone is less obtrusive. A wild grain pattern can introduce a sense of vigour.

Turned bowl
Flaming the workpiece part way through the turning process accentuates the natural colour and texture of an elm burr.

Distinctive colour *(below)*
A hand-painted tour de force, equally striking open and closed. The base gives the impression of a cabinet poised like a dancer on tiptoe.

Bar stool *(below)*
This purely functional object constructed from simple beech laminations is enhanced by coloured wood dyes and clear catalysed lacquer.

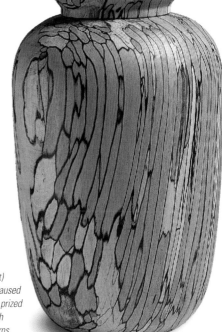

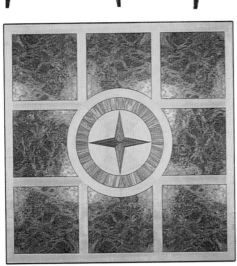

Richly decorated table *(left)*
Marquetry combines colour and texture for this exotic table top.

Lidded container *(right)*
Spalted wood, which is caused by fungal attack, is much prized by woodturners for its rich texture and natural patterns.

Dressing tower (right)
You don't have to sit down to apply make-up or brush your hair. When folded, the mirror is stored behind the cabinet.

Display shelving (far right)
A pair of beautifully finished laminated components linked by plate-glass shelves.

Duck-pond table (below)
Dipping ducks support a glass table top that represents the surface of water.

Developing your own style

The ultimate goal of most serious woodworkers is to develop a visual style that stamps their work with individuality. In order to be distinctive, your style does not have to be flamboyant or eccentric. For instance, you may draw your inspiration from a recognized historical style – not copying pieces faithfully in every detail, but using the essence of that style as a starting point or springboard for your own ideas. On the other hand, it may be that a particular method of production holds a special fascination for you and has a strong influence on the forms and shapes you create. Designing for the woodturning lathe, for example, or using only curved components made from laminated veneers are both ways of channelling your thoughts and energies in a particular direction.

Perhaps the most difficult approach of all is deliberately setting out to break the rules. Challenging preconceived notions of what something is supposed to look like takes imagination and skill, as well as the courage to pull it off successfully. We take it for granted that storage units usually stand against a wall, but it is perfectly possible to make a freestanding unit with access from all sides. By convention, most tables have four legs, but a three-legged table would look arresting and, incidentally, be more stable on an uneven floor. And why take up valuable floor space with a bed when it may be possible to suspend it from the ceiling? Addressing such questions will not always elicit original answers. You may be drawn back to the accepted ways of making things again and again simply because they happen to work best – but just occasionally you may hit upon the germ of an idea that will lead to a truly original piece of work.

Decorated cabinet (right)
Polka-dot effect created by inlaid patinated-copper discs.

Collector's cabinet (left)
An exquisitely proportioned walnut cabinet, given a subtle sheen by applying a simple wax dressing.

Chaise longue (above)
A traditional concept given fresh impetus. The one-piece seat and backrest is supported by a laminated beech underframe which also forms the armrests.

Playful stool (right)
The designer's sense of fun is apparent from this delightfully whimsical stool. It is perched on Dumbo-like feet decorated with polished-metal toenails.

Occasional table (below)
Utter simplicity – often attempted but rarely accomplished. A design that could be modified for mass production with very little effort.

Dressing table (left)
Compact dressing table and matching stool with echoes of utilitarian 1940s furniture.

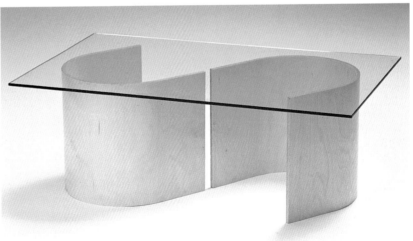

79

CHAIR CONSTRUCTION

In one form or another the upright dining chair has been with us for centuries, and yet the basic design requirements remain unchanged. A chair must support the user in such a position that he or she can eat or work at a table comfortably and, if it has arms, sit down and get up without difficulty. It must be strong enough to bear the weight of the person yet light enough to be moved without effort. This may seem a tall order, but there are traditional 'themes' that solve the problem admirably, to which designers and craftsmen return again and again. Although there are endless combinations, the examples of chair construction that follow provide a useful starting point from which to develop your own designs.

DESIGNING A COMFORTABLE CHAIR

So that a chair will be comfortable for almost everyone, designers generally base their work on standard recommended dimensions. However, to confirm the precise height, shape and angle of a chair's components it may be necessary to make a mock-up of the critical elements or to test and modify certain details as the work progresses.

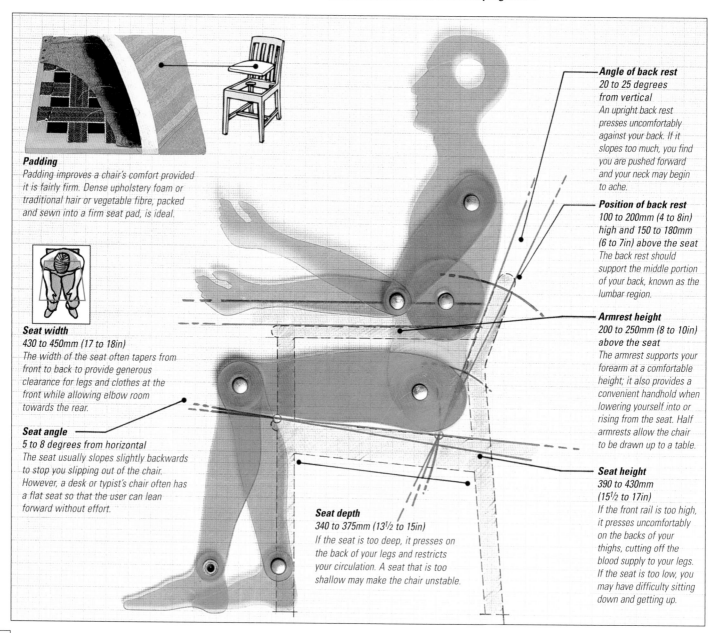

Padding
Padding improves a chair's comfort provided it is fairly firm. Dense upholstery foam or traditional hair or vegetable fibre, packed and sewn into a firm seat pad, is ideal.

Seat width
430 to 450mm (17 to 18in)
The width of the seat often tapers from front to back to provide generous clearance for legs and clothes at the front while allowing elbow room towards the rear.

Seat angle
5 to 8 degrees from horizontal
The seat usually slopes slightly backwards to stop you slipping out of the chair. However, a desk or typist's chair often has a flat seat so that the user can lean forward without effort.

Seat depth
340 to 375mm (13½ to 15in)
If the seat is too deep, it presses on the back of your legs and restricts your circulation. A seat that is too shallow may make the chair unstable.

Angle of back rest
20 to 25 degrees from vertical
An upright back rest presses uncomfortably against your back. If it slopes too much, you find you are pushed forward and your neck may begin to ache.

Position of back rest
100 to 200mm (4 to 8in) high and 150 to 180mm (6 to 7in) above the seat
The back rest should support the middle portion of your back, known as the lumbar region.

Armrest height
200 to 250mm (8 to 10in) above the seat
The armrest supports your forearm at a comfortable height; it also provides a convenient handhold when lowering yourself into or rising from the seat. Half armrests allow the chair to be drawn up to a table.

Seat height
390 to 430mm (15½ to 17in)
If the front rail is too high, it presses uncomfortably on the backs of your thighs, cutting off the blood supply to your legs. If the seat is too low, you may have difficulty sitting down and getting up.

FRAME CHAIRS

The frame chair is the most versatile form of dining chair. The four rails of the seat frame are jointed into a leg at each corner of the structure, while the back legs extend upwards to form the main support of the back rest. The seat itself may be upholstered, caned, rush-covered, or made from solid wood.

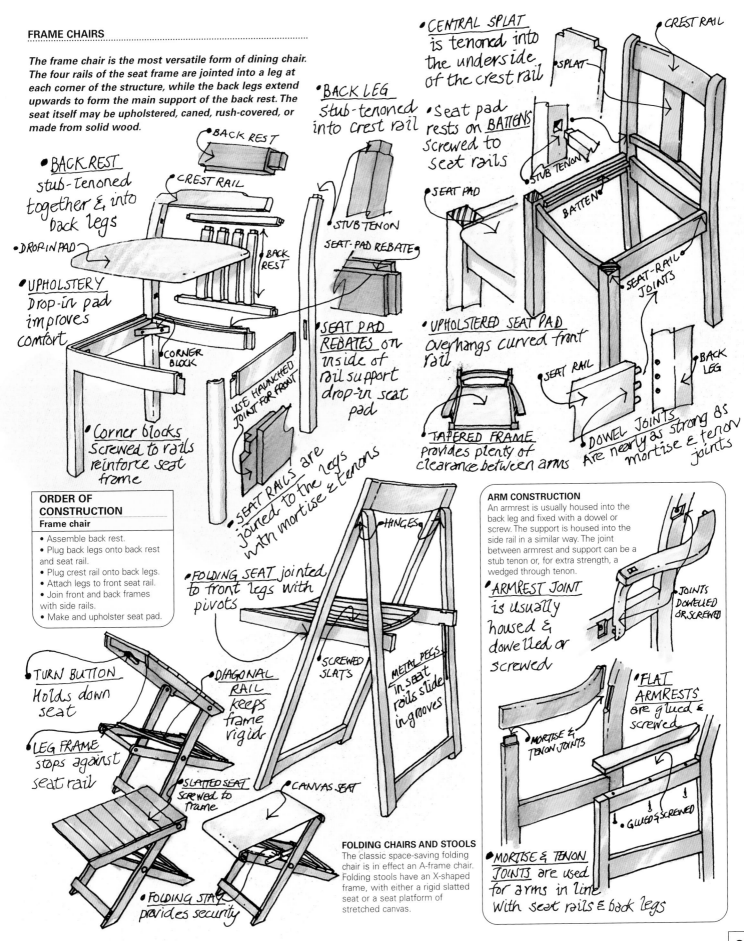

• BACK REST stub-tenoned together & into back legs

• DROP-IN PAD

• UPHOLSTERY Drop-in pad improves comfort

• Corner blocks screwed to rails reinforce seat frame

BACK REST

CREST RAIL

BACK REST

CORNER BLOCK

USE HAUNCHED JOINT FOR FRONT

• SEAT RAILS are jointed to the legs with mortise & tenons

• BACK LEG stub-tenoned into crest rail

STUB TENON

SEAT-PAD REBATE

• SEAT PAD REBATES on inside of rail support drop-in seat pad

• CENTRAL SPLAT is tenoned into the underside of the crest rail

SPLAT

CREST RAIL

• Seat pad rests on BATTENS screwed to seat rails

SEAT PAD

STUB TENON

BATTEN

SEAT-RAIL JOINTS

• UPHOLSTERED SEAT PAD overhangs curved front rail

• TAPERED FRAME provides plenty of clearance between arms

SEAT RAIL

BACK LEG

• DOWEL JOINTS are nearly as strong as mortise & tenon joints

ORDER OF CONSTRUCTION
Frame chair

• Assemble back rest.
• Plug back legs onto back rest and seat rail.
• Plug crest rail onto back legs.
• Attach legs to front seat rail.
• Join front and back frames with side rails.
• Make and upholster seat pad.

HINGES

• FOLDING SEAT jointed to front legs with pivots

• SCREWED SLATS

METAL PEGS in seat rails slide in grooves

• TURN BUTTON Holds down seat

• DIAGONAL RAIL keeps frame rigid

• LEG FRAME stops against seat rail

• SLATTED SEAT screwed to frame

• CANVAS SEAT

• FOLDING STAY provides security

FOLDING CHAIRS AND STOOLS
The classic space-saving folding chair is in effect an A-frame chair. Folding stools have an X-shaped frame, with either a rigid slatted seat or a seat platform of stretched canvas.

ARM CONSTRUCTION
An armrest is usually housed into the back leg and fixed with a dowel or screw. The support is housed into the side rail in a similar way. The joint between armrest and support can be a stub tenon or, for extra strength, a wedged through tenon.

• ARMREST JOINT is usually housed & dowelled or screwed

JOINTS DOWELLED OR SCREWED

• FLAT ARMRESTS are glued & screwed

MORTISE & TENON JOINTS

• GLUED & SCREWED

• MORTISE & TENON JOINTS are used for arms in line with seat rails & back legs

STACKING CHAIRS

The narrow seat frames provide clearance for the back legs when stacking chairs are piled one on top of another for storage.

ORDER OF CONSTRUCTION
Stacking chair

• Join back legs to back rail, then fit crest rail.
• Attach front legs to front seat rail.
• Join front and back frames with side rails.
• Glue back rest to crest rail, and plywood seat panel to chair frame.

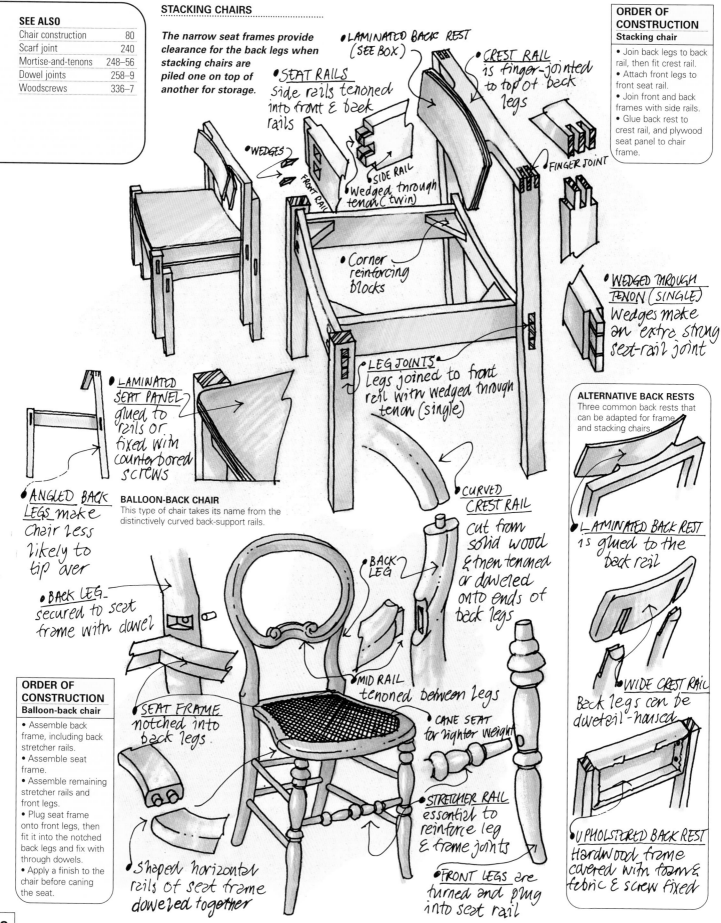

• LAMINATED BACK REST (SEE BOX)

• SEAT RAILS Side rails tenoned into front & back rails

• CREST RAIL is finger-jointed to top of back legs

FINGER JOINT

• WEDGES

SIDE RAIL

FRONT RAIL

Wedged through tenon (twin)

• Corner reinforcing blocks

• WEDGED THROUGH TENON (SINGLE) Wedges make an extra strong seat-rail joint

• LAMINATED SEAT PANEL glued to rails or fixed with counterbored screws

• LEG JOINTS Legs joined to front rail with wedged through tenon (single)

• ANGLED BACK LEGS make chair less likely to tip over

• BACK LEG secured to seat frame with dowel

BALLOON-BACK CHAIR
This type of chair takes its name from the distinctively curved back-support rails.

ALTERNATIVE BACK RESTS
Three common back rests that can be adapted for frame and stacking chairs.

• LAMINATED BACK REST is glued to the back rail

• BACK LEG

• CURVED CREST RAIL cut from solid wood & then tenoned or dowelled onto ends of back legs

• MID RAIL tenoned between legs

• CANE SEAT for lighter weight

• WIDE CREST RAIL Back legs can be dovetail-housed

ORDER OF CONSTRUCTION
Balloon-back chair

• Assemble back frame, including back stretcher rails.
• Assemble seat frame.
• Assemble remaining stretcher rails and front legs.
• Plug seat frame onto front legs, then fit it into the notched back legs and fix with through dowels.
• Apply a finish to the chair before caning the seat.

• SEAT FRAME notched into back legs

• Shaped horizontal rails of seat frame dowelled together

• STRETCHER RAIL essential to reinforce leg & frame joints

• FRONT LEGS are turned and plug into seat rail

• UPHOLSTERED BACK REST Hardwood frame covered with foam & fabric & screw fixed

BENTWOOD CHAIRS

Bentwood chairs are constructed by bolting and screwing together steam-bent beech components. This type of chair is extremely tough and resilient provided the fixings are not allowed to work loose.

LAMINATED CHAIRS

Structurally weak short grain is avoided by making chair frames from thick laminated veneers. This type of structure is strong and resilient.

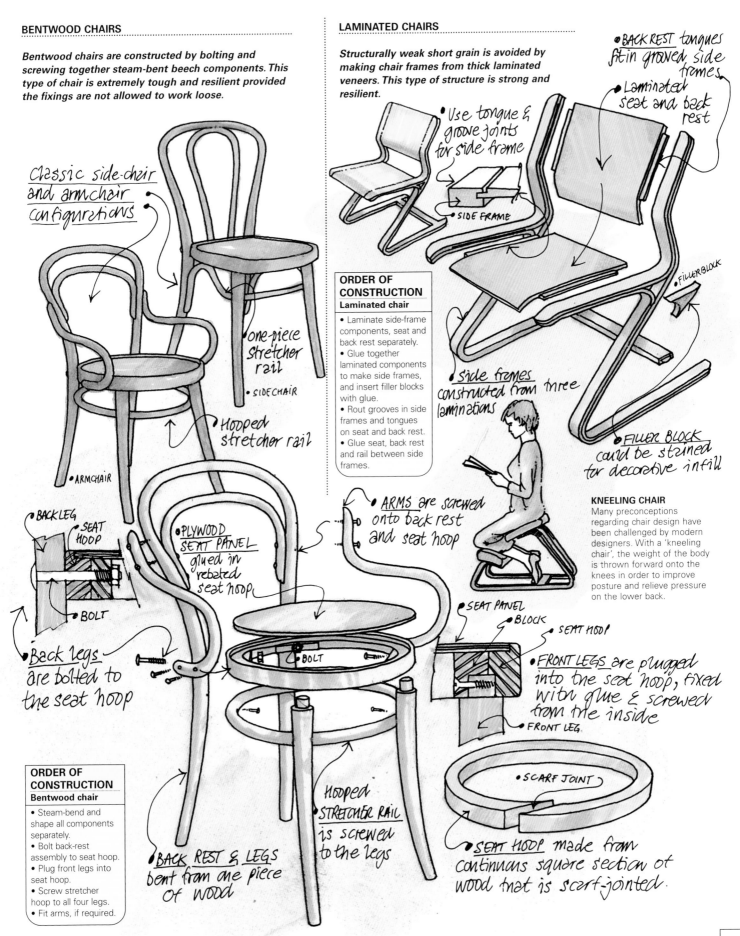

Classic side-chair and armchair configurations

• one-piece stretcher rail
• SIDECHAIR

Hooped stretcher rail

• ARMCHAIR

• BACKLEG
SEAT HOOP
• BOLT

Back legs are bolted to the seat hoop

• PLYWOOD SEAT PANEL glued in rebated seat hoop

• BOLT

Hooped STRETCHER RAIL is screwed to the legs

• BACK REST & LEGS bent from one piece of wood

ORDER OF CONSTRUCTION
Bentwood chair

• Steam-bend and shape all components separately.
• Bolt back-rest assembly to seat hoop.
• Plug front legs into seat hoop.
• Screw stretcher hoop to all four legs.
• Fit arms, if required.

• Use tongue & groove joints for side frame
← SIDE FRAME

• BACK REST tongues fit in grooved side frames
• Laminated seat and back rest

• FILLERBLOCK

side frames constructed from three laminations

• FILLER BLOCK could be stained for decorative infill

ORDER OF CONSTRUCTION
Laminated chair

• Laminate side-frame components, seat and back rest separately.
• Glue together laminated components to make side frames, and insert filler blocks with glue.
• Rout grooves in side frames and tongues on seat and back rest.
• Glue seat, back rest and rail between side frames.

• ARMS are screwed onto back rest and seat hoop

• SEAT PANEL
• BLOCK
• SEAT HOOP

• FRONT LEGS are plugged into the seat hoop, fixed with glue & screwed from the inside
• FRONT LEG

• SCARF JOINT

• SEAT HOOP made from continuous square section of wood that is scarf-jointed.

KNEELING CHAIR

Many preconceptions regarding chair design have been challenged by modern designers. With a 'kneeling chair', the weight of the body is thrown forward onto the knees in order to improve posture and relieve pressure on the lower back.

83

STICK CHAIRS

The stick chair in its countless variations is a beautifully proportioned and functional piece of furniture that has evolved under the trained eye and experienced hands of craftsmen from all over Europe and America. It relies for its strength and rigidity on the fact that the large number of components share the load in such a way that the forces applied to the structure do not attempt to pull it apart. Stick chairs have always been made from tough dense native timbers such as beech, oak, ash and elm.

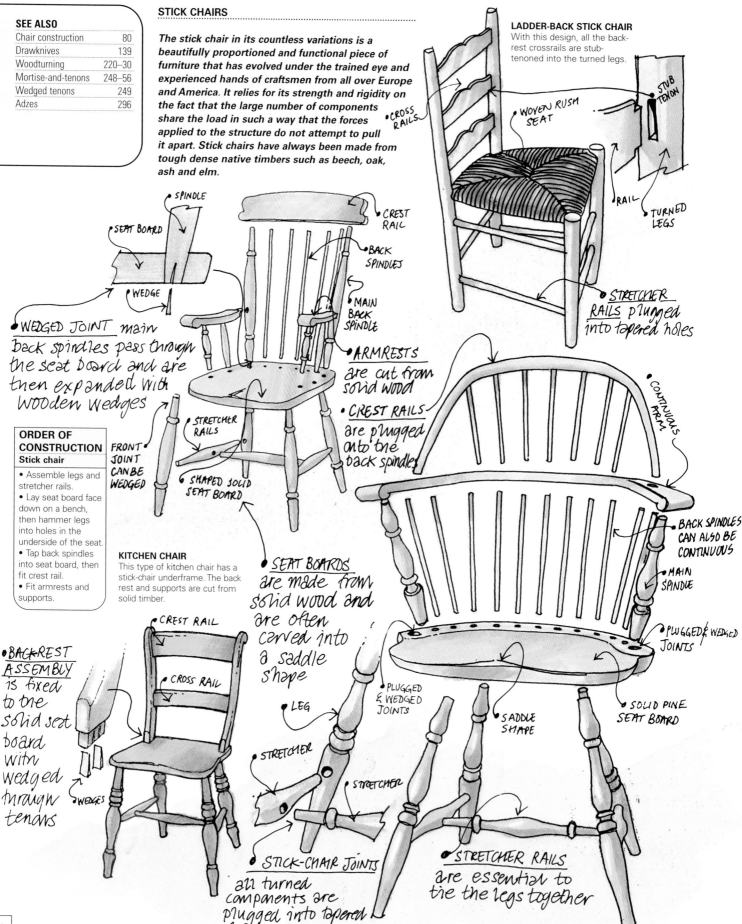

LADDER-BACK STICK CHAIR
With this design, all the back-rest crossrails are stub-tenoned into the turned legs.

CROSS RAILS

WOVEN RUSH SEAT

STUB TENON

RAIL

TURNED LEGS

STRETCHER RAILS plugged into tapered holes

SPINDLE

SEAT BOARD

WEDGE

CREST RAIL

BACK SPINDLES

MAIN BACK SPINDLE

• WEDGED JOINT main back spindles pass through the seat board and are then expanded with wooden wedges

• ARMRESTS are cut from solid wood

• CREST RAILS are plugged onto the back spindles

STRETCHER RAILS

FRONT JOINT CAN BE WEDGED

SHAPED SOLID SEAT BOARD

CONTINUOUS ARM

BACK SPINDLES CAN ALSO BE CONTINUOUS

MAIN SPINDLE

PLUGGED & WEDGED JOINTS

ORDER OF CONSTRUCTION
Stick chair

• Assemble legs and stretcher rails.
• Lay seat board face down on a bench, then hammer legs into holes in the underside of the seat.
• Tap back spindles into seat board, then fit crest rail.
• Fit armrests and supports.

KITCHEN CHAIR
This type of kitchen chair has a stick-chair underframe. The back rest and supports are cut from solid timber.

SEAT BOARDS are made from solid wood and are often carved into a saddle shape

SADDLE SHAPE

SOLID PINE SEAT BOARD

CREST RAIL

CROSS RAIL

• BACKREST ASSEMBLY is fixed to the solid seat board with wedged through tenons

WEDGES

• LEG

• STRETCHER

PLUGGED & WEDGED JOINTS

STRETCHER

• STICK-CHAIR JOINTS all turned components are plugged into tapered holes

• STRETCHER RAILS are essential to tie the legs together

TABLE CONSTRUCTION

A table need be no more than a flat surface supported at a height that's convenient for dining, studying, typing or serving coffee – and yet designers have expended considerable creative energy on this seemingly simple category of furniture. They have experimented with table tops to see what is the best shape and size to accommodate the average dinner party; underframes range from straightforward structures designed to provide maximum leg room to exercises in functional sculpture; and perhaps most ingenuity has been invested in finding easy ways of increasing the size of compact tables when it's necessary to seat a large group of people. The examples that follow illustrate traditional methods and are applicable to both large and small tables. Basic folding and extending mechanisms are also described.

DESIGNING A FUNCTIONAL TABLE

Eating at a dining table can be either an enjoyable social occasion or a nightmare of cramped knees and colliding elbows, depending on the amount of room provided by the designer. Most people are able to write or draw comfortably at dining-table height – but before designing a table for someone to work at, find out whether he or she will be using a computer, because at least part of the table top must be lowered to present a keyboard at the optimum level.

DINING TABLES

Moving a chair
700mm (2ft 4in)
A diner needs a space of this size in order to move a chair and stand up from the table.

Dining-table height
700mm (2ft 4in)
This is a comfortable height for a dining table, though eating from a bowl with chopsticks is easier either at a table closer to the height of a kitchen worktop or sitting cross-legged at a low table little more than 300mm (1ft) from the ground.

Elbow room
600mm (2ft)
This is sufficient space for you to wield a knife and fork without obstructing your neighbour.

Leg room
600mm (2ft)
Allow at least this dimension between the edge of the table rail and the floor.

Knee clearance
250mm (10in)
This is the minimum distance from the edge of the top to a table leg in order to provide clearance for your knees when your chair is drawn up to the table.

Rectangular dining table
To seat six people comfortably, a rectangular dining table should be at least 1.5 x 1m (5ft x 3ft 3in).

Circular dining table
A circular dining table of only 1m (3ft 3in) diameter will seat up to four persons. Increase the diameter to 1.2m (4ft) for six diners, and to about 1.5m (5ft) to seat eight.

WORKTABLES

Desk height
700mm (2ft 4in)
A desk should be the same height as a dining table.

Word processing
650mm (2ft 2in)
Ideally, a worktable used for word processing or other keyboard work should be 50mm (2in) lower than the average desk.

Maximum reach
475mm (1ft 7in)
Sitting at a desk, you can reach a shelf at this height above it.

OCCASIONAL TABLES

300 to 600mm (1 to 2ft)
Occasional tables vary in height a great deal. The lowest ones often look stylish, but can be a bit too low for comfort.

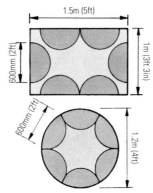

Dining table seating arrangements

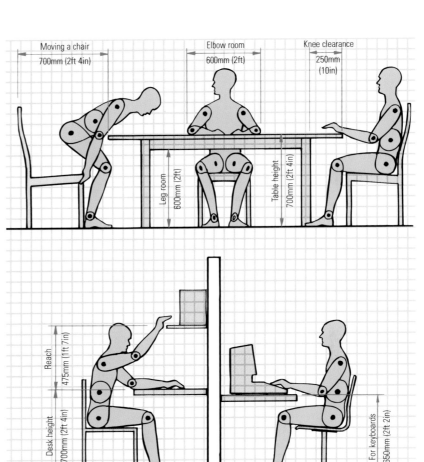

A frame table has four legs, one at each corner. For all its simplicity, a basic frame table can be modified in numerous ways to create a variety of dining tables, side tables and desks With strong mortise-and-tenon or dowel joints, the classic design can be adapted successfully for tables of practically any size. You can make the top from strips of solid timber glued edge to edge, but for stability the larger tops are often constructed from lipped and veneered blockboard or MDF.

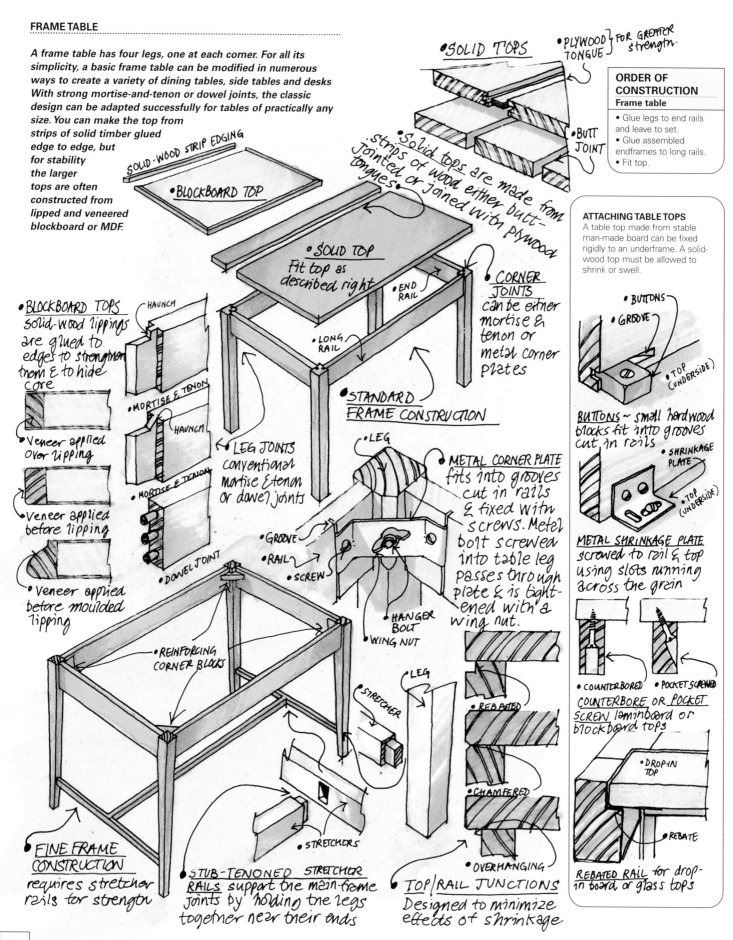

• SOLID TOPS

• PLYWOOD TONGUE } FOR GREATER strength.

• BUTT JOINT

ORDER OF CONSTRUCTION
Frame table
• Glue legs to end rails and leave to set.
• Glue assembled endframes to long rails.
• Fit top.

• Solid tops are made from strips of wood either butt-jointed or joined with plywood tongues.

• SOLID-WOOD STRIP EDGING

• BLOCKBOARD TOP

• SOLID TOP
Fit top as described right

• END RAIL

• LONG RAIL

STANDARD FRAME CONSTRUCTION

CORNER JOINTS can be either mortise & tenon or metal corner plates

ATTACHING TABLE TOPS
A table top made from stable man-made board can be fixed rigidly to an underframe. A solid-wood top must be allowed to shrink or swell.

• BUTTONS
• GROOVE
• TOP (UNDERSIDE)

BUTTONS ~ small hardwood blocks fit into grooves cut in rails

• SHRINKAGE PLATE
• TOP (UNDERSIDE)

METAL SHRINKAGE PLATE screwed to rail & top using slots running across the grain

• BLOCKBOARD TOPS solid-wood lippings are glued to edges to strengthen them & to hide core

HAUNCH
• MORTISE & TENON
HAUNCH
• MORTISE & TENON
• DOWEL JOINT

• Veneer applied over lipping
• Veneer applied before lipping
• Veneer applied before moulded lipping

LEG JOINTS conventional mortise & tenon or dowel joints

• LEG
• GROOVE
• RAIL
• SCREW

METAL CORNER PLATE fits into grooves cut in rails & fixed with screws. Metal bolt screwed into table leg passes through plate & is tightened with a wing nut.

• HANGER BOLT
• WING NUT

• COUNTERBORED
• POCKET SCREWED

COUNTERBORE OR POCKET SCREW laminboard or blockboard tops

• REINFORCING CORNER BLOCKS

• STRETCHER

• LEG

• REBATED
• CHAMFERED

• DROP-IN TOP

• REBATE

REBATED RAIL for drop-in board or glass tops

FINE FRAME CONSTRUCTION requires stretcher rails for strength

STUB-TENONED STRETCHER RAILS support the main-frame joints by holding the legs together near their ends

• STRETCHERS

TOP/RAIL JUNCTIONS Designed to minimize effects of shrinkage

• OVERHANGING

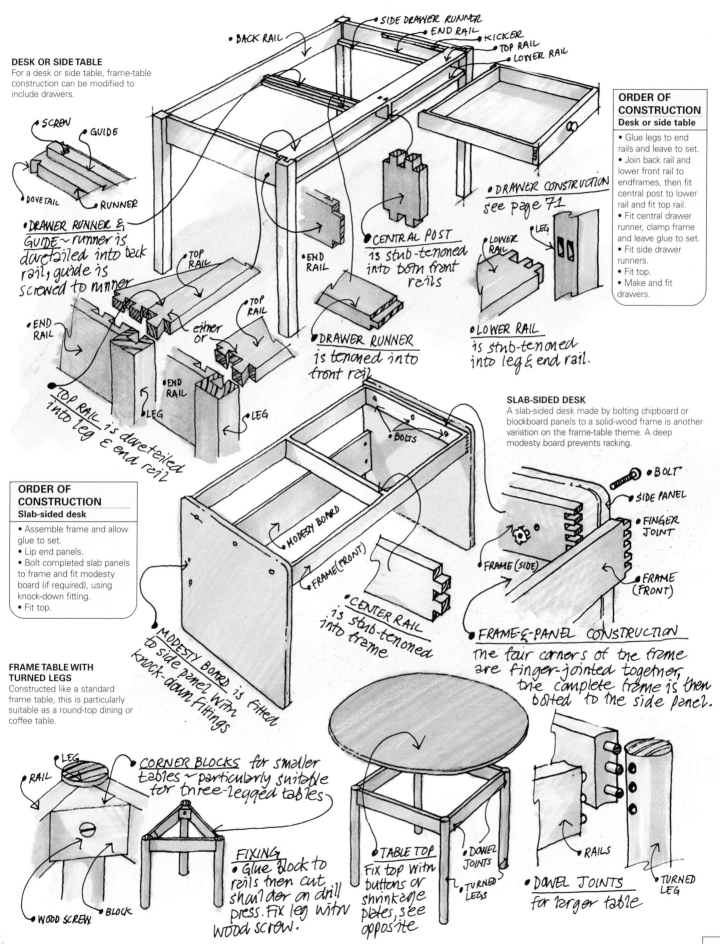

DESK OR SIDE TABLE
For a desk or side table, frame-table construction can be modified to include drawers.

• SCREW
• GUIDE
• DOVETAIL
• RUNNER

• DRAWER RUNNER & GUIDE ~ runner is dovetailed into back rail, guide is screwed to runner

• END RAIL
• TOP RAIL
TOP RAIL is dovetailed into leg & end rail
either or
• END RAIL
• END RAIL
• LEG
• LEG
• TOP RAIL

• BACK RAIL
• SIDE DRAWER RUNNER
• END RAIL
• KICKER
• TOP RAIL
• LOWER RAIL

• END RAIL
• CENTRAL POST is stub-tenoned into both front rails
• DRAWER RUNNER is tenoned into front rail

• DRAWER CONSTRUCTION see page 71

• LOWER RAIL
• LEG
• LOWER RAIL is stub-tenoned into leg & end rail.

ORDER OF CONSTRUCTION
Desk or side table
• Glue legs to end rails and leave to set.
• Join back rail and lower front rail to endframes, then fit central post to lower rail and fit top rail.
• Fit central drawer runner, clamp frame and leave glue to set.
• Fit side drawer runners.
• Fit top.
• Make and fit drawers.

ORDER OF CONSTRUCTION
Slab-sided desk
• Assemble frame and allow glue to set.
• Lip end panels.
• Bolt completed slab panels to frame and fit modesty board (if required), using knock-down fitting.
• Fit top.

• BOLTS
• MODESTY BOARD
• FRAME (FRONT)
• CENTER RAIL is stub-tenoned into frame
MODESTY BOARD is fitted to side panel with knock-down fittings

SLAB-SIDED DESK
A slab-sided desk made by bolting chipboard or blockboard panels to a solid-wood frame is another variation on the frame-table theme. A deep modesty board prevents racking.

• BOLT
• SIDE PANEL
• FINGER JOINT
• FRAME (SIDE)
• FRAME (FRONT)

FRAME-&-PANEL CONSTRUCTION
The four corners of the frame are finger-jointed together, the complete frame is then bolted to the side panel.

FRAME TABLE WITH TURNED LEGS
Constructed like a standard frame table, this is particularly suitable as a round-top dining or coffee table.

• LEG
• RAIL
CORNER BLOCKS for smaller tables ~ particularly suitable for three-legged tables
FIXING
• Glue block to rails then cut shoulder on drill press. Fix leg with wood screw.
• WOOD SCREW
• BLOCK

• TABLE TOP
FIX top with buttons or shrinkage plates, see opposite
• DOWEL JOINTS
• TURNED LEGS

• RAILS
• DOWEL JOINTS for larger table
• TURNED LEG

87

REFECTORY TABLE

This type of underframe is suitable for dining and coffee tables. It is usually made to 'knock down' for transportation. Larger frames, especially, must be strongly constructed to prevent racking. Attach a solid top to the endframes, using shrinkage plates. A blockboard top can be attached with screws passed through the top rails of the endframes.

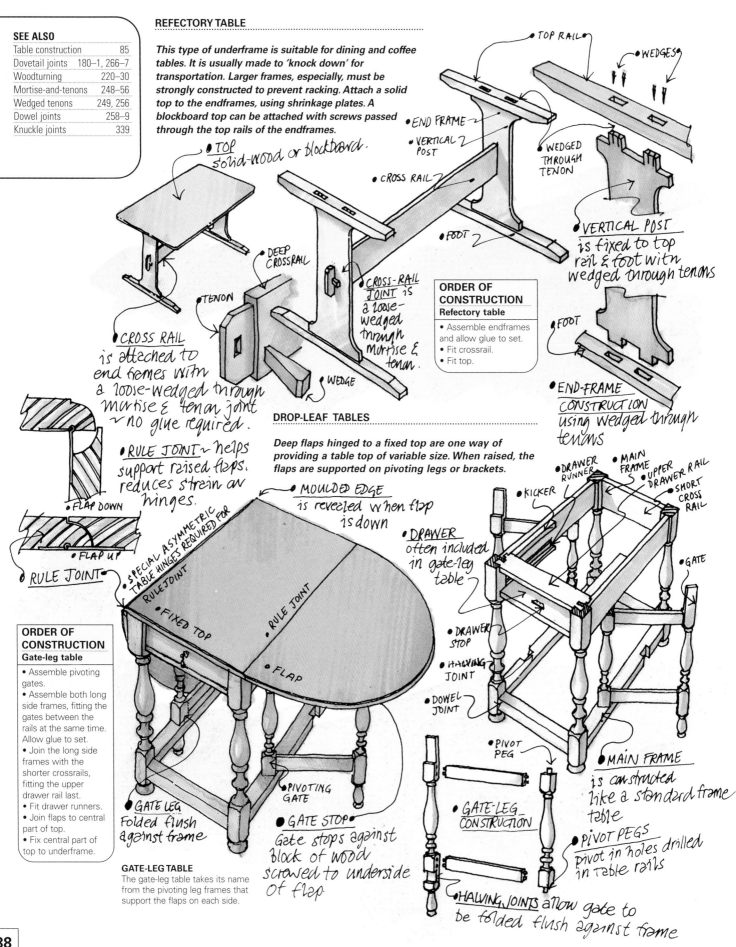

ORDER OF CONSTRUCTION
Refectory table
• Assemble endframes and allow glue to set.
• Fit crossrail.
• Fit top.

DROP-LEAF TABLES

Deep flaps hinged to a fixed top are one way of providing a table top of variable size. When raised, the flaps are supported on pivoting legs or brackets.

ORDER OF CONSTRUCTION
Gate-leg table
• Assemble pivoting gates.
• Assemble both long side frames, fitting the gates between the rails at the same time. Allow glue to set.
• Join the long side frames with the shorter crossrails, fitting the upper drawer rail last.
• Fit drawer runners.
• Join flaps to central part of top.
• Fix central part of top to underframe.

GATE-LEG TABLE
The gate-leg table takes its name from the pivoting leg frames that support the flaps on each side.

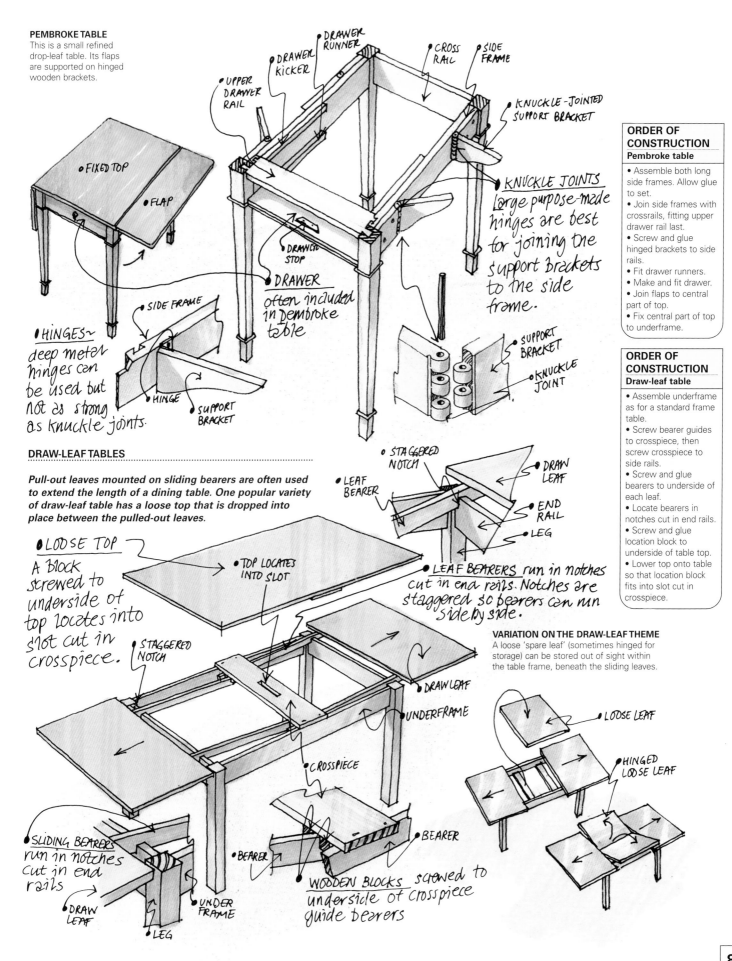

PEMBROKE TABLE
This is a small refined drop-leaf table. Its flaps are supported on hinged wooden brackets.

DRAWER RUNNER

DRAWER KICKER

CROSS RAIL

SIDE FRAME

UPPER DRAWER RAIL

KNUCKLE-JOINTED SUPPORT BRACKET

• FIXED TOP

• FLAP

• KNUCKLE JOINTS
Large purpose-made hinges are best for joining the support brackets to the side frame.

• SIDE FRAME

• DRAWER STOP

• DRAWER
often included in Pembroke table

• HINGES~
deep metal hinges can be used but not as strong as knuckle joints.

• HINGE

SUPPORT BRACKET

SUPPORT BRACKET

KNUCKLE JOINT

ORDER OF CONSTRUCTION
Pembroke table
• Assemble both long side frames. Allow glue to set.
• Join side frames with crossrails, fitting upper drawer rail last.
• Screw and glue hinged brackets to side rails.
• Fit drawer runners.
• Make and fit drawer.
• Join flaps to central part of top.
• Fix central part of top to underframe.

ORDER OF CONSTRUCTION
Draw-leaf table
• Assemble underframe as for a standard frame table.
• Screw bearer guides to crosspiece, then screw crosspiece to side rails.
• Screw and glue bearers to underside of each leaf.
• Locate bearers in notches cut in end rails.
• Screw and glue location block to underside of table top.
• Lower top onto table so that location block fits into slot cut in crosspiece.

DRAW-LEAF TABLES

Pull-out leaves mounted on sliding bearers are often used to extend the length of a dining table. One popular variety of draw-leaf table has a loose top that is dropped into place between the pulled-out leaves.

• STAGGERED NOTCH

• LEAF BEARER

• DRAW LEAF

END RAIL

LEG

• LOOSE TOP
A block screwed to underside of top locates into slot cut in crosspiece.

• TOP LOCATES INTO SLOT

• LEAF BEARERS run in notches cut in end rails. Notches are staggered so bearers can run side by side.

STAGGERED NOTCH

DRAW LEAF

UNDERFRAME

CROSSPIECE

• SLIDING BEARERS run in notches cut in end rails

• DRAW LEAF

• LEG

• UNDER FRAME

• BEARER

• BEARER

WOODEN BLOCKS screwed to underside of crosspiece guide bearers

VARIATION ON THE DRAW-LEAF THEME
A loose 'spare leaf' (sometimes hinged for storage) can be stored out of sight within the table frame, beneath the sliding leaves.

• LOOSE LEAF

• HINGED LOOSE LEAF

FOLDING-TOP TABLES

One way to reduce the area of a table top when it is not in use is to split it down the middle and hinge it, so that one half can be folded over to lie on top of the other.

SIDE TABLE

A side table can be converted into a card table or small dining table by swivelling the two back legs on knuckle joints and opening the hinged top.

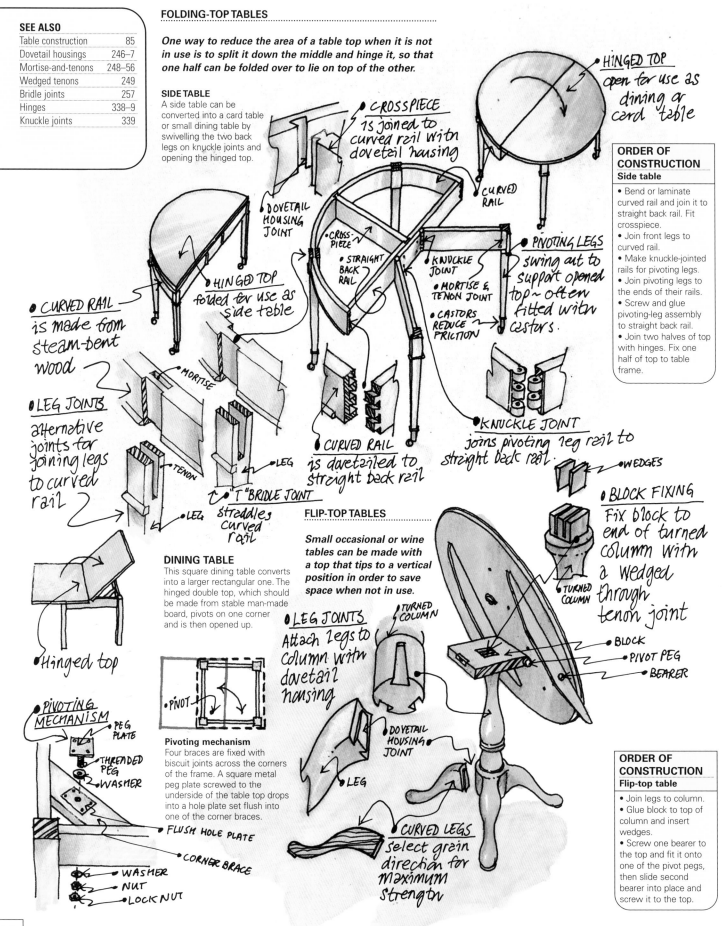

HINGED TOP open for use as dining or card table

CROSSPIECE is joined to curved rail with dovetail housing

DOVETAIL HOUSING JOINT

CURVED RAIL

CROSSPIECE

STRAIGHT BACK RAIL

KNUCKLE JOINT

MORTISE & TENON JOINT

CASTORS REDUCE FRICTION

PIVOTING LEGS swing out to support opened top ~ often fitted with castors.

HINGED TOP folded for use as side table

• CURVED RAIL is made from steam-bent wood

• LEG JOINTS alternative joints for joining legs to curved rail

MORTISE

TENON

LEG

LEG

"T" BRIDLE JOINT straddles curved rail

• CURVED RAIL is dovetailed to straight back rail

KNUCKLE JOINT joins pivoting leg rail to straight back rail

WEDGES

• BLOCK FIXING Fix block to end of turned column with a wedged through tenon joint

TURNED COLUMN

BLOCK

PIVOT PEG

BEARER

ORDER OF CONSTRUCTION
Side table

• Bend or laminate curved rail and join it to straight back rail. Fit crosspiece.
• Join front legs to curved rail.
• Make knuckle-jointed rails for pivoting legs.
• Join pivoting legs to the ends of their rails.
• Screw and glue pivoting-leg assembly to straight back rail.
• Join two halves of top with hinges. Fix one half of top to table frame.

DINING TABLE

This square dining table converts into a larger rectangular one. The hinged double top, which should be made from stable man-made board, pivots on one corner and is then opened up.

Hinged top

PIVOT

Pivoting mechanism
Four braces are fixed with biscuit joints across the corners of the frame. A square metal peg plate screwed to the underside of the table top drops into a hole plate set flush into one of the corner braces.

FLIP-TOP TABLES

Small occasional or wine tables can be made with a top that tips to a vertical position in order to save space when not in use.

• LEG JOINTS Attach legs to column with dovetail housing

TURNED COLUMN

DOVETAIL HOUSING JOINT

LEG

CURVED LEGS select grain direction for maximum strength

PIVOTING MECHANISM

PEG PLATE

THREADED PEG

WASHER

FLUSH HOLE PLATE

CORNER BRACE

WASHER

NUT

LOCK NUT

ORDER OF CONSTRUCTION
Flip-top table

• Join legs to column.
• Glue block to top of column and insert wedges.
• Screw one bearer to the top and fit it onto one of the pivot pegs, then slide second bearer into place and screw it to the top.

STORAGE-UNIT CONSTRUCTION

As a rule, we require an immense range of storage to keep our belongings hidden from view. Even collections of books, CDs or DVDs kept on open shelves need to be stored systematically, so you can lay hands on a particular one without a prolonged search. Customarily, when we talk about the various kinds of furniture used for storage we refer to them by specific names – such as wardrobe, bookcase or dresser – that indicate their function and also their place in the home. Nowadays, many designers regard these traditional classifications as limiting and prefer to employ shelves, drawers and cupboards in whatever combination provides the most effective use of space. In the following pages some of the many ways of constructing cupboard, drawer and shelf units are illustrated and described, so you can use them, either individually or in combination, to design storage to meet your own needs.

DESIGNING ACCESSIBLE STORAGE

Plan storage systems using recommended dimensions that permit someone of average build to reach the top shelf or gain access to the back of a cupboard or drawer without stretching.

Maximum shelf height
1.8 to 2m (6ft to 6ft 6in)
You can reach a shelf this distance from the floor.

Eye-level shelf
1.5 to 1.7m (5ft to 5ft 8in)
Mount a shelf at this height for books, box files, DVDs or other objects that you want to find easily.

Maximum reach above worktop
1.05m (3ft 6in)
You can just reach a shelf at this height when leaning across a standard kitchen worktop.

Optimum reach above worktop
900mm (3ft)
Store frequently used objects at this height.

Lowest shelf above worktop
450mm (1ft 6in)
Shelves and cupboards mounted lower than this begin to obscure your view of the back of the worktop and may obstruct use of food mixers and blenders.

Standard worktop height
900mm (3ft)
You can work comfortably at a counter top fitted at this height.

Worktop depth
600mm (2ft)
Major electrical appliances (dishwashers, washing machines, etc.) are designed to fit beneath a worktop of this depth. These appliances can be concealed behind door panels that match kitchen units.

Wall-cabinet depth
300mm (1ft)
This is the optimum depth for a wall-hung cupboard mounted above a worktop.

Crouching at a cupboard
1m (3ft 3in)
Allow this space in front of a low cupboard.

Safe passing space
900mm (3ft)
Cramped kitchens and workshops cause accidents. Allow this width as a safe access corridor, plus an additional 450mm (1ft 6in) to provide room for someone standing at a worktop.

Access to drawers
1.25m (4ft 2in)
This amount of space is required for someone kneeling at an open drawer.

Hanging space
1.45 to 1.6m (4ft 10in to 5ft 4in)
Allow this space below a hanging rail to accommodate long coats and dresses.

850mm (2ft 10in)
Jackets and shirts will hang in this space.

600mm (2ft)
A storage unit of this depth will accommodate clothing hung on a rail.

Drawer size
425 to 500mm (1ft 5in to 1ft 8in)
Make drawers or trays this depth for folded shirts, sweaters or towels.

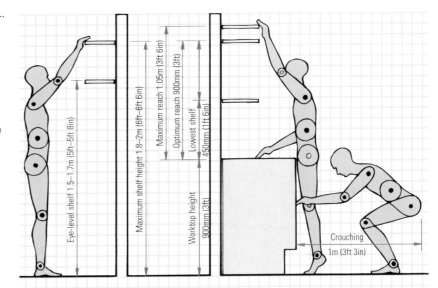

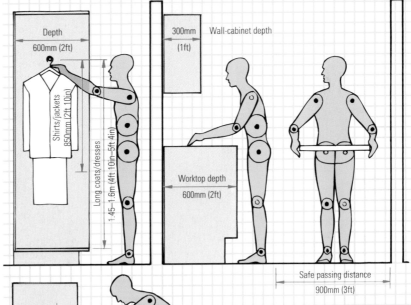

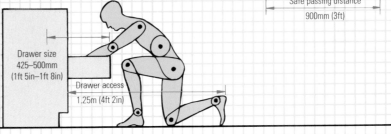

SHELF UNITS

Simple open shelf units constructed from solid timber or man-made boards are suitable for storing books, CDs or DVDs and for displaying collections. Similar forms of construction are used when shelving is incorporated in more complex storage units.

SOLID-WOOD UNIT

Well-made shelf units constructed from solid softwood and hardwood are generally stronger and more attractive than units constructed from man-made boards.

ORDER OF CONSTRUCTION
Solid-wood unit

• Fit fixed bottom shelf into housing in side panels.
• Tap dovetailed top into side panels, then square up and allow glue to set.
• Fix back in rebate with fillets.
• Fit adjustable shelves.

• MITRED DOVETAIL JOINT

DOVETAIL JOINTS FOR TOP

• LAPPED DOVETAIL JOINT

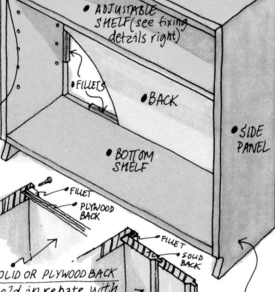

• FIXED TOP

• ADJUSTABLE SHELF (see fixing details right)

• FILLETS

• BACK

• SIDE PANEL

• BOTTOM SHELF

• FILLET
PLYWOOD BACK

SOLID OR PLYWOOD BACK
held in rebate with screwed fillet

• FILLET
SOLID BACK

• DECORATIVE T&G BACK
held in rebate by fillets pinned to side panel

• ADJUSTABLE SHELVES
proprietary adjustable shelving can be used for intermediate shelves

SHELF STUDS

SHELF WIRES

SYSTEM SHELVING

• STRENGTHENING
Books & magazines impose heavy loads strengthening is needed

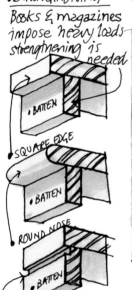

• BATTEN
SQUARE EDGE

• BATTEN
ROUND NOSE

• BATTEN
• REBATED

• FIXED SHELF

• TALL UNIT
An intermediate fixed shelf is needed to hold sides together

• INTERMEDIATE SUPPORT

• STOPPED HOUSING JOINT

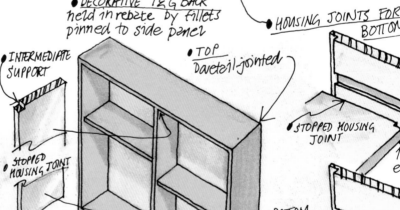

• TOP
Dovetail-jointed

• WIDE UNIT
needs an intermediate vertical support

• BACK
spans width of cabinet & is screwed to vertical support

HOUSING JOINTS FOR BOTTOM

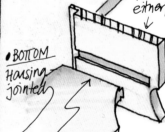

STOPPED HOUSING JOINT

either/or

• BOTTOM Housing jointed

• DOVETAIL HOUSING JOINT

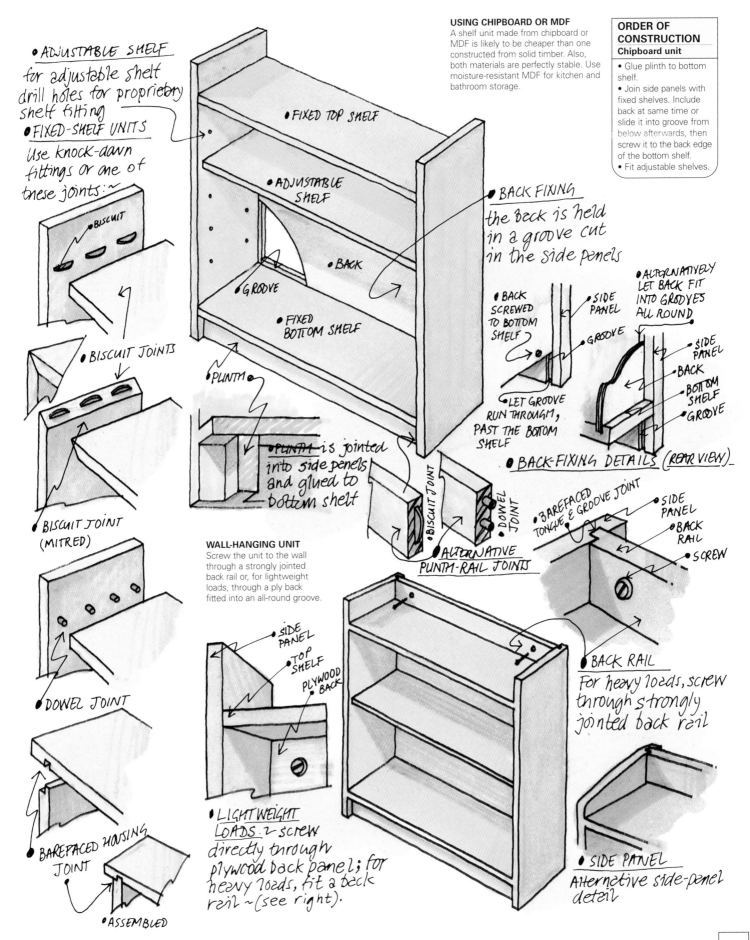

• **ADJUSTABLE SHELF**
for adjustable shelf
drill holes for proprietary
shelf fitting

• **FIXED-SHELF UNITS**
Use knock-down
fittings or one of
these joints:~

BISCUIT

• **BISCUIT JOINTS**

• **BISCUIT JOINT
(MITRED)**

• **DOWEL JOINT**

• **BAREFACED HOUSING
JOINT**

• **ASSEMBLED**

• FIXED TOP SHELF

• ADJUSTABLE
SHELF

• BACK

• GROOVE

• FIXED
BOTTOM SHELF

• PLINTH

• PLINTH is jointed
into side panels
and glued to
bottom shelf

WALL-HANGING UNIT
Screw the unit to the wall
through a strongly jointed
back rail or, for lightweight
loads, through a ply back
fitted into an all-round groove.

• SIDE PANEL
• TOP SHELF
• PLYWOOD BACK

• **LIGHTWEIGHT
LOADS.** 2 screw
directly through
plywood back panel; for
heavy loads, fit a back
rail ~(see right).

USING CHIPBOARD OR MDF
A shelf unit made from chipboard or
MDF is likely to be cheaper than one
constructed from solid timber. Also,
both materials are perfectly stable. Use
moisture-resistant MDF for kitchen and
bathroom storage.

**ORDER OF
CONSTRUCTION**
Chipboard unit
• Glue plinth to bottom
shelf.
• Join side panels with
fixed shelves. Include
back at same time or
slide it into groove from
below afterwards, then
screw it to the back edge
of the bottom shelf.
• Fit adjustable shelves.

• **BACK FIXING**
the back is held
in a groove cut
in the side panels

• BACK
SCREWED
TO BOTTOM
SHELF

• SIDE
PANEL

• GROOVE

• LET GROOVE
RUN THROUGH,
PAST THE BOTTOM
SHELF

• ALTERNATIVELY
LET BACK FIT
INTO GROOVES
ALL ROUND

• SIDE
PANEL
• BACK
• BOTTOM
SHELF
• GROOVE

• **BACK-FIXING DETAILS** (REAR VIEW)

BISCUIT JOINT

DOWEL
JOINT

• **ALTERNATIVE
PLINTH-RAIL JOINTS**

• BAREFACED
TONGUE & GROOVE JOINT

• SIDE
PANEL
• BACK
RAIL
• SCREW

• **BACK RAIL**
For heavy loads, screw
through strongly
jointed back rail

• **SIDE PANEL**
Alternative side-panel
detail

CUPBOARDS

Traditional and modern methods of construction can be used to make free-standing cupboards and also, with modifications, as a basis for building kitchen storage units.

TRADITIONAL CABINET CONSTRUCTION

Constructing a cabinet from solid timber requires considerable thought and careful making, in order to allow for the movement of the wood. It is also necessary to make up wide panels from relatively narrow boards – a task that is made easier if you have access to woodworking machinery.

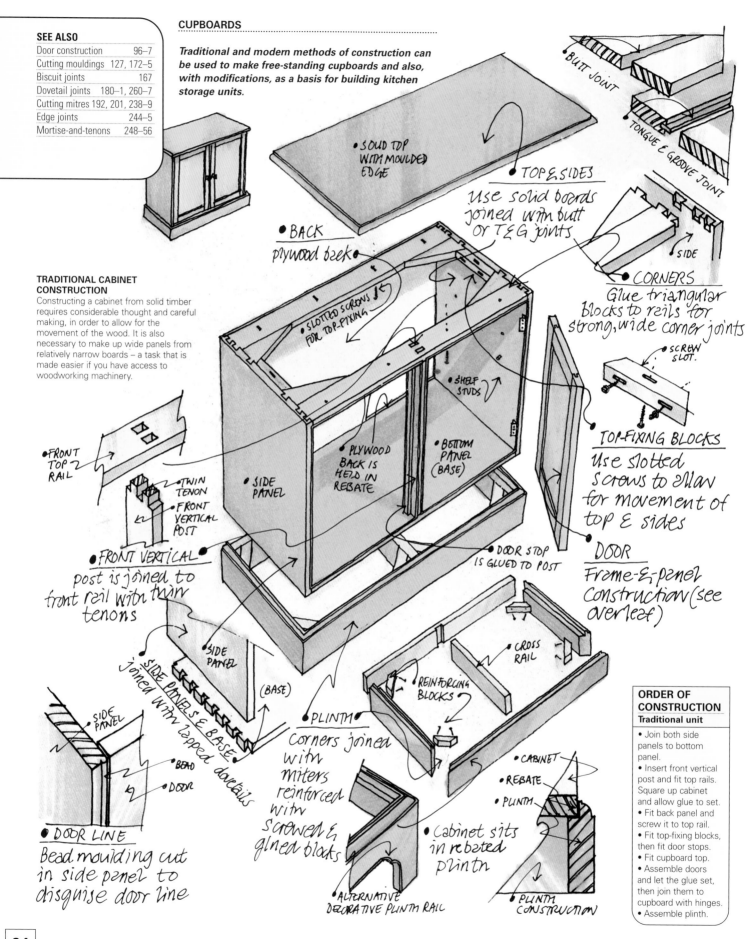

- SOLID TOP WITH MOULDED EDGE
- TOP & SIDES
  Use solid boards joined with butt or T&G joints
- BUTT JOINT
- TONGUE & GROOVE JOINT
- BACK
  plywood back
- SLOTTED SCREWS FOR TOP-FIXING
- SIDE
- CORNERS
  Glue triangular blocks to rails for strong, wide corner joints
- SCREW SLOT.
- SHELF STUDS
- PLYWOOD BACK IS HELD IN REBATE
- BOTTOM PANEL (BASE)
- SIDE PANEL
- TOP-FIXING BLOCKS
  Use slotted screws to allow for movement of top & sides
- FRONT TOP RAIL
- TWIN TENON
- FRONT VERTICAL POST
- FRONT VERTICAL
  post is joined to front rail with twin tenons
- SIDE PANEL
- DOOR STOP IS GLUED TO POST
- DOOR
  Frame-&-panel construction (see overleaf)
- SIDE PANEL (BASE)
- SIDE PANELS & BASE joined with lapped dovetails
- PLINTH
  Corners joined with miters reinforced with screwed & glued blocks
- CROSS RAIL
- REINFORCING BLOCKS
- CABINET
- REBATE
- PLINTH
- SIDE PANEL
- BEAD
- DOOR
- DOOR LINE
  Bead moulding cut in side panel to disguise door line
- ALTERNATIVE DECORATIVE PLINTH RAIL
- Cabinet sits in rebated plinth
- PLINTH CONSTRUCTION

ORDER OF CONSTRUCTION
Traditional unit

- Join both side panels to bottom panel.
- Insert front vertical post and fit top rails. Square up cabinet and allow glue to set.
- Fit back panel and screw it to top rail.
- Fit top-fixing blocks, then fit door stops.
- Fit cupboard top.
- Assemble doors and let the glue set, then join them to cupboard with hinges.
- Assemble plinth.

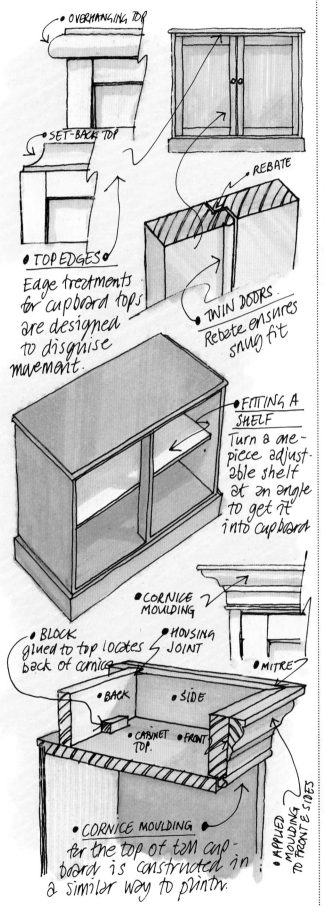

● OVERHANGING TOP

● SET-BACK TOP

● TOP EDGES ●
Edge treatments for cupboard tops are designed to disguise movement.

REBATE

● TWIN DOORS.
Rebate ensures snug fit

● FITTING A SHELF
Turn a one-piece adjustable shelf at an angle to get it into cupboard

● CORNICE MOULDING

● BLOCK glued to top locates back of cornice

● HOUSING JOINT

● MITRE

● BACK   ● SIDE

● CABINET TOP.   ● FRONT

● CORNICE MOULDING ●
for the top of tall cupboard is constructed in a similar way to plinth.

APPLIED MOULDING TO FRONT & SIDES

MODERN CABINET CONSTRUCTION

Constructing a cabinet from man-made boards is relatively simple since the materials are stable. If you are planning to make several identical cupboards, consider using machine-made joints for speed, accuracy and strength. Make entire cupboards from boards faced with veneers or plastic laminates, or save money by using these decorative boards just for the doors.

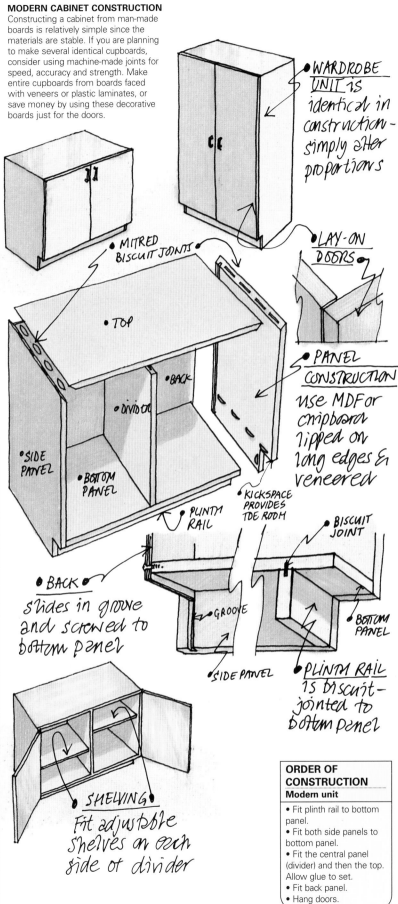

● WARDROBE UNIT is identical in construction— simply alter proportions

● MITRED BISCUIT JOINTS

● TOP

● BACK

● DIVIDER

● SIDE PANEL

● BOTTOM PANEL

● PLINTH RAIL

KICKSPACE PROVIDES TOE ROOM

● LAY-ON DOORS ●

● PANEL CONSTRUCTION
use MDF or chipboard lipped on long edges & veneered

● BISCUIT JOINT

● GROOVE

● SIDE PANEL

● BOTTOM PANEL

● BACK ●
slides in groove and screwed to bottom panel

● PLINTH RAIL is biscuit-jointed to bottom panel

● SHELVING ●
Fit adjustable shelves on each side of divider

ORDER OF CONSTRUCTION
Modern unit

● Fit plinth rail to bottom panel.
● Fit both side panels to bottom panel.
● Fit the central panel (divider) and then the top. Allow glue to set.
● Fit back panel.
● Hang doors.

95

All sorts of doors and flaps can be fitted to cupboards, storage units and other kinds of furniture. The most common forms of door construction are described and illustrated here.

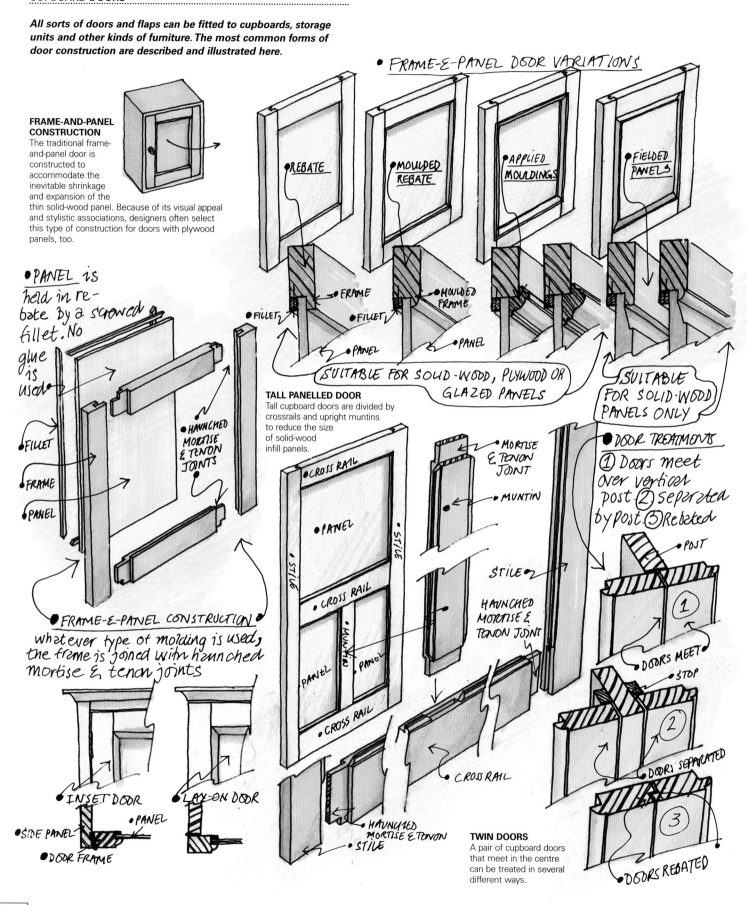

FRAME-AND-PANEL CONSTRUCTION

The traditional frame-and-panel door is constructed to accommodate the inevitable shrinkage and expansion of the thin solid-wood panel. Because of its visual appeal and stylistic associations, designers often select this type of construction for doors with plywood panels, too.

● FRAME-&-PANEL DOOR VARIATIONS

REBATE
MOULDED REBATE
APPLIED MOULDINGS
FIELDED PANELS

● FRAME
● FILLET
● MOULDED FRAME
● FILLET
● PANEL
● PANEL

SUITABLE FOR SOLID-WOOD, PLYWOOD OR GLAZED PANELS

SUITABLE FOR SOLID-WOOD PANELS ONLY

● PANEL is held in rebate by a screwed fillet. No glue is used ●

● FILLET
● FRAME
● PANEL
● HAUNCHED MORTISE & TENON JOINTS

● FRAME-&-PANEL CONSTRUCTION ●
whatever type of molding is used, the frame is joined with haunched mortise & tenon joints

● INSET DOOR
● LAY-ON DOOR
● SIDE PANEL
● PANEL
● DOOR FRAME

TALL PANELLED DOOR

Tall cupboard doors are divided by crossrails and upright muntins to reduce the size of solid-wood infill panels.

● CROSS RAIL
● PANEL
● STILE
● CROSS RAIL
● MUNTIN
● PANEL
● PANEL
● CROSS RAIL

● MORTISE & TENON JOINT
● MUNTIN
● STILE
● HAUNCHED MORTISE & TENON JOINT
● CROSS RAIL
● HAUNCHED MORTISE & TENON
● STILE

● DOOR TREATMENTS
① Doors meet over vertical post ② separated by post ③ Rebated

● POST
① DOORS MEET
● STOP
② DOORS SEPARATED
③ DOORS REBATED

TWIN DOORS

A pair of cupboard doors that meet in the centre can be treated in several different ways.

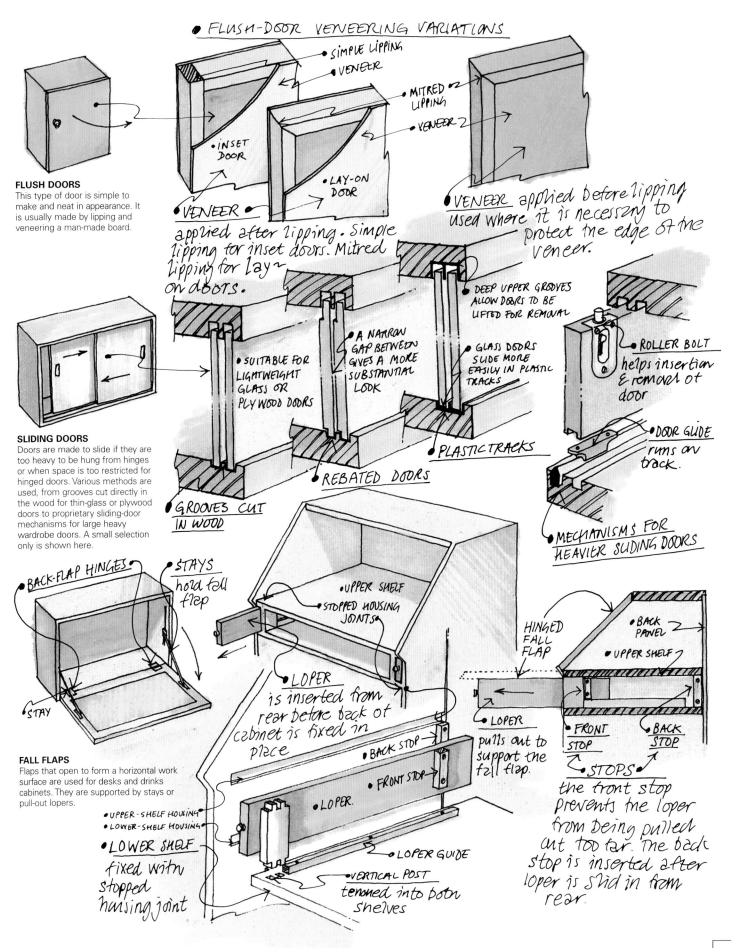

FLUSH-DOOR VENEERING VARIATIONS

- SIMPLE LIPPING
- VENEER
- MITRED LIPPING
- VENEER 2
- INSET DOOR
- LAY-ON DOOR

VENEER applied after lipping. Simple lipping for inset doors. Mitred lipping for lay-on doors.

VENEER applied before lipping used where it is necessary to protect the edge of the veneer.

FLUSH DOORS

This type of door is simple to make and neat in appearance. It is usually made by lipping and veneering a man-made board.

- DEEP UPPER GROOVES ALLOW DOORS TO BE LIFTED FOR REMOVAL
- A NARROW GAP BETWEEN GIVES A MORE SUBSTANTIAL LOOK
- GLASS DOORS SLIDE MORE EASILY IN PLASTIC TRACKS
- SUITABLE FOR LIGHTWEIGHT GLASS OR PLYWOOD DOORS
- ROLLER BOLT helps insertion & removal of door
- DOOR GUIDE runs on track.

SLIDING DOORS

Doors are made to slide if they are too heavy to be hung from hinges or when space is too restricted for hinged doors. Various methods are used, from grooves cut directly in the wood for thin-glass or plywood doors to proprietary sliding-door mechanisms for large heavy wardrobe doors. A small selection only is shown here.

GROOVES CUT IN WOOD

REBATED DOORS

PLASTIC TRACKS

MECHANISMS FOR HEAVIER SLIDING DOORS

- BACK-FLAP HINGES
- STAYS hold fall flap
- STAY
- UPPER SHELF
- STOPPED HOUSING JOINTS
- HINGED FALL FLAP
- BACK PANEL
- UPPER SHELF

FALL FLAPS

Flaps that open to form a horizontal work surface are used for desks and drinks cabinets. They are supported by stays or pull-out lopers.

LOPER is inserted from rear before back of cabinet is fixed in place

- BACK STOP
- FRONT STOP
- LOPER.

LOPER pulls out to support the fall flap.

- FRONT STOP
- BACK STOP

STOPS the front stop prevents the loper from being pulled out too far. The back stop is inserted after loper is slid in from rear.

- UPPER-SHELF HOUSING
- LOWER-SHELF HOUSING
- **LOWER SHELF** fixed with stopped housing joint
- LOPER GUIDE
- VERTICAL POST tenoned into both shelves

CUPBOARD DOORS

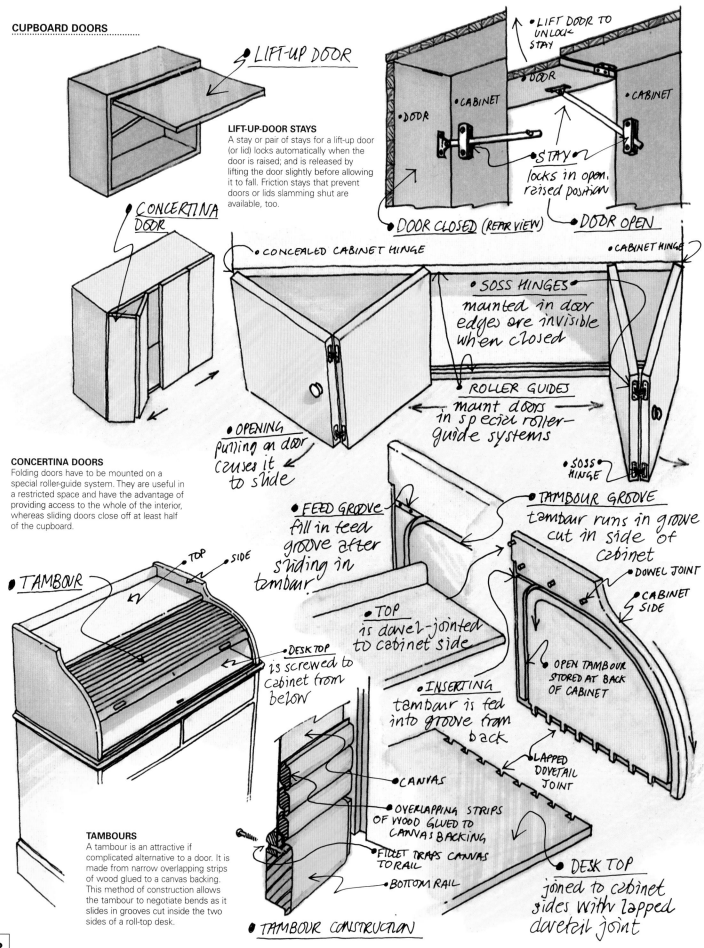

LIFT-UP DOOR

• LIFT DOOR TO UNLOCK STAY

• DOOR   • CABINET

• DOOR   • CABINET

• STAY
locks in open, raised position

• DOOR CLOSED (REAR VIEW)   • DOOR OPEN

LIFT-UP-DOOR STAYS
A stay or pair of stays for a lift-up door (or lid) locks automatically when the door is raised; and is released by lifting the door slightly before allowing it to fall. Friction stays that prevent doors or lids slamming shut are available, too.

CONCERTINA DOOR

• CONCEALED CABINET HINGE   • CABINET HINGE

• SOSS HINGES
mounted in door edges are invisible when closed

• OPENING
pulling on door causes it to slide

• ROLLER GUIDES
mount doors in special roller-guide systems

• SOSS HINGE

CONCERTINA DOORS
Folding doors have to be mounted on a special roller-guide system. They are useful in a restricted space and have the advantage of providing access to the whole of the interior, whereas sliding doors close off at least half of the cupboard.

• FEED GROOVE
fill in feed groove after sliding in tambour

• TAMBOUR GROOVE
tambour runs in groove cut in side of cabinet

• DOWEL JOINT

• CABINET SIDE

• TOP
is dowel-jointed to cabinet side

• OPEN TAMBOUR STORED AT BACK OF CABINET

TOP   SIDE

• TAMBOUR

• DESK TOP
is screwed to cabinet from below

• INSERTING
tambour is fed into groove from back

• CANVAS

• OVERLAPPING STRIPS OF WOOD GLUED TO CANVAS BACKING

• FILLET TRAPS CANVAS TO RAIL

• BOTTOM RAIL

• LAPPED DOVETAIL JOINT

• DESK TOP
joined to cabinet sides with lapped dovetail joint

TAMBOURS
A tambour is an attractive if complicated alternative to a door. It is made from narrow overlapping strips of wood glued to a canvas backing. This method of construction allows the tambour to negotiate bends as it slides in grooves cut inside the two sides of a roll-top desk.

• TAMBOUR CONSTRUCTION

Constructing a drawer unit, especially one made from solid timber, is much more complicated than making a cupboard unit of similar size and construction. Also, greater accuracy is required, to ensure the drawers fit snugly and will continue to run smoothly.

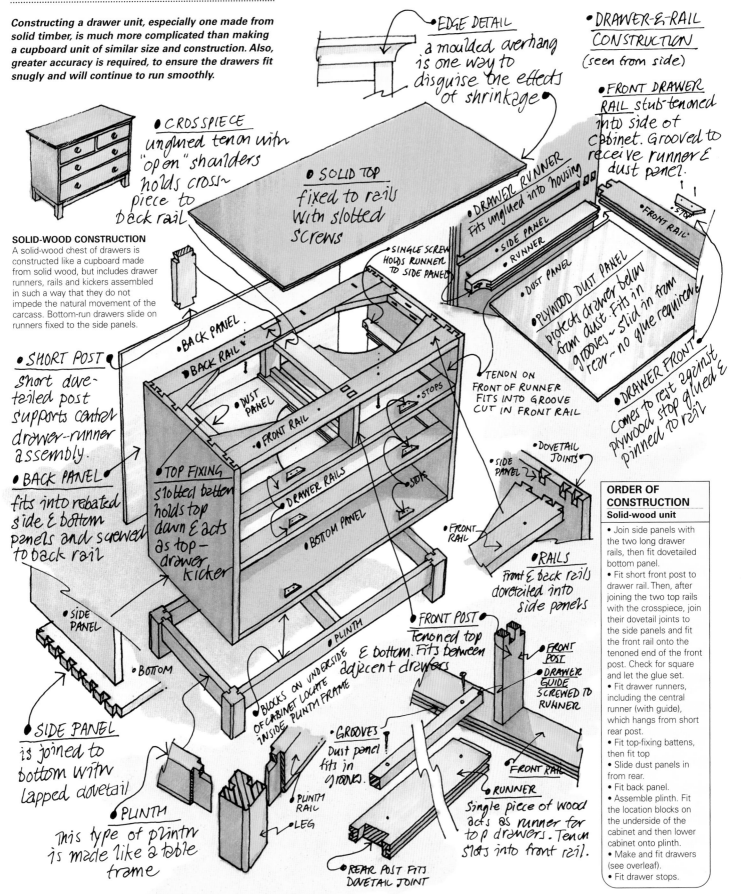

• EDGE DETAIL
a moulded overhang is one way to disguise the effects of shrinkage.

• DRAWER-&-RAIL CONSTRUCTION (seen from side)

• FRONT DRAWER RAIL stub-tenoned into side of cabinet. Grooved to receive runner & dust panel.

• CROSS PIECE unglued tenon with "open" shoulders holds crosspiece to back rail

SOLID-WOOD CONSTRUCTION
A solid-wood chest of drawers is constructed like a cupboard made from solid wood, but includes drawer runners, rails and kickers assembled in such a way that they do not impede the natural movement of the carcass. Bottom-run drawers slide on runners fixed to the side panels.

• SOLID TOP fixed to rails with slotted screws

• SINGLE SCREW HOLDS RUNNER TO SIDE PANEL

• DRAWER RUNNER fits unglued into housing

• SIDE PANEL
• RUNNER
• DUST PANEL

PLYWOOD DUST PANEL protects drawer below from dust. Fits in from grooves – slid in from rear – no glue required

• FRONT RAIL • STOP

• BACK PANEL
• BACK RAIL

• SHORT POST short dovetailed post supports central drawer-runner assembly.

• DUST PANEL
• FRONT RAIL

TENON ON FRONT OF RUNNER FITS INTO GROOVE CUT IN FRONT RAIL

• DRAWER FRONT comes to rest against plywood stop glued & pinned to rail

• BACK PANEL fits into rebated side & bottom panels and screwed to back rail

• TOP FIXING slotted batten holds top down & acts as top-drawer kicker

• STOPS

• DRAWER RAILS

• SLOTS

• BOTTOM PANEL

• SIDE PANEL

• DOVETAIL JOINTS

• FRONT RAIL

• RAILS front & back rails dovetailed into side panels

ORDER OF CONSTRUCTION
Solid-wood unit
• Join side panels with the two long drawer rails, then fit dovetailed bottom panel.
• Fit short front post to drawer rail. Then, after joining the two top rails with the crosspiece, join their dovetail joints to the side panels and fit the front rail onto the tenoned end of the front post. Check for square and let the glue set.
• Fit drawer runners, including the central runner (with guide), which hangs from short rear post.
• Fit top-fixing battens, then fit top
• Slide dust panels in from rear.
• Fit back panel.
• Assemble plinth. Fit the location blocks on the underside of the cabinet and then lower cabinet onto plinth.
• Make and fit drawers (see overleaf).
• Fit drawer stops.

• SIDE PANEL
• BOTTOM

BLOCKS ON UNDERSIDE OF CABINET LOCATE adjacent drawers INSIDE PLINTH FRAME

• FRONT POST Tenoned top & bottom. Fits between adjacent drawers

• FRONT POST
• DRAWER GUIDE SCREWED TO RUNNER

• PLINTH

• SIDE PANEL is joined to bottom with lapped dovetail

• PLINTH This type of plinth is made like a table frame

• GROOVES Dust panel fits in grooves.

• PLINTH RAIL
• LEG

• FRONT RAIL
• RUNNER

Single piece of wood acts as runner for top drawers. Tenon slots into front rail.

• REAR POST FITS DOVETAIL JOINT

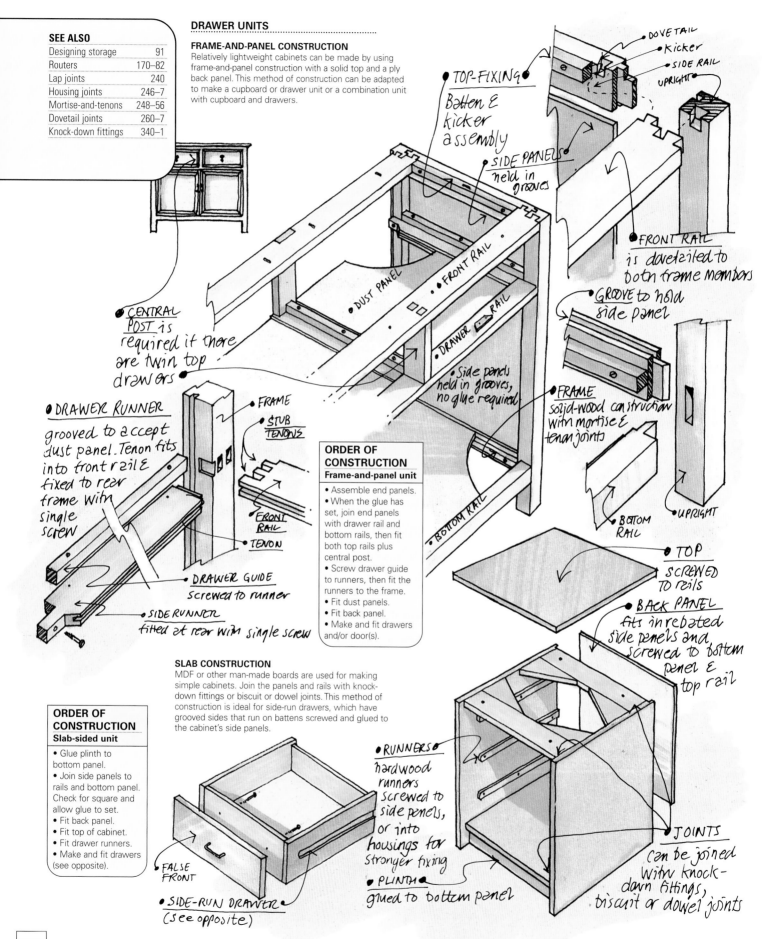

DRAWER UNITS

FRAME-AND-PANEL CONSTRUCTION

Relatively lightweight cabinets can be made by using frame-and-panel construction with a solid top and a ply back panel. This method of construction can be adapted to make a cupboard or drawer unit or a combination unit with cupboard and drawers.

TOP-FIXING
Batten & kicker assembly

DOVETAIL
KICKER
SIDE RAIL
UPRIGHT

SIDE PANELS held in grooves

FRONT RAIL is dovetailed to both frame members

GROOVE to hold side panel

CENTRAL POST is required if there are twin top drawers

DUST PANEL

FRONT RAIL

DRAWER RAIL

Side panels held in grooves, no glue required

FRAME solid-wood construction with mortise & tenon joints

DRAWER RUNNER grooved to accept dust panel. Tenon fits into front rail & fixed to rear frame with single screw

FRAME
STUB TENONS
FRONT RAIL
TENON

DRAWER GUIDE screwed to runner

SIDE RUNNER fitted at rear with single screw

BOTTOM RAIL

UPRIGHT

BOTTOM RAIL

TOP SCREWED TO RAILS

BACK PANEL fits in rebated side panels and screwed to bottom panel & top rail

ORDER OF CONSTRUCTION
Frame-and-panel unit

- Assemble end panels.
- When the glue has set, join end panels with drawer rail and bottom rails, then fit both top rails plus central post.
- Screw drawer guide to runners, then fit the runners to the frame.
- Fit dust panels.
- Fit back panel.
- Make and fit drawers and/or door(s).

SLAB CONSTRUCTION

MDF or other man-made boards are used for making simple cabinets. Join the panels and rails with knock-down fittings or biscuit or dowel joints. This method of construction is ideal for side-run drawers, which have grooved sides that run on battens screwed and glued to the cabinet's side panels.

ORDER OF CONSTRUCTION
Slab-sided unit

- Glue plinth to bottom panel.
- Join side panels to rails and bottom panel. Check for square and allow glue to set.
- Fit back panel.
- Fit top of cabinet.
- Fit drawer runners.
- Make and fit drawers (see opposite).

FALSE FRONT

SIDE-RUN DRAWER (see opposite)

RUNNERS hardwood runners screwed to side panels, or into housings for stronger fixing

PLINTH glued to bottom panel

JOINTS can be joined with knock-down fittings, biscuit or dowel joints

DRAWERS

Drawers are designed to slide in and out of a cabinet to facilitate access. The drawer front protects the contents by filling the opening. Shallow widely spaced drawers or trays are often used as an alternative to shelves behind cupboard doors, especially in wardrobes or built-in storage units. Tray construction is usually very simple, often comprising no more than a finger-jointed box with a plywood bottom.

TRADITIONAL BOTTOM-RUN DRAWER

A traditional bottom-run drawer has thin hardwood sides jointed with finely cut lapped dovetails at the front and through dovetails at the back. The bottom panel is set in a groove at the front and has a grooved slip moulding at each side. Use plywood or MDF for the bottom panel and solid wood for the slip mouldings.

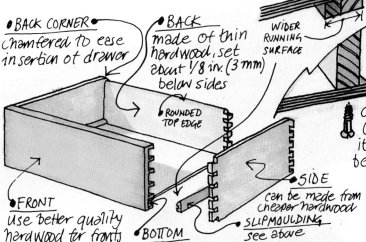

●BOTTOM
often made of plywood. If solid wood is used, grain must run side to side.

●SLIP MOULDINGS glued to each drawer side. End is notched to allow it to run under drawer back.

●FITTING slide bottom into place from rear. Screw to drawer back (do not glue); if it shrinks, it can be moved forward.

WIDER RUNNING SURFACE

●BACK CORNER● chamfered to ease insertion of drawer

●BACK made of thin hardwood, set about 1/8 in. (3 mm) below sides

●ROUNDED TOP EDGE

●FRONT use better quality hardwood for fronts

●SIDE can be made from cheaper hardwood

SLIPMOULDING see above

●BOTTOM groove is concealed by bottom dovetail

Bottom-run drawers
The bottom edges of the drawer's sides run on strips of hardwood fixed to the cabinet's side panels. The strips also act as 'kickers', which prevent the drawer below tipping when it is pulled out.

●BOTTOM-RUN

Side-run drawers
A stopped groove cut in each side of the drawer fits onto a hardwood batten screwed and glued to the cabinet. For a stronger fixing, cut a shallow housing in the sides of the cabinet for each runner.

●SIDE-RUN

Drawer slides
You can buy ready-made drawer-slide systems for screwing to the sides of heavier drawers. The drawer front must overlap at each side to cover the space needed for these fittings.

●DRAWER SLIDE

Inset drawers
Drawers of this type close flush with the face of the cabinet. They need to fit snugly.

●INSET

Overlapping drawers
Overlapping drawer fronts cover the leading edges of the cabinet.

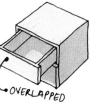

●OVERLAPPED

False front
Overlapping drawers are often made with a false front screwed to each drawer, which makes for much easier fitting.

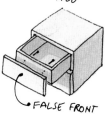

●FALSE FRONT

STIFFENING A WIDE DRAWER BOTTOM

A hardwood crosspiece known as a muntin is used to separate and support the two sections of a wide drawer bottom.

●MUNTIN

●MUNTIN

either

●MUNTIN

or

●BACK

SCREW muntin to drawer back

FITTING A DRAWER

First plane the drawer front to fit snugly in its opening. Make the other components to match the front, then assemble. If the finished drawer is a tight fit, look for shiny spots along the sides that indicate areas of friction. Skim them lightly with a plane, then lubricate all sliding surfaces by rubbing them with a candle.

LAPPED-AND-HOUSED DRAWER

For cheaper-quality furniture, drawers can be made with simple lap joints at the front and housing joints at the back. The strength of the joints relies on the glue, but they can be reinforced with panel pins.

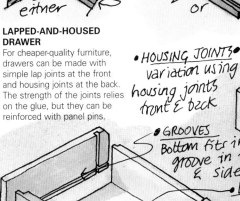

●HOUSING JOINTS● variation using housing joints front & back

●GROOVES bottom fits in groove in front & sides

●FRONT

●BOTTOM made from plywood or hardboard

●FIXING screw bottom to back as on dovetailed drawer

EXTENDED SIDES● can be used as drawer pulls

●FRONT

●PULL RAIL made from dowel or metal tube

SIDE-RUN VERSION

BUILT-IN STORAGE UNITS

Built-in units fitted from wall to wall are relatively cheap to make. An alternative method is to construct 'modules' bolted side by side. Always make sure you can transport the units from your workshop and through doorways or up stairs. If need be, assemble the components on site or construct sub-assemblies that can be joined with screws or bolts. If the units are to be painted, nails and screw-fixings can be disguised with filler.

ORDER OF CONSTRUCTION
Alcove unit

• Stand bottom panel in position after gluing the plinth rails to it.
• Screw the rails and posts to the wall on each side of the cupboard.
• Screw the top to the rails directly, or screw a batten to each rail then screw the battens to the top.
• Scribe upright cover strips to the walls and fix them to the posts. Check they are plumb, using a spirit level.
• Pin and glue moulding along front edge of top.
• Assemble doors and attach with hinges to cover strips.
• Pin battens to underside of top to act as door stop.

• DECORATIVE MOULDING pinned and glued to front edge

• DOOR STOP battens on underside act as door-stop

TOP

RAIL either/or

TOP

RAIL

• STOPS SHORT OF CEILING

• TOP-FIXING DETAILS

• RAIL & POST screwed to wall

• HINGES are attached to cover strip

• TOP

• BOTTOM

• PLINTH RAILS glued to bottom

• COVER STRIP scribed to wall

• DOOR Frame-&-panel construction

ALCOVE UNIT

Make the most of the space available by hanging hinged doors from wall-mounted posts. To avoid damaging cornice mouldings, stop short of the ceiling.

ORDER OF CONSTRUCTION
Modular unit

• Assemble frames in workshop, then bolt them between upright dividing panels on site, working from one end. If there isn't enough room to fit bolts, screw the last panel to its frames from inside. Anchor assembly to wall with screws passed through the top frames.
• Pin plinth cover strip to front edge of every upright panel.
• Drop plywood lids into rebates cut in the top frames.
• Attach doors to upright panels with hinges.
• Make and fit trays and/or other interior fittings.

MODULAR UNIT

Sub-assembled frames are bolted between dividing panels. You can fit full-length doors (perhaps with trays or shelves behind some and hanging space only behind others) or have one or two short doors, too, with drawers below.

SIDE PANEL

• PLINTH COVER STRIP pinned to front of panels. Floor covering can run up front of cover strip.

FLOOR COVERING

• LID plywood lid drops in

• REBATE

• CONCEALED HINGES

• FRAME

• REBATE

• TONGUE-REINFORCED MITRE JOINT

• FRAME with rebate to accept plywood lid.

• UPRIGHT PANELS are bolted to frame

FITTED-FRAME UNIT

Careful planning is required when designing a storage unit that fits wall to wall. The walls in any house, including a newly built one, are bound to be uneven, and you should allow for this when designing built-in storage. Assemble the frame on site and screw it to the wall at each end, then scribe a filling strip to the ceiling. Use sliding doors across wide cupboard openings.

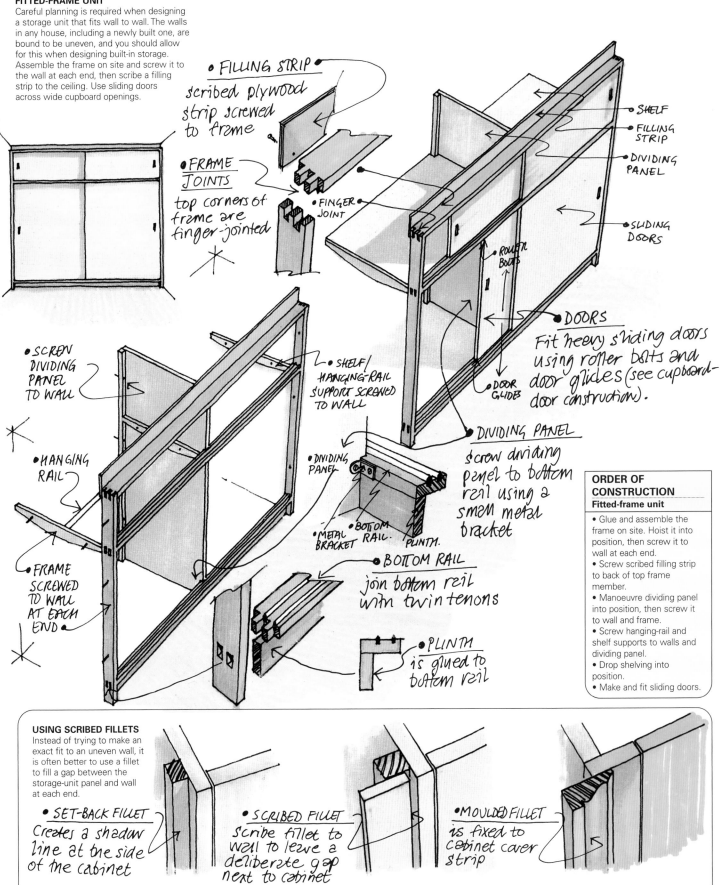

• FILLING STRIP
scribed plywood strip screwed to frame

• FRAME JOINTS
top corners of frame are finger-jointed

• FINGER JOINT

• SHELF

• FILLING STRIP

• DIVIDING PANEL

• SLIDING DOORS

• ROLLER BOLTS

• DOORS
Fit heavy sliding doors using roller bolts and door glides (see cupboard-door construction).

• DOOR GLIDE

• SCREW DIVIDING PANEL TO WALL

• HANGING RAIL

• FRAME SCREWED TO WALL AT EACH END

• SHELF/HANGING-RAIL SUPPORT SCREWED TO WALL

• DIVIDING PANEL

• METAL BRACKET

• BOTTOM RAIL

• PLINTH

• DIVIDING PANEL
Screw dividing panel to bottom rail using a small metal bracket

• BOTTOM RAIL
join bottom rail with twin tenons

• PLINTH
is glued to bottom rail

ORDER OF CONSTRUCTION
Fitted-frame unit

• Glue and assemble the frame on site. Hoist it into position, then screw it to wall at each end.
• Screw scribed filling strip to back of top frame member.
• Manoeuvre dividing panel into position, then screw it to wall and frame.
• Screw hanging-rail and shelf supports to walls and dividing panel.
• Drop shelving into position.
• Make and fit sliding doors.

USING SCRIBED FILLETS
Instead of trying to make an exact fit to an uneven wall, it is often better to use a fillet to fill a gap between the storage-unit panel and wall at each end.

• SET-BACK FILLET
Creates a shadow line at the side of the cabinet

• SCRIBED FILLET
scribe fillet to wall to leave a deliberate gap next to cabinet

• MOULDED FILLET
is fixed to cabinet cover strip

MAKING PLANS

A gifted woodworker may be able to transform an idea into reality on the bench, but most people find it necessary to plan a design in detail on paper and perhaps try it out in three dimensions, too.

Sketch drawings

In order to conceive the shape and general construction of a new workpiece, a designer will normally put down his or her first thoughts on paper in the form of sketches. These are visual notes (similar to those shown on the preceding pages) used to explore the various possibilities until the designer arrives at a solution that appears to satisfy all the requirements. Unfortunately it is all too easy to fool oneself with a sketch, either by underestimating the overall size of the piece or by exaggerating the section of a component. A prudent designer will make a measured scale drawing to check the proportions and constructional detail.

Scale drawings

A professional designer uses scale drawings to communicate information to the workshop or factory where an item is to be manufactured. It is convenient to use a similar system to work up your own sketch ideas. By convention a designer normally adopts a scale of 1:5 (10mm represents 50mm) when using the metric system, and 1:4 ($\frac{1}{2}$in represents 2in) when using imperial measurements. You can use either system, but don't attempt to mix them. Smaller scales, typically 1:20 for metric and 1:24 for imperial, are more convenient when designing built-in furniture. Chairs and other relatively small items are usually drawn full size.

Specific views of a workpiece are drawn side by side. They represent the front elevation (front view), side elevation (side view) and plan (top view); in addition, drawn sections (i.e. slices through the workpiece) show the internal structure. Areas that are unusually complex are often drawn full size to clarify their construction.

Professional draughtsman's equipment is expensive, but you cannot make accurate drawings without a drawing board (any square-cut flat board will do), a T-square for drawing horizontal lines, and a large set square for the vertical ones. In addition, you will need a scale rule marked in increments representing all the common scale measurements and a protractor for measuring angles. Although not essential, it is worth investing in plastic guides known as French curves for drawing curved lines, a circle template for drawing small radii, and a well-made compass for larger circles. Make scale drawings on tracing paper (using a sharp, reasonably hard pencil), so you can overlay subsequent drawings as the design develops.

Scale models

Having made a scale drawing, use it to construct a model of the workpiece out of balsawood and card, so you can see what your design looks like in three dimensions. Some designers like to make a fully detailed model using the actual materials specified for the full-size piece – but this is hardly ever necessary unless you want to impress a client.

Mock-ups

Making a full-size mock-up from workshop scraps and cheap materials can be extremely informative. It is the only way, for example, to make sure a chair is as comfortable or structurally sound as you imagine.

Erecting a visual mock-up made from lightweight materials such as fibreboard or even corrugated cardboard is the ideal way to check the proportions of a large workpiece, especially if you can assemble it on site to see how it fits into its intended environment.

Cutting lists

Before ordering materials from a timber supplier, write out a cutting list specifying the length, width and thickness of every component in a workpiece. The list should also state the material from which each component is to be made and the quantity required. Make sure your supplier is aware that the list specifies finished sizes, so that he or she knows how much to allow for wastage.

Front elevation

Side elevation

Plan

Section

Drawing equipment
1 *Drawing board*
2 *Compass*
3 *Set square*
4 *T-square*
5 *French curves*
6 *Protractor*
7 *Circle template*
8 *Scale rule*

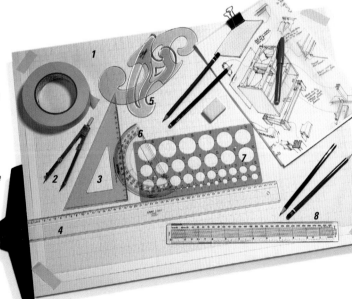

SURVEYING A ROOM

Before you start to design built-in furniture, measure the room carefully and make notes of all the important features.

- Use a long tape measure to take the main dimensions of the room, including the diagonals, in order to check whether it is square in plan. Don't assume the walls are perpendicular – where a good fit may be crucial, take measurements at different heights.
- Measure the size and height of architectural features such as ceiling cornices, skirting boards, dadoes and picture rails.
- Measure windows and doors, and make a note or sketch of how they open.
- Note the position of fireplaces and radiators.
- Make a note of electrical sockets, switches and lighting fixtures that may have to be relocated to accommodate your design.

CHAPTER THREE

HANDTOOLS

Nowadays, when more and more woodworkers are turning to power tools and machinery for convenience or greater accuracy, someone coming fresh to woodwork might assume handtools were merely relics from the past. However, a competent woodworker can often finish a job by hand in the time it takes to set up a machine for the same purpose. Working wood by hand also gives a feel for the material that cannot be derived from power tools – the way different grains respond to the blade, for example, and how some woods are more forgiving while others show up the slightest error on the part of the woodworker. For these and other reasons – not least for the pleasure of using them – a comprehensive set of handtools will be found in even the most sophisticated workshop.

MEASURING AND MARKING TOOLS

It generally makes sense to buy rules and tape measures that have both metric and imperial graduations – but take care not to confuse one system with the other once you have begun to mark out a workpiece. To ensure that several identical components are exactly the same size, measure one of them accurately, then use that piece of wood as a template to mark out the others.

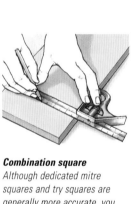

Combination square
Although dedicated mitre squares and try squares are generally more accurate, you can buy a combination square that will serve both functions. The all-metal tool has a sliding 300mm (1ft) blade that is locked in position by a knurled nut. Most models have a spirit level built into the stock or head.

Four-fold rule
The folding carpenter's rule, made from boxwood with brass hinges and endcaps, is still popular among traditionalists. Most folding rules are 1m (3ft) in length when fully extended. Because a wooden rule is relatively thick, you have to stand it on edge in order to transfer measurements accurately to the work. Similar rules made from plastic are sometimes made with bevelled edges to overcome this problem.

Steel rule
A 300mm (1ft) stainless-steel rule is useful for marking out small workpieces and for setting marking gauges and power-tool fences. A steel rule also doubles as a short straightedge.

Straightedge
Every workshop needs at least one sturdy metal straightedge, between 500mm (1ft 8in) and 2m (6ft 6in) long. A bevelled straightedge is ideal for making accurate cuts with a marking knife and for checking that a planed surface is perfectly flat. Some straightedges are etched with metric or imperial graduations.

Retractable tape measure
Retractable steel tapes, from 2 to 5m (6 to 16ft) long, are usually graduated along both edges. The hook at the tip of the tape is intentionally loose on its rivets, so that it can move fractionally to take internal and external measurements. This hook can become displaced if you allow the tape to snap back into its case. A lock button prevents the tape retracting automatically. Refills are usually available for replacing damaged tapes.

Try square
The finest try squares, used to mark and check right angles, have a blued-steel metal blade riveted at 90 degrees to a rosewood stock edged with brass. A square with a 300mm (1ft) blade is best for general woodwork, but you might find a smaller, all-metal engineer's square useful for fine work and for setting-up power tools.

Dovetail template
A special template is used to mark out dovetail joints. One tapered blade, with a slope of 1-6, is for tails in softwood; the other has a ratio of 1-8 for hardwood tails.

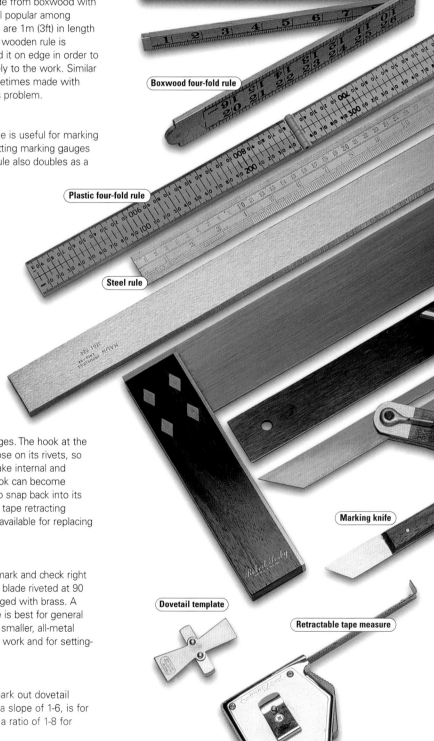

Boxwood four-fold rule

Plastic four-fold rule

Steel rule

Marking knife

Dovetail template

Retractable tape measure

USING MEASURING AND MARKING TOOLS

Since even the best measuring tools are relatively inexpensive, most woodworkers acquire a variety of rules and tape measures to meet different needs.

Dividing a workpiece into equal parts
You can divide a workpiece into equal parts using any rule or tape measure. To divide a board into quarters, for example, align the tip of the rule with one edge and the fourth division with the opposite edge, then mark off the divisions between.

Checking for winding
If you suspect a board is twisted or 'winding', hold a steel rule across each end; if the rules appear to be parallel, the board is flat.

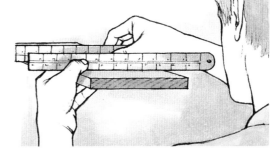

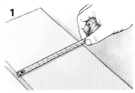

Using a tape measure
When taking external measurements with a retractable tape measure, hook the tip over one edge of the workpiece and read off the dimension against the opposite edge (**1**).

When measuring between two components, read off the measurement where the tape enters its case (**2**), then add the length of the case to arrive at the true dimension.

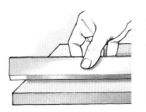

Checking a surface is flat
To check that a panel is flat, place a metal straightedge on the surface. A bump will cause the tool to rock; chinks of light showing beneath the straightedge indicate hollows. By turning the straightedge to various angles you can gauge whether the entire surface is flat. Mark bumps and hollows with a pencil.

Checking the accuracy of a try square
To check the accuracy of a try square, use it to draw a line at right angles to the edge of a workpiece; then turn the square over and slide the blade up to the marked line. If the square is accurate, the blade and the pencil mark will align precisely.

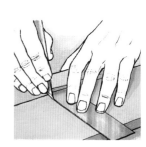

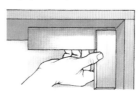

Checking a joint is square
When assembling corner joints, use a try square to check that the two components meet exactly at right angles.

Marking with a try square
Mark out square shoulders with a pencil and try square. Place the tip of a marking knife on the marked line, and slide the square up to the flat side of the blade. Holding the try square firmly against the face edge of the workpiece, draw the knife along the line.

Checking a mitre or bevel
Place a mitre square or sliding bevel, as appropriate, over the bevelled face of the workpiece. Keeping the blade in contact with the wood, slide the tool along the bevelled face to check the angle is accurate across the width of the workpiece.

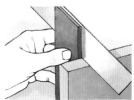

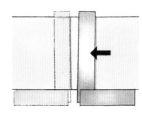

Steel straightedge

Try square

Mitre square

Sliding bevel

Mitre square
The blade of a mitre square, specifically made for marking out and checking the accuracy of mitre joints, is fixed at 45 degrees to the stock.

Sliding bevel
A sliding bevel can be employed to mark or check any angle. The adjustable blade is secured with a short brass lever or wing nut.

Marking knife
Use a pencil for the preliminary marking of joints, but always complete the marking with a knife – as severing the wood fibres ensures a clean edge when you saw to the line. A marking-knife blade is bevelled on one side only; use the knife on the waste side of the line, running the flat face of the blade against a try square.

MARKING GAUGES

Gauges are designed to score fine lines parallel with an edge of a workpiece, usually for marking out joints or scribing rebates. They are also essential for marking out timber before it is cut to size.

Marking gauge

A marking gauge has an adjustable fence or stock that slides along a hardwood beam, which has a sharp steel pin driven through one end. A thumbscrew clamps the stock at any point along the beam. Better-quality gauges have brass strips set flush with the running face of the stock to prevent wear. A standard beam is 200mm (8in) long, but you can get a 300mm (1ft) beam for marking wide boards.

Cutting gauge

A cutting gauge is fitted with a miniature blade instead of a pointed pin, enabling you to mark a line across the grain without tearing the wood fibres. The blade, which is held in place with a brass wedge, can be removed for sharpening. A standard scribing blade, used for marking various corner joints, has a rounded cutting tip. Substitute a pointed knife-edge blade for trimming strips of veneer.

Mortise gauge

A mortise gauge has two pins, one fixed and the other adjustable, so that you can score both sides of a mortise simultaneously. On the best gauges the movable pin is adjustable to very fine tolerances, using a thumbscrew located at the end of the beam. Most mortise gauges have a second fixed pin on the back of the beam, so the tool can double as a standard marking gauge.

Curved-edge gauge

It is practically impossible to score a line parallel to a curved edge with an ordinary marking gauge. A curved-edge gauge has a brass fence that rests on two points, preventing the stock rocking as it follows the edge of the work.

Wheel marking gauge
This all-metal gauge is fitted with a hardened-steel bevelled disc or 'wheel', instead of the usual marking pin. Since the disc is unlikely to tear the grain, this gauge can be used for marking either with or across the grain.

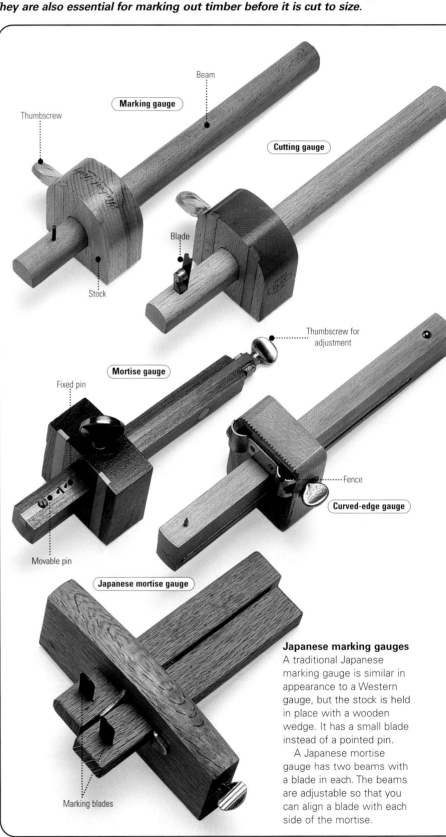

Marking gauge
Thumbscrew
Beam
Stock
Cutting gauge
Blade
Mortise gauge
Fixed pin
Movable pin
Thumbscrew for adjustment
Fence
Curved-edge gauge
Japanese mortise gauge
Marking blades

Japanese marking gauges

A traditional Japanese marking gauge is similar in appearance to a Western gauge, but the stock is held in place with a wooden wedge. It has a small blade instead of a pointed pin.

A Japanese mortise gauge has two beams with a blade in each. The beams are adjustable so that you can align a blade with each side of the mortise.

IRREGULAR PROFILES

None of the gauges described opposite will enable you to mark out workpieces that have irregular edges.

Profile gauge

A profile gauge has a row of metal pins or plastic blades which, when pressed against a moulding, slide back to reproduce its shape exactly. Copy the shape of the moulding onto another piece of wood by drawing carefully along the edge of the gauge.

Chalked line

You can't use a marking gauge to scribe a straight line on a board with a waney edge – but you can use a chalked length of string instead. In a purpose-made tool, the string is wound into a case containing coloured chalk, which coats the string each time it is pulled out. Stretch the string taut along the intended line, then pluck it like a bowstring against the wood to deposit a chalked impression on its surface.

USING MARKING AND CUTTING GAUGES

When using a marking gauge, the intention is to leave a clear but fine line on the work. Scoring a deep line can tear the wood, leading to inaccuracy.

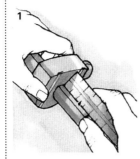

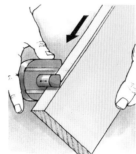

Adjusting a marking gauge

Align the stock using a rule (**1**), then tighten the thumbscrew. Check the measurement and make fine adjustments by tapping the base of the beam on a bench to increase the distance between pin and stock (**2**). To reduce the distance, tap the tip (**3**).

Adjusting a mortise gauge

Adjust the distance between the pins to match the width of a mortise chisel, then set the stock to suit the thickness of the leg or stile.

Gauging a centre line

To find the exact centre of a rail or stile, set a marking gauge as accurately as possible then check the measurement by making a single pinprick, first from one side of the workpiece and then from the other. If the pinpricks fall short or overshoot the centre line, adjust the gauge until they coincide.

Scribing with a gauge

With the pin pointing towards you, slide the stock up against the side of the workpiece. Push the gauge away from you to scribe the line parallel to the edge.

Cutting strips of veneer

Place the veneer on a straight-edged board and align one of the planed edges of the veneer with the edge of the board. Holding the veneer down with a stout batten, use a cutting gauge to slice off a parallel-sided strip. If the veneer does not cut cleanly, sharpen the blade.

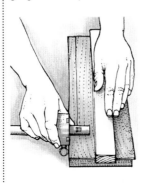

DIMENSIONING TIMBER

When preparing a piece of timber, you need to ensure that adjacent surfaces are cut and planed at right angles to one another.

Squaring-up

Select the most attractive and blemish-free face and plane it flat. Designate this planed surface as the 'face side' by marking it with a loop that trails off to one edge (**1**). Plane this edge square to the face side, checking it with a try square, and mark it as the 'face edge' by drawing an arrowhead pointing to the face-side loop (**2**). All other dimensions should now be measured and gauged from these two prepared surfaces. Set a marking gauge to the required thickness and scribe a line on both edges, working from the face side (**3**). Plane the unfinished surface down to these lines (**4**). Mark the width on both sides of the wood, working from the face edge (**5**), then plane down to these lines (**6**).

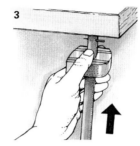
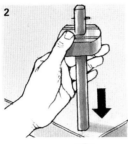

1 *Mark face side* **2** *Mark face edge* **3** *Gauge the thickness*

4 *Plane to lines* **5** *Gauge the width* **6** *Plane to size*

IMPROVISING A GAUGE

For carpentry that does not require absolute precision, you can gauge lines with a pencil. Run a fingertip against the edge of the work-piece to keep the pencil point on a parallel path (**1**).

For slightly wider dimensions, follow the edge of the work with the head of a combination square, using the tip of the blade to guide the pencil point (**2**).

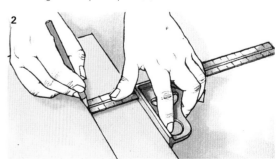

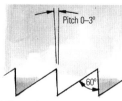

The set

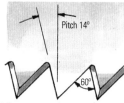

Pitch 0–3°

60°

1 Rip teeth

Pitch 14°

60°

2 Crosscut teeth

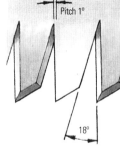

Pitch 1°

18°

3 Japanese crosscut teeth

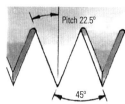

Pitch 22.5°

45°

4 Fleam teeth

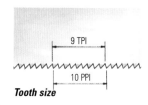

9 TPI

10 PPI

Tooth size

HOW SAWS WORK

Whether they are made for fast cutting, designed to cut curved shapes, operated by hand or powered with electricity, all saws sever wood in basically the same way. Depending on the type of saw, the pointed teeth act like miniature chisels or knife blades – removing minute shavings or slivers of wood, which fall to the floor as sawdust, leaving a slot or 'kerf' slightly wider than the thickness of the saw blade.

The set of saw teeth

If saw teeth were simply stacked one behind the other, the blade would jam in the cut after a few minutes' work. Consequently all but the finest teeth are 'set', or bent to the right or left, to cut a kerf that is wider than the thickness of the blade. This prevents the saw jamming in the wood.

The shape of saw teeth

Saw teeth are shaped differently according to the job they are required to do.

Ripsaw teeth (**1**) are for cutting with the grain – for tasks such as sawing a plank to width. These are large teeth with almost vertical leading edges, and each tooth is filed straight across to produce a chisel-like cutting tip.

Crosscut teeth (**2**) are designed for severing solid timber across the grain without tearing the wood fibres. This is necessary when cutting most joints or for sawing a plank to length. The leading edge of each tooth leans backward slightly and is filed at an angle to form a sharp cutting edge and tip. The teeth act like knives, scoring the wood on each side of the kerf, leaving the waste to fall out as it is cleared by the passage of the blade.

The Japanese crosscut tooth (**3**) is taller and narrower than the Western version and has a third bevel filed across the top. Some manufacturers have adopted this style of tooth for conventional handsaws that cut on the forward stroke.

Symmetrical 'fleam' teeth (**4**) are particularly efficient, as they sever the wood on the return stroke as well as the forward.

The size of saw teeth

A saw designed for fine work – such as cutting a dovetail joint – will have small finely set teeth. However, small teeth cut slowly. To be able to cut through timber quickly, especially resinous softwoods, a saw must have relatively large teeth with deep 'gullets' (spaces between the teeth) that are capable of clearing large amounts of sawdust from the kerf.

Despite metrication, saw-tooth sizes are generally specified by the number of teeth that fit into 1 inch – TPI (teeth per inch) – measuring from the base of one tooth to the base of another. Alternatively, they may be specified by PPI (points per inch) counting the number of saw-tooth tips in 1 inch of blade. When compared, there is always one more PPI than TPI.

Occasionally saws have rising-pitch teeth – the teeth get progressively larger towards the handle. The cut is started using the small teeth, but once the kerf is established the full length of the blade is utilized.

Hardened teeth

Saws are sometimes subjected to a high-frequency hardening process. A hardpoint saw, which is distinguishable by its blue-black toothed edge, stays sharp longer than an untreated saw, but the metal is so hard the teeth have to be sharpened by a specialist.

HANDSAWS

Handsaws are designed for converting solid wood and man-made boards into smaller components, ready for planing. The very best handsaws are skew-backed, having a gentle S-shaped curve to the top of the blade, which reduces the weight of the saw and improves its balance. The same blades are usually hollow-ground, being reduced in thickness above the cutting edge to provide better clearance in the kerf. Blades are sometimes covered with polytetrafluoroethylene (PTFE) to reduce friction.

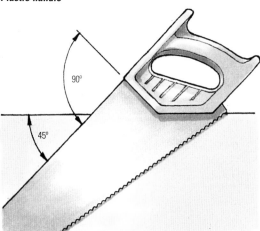

Skew-back hollow-ground handsaw

SAW HANDLES

The handle is set low behind the saw blade, for maximum thrust midway along the row of teeth.

Pistol-grip handle

Closed wooden handle

Plastic handle

Although a few handsaws are still made with the pistol-grip handle, most are fitted with a stronger closed handgrip. The traditional horned handle is functional and comfortable to use, but the majority of handsaws now have moulded-plastic grips that are more economical to manufacture. Plastic grips are often designed in such a way that the long straight back of the blade can be used as an extra-large try square.

90°

45°

Using a saw as a mitre square

Ripsaw

The ripsaw is the largest of the handsaws, with a 650mm (2ft 2in) blade designed specifically for cutting solid timber in the direction of the grain. Ripsaw blades are made with 5 or 6 PPI.

Crosscut saw

The crosscut saw is ideal for cutting solid planks or balks of timber to length, but it is rather coarse for man-made boards. Blades are between 600 and 650mm (2 and 2ft 2in) long, with 7 to 8 PPI.

Panel saw

Having relatively small (10 PPI) crosscut teeth, a panel saw is designed primarily for cutting man-made boards to size, but can double as a crosscut saw for severing solid wood. The blades are between 500 and 550mm (1ft 8in and 1ft 10in) long.

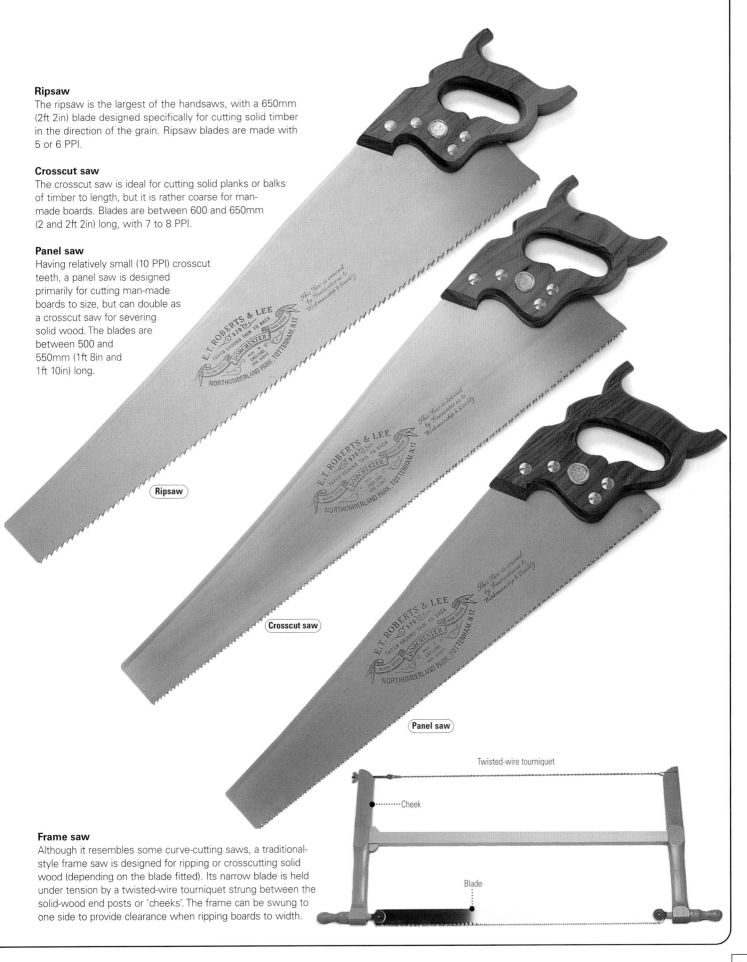

Ripsaw

Crosscut saw

Panel saw

Twisted-wire tourniquet

Cheek

Blade

Frame saw

Although it resembles some curve-cutting saws, a traditional-style frame saw is designed for ripping or crosscutting solid wood (depending on the blade fitted). Its narrow blade is held under tension by a twisted-wire tourniquet strung between the solid-wood end posts or 'cheeks'. The frame can be swung to one side to provide clearance when ripping boards to width.

USING HANDSAWS

Provided the saw is sharp and the teeth have been set properly, it is possible to work for long periods with a handsaw without tiring.

Controlling a handsaw

Hold a handsaw with your forefinger extended towards the toe of the blade (**1**). This grip provides optimum control over the direction of cut and prevents the handle twisting in the palm of your hand.

Place the cutting edge of the saw just to the waste side of the marked line. Guiding the saw with your thumb held against the flat of the blade (**2**), make short backward strokes to establish the cut.

Saw with slow steady strokes, using the full length of the blade – fast or erratic movements can be tiring, and the saw is more inclined to jam or wander off line.

If the cut does begin to deviate from the intended course, twist the blade slightly to bring it back on line. If you find a saw consistently wanders, check that the teeth are set accurately.

If the kerf begins to close on the blade, drive a small wedge into the cut to keep it open (**3**). Otherwise, lubricate the saw by rubbing a candle on both sides of the blade.

Finishing the cut

As you finish sawing a plank to length, support the offcut with your free hand (**4**). Work slowly and gently to sever the last few fibres without splitting the wood.

As you approach the end of a long plank of wood, turn round and saw back towards the kerf you have just made. Alternatively, use a two-handed grip to control the saw (**5**), continuing the kerf in the same direction but with the saw teeth facing away from you.

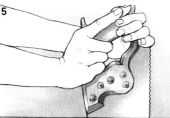

Caring for handsaws

Before you put your saw away, slip a plastic guard over the teeth to protect them. For long-term storage, wipe an oily rag over the blade to keep it rust free. You can remove rust spots with wire wool dipped in white spirit.

SUPPORTING THE WORK

You can't cut a workpiece with accuracy unless you support it properly. Sawhorses (trestles) about 600mm (2ft) high will allow you to hold the work down with one hand and use your knee to stop a plank of wood swivelling.

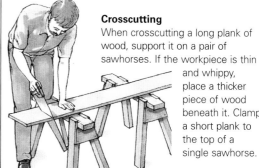

Crosscutting

When crosscutting a long plank of wood, support it on a pair of sawhorses. If the workpiece is thin and whippy, place a thicker piece of wood beneath it. Clamp a short plank to the top of a single sawhorse.

Ripsawing

Similarly, when ripping a plank lengthways support it on sawhorses, moving each one in turn to provide a clear path for the blade. Prevent a wide man-made panel from flexing by placing two planks under the board, one on each side of the saw kerf.

Crosscutting with a frame saw

When severing a plank of wood with a frame saw, cant the frame slightly to one side so you can see the cut line clearly. To support offcuts, pass your free hand through the frame and behind the blade.

Ripsawing with a frame saw

Clamp the work to a sturdy bench – so that you can use two hands to control the saw – and turn the blade at 90 degrees to the frame. Grip one of the end posts with both hands ensuring that the narrow blade cannot twist and cause the saw to wander off line.

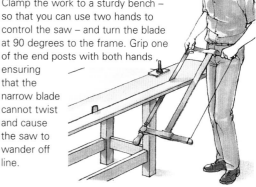

BACKSAWS

Backsaws are made with relatively small crosscut teeth for trimming lengths of wood to size and for cutting woodworking joints. The special feature of all backsaws is the heavy strip of brass or steel folded over the top of the blade. This strip not only keeps the blade straight but provides sufficient weight to keep the teeth in contact with the wood without having to force the blade into the work.

Tenon saw

A tenon saw, having 13 to 15 PPI along a 250 to 350mm (10 to 14in) blade, is the largest and most versatile of the backsaw family. While it is possible to sever quite hefty sections of timber with a tenon saw, it is also suitable for precise work such as cutting tenons and other woodworking joints.

Dovetail saw

A dovetail saw is a smaller version of the tenon saw, but the teeth are too fine (16 to 22 PPI) to be set conventionally. Instead, it relies on the burr produced by file-sharpening to provide the extremely narrow kerf required for cutting dovetails and similar joints. Dovetail saws that have a traditional handle, either closed or pistol-grip, are generally made with a 200mm (8in) blade. An alternative pattern, with a longer blade, has a straight handle in line with the folded metal strip.

Offset dovetail saw

A straight dovetail saw with a handle cranked to one side is made for trimming dowels and through tenons flush with the surface of the wood.

Bead saw

A miniature backsaw with about 26 PPI, the bead saw is ideal for cutting very fine joints and for model-making.

Blitz saw

The blitz saw is an extremely fine backsaw suitable for model-making. At 33 PPI, the teeth are so small that they cannot be sharpened. Consequently, the blades are replaceable.

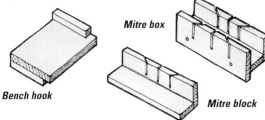

Mitre box

Bench hook

Mitre block

Accessories

A bench hook is used for crosscutting short lengths of timber with a backsaw. A mitre box is a jig for cutting mitres; the saw blade locates in slots in each side. A mitre block is a cheaper one-sided version.

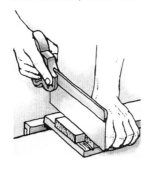

Using a backsaw
Make short backward strokes on the waste side of the line until the cut is established. Then gradually lower the blade to the horizontal as you extend the kerf.

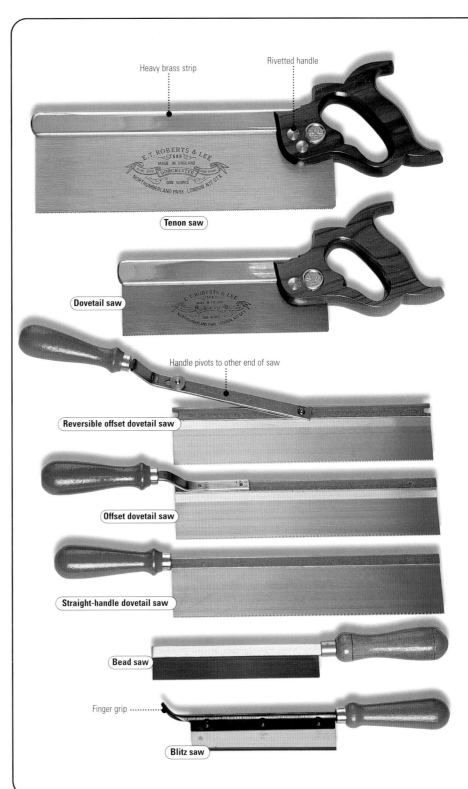

Heavy brass strip

Rivetted handle

E.T. ROBERTS & LEE

Tenon saw

Dovetail saw

Handle pivots to other end of saw

Reversible offset dovetail saw

Offset dovetail saw

Straight-handle dovetail saw

Bead saw

Finger grip

Blitz saw

CURVE-CUTTING SAWS

A group of saws with narrow blades is made specifically for cutting curved shapes or holes in solid wood and boards. Various sizes and designs are available; your choice will depend on the material to be cut and the scale of the work.

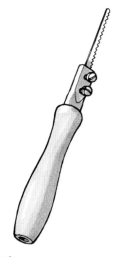

Padsaw

This type of compass saw has a retractable blade clamped in place by slotted screws in the ferrule. The straight handle is convenient for turning the saw to cut in any direction.

Bow saw

A medium-weight frame saw suitable for cutting relatively thick pieces of wood, the bow saw is fitted with a 200 to 300mm (8 to 12in) blade held under tension by a tourniquet strung between the saw's end posts. The 9 to 17 PPI blades can be turned through 360 degrees to swing the frame aside.

Coping saw

The very narrow blade of a 150mm (6in) coping saw is held under tension by the spring of its metal frame. The 15 to 17 PPI blades are too narrow to sharpen, and are simply replaced when they break or become blunt. A coping saw blade can be turned to swing the frame out of the way, to facilitate cutting curves in either solid wood or man-made boards.

Fret saw

A fret saw, with its 32 PPI blades, is used for cutting thin pieces of wood and board or shaping a sandwich of marquetry veneers. A fret saw cuts on the pull stroke, to prevent the blade buckling.

Compass saw

Most curve-cutting saws are limited by their frames to cutting holes relatively close to the edges of a workpiece. A compass saw has a narrow tapered blade that is stiff enough to hold its shape without being held under tension, and can therefore be used to cut a hole in a board of any thickness as far from the edges as required. The 8 to 10 PPI blades are either bolted into a pistol-grip handle or fitted into a straight wooden handle.

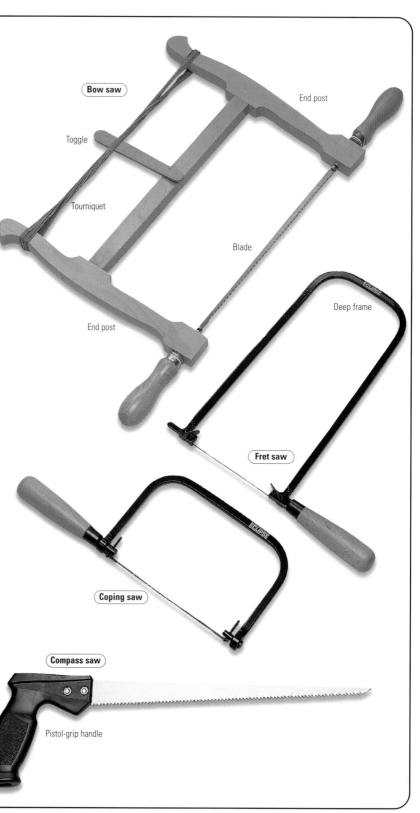

Bow saw

End post

Toggle

Tourniquet

Blade

End post

Deep frame

Fret saw

Coping saw

Compass saw

Pistol-grip handle

Curve-cutting saws are designed to enable quick and easy replacement of blunt, broken or bent blades.

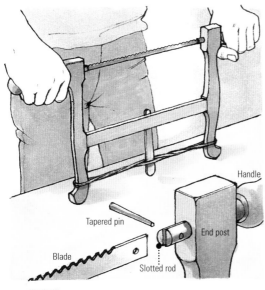

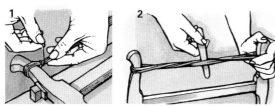

Handle

Tapered pin

End post

Blade

Slotted rod

Changing a bow-saw blade.

Unwind the toggle to slacken the tourniquet, then locate each end of the blade in the slotted metal rods that extend from the handles. Pass the tapered retaining pins through the rods and blade at both ends. Tighten the tourniquet again and rotate both handles to straighten the blade.

Replacing a tourniquet

With the blade in position, lightly clamp the end posts of the saw between bench stops. Tie the new string to one cheek, then make a cord by winding it end-to-end about four times. Bind the loose end around the cord near one cheek and tie a knot through the strings (**1**).

Pass the wooden toggle through the centre of the cord (**2**) and wind it up until the blade is taut.

Fitting a coping-saw blade

Each end of a coping-saw blade fits into a slotted retaining pin. To replace a damaged blade, reduce the distance between the retaining pins by turning the saw's handle anticlockwise.

Attach the blade to the toe of the saw, with the teeth facing away from the handle. Flex the frame against the edge of a bench until you can locate the other end of the blade. Tighten the saw's handle to tension the blade; then align both retaining pins by eye.

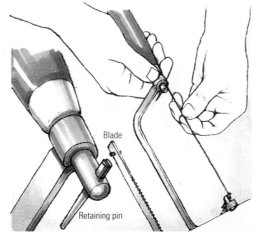

Blade

Retaining pin

Fitting a fret-saw blade

Fret-saw blades are fitted in a similar way, but instead of retaining pins a thumbscrew clamps the flat section at each end of a blade. With the teeth facing the handle, clamp the toe end of the blade, then flex the frame against a bench so you can clamp the other end of the blade. Releasing pressure on the frame is sufficient to put the blade under tension.

Fitting a compass-saw blade

To change a compass-saw blade, slacken the clamping screws and slide the slotted end of the blade into the handle. Then tighten the screws.

Thumbscrew

Handle

Blade

Blade

Clamping screws

Most curve-cutting saws require special techniques to counter the tendency for the weight of their frames to make the blade wander off line.

Cutting with a bow saw

A bow saw requires a two-handed grip to compensate for the twisting force of the frame. Grip the straight handle with one hand, extending your forefinger in line with the blade. Place your free hand alongside the other, wrapping the forefinger and middle finger around the saw's end post, one on each side of the blade.

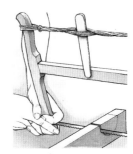

Controlling a coping saw

To prevent the blade wandering off line, place the first joint of your extended forefinger on the coping saw's frame. If it feels more comfortable, close your other hand around the first to form a double-handed grip (**1**).

When sawing a hole, first bore a small access hole for the blade, just inside the waste. Pass the saw blade through the hole and connect it to the frame (**2**).

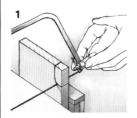

Cutting with a fret saw

Thin workpieces tend to vibrate unless they are supported from below by a strip of plywood, screwed to the bench top and overhanging the front edge. Cut a V-shape notch in the plywood to provide clearance for the fret-saw blade. Sit on a low stool so that you can cut downwards on the pull stroke.

Cutting holes with a compass saw

When cutting holes and apertures, drill a small starter hole for the tip of the saw blade. Saw steadily to avoid buckling the narrow blade on the forward stroke.

JAPANESE SAWS

Because Japanese saws are designed to cut on the pull stroke, they can be made with blades that are thinner than their Western equivalents. Since their teeth are also finely set, these saws are capable of cutting relatively narrow kerfs. The best blades are taper-ground to reduce friction.

Using a hugihiki
Flex the saw blade against the work to cut a dowel flush with the surface.

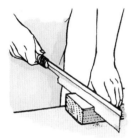

Cutting with a dozuki
Saw with the blade parallel to the bench. Some woodworkers like to saw a kerf on all four sides before cutting through the work.

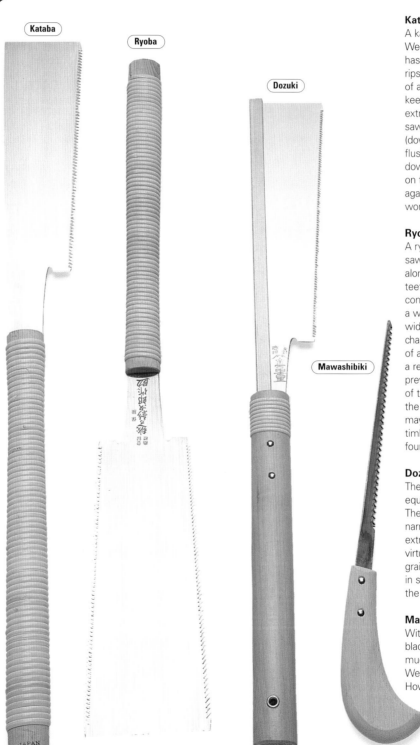

Kataba

Ryoba

Dozuki

Mawashibiki

JAPAN

Kataba
A kataba is similar to a Western handsaw in that it has a row of crosscut or ripsaw teeth along one edge of a broad blade that helps keep the saw on course. An extra-flexible version of the saw, known as a hugihiki (dowel saw), is used to flush-cut through tenons or dowel joints. It has no set on the teeth and is flexed against the surface of the work like a spatula.

Ryoba
A ryoba is a combination saw with crosscut teeth along one edge and ripsaw teeth along the other. It is convenient to be able to cut a workpiece to length and width without having to change saws, but the blade of a ryoba has to be held at a relatively shallow angle to prevent the uppermost row of teeth scoring the sides of the kerf. Consequently, you may have to sever a balk of timber by sawing from all four sides.

Dozuki
The dozuki is the Japanese equivalent of the backsaw. The dovetail version has a narrow blade that cuts an extremely fine kerf with virtually no tearing of the grain. The teeth are graded in size towards the heel of the saw, for starting the cut.

Mawashibiki
With its narrow tapered blade, the mawashibiki has much in common with the Western compass saw. However, there is less danger of buckling a blade that cuts on the back stroke.

SHARPENING SAWS

Reconditioning a saw, including topping, setting and filing the teeth, takes time to perfect – which is why many woodworkers send a saw away to be sharpened professionally. However, it is not necessary to put a saw through the whole process each time you feel it is not cutting at its best. A few strokes with a saw file may be all that is required to put a blunt saw back into perfect working order.

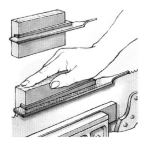

SELECTING A SAW FILE

SAW	PPI	FILE LENGTH
Ripsaw	5 to 7	250mm (10in)
Crosscut saw	6 to 8	230mm (9in)
Panel saw	10 to 12	200mm (8in)
Tenon saw	13 to 15	180mm (7in)
Dovetail saw	16 to 22	150mm (6in)

Saw files

The cutting edges of saw teeth are sharpened with a special triangular file. Each face of the file should be approximately twice the height of the saw tooth. Use the chart above as a rough guide to selecting a saw file.

Knife-edge files are available for sharpening Japanese saws, but resetting and sharpening these saws is an exacting task best left to a professional.

Saw file

Saw set

Saw set

This tool is designed to bend individual saw teeth precisely to the required angle. Squeezing the handles operates a plunger that presses each tooth against an angled anvil, which is adjustable for different-size teeth. The standard saw set copes with teeth up to 12 PPI; a fine saw set is also available. Some saw sets are made with a magnifying lens.

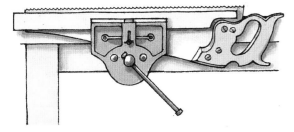

Clamping a saw

To prevent a saw vibrating while being sharpened, the blade must be held rigidly between stiff battens clamped just below the row of teeth. Cut a pair of hardwood battens long enough to support your largest handsaw, and shape them at one end to accommodate the saw handle. Sandwich the blade between the battens clamped in a bench vice: if necessary, use a small G-cramp to pinch the battens together near the toe of the saw.

Topping a saw

Running a file lightly along the cutting edge of a saw puts a tiny bright spot on the point of each tooth. These will serve as an invaluable guide to accurate sharpening (see below). Topping is essential to reduce all the teeth to the same level when repairing a damaged saw.

Make a jig to carry a smooth metal file, by cutting a narrow tapered housing across a block of hardwood. Wedge the file in the housing. Rubbing the block against the face of the saw, make two or three passes with the file, covering the entire length of the blade each time.

Filing ripsaw teeth

Clamp a ripsaw between battens, with its handle to your right. Starting near the toe of the saw, place the saw file on the first tooth bent away from you and against the leading edge of the tooth next to it. Steadying the file with both hands, hold it horizontal and square to the blade. Make two or three strokes, applying pressure on the forward pass only, until about half the bright spot on the tooth point is removed. Working towards the handle, place the file in alternate gullets until you have sharpened half the saw's teeth. Turn the saw around and file the remaining teeth until the bright spots disappear.

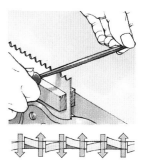

Filing crosscut teeth

Sharpen a crosscut saw the same way as a ripsaw, but turn the file to an angle of about 65 degrees to the blade, with the tip of the file pointing in the direction of the saw handle. Drawing 65-degree parallel lines across the top of both clamp battens may help you orientate the file.

Setting the teeth

Reset the teeth if your saw has been binding in the kerf or wandering off line. Adjust the saw set by releasing the locking screw on the end of the tool and turning the anvil until the required PPI figure marked on its edge aligns with the indicator. Then retighten the screw. Working from either end of the blade, locate the saw set over the cutting edge and bend each tooth that leans away from you (**1**). Turn the saw around and set the remaining teeth.

Holding the saw at eye level with the teeth facing away from you, check that you have not missed any of the teeth (**2**).

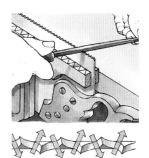

1

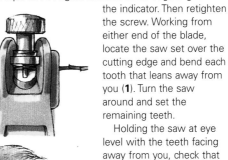

2

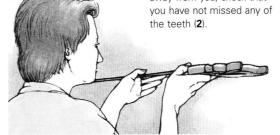

Using a saw-file guide

Using a saw-file guide guarantees consistency of angle and depth when sharpening ripsaw and crosscut teeth. The jig fits onto the toothed edge of a saw, holding the captive file either square to the blade or at the appropriate angle.

117

BENCH PLANES

The basic bench plane is available in a range of sizes, providing the woodworker with the means to smooth workpieces of various lengths and widths. The replaceable-blade bench plane is a relatively new concept. When blunt, its narrow cutter is discarded and a new one substituted.

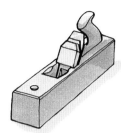

Traditional jack plane
Even though its wedged blade is difficult to adjust, this type of bench plane is popular with old-tool enthusiasts. New ones are still available from specialist suppliers.

Scrub plane
The scrub plane has a blade with a convex cutting edge that will quickly reduce a workpiece to size, prior to smoothing the surface with a conventional bench plane. Planing diagonally across the grain from two directions with a scrub plane leaves a relatively rough but flat surface. Now that more woodworkers own or have access to machinery, this type of plane is rarely used in home workshops.

Extra-long soles for
planing straight edges

Wooden try plane

Metal try plane

Scrub-plane blade

Scrub plane

Try plane

A try or jointer plane is made with a sole up to about 600mm (2ft) long, enabling it to bridge minor undulations on the surface of the work. As a result, a try plane is the ideal tool for planing long straight butt joints between boards and for flattening the surfaces of wide panels. Being mass-produced, metal bench planes are usually cheaper than wooden ones.

Jack plane

With a sole 380mm (1ft 3in) long, the jack plane is a good general-purpose plane – long enough to make reasonably accurate edge joints, but not so unwieldy that it cannot be used to finish most workpieces square and flat.

Replaceable-blade bench plane

Smoothing plane

The relatively short smoothing plane is used to take very fine shavings as a means of producing the final planed surface on a workpiece. The best wooden smoothing planes have self-lubricating lignum vitae soles.

Wooden jack plane

Medium-length soles for general-purpose woodwork

Metal jack plane

Short soles for smoothing workpieces

Wooden smoothing plane

Metal smoothing plane

DISMANTLING AND ADJUSTING BENCH PLANES

All metal bench planes are made with similar components and dismantled in the same way. Although on some bench planes the blade is held in place with a wedge, most modern planes are fitted with capped blades and depth-adjustment screws.

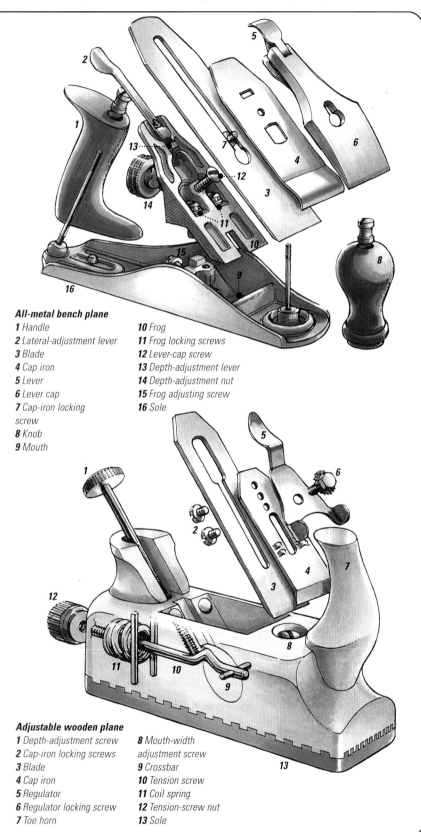

All-metal bench plane
1 *Handle*
2 *Lateral-adjustment lever*
3 *Blade*
4 *Cap iron*
5 *Lever*
6 *Lever cap*
7 *Cap-iron locking screw*
8 *Knob*
9 *Mouth*
10 *Frog*
11 *Frog locking screws*
12 *Lever-cap screw*
13 *Depth-adjustment lever*
14 *Depth-adjustment nut*
15 *Frog adjusting screw*
16 *Sole*

Adjustable wooden plane
1 *Depth-adjustment screw*
2 *Cap-iron locking screws*
3 *Blade*
4 *Cap iron*
5 *Regulator*
6 *Regulator locking screw*
7 *Toe horn*
8 *Mouth-width adjustment screw*
9 *Crossbar*
10 *Tension screw*
11 *Coil spring*
12 *Tension-screw nut*
13 *Sole*

Removing the blade and cap iron of a metal plane

In order to remove the blade of a metal bench plane for sharpening or to make other adjustments, first take off the lever cap by lifting its lever and sliding the cap backward to release it from its locking screw. Lift the blade and cap iron out of the plane, revealing the wedge-shaped casting known as the frog, which incorporates the blade-depth and lateral-adjustment controls.

To separate the cap iron and blade, use a large screwdriver to loosen the locking screw, then slide the cap iron towards the cutting edge until the screw head can pass through the hole in the blade.

Assembling the plane

1 Lay cap iron across blade

2 Align cap iron and blade

3 Slide cap iron towards the cutting edge

Having sharpened the blade, hold it bevel-downwards and lay the cap iron across it, locating the head of the captive locking screw in the hole in the blade (**1**).

Sliding the screw along the slot in the blade, swivel the cap iron until it aligns with the blade (**2**). Don't drag the cap iron across the cutting edge.

Slide the cap iron to within 1mm ($^1/_{16}$in) or less of the cutting edge (**3**), then tighten the locking screw.

Lower the blade assembly into the plane, fitting it over the projecting lever-cap screw and onto the stub of the depth-adjustment lever. Replace the lever cap.

Turn the depth-adjustment nut until the blade protrudes from the mouth. Move the lateral-adjustment lever until the cutting edge appears to be parallel with the sole. Set the depth of cut.

Removing the blade from a wooden plane

Back off the depth-adjustment screw by about 10mm ($1^1/_2$in), and loosen the tension-screw nut at the heel of the plane. Turn the tension screw's crossbar through 90 degrees to release the blade assembly, which includes the cap iron and regulator. To dismantle the assembly for sharpening, remove the two screws at the back of the blade.

Assembling and adjusting a wooden plane

Having sharpened the blade, replace the cap iron and lower the assembly into the plane. Pass the crossbar through the slot in the assembly, turning the bar to locate it in its seat in the cap iron, then slightly tighten the tension-screw nut.

Adjust the depth screw until the blade protrudes through the mouth of the blade, and use the regulator to ensure the cutting edge is parallel with the sole. Back off the depth adjuster to the required setting, and then finally tighten the tension-screw nut. To open or close the mouth on a wooden plane, adjust the screw behind the toe horn.

Having assembled a bench plane, take a few trial shavings to make sure the tool is adjusted properly.

USING BENCH PLANES

When setting up a workpiece for planing, inspect the wood to ascertain the general direction of the grain. Planing with the grain is always preferable, since planing against the grain tends to tear the wood fibres. If you are planing wood with irregular grain, adjust the plane to take very fine shavings.

Handling bench planes

When using a wooden smoothing plane, nestle your hand into the shaped crotch just above the heel of the plane, grasping the body with your fingers and thumb. Use the ergonomic horn to provide downward pressure (**1**).

Hold the handle of a metal bench plane with your forefinger extending towards the toe of the tool – this guarantees control over the direction of the plane. Place your free hand on the round knob to keep the toe in contact with the work (**2**).

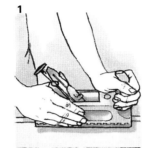

Planing edges

Maintain a square edge by putting pressure on the toe with your thumb, curling your fingers under the plane to act as a guide fence against the side of the work. Use a similar grip to hold the plane at an angle when planing chamfers along a workpiece.

Using a slicing action

It is sometimes easier to smooth irregular grain if you create a slicing action by turning the plane at a slight angle to the direction of travel. Make sure you don't allow the plane to rock.

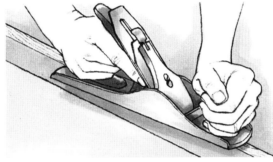

Planing a board flat

Begin by planing at a slight angle across the board from two directions. Check the surface with a straightedge, then adjust the plane to take thinner shavings and finish with strokes parallel to the edges of the workpiece (**1**).

To prevent the plane rounding off the work at either end, keep the weight on the toe of the plane as you begin each stroke and gradually transfer pressure to the heel (**2**).

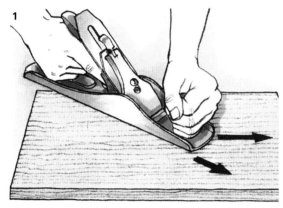

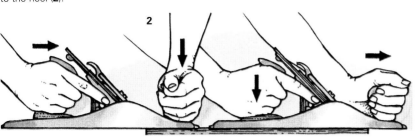

SERVICING BENCH PLANES

Although you may experience minor difficulties from time to time, provided you take reasonable care of your bench planes they should require very little servicing. Keep planes clean and well lubricated, and occasionally wipe exposed metal surfaces with an oily rag. Store bench planes on their sides, with their blades withdrawn.

Lubricating a sticky sole

If you feel that a metal plane is not gliding across the work as it should, lightly rub a stub of white candle across the sole.

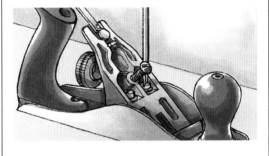

Correcting blade chatter

If your plane vibrates or 'chatters', instead of taking a shaving smoothly, check that the blade is held securely. Tighten the lever-cap screw or, if you are using a wooden plane, the tension-screw nut.

If the fault persists, check there are no foreign bodies trapped behind the blade and, in the case of a metal bench plane, tighten the frog's fixing screws.

Preventing shavings jamming

Shavings get caught between the leading edge of the cap iron and the blade when these are not fitting snugly against one another. Check whether deposits of resin are preventing the cap iron from bedding down. If necessary, re-dress the leading edge of the cap iron on an oilstone, taking care to hone the edge flat and at the original angle.

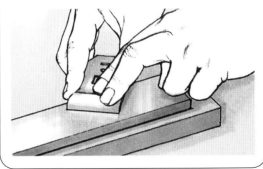

REBATE AND SHOULDER PLANES

Various planes are made for cutting and trimming rebates and other similar square-section recesses, such as housings and the shoulders of large joints. As they are somewhat specialized, you may not want to include all of them in your tool kit, but they can be invaluable when the need arises.

Bench rebate plane
The bench rebate plane is similar to other bench planes in every respect except for the blade, which extends across the entire width of the sole. Since it has neither depth gauge nor fence, it is necessary to use a batten to guide a bench rebate plane on the intended path.

Rebate-and-filister plane
Fitted with an adjustable depth stop and side fence, the rebate-and-filister plane has two mountings for the blade, one to the rear for normal use and a second one near the toe for planing up to the end of stopped rebates. This type of plane also has a spur – a short knife blade – that scores the wood ahead of the plane blade when cutting rebates across the grain.

Shoulder plane
An accurately engineered shoulder plane can be used like a narrow bench rebate plane, but it is primarily intended for trimming the shoulders of large tenons or lap joints. The blade is set at a low angle so that it will shave end grain cleanly. Some shoulder planes have a detachable nose, to convert the plane for bullnose work.

Bullnose plane
A bullnose plane is handy for trimming stopped rebates or small joints.

Side rebate plane
This lightweight tool is fitted with a pair of blades facing in opposite directions so you are always able to plane with the grain. It is designed for trimming rebates or easing narrow grooves. Having a detachable nose at each end, it can be used to shave right up to the ends of stopped housings.

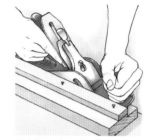

Guiding a bench rebate plane
Temporarily nail or clamp a straight batten to the work when using a bench rebate plane. Holding the side of the plane hard up against the batten, start planing at the far end of the workpiece and gradually work backward as the rebate begins to form.

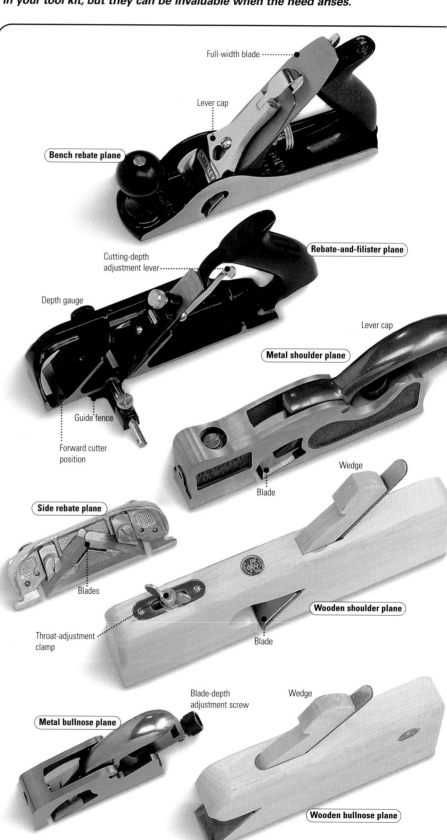

Full-width blade

Lever cap

Bench rebate plane

Cutting-depth adjustment lever

Rebate-and-filister plane

Depth gauge

Lever cap

Metal shoulder plane

Guide fence

Forward cutter position

Wedge

Blade

Side rebate plane

Blades

Wooden shoulder plane

Throat-adjustment clamp

Blade

Blade-depth adjustment screw

Wedge

Metal bullnose plane

Wooden bullnose plane

BLOCK PLANES

The block plane is a lightweight tool primarily for trimming end grain. It is designed to be held in one hand, though pressure is applied to the toe of the plane with the other.

Using a rebate-and-filister plane
Having set the depth gauge and fence, start planing at the far end of the workpiece and work backward, gradually lengthening the strokes. To prevent cross-grain wood from splintering, lower the spur until its point can slice the fibres just ahead of the plane.

Trimming large shoulders
Holding the work on a bench hook, lay the plane on its side to pare the shoulder's end grain. Use a strip of wood to prevent the work splitting along the back edge.

Easing a groove
Holding the side rebate plane on edge in the groove (or rebate), adjust the depth gauge until it comes to rest on the top surface of the work. Run the plane against the vertical wall to trim the recess to size.

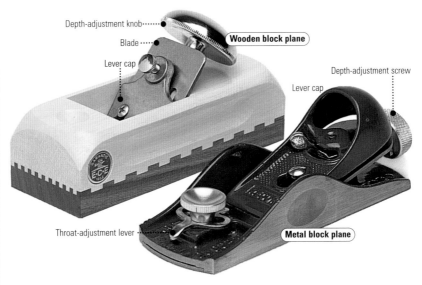

Depth-adjustment knob · · · · · ·
Blade · · · ·
Lever cap
Wooden block plane
Depth-adjustment screw
Lever cap
Throat-adjustment lever · · · · · ·
Metal block plane

PLANING END GRAIN

It is comparatively easy to skim end grain with a block plane – but for precise trimming use a bench plane on a shooting board.

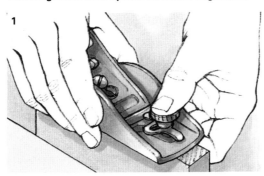

1

2

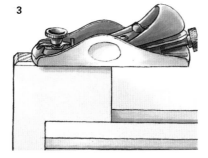

3   **4**

Using a block plane
Cup the bulbous lever cap or domed depth-adjusting knob in the palm of your hand, gripping the sides of the plane between fingers and thumb. While advancing the plane across the work, exert pressure on the toe with the thumb or fingertips of your free hand (**1**). Plane from both ends towards the middle (**2**), to avoid splitting wood from the edge of the work. Alternatively, plane off one corner down to the marked line, then plane the end grain towards the chamfered edge (**3**) or clamp a strip of wood flush with the end of the workpiece to support the edge and prevent it splitting off (**4**).

Removing the lever cap from a block plane reveals the blade, which is fitted bevel uppermost and presented at a relatively shallow angle to the work surface to produce a paring action. Both wooden and metal block planes have comparatively sophisticated control over cutting depth and over lateral movement of the blade. The mouth of either type can be adjusted to take fine shavings. Good-quality wooden planes are made with hardwood bodies and lignum vitae soles.

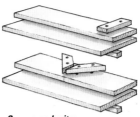

Square and mitre shooting boards

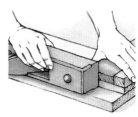

Using a bench plane and shooting board
A shooting board is used to jig the work when planing end grain with a bench plane. Square and mitre shooting boards are available. The workpiece is held against the stop block, which prevents the wood splitting as the plane is slid along the jig to take a fine shaving. Rub candle wax on the board for smooth running.

JAPANESE PLANES

A Japanese woodworking plane consists of a simple hardwood body accommodating a laminated-steel blade and a cap iron that breaks and curls the shavings to prevent the wood fibres tearing in advance of the blade. A steel retaining pin keeps the cap iron pressed against the blade. Although these tools are not dissimilar to traditional Western bench planes and moulding planes, the Japanese technique for planing wood is quite distinctive. Japanese woodworkers plane backwards, on the pull stroke, and with a finely set tool will cut a continuous wafer-thin shaving from one end of a workpiece to the other.

A hollowed sole
The sole of a kanna is hollowed to leave three points of contact with a workpiece.

Using a kirimen-kanna
The kirimen-kanna is placed on the corner of the workpiece, with one fence running against each face.

Kanna

The full range of what we would call bench planes varies from 600 to 75mm (2ft to 3in) in length. The sole of the larger planes is hollowed behind and in front of the blade to reduce friction. The blades are made with a thin layer of high-carbon steel, which forms the actual cutting edge, backed by a comparatively soft shock-absorbing strip of low-carbon steel. The back face of each blade is hollowed out, to make it easier to grind the back flat on a lapping plate or stone. There is a knack to adjusting the blade, which is acquired with experience. To take a thicker shaving, for example, the top edge of the blade is tapped with a soft hammer or mallet; tapping the heel of the plane reduces the depth of cut.

Kirimen-kanna

The Japanese make a great many specialized moulding planes – including the chamfer plane with its pair of adjustable fences that expose more or less of the cutting edge depending on the width of the chamfer required. The plane body, which carries the blade, is inserted from the side to bridge the fences.

Sakuri-kanna

Japanese shoulder planes have a blade that extends across the width of a narrow oak body.

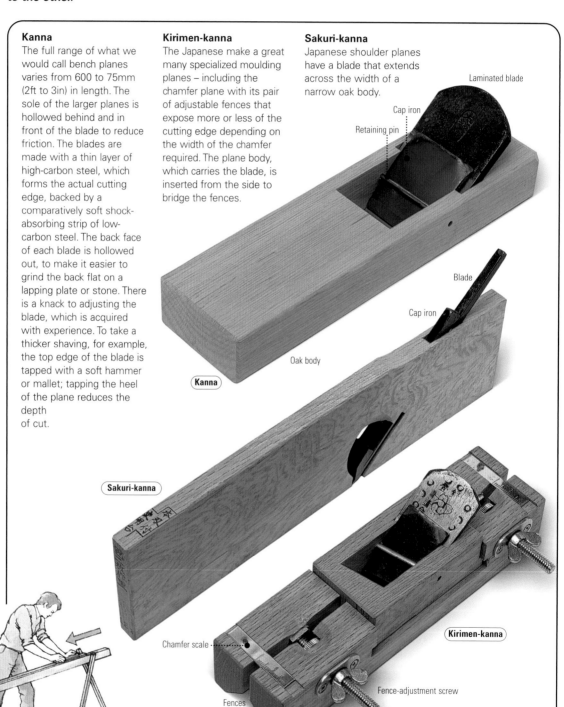

Laminated blade

Cap iron

Retaining pin

Blade

Cap iron

Oak body

Kanna

Sakuri-kanna

Kirimen-kanna

Chamfer scale

Fences

Fence-adjustment screw

Japanese planes cut on the pull stroke

SPECIALIZED PLANES

Power tools have virtually replaced certain planes that were once found in every workshop. Nevertheless, compass planes and router planes are still being manufactured for woodworkers who prefer to use handtools for jobs that can be completed in less time than it takes to set up a power tool.

Compass plane

The sole of a compass plane is made from flexible steel and can be adjusted by means of a large knurled nut to form a concave or convex curve. Its blade, cap iron and lever cap are identical to those of standard bench planes.

A compass plane is especially useful for trimming gentle curves, such as the edge of a round table. After sawing the wood roughly to shape, either set the sole of the plane to match the cut edge or draw the intended curve on a board as a guide to adjusting the sole to the required shape.

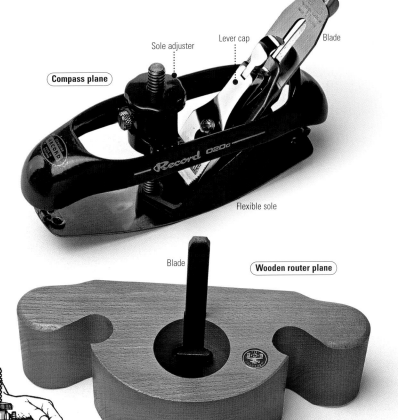

(Compass plane)

Sole adjuster   Lever cap   Blade

Flexible sole

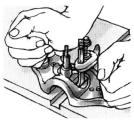

Cutting a housing
First, on both sides, saw down the line to the depth of the housing. Then use the router-plane, adjusting the cutter depth little by little to remove the waste in stages.

Blade   **(Wooden router plane)**

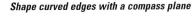

Shape curved edges with a compass plane

Sharpening cutters
To sharpen a router-plane cutter on an oilstone, place the stone near the edge of a bench to provide clearance for the cutter shaft.

Router plane

Owing to its relative cheapness and simplicity, a router plane is often the preferred tool for cutting small recesses for locks and hinges. A very basic wooden router plane is available from European suppliers, but a metal plane with screw-adjustable cutters is far more adaptable. Chisel-like cutters are used to level square-sided recesses, and there is a pointed cutter for working into tight corners and for shaping the undercut sides of dovetail housings.

You can level a through housing with a cutter mounted in the forward position of the cutter clamp. With a cutter mounted in the rear position, you can use the plane in reverse to work up to the end of a stopped housing.

A small fence, screwed to the sole, is designed to guide cutters at a set distance from straight or curved edges. A depth gauge fitted in the open throat of the plane allows the tool to be used on a narrow edge.

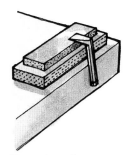

(Metal router plane)

Fence

Blade-depth adjuster

Standard cutter

Pointed cutter

Depth gauge

PLOUGH AND COMBINATION PLANES

The invention of a single tool combining the functions of dozens of grooving, rebating and moulding planes was in its day no less radical than the introduction of the power router – which was in turn destined to limit the appeal of these ingenious planes. Much loved by traditionalists, the simple plough plane, the more versatile combination plane and the multi-plane are all still available from specialist tool suppliers.

Plough plane

Supplied with a range of straight square-edged blades, the plough plane is designed specifically for cutting grooves or narrow housings. It comes with a depth gauge and side fence.

Combination plane

Similar in appearance to the plough plane, the combination plane includes a sliding clamp to hold the blade in place and a knurled screw to adjust the cutting depth. In addition to the usual depth gauge and side fence, the combination plane is equipped with a special narrow fence that facilitates the planing of a bead along a tongued edge – a feature that is often required for matchboarding. As well as standard blades, it can take a range of shaped cutters.

Multi-plane

A multi-plane is a combination plane with an even wider range of cutters, including a slitting knife for slicing off strips of timber or cutting finished mouldings off a board. The kit includes a cam steady, a device that prevents the fence supports sagging when you are planing mouldings some distance from the edge of a workpiece.

Scratch stock

A scratch stock is a homemade moulding tool. To make the cutter, take a piece of broken hacksaw blade and file it to the reverse shape of the required moulding.

Using a scratch stock

Clamp the cutter between two identical pieces of plywood screwed together to form a simple stock with a built-in guide fence. Leaning the tool away from you, scrape the wood with the projecting part of the cutter until the stock comes to rest on the work.

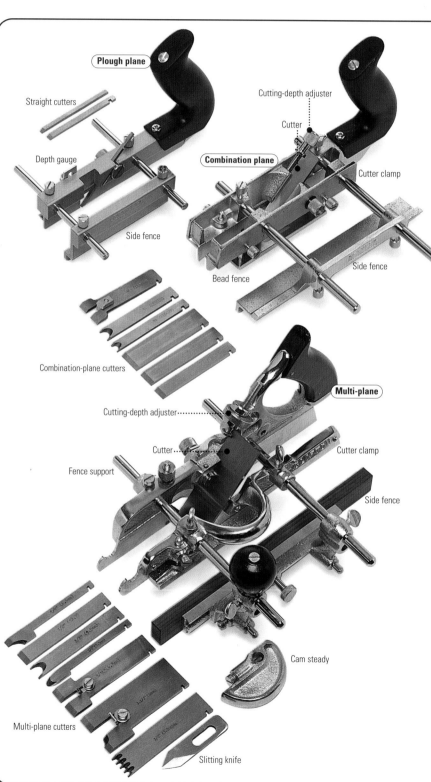

Plough plane

Straight cutters

Depth gauge

Side fence

Combination plane

Cutting-depth adjuster

Cutter

Cutter clamp

Side fence

Bead fence

Combination-plane cutters

Multi-plane

Cutting-depth adjuster

Cutter

Cutter clamp

Fence support

Side fence

Cam steady

Multi-plane cutters

Slitting knife

PLANE CUTTERS

The full range of cutters is shown right, together with the shape each is designed to cut.

A **tongue cutter**, in combination with a matching straight cutter, makes a tongue-and-groove joint. The tongue cutter has its own adjustable depth stop.

A **sash-moulding cutter** shapes one half of a sash-window moulding on the edge of a plank. The shape is then repeated on the other side before the slitting knife is used to cut the finished moulding from the plank.

An **ovolo cutter** can be used to shape the edges of straight boards or all four sides of a panel.

A **bead cutter** is often used to disguise the joint between two boards.

A single **reed cutter** produces a series of beads, side by side.

A **flute cutter** shapes hollows for finger pulls, pen holders, and so on.

Straight cutters can be used for planing rebates and grooves.

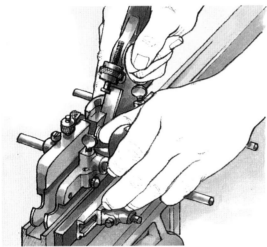

Controlling the planes

Plough planes, combination planes and multi-planes are all held and controlled in a similar fashion. Keeping the side fence pressed against the work with your left hand, start to plane at the far end with short strokes, gradually working backward until the plane is taking full-length shavings.

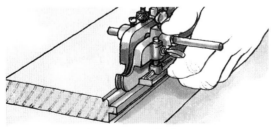

Cutting a bead along a tongued edge

Replace the standard side fence with the narrow bead fence – which runs against the edge of the work, just above the tongue. Set the depth gauge to ensure the top of the bead remains almost flush with the surface of the work.

Cutting matching tongues and grooves

Set the depth stop on the tongue cutter and adjust the side fence to centre the tongue on the edge of one of the workpieces. Plane the tongue, then substitute a straight blade and plane a matching but slightly deeper groove in the other workpiece.

Multi-plane cutters
1 Tongue cutter
2 Sash-moulding cutter
3 Ovolo cutter
4 Bead cutter
5 Reed cutter
6 Flute cutter
7 Straight cutter (rebate)
8 Straight cutter (groove)

CHISELS AND GOUGES

A set of chisels and a selection of basic gouges are essential for every workshop. They are used primarily for removing the waste from joints and for shaping and trimming workpieces.

Corner chisel
A corner chisel, which has a blade with two cutting edges at right angles to one another, is used for squaring off routed hinge recesses. Having chopped out the corners of the recess, pare out the waste before inserting the hinge.

USING CHISELS SAFELY

• Keep your chisels sharp. You have to apply more force to drive a blunt chisel — which can make it suddenly slip without warning.
• Never pare towards your body.
• Keep both hands behind the cutting edge.
• The long edges of new chisels can be sharp enough to cut your fingers while paring. Blunt them with an oiled slipstone.

Firmer chisel
The firmer chisel, with its relatively thick rectangular-section blade, is the woodworker's general-purpose chisel. It is strong enough to be driven with a mallet through the toughest hardwood. Blade widths range from 3 to 38mm ($\frac{1}{8}$ to $1\frac{1}{2}$in), but basic sets of chisels offered for sale hardly ever include one that is wider than 25mm (1in).

Bevel-edge chisel
This is a comparatively lightweight chisel, designed for trimming and shaping workpieces by hand. The blade is flat on the underside, like a firmer chisel, but shallow bevels are ground along both long edges on the upper face so that you can trim dovetailed undercuts. Bevel-edge chisels are made in the same range of sizes as firmer chisels.

Paring chisel
This is a specialized bevel-edge chisel with an extra-long blade for removing waste from housing joints. A paring chisel with a cranked neck allows you to keep the blade flat on the work even when removing wood from the centre of a wide panel or board.

Skew chisel
The end of the blade is ground to an angle of 60 degrees in order to produce a slicing action as the chisel is driven forward. This makes for smooth cutting, even through wild grain or knotty timber. Blades are 12, 18 and 25mm ($\frac{1}{2}$, $\frac{3}{4}$ and 1in) wide.

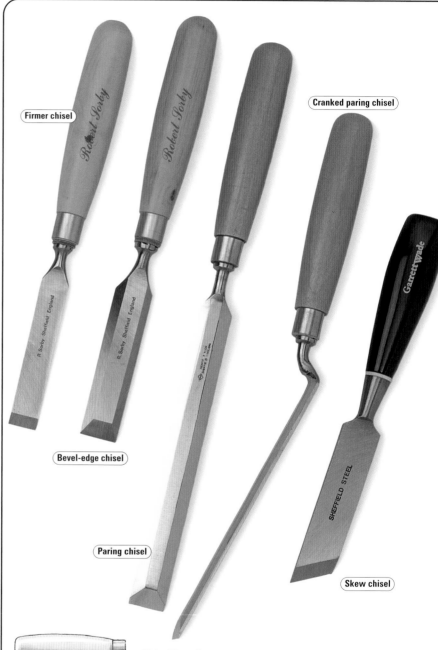

Firmer chisel

Cranked paring chisel

Bevel-edge chisel

Paring chisel

Skew chisel

Carver's-pattern handle

Octagonal handle

Oval handle

Registered handle

Chisel handles
A great many chisels are still made with tough hardwood handles, but moulded plastic handles are becoming increasingly popular. These are practically indestructible, even when driven with a metal hammer – a practice that would ruin a wooden handle.

Traditional cylindrical carver's-pattern handles provide a comfortable ergonomic grip. An octagonal handle prevents a chisel rolling off the bench – as does the more common oval grip, usually moulded from plastic. A registered handle is reinforced at the butt end with a metal hoop to prevent the wood splitting under constant hammering from a mallet.

CHISEL CONSTRUCTION

Construction varies according to the type of chisel and from one manufacturer to another, but essentially all chisels have a stiff metal blade attached to a straight roughly cylindrical handle. The design of the joint between the blade and the handle is critical.

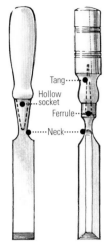

Tang

Hollow socket

Ferrule

Neck

How handles are fitted

Blades

The average bench chisel has a blade 125 to 175mm (5 to 7in) long. Some woodworkers prefer the feel of the butt chisel, a shorter and heftier version with a blade length of 75 to 100mm (3 to 4in). Special-purpose chisels have blades up to 250mm (10in) long. Manufacturers grind a single bevel on the end of each chisel – you have to hone the actual cutting edge yourself.

The critical joint

A chisel blade narrows noticeably at the 'neck', just before the handle. At this point, on most chisels, the blade is forged into a spike or 'tang', which is either driven into a wooden handle or moulded into a plastic one. The junction between handle and blade is usually reinforced with a metal collar known as a ferrule.

Alternatively, the neck may flare out again to form a hollow socket into which the handle fits.

USING CHISELS

Provided your chisels and gouges are kept sharp, you can drive them through the wood using hand pressure only – though sometimes it may be necessary to use a carpenter's mallet, especially when there's a lot of waste to be removed.

Paring with a chisel

Clamp the work to a bench or steady it against a bench hook. Grip the chisel handle in one hand, with your index finger extended towards the blade. Keep your forearm in line with the chisel and tuck your elbow into your side. With your free hand, grip the blade behind the cutting edge between index finger and thumb. As you apply pressure to the handle, use the other hand to guide the blade and control the force applied to the cutting edge (**1**)

1

If you need to apply extra force when paring wood from a recess, either tap the chisel with a mallet or, keeping your forearm in line with the blade, strike the end of the handle with the ball of your hand (**2**).

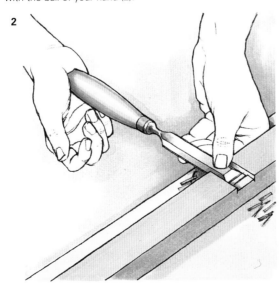

2

Wall-storage rack
You can buy a magnetic tool rack, or make your own rack from two strips of wood or plywood separated by short spacer blocks. Screw it to the wall and drop the chisel blades into the slot between the strips.

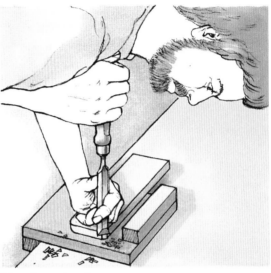

Trimming end grain

To shape the end of a workpiece, place the wood flat on a bench hook or on a piece of scrap board. Hold the chisel upright, with your thumb curled over the butt end of the handle. Rest your free hand on the work, controlling the blade by allowing it to slide between your index finger and thumb. Apply firm, steady pressure to the chisel with your shoulder.

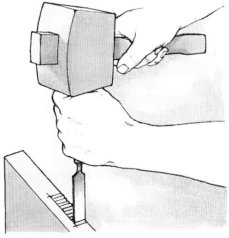

Driving a chisel with a mallet

To drive a chisel through tough hardwood or chop the waste from deep joints, place the cutting edge on the work then strike the butt end of the handle with a carpenter's mallet. For more delicate work, such as removing the waste from a hinge recess, grip the mallet shaft just below the head and tap the handle, letting the weight of the mallet do the work.

129

MORTISE CHISELS

Cutting deep mortises requires a chisel that will not jam in the work and which is strong enough to be used as a lever to remove the waste. Many mortise chisels are fitted with a leather shock-absorbing washer between the handle and the blade.

Gouge profiles

Sash-mortise chisel
To cut deep but narrow mortises, choose a sash-mortise chisel with a thick tapered blade up to 12mm (1/2in) wide.

Registered mortise chisel
This type of chisel is similar in appearance to an ordinary firmer chisel, but the blade tapers in thickness towards the cutting edge so that it will not become jammed in a deep mortise. Registered mortise chisels are available in widths up to 50mm (2in).

Lock-mortise chisel
A swan-neck lock-mortise chisel is used to level the bottom of a deep mortise cut with a sash-mortise chisel. Use one that is either the same size or slightly smaller than the chisel used to cut the mortise.

Drawer-lock chisel
A cranked all-metal drawer-lock chisel is designed for working in confined spaces where it would be impossible to wield an ordinary chisel and mallet. It has two cutting edges, one parallel to the shaft and the other at right angles to it. Strike the cranked shaft with a hammer, close to one of the cutting edges.

Sash-mortise chisel

Registered mortise chisel

Drawer-lock chisel

Lock-mortise chisel

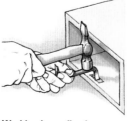

Working in confined spaces
Use a drawer-lock chisel

FIRMER GOUGES

A gouge is a chisel with a blade that is curved in cross section.

An out-cannel gouge (one with the cutting edge ground on the back of the blade) is used to scoop out hollows. An in-cannel gouge (which has the cutting edge ground on the top face of the blade) is used for trimming curved shoulders – such as those on a chair rail joining turned legs. Gouges range from 6 to 25mm (1/4 to 1in) in width.

Out-cannel gouge

In-cannel gouge

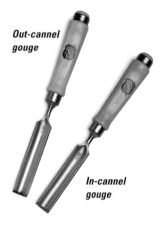

Scooping out hollows
Use an out-cannel gouge

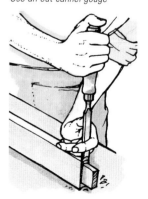

Trimming shoulders
Use an in-cannel gouge

JAPANESE CHISELS

As with Japanese plane blades, a laminated-steel construction is used for the manufacture of Japanese chisels. The hollow-ground blade and the socket and tang are forged in one piece, forming the strongest possible joint with the hardwood handle, which is reinforced with a deep tapered ferrule. At one time, Japanese tools were expensive and difficult to obtain, but nowadays most good mail-order companies offer a wide range of chisels.

Oire-nomi
The oire-nomi is the Japanese equivalent of the firmer chisel. It is strong enough to be driven with a mallet, despite having a bevel-edged blade. The blade width varies from 3 to 42mm (1/8 to 1 3/4in).

Umeki-nomi
The triangular cross section of the blade makes it ideal for chopping out the waste from between the pins and tails of dovetail joints. The blades are 3 to 12mm (1/8 to 1/2in) wide.

Kinari-nomi
The comparatively lightweight kinari-nomi is a paring chisel designed to be used with a two-handed grip. The blades, thinner than those of oire-nomis, range from 6 to 25mm (1/4 to 1in).

Kote-nomi
The cranked neck of this paring chisel allows you to clean up long rebates and housings. The blades are 6 to 18mm (1/4 to 3/4in) wide.

Tateguya-nomi
This is very similar to a Western mortise chisel, having a thick rectangular-section blade for cutting deep recesses. It is available from 3 to 18mm (1/8 to 3/4in) wide.

Mori-nomi and sokozarai-nomi
Used to clean up the sides and bottom of a mortise, these specialized chisels have a hook for clearing out the waste.

Chokkatu-nomi
This chisel is designed for cleaning up the corners of large mortises. Each half of the 90-degree cutting edge is 9, 16 or 25mm (3/8, 5/8 or 1in) wide.

Uchi-hagane-nomi
Like Western chisels that are mallet-driven, Japanese out-cannel firmer gouges are fitted with a metal collar to prevent the handle splitting. Blade widths range from 3 to 30mm (1/8 to 1 1/4in).

Oiri-uramaru-nomi
This in-cannel gouge, made for scribing rounded shoulders, has a thick blade ground with a flat bevel. Blade sizes are identical to those of out-cannel gouges.

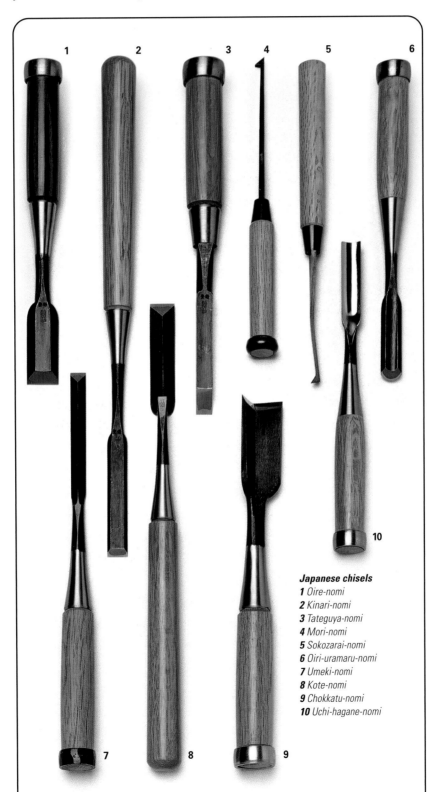

Japanese chisels
1 *Oire-nomi*
2 *Kinari-nomi*
3 *Tateguya-nomi*
4 *Mori-nomi*
5 *Sokozarai-nomi*
6 *Oiri-uramaru-nomi*
7 *Umeki-nomi*
8 *Kote-nomi*
9 *Chokkatu-nomi*
10 *Uchi-hagane-nomi*

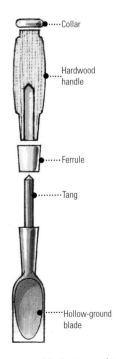

Collar
Hardwood handle
Ferrule
Tang
Hollow-ground blade

Japanese chisel construction

SHARPENING STONES

Woodworking blades are kept sharp by using abrasive stones to wear the metal to a narrow cutting edge. The better-quality natural stones are expensive, but you can get very satisfactory results from cheaper synthetic stones. As part of the sharpening process, stones are usually lubricated with water or oil to ensure the steel does not overheat and to prevent fine particles of metal and stone clogging the abrasive surface of the stone. Generally, sharpening stones are sold as rectangular blocks – bench stones – for sharpening everyday edged tools or as small knife-edge or teardrop-section stones for honing gouges and carving chisels. Some discerning woodworkers prefer to sharpen blades on a diamond-impregnated stone or on a perfectly flat metal plate dusted with abrasive powder.

Oilstones

Most woodworkers lap and hone their chisel and plane blades on a rectangular bench stone lubricated with oil. Novaculite, a compact silica crystal generally considered to be the finest oilstone available, is found only in Arkansas, USA. It occurs naturally in various grades. The coarse mottled-grey Soft Arkansas stone removes metal quickly and is used for the preliminary shaping of edged tools. The white Hard Arkansas stone puts the honing angle on the cutting edge, which is then refined and polished with Black Arkansas stone. Even finer is the rare translucent variety.

Synthetic oilstones are made from sintered aluminium oxide or silicon carbide. Categorized as coarse, medium and fine, man-made sharpening stones are far cheaper than their natural equivalents.

Some woodworkers like to have separate stones for each stage of the sharpening process, but it is more economical to buy oilstones featuring different grades of abrasive glued back to back. Dual stones of this kind are made from both natural and synthetic abrasives.

Carver's stones

Waterstones moulded with shaped profiles to match the most common carving tools are made in coarse, medium and fine grades.

Diamond stones

Extremely durable coarse and fine-grade sharpening 'stones' comprise a nickel-plated steel plate that is embedded with monocrystalline diamond particles and bonded to a rigid polycarbonate base. These fast-cutting sharpening tools, available as bench stones and narrow files, can be used dry or lubricated with water. Diamond stones will sharpen steel and carbide tools.

Combination oilstone

Dressing stone

Diamond stone

Waterstone

Black Arkansas

Hard Arkansas

Carver's stone

Cone slip

Soft Arkansas

Stone files

Metal lapping plates

Available as alternatives to conventional sharpening stones, metal plates sprinkled with successively finer particles of carborundum produce absolutely flat polished backs to plane and chisel blades as well as razor-sharp cutting edges. For the ultimate cutting edge on steel tools, finish with diamond-grit compound spread on a flat steel plate. Diamond abrasives are also used for honing carbide-tipped tools.

Slipstones and stone files

Small shaped stones are made for sharpening gouges, carving chisels and woodturning tools. Teardrop-section slipstones and tapered cones are the most useful, but there are also knife-edge, square and triangular-section stones for honing small carving chisels, drill bits and router cutters.

Natural and man-made waterstones and oilstones are available as slipstones, and in the usual range of grades. Combination waterstone slips are made for honing drawknives, axes and garden tools.

Waterstones

Because it is relatively soft and friable, a sharpening stone lubricated with water cuts faster than an equivalent oilstone; as a metal blade is rubbed across the surface, fresh abrasive particles are constantly exposed and released. However, this soft bond also makes a waterstone vulnerable to accidental damage – in particular, when honing narrow chisels it is easy to score the surface. Naturally occurring waterstones are so costly that most tool suppliers offer only synthetic varieties, which are almost as efficient.

Waterstones range from 800 grit at the coarse end, through 1000 and 1200 grit as medium grades, to something like 4000 to 6000 grit for final honing. Even finer, 8000-grit stones are available for polishing cutting edges. Extra-coarse 100 and 220 grits are used to repair damaged or very worn blades.

Chalk-like dressing stones are rubbed across the face of wet finishing-grade stones to raise a slurry that improves their cutting action.

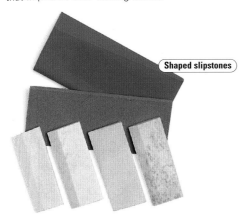

Shaped slipstones

CARING FOR SHARPENING STONES

Oilstones are often supplied in wooden boxes for mounting side by side on a bench. Waterstones can be clamped into special adjustable holders that prevent them sliding on the workbench.

Leave relatively coarse waterstones immersed in water for at least 5 minutes before you use them. Finer stones require less soaking; the very finest grades should only be sprinkled with water just before you start honing a blade.

So that your waterstones are always ready for use, store them in fitted vinyl boxes to prevent moisture evaporating. Some woodworkers keep their coarse stones immersed permanently in water, at a temperature above freezing.

Keep an oilstone covered, to prevent dust sticking to it, and clean the surface from time to time with paraffin applied with a coarse cloth.

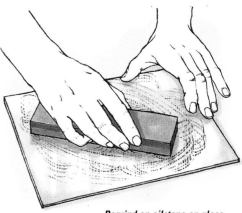

Regrind an oilstone on glass

Regrinding stones

Eventually, all sharpening stones become concave through constant use. Flatten an oilstone by rubbing it on an oiled sheet of glass sprinkled with silicon-carbide powder. Regrind the surface of a waterstone on a sheet of 200-grit wet-and-dry paper taped to a sheet of glass.

Sharpening-stone grades

The various methods by which sharpening stones are graded are listed below. Every woodworker needs at least one medium and one fine stone.

GRADE	MAN-MADE OILSTONES	NATURAL OILSTONES	WATERSTONES
Extra-coarse			100 and 200 grits
Coarse	Coarse	Soft Arkansas	800 grit
Medium	Medium	Hard Arkansas	1000 grit
Fine	Fine	Black Arkansas	1200 grit
Extra-fine			6000 and 8000 grit

STROPS

Having honed your tools on a sharpening stone, use a strop to remove any remaining trace of a burr, leaving the cutting edge razor-sharp.

Use a simple strip of thick hide or a proprietary combination strop that has one side covered in fine emery stone and the other three with coarse to fine leather. Lubricate all but the final leather surface with fine stropping paste.

Graded-leather surfaces

Combination strop

Stropping paste

SHARPENING CHISELS AND PLANES

A new plane iron or chisel is ground at the factory with a 25-degree bevel across its width. Although some woodworkers like to hone this bevel to a sharp edge for working softwood, such an edge is too weak to stay sharp for long when cutting hardwoods, so it is usual to hone a secondary bevel on a bench stone.

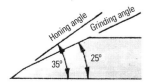

The cutting edge

The exact honing angle for this secondary bevel depends on the tool and the type of work you intend to do with it. A bench plane, for example, works best with a honing angle of between 30 and 35 degrees. A paring chisel, which should never need driving through the wood with a mallet, can be honed to an angle as shallow as 20 degrees. In contrast, cutting a mortise in dense hardwood might merit a chisel with a cutting edge honed to 35 degrees.

Lapping the back of a blade

Grinding a blade leaves minute scratches on the back and bevel, creating a serrated cutting edge that can never be truly sharp, even after honing. Consequently, the first stage of sharpening a new blade should be to flatten the back on a medium-grade bench stone or metal lapping plate.

Lubricate the stone and hold the blade flat on the surface, bevel side up (**1**). Rub the blade back and forth, maintaining pressure with your fingertips to prevent the blade rocking. Concentrate on the 50mm (2in) of blade directly behind the cutting edge – the rest of the blade can be left with its factory finish. Repeat the process on a fine whetstone until the metal shines.

Honing a plane blade

Grasp the blade, bevel side down, with your index finger extending along one edge. Place the fingertips of your free hand on top of the blade, just behind the cutting edge. Place the grinding bevel on a lubricated medium-grade bench

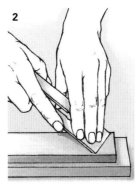

stone, rocking the blade gently until you can feel that the bevel is flat on the surface. Turn a wide blade to one side, so that the whole of the cutting edge is in contact with the stone (**2**).

Tilt the blade up onto its cutting edge and rub it back and forth along the entire length of the stone to hone the secondary angle. Keep your wrists firm, to maintain a constant angle.

Removing the wire edge

Having honed a bevel about 1mm ($^1/_{32}$in) wide, continue with sharpening the blade on a fine-grade whetstone. Eventually the process wears a 'wire edge' on the back of the blade – a burr that you can feel with your thumb (**3**). To remove the burr, lap the back of the blade on the fine stone, hone the bevel again with a few light strokes, and then lap once more until the burr breaks off, leaving a sharp edge.

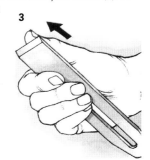

Finally, polish the cutting edge by honing on an extra-fine stone or on a leather strop lubricated with a small cake of fine stropping paste.

Honing a chisel

Sharpen a chisel exactly as described left and above – but because most chisel blades are relatively narrow, while you are honing the blade move the cutting edge from one side of the bench stone to the other, to avoid wearing a hollow down the middle.

USING A HONING GUIDE

If you have trouble maintaining an accurate bevel when sharpening chisels and planes, try clamping

the blade in a proprietary honing guide – a simple jig (of which there are numerous different styles) that holds the blade at the required angle. A honing guide is convenient for sharpening short spokeshave blades, which are difficult to manipulate by hand.

SHARPENING GOUGES

To hone an out-cannel gouge, rub the tool crossways on a bench stone – describing a figure-of-eight stroke while rocking the blade from side to side (**1**). This brings the whole of the curved edge into contact with the stone and evens out the wear. Remove the burr raised on the inside of the blade with a lubricated slipstone (**2**). Finally, strop the edge, having first wrapped the stone with a strip of soft leather.

Use a similar slipstone to hone the bevel on the concave edge of an in-cannel gouge (**3**). Rub the back of the gouge along a lubricated bench stone to remove the wire edge. Keep the back of the gouge flat on the stone while rocking the tool from side to side (**4**).

Carving gouges are sharpened in a similar way. Use knife-edge slipstones or stone files to hone the cutting edges of special carving chisels such as V-shaped parting tools and the squarish gouge-like macaronis and fluteronis.

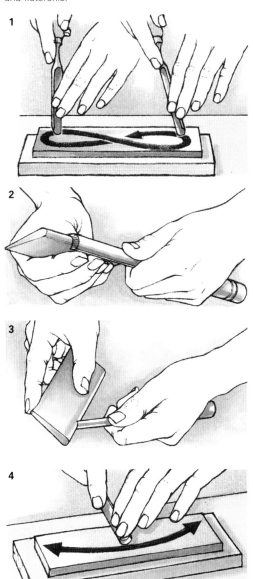

SHARPENING JAPANESE BLADES

Although Japanese planes and chisels are sharpened in a similar way to Western blades, there are significant differences, resulting from their construction. Because each blade is laminated with a hard-steel cutting edge, there is no need to hone a secondary bevel to strengthen it.

The hollow grinding on the back of every blade creates a narrow border of metal, which is easy to keep flat on a stone. Eventually, repeated honing of the bevel wears into this hollow so that the cutting edge is no longer continuous. Maintaining this hollow can be achieved by flattening the back after every honing. However, this wears away the blade relatively quickly, so Japanese craftsmen prefer to recreate the hollow periodically by hammering some metal into the narrow border behind the cutting edge.

Flattening a new blade
As with Western blades, the back of a new chisel or plane is flattened before honing the bevel for the first time. Because the metal is so hard, this is done by grinding on a steel lapping plate, using a pinch of coarse carborundum powder mixed with a little water.

Hold the blade flat on the surface at right angles to the plate and use a short length of softwood to apply pressure. When the narrow border surrounding the hollow is an even colour and texture, repeat the process with finer powder.

Wipe the blade clean and move on to a medium sharpening stone to continue flattening the back. Finish the job on a fine stone until the metal shines.

Sharpening the edge
Sharpen the cutting edge of Japanese blades in the same manner as their Western equivalents, but hone the whole width of the bevel. Do not hone a secondary bevel on the cutting edge.

Blade-hammering jig
Because hammering a blade by hand is a tricky process (see right), some wood-workers use a special proprietary jig to do the job. A heavy metal bar, guided by a hollow tube, is dropped onto the bevelled edge, of the blade, which is backed up by a metal anvil.

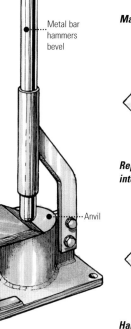

Metal bar hammers bevel

Blade

Anvil

Blade clamp

Blade-hammering jig

MAINTAINING THE HOLLOW BACK

Re-creating the leading edge of the hollow back is a skilled process. Traditionalists rest the back of the blade on the edge of a block of wood. A square hammer is used to tap the bevel, pushing metal out of the back to fill the hollow edge. Blows must be within the soft part of the bevel – as the hard cutting edge is brittle and will chip if struck with the hammer.

Once the hollow is refilled, the back is flattened on a grinding plate as already described.

Maintaining a hollow back

Repeated honing wears into the blade hollow

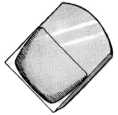

Hammering the bevel reforms the edge

GRINDERS

It soon becomes impossible to work with blades that have worn unevenly or when the cutting edge is chipped. Eventually they have to be repaired by accurately regrinding the bevel to an angle of 25 degrees. You can repair a blade on a coarse bench stone, but most woodworkers prefer to use a power grinder or motorized whetstone.

Grinding on a motorized whetstone

High-speed grinders

A standard bench grinder drives two relatively small grinding wheels or discs at about 3000rpm. There are grinders that run at half that speed, to avoid overheating tool blades. Wheels are interchangeable, but most machines are supplied with a coarse wheel for regrinding the bevel and a fine-grade wheel for honing the cutting edge. When you are using a high-speed grinder, the tool blade has to be cooled at regular intervals by dipping it in water. All grinders must be bolted firmly to a bench.

Wheels and discs

High-speed aluminium-oxide grinding wheels for repairing and honing tools are made in coarse, medium and fine grades. Some are engineered with a soft vitrified bond to reduce the problem of overheating. Neoprene-rubber wheels impregnated with silicon-carbide abrasives are especially recommended for honing narrow chisels and carving tools. There are also leather or hard-felt stropping wheels; and cloth discs dressed with honing and buffing compound for putting the final polished edge on cutting tools. Discs made from these relatively soft materials must be made to rotate away from cutting edges.

Combination grinders

There are machines that combine the advantages of high-speed grinding with slow whetstone sharpening. One common combination is a vertically mounted stone disc that runs through a bath of water, at one end of the machine, coupled with an aluminium-oxide wheel turning at a higher speed at the other. Similar machines are made with replaceable abrasive belts instead of a whetstone, or with a wide leather stropping wheel for honing blades.

Water reservoir

Stone disc

Tap

Motorized whetstone

Tool rest

Low-speed whetstone

High-speed wheel

Coarse-grade wheel

Combination grinder

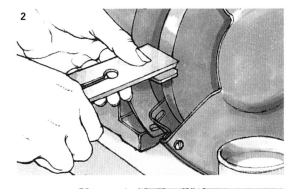

A grinding wheel that has become 'glazed' cuts slowly and is much more likely to overheat woodworking tools.

Wearing a dust mask and safety goggles, switch on the grinder and run a dressing tool or silicon-carbide stick from side to side across the edge of the grinding wheel to clean the surface. The same process is used to reshape a worn or unbalanced wheel.

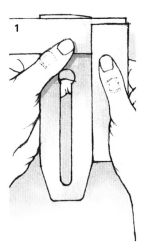

1

Motorized whetstones

Heat generated by grinding with a high-speed disc can ruin a blade – which is why a water-cooled motorized whetstone that turns at only 500rpm is a popular machine for regrinding woodworking tools. A traditional grindstone is mounted vertically and tools are ground on the edge of the stone, but a horizontally mounted stone is sometimes preferred because it enables you to grind a bevel with a perfectly flat face. A synthetic 1000-grit general-purpose stone is fitted as standard, but you can swap it for a coarse or fine stone in seconds.

REGRINDING BLADES

Use a coarse grinding wheel to reshape a badly worn blade, then change to a finer grade.

Marking a worn blade

Before regrinding a chisel or plane blade, check the cutting edge with a try square (**1**). Use a fine felt-tip pen to mark a guide line square to the long edges of the blade.

Grinding the blade square

Set the tool rest of your bench grinder about 3mm (¹⁄₈in) from the edge of the grinding wheel. Check that all clamps are tight, then switch on the machine. Wearing eye protection, dip the tip of the blade in water and place it bevel downwards on the tool rest (**2**). Feed the blade steadily against the wheel and, to prevent the metal overheating, move the blade from side to side as soon as it comes into contact with the abrasive surface.

Regrinding the bevel

Once the blade is square, switch off the grinder and adjust the tool rest to present the blade at an angle of 25 degrees to the wheel (**3**). Switch on, and grind the bevel across the width of the blade – once again keeping it cool by dipping the tip in water every few seconds.

2

High-speed grinder

Spark deflector

Fine-grade wheel

Tool rest

Star-wheel dressing tool

Grinding wheels

If you inadvertently allow the metal to heat to a temperature at which it turns blue, the blade will not be able to hold a sharp cutting edge for very long. The only remedy for this is to grind the blade square beyond the blued area and then regrind the bevel.

3

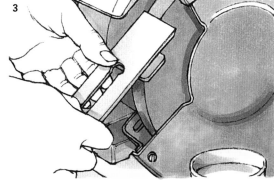

SPOKESHAVES

A spokeshave is essentially a specialized plane for finishing curved workpieces. Once you get the hang of it, smoothing with a spokeshave is both fast and efficient. Every tool kit should include at least straight-face and round-face versions of the standard spokeshave. Other, less essential, models can be acquired as and when you need them.

Standard spokeshave

A spokeshave is controlled by straight handles, mounted on each side of a short plane-like blade. The cutting depth and angle of the blade, which is held in place by a cast-metal cap iron, can be adjusted by means of two knurled screws. In cheaper spokeshaves, the blades have no means of adjustment and are simply positioned by eye before the cap iron is inserted. Use a straight-face spokeshave to shape convex curves, and a round-face one for concave edges.

Combination spokeshave

A dual-purpose spokeshave – equipped with a standard blade mounted alongside a blade with a half-round cutting edge – saves having to swap one tool for another when working components with ever-changing profiles.

Chamfer spokeshave

This spokeshave is fitted with a pair of adjustable fences that allow you to cut accurate chamfers along a workpiece that has 90-degree corners.

Half-round spokeshave

This is a hollow-face spokeshave with a concave cutting edge – ideal for smoothing rounded edges of rails and legs.

Radius spokeshave

The markedly convex cutting edge makes this an ideal tool for finishing hollows – such as those in solid-wood seats for traditional stick-back chairs.

USING SPOKESHAVES

Until you develop the right 'feel', a spokeshave tends to either skid across the surface, without taking a shaving, or bury its cutter in the wood.

Controlling a spokeshave

To cut smoothly, it is essential to have precise control over the angle of the blade. This is achieved by taking hold of the tool with your thumbs resting on the back edges of the handles. With the face of the spokeshave resting on the work, push the tool forward, rocking it back and forth until you begin to take a shaving cleanly. Shave a curve in two directions, to ensure you are always cutting with the grain.

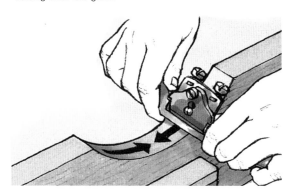

Straight-face spokeshave

Round-face spokeshave

Sharpening a spokeshave
Spokeshave cutters are ground and sharpened in much the same way as plane and chisel blades. Clamp a worn or chipped cutter in a plier wrench to hold it firmly for power grinding.

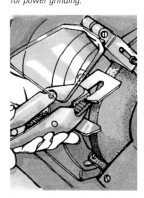

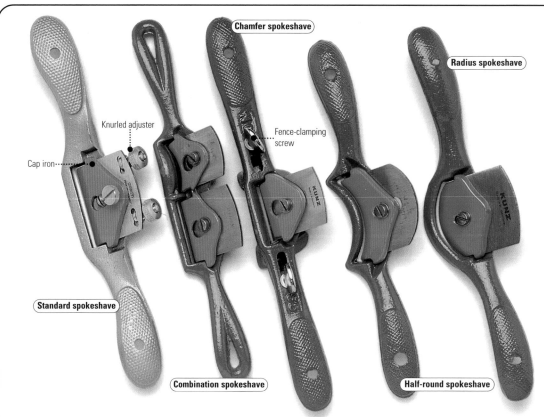

Chamfer spokeshave

Radius spokeshave

Knurled adjuster

Fence-clamping screw

Cap iron

Standard spokeshave

Combination spokeshave

Half-round spokeshave

DRAWKNIVES

Like the axe and the adze, the drawknife is a tool that was adopted by a wide variety of tradesmen from earliest times. Today it is rarely used except by woodworkers who appreciate the speed with which a drawknife can reduce a blank to size for carving or turning. It is, however, a versatile tool which in the hands of a skilled woodworker can be used to make curved backs and shaped arms for chairs.

Drawknife
Although all drawknives function in a similar way, different styles have evolved to meet the needs of specialist craftsmen or as a result of local tradition. The blade of a basic drawknife may be either straight or curved and is bevelled on one edge. The metal at each end of the blade is forged into a pointed tang, which is bent at right angles and fitted with a turned wooden handle.

Curved-edge blade

Continental-pattern drawknife

Forged tang

Push knife

British-pattern drawknife

Cutting edge

Inshave

Scorp

Deeply curved cutting edge

Push knife
A modern derivation from the drawknife, this tool has a short razor-sharp blade measuring 100 x 25mm (4 x 1in). It has two straight handles, and you can use it with both push and pull strokes.

Inshave
This is a tightly curved drawknife for working deep hollows. Inshaves are usually bevelled on the outside of the curve.

Scorp
A scorp is a one-handed inshave for shaping small items, such as wooden bowls and spoons.

USING A DRAWKNIFE

Drawknives are designed to cut on the pull stroke, using the handles to control the depth of cut by presenting the cutting edge at just the right angle to the work. Extending your thumbs along the handles prevents the tool twisting in your hands.

Shaping wood
Strokes with a drawknife should always be in the direction of the grain. Pulling the blade diagonally across the work produces a slicing action to facilitate cutting cross-grain wood.

If you are working a convex shape, hold the tool with the bevel upwards. Turn the tool over when cutting a concave shape, to prevent the bevel driving the blade deeply into the wood.

> ### Sharpening a drawknife
> Hold the drawknife on end with one handle located in the half-open jaws of a bench vice. Hone the cutting edge with a lubricated sharpening stone, using small circular strokes.

1

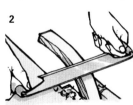

2

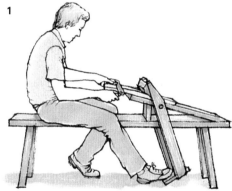

3

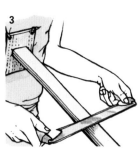

Holding the work
Traditionally, wood being worked with a drawknife is held on a shaving horse – a purpose-made stool with a foot-operated cramp (**1**). However, you can stand at the end of an ordinary workbench and shave work clamped in a vice (**2**). Alternatively, use a breast bib – a small sawn board suspended on a string hung round your neck. So that the work is firmly held, support one end of the workpiece on the edge of a bench and press against the opposite end with the breast bib (**3**).

SCRAPERS

Even though sanding is the most frequently used method for smoothing timber, scraping the surface – which removes minute shavings instead of dust particles – produces a superior finish. And because a scraper can take such a fine cut, you can use it on areas of wild grain that are difficult to plane well.

SHARPENING A SCRAPER

To get a new cabinet scraper working efficiently (or to sharpen a blunt one) it is necessary to prepare each cutting edge carefully and then raise a tiny burr on the metal, which acts like a miniature plane iron.

Filing the edges
Clamp the scraper in a bench vice and draw-file its two long edges to make them perfectly square. Use your fingertips to guide the file and stop it rocking (**1**).

Honing the scraper
Filing leaves rough edges that must be rubbed down with an oiled slipstone. Rub the stone along both sides of each cutting edge (**2**), keeping the stone flat against the face of the scraper.

Raising a burr
Create a burr along both cutting edges with a smooth metal burnisher. To do this, hold the scraper on the bench top and strop each edge firmly four or five times, drawing the burnisher towards you (**3**) while keeping it flat on the scraper.

Turning the burr
For the scraper to function, the raised burrs must be folded over at right angles. Holding the burnisher at a slight angle to the burred edge, draw the tool firmly along the scraper two or three times (**4**).

Blade — **Curve adjuster**

Scraper holder
Scraping wood is hard on the thumbs, especially when the metal gets hot. A glass-reinforced nylon holder puts the optimum curve on the scraper and takes the strain off your thumbs.

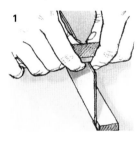
1

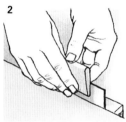
2

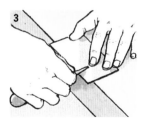
3

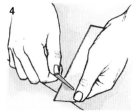
4

Cabinet scrapers
The basic scraper is a simple rectangle of tempered steel. It is supplied as a cropped blank upon which a scraping edge must be raised before it is ready for use. Goose-neck and concave/convex scrapers are made for finishing mouldings and other shaped work.

Hook scrapers
A hook scraper with a wooden handle is easy to use and comfortable to hold. Replace the disposable blades as soon as they become blunt. When using a hook scraper (which cuts on the pull stroke only), hold it at an angle to the surface.

Scraper plane
A scraper plane is a simple cast-metal jig designed to make scraping easier and more comfortable. The blade is clamped to the stock at the optimum angle and is bent into a curve by a centrally placed thumbscrew.
  Unlike a standard cabinet scraper (which is cropped with a square edge all round), scraper-plane blades are ground on two edges, at an angle of 45 degrees. Hone these edges on a stone and raise a scraping burr as for a cabinet scraper.

Burnishers
Burnishers made from hardened steel, with a round, oval or triangular section, are used to raise a burr on a scraper.

Bench-plane insert
A proprietary insert with a scraper blade can be fitted to a standard bench plane. The plane's own controls are used to adjust the depth of cut and lateral movement of the blade.

Basic — Concave/convex — Goose-neck — **Cabinet scrapers**

Blade — Blade-clamping bar — Thumbscrew — **Scraper plane**

Hook scrapers

Blade

Blade — **Burnishers**

WOOD RASPS AND FILES

Rasps and files are used rarely for woodwork except by carvers. A rasp removes wood very quickly and is frequently used by carvers for preliminary shaping – especially as it can cut both with and against the grain. Rasps leave a rough surface, and files of the same shape are employed to improve the finish.

USING A SCRAPER

By experimenting with different curvatures and angles, you can vary the action and cutting depth to suit the particular task.

Holding the scraper in both hands, lean it away from you and push the tool forwards (**1**). Bending the tool – by pressing with your thumbs near the bottom edge – concentrates the forces in a narrow band so that you can scrape small blemishes from the wood.

To scrape a panel flat and level, work in two directions at a slight angle to the general direction of the grain. Then to finish, smooth the wood by scraping parallel with the grain (**2**).

To scrape away from an edge or smooth the inside of a rebate, pull the scraper towards you (**3**).

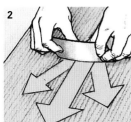

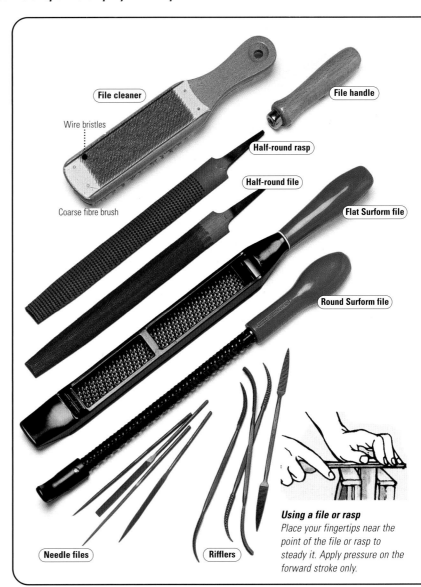

Rasps
The surface of a rasp is covered with individual teeth, which cut on the forward stroke. The size and distribution of the teeth determine the degree of coarseness, or 'cut', of the rasp. Manufacturers describe the cut in slightly different ways, but broadly speaking there are bastard, second-cut and smooth rasps — the bastard cut being the most coarse.

There are flat and round rasps, but the most versatile is the half-round rasp.

Wood files
A wood file has rows of closely packed sharp ridges, which smooth off the high points of the roughened timber left by a rasp. Although file cuts are described as bastard, second-cut and smooth, they are all relatively fine compared with rasps.

Surform tools
The thin perforated blades are made by punching out regularly spaced teeth with sharp cutting edges facing forward, leaving holes in the metal through which the wood shavings pass. This enables the tool to cut faster than a regular rasp, without clogging.

Rifflers
Rifflers are miniature double-ended files for working in tight corners and confined spaces. Choose rifflers with a rasp head at one end and a file head at the other.

File cleaners
The wire bristles on a file cleaner loosen the dust, packed in file and rasp teeth. The dust is then cleaned out with the coarse brush on the other side.

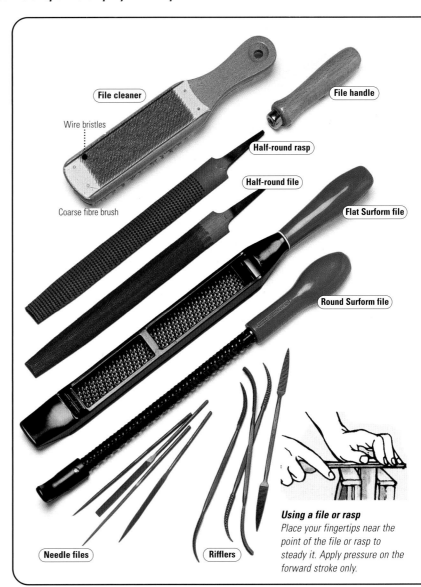

File cleaner

Wire bristles

Coarse fibre brush

File handle

Half-round rasp

Half-round file

Flat Surform file

Round Surform file

Needle files

Rifflers

Using a file or rasp
Place your fingertips near the point of the file or rasp to steady it. Apply pressure on the forward stroke only.

Fitting a file handle
Never use a file or rasp without a handle – if the tool catches and stops suddenly, the pointed tang could be driven through the palm of your hand.

Remove a damaged handle by holding the file in one hand and striking the front edge of the ferrule with a block of wood (**1**). Drive a new handle onto the tang by tapping the rounded end of the handle on a bench (**2**).

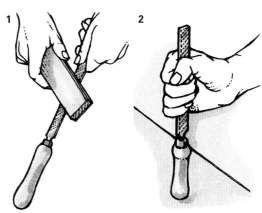

HAND DRILLS AND BRACES

The availability of power drills, especially the improved range of cordless tools, has reduced the need for hand-operated drills and ratchet braces. However, electric drills have not completely eradicated the demand for these tools – which are inexpensive, quiet, and perfectly safe in the hands of young woodworkers.

Using a bradawl
To open up a starter hole for a screw, twist the bradawl from side to side as you push it into the wood.

Bradawl

The bradawl is perhaps the simplest hole borer of all. Unlike a drill, it does not remove wood but merely displaces it by forcing the fibres apart. It is the ideal tool for making a starter hole, either for inserting a screw or to hold the point of a drill on its centre mark.

Placed across the grain, the sharp screwdriver-like tip severs the fibres as the awl is pushed into the wood; twisting the tool opens up the hole.

Sharpen the tip on the edge of a bench stone.

Gimlet

A gimlet does a similar job to a bradawl but, having a spiral flute, it is capable of making deeper holes by cutting and removing wood like a drill bit.

Hand drill

Cranking the tool's handle causes the chuck to rotate at relatively high speeds, via a system of gear wheels. With some models, the drive mechanism is encased in a cast-metal shell. The chuck will accommodate a wide range of twist drills and dowel bits.

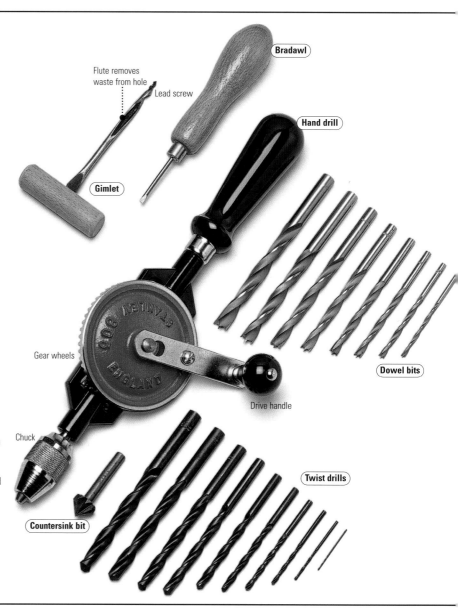

Flute removes waste from hole

Lead screw

Bradawl

Gimlet

Hand drill

Gear wheels

Dowel bits

Drive handle

Chuck

Twist drills

Countersink bit

HAND-DRILL BITS

The jaws of a hand drill take cylindrical twist drills and dowel bits. Buy good-quality drill bits only – cheap drills not only blunt quickly but are often ground inaccurately.

Twist drills

Twist drills are made with a pair of helical flutes that clear the waste from the hole as the drill bores into the wood. The flutes culminate in two cutting edges at the pointed tip.

Dowel bits

These are specialized wood-boring twist drills with a sharp lead point – designed to prevent them wandering off line – and two sharp spurs that cut a clean-edged hole.

Countersink bit

A countersink bit cuts a shallow tapered recess to accommodate the head of a woodscrew so that it lies flush with the surface of the work. A clearance hole is bored first to centre the bit.

Twist-drill tip

Dowel-bit tip

Countersink tip

BRACE BITS

The jaws of a brace chuck are designed to hold special-purpose square-shanked bits. Some braces are made with universal jaws, which will also accept round-shanked twist drills.

Auger bits
A solid-centre auger bit for a ratchet brace has a single helical twist that brings the waste to the surface and keeps the bit on line when boring deep holes. It has a pair of spurs at the cutting tip that score the wood ahead of the cutting edges to ensure a crisp edge to the hole. The central lead screw pulls the bit into the wood. The similar Jennings-pattern auger bit has a double helical twist. Auger bits range from 6 to 38mm (1/4 to 1 1/2in) in diameter.

Expansive bits
An adjustable expansive bit will cut a hole of any size between limits. The calibrated spurred cutter is held in place by a spring-loaded packing piece or, on some bits, by a toothed dial. Depending on the model, an expansive bit is capable of cutting holes either between 12 and 38mm (1/2 and 1 1/2in) in diameter or between 22 and 75mm (7/8 and 3in).

Centre bits
These are designed to bore relatively shallow holes, from 68 to 112mm (2 3/4 to 4 1/2in) deep. The single spur on one side of the bit scores the edge of the hole before the cutting edge on the other side enters the work. Centre bits are simpler and therefore cheaper than equivalent auger bits.

Countersink bit
Similar to the countersink bit for a hand drill, this has a square shank to suit the standard brace chuck.

Screwdriver bits
Special double-ended bits convert a brace into a heavy-duty screwdriver.

Ratchet brace
Tool manufacturers still offer a variety of braces – including a special ratchet brace for boring holes through ceiling and floor joists to accommodate pipes or electrical wiring.

An ordinary woodworker's brace is driven by cranking the frame clockwise while pressure is applied to the round handle. The circle described by the moving frame is known as the 'sweep'. Braces are listed in tool catalogues according to the diameter of their sweep, though 250mm (10in) is more or less standard.

A ratchet mechanism makes it possible to use a brace in confined spaces where a complete sweep is impossible. Having cranked the handle as far as possible, the ratchet allows for movement in the opposite direction, leaving the chuck stationary until clockwise rotation is resumed. Operating a cam ring reverses the ratchet mechanism, so you can withdraw the drill bit.

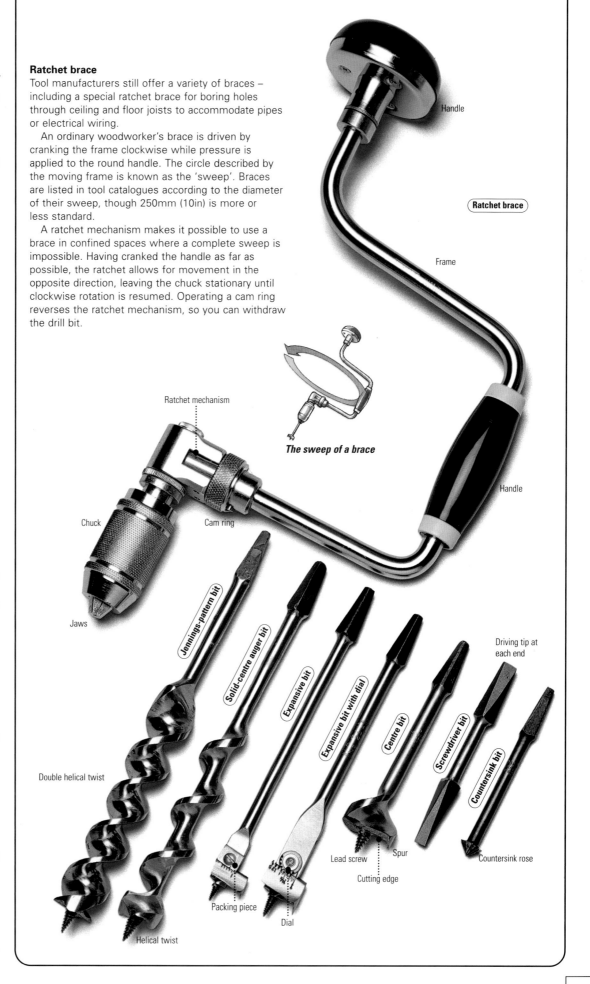

Ratchet brace

Handle

Frame

Ratchet mechanism

The sweep of a brace

Chuck

Cam ring

Handle

Jaws

Jennings-pattern bit

Solid-centre auger bit

Expansive bit

Expansive bit with dial

Centre bit

Screwdriver bit

Countersink bit

Driving tip at each end

Double helical twist

Packing piece

Dial

Lead screw

Cutting edge

Spur

Countersink rose

Helical twist

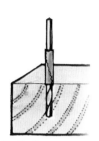

Depth stop
Wrap a strip of coloured tape around a twist drill as a guide to the depth of a hole.

USING A HAND DRILL

A hand drill is primarily used to bore small holes for woodscrews or dowels.

Operating a hand drill
Place the tip of the drill bit on the workpiece, and gently move the handle back and forth until the bit begins to bite into the wood. Crank the handle at speed to bore a hole to the required depth. Don't apply too much pressure when using small twist drills: the weight of the tool alone will be sufficient to encourage the drill to penetrate the wood.

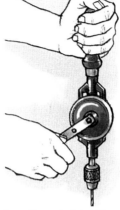

Inserting a twist drill
To open the jaws of a hand drill, hold the chuck in one hand and crank the handle anticlockwise. Load the drill bit, then grip the chuck and turn the handle clockwise to tighten the jaws. Before using the tool, check that the twist drill is centred in the jaws.

USING A RATCHET BRACE

Despite its simplicity, a ratchet brace is a versatile tool. It is capable or boring large-diameter holes and can be used to drive woodscrews effortlessly.

Fitting a brace bit
Lock the brace ratchet by centring the cam ring, then grip the chuck in one hand and turn the frame clockwise. Drop a bit into the chuck, then reverse the action to close the jaws.

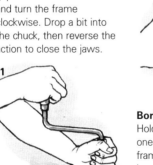

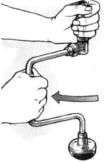

Boring with a brace
Hold the brace upright with one hand while cranking the frame with the other (**1**). To bore horizontally, steady the round handle against your body. To retrieve the bit, lock the ratchet and reverse the action a couple of turns to release the lead screw; then pull on the tool while moving the frame back and forth.

When drilling right through the wood, turn the work around as soon as the lead screw appears and finish the hole from that side (**2**).

SHARPENING DRILL BITS

Although woodworkers are used to sharpening chisels and planes regularly, brace bits and twist drills tend to be neglected, simply because a little extra pressure overcomes the problem of boring with blunt tools. However, a sharp drill bit works faster and makes cleaner, more accurate holes.

Sharpening brace bits
Auger bits and centre bits are sharpened similarly, using a small flat needle file. Start by stroking the inner face of each spur with the file (**1**). Don't under any circumstances try to sharpen the outer edges, because that would change the diameter of the bit. Resting the lead screw on your bench, file the bit's cutting edges (**2**). Take care not to damage the screw when filing.

Sharpen the cutter and spur of an expansive bit with a similar file.

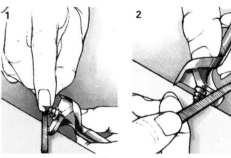

Sharpening twist drills
There are a number of proprietary sharpening jigs that hold a drill bit at the required angle to a small powered grinding wheel. Some sharpeners are designed for use with an electric drill, others have built-in motors. The better jigs, which will accommodate twist drills up to 12mm ($\frac{1}{2}$in) in diameter, are supplied with a wheel made from silicon carbide for sharpening masonry drills, in addition to the standard aluminium-oxide wheel.

You can also sharpen twist drills on a bench grinder. Rotate the tip against the rotating wheel (**3**), making sure you grind both sides evenly to keep the point accurately centred.

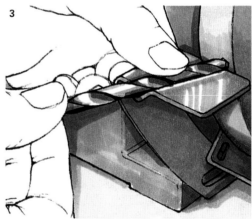

Dowel bits
Touch up the cutting edges and spurs of a dowel bit with a pointed needle file – taking care to sharpen both sides equally.

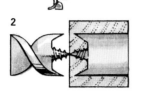

HAMMERS

Although nail fixings are rarely used for fine woodwork, they are often employed when constructing mock-ups and for joinery. Consequently, most tool kits boast a range of hammers of different weights.

Cross-peen hammer

A medium-weight – 280 to 340g (10 to 12oz) – cross-peen hammer is adequate as a general-purpose woodworking hammer. The wedge-shaped peen (the rear end of the head, opposite the striking face) is used to start small nails held between finger and thumb.

As with most good hammers, the top end of the ash or hickory shaft is preshrunk and sealed in oil before being driven into the hammer head and expanded with hornbeam and iron wedges to lock the head securely on the shaft.

Pin hammer

A pin hammer is a lightweight cross-peen hammer for driving small nails, panel pins and tacks.

Claw hammer

Most woodworkers choose a 570 or 680g (20 or 24oz) claw hammer for driving large nails. Its split peen, or 'claw', is used to lever bent nails out of wood, which puts considerable strain on the shaft. A tough wooden shaft driven into a deep socket in the hammer head will be more than adequate for most purposes. Even stronger is a tubular-steel or fibreglass shaft permanently fixed to the head; a vinyl or rubber sleeve moulded onto the shaft provides a comfortable non-slip handgrip.

Peen

Cross-peen hammer

Striking face

Continental-pattern cross-peen hammer

Pin hammer

Continental-pattern pin hammer

Claw

Adze-eye claw hammer

Socket

Claw

Steel-shafted claw hammer

Tubular-steel shaft

Non-slip handgrip

Nail set

This square-tipped punch is for driving panel pins and nails below the surface of the timber. Point diameters range from 1.5 to 4mm ($^1/_{16}$ to $^5/_{32}$ in). Use a punch that is slightly smaller than the head of the nail.

MALLETS

Mallets and 'soft' hammers are required for driving wood chisels and gouges, and for assembling or dismantling joints.

Carpenter's mallet

A solid or laminated-beech mallet head is tapered so that swinging the mallet automatically presents the striking faces square to the work or to the butt end of a chisel. The socket within the head is also tapered to match the flared end of the shaft: with each swing of the mallet, centrifugal force tends to tighten the head onto the shaft.

Solid-beech head

Carpenter's mallet

Flared shaft

Soft mallet

Soft hammers and mallets

Soft hammers and soft mallets have heads or striking faces made from rubber, plastic or coiled rawhide, which will not bruise the wood when dismantling or assembling frames and carcasses.

Rubber head

USING HAMMERS

There's no real trick to using a hammer, but it takes patience and practice before you can drive a nail quickly and surely without bending it or bruising the wood.

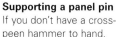

Setting a nail

When starting a nail, hold it upright between finger and thumb and tap the head with the hammer until the point is buried in the wood. Use the peen of a cross-peen or pin hammer to start a small nail or panel pin.

Supporting a panel pin

If you don't have a cross-peen hammer to hand, push a panel pin through a strip of stiff paper or thin card and use it to hold the pin upright while you tap it into the wood. Once the pin is firmly embedded, tear the paper or card free and drive the pin home.

Driving nails with a hammer

With a hammer of the correct weight, you should be able to drive a nail in with the minimum of effort. Holding the tool near the end of the shaft, swing your arm from the elbow. Keep your eye on the nail and strike it square: glancing blows will bend the nail over.

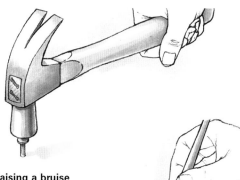

Raising a bruise

If you dent the wood with a misplaced hammer blow, apply a few drops of hot water to the bruise and wait for the fibres to swell. Once the wood is dry, you can sand it smooth.

Sinking a nail head

To ensure that you don't dent the wood with the final hammer blow, use a nail set to drive the nail head just below the surface of the work. Place the tip of the punch on the nail head and steady the tip with a fingertip while you tap the nail set firmly with the hammer.

Secret nailing

Having buried a nail head as described opposite, you can cover it with filler before painting or polishing the workpiece. Alternatively, use a sharp gouge to lift a sliver of wood, then drive in the nail before gluing and clamping the sliver down to conceal the fixing.

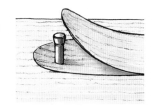

Preventing split wood

To prevent a piece of softwood splitting, blunt the point of a nail by tapping it with a hammer. This makes the nail punch its way through the wood, instead of wedging the fibres aside. When nailing hardwood, it pays to drill a pilot hole that is very slightly narrower than the nail shank.

MAINTAINING HAMMERS

If the face of a hammer gets dirty and greasy it tends to skid off a nailhead, bending the nail and bruising the wood. Keep the face of the hammer clean by rubbing it on a piece of fine emery cloth. Keep a vinyl or rubber handgrip clean by scrubbing it with a nailbrush dipped in a solution of mild detergent and warm water.

Fitting a new shaft

If you break a wooden hammer shaft, chisel or knock out the remaining stump, then plane the tip of a new shaft to make a tight fit in the 'eye' of the hammer head.

Make two or three sawcuts (depending on the size of the hammer) across the top of the shaft and at a slight angle (**1**). Saw down about two-thirds the depth of the eye. Fit the head on the shaft and tap the other end of the shaft firmly on the bench to set the head (**2**). Saw off any part of the shaft protruding from the top of the head, then drive iron hammer wedges into each sawcut to spread the shaft (**3**). If the wedges do not lie flush with the tip of the shaft, grind them down on a bench grinder.

EXTRACTING NAILS

No matter how experienced you become, you will occasionally mishit a nail and bend it over. Don't try to straighten it in situ, as the next blow will almost certainly bend it again and probably drive it sideways into the wood. Instead, extract the bent nail and replace it with a new one.

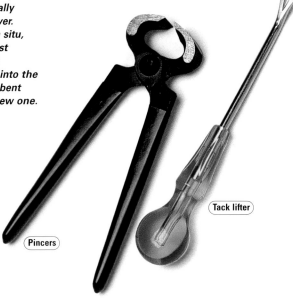

(Pincers) (Tack lifter)

Pincers

Panel pins and nails that are too small to be removed with a hammer can be extracted with pincers.

Tack lifter

The small curved claw of a tack lifter is for prising tacks holding upholstery fabric and webbing in place.

Using a claw hammer

To draw a partially driven nail, slip the split peen of a claw hammer under the nail head, then use the shaft as a lever to extract the nail. To protect the surface of the work, slip a strip of card or veneer under the hammer head (**1**).

To draw an extra-long nail, substitute a small block of wood for the card or veneer (**2**).

One way of removing old nails from dismantled framing is to tap the points to drive the heads clear of the surface. Alternatively, jam the claw of a hammer onto the protruding shaft of a nail so that the claw bites into the metal, then pull the nailhead right through the timber.

Removing upholstery tacks

Work the claw of a tack lifter under the fabric or webbing beneath the head of each tack, then push down on the handle to lever the tack out.

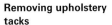

Pulling out a nail with pincers

When you grip the shaft of the nail, rest the jaws of the pincers on the work. Squeeze the handles together and rock the pincers away from you, protecting the wood surface by slipping card beneath the jaws.

Draw a long nail in stages rather than risk bruising the wood by levering the nail sideways.

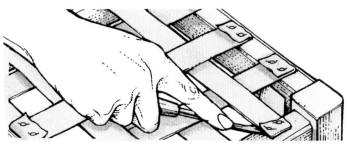

SCREWDRIVERS

In order to insert or remove a woodscrew successfully, you need to select a screwdriver that fits snugly in the screw slot. To do otherwise is to run the risk of damaging the screw head or the work itself. Since there are a number of different types and sizes of screw slot, it follows that you are going to need a whole family of screwdrivers. One solution is to buy a power screwdriver with an extensive range of bits.

Cabinet screwdriver

Traditional woodworking screwdrivers have a bulbous wooden handle that nestles comfortably in the palm of the hand. Similar grips are now moulded from plastic. Custom also dictates that the blade has a wide, flat heel that fits into a deep slot in the metal ferrule, but the cylindrical shaft on many modern cabinet screwdrivers passes straight through the ferrule into the handle.

Engineer's screwdriver

Screwdrivers with relatively slim fluted handles were originally developed for the automotive and electrical industries. They are useful for delicate jobs where you might want to spin the handle with your fingertips, and the slim long shaft is ideal for reaching a screw at the bottom of a deep hole. However, a parallel-sided handle with fluting does not provide as good a grip as a smooth bulbous one when you want to deliver maximum torque at the driving end.

Ratchet screwdriver

With a ratchet screwdriver, you can insert or remove screws without changing your grip on the handle. A small thumb slide engages the ratchet for forward or reverse action; centralizing the slide immobilizes the mechanism so that the tool can be used as a conventional screwdriver.

The tip of a spiral-ratchet or pump-action screwdriver is driven clockwise or anticlockwise by applying pressure to the handle (the spring-loaded shaft extends each time pressure is released). The chuck takes interchangeable bits.

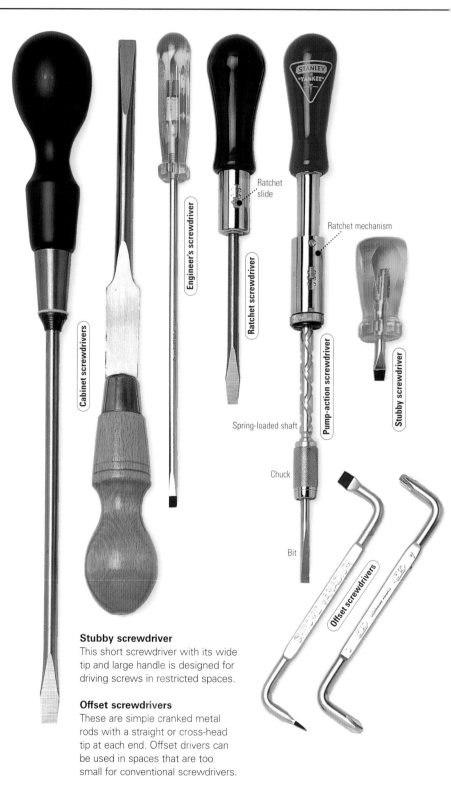

Cabinet screwdrivers

Engineer's screwdriver

Ratchet screwdriver

Ratchet slide

Ratchet mechanism

Pump-action screwdriver

Spring-loaded shaft

Chuck

Bit

Stubby screwdriver

Offset screwdrivers

Stubby screwdriver

This short screwdriver with its wide tip and large handle is designed for driving screws in restricted spaces.

Offset screwdrivers

These are simple cranked metal rods with a straight or cross-head tip at each end. Offset drivers can be used in spaces that are too small for conventional screwdrivers.

SCREWDRIVER TIPS

Screwdrivers for straight-slot screws have either a parallel-sided tip or a flared tip that is sometimes tapered by grinding away both edges.

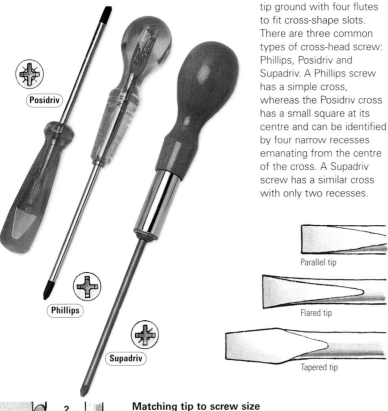

Posidriv

Phillips

Supadriv

For improved grip between screw and tool, some screwdrivers have a pointed tip ground with four flutes to fit cross-shape slots. There are three common types of cross-head screw: Phillips, Posidriv and Supadriv. A Phillips screw has a simple cross, whereas the Posidriv cross has a small square at its centre and can be identified by four narrow recesses emanating from the centre of the cross. A Supadriv screw has a similar cross with only two recesses.

Parallel tip

Flared tip

Tapered tip

Matching tip to screw size

A screwdriver tip that is too wide for the slot (**1**) will score the surrounding wood as the screw is driven home. If the tip is too narrow (**2**), it may not generate enough torque to loosen a stubborn screw but will gouge the metal on each side of the slot.

Cross-head screwdrivers are designated by point size. The chart below matches tip size to screw gauges.

Screw gauge	3–4	5–10	12–14	16 plus
Driver point	1	2	3	4

POWER SCREWDRIVERS

Cordless screwdrivers take much of the effort out of inserting woodscrews, especially in awkward corners where it can be difficult to produce the necessary turning force. They invariably have a spindle lock, which is automatic on some models, so that you can use the tool manually to put the final turn on a screw or loosen it before you apply power. If the screwdriver is fitted with torque control, you have the option of a low setting to stop you overtightening small screws and a higher setting for large fixings. When using a power screwdriver, it is just as important to maintain pressure on the tool when removing screws as it is when driving them home.

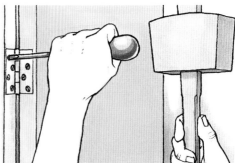

Torque control

Trigger

INSERTING A WOODSCREW

The shanks of newer-generation twin-thread screws are relatively thin, which generally allows them to be driven into the wood without the need for clearance holes or even pilot holes. However, when using conventional woodscrews it pays to drill a narrow pilot hole to guide the screw on its intended path, and a wider clearance hole to prevent the shank splitting the wood or jamming before you can drive the screw home.

Drilling pilot and clearance holes

Bore the pilot hole, using a drill bit that is slightly narrower than the threaded portion of the screw; then, to reduce friction, enlarge the first part of the hole with a bit that matches the shank diameter. Countersink the clearance hole before inserting the screw.

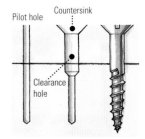

Pilot hole   Countersink

Clearance hole

Counterboring a screw

If you need to drive a screw below the surface of a workpiece – to hold a deep rail in place, for example – bore a hole the same diameter as the screw head before you drill the pilot and clearance holes.

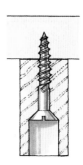

Removing woodscrews

Using a snug-fitting screwdriver with a large, comfortable handgrip, it should be possible to remove most woodscrews without too much trouble. However, an old screw may resist your initial efforts, especially if it has been in place for a long time or has been painted over at some time.

First, clean out the slot; then try tapping the butt end of the screwdriver with a mallet (the shock sometimes frees a stubborn screw). Alternatively, heat the head of the screw with a soldering iron and then remove the screw once the metal has cooled.

Repairing screwdriver tips

A tip that is worn tends to ride out of the screw slot. Regrind each side of a straight-tip screwdriver, then grind the tip square. If the tip of a cross-head screwdriver is badly worn, replace it.

CRAMPS

Every workshop needs a variety of cramps – long bar or pipe cramps for assembling large constructions, web or mitre cramps for mitred picture frames, and several fast-action or G-cramps for gluing up small jobs or to provide an 'extra hand' to help with a complicated assembly. Complete sets of cramps are relatively expensive, but you can acquire them over a period of time or hire them as required.

Making rubbed joints
Small accurately cut edge-to-edge joints can be assembled without cramps. Apply glue to both parts and rub them together, squeezing out air and adhesive until atmospheric pressure holds the surfaces in contact while the glue sets.

Quick-grip ratchet cramp
Available in a wide range of sizes, these cramps are invaluable when fast assembly is important. The movable jaw is designed to slide quickly into position; you then simply squeeze the cramp's trigger to apply the clamping force. Some models can be reversed and used to pull frames and other similar constructions apart.

Bar cramp

Bar cramps are used for assembling large frames, panels and carcasses. Attached to one end of the flat steel bar is a screw-adjustable jaw. To accommodate assemblies of different sizes, a second movable jaw or tail slide is free to move along the bar and is secured at the required position with a tapered steel pin that passes behind the jaw into one of a series of holes in the bar. The cramps generally range from 450 to 1200mm (1ft 6in to 4ft) in length, but you can hire longer cramps that have T-section bars for extra rigidity.

Cramp heads

Custom-made bar cramps can be made for exceptionally large assemblies, using cast-iron cramp heads designed to fit onto a piece of timber 25mm (1in) thick.

Fast-action bar cramp

These cramps can be adjusted quickly to fit the size of the workpiece. They have two movable jaws, one of which is also screw-adjustable. As the screw is tightened on the work, both jaws rock over and jam on the bar.

Pipe cramp

This is similar to a bar cramp but the jaws are attached to a length of round steel pipe. Operating a cam-action lever on the movable tail slide locks it at any point along the pipe. Other models have a one-way clutch mechanism that tightens as load is applied to the tail slide. The cramp heads are made in two sizes, to fit a 12 or 18mm (½ or ¾in) pipe.

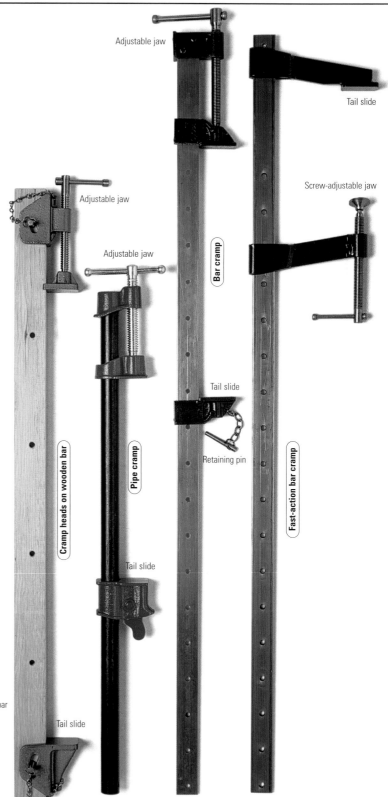

Adjustable jaw

Tail slide

Adjustable jaw

Adjustable jaw

Screw-adjustable jaw

Bar cramp

Cramp heads on wooden bar

Pipe cramp

Tail slide

Retaining pin

Fast-action bar cramp

Tail slide

Wooden bar

Tail slide

The majority of frames (and carcasses) need clamping in order to hold the assembly square until the adhesive sets.

Dry assembly

When gluing up any assembly, it pays to prepare the work area and rehearse the procedure in advance. This avoids delays that could lead to complications, especially when using a fast-setting adhesive. Assemble the parts without glue, to work out how many cramps you need and so you can adjust them to fit the work. You will find a helper invaluable when clamping large or complicated assemblies.

It isn't necessary to glue every joint at once. For example, glue the legs and end rails of a table frame first; and when these are set, glue the side rails between them.

Setting up

Prepare a pair of bar cramps, adjusting them so that the assembled frame fits between the jaws and allowing for softwood blocks to protect the work from the metal cramp heads. Carefully position the blocks to align with each joint (**1**); a misplaced or undersize block can distort the joint and bruise the wood (**2**)

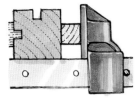

1 Align block with the joint

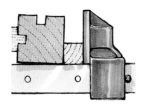

2 Misplaced block distorts joint

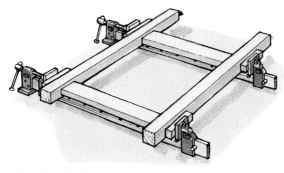

Clamping the frame

Apply adhesive evenly to both parts of each joint. Assemble the frame, ensuring that the cramps are perfectly aligned with their respective rails; then gradually tighten the jaws to close the joints. Using a damp cloth, wipe off excess adhesive squeezed from the joints.

To check that the frame is not 'in wind' (twisted), look across it to see if one rail seems to be aligned with the other. To straighten out a twisted frame, lift one end of a cramp to correct the distortion, then check for alignment again. If necessary, slacken the cramps slightly and force the frame back in line.

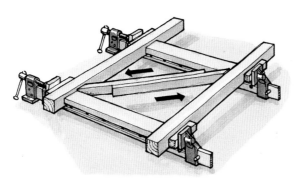

Checking for square

You can use a try square to check that each corner of a small frame is truly square. For larger frames, measure the diagonals to ensure they are identical. Make a pair of pinch rods from slim battens, planing a bevel on one end of each rod. Holding the rods back to back, slide them sideways until they fit diagonally across the frame, with a bevelled end tucked into each corner. Holding the pinch rods together firmly, lift them out of the frame and check whether they fit the other diagonal exactly.

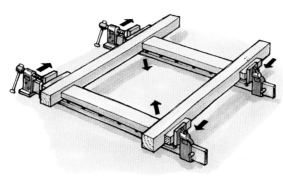

Adjusting the frame

If the diagonals are different, slacken the cramps and set them at a slight angle to pull the frame square, then check the diagonals again.

Web cramp

This consists of a length of nylon webbing 25mm (1in) wide that's wound around a workpiece and pulled taut by a ratchet mechanism. The web applies equal pressure to the four corners of a mitred frame and can be used to clamp a stool or chair with turned legs – a difficult job with bar cramps. Tighten the cramp by turning the small ratchet nut with a spanner or screwdriver. Wait till the glue has set, then release the tension by pressing the lever.

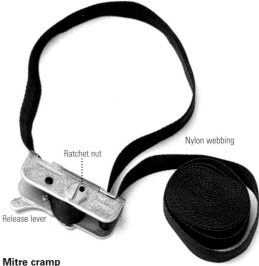

Nylon webbing

Ratchet nut

Release lever

Mitre cramp

This special cramp holds glued mitre joints at right angles, preventing the components from slipping while reinforcing nails are being inserted.

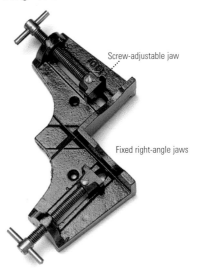

Screw-adjustable jaw

Fixed right-angle jaws

Shorter fast-actions cramps and quick-grip ratchet cramps are practically identical to the larger models used for frame and carcass assembly. Other cramps are purpose-made for gripping and assembling small components.

G-cramp

The G-cramp is an excellent general-purpose cramp that is often used to hold wood firmly on a bench while you work on it. Usually made from cast iron, the frame forms a fixed jaw. Clamping force is applied by a screw fitted with a ball-jointed shoe. G-cramps are manufactured in many sizes.

Long-reach G-cramp

With its deep frame, this cramp is designed for applying pressure to components clamped well in from the edge.

Edge cramp

These special-purpose G-cramps made for clamping edge lippings onto boards are particularly useful on curved edges, which are difficult to clamp with bar or pipe cramps. With the edge screw retracted, they can be used as normal G-cramps.

Fast-action cramp

These short fast-action bar cramps are used in situations where you could also use G-cramps, but are especially handy when adhesive is rapidly setting.

Cam cramp

The cam cramp is a fast-action lightweight cramp with wooden jaws. Having slid the movable jaw up to the workpiece, you apply clamping force by cocking the cam lever. Each jaw is cork-lined to protect the work.

Handscrew

The wide wooden jaws of this traditional cramp can be set to apply even pressure over a broad area. A handscrew is particularly useful when assembling out-of-square frames or for clamping tapered workpieces.

Spring cramp
Simple spring-loaded cramps are useful when you need to hold something in place temporarily.

Operating a G-cramp
To adjust a G-cramp, spin the threaded screw between fingers and thumb to close the gap between the circular 'shoe' and the fixed jaw. Then, with the jaw in contact with the work, apply pressure by screwing up the tommy bar or thumbscrew. Being attached with a ball joint, the shoe adjusts automatically to accommodate angled work. If necessary, use softening blocks to protect the wood.

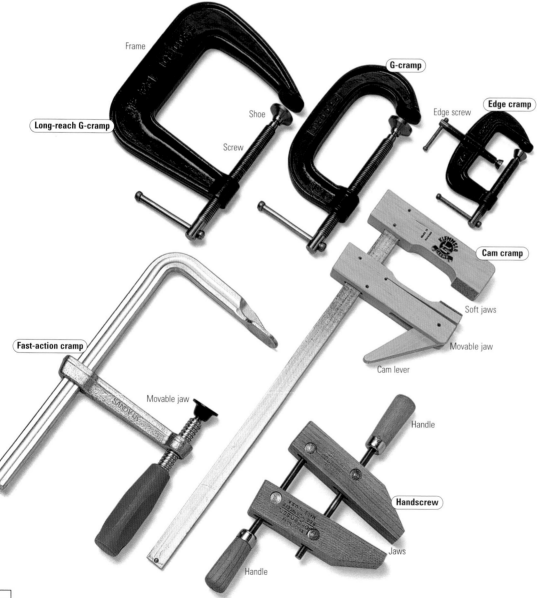

Frame

Shoe

Screw

Long-reach G-cramp

G-cramp

Edge screw

Edge cramp

Soft jaws

Cam cramp

Movable jaw

Cam lever

Fast-action cramp

Movable jaw

Handle

Handscrew

Jaws

Handle

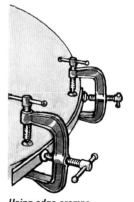

Using edge cramps
Clamp a lipping onto a curved-edge workpiece, using special-purpose G-cramps.

CHAPTER FOUR

POWER TOOLS

At one time home workshops were equipped with little more than a power drill and a few attachments to convert it into a circular saw, jigsaw or orbital sander. Today the picture is completely different. Woodworkers can invest in purpose-made mains-powered power tools with lightweight insulated bodies. They are better designed and more powerful than their predecessors, and most of them can be bench-mounted to create what is in effect a serviceable miniature machine shop. Another important development has been the widespread use of battery-powered cordless tools. The first battery packs could not store sufficient electricity to drive powerful motors for long periods, but more recent improvements have revolutionized the power-tool industry with the introduction of cordless tools that are quiet, efficient and convenient to use.

POWER DRILLS

The electric drill is the most widely sold and used power tool on the market. Not only is it invaluable for woodwork, it is also an indispensable DIY tool found in nearly every home for general household maintenance. Manufacturers try to satisfy the huge demand for power drills by producing an immense range of tools, from cheap 'throwaway' drills to more sophisticated and powerful professional models. The woodworker needs a drill falling somewhere in the middle of the range – a tool that is accurate and reasonably versatile. Most people still buy one powered by mains electricity, although today's 18V or 24V cordless drills provide plenty of power and dispense with the awkward trailing flex.

MAINS-POWERED DRILLS

Drills that run on mains electricity may be relatively heavy and bulky, but they are extremely tough and reliable tools, capable of running more or less continuously for hours on end. Consequently, many woodworkers continue to opt for a mains-powered drill.

Depth stop
All-plastic body
Hammer-action switch
Automatic-locking keyless chuck
Gear selector
Secondary handle

BOS

PSB

Mains-powered electric drill

Motor size
Manufacturers normally specify the drill's motor as having a power input of so many watts. A 500 to 800W drill capable of producing about 3000rpm is suitable for woodwork.

Drill chucks
Most chucks have three self-centring jaws that grip the shank of a drill bit. Some chucks need tightening with a special toothed key to ensure that the drill bit is held securely by the jaws and will not slip in use, but a great many drills are made with 'keyless' chucks that take a firm grip on the bit simply by turning a cylindrical collar that surrounds the mechanism. Certain drills have an automatic-locking keyless chuck that can be tightened and loosened with just one hand on the chuck.

Professional models may feature a fast-action chuck. When the chuck is pulled back, it opens automatically and special bits with grooved shanks are inserted; when the chuck is released, it grips the bit. Bits for this type of drill are made in a range of sizes, but all with the same shank size. A chuck adapter accepts ordinary bits.

Speed selection
Although a few basic drills have a limited range of fixed speeds selected by operating a switch, the majority of drills are variable-speed tools, controlled by the amount of pressure applied to the trigger. On most models, it is also possible to select the maximum rotational speed by turning a small dial that limits the movement of the trigger. Many drills also incorporate an electronic speed-control system that maintains optimum speed when the load applied to the drill bit changes. A system of this kind can protect the motor from damage if the bit jams in the work and may also minimize the initial jolt as the high-speed electric motor starts up.

Manufacturers recommend a range of speeds at which their drills will perform best; however, as a rule of thumb, select a fast speed for boring into wood, but slower speeds for drilling metal or masonry and to drive woodscrews. Some models have a small screen that displays the recommended torque and speed settings for boring into various materials; and there may be a similar screen displaying a levelling device that tells you when the bit is perfectly horizontal.

Reverse action
A reverse-action switch changes the direction of rotation so that the drill can be used to extract woodscrews.

USING POWER TOOLS SAFELY

If you treat power tools with respect and handle them carefully, you should never have an accident. Always follow these basic safety procedures, whatever tool you are using.

- Don't wear loose clothing or jewellery that could get caught in the moving parts of a tool. Tie back loose hair.
- Wear protective eye shields whenever you are doing work that could throw up debris.
- Never carry a power tool by its flex or use the flex to pull the plug out of a socket.
- Regularly check the flex, casing and three-pin plug for signs of wear or damage.
- Unplug power tools before making adjustments or changing accessories and attachments.

- With certain tools, make sure you have removed the chuck key before plugging in.
- Keep children away from areas where power tools are in use. When you have finished work, lock your tools away.
- Always clamp work securely.
- Don't use mains-powered tools in the rain or in very damp conditions.
- Keep handles and grips dry and grease-free.
- Never throw used batteries from cordless tools into water or a fire. And don't put them in an ordinary household waste bin. Ask your local authority to recommend an alternative method of disposal.

Speed selector/torque limiter

Hammer action
Throwing a switch engages the drill's hammer action, which delivers several hundred blows per second behind the bit to help break up masonry when boring into stone or brick walls.

Collar size
A drill that has a 43mm-diameter collar (the international standard) directly behind the chuck will fit accessories or attachments made by other manufacturers subscribing to the same system. This gives you the option to buy cheaper or better-quality equipment than is made by the drill's manufacturer.

Secondary handle and depth stop
Most drills can be fitted with an additional handle that clamps onto the collar at the most convenient angle. The best ones have teeth moulded on the inside of the collar of the handle, which mate with similar teeth on the drill collar. This simple device stops the handle slipping under load. Ideally the handle should incorporate an integral depth stop that comes to rest against the work when the drill bit has bored to the required depth. On some models, the secondary handle also serves as a storage magazine for spare drill bits.

Electrical insulation
The all-plastic body of a power drill protects the user from electric shock should a fault occur within the tool. This is known as 'double insulation'. When a tool is described as having 'full insulation', not only are you protected but the motor is safe from damage even if you inadvertently drill into an electric cable.

Trigger lock
Depressing a button on the drill's handle locks the trigger for continuous running. Squeezing the trigger again releases the lock button.

Reverse-action switch

Trigger-lock button

Variable-speed trigger

CORDLESS DRILLS

In terms of performance, most modern cordless drills compare well with mains-powered drills. Cordless drills are also comparatively lightweight and make less noise.

Most cordless drills have a chuck capacity of between 10 and 13mm (³⁄₈ and ¹⁄₂in) but, using specialized bits, will bore holes up to 30mm (1¹⁄₄in) in diameter in wood. Power drills fitted with hammer action (combi drills) will bore into masonry as well as wood. The majority of cordless drills have keyless chucks.

There are both fixed-speed and variable-speed models, and some have electronic control. All cordless drills have reverse action for removing screws: a drill with a torque setting allows you to drive a screw flush without overriding and damaging the screw slot.

Some drills are supplied with a wall-hung charging unit: when the drill is returned to the unit after use, it is recharged automatically. However, most cordless drills have removable battery packs that are inserted into a separate plug-in charger, which may indicate how much power is left in the battery pack and tell you if the battery is no longer capable of taking a charge.

It usually takes about an hour to fully recharge a battery, but you can buy rapid chargers that will do the job in 15 minutes or less. Most battery packs can be recharged several thousand times before they need replacing.

Battery packs are usually made with NiCd (nickel/cadmium) cells, though more manufacturers are now incorporating NiMh (nickel/metal hydride) cells, which are better for the environment and do not suffer from a progressive reduction of charging capacity (sometimes referred to as 'memory effect'). Long exposure to excessive heat or freezing conditions can ruin a cordless drill.

Gear selector

Speed selector/torque limiter

Keyless chuck

Reverse-action switch

Trigger

Screwdriver bit

Battery pack

Cordless drill

Screwdriver bits
Different bits are needed for slotted and cross-head screws. Locate the screwdriver bit in the screw slot before switching on. Maintain pressure on the drill the whole time, to prevent the bit slipping.

POWER-DRILL BITS

Most power drills have a chuck capacity – the maximum size of drill-bit shank that the chuck will accommodate – of 10 or 13mm (³⁄₈ or ¹⁄₂in). The shank size of an ordinary twist drill or dowel bit corresponds exactly to the size of hole that particular bit will bore. However, a great many woodboring bits are capable of making holes larger than their shank diameter.

Twist drills
Although twist drills are designed for metalwork, they also serve as good general-purpose woodboring bits. Carbon-steel twist drills are perfectly adequate for woodwork but, since you will almost certainly want to drill metal at some time, it is worth investing in the more expensive high-speed-steel bits. Twist drills ranging from 13 to 25mm (¹⁄₂ to 1in) in diameter are made with reduced shanks to fit standard power-drill chucks.

Keep twist drills sharp and, before use, pick out any wood dust that has become packed into the flutes.

Twist drills are not easy to locate on the dead centre of a hole – so, particularly when drilling hardwoods, it pays to mark the centre of the hole first, using a metalworking punch. To avoid splintering the wood, take the pressure off the drill as the bit emerges from the far side of the work. Alternatively, clamp a piece of scrap timber to the back face.

Dowel bits
The dowel bit is a twist drill that has a centre point, to prevent it wandering off line, and two spurs that cut a clean-edged hole.

Spade bits
These are inexpensive drill bits made for power-drilling large holes from 6 to 38mm (¹⁄₄ to 1¹⁄₂in) in diameter. A long lead point makes for positive location even when drilling at an angle to the face of the work.

Masonry drills
Masonry drills are steel twist drills with a brazed tungsten-carbide tip designed to bore into brick, stone or concrete.

Percussion drills
These masonry drills have a shatter-proof tip designed to withstand the vibration produced by hammer action.

Forstner bits
Forstner bits leave exceptionally clean flat-bottomed holes up to 50mm (2in) in diameter. These bits will not be deflected even by wild grain or knots. This enables you to bore overlapping holes – and also holes that run out to the edge of the work – without difficulty.

Countersink bits
Similar to the countersink bits made for hand drills and braces, these drill bits are used to make tapered recesses for the heads of woodscrews. Centre the bit on a clearance hole bored in the wood, and run the power drill at a high speed for a clean finish.

Drill-and-countersink bits
These specialized bits cut a pilot hole, clearance hole and countersink for a woodscrew in one operation. Each bit is matched to a particular screw size.

Drill-and-counterbore bits
Instead of cutting a tapered recess for a screw head, this type of bit leaves a neat hole that allows the screw to be driven below the face of the workpiece.

Plug cutters
Driving a plug cutter into side grain cuts a cylindrical plug of wood to match the hole left by a drill-and-counterbore bit. Cut plugs from timber that closely matches the colour and grain pattern of the work.

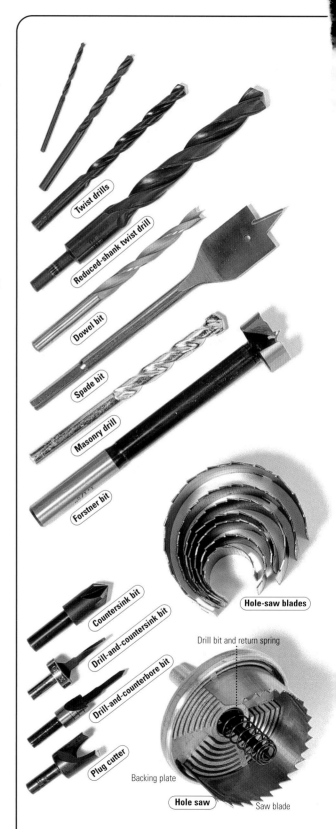

Twist drills

Reduced-shank twist drill

Dowel bit

Spade bit

Masonry drill

Forstner bit

Countersink bit

Drill-and-countersink bit

Drill-and-counterbore bit

Plug cutter

Hole-saw blades

Drill bit and return spring

Backing plate

Hole saw

Saw blade

POWER-DRILL ACCESSORIES

Accessories merely extend the usefulness of a power drill and are not generally considered essential workshop equipment. One exception is a vertical drill stand – which, unless you have a pillar drill, is necessary for drilling accurately and square to the face of the work.

Hole saws
A hole saw is a cylindrical saw blade held in a plastic or metal backing plate, which is clamped to a twist drill passing through its centre. Hole saws are sold in sets ranging from 25 to 89mm (1 to 3½in) in diameter.

The saw blade rotates very much faster than the drill bit – so select a slower speed than you would normally use for boring into wood. Clamp the shank of the bit securely in the chuck, and feed the blade into the work at a steady rate.

Flexible drive
A flexible drive enables you to work with drill bits and rotary files or rasps in areas that would be inaccessible with a full-size drill. It consists of a drive cable sheathed in a flexible casing, with a spindle at one end and a small chuck at the other. The spindle end fits into the chuck of a standard power drill – which should, ideally, be clamped in a bench stand. Flexible drives have chuck capacities of 6 to 8mm (¼ to ⁵⁄₁₆in).

Sheathed drive cable

(Flexible drive)

Chuck

Spindle

Separate end cramp

Guide bush

Workpiece cramp

(Dowelling jig)

Dowelling jigs
A proprietary dowelling jig provides a means of repeating hole spacing for the two components of a dowel joint by guiding a drill bit square and true. Choose a jig that is sturdy, well made and capable of jigging solid-wood rails and wide boards for cabinet-making.

Better-quality jigs are supplied with metal guide bushes to accommodate a range of drill-bit sizes. A separate cramp holds the workpieces firmly so you can move the jig to another position.

Pocket-hole jigs
Instead of dowelling a butt joint, it is possible to reinforce the joint with self-tapping pocket screws driven at a shallow angle through both parts of the joint. Purpose-made jigs enable you to drill accurate clearance holes (pockets) for the screws.

This type of joint is suitable for assembling cabinets where the pockets can be situated, unseen, on the inside of the framework.

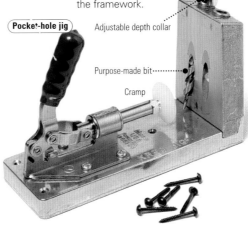

(Pocket-hole jig)   Adjustable depth collar

Purpose-made bit

Cramp

Rotary rasps
Coarse rotary rasps designed for use with a flexible drive are ideal for grinding hollows and complicated curves.

Vertical drill stand
A vertical stand converts a portable power drill into a serviceable pillar drill. Pulling down on the feed lever lowers the drill bit into the work. When you release the feed lever, a spring automatically returns the drill to its starting position.

Make sure the stand you choose has a sturdy, rigid column, and a positive clamp to hold the drill. Look for a stand with a wide, heavy base that can be bolted to your workbench. Slots in the base enable you to attach small vices to hold metal components for drilling. You can use the same slots for bolting on a home-made wooden fence to help position the work directly below the drill bit when boring a row of identical holes.

A depth gauge on the stand limits the travel of the drill when you want to bore a stopped hole.

When drilling right through the workpiece, place a piece of chipboard or MDF under the wood, to prevent splintering on the underside as the drill bit emerges.

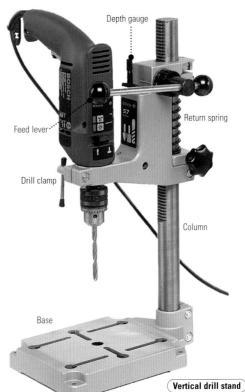

Depth gauge

Return spring

Feed lever

Drill clamp

Column

Base

(Vertical drill stand)

JIGSAWS

Although you can make straight cuts using a side fence or straightedge as a guide, you only really begin to appreciate the advantages of a power jigsaw when you come to cut curves and apertures – tasks it can perform effortlessly, whether sawing through solid wood or man-made boards. With the right blade, you can even saw through sheet metal and plastics.

Scorched wood

If the wood starts to char and smoke when you are sawing, fit a new blade immediately and apply less pressure when feeding the saw into the work. Increasing the blade's pendulum action may prevent sawdust clogging the kerf – check your user's handbook for optimum settings.

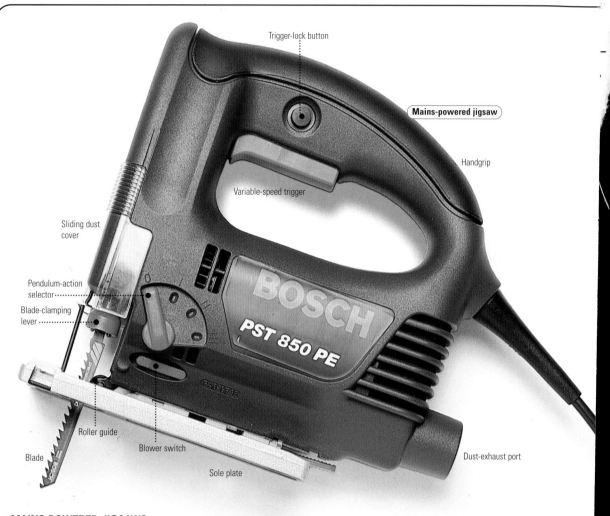

Trigger-lock button

Mains-powered jigsaw

Handgrip

Variable-speed trigger

Sliding dust cover

Pendulum-action selector

Blade-clamping lever

BOSCH

PST 850 PE

Roller guide

Blade

Blower switch

Sole plate

Dust-exhaust port

MAINS-POWERED JIGSAWS

When you buy a portable jigsaw these days, you get a lot for your money. Variable speed control and pendulum action are more or less standard, and many saws incorporate electronics that regulate the saw's performance for optimum effect. Fitted with dust extraction and an electric motor able to run continuously for long periods with very little noise or vibration, a well-made power jigsaw is comfortable to use and easy to control.

Motor size

Jigsaws are fitted with a precisely balanced 350 to 600W electric motor capable of a maximum speed of about 3000 strokes per minute. The larger motors are intended for cutting thicker material rather than to produce a higher stroke rate.

Pendulum action

As well as moving the saw blade up and down, jigsaws with pendulum or orbital action cause the blade to cut faster by advancing it into the work on the upstroke and moving it backward on the downstroke to help clear sawdust from the kerf.

Select maximum advance for softwood and plastics, progressively reducing the degree of oscillation for hardwoods, chipboard and soft metals. Select zero movement for steel and use the same setting when cutting thin sheet materials in order to prevent them vibrating.

Depth of cut

Fitted with the appropriate blade, the average mains-powered jigsaw will cut solid wood and man-made boards up to 70mm (2^3/$_4$in) thick. It can also cope with non-ferrous metals up to 18mm (^{3}/$_4$in) thick, and sheet steel up to 3mm (^{1}/$_8$in) thick.

Cordless jigsaw

Lock-off button prevents accidental start-up

Pendulum-action selector

2.6 Ah

Dust-exhaust port

Battery pack

USING A JIGSAW SAFELY

Follow the basic safety procedures for power tools, but take extra care with a jigsaw.

- Check that the intended path of the blade is clear below the work.
- Make sure the flex trails behind the tool, not in front of the blade.
- Use sharp blades only. Blunt blades have to be forced through the work.
- Never curl your fingers around the workpiece near the line of cut.
- Relieve the pressure on the saw as you are about to finish a cut – to avoid sudden acceleration as the blade leaves the kerf.
- Switch off and wait until the blade has completely stopped moving before you put the saw down.

Dust extraction

Sawdust constitutes a health risk and fire hazard. So either fit a dust-collecting bag to your jigsaw or attach a flexible hose between the saw's exhaust port and an industrial vacuum cleaner to suck up the dust as soon as it is created.

On most jigsaws, the motor-cooling fan generates a jet of air from behind the blade to blow sawdust away from the cutting line.

Working light

Some saws have a miniature spotlight mounted near the front to illuminate the cutting line. This feature is especially useful when working inside fitted cupboards and other enclosed spaces.

Sole plate

On nearly all jigsaws the sole plate tilts to any angle up to 45 degrees for cutting bevels. On some models, it also slides backwards to allow the blade to cut right up to a vertical surface.

Electrical insulation

Choose a jigsaw with an all-plastic casing that insulates the user from electric shock.

Speed selection

The majority of jigsaws have some form of speed control so you can select the optimum stroke rate for the material you are cutting. This may take the form of a dial that allows you to preselect a speed ranging from 500 to 3000 strokes per minute. But on a true variable-speed jigsaw the speed is controlled according to how much pressure you apply to the trigger – though this can be limited to a maximum stroke rate, usually by means of a built-in dial.

In general, it is best to select the higher speeds for woodwork and the middle range for aluminium and plastics, reserving the lowest stroke rates for cutting sheet steel or ceramic tiles. Constant-speed electronics monitor the stroke rate, maintaining the selected speed within reasonable limits.

Trigger lock

When making long or complicated cuts, switch on and depress the trigger-lock button to keep the saw running continuously. Switch off again by squeezing the trigger.

CORDLESS JIGSAWS

Powerful cordless jigsaws are available for the professional workshop, but relatively few manufacturers make models specifically for amateur woodworkers. Consequently, most cordless jigsaws are expensive, compared with mains-powered saws.

Although the advantages of a saw without a trailing flex are obvious, a cordless jigsaw may not be as powerful as one operated on mains electricity. Its depth-cutting capacity for all materials is invariably less than that of a mains-powered saw; and when cutting dense materials like chipboard, it will run efficiently for only a relatively short period before it needs recharging.

Look for a model with a battery capacity of at least 2Ah (the capacity can be found on the saw's specification label). And make sure the saw is supplied with two battery packs and a 1-hour charger, so you never have to wait for the batteries to recharge. When buying a cordless saw, check that it can't be switched on accidentally.

Splinter control

The reciprocal action of a jigsaw blade tends to splinter the kerf on the upper surface of a workpiece. On some saws, the sole plate can be adjusted fore and aft to locate the blade within a narrow slot in the metal – which reduces the clearance on each side of the blade, minimizing breakout along the kerf. On other saws, this is achieved by fitting a plastic insert that surrounds the blade.

Changing jigsaw blades
Jigsaw blades are never sharpened: they are simply discarded when they break or become blunt. Consequently, all jigsaws are designed for easy blade replacement. Either the blade is held in place by a clamp that is adjusted with an Allen key, or the saw has a built-in clamp-release mechanism. Before changing blades, unplug the saw.

JIGSAW BLADES

Different types of jigsaw blade are available for cutting a variety of materials. You can also buy blades designed specifically for cutting faster or more cleanly, or for making particularly tight turns.

Although manufacturers describe their blades in different ways, a basic understanding of their construction and specification will help you select the appropriate blade for a particular job.

Blade length
Blade size is specified according to the length of the cutting edge. Mostly you will be using just the top section of a blade, but make sure any blade you buy for a specific task is at least 15 to 18mm (5/8 to 3/4in) longer than the maximum thickness of the wood or other material you intend to saw.

Set of tooth
Jigsaw-blade teeth are sometimes side-set in the conventional manner – alternate teeth being bent to the right and left. This can only be achieved with relatively large teeth and is reserved for blades designed to cut quickly, leaving a rough-edged kerf.

For making finer cuts, the teeth are not set but the blade is ground to a thinner section behind the row of teeth to provide a clearance in the kerf. Ground blades cut very clean kerfs in man-made boards as well as solid timber. A blade that is slightly side-set in addition to being taper-ground will cut a little faster.

Blades with extremely fine teeth are wavy-set. These blades have a serpentine cutting edge that produces a wider kerf than the true thickness of the blade. Wavy-set blades are designed for cutting metal but are also useful for making a clean, narrow kerf in plywood, MDF and blockboard.

Size of teeth
As with most saw blades, jigsaw-tooth size can be specified as teeth per inch (TPI); but sometimes the term 'pitch' is used, which describes the distance in millimetres between the point of one tooth and another. For example, the same blade may be described as having 10 TPI or a pitch of 2.5mm. As a rough guide, the smaller the teeth the finer the cut.

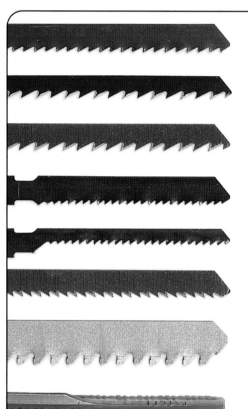

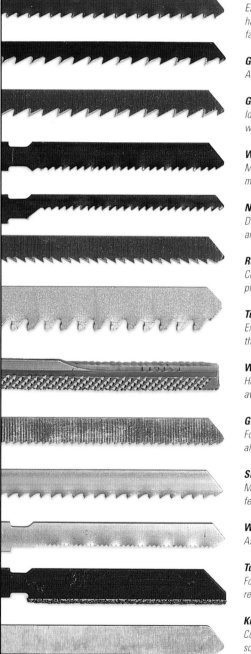

Side-set wood blade
Especially good for cutting softwoods and hardwoods with the grain. Produces a fairly rough cut.

Ground and side-set blade
As above, but produces a cleaner cut.

Ground wood blade
Ideal for making very clean cuts in solid wood and man-made boards.

Wavy-set blade
Makes a very fine kerf when cutting man-made boards.

Narrow wavy-set blade
Designed for cutting tight curves in wood and man-made boards.

Reverse-tooth blade
Cuts on the downstroke to avoid chipping plastic-laminated boards.

Tungsten-carbide-tipped blade
Excellent for chipboard and other boards that have a high glue content.

Wood files
Half-round, flat and triangular files are available for fitting in a jigsaw.

Ground metal blade
For cutting non-ferrous metals, such as aluminium.

Side-set metal blade
Made from high-speed steel. Cuts non-ferrous metals and mild steel.

Wavy-set metal blade
As above, but for thin sheet metal only.

Tungsten-carbide-coated blade
For cutting ceramic tiles and glass-reinforced plastic (GRP).

Knife-ground blade
Cuts cardboard, carpet, cork, plastics and soft rubber.

USING A JIGSAW

When cutting with a jigsaw, clamp the work so that it overhangs the edge of a bench or bridges a pair of sawhorses. Unless it is held firmly, thin sheet material will vibrate and throw the blade off course. Make sure that the lead from a mains-powered jigsaw trails behind the blade and cannot get caught on an obstruction as you feed the saw across the surface of the workpiece.

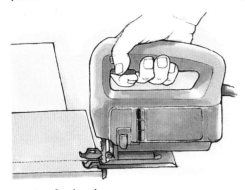

Sawing freehand
Rest the front of the sole plate on the work, aligning the blade with a line marked on the work. Switch on and feed the blade steadily into the work. Follow the line, maintaining a constant feed rate without forcing the pace. Relieve the pressure on the blade as you approach the end of the marked line to avoid a sudden acceleration as you sever the offcut.

Using a straightedge
Since it is practically impossible to follow a straight line accurately when sawing freehand, run the saw's sole plate against a wooden straightedge clamped across the work. Maintain side pressure against the straightedge as you continue to feed the blade at a steady rate.

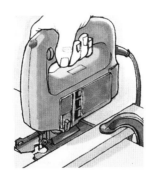

Sawing parallel to an edge
When the intended line of cut is close to the edge of a workpiece, you can fit the side fence supplied with the saw. A hardwood strip screwed to the face of the fence will help keep the blade on course.

To set the fence, align the blade with the marked line, then slide the fence up against the guide edge and tighten the fence clamp. Keep the fence pressed against the guide edge while feeding the saw through the work.

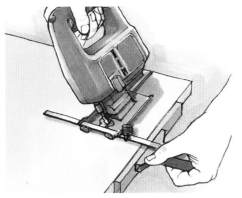

Cutting bevels
Use a guide fence or a straightedge to guide the saw when making bevelled cuts. To adjust the angle of the blade, slacken the sole-plate clamping screws and tap the shoe with a screwdriver handle until the required angle is indicated on the saw's tilt gauge. Retighten the clamps and make a test cut to check the setting.

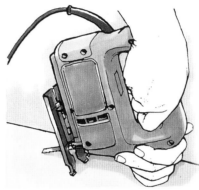

Plunge-cutting with a jigsaw
Plunge-cutting, a technique that requires a little practice to perfect, saves you having to drill starter holes when sawing apertures in man-made boards. Tip the saw onto the front edge of its sole plate, with the blade held clear of the work. Switch on and gradually pivot the saw on the sole plate until the point of the blade cuts its way through the wood. Once the sole plate is flat on the work, continue to saw in the normal way. Always plunge-cut well within the waste wood and not too close to your marked lines.

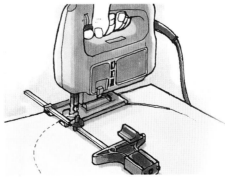

Cutting circles
To cut a perfectly circular aperture, convert your side fence into a trammel, using the detachable point supplied with the fence. Press the point into the centre of the waste wood, and pivot the saw about it.

If you want to cut a disc, press the trammel point into a small patch of plywood stuck over the centre of the disc with double-sided adhesive tape.

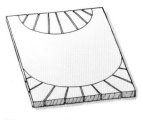

Making curved cuts
Most gentle curves can be followed freehand, but forcing a blade round a tight bend will result in the blade breaking or the edge of the work being scorched. To relieve the blade in a tight kerf, make a series of straight cuts through the waste up to the marked line. As you proceed with cutting the curve, the waste will fall off in sections, providing sufficient clearance for the blade.

Cutting a rectangular aperture
When cutting an aperture with rounded corners, drill a starter hole in the waste, then lower the blade into the hole and make one continuous pass with the saw. To cut an aperture with square corners, feed the blade into each corner in turn, then back off about 25mm (1in) and cut a curve that intercepts the next straight section. When you have cut all four sides, turn the jigsaw around and saw back into each corner from the opposite direction to sever the remaining waste.

CIRCULAR SAWS

When fitted with the appropriate blades, an electric circular saw combines all the functions of a complete set of handsaws. A mains-powered saw may be a trifle unwieldy for crosscutting smaller pieces of wood, but there is no disputing the fact that it is ideal for converting large numbers of solid-wood workpieces and full-size man-made panels.

Riving knife
A riving knife – the metal strip mounted directly behind the saw blade – prevents the kerf closing up and constricting the blade. The riving knife should be adjusted to within 2 to 3mm (1/8in) of the saw teeth, and the tip of the knife should be about the same distance above the bottom edge of the blade.

2–3mm (1/8in)

2–3mm (1/8in)

Saws for man-made boards
Some circular saws are now made without riving knives. These saws are designed primarily for cutting man-made boards that do not move and clamp the blade as it is fed into the work.

MAINS-POWERED CIRCULAR SAWS

A poorly made circular saw is a potentially dangerous tool – so choose a good-quality branded one with a sturdy fence and blade guard. Check that it is well balanced and not too heavy, so you can work for prolonged periods without becoming tired. Some saws have built-in electronic systems that provide variable-speed control and supply additional power when the tool is under load. The initial kick that you normally feel when switching on a circular saw is also eradicated with electronic monitoring.

Dust extraction
The fixed guard mounted above the blade is fitted with a dust-extraction port. This either deposits sawdust into a lightweight bag or is connected to the hose of a portable dust extractor/vacuum cleaner.

Safety lock
To prevent a circular saw being switched on accidentally, a small button mounted on the main handgrip has to be depressed with your thumb before the trigger will operate.

Retractable guard
A circular saw is fitted with a retractable guard that is pushed back by the edge of the work as the blade is fed into the wood. A strong spring returns the guard, ensuring that the saw teeth are enclosed as soon as the blade is clear of the work. Before using a circular saw, always check that the blade guard is operating smoothly.

Anti-locking clutch
Clamping flanges on each side of the blade act as an anti-locking clutch. Should the blade jam they allow it to slip, protecting the drive mechanism from damage.

Insulating plastic body
All good power tools are made with non-conductive plastic casing to protect the user from electric shock should a fault occur.

Handgrips
The saw's main handgrip houses the trigger. A secondary handle, mounted near the toe of the saw, provides positive control over the saw.

Side fence
An adjustable fence guides the blade on a path parallel to the edge of the work. Extend a relatively short fence by attaching a batten to it with woodscrews.

Fixed guard

Handgrip

Sawdust-exhaust port

Trigger

Secondary handle

makita

Sole plate

Tilt scale and clamp

Pivoting blade guard

Riving knife

Blade

Cut-line sight

Mains-powered circular saw

Blade-tilt facility

The sole plate of a circular saw can be adjusted to present the blade at any angle up to 45 degrees to the work surface. Although the angle is usually indicated on a quadrant scale, it's advisable to make a trial cut in scrap wood and to check the angle with a mitre square or sliding bevel.

DEPTH OF CUT

Blade size should not be confused with cutting depth. A 130mm (5in) blade, for example, will only cut to a depth of about 40mm (1$\frac{1}{2}$in) – considerably less than half its diameter. As a guide, the chart below shows the maximum cutting depth of typical circular-saw blades. The maximum depth of cut is reduced when the blade is tilted for making bevelled cuts.

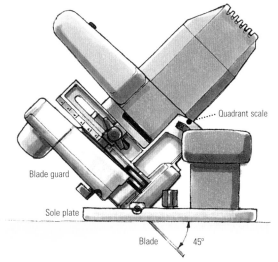

Quadrant scale

Blade guard

Sole plate

Blade 45°

CUTTING DEPTH OF TYPICAL BLADES	
Blade diameter	**Cutting depth**
130mm (5in)	40mm (1$\frac{1}{2}$in)
150mm (6in)	46mm (1$\frac{7}{8}$in)
160mm (6$\frac{1}{2}$in)	54mm (2$\frac{1}{8}$in)
190mm (7$\frac{1}{2}$in)	66mm (2$\frac{5}{8}$in)
210mm (8$\frac{1}{2}$in)	75mm (3in)
230mm (9in)	85mm (3$\frac{3}{8}$in)

Most woodworkers require a saw that can cut to a depth of not less than 50mm (2in). However, if you need a saw primarily for cutting man-made boards, you may want to opt for a smaller model – especially as saws at the upper end of the scale can be cumbersome.

Adjusting the saw

You adjust the depth of cut by raising or lowering the body of the tool in relation to the sole plate. A depth scale is usually provided – but, as with most power-tool settings, it is often better to use the work itself as a guide when accuracy is important. Always unplug the saw before making any adjustments.

To sever a workpiece, withdraw the retractable guard and lay the sole plate on the work, with the blade resting against one edge. Release the clamp on the depth scale and lower the blade until the teeth project about 2mm ($\frac{1}{8}$in) below the workpiece (**1**). Tighten the clamp before lifting the saw off the work.

To make a partial cut, mark the required cutting depth on the side of the workpiece, then adjust the blade until the saw teeth coincide with the mark (**2**).

1

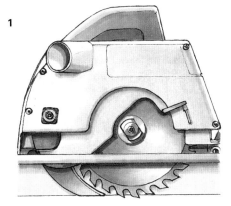

2

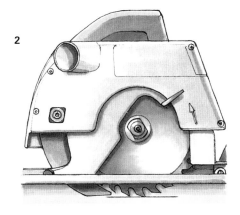

USING A CIRCULAR SAW SAFELY

A circular saw is capable of inflicting serious injury. However, accidents rarely happen if safety procedures are strictly observed. Follow the basic rules that apply to all power tools, but be especially careful with a circular saw and never be tempted to bend the rules.

• Before sawing, check the wood for nails and screws – which would blunt or knock a tooth off the saw blade.
• Look for loose knots, which could be dislodged and thrown into the air.
• Don't rely on switching off at the socket before changing or adjusting a blade – always unplug the tool first.
• Use sharp blades and always replace a cracked or bent one.
• Never be tempted to remove the riving knife if one is fitted.
• Never tape or wedge a pivoting guard in the open position, except when bolted to a table-saw attachment where another guard and riving knife is substituted.
• Don't force the blade through the work. If it doesn't feed smoothly, the blade is blunt and needs to be replaced.
• Don't stop a spinning blade by applying sideways pressure to it.

CORDLESS CIRCULAR SAWS

Cordless-tool technology has not yet developed sufficiently to produce a battery that allows you to work continuously with a circular saw for long periods. However, one of the latest 18V and 24V saws is perfectly suitable for the home workshop, provided it comes with a spare battery pack.

You will find a cordless circular saw useful for cutting down large man-made panels that are too large to carry conveniently into the house or workshop.

As a precaution, always remove the battery pack from a cordless circular saw when changing the blade.

Feeding a cordless saw
Operate a cordless saw like a mains-powered model – don't try to force the pace, especially when sawing chipboard.

CIRCULAR-SAW BLADES

Provided it is sharp, a good-quality circular-saw blade makes such a clean cut that the wood surface needs nothing more than a light skimming with a plane before sanding. Blades with tungsten-carbide-tipped teeth produce the best finish and stay sharp longer than ordinary blades. A PTFE (non-stick) coating reduces friction, increasing both the life of the blade and the life of the saw's drive mechanism. It also minimizes the risk of scorching the wood.

1 Pointed-tooth blade
Designed primarily for crosscutting solid wood.

2 Fine-tooth blade
Intended for making fine cuts in chipboard and plastic-laminated panels. Cuts relatively slowly.

3 Ripsaw blade
A blade with large tungsten-carbide-tipped teeth and wide gullets that clear the copious amounts of resinous sawdust created by ripping softwoods. Will also rip hardwoods and man-made boards, but is not capable of producing a first-class finish.

4 Chisel-tooth blade
A medium-priced, all-purpose saw blade suitable for ripping and crosscutting solid timber. It also copes with man-made boards.

5 Carbide-tipped universal saw
An excellent general-purpose saw blade for all solid wood and wood-based materials, including laminated boards. Leaves a fine finish when ripping or crosscutting softwood and hardwoods.

Changing saw blades
Always unplug a portable circular saw before changing the blade. When fitting a blade, check that the hole in the centre is the correct diameter for the saw's arbor (rotating shaft) and ensure that the teeth face away from the riving knife. Have blunt blades sharpened professionally, and discard any that appear to be cracked or distorted.

USING A CIRCULAR SAW

The teeth of a circular-saw blade move forward and upward when cutting timber and board, so any tearing of the grain will appear on the uppermost surface of the workpiece. Consequently, always lay the workpiece with its face side down when ripping or crosscutting.

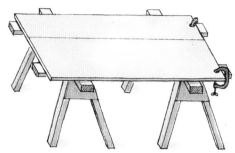

Supporting the work
Since you need both hands to control the saw, clamp the workpiece securely, either overhanging a bench top or to a pair of sawhorses. So that you can make one continuous pass with the saw, nail two stout battens across the top of the sawhorses, leaving a space between the battens for the saw blade. Whatever method you use to support the wood, check there are no obstructions beneath the workpiece that might impede the safe passage of the blade.

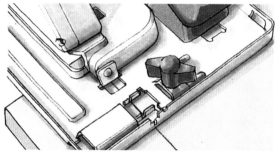

Sawing freehand
Circular saws have a small notch in the front edge of the sole plate, which acts as a sight when cutting workpieces roughly to size. Rest the front part of the sole plate on the work, aligning the notch with a cut line pencilled clearly on the wood. Switch on and feed the saw blade steadily into the work, following the marked line throughout the pass. Release the trigger and allow the retractable guard to snap closed before lifting the saw off the work.

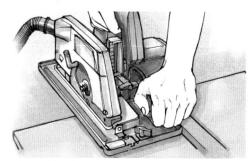

Crosscutting with a batten
When you need to make a cut across a wide board, run the edge of the sole plate against a straight batten clamped to the work. Most often the batten will be set at 90 degrees to the front edge, but you can clamp the batten to whatever angle is required.

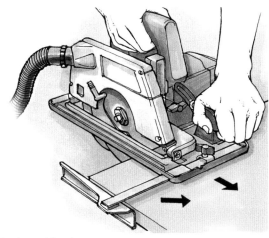

Ripping with a fence

All saws are supplied with an adjustable side fence to guide the blade on a path parallel to the edge of a workpiece. The fence can be mounted on either side of the saw and, although the fence should be sturdy enough as supplied, you can extend it by screwing a hardwood batten to its face.

Set the fence (a scale is sometimes marked on its mounting arm), then make a trial cut to check the setting before ripping the workpiece itself. Advance the saw into the wood at a steady rate, keeping the fence pressed against the edge of the workpiece.

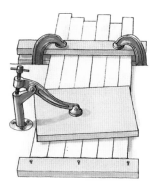

Cutting workpieces to the same length

To cut a number of similar workpieces to the same length, trim one end of each piece square and butt all the trimmed ends against a stop batten nailed to the bench. Clamp a guide batten across the workpieces and cut them all to length with one pass of the saw.

Cutting grooves and rebates

Although not the most obvious tool for the job, it is possible to cut grooves and rebates with a circular saw. Set the fence to cut both sides of a groove (**1**) or the inner edge of a rebate (**2**). Then reset the fence to remove the waste in stages – (**3**) and (**4**).

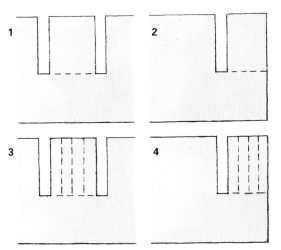

Making a crosscutting T-square

Construct a T-square to use as a permanent guide for crosscutting timber and boards. Screw and glue an MDF straightedge to a solid-wood or MDF stock, checking that they form a perfect right angle (**1**).

Clamp the T-square to a piece of scrap board and run the saw's sole plate against the straightedge to trim the end off the stock (**2**).

When you come to use the T-square for crosscutting, hold the stock against the edge of the workpiece, aligning the trimmed end of the stock with a cut line marked across the wood or board (**3**).

Clamp the straightedge to prevent the T-square moving, and sever the workpiece on the waste side of the line with one pass of the circular saw.

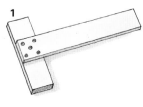

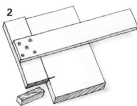

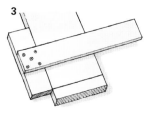

TABLE-SAW CONVERSIONS

Most tool manufacturers can supply a bench to convert a portable circular saw into a table saw. Usually, the saw is bolted upside down to the underside of the bench with its blade protruding through the table top.

A table saw has certain advantages. It leaves both hands free to control the work, and it should have better guides and fences. Unfortunately, however, most bench conversions are much too small to be practical and, unless they are supplied with extensions, there is no possibility of passing man-made boards across them. Moreover, the guides and fences are often flimsy or do not slide smoothly.

A serious woodworker would be better advised to spend a little extra to purchase a good-quality workcentre, which will not only serve as an excellent table-saw base but will also convert to a spindle moulder or shaper table by swapping the saw for an electric router.

A good workcentre converts a portable saw into a table saw

BISCUIT JOINTERS

A biscuit jointer is a miniature plunge saw developed to make a form of tongue-and-groove joint. The joint works like a dowel joint but, instead of gluing a peg into a pair of holes bored in the wood, you insert a flat oval plate or 'biscuit' of compressed beech into slots cut by a circular-saw blade. When water-based PVA glue is introduced into the joint, the wooden plate expands to fill the slot and forms an extremely strong bond. A combined biscuit jointer and groover is ideal for cutting grooves for drawer bottoms or to trim wall cladding, panelling or floorboards.

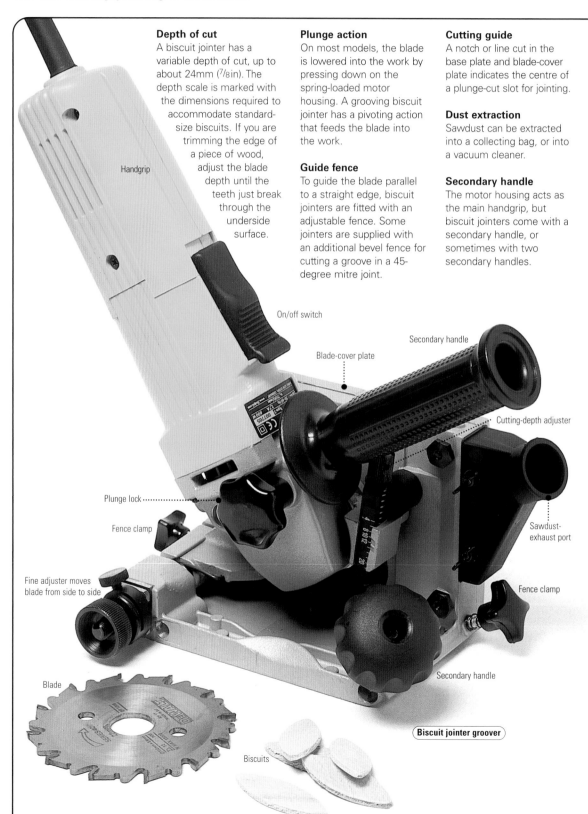

Depth of cut
A biscuit jointer has a variable depth of cut, up to about 24mm ($^7/_8$in). The depth scale is marked with the dimensions required to accommodate standard-size biscuits. If you are trimming the edge of a piece of wood, adjust the blade depth until the teeth just break through the underside surface.

Plunge action
On most models, the blade is lowered into the work by pressing down on the spring-loaded motor housing. A grooving biscuit jointer has a pivoting action that feeds the blade into the work.

Guide fence
To guide the blade parallel to a straight edge, biscuit jointers are fitted with an adjustable fence. Some jointers are supplied with an additional bevel fence for cutting a groove in a 45-degree mitre joint.

Cutting guide
A notch or line cut in the base plate and blade-cover plate indicates the centre of a plunge-cut slot for jointing.

Dust extraction
Sawdust can be extracted into a collecting bag, or into a vacuum cleaner.

Secondary handle
The motor housing acts as the main handgrip, but biscuit jointers come with a secondary handle, or sometimes with two secondary handles.

Handgrip

On/off switch

Blade-cover plate

Secondary handle

Cutting-depth adjuster

Plunge lock

Fence clamp

Sawdust-exhaust port

Fine adjuster moves blade from side to side

Fence clamp

Secondary handle

Blade

Biscuits

Biscuit jointer groover

USING A BISCUIT JOINTER SAFELY

Follow the usual safety procedures recommended for power tools. In addition:

- Don't attempt to plunge the jointer blade into the wood until the motor is running.
- Use sharp blades only. Inspect blades regularly and discard any that are cracked or bent.
- Don't apply side pressure to a spinning blade in order to slow it down or bring it to a stop.
- Never run the tool with the cover plate removed.
- When cutting a groove, feed the jointer at a steady rate away from you against the rotation of the blade.

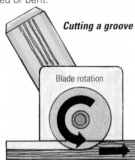

Cutting a groove

Blade rotation

Direction of feed

On/off switch
The on/off switch is situated on the motor housing, either underneath for index-finger operation or on top for thumb operation.

Blades
Biscuit jointers are fitted with miniature circular-saw blades, 100 to 105mm (4 to 4^1/$_4$in) in diameter, with tungsten-carbide-tipped teeth. Jointing and grooving blades cut a 4mm (^{5}/$_{32}$in) slot. Slimmer blades are available for trimming wood to length.

Biscuits
The compressed-beech biscuits are manufactured in three sizes: for board thicknesses of 10 to 12mm (^{3}/$_8$ to ^{1}/$_2$in); 13 to 18mm (^{1}/$_2$ to ^{3}/$_4$in); and 19mm (^{3}/$_4$in) and over. Barbed plastic biscuits are available for test assemblies.

Straight-plunging biscuit jointer

CUTTING BISCUIT JOINTS

Biscuit jointing is suitable for cabinet and frame construction, using man-made boards and solid timber with butt, mitre or edge-to-edge joints.

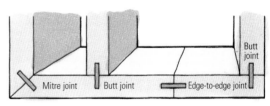

Mitre joint   Butt joint   Edge-to-edge joint   Butt joint

Jointing methods

Making a butt joint
Having drawn the centre line of the joint on the work, mark along it the central points of the biscuit slots, spaced about 100mm (4in) apart. Set the cutting depth to suit the biscuits you are using and adjust the guide fence to align the blade with the centre line.

Align the cutting guide with the central point of each slot and press the fence against the edge of the work, then plunge the blade to make the cut (**1**).

To cut a slot in the edge of a matching component, place the workpiece on a flat surface and lay the jointer on its side (**2**). Edge-to-edge joints are cut in the same way.

To cut slots across the central part of a board, hold the matching component on edge and draw a line along one side. Tip the component to that side of the line and use the component as a fence to plunge the slots across the board (**3**); then, without moving the matching component, cut slots in its edge as described above.

Cutting a mitre joint
If the biscuit jointer is supplied with a bevel fence, you can cut slots for a mitre joint, with the workpiece laid flat on the bench (**4**).

A straight-plunging jointer with an adjustable fence can be used to cut mitre joints in a similar way (**5**).

Cutting a groove
To cut a continuous groove, adjust the jointer as if you were cutting a butt joint. Place the tool at one end of the work, switch on, and plunge the saw. Feed the tool to the end of the groove, raise the blade, and then switch off.

1
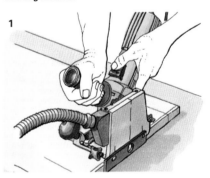

2
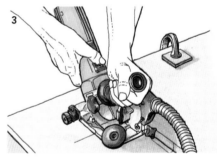

3
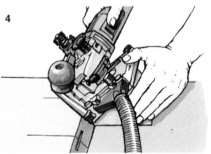

4
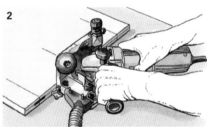

5
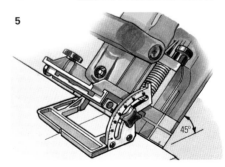

PORTABLE PLANERS

A portable planer can't do the work of a finely set hand plane or take the place of a stand-alone planer/thicknesser – but it does reduce the work involved in planing large sections of timber to size and it's a boon if you need to skim the closing edge of a door or plane a bevelled rebate on a hardwood windowsill. A few cordless planers are made for the professional market, but they tend to be prohibitively expensive.

Rebating depth and width

An adjustable depth gauge determines the maximum depth of rebate that can be cut with a planer. This will be between 20 and 24mm (^{3}/$_4$ and 1in) with most planers, although some of the smaller tools may not be able to rebate any deeper than 8mm (^{5}/$_{16}$in). On better-quality planers, a side fence regulates the rebate width. On some models, the normally square face of the fence can be adjusted to any angle up to 45 degrees for planing bevels accurately.

Cutting depth

The sole of a planer is made in two sections, separated by the cylindrical cutter block. Raising the front or in-feed section increases the amount of wood the cutters can remove in one pass. Smaller planers have a maximum cutting depth of no more than 1mm (^{1}/$_{32}$in), whereas large professional models will cut up to 3.5mm (^{5}/$_{32}$in) deep. You can expect a good middle-range planer to remove up to 2.5mm (^{1}/$_8$in).

Usually, cutting depth is selected by adjusting a dial or knob mounted near the toe of the tool.

Planing width

The cutters run the full width of the sole, which on the majority of planers is 82mm (3^1/$_4$in) wide.

Handgrip

The weight of the tool is taken with the main handgrip. This also incorporates the trigger and the lock button, which when depressed allows the machine to run continuously. Before you plug it in, check that the planer is not locked for continuous running.

Secondary handle

A secondary handle mounted above the toe helps to control the planer. This handle often doubles as the cutting-depth adjuster. Always use the handgrip and handle to control the tool; never curl your fingers around the edge of the sole.

Handgrip

Trigger-lock button

Trigger

Drive-belt cover

Secondary handle and cutting-depth adjuster

Rebate depth gauge

Infeed sole

Chamfer-cutting groove

Side fence

SKIL PROFESSIONAL 1525

(Portable electric planer)

Dust extractor

While the machine is running, it ejects a considerable amount of shavings from its exhaust port. It pays to catch them in a purpose-made bag or, better still, to attach a flexible hose connected to an industrial vacuum cleaner. For clarity, the dust bag has been omitted from the illustrations right.

Cutter-block protection

On some models, a spring-loaded guard covers the cutter block completely until it is retracted automatically by the end of the workpiece as the planer is fed forward. On other models a plastic 'foot', mounted at the rear end of the sole, holds the cutter block off the surface of the bench when the planer is put down.

Chamfer-cutting groove

A V-groove machined down the centre of the in-feed section of the sole positively locates the planer on a 90-degree corner for planing chamfers along workpieces.

Electrical insulation

A double-insulated plastic casing protects the woodworker from electric shock.

PLANER CUTTERS

The cylindrical cutter block usually holds a balanced pair of cutters or blades, though some planers are designed to take a single cutter.

There are straight general-purpose blades, usually tipped with tungsten carbide and often reversible. Straight cutters with rounded corners allow you to plane surfaces wider than the sole without leaving ridges in the wood. There are also wavy-edge cutters that simulate the tooled surface of 'rustic' joinery.

Replacing cutters

A good planer is designed to make changing the cutters as easy as possible. A cutter should be replaced when both edges are blunt.

Your planer may have its own system for changing cutters, but the usual practice is to slide each blunt blade from a groove machined across the block and either reverse the blade or replace it with a new one (**1**).

Use a straight block of wood to align the end of each cutter with the edge of the sole (**2**), then tighten the clamping screws that secure the cutter in its groove.

Straight cutter

Straight cutter with rounded corners

Wavy-edge cutter

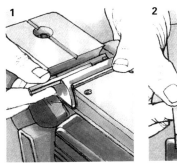

POWER PLANING

As with any plane, it is always preferable to cut in the general direction of the grain; when planing wild grain, adjust the planer to take a finer cut. In any case, you will achieve a better finish if you plane down to the required depth in stages, rather than try to remove the same amount of wood with a single pass.

Handling a power planer

With the in-feed section of the sole resting on the work, switch on and advance the plane at a steady rate. Keep your weight on the toe of the tool until the entire sole is in contact with the wood. Near the end of each pass, transfer your weight to the rear of the planer to maintain a flat surface.

If possible, fit a side fence to help keep the planer square to the work; if your plane is not fitted with a fence, check the work with a try square after planing. To flatten a board, plane diagonally across the work in two directions, overlapping the passes each time. Finally, plane parallel with the long edges.

Planing a chamfer

Locate the V-groove in the in-feed sole on the square corner of the workpiece. Switch on and pass the plane from end to end, removing wood to the required depth in stages. If possible, fit an angled side fence when planing a wide chamfer.

Planing a rebate

To plane a rebate along one edge of a workpiece, first set the side fence and depth gauge to the required dimensions. Keep sideways pressure against the fence during each pass, until the depth gauge comes to rest on the top surface of the work. If your planer is not fitted with a fence or depth gauge, guide the planer with a straight batten like a hand-held rebate plane.

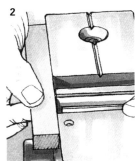

Planing a bevelled rebate

To plane a bevelled rebate, adjust the face of the fence to tilt the whole plane at the required angle. It is absolutely vital to keep sideways pressure on the fence to prevent the planer sliding down the slope.

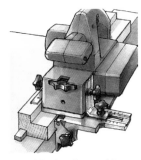

Converting to a jointer

Most portable planers can be converted to a bench-mounted planer/jointer by clamping the tool into a purpose-made accessory that comes with the requisite adjustable guide fence and in some cases with a retractable cutter-block guard, too. Never try to improvise – by clamping the planer's handle in a bench vice, for example.

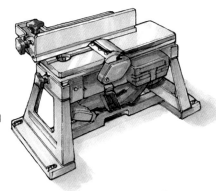

POWER ROUTERS

A remarkably versatile machine, the router has made more impact on woodworking than any other power tool since the introduction of the electric drill.

You can set up a power router in about the time it takes to adjust a handtool to do a similar job; and because the router cutter is driven at relatively high speeds, the results are invariably precise and professional in appearance.

Regardless of size or style, the majority of modern routers are fundamentally very similar: a precision-ground cutter is fitted into the bottom of a motor housing, which has a handgrip mounted on each side. The housing rides up and down on a pair of metal columns attached to the tool's base plate. Pressing down on the handgrips plunges the cutter through a hole in the base plate and into the wood; strong coil springs raise the housing automatically as soon as you release the pressure on the handgrips.

Lightweight plastic body
Modern routers have a lightweight plastic motor housing that insulates the user from contact with live components.

Collet capacity
The shank of a router cutter fits into a tapered collet mounted directly below the electric motor. Tightening the collet nut locks the cutter in place. Most router collets are designed to accommodate 6 or 8mm (1/4 or 3/8in) diameter shanks, but larger routers have a collet capacity of 12mm (1/2in).

Some routers can be fitted with interchangeable collets of different sizes. Collet capacity is not the same as cutter diameter, which varies considerably, according to a particular cutter's shape and function.

Motor housing

Variable-speed control

Depth stop

trend *routing technology*

On/off switch

Plunge lock

Handgrip

Collet

Spindle lock

Turret stop

Base plate

Dust-extraction spout

Power router

Side fence

Light-duty routers

Inexpensive low-power (up to 750W) light-duty plunge routers are able to carry out most operations, including grooving, rebating and decorative moulding.

On many light-duty plunge routers, the motor housing can be separated from the base, allowing you to mount the motor in an overhead stand or pillar drill.

Handgrips

These generally consist of two side handles for gripping and guiding the router. For good control and balance, the handgrips should be positioned as near to the base of the router as possible.

Variable speed control

The majority of routers are available with variable speed control, so that you can select the optimum spindle speed for the job in hand. For most operations, you can operate a router at maximum speed (20,000 to 30,000rpm, depending on the tool's power output) – but it is necessary to reduce the speed when using a large-diameter cutter, for example. Similarly, relatively low spindle speeds are required when machining soft metals and plastics, and also to reduce the risk of scorching wood when making intricate freehand cuts. Router manufacturers supply recommended operating speeds for particular models.

Electronic monitoring maintains a constant speed, even when the feed rate changes or you encounter a tough section of timber. It also eliminates the familiar 'kick' on starting up. Spindle speed is usually selected by turning a dial before switching on the router.

On/off switch

A router's on/off switch should be in reach without having to release your grip on the handles. Some models have a double-switch trigger on one side, which cuts the power when the trigger is released.

Plunge lock

A mechanism that enables you to lock the cutter at any height is usually built into one of the handgrips.

Depth stop

The depth stop determines how far a cutter projects from the base of the router, and therefore how deeply it can cut into the wood. Because it is good practice to make deep cuts in stages, most routers incorporate a turret stop that enables you to preset up to three different cutting depths.

Spindle lock

On most modern routers the spindle is immobilized by pressing a button, enabling you to turn the collet nut with a spanner when changing a cutter. On some models a second spanner is required to lock the spindle.

Base plate

The base plate carries all the clamps that secure the various accessories, including the side fence and dust-extraction hood. A replaceable plastic facing prevents the metal base plate marking the wood.

Side fence

An adjustable side fence, used to guide the cutter on a path parallel to the straight edge of a workpiece, is virtually standard equipment, often supplied with the router as part of the kit.

Dust extraction

Dust-extraction facilities are available for all power routers. On some models the extraction unit comes as a permanent fixture, but on most it takes the form of a transparent plastic hood that encloses the cutter. The hood is connected to a flexible hose that diverts the waste to an industrial vacuum cleaner. For clarity, the dust-extraction hood and hose have been omitted from many of the illustrations in this book.

Dust-extraction hose

Guide bushes

Most routers come with at least one guide bush that enables the router to be used with templates and jigs. There are so many guide bushes to choose from that it makes sense to buy them as need dictates.

Medium-duty routers

A good-quality plunge router of around 800 to 1200W is ideal for furniture-making, machining wood and some joinery work. These relatively compact machines are also suitable for inverted or overhead-table routing, and many accessories, jigs and templates are produced for this size of router.

Heavy-duty routers

With power-input ratings of up to 1850W, heavy-duty routers can take large cutters for joinery work, such as constructing windows and doors. There is little risk of overloading the motor, and you can make relatively deep, wide cuts.

Plain or fence-guided cutters

This type of cutter has to be guided on its intended path either by means of the adjustable side fence or a trammel or by running the router's base plate against a straightedge. Plain cutters are also used when routing freehand, or with a guide bush and template.

Self-guiding cutters

This type of cutter is manufactured with a solid pin ground on its tip or with a bearing race mounted on the tip or the shank, just above the cutting edges. With their pilot tip or bearings running against the edge of a workpiece or template, self-guiding cutters can be used to machine a variety of edge mouldings and rebates. Self-guiding cutters are also made for trimming veneers and plastic laminates flush with a workpiece.

ROUTER CUTTERS

Router cutters are expensive – especially those with large or complex profiles – and, since no woodworker needs to acquire the full range available, it makes sense to buy them as the need arises, spending as much as you can afford at the time in order to get good-quality cutters.

1 Cutting edges
Each cutting edge must be ground to exactly the same angle, size and shape.

2 Rake angle
The angle at which the cutting edge meets the surface of the wood.

3 Clearance angle
Amount of clearance behind the cutting edge.

4 Radial relief
The back face of the cutter is ground away to prevent friction between the cutter and the face of the wood.

5 Shank
Steel shaft that is clamped in the router collet.

6 Flute or gullet
The gap between the cutting face and the body of the cutter.

7 Cutting angle
Angle ground on cutting edge.

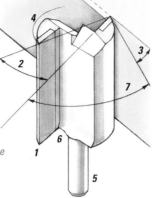

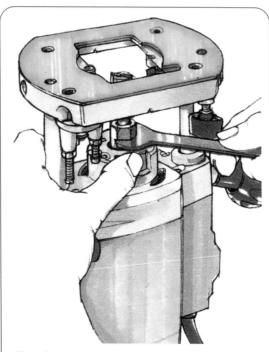

Changing router cutters
To remove a cutter, unplug the router, then depress the spindle lock and loosen the collet nut with a spanner. When inserting another cutter, ensure that at least three-quarters of the shank is held in the collet. When changing cutters, always turn your router upside down, to prevent the cutter dropping onto the bench when you loosen the collet nut.

GROOVING CUTTERS

The following selection of plain or fence-guided router cutters can machine recesses both parallel with or across the grain. For plunge cutting, it is essential that cutting edges extend across the bottom of the cutter. Cutters without a bottom-cutting facility must be fed into the work from one edge.

Straight cutters
The basic router cutter machines square-section grooves or housings. Most straight cutters are manufactured with either one or two cutting edges. The latter (known as two-flute cutters) leave a better finish, but a single-flute cutter clears waste more efficiently.

Dovetail cutters
Designed primarily for machining dovetail joints, these cutters are also useful for making dovetail housings.

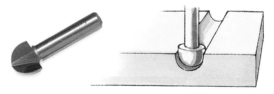

Radius or core-box cutters
These cutters can be used to machine single round-bottomed grooves or a series of parallel flutes.

Veining cutters
Create narrow and relatively deep round-bottomed grooves with a veining cutter.

V-groove cutters
Used primarily for decorative low-relief carving and for freehand lettering.

EDGE-FORMING CUTTERS

Grooving cutters can be used in conjunction with a guide fence to machine the edges of a workpiece, but the majority of edge-forming cutters are made with a self-guiding tip or bearing. On bearing-guided cutters, the mounting pin or spigot must be strong enough not to snap off under load. You must be able to tighten the holding screw sufficiently, without stripping the thread, to prevent it undoing when routing.

Rebate cutters
Depth of cut is determined by how far the cutter projects from the router base. Some cutters can be fitted with different-size bearings to alter the rebate width.

Chamfer cutters
Used to machine 45-degree bevels along the edges of the work. The same cutter can be used to cut different-size chamfers simply by adjusting the router's depth stop.

Rounding-over cutters
These cutters produce a simple rounded edge or, when set lower, a stepped ovolo bead.

Cove cutters
You can produce decorative scalloped edges with a cove cutter or, in combination with a similar rounding-over cutter, machine a rule joint for a drop-leaf table.

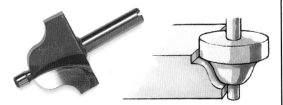

Decorative-moulding cutters
There are a great many cutters designed to produce moulded edges on frames or panels.

MAINTAINING CUTTERS

Overheating, rather than blade wear, is the main cause of router cutters becoming blunt. Feeding the router too slowly or inconsistently will overheat a cutter. Waste packed tightly in the cutter flutes has a similar effect. Once a cutter has started to dull it rapidly loses its tempering, so that it is no longer able to hold a keen edge.

Cleaning cutters
Scrape any traces of resin or sawdust from the cutting faces and from the corners of the flutes.

Checking for a worn collet
Worn or damaged collets run cutters out of true – radial scoring on the shanks of your cutters may mean that they are slipping in a worn collet. Multi-slit collets grip better than the simpler split-cone types. When tightening a collet, take care not to cross the thread, and don't overtighten the nut.

Storing cutters
Store cutters in a plastic case with foam padding, or in a wooden cabinet with drilled racks. Don't keep your cutters on the bench or near areas where they can get knocked against other tools. If you do not intend to use router cutters for a while, spray them with a thin oil.

SHARPENING CUTTERS

To sharpen HSS cutters, use the same oilstones that are employed to hone chisels and plane irons. TCT cutters must be honed on hard stones (such as diamond-impregnated or ceramic stones), used dry or lubricated with a little water. Keep a pocket slipstone handy for touching up the edges regularly. You can also use these stones to hone HSS cutters.

Honing cutting edges
Hone only the flat faces of the cutting edges. Keep each face flat on the stone and rub it back and forth several times. Don't attempt to grind or hone the bevelled cutting edge.

When sharpening cutters that have more than one edge, hone each one an equal number of times – if cutting edges are not the same profile and size, their effectiveness is reduced.

Honing self-guiding cutters
When honing fixed-pin self-guiding cutters, take care not to run the pin against the edge of the stone. Remove the bearings from bearing-guided cutters before honing.

Materials used for cutters
High-speed-steel (HSS) cutters are perfectly adequate for most woodworking applications, but you will find that the more expensive tungsten-carbide-tipped (TCT) or solid tungsten-carbide (STC) cutters are more cost effective in the long run because they hold their edges longer, especially when routing tough hardwoods and abrasive man-made boards. Some cutters are made with replaceable STC blades held in place by small screws.

ROUTING GROOVES AND HOUSINGS

Cutting a groove accurately is essential when fitting drawer bottoms and when fixing the back panel into a cupboard. A true groove runs parallel with the grain; when a groove is cut across the grain, it is known as a housing. Housings are used a great deal for fixed shelving and for attaching drawer runners on the inside of a cabinet. Used with a side fence or a straightedge guide, a power router is the ideal tool for machining both grooves and housings.

Grooving with a side fence

When machining a groove relatively close to the edge of a panel, first place the router on the surface, aligning the cutter with a pencil mark drawn across the workpiece. Slide the fence up against the edge of the work and tighten the fence clamps.

To cut a through groove, plunge and lock the cutter, then rest the front half of the base plate on the work with the cutter clear of the edge. Switch on and feed the cutter into the work, keeping the fence held firmly against the guide edge. Continue with the pass until the cutter emerges from the opposite edge of the work, then switch off before releasing the plunge lock.

Clearly mark the ends of a stopped groove with a pencil and position the router as described above. Switch on and plunge the cutter into the work, then feed it forwards at a steady rate until you reach the other end of the groove. Back off slightly before lifting the cutter clear and switching off.

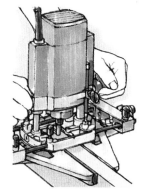

Grooving an edge
Fit a second side fence to prevent the router rocking when machining a narrow workpiece. Set the distance between the fences to leave minimal side play – but before switching on, check that you can feed the router smoothly.

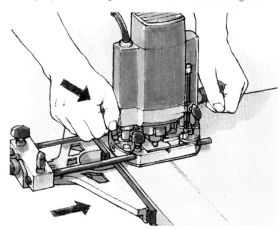

Cutting curved grooves

A trammel – a rigid metal rod or bar with a pin at one end – is used to rotate a router about a centre point for cutting arcs or circles. A trammel rod locates in the side-fence clamps. In order to prevent the trammel pin marking the work, use double-sided adhesive tape to stick a small plywood or MDF patch over the centre point.

Cutting a housing

When a housing is too far from the edge of a workpiece to use a side fence, clamp a straight batten across the work to guide the edge of the base plate. Most housings are square to the edges of the workpiece, but you can clamp a batten at any angle.

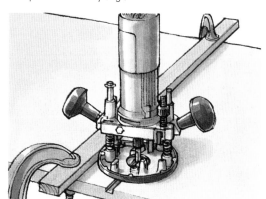

Cutting a wide housing

To machine a housing that is wider than the router cutter, use a pair of parallel guide battens to align a cutting edge with each side of the housing. Machine one side of the housing, then move the router across to the other batten to make a second pass in the opposite direction. Make each pass against the rotation of the cutter; this helps to keep the base plate pressed against the guide battens.

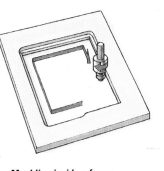

Shaping the edges of a workpiece, either to form rebates or cut decorative mouldings, is a straightforward procedure using a power router. You can use plain or self-guiding cutters.

Feeding the router

When cutting rebates and edge mouldings, always feed the power router against the direction of cutter rotation, so that the rotational force will tend to pull the cutter into the workpiece.

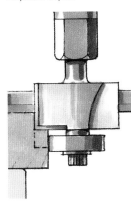

Moulding a straight edge

Ensure that the edge of the work is square and smooth. Fit a plain moulding cutter and set the face of the side fence to align with the central axis of the cutter. Adjust the depth of cut for the first pass, increasing the depth setting as the work progresses.

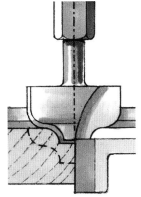

Rebating with a straight cutter

Fit a straight router cutter with a diameter that is larger than the width of the rebate. Adjust the side fence to align the cutting edge with the inner face of the rebate. Cut in a series of shallow steps, until you reach the required depth.

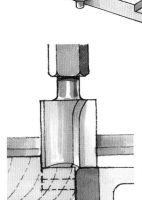

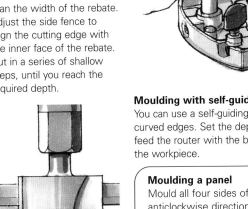

Moulding with self-guiding cutters

You can use a self-guiding cutter to mould straight and curved edges. Set the depth of cut for the first pass, and feed the router with the bearing running against the edge of the workpiece.

Moulding inside a frame

When you are moulding (or rebating) the inside of a frame, feed the router clockwise. Router cutters leave rebates with rounded corners, but you can trim them square with a corner chisel.

Rebating with a self-guiding cutter

Self-guiding rebate cutters can be used on straight or curved edges. Run the bearing tip against the edge of the work, adjusting the cutting depth between passes until the rebate is complete.

Providing bearing clearance

In most cases, allowing the workpiece to overhang the edge of the bench provides sufficient clearance for the bearing of a self-guiding cutter. However, if that is inconvenient (such as when machining a curved or shaped edge), provide clearance for the bearing by raising the work on a panel. Make sure the work and panel are clamped securely before cutting.

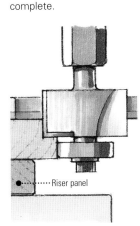

Riser panel

Moulding a panel

Mould all four sides of an MDF panel in an anticlockwise direction (**1**). If the panel is made from solid wood, machine the end grain first; any split edges will be removed when you mould the side grain (**2**).

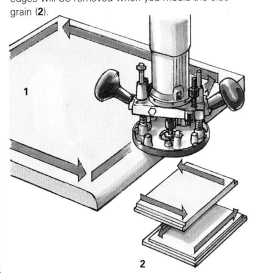

ROUTING WITH TEMPLATES

Using a template to guide the router is a quick and accurate method of performing repetitive tasks, such as cutting woodworking joints or the demanding task of cutting identical decorative panels.

You can cut a template from any scrap piece of smooth sheet material that is thick enough to keep a guide bush clear of the work. MDF is ideal for most operations, but you might consider using polycarbonate sheet for intricate or frequently used templates. A power router is without doubt the best tool to use for manufacturing templates with clean perfectly square edges.

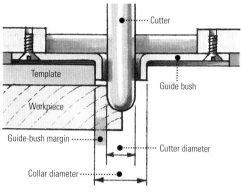

Guide bushes
A guide bush projects through the router's base plate and forms a metal collar or ring fence surrounding the cutter. Its function is to maintain a constant distance between the cutter and a template or edge guide.

Guide-bush margin
The guide-bush collar runs against the edge of the template, and the cutter faithfully reproduces its profile. When designing and making templates, you need to allow for the guide-bush 'margin' – the difference between the diameter of the collar and the diameter of the cutter itself.

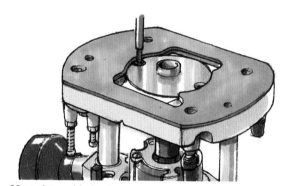

Mounting guide bushes
Router manufacturers utilize various methods for mounting guide bushes, but most are designed to be located within a recess machined in the base plate and held securely with countersunk screws or with round-head clamping screws that grip the edge of the bush. With some routers, guide bushes are attached with a bayonet fitting that works with a simple twist-and-lock action.

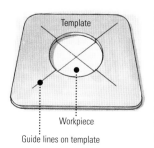

Guide lines on template

Registering a template
If the effort is to be worthwhile, every template must be registered accurately on the work. You can glue or screw locating battens, blocks or dowels to the template, but the simplest method is to draw registration lines on the template and align them with similar lines or marks drawn on the workpiece.

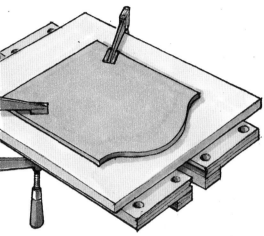

Securing templates
Always mount templates securely. You can pin or screw a template to a workpiece that is to be painted or concealed in some way. Provided the surfaces are flat, clean and grease-free, you could use double-sided adhesive tape to fix a template in place. However, cramps are invariably the easier option, so long as they don't interfere with the passage of the router.

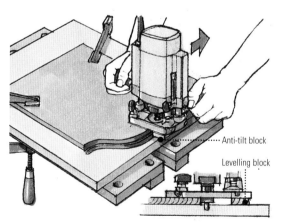

Supporting the router
Most of the router's weight should be supported by the template itself, but where the router overhangs the edge of the template, locate levelling blocks around the workpiece or, better still, attach an anti-tilt foot or block to the underside of the router's base.

Once you have machined the edges of a lock or hinge recess, or perhaps cut the shoulders of a tenon or lap joint, it is a simple task to remove the remaining waste wood, using the router freehand. However, there are more creative applications for freehand routing, including lettering and low-relief carving.

Controlling the router

The action of a rotating cutter tends to pull the router sideways across the workpiece. In normal use, this tendency is restrained by a guide edge or fence, which keeps the router on course. When routing freehand, however, you have to exert more control over the router to prevent the cutter wandering, particularly when cutting through tough patches of grain and knots. To brace the machine against sudden changes of direction, hold the router by its base plate, keeping your hands lightly in contact with the surface of the work.

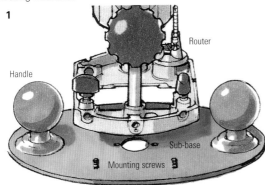

Fitting a sub-base

Increase your control over the router with a clear-plastic or MDF sub-base fixed to the base plate (**1**). Cut a 40mm (1⁵⁄₈in) hole through the centre of the sub-base, and drill and countersink holes to take the mounting screws. Fit a simple handle on each side of the sub-base.

Because it is wider than the router's base plate, using a sub-base (**2**) reduces the tendency for the router to tip when routing freehand.

1

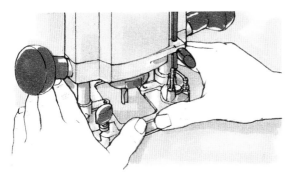

Handle

Router

Sub-base

Mounting screws

2

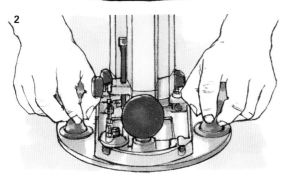

Supporting the router base plate

To keep the base plate on an even keel, work out in advance a cutting sequence that leaves some areas of the wood intact until most of the waste has been removed. Where this is not practicable, stick levelling blocks temporarily to the work with double-sided tape.

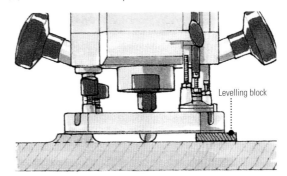

Levelling block

FREEHAND LETTERING

It is relatively easy to cut a nameplate for your house or boat using a router freehand. The simplest method is to remove the background, leaving the letters, numerals or decorative motifs standing proud, in relief.

Draw your design on tracing paper. To transfer the design to the wood, rub the back of the paper with a soft pencil and then, with the pattern taped to the work, trace over the lines to imprint them on the surface (**1**).

Follow the outlines of the design (**2**), using the procedures for freehand routing described left.

1

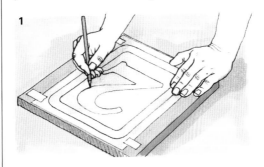

2

Cutters for freehand work

In addition to the range of straight, radius and V-groove cutters that can be used for freehand work, there are also rotary burrs and rasps, which are useful for shaping and smoothing wood. As with other operations, feed the cutter against the direction of rotation and cut in shallow steps.

Carving with a router

If it can be detached from its base plate, you can use the motor housing of a lightweight router as a handy carving tool. Fit a rotary burr or rasp and, holding the motor housing with both hands, grind away sufficient waste to allow you to carve detail into the workpiece using chisels and gouges.

CUTTING JOINTS WITH A ROUTER

It is possible to make simple joints, such as housings, rebates and grooves, following the basic procedures described earlier. In addition, using appropriate jigs and guides, you can make special joints for cabinet-making and joinery accurately and relatively quickly, some of which can be quite laborious to construct by hand.

HALVING JOINTS

The halving joint is used exclusively for framing made from components of equal thickness. Although it is not an especially strong joint, it is extremely simple to make, and the basic joint can be adapted to make right-angle corners, T-joints and cross frames. As with all halving joints, an equal amount of wood is cut from each workpiece, so the components lie flush when the joints are assembled.

Cross halving joint

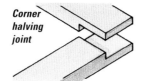

Corner halving joint

T-halving joint

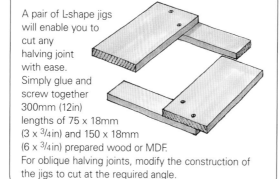

Lap joints
Cut the rebate for a lap joint the same way as a simple halving joint.

MAKING RIGHT-ANGLE JIGS

A pair of L-shape jigs will enable you to cut any halving joint with ease. Simply glue and screw together 300mm (12in) lengths of 75 x 18mm (3 x ¾in) and 150 x 18mm (6 x ¾in) prepared wood or MDF. For oblique halving joints, modify the construction of the jigs to cut at the required angle.

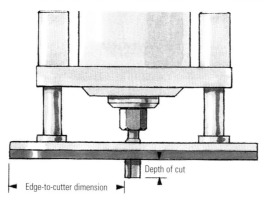

Depth of cut

◄— Edge-to-cutter dimension —►

Setting up the router
Set the maximum depth of cut to half the thickness of the timber, and set the turret stop to cut in two or more passes. Measure from the edge of the base to the side of the cutter – use this edge-to-cutter dimension to position the L-shape jigs on the work.

Cutting a corner halving joint
Draw the shoulder line across the work, and mark another line – the edge-to-cutter dimension (see below left) – from the shoulder line. Align an L-shape jig with this second line, and clamp both the jig and work to the bench.

To cut the halving joint, run the edge of the router base against the jig to form the shoulder, then remove the rest of the waste freehand. The jig itself will prevent break out – but if you want to avoid cutting into the jig, place a strip of scrap wood behind the work.

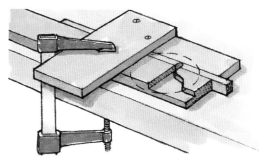

Cutting a T-halving joint
One of the components of a T-halving joint is cut like a corner halving joint (see above).

To cut the recess in the other component, mark two shoulder lines and clamp two jigs on top of the work, allowing for the edge-to-cutter dimension. Without altering the depth setting on the router, use the left-hand jig to cut one shoulder and then move the router to the right-hand jig to cut the other. Clean out the waste in between.

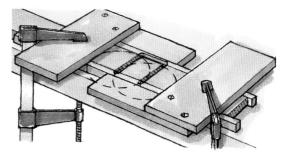

Making cross halving joints
Clamp the two components of a cross halving joint together, then cut both recesses simultaneously.

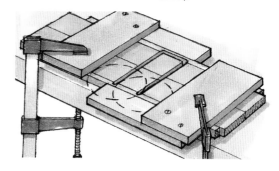

MORTISE-AND-TENON JOINT

A mortise is really nothing more than a deep groove. However, you will have to chisel the rounded ends square to match the tenon.

You can cut tenons using a method similar to that described for making halving joints. Cut one face, then turn the workpiece over and cut the second one. It is generally best to cut haunches (whether square or sloping) by hand, after you have machined the tenons.

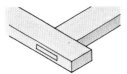 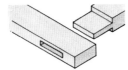

Using a right-angle jig to cut a tenon
Make an L-shape jig (similar to the one described for cutting a halving joint) by gluing and screwing together two pieces of prepared wood or MDF at right angles.

Lay the jig on the rail and clamp the assembly to the bench. Set the maximum depth of cut and, if necessary, adjust the turret stop to cut in two or more passes. Use the jig to cut the shoulder, then remove the remaining waste by cutting freehand.

When cutting a narrow tenon, you may need to support it on a piece of timber, to prevent the wood vibrating as you cut the second face.

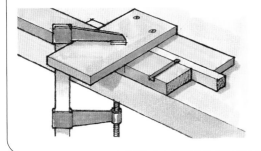

DOVETAIL HOUSING JOINT

Cutting a dovetail housing joint by hand is a laborious process – whereas cutting both components with a power router and a dovetail cutter is extremely simple.

Cutting the tongue
Machine the housing by running the tool against a guide batten, then clamp the mating component between two pieces of scrap timber. Use a side fence to guide the cutter along one or both sides of the component, leaving a dovetail-shape tongue that matches the housing exactly.

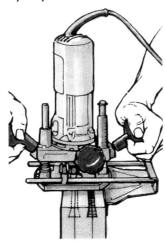

RULE JOINT

A rule joint is not a woodworking joint in the conventional sense, since it does not physically attach one component to another.

The joint comprises two moulded edges, one on a fixed table top and the other on a hinged leaf, designed to pivot one around the other as the leaf is raised and lowered. Its function is to conceal special backflap hinges screwed to the undersides of the top and leaf. This type of hinge has flaps of different length, the longer one being screwed to the leaf. You can use a routing table to machine both edge profiles; but cut large tops and flaps on a bench, using a hand-held router.

Before you machine the actual table top and folding leaves, make a trial piece to check the fit of the rule joint, making a careful note of the settings.

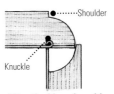

Align the hinge knuckle with the shoulder

RULE-JOINT CUTTERS

Rule-joint sets are available for timber ranging from 9mm (³/8in) to 18mm (³/4in) minimum thickness. Each set comprises a rounding-over cutter and a matching cove cutter. Fit a side fence with extended faces to guide a set of plain cutters. Run the bearings of self-guiding cutters along the uncut shoulder of each profile. If necessary, clamp a batten flush with the guide edge to provide sufficient running surface for the bearing.

Cutting a rule joint
Clamp the leaf on the bench, face down. Fit a plain cove cutter in the router and set the depth of cut to leave a suitable shoulder along the top edge. This shoulder not only forms the guide edge for the fence or guide bearing, but also forms the visible, and most vulnerable, edge on the flap.

Set the fence in line with, or very slightly forward of, the axis of the cutter.

Set the depth of cut using the turret stop, finishing slightly less than the full depth. This gives you the opportunity to make a very fine cut on the final pass. Gradually lowering the cutter between passes, machine the profile against the rotation of the cutter (**1**).

To machine the fixed table top, clamp it face up, fit a rounding-over cutter in the router, and set the full depth of cut to match the previously cut profile (**2**).

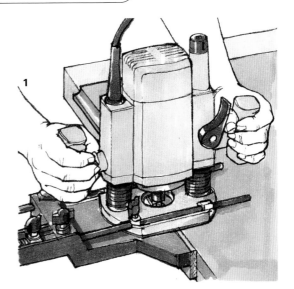

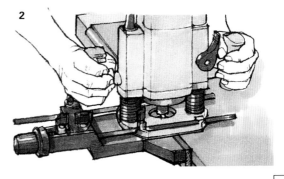

THROUGH DOVETAIL JOINT

Through dovetail joints can be cut easily and quickly using special factory-made jigs together with a power router fitted with a guide bush and cutter that ensure the size and pitch of the pin and tail match exactly.

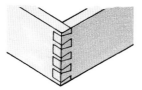
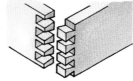

Adjustable-finger jigs

You can tailor a through dovetail joint to suit any width of workpiece, using a jig that features individually adjustable fingers for guiding the router cutter. The setting of the finger assembly governs the size and spacing of the tails and pins. Adjusting the fingers for the pins along one side of the assembly automatically sets the fingers for matching tails on the opposite side. There is also a device for fine fore-and-aft adjustment of the finger assembly.

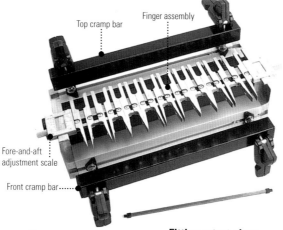

Top cramp bar
Finger assembly
Fore-and-aft adjustment scale
Front cramp bar

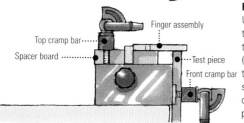

Top cramp bar
Spacer board
Finger assembly
Test piece
Front cramp bar

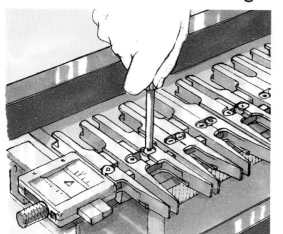

Fitting a test piece

Use test pieces to set up the jig and check the fit of the parts. Place an 18mm ($3/4$ in) spacer board under the finger assembly and secure it with the jig's top cramp bar. Clamp a test piece of the correct width to the front of the jig, making sure it butts against the side stop and the underside of the finger assembly.

Adjusting the finger assembly

You need one pair of fingers for each dovetail and a single finger at both ends of the row. First, set these single fingers so that they are flush with each edge of the test piece; then space the pairs of fingers at regular intervals between them. Finally, tighten the clamping screws.

Rotating the fingers

Once you have adjusted one half of the assembly, all that is required to utilize the other set of fingers is to unclamp the entire assembly, rotate it and clamp it down again.

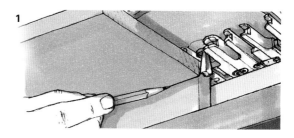

Cutting the joint

Set the assembly with the straight-sided tail fingers pointing towards you. Fit a compatible dovetail cutter and guide bush into the router. Using the other component as a template, mark the depth of cut on the tail member (**1**), then adjust the router cutter down to the marked line.

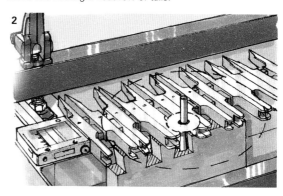

Before switching on the router, always check that all parts of the jig and the test piece are securely clamped. Then run the cutter between each set of fingers (**2**), cutting out the waste wood and leaving a neat row of tails.

Rotate the assembly to present the pin fingers to the front of the jig, and clamp a second test piece in the jig. Mark the depth of cut as before, using the tail member you have just cut as a template (**3**). Fit a straight cutter in the router and adjust it down to the marked line.

With the router placed flat on the finger assembly, switch on and then rout out the waste between each pair of fingers (**4**).

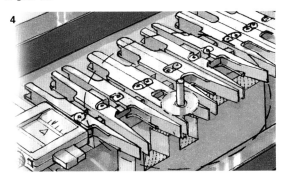

Assemble the joint to check whether it fits snugly. If it is slack, use the jig's fine-adjustment scale to move the finger assembly forward (**5**). If the joint is too tight, adjust the finger assembly backwards. Before proceeding with the actual workpieces, cut another pair of test pieces to make sure that the joint fits satisfactorily.

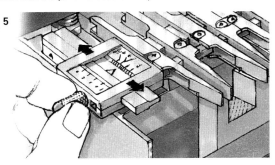

LAPPED DOVETAIL JOINT

You can cut a lapped dovetail joint with a router, using a fixed-finger dovetail jig that enables the pins and tails to be cut simultaneously. It is a relatively inexpensive jig that produces regularly spaced equal-size pins and tails. The joint is perfectly functional, but it is necessary to design the width of the components to suit the finger spacing of the jig. Test the jig's settings by cutting test pieces before you proceed with the actual work.

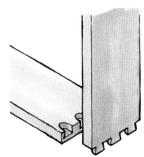

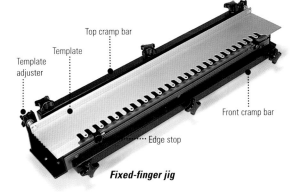

Template adjuster · Template · Top cramp bar · Front cramp bar · Edge stop

Fixed-finger jig

Cutting the joint

Mount the tail member vertically in the jig, face side inward, then insert the pin member (usually the drawer front) face down and butt its end grain against the tail member. Slide the pin member up to the jig's edge stop, then offset the tail member sideways by half the finger spacing (**1**). Now fit the finger template, which is marked with a 'sight line' that runs centrally down the row of fingers. Adjust it until the sight line corresponds to the butt joint between the two components.

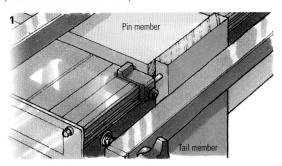

Pin member

Tail member

Fit the recommended guide bush and dovetail cutter. Make a light back cut from right to left, to leave a clean shoulder; then feed the cutter from left to right between each pair of fingers, keeping the router level and following the template with the guide bush (**2**).

Unclamp the test pieces and rotate one of them through 180 degrees to mate their jointed ends (**3**). If the joint fits snugly, cut a similar joint for the other end of the pin member (drawer front), butting it against the edge stop at the other end of the jig. If you find the joint is loose, increase the cutting depth of the router slightly. If the joint is too tight, raise the cutter (**4**).

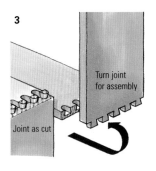

Turn joint for assembly

Joint as cut

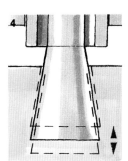

If the sockets are too deep, adjust the finger template forward. If the tail member projects slightly, set the template backwards (**5**).

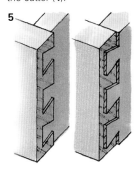

INVERTED-ROUTER TABLES

Mounting a router upside down in a purpose-made table offers a higher degree of control and precision than you could achieve using a hand-held router.

1 Guide fence
The fence should be adjustable fore and aft.

2 Cutter guard
A clear-plastic pivoting guard encloses the exposed cutter.

3 Spring-pressure cramps
These prevent the workpiece lifting from the table surface.

4 Mitre fence
A sliding mitre fence allows you to machine the ends of narrow workpieces.

5 Sliding push block
This allows you to machine the ends of workpieces held vertically.

6 Remote switch
Avoids having to reach under the table to switch off the router.

7 Fine-depth adjuster
Provides precise cutter settings. Particularly useful because the plunge action is not accessible with the router inverted.

Proprietary tables

A basic inverted-router table consists of a flat top to support the workpiece being passed over the cutter and a straight guide fence. Other essentials are adequate cutter guards and – for ease of working as well as safety – efficient hold-down cramps.

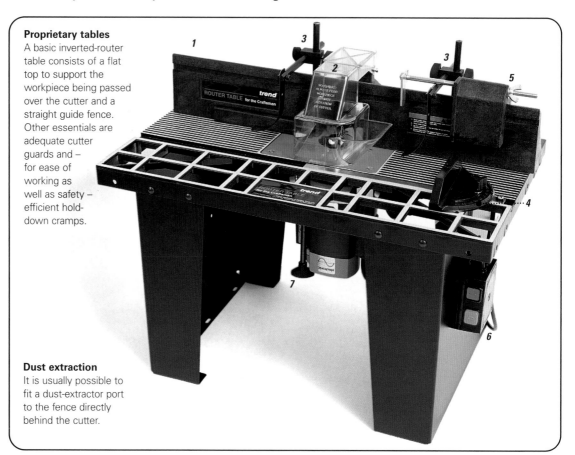

Dust extraction

It is usually possible to fit a dust-extractor port to the fence directly behind the cutter.

MAKING A ROUTING TABLE

Although most proprietary router tables are made of aluminium or steel, man-made boards such as MDF and dense particle board are perfectly adequate for a home-made routing table. Plastic-faced board is particularly suitable, as it is stable and easy to work and has a relatively low-friction surface. It is also inexpensive – offcuts of kitchen worktop are ideal. Make sure there is a balancing laminate on the reverse side to prevent bowing. Mount the table on a sturdy underframe, or make a box from man-made board.

Mounting the router

If you use relatively thick board for the table, you will have to set the router into the thickness of the board, rather than simply bolt it on. Cut a hole larger than the router through the table and mount the router on a metal plate, 3mm (1/8in) thick, inset flush with the table surface. Most router base plates are drilled and threaded to take fixing screws for table and jig mounting.

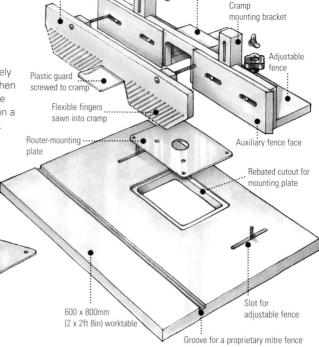

Hold-down cramp
Folded-aluminium dust hood
Cramp mounting bracket
Adjustable fence
Plastic guard screwed to cramp
Flexible fingers sawn into cramp
Router-mounting plate
Auxiliary fence face
Rebated cutout for mounting plate
600 x 800mm (2 x 2ft 8in) worktable
Slot for adjustable fence
Groove for a proprietary mitre fence

BELT SANDERS

Portable machines take a lot of the drudgery out of sanding wood smooth, and a good finishing sander will produce a surface that to all intents and purposes is ready for finishing. However, for top-class work examine a power-sanded surface to ensure there are no scratches that will show up when you apply a clear finish. Then finally, to be absolutely sure, dampen the wood and rub down by hand.

PORTABLE BELT SANDERS

A sander that removes wood so quickly that you can use it to smooth rough-sawn timber is not a tool for cabinet-making. However, a powerful belt sander can be a boon to the joiner and is a handy bench-mounted machine for shaping workpieces.

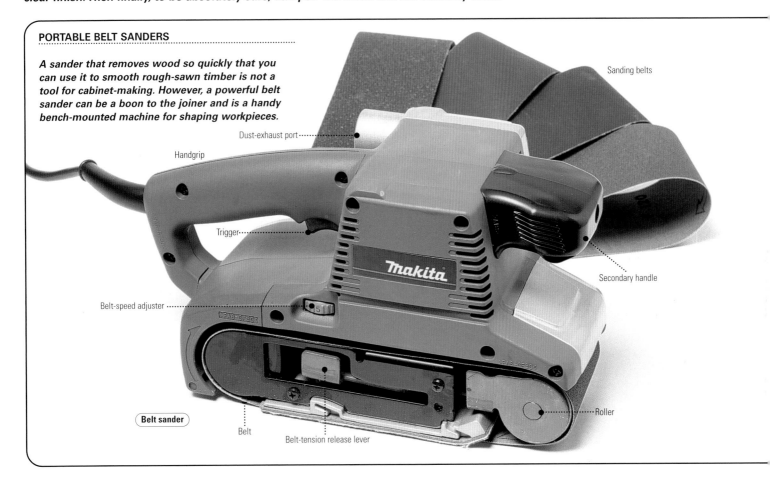

Sanding belts

Dust-exhaust port

Handgrip

Trigger

Secondary handle

Belt-speed adjuster

Belt sander

Belt

Belt-tension release lever

Roller

A belt sander uses a continuous loop of abrasive-covered paper or cloth, held taut between a pair of rollers. An electric motor drives the rear roller, while the front one is adjustable, to control the tension and tracking of the belt. Some models feature automatic belt control, which eradicates the need for manual tracking. A platen (metal bed) mounted between the rollers holds the belt flat on the work. Sanding belts are between 60 and 100mm ($2^3/_8$ and 4in) wide. Large belt sanders are heavy, and can be tiring to use for prolonged periods.

No-load speeds
Most belt sanders run at no-load speeds of between 190 and 360m (617 to 1170ft) per minute. On some models, electronic monitoring maintains optimum speed. If your work requires a more powerful machine, consider buying a professional-grade variable-speed sander with a top speed of around 450m (1462ft) per minute.

Dust extraction
Belt sanding creates inordinate amounts of dust. All machines have a dust port for attaching a collecting bag – though it's better to connect your sander to an industrial vacuum cleaner.

Electrical insulation
Choose a sander with a plastic body that insulates the user from electric shock.

Handgrips
You need both hands to wield a belt sander. The main handgrip incorporates the trigger and lock button, while the secondary handle on the front end of the sander enables you to lower the machine onto the work and remove it after sanding. It is easier to control a well-balanced sander and you are less likely to leave deep scratches in the wood.

Continuous running
When you switch on and press the lock button, the machine will run continuously until you squeeze the trigger a second time. Continuous running is an essential feature of all power sanders.

Sanding frame
On some machines it is possible to fit an adjustable sanding frame that surrounds the belt. This prevents the sander tilting accidentally, which could score the surface.

SAFE SANDING
Belt sanders are not particularly dangerous, but a coarse-grade belt running at high speed can cause a very painful wound. Follow the general rules for power-tool safety. In addition:

• Hold a sander with both hands; and do not lay it aside until the belt has stopped moving.
• Fit a dust bag whenever you are sanding wood; and if the extraction system cannot cope with the amount of dust being created, wear a face mask that covers your nose and mouth.

ABRASIVE BELTS

Use a coarse-grade belt on rough work, following up with a medium-grade and, finally, a fine-grade belt to remove the scratches left by the previous grade.

Changing sanding belts

A torn or clogged belt can damage the surface of the wood, so discard a belt as soon as it begins to show signs of wear.

With the sander unplugged, adjust the rollers to reduce the distance between them, so you can remove the worn belt and replace it with a new one. Switch the machine on and, if your machine requires manual tracking, adjust the control to centre the belt on the rollers.

TYPICAL SANDING-BELT GRADES

Grit 40	Very coarse
Grit 60	Coarse
Grit 80	Medium
Grit 100	Medium
Grit 150	Fine
Grit 240	Very fine

USING BELT SANDERS

Although it is simple to operate, there is a knack to handling a belt sander safely and efficiently. It's a technique that can be learned quickly, but if you are inexperienced, you can inflict considerable damage in seconds. If you have never handled a belt sander before, it pays to practise for a few minutes on scrap timber or board.

FILING SANDERS

These are specialized belt sanders for shaping and smoothing inside narrow apertures. A belt 6 to 9mm ($1/4$ to $3/8$in) wide is held under tension on an arm projecting from the front of the tool. Some models have an extendable cranked arm, for extra reach. Filing sanders are not ideal for fine woodworking, though they are useful for tasks such as removing waste wood from inside deep lock mortises and for shaping small components for toys or models. They also have their uses for DIY projects such as sanding rust from metal railings and for smoothing the cut edges of ceramic tiles.

Handling a belt sander

Switch on and gradually lower the sander onto the work. As soon as the belt touches the wood, allow the sander to move forward under control – holding a machine stationary for any length of time may score the work or sand a deep hollow. Move the sander across the surface, using parallel, overlapping strokes, following the general direction of the grain. Lift the sander off the work before switching off.

Sanding up to an edge

Take care to keep the platen flat on the work, especially as you approach the edges of a board or panel: if you allow the machine to tilt sideways at this point, you will wear away a sharp edge in seconds. With veneered boards in particular, take the precaution of temporarily pinning battens around the edges, flush with the surface, to prevent the sander accidentally wearing through to the core.

Using bench-mounted sanders

Clamping a belt sander to the bench leaves both hands free to control the work. A bench-mounting attachment includes an adjustable fence that helps you sand long edges accurately (**1**).

Clamped on end (**2**) or laid on its side (**3**), the sander can be used to shape workpieces. Change a belt as soon as the abrasive stops cutting efficiently, or you risk scorching the end grain.

Abrasive sheets

For no obvious reason, sheets of abrasive paper made specifically for finishing sanders are a proportion of the standard-size sheets made for hand sanding. Specified as quarter, third or half sheets, these proportions govern the size of orbital sanders; quarter-sheet palm-grip sanders are designed to be operated with one hand.

Self-adhesive or velour-backed sheets of sandpaper can be peeled off the base plate when they need replacing. On some orbital sanders, abrasive sheets are wrapped around the base plate and held in place at each end by a wire or metal clamp.

Cordless sanders

Very few manufacturers include a sander in their range of cordless tools – despite the obvious advantages offered by a sander that has no electrical flex to get caught on the workpiece or other obstructions.

1

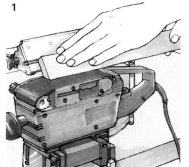

2

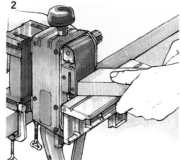

3

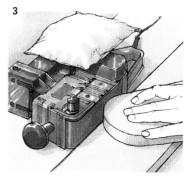

FINISHING SANDERS

Designed to leave a smooth, flat and virtually scratch-free surface, orbital sanders have a foam-covered base plate faced with sheets of abrasive paper. Under power, the base plate describes a tight elliptical motion, which removes wood relatively quickly but invariably leaves the surface covered with a pattern of tiny swirling scratches. Some machines can be switched to a straight reciprocal stroke to eradicate any visible scratches after the wood has been sanded flat.

Sanding rates
The sanding rate of orbital sanders is given as orbits per minute. Fixed rates of between 20,000 and 25,000opm are commonplace, but there are also variable-speed sanders that can be operated at much slower speeds for finishing paintwork and heat-sensitive plastics.

Dust extraction
Efficient dust extraction is not only desirable for your health, it also reduces clogging of the abrasive paper. On some models, the base plate and sandpaper are perforated so that the dust is sucked from beneath the sander directly into a collecting bag or vacuum cleaner.

Electrical insulation
Lightweight plastic casings insulate the user from live electrical components.

DELTA SANDERS

With its triangular base plate, a delta sander is an orbital sander designed for sanding into tight corners, narrow rebates and other awkward recesses. On most models you can preselect the optimum speed for the material you are sanding. Swapping the peel-off abrasive sheet for a felt pad turns a delta sander into a handy polishing machine.

RANDOM-ORBITAL SANDERS

This type of sander combines the characteristics of a disc sander with an eccentric orbital motion, which practically eliminates surface scratching. Some models have flexible sanding pads that can cope with curves as well as flat surfaces, but you need to switch to a delta sander to reach inaccessible corners.

Motor housing

On/off button

Orbital sander

Handgrip

On/off switch

Handgrip

Palm sander

Dust-exhaust port

Secondary handle

SKIL
475 Watt

Half sanding sheets

Paper clamp

Quarter sanding sheets

Paper clamp

Paper-release lever

Foam-rubber pad

ABRASIVES FOR POWER SANDING

A piece of wood is gradually reduced to a smooth surface ready for finishing by working through ever finer grades of abrasive grit resin-bonded either to paper or to fabric backing sheets. Aluminium oxide is widely used in the manufacture of sheets, belts and discs for power sanders. Silicon carbide, the hardest and most expensive woodworking abrasive, is another excellent material for sanding hardwoods, MDF and chipboard. Silicon carbide is also used extensively as an abrasive for rubbing down surface finishes such as paint or varnish.

Abrasive grades
Coarse grades are suitable for sanding sawn softwood and for other rough work. Medium to fine grades produce a good finish ready for a light hand sanding. On thin veneers, use very fine grades only.

On 'closed-coat' paper, for fast general-purpose sanding, the abrasive grit is packed closely together. 'Open-coat' papers have widely spaced grit for sanding resinous softwoods, which would clog other papers very quickly.

Perforated sheets
Some sanding sheets are ready-perforated to increase the efficiency of dust extraction. Alternatively, you can buy templates for punching holes in standard sheets of abrasive paper.

Antistatic additives
Antistatic additives included during the manufacture of bonded abrasives retard clogging dramatically and increase the efficiency of extractors. You may not be able to obtain ready-cut antistatic sheets for power sanders, but you can cut your own from rolls of a suitable width.

Lubricants
Silicon carbide, in the form of traditional wet-and-dry paper, is lubricated with water to prevent the abrasive grains becoming clogged with particles of paint or varnish. Abrasives are also coated with dry lubricants or stearates to reduce premature clogging with wood dust and finishes.

TYPICAL ABRASIVE GRADES

Grit 40	Very coarse
Grit 50	Very coarse
Grit 60	Coarse
Grit 80	Coarse
Grit 100	Medium
Grit 120	Medium
Grit 150	Fine
Grit 180	Fine
Grit 240	Very fine
Grit 280	Very fine
Grit 320	Very fine
Grit 400	Very fine

USING FINISHING SANDERS

Once you get the hang of keeping the tool moving while it's in contact with the work, there is nothing difficult about operating finishing sanders.

Operating an orbital sander
Move the sander back and forth along the grain, covering the surface evenly with overlapping parallel strokes. Keep the tool moving the whole time it is in contact with the work, and don't press too hard. Excessive pressure merely serves to generate heat, which causes wood dust and resin to clog the abrasive.

Working overhead
Even though it makes sense to choose the largest available machine when sanding sizeable workpieces, you will find a lightweight palm-grip sander convenient for applications where a heavier tool would be cumbersome.

SAFETY AND SANDING
Provided you follow the basic safety procedures recommended for power tools, finishing sanders are safe to operate.

- Wear safety goggles and a lightweight face mask when sanding overhead.
- Always unplug a sander before changing the paper.

DISC SANDERS

With the exception of bench-mounted machines, cabinet-makers seldom have use for disc sanders, which can cause deep cross-grain scratches in the wood. However, miniature disc sanders are ideal for intricate woodwork such as carving and model-making – and they are especially suited to woodturners, who employ the combined actions of disc and lathe to advantage when sanding bowls and platters. The soft-foam backing pads of a miniature disc sander are able to conform to the changing contours of a wooden bowl, ensuring even distribution of pressure without generating too much heat. Also, with the disc and workpiece rotating simultaneously, tool marks can be removed rapidly without scratching the wood.

Flexible-shaft sanders
Arbor-mounted foam pads, from 25 to 75mm (1 to 3in) in diameter, are made for use with a portable power drill or, better still, for flexible-shaft sanders, which are highly manoeuvrable. Velour-lined or self-adhesive abrasive discs, with cloth or paper backing, come ready-made to fit every size of foam pad.

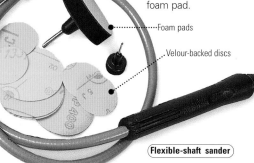

Foam pads

Velour-backed discs

Flexible-shaft sander

CHAPTER FIVE

MACHINE TOOLS

Not every woodworker has the space or budget to set up a fully equipped machine shop, but even one or two well-chosen machines make light work of ripping, crosscutting, and planing heavy baulks of timber to size. Most woodworking machines are designed to make the production of identical components easy and precise, and the quality of finish is so fine that they provide an incentive to attempt projects that would be daunting by hand.

Because virtually all woodworking machines are potentially hazardous, it is essential to follow safety procedures to the letter and to fit some form of dust extraction in your workshop. Also, never allow your concentration to lapse, nor be tempted to push a machine beyond safe limits.

TABLE SAWS

In its basic form, a table saw comprises a rotary saw blade protruding through the centre of a flat worktable. Fitted with fences and guides, it is primarily used to cut solid timber and man-made boards to size. Despite its seemingly limited function, a table saw is likely to become the centre of machine-shop activity, since workpieces are returned to the saw again and again as they are squared, shaped, grooved and mitred.

Riving knife

When timber is seasoned unevenly, it can become 'case-hardened' as a result of the moisture content varying throughout its thickness. As soon as case-hardened timber is cut it begins to move, due to the release of stresses created within it. If this movement causes partially sawn timber to close up and pinch a revolving saw blade, the workpiece will be thrown back towards the operator with considerable velocity. For this reason, a curved metal blade known as a riving knife is bolted directly behind the saw blade, to keep the kerf open. The riving knife is adjustable to suit blades of different diameters. When set correctly, it should be approximately 3mm (1/8in) from the saw teeth at its lowest point; no more than 8 or 9mm (3/8in) from the teeth at its tip; and a maximum of 2 to 3mm (1/8in) below the highest point of the saw blade.

Saw-blade diameter

Table saws for the home workshop are made with blades ranging from 140 to 300mm (5½in to 1ft) in diameter. The maximum depth of cut – which is determined by how much of the blade can protrude above the table – is only about one-third of the blade's diameter. For serious woodworking, consider buying a saw with a 250mm (10in) or preferably a 300mm (1ft) blade.

The blade is usually raised or lowered by means of a handwheel or crank handle. For the cleanest cut and to prolong the life of the blade, adjust its height so that the teeth are about 6 to 9mm (1/4 to 3/8in) above the surface of the work.

Saw-blade angle

By operating another handwheel or crank, the blade can be tilted to any angle from vertical to 45 degrees to the table. Having adjusted the blade, before switching on always check the position of the guard and fences, to make sure they won't retard its movement. Also, read the manufacturer's instructions to see whether you should remove the table insert or lower the blade before adjustment. Saws have a graduated scale that indicates the angle of the blade.

Table insert

A small section of the table immediately surrounding the blade is usually removable, so you can change blades.

Blade guard

A sturdy metal or plastic guard is suspended directly over the blade to prevent the operator touching it accidentally, and also to restrain the workpiece if it is lifted from the table by the motion of the saw. The guard is either bolted onto the riving knife or suspended from an adjustable arm. Adjust the guard as close to the work as is practicable.

MACHINE-SHOP SAFETY

It is important to maintain a safe working environment in any workshop, but safety is paramount in a shop where woodworking machinery is being operated. Periodically tidy up your machine shop to prevent offcuts cluttering the workspace.

• Don't store materials or equipment above a machine in such a way that they could fall onto it.
• Keep the area around every machine clean and free from clutter. Cutting plastic-coated boards leaves especially slippery dust on the floor.
• Fit dust extraction or wear a face mask.
• Before switching on, check that spanners and adjusting keys have been removed.
• Periodically check that all nuts, bolts and other fixings are tightened properly.
• Check your machine settings and run through the procedure in your mind before you switch on.
• When you have finished working, disconnect machines and lock your workshop. Keep unsupervised children well away from all machinery, even when it is not in use.

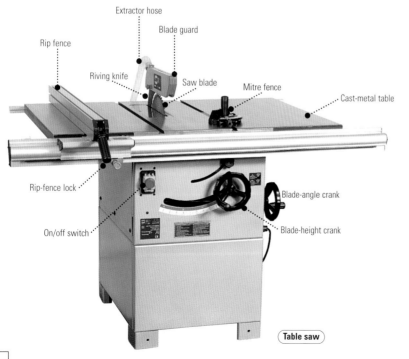

Rip fence
Extractor hose
Blade guard
Riving knife
Saw blade
Mitre fence
Cast-metal table
Rip-fence lock
Blade-angle crank
On/off switch
Blade-height crank

(Table saw)

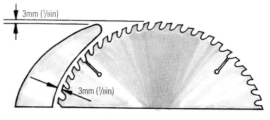

3mm (1/8in)

3mm (1/8in)

Recommended riving-knife settings

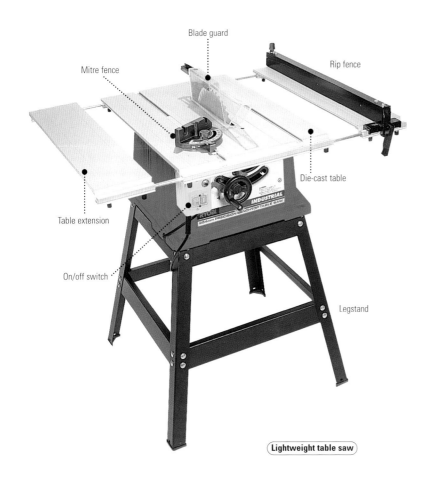

Blade guard

Mitre fence

Rip fence

Die-cast table

Table extension

On/off switch

Legstand

Lightweight table saw

Mitre fence
An adjustable mitre fence slides in a slot machined in the table, on a path that's parallel to the blade. It is used when crosscutting timber from 90 to 45 degrees. The fence must run smoothly without being slack, and it should be marked with a clear scale to indicate its angle.

Sliding table
A standard mitre fence is adequate for relatively small-scale work, but it is difficult to crosscut a wide board unless the table has an adjustable fence attached to a section that slides parallel to the blade. Sliding crosscut tables are sometimes supplied as accessories to saws made for the home workshop.

On/off switches
Choose a saw with easily accessible on/off switches that will be close at hand when you are working on the saw. All new machines come with a no-volt release switch, which will automatically stop the machine from operating if the power is suddenly cut. The switch must be manually reset when the power is restored.

Worktable
The main requisite of any saw table is that it should be rigid and flat. Consequently, the best saws are made with cast-metal or ground fabricated-steel tables. A cheaper folded-metal table is acceptable provided it is rigidly braced. Choose a saw with a generous-size table, or one that is equipped with extension pieces to support man-made boards.

Electric motor
Being stationary machines, table saws are equipped with relatively large electric motors that are more than capable of driving a blade fast enough to leave a clean-cut edge on the work. However, the larger table-saw motors are less likely to be strained by cutting thick, dense hardwood. A 1.5kW motor is adequate for a machine fitted with a 250 to 300mm (10 to 12in) blade.

Rip fence
To guide it on a straight path, a workpiece is run against a rip fence as it is sawn from end to end. It is essential that the fence is sturdy and inflexible. Some fences are secured at both the front and the back of the saw table, but this is not essential provided the fence is constructed with a well-designed single mounting. The fence should be capable of very fine adjustment from side to side, with a clear graduated scale. Fore and aft adjustment is a useful feature found on a few of the table saws designed for the home workshop.

The rip capacity — the distance between the fence and the blade – varies considerably from saw to saw. Ideally, choose a saw capable of halving a full-size man-made board (many perfectly good saws have a smaller capacity).

Finely adjustable rip fence

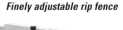

Chisel-like teeth

Deep gullet

Ripsaw blade

Crosscut blade

•Cleaning a saw blade
Clean wood resin from a saw
blade with a rag soaked in
cellulose thinner or white spirit.
Alternatively, you can use a
proprietary resin-removing spray.

Universal blade

Carbide tip

Carbide-tipped blade

Slot prevents distortion

TABLE-SAW BLADES

Special-purpose ripsaw or crosscut blades are used when a table saw is set up to perform a particular function for a period of time. A universal or combination-tooth blade is a better choice for the average home workshop, since the chore of repeatedly changing the blade would soon become tedious. Despite its additional cost, a carbide-tipped universal blade is an even better choice. It rips and crosscuts solid timber, leaving a superb finish, and is ideal for cutting chipboard and plywood, which quickly blunt ordinary steel blades. Always follow the saw manufacturer's instructions for changing blades.

Ripsaw blade
A ripsaw blade has large alternately set chisel-like teeth, with deep gullets between them for clearing large amounts of waste. It is designed to cut with the grain only.

Crosscut blade
Crosscut teeth are much smaller than those on a rip-saw blade and are shaped to saw across the grain without tearing it out. Hollow-ground blades, which are reduced in thickness towards the centre, are made to produce a top-quality finish and are sometimes known as 'planer blades'.

Universal blade
Universal blades, which are made to cut both with and across the grain, have groups of crosscut teeth separated by a rip tooth and a deep gullet. They do not perform quite as well as special-purpose blades.

Carbide-tipped blade
This blade has no 'set', in the conventional sense. Instead, a wide tip of tungsten carbide is brazed to each tooth to provide the necessary clearance in the kerf or sawcut. Carbide-tipped blades are often slotted to prevent distortion as the blade expands through heating. To reduce whistling, caused by the blade moving through the air at speed, the hole at the root of each slot is plugged with soft metal.

Sharpening table-saw blades
When a blade becomes blunt, you will smell burning and find that it is more difficult to feed the work. A blunt blade is also more likely to jam and throw the work back towards the operator. Take a blunt blade to a specialist for sharpening or for the replacement of a damaged carbide tip.

Overhead blade guards
Every table saw is supplied with a blade guard, often bolted to the riving knife. However, to perform certain functions, it is necessary to remove the riving knife – which means having to provide a safe alternative to a knife-mounted guard. One solution is a counter-weighted guard suspended  from an adjustable floor-standing mast with a boom that also carries a dust-extracting hose to the guard. For clarity, the blade guard has been omitted from some illustrations in this chapter, but this does not imply that it's safe to operate a saw without an adequate guard.

Ripsawing is used to reduce solid timber to width by cutting more or less parallel to the grain. The work is always run against the rip fence and never cut freehand, in order to avoid the risk of twisting the workpiece and jamming the blade in the kerf. Man-made boards are ripped in a similar way. The riving knife and blade guard must be in position when ripsawing.

Adjusting the rip fence

A rip fence that extends in one piece across the saw table is ideal for cutting stable man-made boards. However, when sawing solid timber there is always a chance that this type of fence will cause an accident. Stresses locked in the timber can make the kerf spring open until pressure against the rip fence forces the workpiece against the side of the blade, causing it to jam and throw the workpiece.

If the fence is capable of fore-and-aft adjustment, it should be withdrawn until its far end is about 25mm (1in) behind the leading edge of the exposed part of the blade (**1**), providing clearance to the right of the blade. Alternatively, clamp or screw a block of timber to a one-piece fence (**2**) to provide similar clearance. Whatever type of fence is fitted, it must be set parallel to the blade.

Using the graduated scale as a guide, adjust the fence to the required width of cut, then make a test cut in the end of a piece of scrap timber to check the setting. If you cannot trust the scale, use a rule to measure from the fence to one of the saw teeth set towards the fence. Before you switch on, check that the fence is securely clamped.

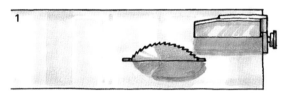

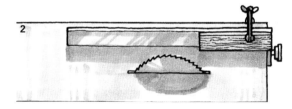

Ripping a wide board

Use both hands to rip a wide board – applying pressure with one hand directly behind the work but out of line with the blade, while holding the work against the fence and down onto the table with the other. Feed the work at a steady rate, and do not attempt to retrieve the offcut until the blade has stopped moving.

When ripping a very wide board, have an assistant help you support the board – making it clear that you will guide the workpiece and control the feed rate.

Ripping a narrow board

As you approach the end of a ripcut in a narrow board, feed the work with a push stick – a strip of hardwood notched at one end, with a rounded handgrip at the other – and use a second push stick to apply pressure against the rip fence.

Proprietary plastic push sticks are available from tool stockists. Store your push sticks near the table, so they are always to hand when needed.

Bevel ripping

To rip a bevel along a workpiece, before you switch the saw on, tilt the blade to the required angle and check that the blade is not touching the guard or rip fence. Feed the work as for a normal ripcut.

Cutting a tapered workpiece

To saw a tapered workpiece, cut a notch in the side of a plywood or chipboard jig to hold the wood at the required angle to the blade. Keep the jig pressed against the rip fence while feeding it in the normal way.

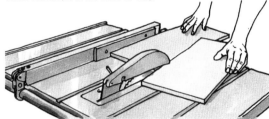

Ripping a waney-edge board

It is impossible to run a waney edge against the rip fence with any certainty of achieving a straight ripcut. Pin a sheet of thin plywood to the underside of the workpiece so that it projects slightly beyond the waney edge and acts as a guide.

CROSSCUTTING WITH A TABLE SAW

When cutting workpieces to length on a table saw, use the mitre fence or a sliding crosscut table to guide the wood past the blade. A sharp blade will produce such a clean cut that the end grain may need no further finishing. Keep the blade guard and riving knife in position, even though the knife is not essential for crosscutting.

Crosscutting with a mitre fence

Although the adjustable mitre fence on the average table saw is relatively short, it is often drilled so that you can

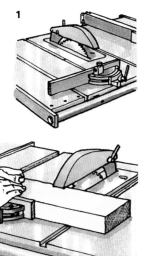

screw a longer hardwood fence to its face (**1**). Once the wooden fence is crosscut on the table saw, it also acts as a backup to the work – to prevent the grain splitting out at the back as the workpiece is fed past the blade. Alternatively, as a temporary backup, sandwich a piece of scrap timber between the factory-made mitre fence and the workpiece.

Hold the work firmly against the fence with both hands (**2**), and feed it relatively slowly into the blade. If the workpiece is too short to be held securely with both hands, clamp it to the fence.

Crosscutting on a sliding table

The friction between a large board or long workpiece and the saw table can make crosscutting with a mitre fence a laborious procedure. A smooth-running, sliding crosscutting action makes for easy and accurate work, regardless of the size or weight of the workpiece. A sliding table is fitted with a longer-than-average crosscut fence that is adjustable to any angle between 90 and 45 degrees to the blade. Most fences are made with an adjustable end stop for use when making identical workpieces.

Cutting a mitre

To cut a mitre on a table saw, adjust the mitre fence to the required angle, then feed the workpiece past the blade in the normal way (**1**). Take care to hold the work firmly against the fence, to prevent it being drawn backwards by the blade.

To cut a compound mitre (one angled in two planes), adjust the mitre fence then tilt the saw blade (**2**). To cut a mitre across the end of a board, tilt the blade to 45 degrees and set the mitre fence at 90 degrees to the blade (**3**).

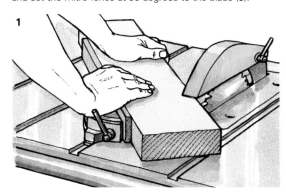

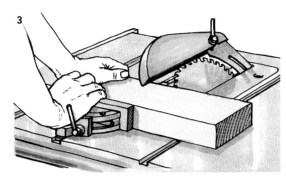

MAKING MULTIPLE CROSSCUTS

Many woodworking projects entail making several identical components. Rather than trying to crosscut individually marked workpieces one at a time, set up one or two stops to locate the wood accurately in relation to the blade, so you can make repetitive cuts quickly and accurately.

Making identical offcuts

It is tempting to butt the end of the work against the rip fence to ensure that offcuts to the right of the blade are of equal length. However, an offcut caught between the fence and the revolving blade can be thrown back into the face of the operator. The correct method is either to withdraw the rip fence clear of the blade or to clamp a spacer block to the fence to act as an end stop for the work, leaving a clearance to the right of the blade (**1**).

To make the cut, slide the work sideways until it butts against the block and feed the wood into the blade – then repeat the process to make identical offcuts.

Making identical workpieces

Using the mitre fence, cut each piece of wood square. Clamp a block of wood to the extended mitre fence to act as a stop for the squared end of each workpiece (**2**), then feed the workpieces past the blade to cut them to length.

CUTTING REBATES AND GROOVES WITH A TABLE SAW

When cutting a groove or rebate, on certain table saws it is necessary to remove the combined riving knife and blade guard. Some table saws can be fitted with special vertical/horizontal hold-down guards, which surround the work in the vicinity of the blade. If this is not possible with your saw, suspend a proprietary dust-extracting guard over the blade when performing such operations.

Fit a hold-down guard when grooving or rebating

Cutting a rebate

Two straightforward ripcuts produce a rebate on a workpiece. Make the first cut in the narrower face of the workpiece (**1**), leaving sufficient wood on each side of the kerf to provide adequate support. Reset the rip fence and blade height, then make the second cut to detach the waste from the workpiece (**2**). Make this second cut with the waste facing away from the fence – since a waste strip trapped between the blade and fence could be thrown back as the last few wood fibres are severed. Stand to one side when feeding work into the blade.

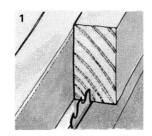

Cutting a groove

To cut a groove that is wider than the kerf cut by the saw blade, make one sawcut to the required depth on each side of the groove (**3**), then adjust the rip fence sideways one kerf-width at a time to remove the waste between (**4**).

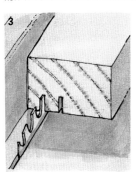

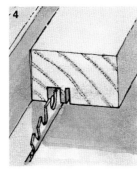

Cutting a tongue and groove

Leave a centrally placed tongue on the edge of one workpiece by cutting two identical rebates. Make the first cut in the narrower face, then turn the wood end for end to cut the other side of the tongue (**5**). Remove the waste from both sides (**6**). To saw a matching groove in another workpiece, adjust the fence to cut one side, then turn the work end for end to make the second cut before removing the waste (see below left).

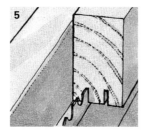

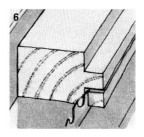

Kerfing with a table saw

Almost severing a strip of wood with regularly spaced sawcuts provides sufficient local flexibility to make a tight bend in a thick workpiece of solid timber. The exact kerf spacing is a matter of experimentation – but as a rough guide, the closer the spacing the tighter the bend. Adjust the height of the blade to leave an intact strip of wood between 2 and 6mm ($\frac{1}{16}$ and $\frac{1}{4}$in) thick, depending on the flexibility of the wood. When performing this operation, fit an overhead blade guard (for clarity, omitted from the illustrations here).

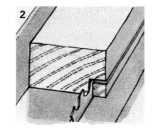

Bend solid timber by kerfing

Accurate spacing is essential if the resulting curve is to be smooth and regular. Screw a temporary wooden fence to the saw's mitre fence. Make one cut through the wooden fence, then drive a nail into it to mark the kerf spacing and cut off the head of the nail (**1**).

Having cut one kerf in the work, slot the first kerf onto the nail and cut your second kerf. Slot that kerf over the nail and make your third cut, and so on (**2**).

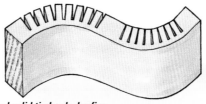

FIT A BLADE GUARD

For clarity, the blade guard has been omitted from some illustrations on this page – but this does not imply that it's safe to operate a table saw without an adequate blade guard.

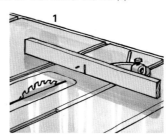

RADIAL-ARM SAWS

The radial-arm saw is first and foremost a crosscut saw for making square, bevelled and mitred cuts. It also makes a passable ripsaw. The blade-and-motor housing on a standard-pattern radial-arm saw is suspended below a metal arm mounted on top of a rigid column. The arm swings from side to side to present the blade at an angle to the work for cutting mitres. In addition, the motor housing and blade can be tilted and pivoted to make compound-angle cuts. On one model, the arm is fixed while the table pivots below it. As the column is mounted to the rear of the worktable, a radial-arm saw can be installed against a wall. Most radial-arm saws stand on a bench or their own legstands, and some can be folded away and hung from wall brackets.

Electric motor
The average radial-arm saw for the home workshop is fitted with an electric induction motor rated at about 1.1kW. This is powerful enough to generate adequate saw-blade speeds of nearly 3000rpm.

Saw-blade diameter
The saws manufactured for the home workshop are usually supplied with 250mm (10in) blades.

Depth of cut
Most radial-arm saws have a possible maximum depth of cut of about 75mm (3in). The blade, along with the machine's arm, is raised or lowered by operating a crank situated either on top of the column or beneath the worktable.

Arm angle
The arm can be rotated left or right, after releasing the mitre clamping lever. A latch positively locates the arm for crosscutting at 90 or 45 degrees. A scale on top of the column indicates the angle of the arm.

Saw-blade angle
Having released the bevel clamping lever, you can tilt the saw blade to any angle between vertical and horizontal. A locating pin engages automatically when the blade is at 90 or 45 degrees. Choose a machine with a scale that indicates the angle of the blade clearly.

Crosscut capacity
The maximum crosscutting width is determined mainly by the length of the arm. The crosscut capacity of home-workshop saws varies from 310 to 465mm (1ft to 1ft 6in). To make cuts up to 600mm (2ft) wide, you need to buy one of the smaller industrial radial-arm saws.

Rip capacity
The width of ripcut – up to a maximum of between 500 and 650mm (1ft 8in and 2ft 2in) – is selected by sliding the motor housing along the arm and locking it in position with a clamping lever or knob. Scales printed along the arm indicate ripcut width.

Blade guard
The blade on a radial-arm saw is enclosed by a 'gravity guard', which is raised automatically by the work during ripping and crosscutting operations. The guard drops back under its own weight at the completion of either process.

Riving knife
When ripping, to prevent case-hardened timber closing on the blade, lower the riving knife into position just behind the blade and secure it with the lock nut. When crosscutting, the knife is pushed back inside the blade guard.

Depth crank
Mitre clamping lever
Mitre latch
Sawdust-exhaust port
Column
Anti-kickback assembly
Fence
Mitre scale
Electrical flex
Radial arm
Blade-pivot latch
Worktable
Blade guard
Legstand

(Radial-arm saw)

ANTI-KICKBACK ASSEMBLY

If a blade jams during a ripcut, it can throw the work back towards the operator. To prevent this happening, an anti-kickback assembly, which has trailing teeth or 'pawls', is mounted on the saw.

The slightest backward movement of the work causes the pointed pawls to pivot downwards to restrain the wood. The anti-kickback assembly also acts as a hold-down device to prevent the workpiece being lifted off the table by the ascending saw teeth.

For ripsawing, raise or lower the anti-kickback assembly until the points of the pawls hang 3mm (1/8in) below the surface of the wood. For crosscutting, raise the assembly clear of the work.

• Setting up the machine
Support a radial-arm saw on a bench at a comfortable working height, and allow enough clearance for your knuckles between the column and the wall when operating the depth-adjustment crank.

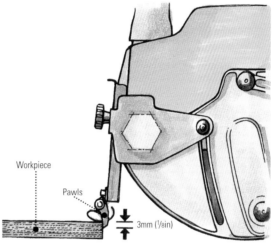

Workpiece

Pawls

3mm (1/8in)

Worktable
A simple worktable of high-density fibreboard or chipboard is fixed to the machine's metal base. Because the blade of a radial-arm saw must cut into the surface of the table, it is worth covering the surface with a thin sheet of plywood or MDF. Attach the MDF or plywood with strips of double-sided self-adhesive tape.

Fence
Workpieces are crosscut against a fence running across the worktable. The same fence is used to guide the work during ripsawing operations.

For crosscutting, the fence is sandwiched between the worktable and a spacer board – the blade being parked behind the fence between cuts. To increase rip capacity, the fence can be placed behind the spacer board.

The fence that comes with the machine is usually made from the same fibrous material as the worktable. However, you can replace it with one made from solid timber – in which case, it's convenient to make it longer than the original fence.

On/off switches
The on/off switches are usually placed either at the end of the radial arm or on the main control handle, where they are within easy reach. Some saws are supplied with removable keys, so they can be rendered inoperable.

Dust extraction
Radial-arm saws create a great deal of dust, which is ejected through a rubber exhaust port on the blade guard. Some form of extraction is required in order to make sure the area surrounding the saw does not become slippery with loose sawdust.

USING A RADIAL-ARM SAW SAFELY
Always follow the general safety recommendations for working in a machine shop and take extra care when operating a radial-arm saw.

• Install the saw sloping backwards very slightly, so the blade and motor housing cannot slide towards the operator under their own weight.
• When crosscutting, make sure the hand holding the work is not in line with the blade.
• Always park the blade and motor housing behind the fence between crosscuts.
• Never rip without using the anti-kickback assembly and riving knife.
• Keep anti-kickback pawls sharp. Take care when ripping plastic-laminated board, since it may not provide sufficient grip for the pawls.
• Do not perform an operation freehand. Always use the fence or some other device that will hold the workpiece still and stop it rotating or twisting.
• Plan a ripcut so that the offcut is free to move sideways away from the blade.
• Do not stand directly in line with the blade when ripping workpieces.
• Have an assistant help you to support a long board.
• Don't rip short pieces of wood that will bring your hands close to the blade. Use a notched push stick to feed narrow workpieces.
• Keep the saw's blade guard in place and in good working order.

SAW BLADES

Blades similar to those used on a table saw are available for radial-arm saws. A general-purpose or universal blade, especially one with tungsten-carbide-tipped teeth, is a good choice for a home workshop. However, there are other, more specialized, blades suitable for a radial-arm saw.

General-purpose anti-kickback blades

Whether crosscutting or ripsawing, these blades leave a good finish on the wood. The small metal 'horn' behind each saw tooth not only reduces kickback when wood is fed too slowly into the blade, but also minimizes the tendency for the blade to 'climb' onto a workpiece being crosscut on a radial-arm saw.

Laminated-panel blades

Having negative-rake (backward-leaning) teeth, these blades cut double-sided laminated panels without chipping the melamine surface. Though relatively expensive, they may be cost-effective if you are planning to make a complete fitted kitchen from laminated boards. The negative-rake teeth also have the advantage of reducing blade climb when crosscutting workpieces.

Metal-cutting blades

Intended primarily for sawing non-ferrous metals, these blades are a slightly cheaper option for cutting melamine-faced boards cleanly.

Tungsten-carbide-tipped saw blade
New radial-arm saws are usually supplied with a general-purpose TCP blade.

Storing saw blades
It is worth investing in purpose-made plastic boxes to protect your circular-saw blades from accidental damage.

• *Changing blades and cutters*
Always follow the saw manufacturer's instructions when fitting blades on your radial-arm saw.

Anti-kickback blade

Laminated-panel blade

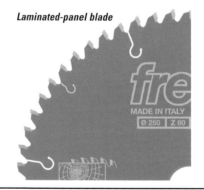

Metal-cutting blade

Dado head

A dado head fitted to the normal saw arbor provides a means of cutting grooves and housings up to 21mm ($^7/_8$in) wide in one pass. A dado head comprises two universal blades, which cut both sides of a groove or housing simultaneously, and a pair of 'chipper' blades sandwiched between them to remove the waste. Paper washers are inserted between the blades to make minute adjustments to the width of cut. Don't fit a dado head to a radial-arm saw that has an electronic braking system, which slows blade rotation after switching off. The braking action can loosen the blades.

Chipper blades are sandwiched between dado saw blades

In order to sever a workpiece completely, the saw blade must cut into the plywood table lining to a depth of about 1mm (1/16in). This scored line passes across the table and through the fence. The notch cut in the fence makes an ideal guide when you need to align the blade with a cut line marked on a workpiece. Both the anti-kickback assembly and riving knife must be withdrawn while crosscutting.

Making a square crosscut

With one hand, hold the work face side uppermost, against the fence, positioning the workpiece so that the blade will cut on the waste side of the marked line. Make sure all clamping levers are tight, except for the one that allows the blade and motor housing to travel along the arm. Switch on and steadily pull the saw towards you to just sever the work (**1**), then push it back and switch off.

Crosscutting is a relatively safe procedure, because the action of the blade tends to hold the work against the fence and down onto the table. However, the blade also has a tendency to 'climb' – pull itself towards the operator – when crosscutting. This tendency must be resisted by keeping your forearm in a straight line with the control handle of the saw.

1

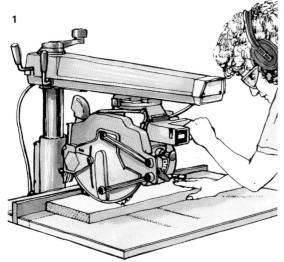

Cutting a wide or thick board

Provided it's not important to preserve a face side, use an end stop when you want to cut a board that is wider than the saw's crosscut capacity or thicker than its maximum depth of cut. Cut just over halfway through the work (**3**), then turn it over, press it against the end stop and sever the wood with a second cut.

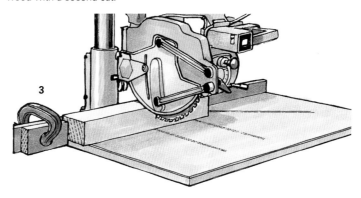

3

Making a bevelled crosscut

To make a bevelled crosscut, first tilt the blade and clamp it at the required angle, then proceed the same way as for a square crosscut (**4**).

4

Making repetitive crosscuts

Aligning the marked lines with a notch in the fence may not be sufficiently accurate when you need to cut a number of identical workpieces to length. Instead, clamp a block of wood to the fence (**2**) to act as an end stop for the workpieces – but never position the end stop so that it restricts the lateral movement of an offcut once it has been severed. Also, always make sure that sawdust does not become trapped between a workpiece and the fence or end stop.

Cutting a mitre

To cut a mitre on the end of a workpiece, swing the arm to the required angle (usually 45 degrees), keeping the blade vertical, then clamp the arm in place. Holding the work firmly against the fence to make sure it cannot move during the operation, cut the mitre by pulling the saw towards the front of the table (**5**).

2

5

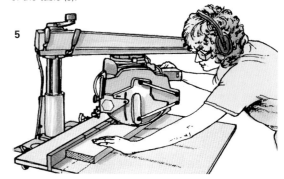

RIPPING WITH A RADIAL-ARM SAW

Radial-arm saws are not ideal for cutting timber to width – it's usually preferable to use a table saw or even a portable circular saw. If you need to perform the operation on a radial-arm saw, turn the blade parallel to the fence. For relatively narrow workpieces, the blade faces the saw's column in what is called the 'inrip' position. To rip wider boards, the blade is turned to the 'outrip' position, facing away from the column.

Feeding the work

A workpiece must be fed into the saw blade against its direction of rotation (**1**). To feed the work in the opposite direction would result in the blade snatching the work, perhaps pulling the operator's hands towards it.

When inripping, the work is fed from one side of the table (usually the right-hand side, but check the manufacturer's instructions). When outripping, the work is fed from the other side since the blade is facing in the opposite direction.

Both the riving knife and the anti-kickback assembly must be deployed whenever you are ripping timber.

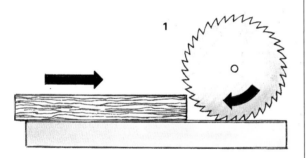

Adjusting the blade

Slide the blade along the arm until the required width of cut is indicated on one of the rip scales. To make sure the setting has not been affected by tightening the clamping lever, make a test cut in the end of a piece of scrap timber. You can increase the rip capacity by placing the fence behind the table's spacer board. To sever a workpiece completely, the blade must be lowered until it cuts into the table lining to a depth of about 1mm ($^1/_{16}$in).

Ripping a workpiece to width

Make sure all clamping levers are tight, then switch on. Keeping the work pressed against the fence, use both hands to feed the work into the blade at a steady rate. Use a notched push stick to feed a narrow workpiece that would bring your hands close to the blade.

Bevel ripping

To cut a bevel along one edge of a workpiece, proceed as for a square ripcut but tilt the blade to the required angle. Follow the saw manufacturer's instructions for setting the anti-kickback pawls for a tilted blade.

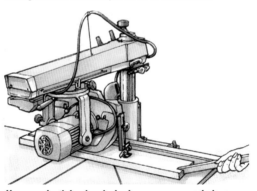

Use a push stick when inripping a narrow workpiece

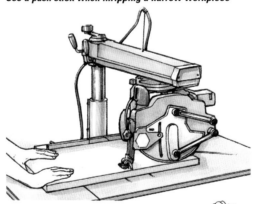

Turn the blade away from the column to outrip a wide board

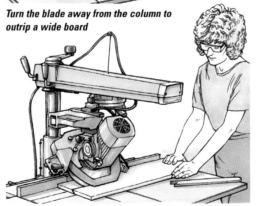

Tilt the blade to cut a bevel

CUTTING HOUSINGS, GROOVES AND REBATES

It is possible to cut a groove or rebate parallel with the grain or a housing across a workpiece by using the standard saw blade to cut along both sides, then resetting the saw to remove the waste one blade-width at a time. However, it is much less laborious to cut grooves, housings and rebates with a dado head. Never fit a dado head to a saw that has an electronic blade-braking system.

Cutting a housing

Using a dado head, cut a housing as if you were making a crosscut or mitre. Being considerably wider than a single saw blade, a dado head may exaggerate the machine's tendency to pull itself towards the operator – so be prepared to resist it. To repeat a housing on more than one workpiece, clamp an end stop to the fence (**1**).

Cutting a groove

Fit a dado-head combination to make up the required width of cut. Remove the riving knife, but keep both the blade guard and anti-kickback assembly in place. Select the inrip or outrip position for the dado head, as appropriate, then proceed as if making a ripcut (**2**).

Cutting a rebate

To cut a rebate along the edge of a workpiece, use the dado head as if you were cutting a groove.

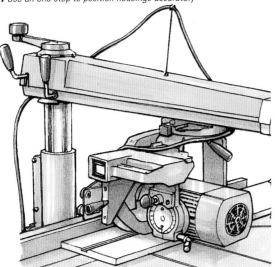

1 *Use an end stop to position housings accurately*

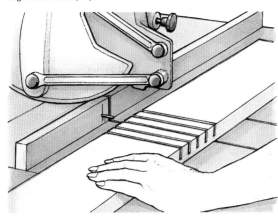

2 *A dado head cuts a wide groove with one pass*

KERFING

Bending a length of solid timber by kerfing is an easy procedure on a radial-arm saw set up for crosscutting.

You can make a simple jig for accurate kerf spacing by driving a nail into the fence and snipping its head off. Having made one kerf, shift the work sideways, then slide the kerf onto the nail and cut the next kerf. Alternatively, instead of using a nail, you can make a pencil mark on the fence and align each cut by eye.

CUTTING JOINTS WITH A RADIAL SAW

Certain simple joints can be cut quickly and accurately on a radial-arm saw. Fit a universal blade, or save time by using a dado head for halving joints, lap joints and tenons – but never fit a dado head to a saw that has an electronic blade-braking system.

Reinforced mitre joint
A plywood tongue is often used to reinforce a mitre joint. Having made two straightforward bevel crosscuts, adjust the blade depth, then turn the work end for end and cut a slot for the tongue in each bevel (**1**). Use an end stop to ensure the slot is identically placed in both halves of the joint.

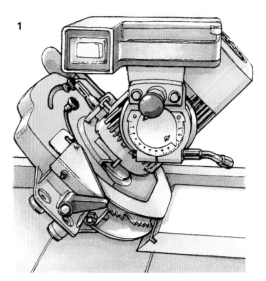

1

Halving joints
For a halving or cross halving joint, first adjust the blade to cut halfway through the work and make crosscuts on the shoulder lines. Slide the work sideways against the fence, making successive crosscuts to remove the waste little by little (**2**). Use an end stop to repeat shoulder-line cuts accurately. In the case of a cross halving joint, clamp end stops at both ends of the fence – one for each of the shoulders.

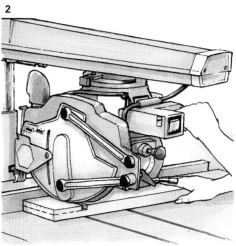

2

Lap joints
Square both halves of the joint with a straightforward crosscut, then adjust the blade height and cut the lap in the same manner as a halving joint.

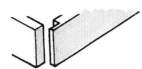

Cutting tenons
With the workpiece butted against an end stop, cut one side of a tenon as you would a lap joint. Then turn it over and cut the other side (**3**).

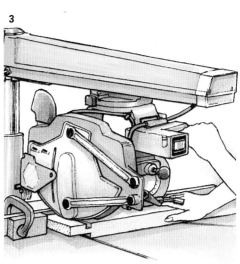

3

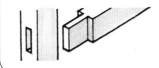

MITRE SAWS

Until recently, mitre saws or 'chop saws' were used almost exclusively by professional woodworkers and site contractors for cutting mitres and compound angles. Now that these saws are available at vastly reduced prices, they have become popular for the home workshop. Basically they consist of a circular saw on a round pivoting base that can be swivelled to make angled cuts up to 45 degrees. With medium-range models, you can also tilt the blade sideways to make bevelled cuts and compound mitres. At the top of the range, the saw body is attached to a sliding carriage that can be moved back and forth. This greatly increases the capacity of the saw, making it possible to cut relatively wide boards, even when making compound cuts.

Electric motor

Mitre saws vary in power from around 1000W to 1800W. Better-quality machines are fitted with soft-start induction motors so the blade does not 'kick' as the tool is switched on.

Fences

A two-part fence supports the work on either side of the blade. The fences on larger compound-mitre machines are adjustable so both halves can be slid out of the way for compound cuts. Fences sometimes have predrilled holes for adding temporary wooden extensions.

Blade guards

All mitre saws have a pivoting guard to cover the raised blade. A locking switch or lever on the handle must be operated before the saw can be lowered. The guard then pivots upward away from the cutting area.

Sliding bars

The cutting capacity of sliding mitre saws is much greater than that of fixed-head models. Some can cut boards 340mm (13$\frac{3}{8}$in) wide, although this is reduced by 100mm (4in) or more when cutting 45-degree mitres. The saw head moves on bearings along a single-bar or double-bar assembly. The sliding action should be smooth, with no side-to-side play in the bearings.

Dust control

Many mitre saws are fitted with dust bags, but these are often too small. A better option is to buy a model that can be connected to a vacuum cleaner or portable dust extractor.

Laser guides

Laser guides are now fitted to a number of woodworking tools, including jigsaws, circular saws and mitre saws. A small laser fixed to the saw assembly throws a narrow red beam onto the table, showing exactly where the blade will cut.

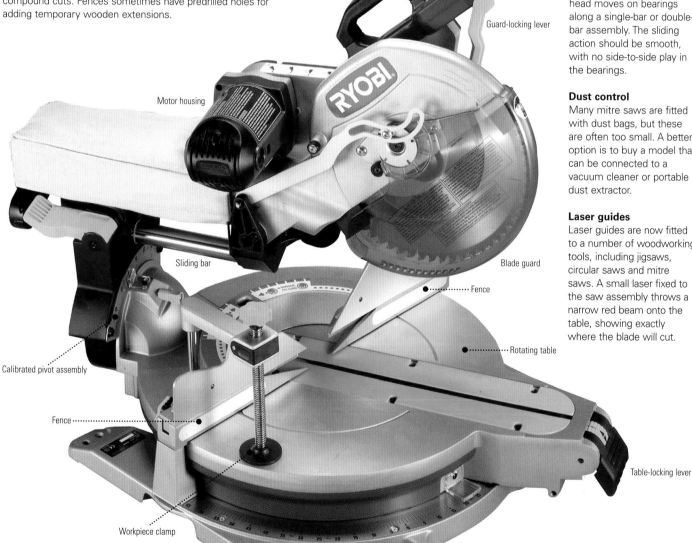

Control handle

Guard-locking lever

Motor housing

Sliding bar

Blade guard

Fence

Rotating table

Calibrated pivot assembly

Fence

Table-locking lever

Workpiece clamp

Sliding mitre saw

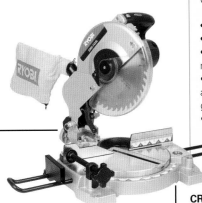

Base

The base of a mitre saw consists of a rotating central table surrounded by a fixed section that is graduated from zero degrees at the centre and up to 45 degrees to the left and right of centre. Most machines have indents or grooves indicating the most commonly used angles (15, 22.5, 30 and 45 degrees). The saw assembly should move smoothly and stop automatically at the required angle.

Saw bases are designed to be bolted securely to a bench or workstation. Some are fitted with sliding extensions that support a long workpiece on both sides of the blade. Most models come with clamps, fitted to the base or fence, which hold the workpiece securely and prevent it moving as the blade cuts into the wood.

Blades

The smaller basic mitre saws are fitted with 200mm (8in) diameter tungsten-carbide-tipped blades. Larger machines may be designed to take 250 or 305mm (10 or 12in) blades.

Teflon-coated high-finish saw blades leave an extremely clean finish on mouldings. Similar blades are essential for mitring picture-frame mouldings with fragile coatings, such as lacquer or gilding.

USING A MITRE SAW SAFELY

As well as following general machine-shop safety recommendations, take the following precautions when using a mitre saw.

- Mount the saw on a sturdy bench or workstation.
- Wear eye protectors.
- Disconnect the saw from the power supply when making adjustments.
- Before switching on, make sure all cramps and adjusters are tightened fully and that the blade guard is operating correctly.
- When holding a workpiece against the fence, keep your hand well away from the blade.
    - Make sure the blade is running at full speed before making a cut.

CROSSCUTTING WITH A MITRE SAW

All mitre saws cut workpieces accurately to length, leaving nicely finished end grain. With the machine secured to a bench or rigid purpose-made stand, lock the blade at 90 degrees to the fence.

Holding the workpiece firmly against the fence, align the cutting line with the saw blade. Release the guard-locking switch or lever and operate the power switch. Allow the blade to run up to speed, then pull down on the saw head to make the cut (**1**). Once the work is severed, lift the blade out of the kerf and then switch off.

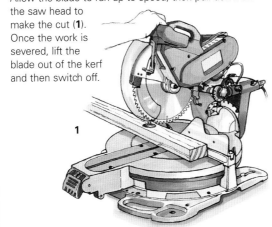

Making a sliding cut

This is possible only with a sliding head. Clamp the workpiece to the table, pull the saw head towards you, then release the guard lock and switch on. Lower the blade into the work and push forwards with slow even pressure (**2**). Don't make sliding cuts for small sections of timber.

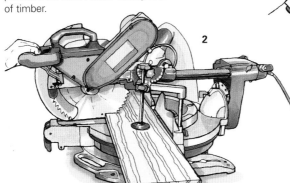

TRENCHING WITH A MITRE SAW

With some sliding mitre saws you can adjust the depth of cut in order to cut a trench (housing) across a workpiece – a feature that enables you to make accurate halving and housing joints.

Cutting a housing

Mark the housing on the workpiece, then adjust the saw's grooving control to the exact depth of cut and set the required cutting angle. Check that all the controls are tightened. Place a piece of scrap timber, about 50mm (2in) wide, between the workpiece and the back fence. Turn on the saw and make a sawcut on each side of the housing, just on the inside of the marked line. Using a paring chisel or router plane, remove the waste between the sawcuts.

CUTTING MITRES

An angled blade can cause the workpiece to creep sideways as it starts to cut – so, when possible, clamp workpieces that are to be mitred.

To cut a basic mitre, set up the saw as for crosscutting but release the locking mechanism that allows you to swivel the blade to 45 degrees (**3**). Tighten the mechanism before making the cut.

Cutting compound mitres

On some saws the blade can swivel and tilt to make compound-angle mitre joints. A calibrated pivot assembly at the back of the saw indicates the angle of tilt. On most models the blade tilts in one direction only (usually to the left) – though double-bevel saws can be tilted to either side of vertical, which is more convenient.

To make a compound cut, set up the mitre angle as described above. If possible, increase the gap between the two halves of the fence. Check that the fence still provides adequate support for the workpiece, then clamp the fence securely.

Loosen the bevel control and set the required angle, then retighten. With the power off, lower the saw to make sure the blade will not foul the fence. Turn on the power and make the compound cut (**4**) as if you were sawing a standard mitre.

BAND SAWS

A band-saw blade is a continuous loop of metal driven over two or three large wheels. Because the thrust of the blade is always downwards onto the saw table, there is no danger of a kickback throwing the work towards the operator. For this reason, many woodworkers prefer the band saw to a radial-arm saw or table saw, even though it neither rips nor crosscuts quite as cleanly or as fast. The band saw has several other advantages. It can be used to cut curved components; it will cut thicker timber than the average circular saw will; the wastage of timber is minimal thanks to the very narrow kerf cut by the blade; and it also costs less than a good table saw. Band saws run relatively quietly – an advantage if your workshop is part of your house.

• Electric motor
Band saws for the non-professional market are made with 550 to 1000W electric motors – quite powerful enough to cope with the demands made on them in a home workshop.

Depth of cut

Many band saws are sold by virtue of the fact that they are capable of cutting thick workpieces. The average home-workshop band saw will cut wood up to 150mm (6in) thick, but the slightly more expensive models have a maximum capacity of 300mm (1ft). This facility makes a band saw the ideal machine for cutting large baulks of wood into planks, or even into veneers.

Width of cut

The band saw's throat – the distance from the blade to the vertical frame member – determines its maximum width of cut. Throat size on most home-workshop band saws is about 300 to 350mm (1ft to 1ft 2in). If you are likely to cut wider boards, choose one of the smaller industrial band saws.

Cutting speed

The cutting speed of a band saw is measured by the number of metres or feet a point on the blade will travel in one minute. Top speed varies considerably from saw to saw, ranging from 220m (720ft) to 1220m (4000ft) per minute. On some band saws, you can select slower speeds for cutting metals and hard plastics. Others are fitted with variable-speed control between limits. Manufacturers normally recommend the highest speeds for cutting wood, but be prepared to reduce speed if you sense the saw is straining when cutting very dense timber.

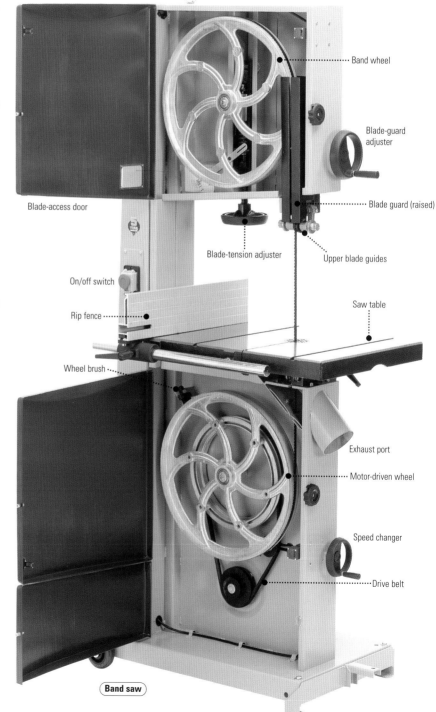

Band wheel

Blade-guard adjuster

Blade-access door

Blade guard (raised)

Blade-tension adjuster

Upper blade guides

On/off switch

Saw table

Rip fence

Wheel brush

Exhaust port

Motor-driven wheel

Speed changer

Drive belt

Band saw

Band wheels

All band saws have at least two wheels for the blade, one mounted directly above the other. The lower wheel is driven by the motor. A few saws have a third wheel – which has the effect of increasing throat width, since the blade travels to one side before returning to the upper wheel. Three-wheel saws put a greater strain on blades, causing them to break more often. Band wheels are fitted with rubber, cork or PVC tyres to preserve the set of the blades.

Accumulated dust can cause the blade to slip – so, if possible, choose a saw with a fixed brush mounted in such a way that it cleans sawdust from the drive-wheel tyre. Also look for band wheels mounted on sealed bearings – they never need lubricating.

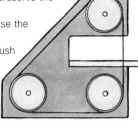

Three-wheel band saw

Blade guides

Bearings or guide blocks support the blade on both sides and from behind so as to resist the tendency for it to be twisted and pushed off the band wheels by the action of cutting a workpiece. One set of bearings, mounted above the saw table, is moved up or down to accommodate the thickness of the work; and a fixed set of bearings is usually mounted below the table. Blade guides must be capable of adjustment to very fine tolerances.

Blade tension and tracking

The blade's tension is adjusted by moving the top band wheel up or down. Some saws are made with a scale that indicates the tension for each blade, but usually the correct blade tension has to be ascertained by experimentation and experience. Some newer models have a cam-action tensioner that automatically resets the tension when you change a blade.

Tracking is usually adjustable to ensure that the blade runs centrally on the band wheels.

Blade guards

Except for the part exposed to the work, the entire band-saw blade is enclosed by the machine's casing. The exposed section is shielded by a vertically adjustable guard.

Saw frame

The best band saws are constructed with a rigid heavy-gauge-steel frame to resist the considerable tension applied to the blade. A saw cannot run true if the frame is flexible.

Saw table

The majority of saw tables are made from cast iron, ground fabricated steel or an aluminium alloy. They are machined perfectly flat or have grooves for faster sawdust clearance.

Every band-saw table tilts to 45 degrees for cutting mitres and bevels. A scale under the table indicates the angle of tilt. The average table is 400 to 450mm (1ft 4in to 1ft 6in) square.

Rip fence

Straight ripcuts are made against a short adjustable fence. Very deep or long workpieces may prove unstable when using the rip fence as supplied – in which case, extend the fence by screwing a higher wooden fence onto it. You will find it advantageous if the rip fence can be mounted on either side of the blade, particularly for bevel ripping – gravity helps to hold the work against the fence on the tilted table. Some saws are made with a depth stop mounted ahead of the rip fence, for cutting tenons and other joints to length.

Mitre fence

A mitre fence slides along a groove machined or cast in the saw table. By adjusting the angle of the fence, it is possible to make square or mitred crosscuts. Mitre fences are often too short, and should be extended with a wooden facing to support long workpieces.

On/off switches

No-volt on/off switches automatically stop the machine from operating if the power is suddenly cut. As an additional safety feature, these switches are sometimes made with a removable key. On some models opening the blade-access doors immobilizes the machine automatically, ensuring that the saw cannot be switched on accidentally when the blade and wheels are exposed.

Foot brake

Floor-standing band saws are sometimes fitted with a brake, to bring the blade to a stop after switching the machine off.

Dust extraction

A sawdust-exhaust port below the table can be attached to the hose of a portable extractor.

Bench-mounted band saw
The larger band saws stand on the workshop floor and have a one-piece frame. The smaller models are designed for mounting on a low bench – you can either buy a bench as an accessory or make your own.

USING A BAND SAW SAFELY

A band saw is a relatively safe woodworking machine provided you follow general safety recommendations and observe the following rules.

• Always adjust the blade guard and top guides as close as possible to the workpiece.

• Do not feed work with your thumbs directly in line with the blade. Use a push stick to feed narrow workpieces.

• To avoid pulling the moving blade off the band wheels, never back out of a deep cut without switching off first.

• Should a blade break or slip from the band wheels while you are using the saw, switch off immediately and stand back. Do not open the blade-access doors until the machine has come to a stop.

• Replace blunt or damaged blades before you find you are having to feed the work with excessive force.

• Wear tough work gloves when coiling or uncoiling band-saw blades.

BAND-SAW BLADES

When you buy a band saw, it will probably be fitted with one of the wider saw blades available for that particular machine. However, a variety of blades is made for every band saw – and even if you decide to continue using one or two blades only, it is worth knowing about the full range in case you want to undertake a task that your standard blades cannot cope with.

Saw-blade materials

Band-saw blades made from tough flexible steel have a hard, brittle cutting edge that stays sharp and keeps its set for long periods, even when sawing man-made boards. Hard-edged blades cannot be file-sharpened and are discarded as soon as they become blunt.

Although relatively soft, nickel-steel blades can be sharpened, reset and even rewelded when broken. However, the cost of professional repair and maintenance is such that the longer-lasting disposable blades are usually a better option.

Tooth size

In spite of metrication, saw-tooth size is specified by the number of teeth that fit into a 1in length of blade. For a given thickness, tough wood, chipboard and plywood require more teeth per inch (TPI) than resinous softwood. Also, bear in mind that small teeth tend to skid when cutting softwoods.

Generally, the best finish is achieved using a blade with relatively fine teeth, a high saw speed and a slow rate of feed. For faster cutting, fit a blade with larger teeth, then increase both the saw speed and feed rate.

Width of blade

Depending on what type of band saw you have, blades are available from 3 to 20mm ($1/8$ to $3/4$in) wide. Wide blades tend to hold a straight line better than narrow ones do, and are recommended for ripping timber and boards to width. When you want to cut curves in timber, select the optimum width of blade to suit the minimum radius – see chart below. To avoid having to change blades, most woodworkers fit a medium-width blade for general-purpose work.

Tooth set

Band-saw teeth are bent sideways to cut a kerf wider than the blade itself. This provides a clearance, which reduces friction in a straight cut and also permits the work to be steered on a curved path.

Standard set

The teeth are bent alternately to left and right, as on the blades of most woodcutting saws.

Raker set

Saw blades designed primarily for cutting curves are raker set, having pairs of standard-set teeth separated by a single unset tooth.

Wavy set

Groups of teeth set alternately to the left and right form a wavy cutting edge on this type of blade. It is the best sort of blade for cutting thin boards.

Special-purpose bands

Occasionally you may want to cut materials that require special-purpose bands, instead of the usual toothed blades. These bands are fitted the same way as conventional saw blades.

Knife-edge bands

To cut upholstery foams, fabrics and cork, fit a straight, scalloped or wavy-edge knife band.

Abrasive bands

These are narrow flexible bands covered with abrasive material for shaping and sanding straight and curved edges. An abrasive band is backed up by a rigid plate bolted in place of the blade guides.

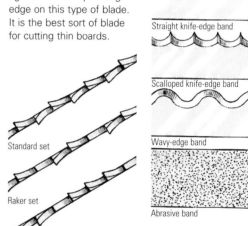

Straight knife-edge band

Scalloped knife-edge band

Wavy-edge band

Abrasive band

Standard set

Raker set

Wavy set

BLADE-WIDTH GUIDE
Select the width of blade that suits the minimum radius of a curved cut

Blade width						
mm	3	6	10	12	15	20
in	$1/8$	$1/4$	$3/8$	$1/2$	$5/8$	$3/4$
Minimum radius						
mm	8	25	38	62	100	136
in	$5/16$	1	$1^1/2$	$2^1/2$	4	$5^1/2$

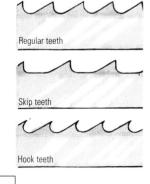

Regular teeth

Skip teeth

Hook teeth

Tooth shape

The shape of the saw tooth is designed either for faster cutting or a clean finish.

Regular tooth

This is the standard type of tooth for most band-saw blades. It will produce a fine, accurate finish on most woods and man-made boards.

Skip tooth

The shape of a skip tooth is similar to that of a regular tooth, but each one is separated by a wide gullet for better chip removal. The finish is relatively rough. Skip-tooth blades are particularly suitable for sawing deep workpieces.

Hook tooth

This kind of tooth has what is known as a 'positive rake' – i.e. the leading edge of each tooth leans at an acute angle. A hook tooth is able to cut hard material quickly.

CHANGING A BAND-SAW BLADE

Use the same procedure to replace blunt blades or simply to swap a blade for one of a different size or tooth configuration.

Replacing the blade

To change a blade, first remove the rip-fence guide rail and blade guard, then withdraw the blade guides. Lower the upper band wheel by turning the blade-tension adjuster, and lift the blade out of the machine.

Carefully place the new saw blade over the top wheel and feed it onto the lower one while turning the wheels slowly by hand. The blade teeth should be facing the operator and pointing downwards towards the saw table.

Tension the blade just enough to take up the slack, then check the tracking by spinning the band wheels by hand. Professional sawyers like to have the blade running close to the front edge of the wheels (**1**), but it is normally safer to position the blade centrally (**2**). However, check the manufacturer's recommendations for tracking adjustment. Adjust the tracking device until the blade runs true.

Raise the top wheel until the correct tension is indicated on the appropriate scale, or until the unsupported section of the blade can flex no more than about 6mm (¼in) to either side.

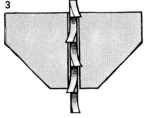

Setting the blade guides

Set both sets of blade guides in the same way. First, adjust the thrust bearing up to the back edge of the blade – leaving the minimum clearance, so contact is made only when load is applied to the saw blade.

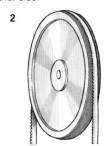

Next, adjust the side bearings to leave a paper-thin clearance on each side of the blade (**3**). When the blade is cutting, each side bearing should be level with the roots of the teeth (**4**). If you advance the bearings too far, they will destroy the set of the blade.

Thrust bearing

Side bearing

Finally, replace the guard and close the blade-access doors. Reassemble the rip fence before you switch the saw on.

FOLDING A BAND-SAW BLADE

To store your band-saw blades, fold them into three coils and hang them on pegs on the workshop wall. Wear gloves to protect your hands and wrists.

With the teeth facing away from you, hold one side of the band in each hand and, at the same time, hold the bottom of the band gently under one foot (**1**). Bring your hands together, allowing the top of the band to bend towards the floor (**2**). Cross the blade over itself to form three coils (**3**), then let it fall lightly to the floor. To unfold a coiled band, hold it securely and separate the coils slowly, allowing the blade to spring open away from you.

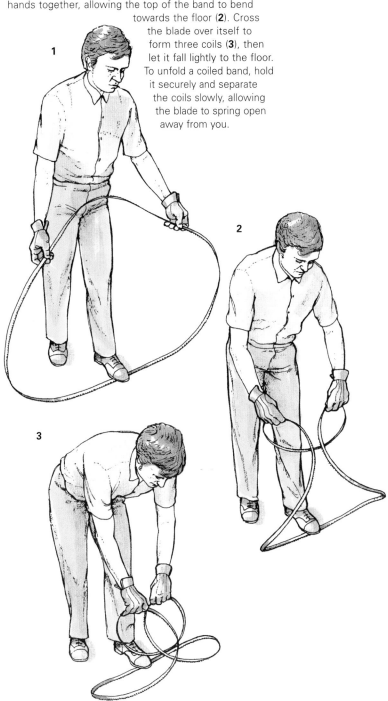
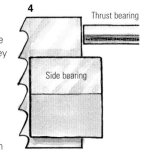

Provided the blade is sharp and accurately set, it is relatively easy to saw freehand, following a line marked on a workpiece. If the blade is blunt or damaged, it is much more likely to wander and you will find yourself constantly correcting the line of cut, which inevitably puts a strain on the blade.

Select the width of blade to suit the minimum radius you want to cut, and plan the procedure to ensure that the bulk of the workpiece is able to pass through the throat of the saw.

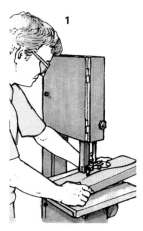

Following a curve freehand

Feed the work into the blade, cutting at a steady rate on the waste side of the line, and follow the curve without twisting the blade in the kerf. As the blade approaches the end of the cut, keep your hands away from the cutting edge and, if need be, pass one hand behind the blade to guide the work (**1**).

Cutting parallel curves

Curved components often have parallel sides. To help cut one curve parallel to another, round over the end of a block of timber and clamp it to the saw table, leaving a clearance between it and the blade equal to the width of the finished workpiece. Run one of the curves against the rounded end of the block while following the other marked line with the saw blade.

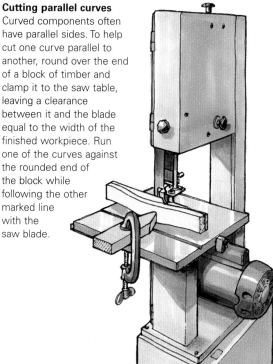

Don't withdraw a blade that begins to bind as you negotiate a tight curve. Instead, allow the kerf to run out through the waste towards the side of the workpiece and start the cut again. It may be necessary to perform the procedure several times to complete a curve (**2**).

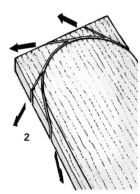

If you suspect in advance that it will be impossible to complete a cut in one flowing movement, make short straight cuts through the waste, so it will fall away in sections as the curved cut progresses (**3**). Alternatively, drill clearance holes at strategic points, so you can turn the blade in another direction (**4**). If there's no escape route for a binding blade, switch off and slowly back out of the kerf.

Cutting three-dimensional curves

To cut a component that has three-dimensional curves (a cabriole leg, for example), mark out its shape on two adjacent sides of a square-section blank. Cut one side freehand, then replace the waste and tape it in position. Turn the workpiece through 90 degrees in order to cut the second curve.

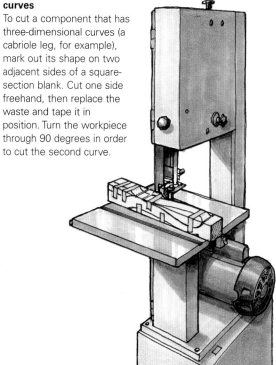

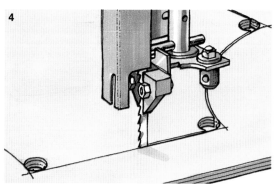

RIPSAWING WITH A BAND SAW

Making a ripcut parallel to another edge is a straightforward procedure – but unless the blade is sharp and set perfectly, it will tend to drift off line even when you are ripping against a fence. Also, make sure the blade guides are adjusted correctly and the tracking is true.

Ripping against the fence
With the work pressed against it, adjust the rip fence sideways until the blade is just on the waste side of the marked line. Clamp the fence in place. Switch on and feed the work at a steady rate, without forcing it. Keep the workpiece pressed against the fence throughout the cut. Finish cutting a narrow workpiece by feeding it with a push stick, pressing diagonally towards the fence.

Ripping against a block
If a blade persists in wandering when you are using the rip fence, employ a rounded guide block, as when cutting parallel curves. Clamp it to the saw table, leaving the required clearance between blade and block; and make the ripcut freehand, so you can compensate for the sideways drift by slightly changing the direction of feed.

Bevel ripping
To cut chamfers along a workpiece, tilt the saw table and position the rip fence below the blade.
If you can't fit your rip fence below the blade, clamp a temporary wooden fence to the saw table for bevel ripping.

CROSSCUTTING WITH A BAND SAW

It is possible to crosscut reasonably accurately on a band saw, but the finish will not be as good as on a table saw. If appearance is important, you will need to plane or sand the end grain.

Holding the work firmly against the mitre fence, feed the workpiece past the blade by sliding the fence along the groove machined in the saw table. Don't force the pace, or you will distort the blade.
If you want to saw several identical offcuts, clamp a block to the rip fence to serve as an end stop (**1**).

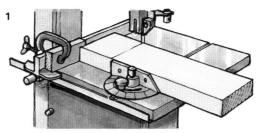

1

To cut a number of workpieces to the same length, extend the saw's mitre fence with a wooden facing and clamp an end stop to it. Butt the squared end of each of the workpieces against the end stop and cut them to length (**2**).
Cut a mitre by adjusting the angle of the fence. To make a compound mitre (one that is angled in two planes), tilt the saw table at the same time.

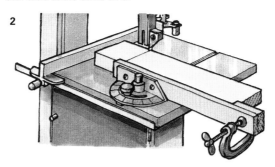

2

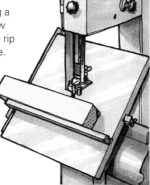

CUTTING JOINTS WITH A BAND SAW

Any joint that incorporates a tongue – a lap joint, barefaced housing, corner halving joint, and so on – can be cut in a similar way to a tenon. The procedure for cutting a tenon is therefore described here. To avoid having to back out of a deep cut, always saw the shoulders first – so that when you cut alongside the tongue, the waste falls away.

Using the mitre fence fitted with an end stop (see above), crosscut the shoulder lines of the tenon.
Adjust the rip fence to saw alongside the tenon, with the waste facing away from the fence. Set the saw's depth stop to complete the cut on the shoulder line. If your saw is not fitted with a depth stop, clamp a block to the fence ahead of the work.
After cutting one side, turn the work over and cut the other, to ensure that the tenon is centred on the rail.

POWERED FRET SAWS

Powered fret saws are generally associated with model-making and lightweight craftwork, but the better-quality saws will cut relatively thick timber with ease and to a superb finish. The saw's reciprocal action derives from the hand-held fret saw, but the powered version leaves both hands free to guide the work – enabling you to work accurately and also to cut very tight curves when required. To a large extent, the fret saw's popularity is due to its safety record, which makes it suitable for young woodworkers. Any blade that cuts wood can cut your fingers, but if you operate the saw with care and observe general machine-shop safety procedures, it is practically impossible to have a serious accident.

Depth of cut
Even a reasonably small powered fret saw is capable of cutting wood 50mm (2in) thick. The heavy-duty ones can handle timber twice that thickness.

Saw table
Whether the saw table is made from cast alloy or pressed metal, it must be flat and rigid. Nearly all tables can be tilted for making bevel cuts, and some can be raised or lowered to utilize another section of the blade when one part becomes worn.

Throat
A fret saw's 'throat' – the distance between the blade and the column behind the saw table – determines the maximum width of cut possible. A small powered fret saw has a throat of about 380mm (1ft 3in) or less, but you can buy larger saws that will cut boards 600mm (2ft) wide. In any case, blades can be turned through 45 or 90 degrees so that a long workpiece can be fed past the column.

Dust extraction
Dust-extraction systems are not normally supplied for powered fret saws – but, as the sawdust produced is very fine, it is advisable to wear a face mask.

Length of stroke
Even though a fret saw will cut quite thick material, the length of stroke – vertical movement of the blade – is relatively short. As a result, if you cut a lot of thin materials, you will blunt a short section of blade just above the table while the rest of the saw teeth remain untouched. To get more use out of the blade, raise the work on a secondary table top made from chipboard or plywood about 18mm ($^3/_4$in) thick.

Blade tensioner
Fret-saw blades are extremely narrow and must therefore be held taut to prevent them bending when load is applied. This is achieved by a strong spring acting on one end of the blade. On some saws, spring tension is adjustable to suit different blade sizes.

• **Electric motor**
The tiny 100W induction motor that powers the average machine fret saw is capable of generating blade speeds of between 2800 and 5750 strokes per minute. Some fret saws are supplied with variable-speed control.

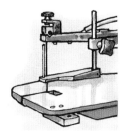

Hold-down
An adjustable hold-down stops thin workpieces vibrating.

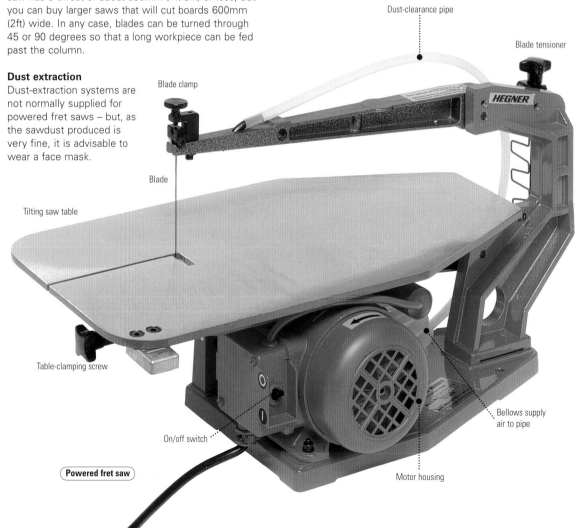

Dust-clearance pipe

Blade tensioner

Blade clamp

HEGNER

Blade

Tilting saw table

Table-clamping screw

On/off switch

Bellows supply air to pipe

Motor housing

(Powered fret saw)

There are coarse 'coping-saw' blades with standard alternate-set teeth for ripping thick timber, but most of the blades made for powered fret saws have a skip-tooth arrangement – a deep gullet between each tooth – or else pairs of teeth separated by deep gullets. Skip-tooth or double-tooth blades will cut wood and soft metals; for cutting hard ferrous metals, you can buy jeweller's blades.

BLADE-SIZE SELECTION

Blade size	TPI	Material thickness
1	25	Veneers and wood up to 6mm ($\frac{1}{4}$in)
2	23	Plastics up to 6mm ($\frac{1}{4}$in)
		Soft metals up to 1.5mm ($\frac{1}{16}$in)
3	20	Hardwoods up to 12mm ($\frac{1}{2}$in)
		Softwoods up to 18mm ($\frac{3}{4}$in)
4	18	Plastics up to 6mm ($\frac{1}{4}$in)
		Soft metals up to 3mm ($\frac{1}{8}$in)
5	16$\frac{1}{2}$	Hardwoods from 6 to 18mm ($\frac{1}{4}$ to $\frac{3}{4}$in)
		Softwoods 6 to 25mm ($\frac{1}{4}$ to 1in)
6	15	Plastics up to 12mm ($\frac{1}{2}$in)
		Soft metals up to 6mm ($\frac{1}{4}$in)
7	14	Hardwoods from 6 to 25mm ($\frac{1}{4}$ to 1in)
8	14	Softwoods 6 to 50mm ($\frac{1}{4}$ to 2in)
9	14	Plastics up to 12mm ($\frac{1}{2}$in)
		Soft metals up to 12mm ($\frac{1}{2}$in)
10	12$\frac{1}{2}$	Hardwoods from 18 to 50mm ($\frac{3}{4}$ to 2in)
11	12$\frac{1}{2}$	Softwoods 18 to 50mm ($\frac{3}{4}$ to 2in)
		Plastics up to 18mm ($\frac{3}{4}$in)
12	12$\frac{1}{2}$	Soft metals up to 12mm ($\frac{1}{2}$in)

Hold-downs
To prevent thin workpieces 'chattering' (vibrating noisily), fret saws are supplied with a hold-down to stop the work being lifted from the table by the action of the blade. A sprung hold-down lifts automatically as thin wood is fed towards the blade, but with thicker wood it may be necessary to lift the hold-down up onto the workpiece manually before you can begin to cut. A vertically adjustable hold-down is set to suit a work-piece before cutting starts.

Blade guard
A blade guard on a fret saw is very simple, usually consisting of one or two vertical wire or plastic rods that form part of the hold-down. This type of guard is designed to stop you pushing your fingers against the blade. However, if you feed the work correctly, this should never happen. When cutting thick timber a fret saw is often operated without a blade guard of any description, especially since with some saws the hold-down with its integral guard is offered only as an optional accessory.

On/off switch
On most fret saws the on/off switch is of the simple toggle variety.

Dust clearance
Many fret saws have a flexible pipe mounted just behind the blade to blow sawdust away from the point of cut before it obscures your view of the marked line.

USING A FRET SAW SAFELY
A fret saw is safe enough to be used by quite young operators provided that they have been trained in general machine-shop safety procedures. Even when a fret-saw blade breaks, it is unlikely to do you any serious harm.

• When you are feeding a workpiece, keep your fingers out of direct line with the blade – and take care that your thumbs are well out of the way as the blade breaks free at the edge of the work.
• Check that the switch is off before you plug a fret saw into an electrical socket.

Selecting the size of blade
Blade size is normally specified by the numbers 1 to 12, although not all manufacturers supply the complete range. Each size of blade is designed to cope with materials of different thicknesses, but the intricacy of cut will also affect your choice. Select a finer blade if the one you are using cannot negotiate a tight curve.

The chart above is intended as a guide to selecting the appropriate blade size, but the final compromise between smoothness of finish, speed of cut and durability of blade must be a matter of experiment and personal preference.

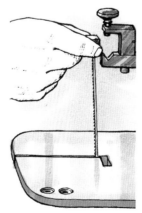

Fitting a blade
Follow the fret-saw manufacturer's instructions for fitting and tensioning a blade. The teeth of the blade should always point downwards towards the saw table.

MAKING CURVED CUTS WITH A FRET SAW

Cutting a curved workpiece – even one that is quite intricately shaped – with a powered fret saw is a commonplace task. So long as you are using a blade of the right width, it is easy enough to follow a marked line freehand, always cutting on the waste side of the line to preserve the shape of the finished piece.

Cutting curves

Feed the work with both hands, holding it flat on the saw table while applying forward pressure into the blade. Keep your hands on either side of the blade, never directly in line with it. Be patient and feed the work slowly and steadily, allowing the blade to cut naturally. If you feel you are having to force the pace, then you need to change the blunt blade for a sharp one.

While concentrating on the point of cut, it is all too easy to distort a narrow blade by unintentional sideways pressure or by twisting the work. To allow the blade to spring back to its natural position, relax fingertip pressure very slightly while continuing to maintain control over the work.

Cutting an aperture

First, drill a small hole in the waste and pass the blade through it; then, with the saw unplugged, connect both ends of the blade to the saw. Switch on and follow your marked line until you have completed the aperture, then switch off and unplug the saw again so that you can release the blade to remove the workpiece.

Making bevel cuts

To make a bevel cut, adjust the angle of the saw table then proceed as if you were cutting a square edge, taking extra care not to distort the blade. To avoid distortion, keep the feed pressure directly in line with the cutting edge.

MAKING STRAIGHT CUTS WITH A FRET SAW

A powered fret saw is not an especially good tool for making straight cuts, but you can clamp a temporary wooden fence (straight batten) to the saw table to guide the work on its intended path.

As most fretwork consists of a combination of straight and curved shapes, it is usually necessary to follow all marked lines by eye. To make a long straight cut, turn the blade – following the saw manufacturer's instructions – to an angle that allows you to feed the work past the saw column at the rear of the table.

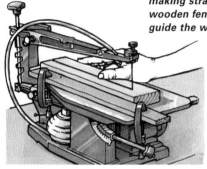

Combining straight and curved cuts

If the combination of straight and curved lines is such that you will need to change one blade for another, drill access holes at strategic points where the wider blade will have to be swapped for a narrow one and vice versa.

PLANERS

Having acquired a table saw or band saw, most woodworkers begin to think about buying a machine that will plane surfaces accurately on all four sides of a workpiece.

A production workshop is often equipped with two planing machines. The first is a surface planer or jointer for dressing the face side and face edge of a workpiece. The same workpiece is then passed through a thicknesser, which planes the remaining surfaces parallel to the face side and face edge.

If there is no room or need for two planers, home woodworkers often opt for a planer/thicknesser that combines both functions in a single machine.

Maximum planing width

Planers are most often specified according to the widest workpiece you can plane on the machine – which is determined by the length of the cutters bolted into the revolving cutter block. Small special-purpose surface planers have short cutters – 150mm (6in) or less – but the average home-workshop planer/thicknesser will have a maximum planing width of about 260mm (10¼in).

Cutter-block speed

The cylindrical block with its two or three balanced cutters revolves at a very high speed in order to produce a clean, smooth surface. Cutter-block speed is sometimes specified in revolutions per minute, but a more telling figure is the number of cuts per minute produced by the cutters.

A three-cutter block will produce more cuts per minute than a two-cutter block revolving at the same speed. For a two-cutter block, 12,000 cuts per minute is a respectable speed.

Combined length of tables

In order to be able to plane a perfectly straight edge on a workpiece, the overall length of the infeed plus outfeed tables should be as long as possible. The overall combined length of the average planer is about 1m (3ft 3in).

Fence

A rigid metal fence is essential for planing true square or bevelled edges on a workpiece. All fences can be tilted to any angle between 90 and 45 degrees to the tables. It is convenient if the fence automatically comes to a stop at both extremes, but check the settings with a try square or sliding bevel.

On/off switches

Ideally, there should be no-volt on/off switches accessible from either end of the planer – so you can turn the machine off quickly in an emergency, no matter whether you happen to be surface-planing or thicknessing.

Secondary cutter-block guard
Fence
Cutter-block guard
Infeed table
Outfeed table
Cutter-depth adjuster
Thicknessing table

Surface-planer mode

Maximum depth of cut

The cutter block is situated between two independently adjustable cast-metal tables. The height of the table to the rear of the cutter block – the outfeed table – should be adjusted so that it is level with the top of the circle described by the revolving cutters. The table in front of the cutter block – the infeed table – is lowered to produce the required depth of cut, up to a maximum of about 3mm ($^1/_8$in). A very shallow 0.5mm ($^1/_{32}$in) cut will produce a superior finish. For speed, make two or three deeper cuts followed by one or more finishing cuts. Depth of cut is indicated by a scale next to the infeed table.

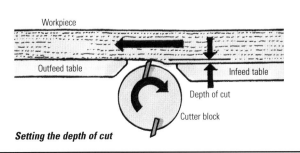

Workpiece
Outfeed table
Infeed table
Depth of cut
Cutter block

Setting the depth of cut

Cutter-block guard

A planer's revolving cutters are capable of severing a fingertip in a fraction of a second – so never operate the machine without the appropriate guard in place.

The ideal form of protection is a bridge guard that is adjustable in height and able to slide across the entire width of the cutter block. Some planers are made with spring-loaded bridge guards that are lifted or pushed aside by the work as it is passed over the cutter block. This type of guard is superior to simpler ones, which merely swing aside to expose the cutters.

In addition, behind the fence there should be a guard that is automatically drawn across the cutter block as the fence is adjusted sideways.

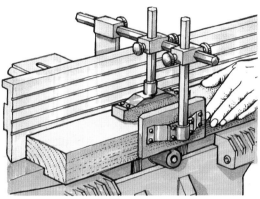

Hold-down guards
Never attempt to rebate a workpiece without a vertical/horizontal hold-down guard in place, so your hands need not approach the cutters.

Planers should have accessible on/off switches

Width of thicknesser table

The average thicknesser table is about 250mm (10in) wide. Never attempt to plane a workpiece that is shorter than the width of the table. If a piece of wood is able to slew sideways, it may be splintered by the feed rollers and cutters – and pieces can be thrown out of the planer with considerable force.

.

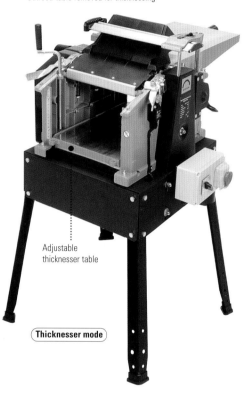

Outfeed table removed for thicknessing

Adjustable
thicknesser table

(Thicknesser mode)

Feed rollers

A thicknesser is equipped with two motor-driven spring-loaded feed rollers that pass the workpiece under the revolving cutter block and out the other end of the machine. The infeed roller (usually a horizontally ribbed steel roller) is situated in front of the cutter block and provides the main driving force. The outfeed roller, which is situated behind the cutter block, is smooth – so as not to mark the planed surface – and exerts less pressure on the work. The parallel bruising left by a ribbed roller is sometimes detectable on the planed surface. For this reason, some planers are made with rubber-covered drive rollers.

Thicknesser feed rollers

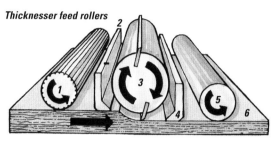

1 Infeed roller   **4** Pressure bar
2 Chip breaker   **5** Outfeed roller
3 Cutter block   **6** Workpiece

Maximum thicknessing depth

When a workpiece is passed through a thicknesser, it travels on a bed situated beneath the same cutter block used for surface planing. The thicknessing table on the average home-workshop machine can be raised or lowered to accommodate workpieces up to a maximum thickness of 160 to 180mm (6 to 7in). Even though the thicknesser is power-driven, never attempt to take more than 3 to 4mm ($\frac{1}{8}$in) in one pass.

Electric motors

A 375W electric motor is powerful enough for a special-purpose surface planer. However, on a thicknesser the motor is used to drive the feed rollers and cutter block simultaneously, so a 1.5 to 2.2kW motor is required. On some models, the drive rollers can be disconnected from the motor so that its entire output is available for surface planing.

Thicknesser feed rate

Because an amateur woodworker is not primarily concerned with a fast throughput of work, he or she is more likely to be attracted by a planer that produces a good finish at the expense of speed – since a slow feed rate combined with a high cutter-block speed produces the best finish. Many thicknessers are therefore designed to feed the work at the relatively slow speed of about 5m (16ft) per minute. However, you can buy a thicknesser with a minimum feed rate of 9m (29ft) per minute, which can be increased to 11m (36ft) per minute. As a general rule, feed hardwoods slowly but increase the feed rate for softwoods.

Anti-kickback device

If for some reason the drive rollers loose their grip on a workpiece, it may be thrown out of the machine by the cutter block and a serious accident can occur if you are feeding the work at the time. To prevent this happening, a row of pointed metal teeth or 'pawls' hang in front of the infeed roller. As the work travels under them, the pawls lift to allow free passage. Should the work begin to travel backwards, the pointed pawls catch in the surface of the wood and restrict its movement.

Dust extractor

Without an extractor, shavings are dumped onto the tables above and below the cutter block, where they impair the efficiency and accuracy of the machine. Consequently, you have to stop the planer regularly to clear the accumulated debris. A hose attachment leading to a portable extractor solves the problem.

USING A PLANER/THICKNESSER SAFELY

Always operate a planer confidently but with extreme caution. An accident can happen so quickly that even the fastest reflexes will not save you from injury. It is therefore essential to observe general machine-shop safety procedures and to cultivate a safe method of working. Modern machines have 'interlock' switches that prevent the thicknesser mode being switched on when the machine is set up for planing, and vice versa. Never attempt to fix electrical problems yourself, as you could interfere with this important safety feature. Have a faulty machine repaired by a service agent.

• Follow the manufacturer's instructions for fitting cutters, and always complete the procedure before you leave the machine. If you are distracted and forget to secure a cutter, a serious accident could result.
• Inspect the machine before you switch on, to make sure nothing is likely to foul the cutter block.
• Never use a surface planer without a properly adjusted guard in position.
• Use a push block to feed a thin workpiece over the cutters. Never attempt to plane a piece of wood less than 10mm (3/8in) thick.
• Don't attempt to surface-plane a workpiece that is too short to be held firmly in both hands.
• Never trail your fingers or thumb behind a workpiece when surface planing.
• Always feed work against the direction of rotation of the cutter block.
• Feed one workpiece at a time through a thicknesser.
• Don't try to force a workpiece through a thicknesser. Let the feed rollers work at their intended rate.
• When planing a workpiece of uneven thickness, set the depth of cut to cope with the thickest section first, then gradually raise the thicknessing table between passes until you are cutting the full length of the board.
• Don't feed work that is shorter than the width of the thicknessing table, nor shorter than the distance between the feed rollers.
• When planing long workpieces, either have an assistant take the weight as they come off the machine or set up a roller stand or trestles to support the work.
• Never put your hands into a thicknesser to retrieve a workpiece or clear away shavings. Use a long push stick instead, to extend your reach.

PLANER CUTTERS

A few planers are made with double-edge disposable cutters, similar to those used in portable power planers. However, the majority of machines are fitted with two or three single-edge cutters or 'knives', which need to be honed and sharpened at regular intervals.

Types of cutter

Planers for the home-workshop market are supplied with high-speed-steel cutters that are perfectly adequate unless you expect to plane a lot of chipboard or 'gritty' timbers like teak. When planing these materials, follow production-workshop practice and fit the more expensive tungsten-carbide-tipped cutters, which will hold a sharp edge much longer but must, when the time comes, be sent to a professional for sharpening. Even high-speed-steel cutters are sent for regrinding, but they can be honed in the meantime by running an oilstone along the cutting edges.

Fitting cutters

It is important to follow the planer manufacturer's instructions for fitting cutters. However, in principle, each cutter fits into a slot in the cylindrical block. In some cases, the cutter rests on springs at the bottom of the slot and height adjustment is simply a matter of holding the cutter down against their compression. The cutter is normally secured with a wedge-shaped bar clamp held tight by adjusting expansion bolts. Before you switch on, always double-check that the cutters are tight.

Adjusting cutters

In order to do its fair share of the work, each cutter must project from the block by exactly the same amount. If one cutter is set higher than another, it will do all the planing but a loss of finish will result. It is possible to buy special equipment for gauging cutter setting, but in a home workshop a straight batten is quite good enough. Always disconnect a planer from the electricity supply before making adjustments to the cutters.

Adjust all the cutters by eye until they appear to project the required amount. Lower the outfeed table slightly, then rest the wooden batten on it, overhanging one end of the cutter block. Mark the edge of the outfeed table on the batten (**1**). Turn the cutter block slowly by hand, allowing the cutter to lift the batten and carry it forward, then mark the edge of the batten again (**2**).

Move the batten to the other end of the cutter block, aligning the first mark with the edge of the table. Turn the block again. The same cutter should move the batten forward by exactly the same amount. If the second mark does not align with the table edge, adjust the height of the cutter at that end until it does.

Tighten the cutter bar clamp, then repeat the gauging process at each end, to make sure that clamping has not altered the setting. Turn the block and set each cutter in the same way. Finally, raise the outfeed table until each cutter just scrapes the underside of the batten.

A typical planer cutter block

Coil spring
Expansion bolt
Cutter
Bar clamp

• Cleaning the cutter block
Before you fit new or reground cutters, clean wood resin from the cutter-block slots and bar clamps with a solvent such as cellulose thinner or white spirit.

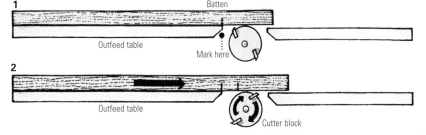

1 Batten
Outfeed table
Mark here

2
Outfeed table
Cutter block

Grain direction
Feed the work with the grain running at an angle away from the cutters.

SURFACE PLANING

To square-up a piece of timber, first prepare the face side and face edge on the surface planer then pass it through the thicknesser to plane the remaining faces.

Inspect the workpiece to select the most suitable faces to plane. If the workpiece is bowed, plane it with the concave face resting on the feed tables – it is virtually impossible to flatten a convex surface on a planer, since the workpiece is sure to rock on the tables as you pass it across the cutters. To achieve a smooth finish, orientate the wood so the grain runs at an angle away from the cutters.

When the grain runs in different directions, the decision may not be quite so straightforward – in which case, take a fine cut and if the planer tears the grain, turn the work round and try again.

Planing the face side
Lower the thicknesser table, then move the fence aside to accommodate the widest face of the workpiece and select the depth of cut by adjusting the infeed table.

Slide the bridge guard to cover the cutter block and, with the wood resting on the infeed table, raise the guard to just clear the workpiece (**1**).

Stand to the side of the infeed table and switch on. With your right hand flat on the work, feed the wood across the cutters (**2**). Apply just enough pressure to control the work. If you press a bowed or twisted workpiece flat on the infeed table, the cutters will remove an even layer from the surface – but as soon as you relieve the pressure, the wood will spring back to its distorted condition. Your intention should be to plane just those points in contact with the table, gradually removing more and more wood until the surface is flat.

As soon as the workpiece passes under the guard, shift your body weight to hold the work on the outfeed table with your left hand (**3**). Continue feeding the work at an even rate, transferring your right hand to the work on the outfeed table (**4**). Keep the work moving until you have completed the first cut. Return the workpiece to the infeed table and repeat the process until the face side is flat, then switch off.

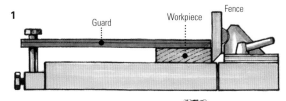

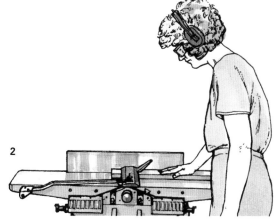

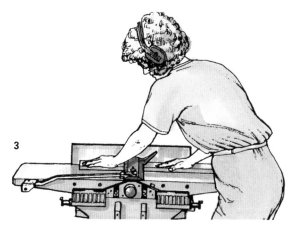

Planing the face edge
Brush any shavings away from the fence, and check that it is perfectly upright.

Lower the guard and slide it sideways to allow the work to pass between the guard and the fence with minimum clearance. Make sure your fingertips cannot slip between the end of the fence and the workpiece.

Switch on and, with the face side held firmly against the fence, pass the work from one hand to the other over the cutter block.

Adjust guard to plane an edge

Pass work from hand to hand

Planing a bevel
To plane a bevel on a workpiece, tilt the fence to the required angle and slide the bridge guard sideways, allowing the minimum clearance for the work.

In order to maintain an accurate bevel, you must prevent the bottom edge of the work sliding away from the fence. Use your left hand as a stationary guide – holding the work against the fence with your index finger and thumb while resting the other three fingers on the outfeed table – and feed the work with your right hand.

Tilt the fence to plane a bevel

Planing a bevel
Support the work with your left hand.

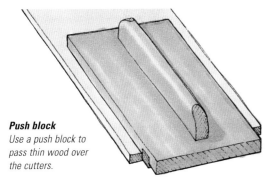

Push block
Use a push block to
pass thin wood over
the cutters.

Planing a thin workpiece

It is never safe to feed a thin piece of wood over the
planer cutters by hand. Instead, make a push block
from softwood, with a batten housed into the
underside for pushing the back edge of the workpiece.
Glue a long handle down the centre, so you can grip
the push block with both hands. Even with a push
block, never attempt to plane a piece of wood that is
less than 10mm (^{3}/$_8$in) thick.

PLANING A STOPPED CHAMFER

*A stopped chamfer is often used as a decorative feature
in furniture-making. A surface planer is the ideal
machine for producing such a detail, but take
professional tuition before attempting the
process yourself.*

It involves lowering
both tables by an
equal amount, so
that you can cut
the chamfer in
one pass. Screw
end stops to a long

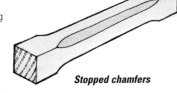

Stopped chamfers

board, clamp the board to the fence, and then tilt the
fence to 45 degrees. Adjust the guard as if you were
planing a normal bevel.

Butt one end of the work firmly against the rearward
end stop, while holding the other end above the cutter
block (**1**). With your fingertips on the very end of the
wood, lower the workpiece slowly onto the cutter block.
There will be considerable rearward force on initial contact
with the cutters. Feed the work along the fence until it
comes to rest against the forward end stop, then carefully
lift the wood off the cutters (**2**) and switch off. For safety,
plane a stopped chamfer on an overlong piece of wood –
then, after machining, cut it to length at each end.

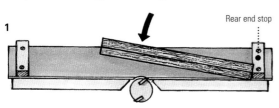

1   Rear end stop

2   Forward end stop

THICKNESSING

*Having planed a flat face side and face edge, the
work is ready for thicknessing – but don't waste
time and money by turning more wood than
necessary into shavings. Band-saw oversize
workpieces close to finished width or thickness,
then return them to the planer.*

Preparing the thicknesser

Remove the fence and then, depending on the
manufacturer's instructions, either remove the outfeed
table or lift and secure one or both tables. Fit the
thicknesser's cutter-block guard and shavings deflector
in position. Select the depth of cut by adjusting the
thicknesser table to the required height, using its depth
scale as a guide.

Feeding the work

Switch on and engage the automatic feed mechanism.
Then, standing slightly to one side of the machine,
pass the end of the workpiece into the thicknesser
until the feed rollers draw it under the cutter block. If
the rollers do not take hold of the work, raise the table
very slightly.

Move to the other end of the machine and withdraw
the work – don't attempt to accelerate the process by
pulling the wood through the thicknesser. Return to the
infeed end of the machine and raise the table to take
another cut. Repeat the process as often as necessary.

Planing a thin board

To plane a board that's thinner than the minimum
depth of cut on a thicknesser, place it on top of a
thicker board already planed to an even thickness and
pass both boards through the machine together.

Planing an edge

If a workpiece is thick enough to be stable, you can
pass it on edge through a thicknesser. However, a thin
workpiece may tip over as it is taken by the rollers,
crushing the corners of the wood. If you suspect there
is a possibility of damaging a workpiece, rip it to within
1mm (^{1}/$_{16}$in) of its final width on a power saw.

If you are preparing several identical components, rip
them all on the same setting. Take one workpiece to
the finely set surface planer and plane the first 25mm
(1in) of the sawn edge. Check the width and, if
necessary, adjust the depth of cut and plane the same
25mm (1in) again. When you are satisfied with the
width of the workpiece, pass the whole sawn edge
over the cutters. Finally, with one pass, plane all the
matching components to an identical width.

• **Cleaning a thicknesser**
*With the machine disconnected
from the electricity supply, clean
wood resin from the thicknesser
table and rollers, using a solvent
such as white spirit or cellulose
thinner. Then polish the table
with a dry cloth.*

Planing end grain
*To plane end grain, construct a
jig to hold the workpiece upright
and prevent it tipping as you
feed it across the cutters. Make
the whole jig from softwood
(man-made boards may chip the
edges of planer cutters). With
the workpiece clamped securely
in the jig, pass it across the
cutter block.*

PILLAR DRILLS

A pillar drill is basically a drilling machine with an adjustable worktable. The drilling head – comprising the chuck for holding the drill bit, the drive-belt mechanism and the electric motor – is mounted on a rigid metal column supported by a heavy cast-metal base. With bench-mounted pillar drills, the base is bolted to the bench – the upper surface of the base is machined flat and is slotted to serve as a second worktable for large workpieces. On floor-standing models, the column is long enough to raise the drill and worktable to a comfortable working height.

Chuck

The chuck of a pillar drill has three self-centring jaws operated by a key. Most pillar-drill chucks accommodate bits with a shank diameter of up to 16mm ($5/8$in).

Electric motor

Pillar drills are made with induction motors rated between 187 and 875W. This type of motor is very efficient – but even so, it is best to buy a drill with at least a 250W motor.

The motor's power is transmitted via a V-belt and pulley-wheel system to the spindle and chuck. Moving the rubber V-belt up or down stepped cone pulleys changes the speed, in at least four increments, between 450 and 3000rpm. Stepless variable speed is a feature of some models, which may also display the selected speed electronically.

NVR switch

For safety, pillar drills are fitted with a no-volt release switch.

Worktable

The cast-metal worktable is cantilevered from the column. A hole in the centre of the table allows the drill bit to pass through a workpiece without damage.

Select a machine with a table that can be tilted to 45 degrees and which can be swung to one side in order to place a larger-than-average workpiece on the pillar-drill base. Fences, vices or jigs can be bolted into the slots machined across the table.

Pillar-drill vice
This small engineer's vice is for holding metal workpieces on the table of a pillar drill.

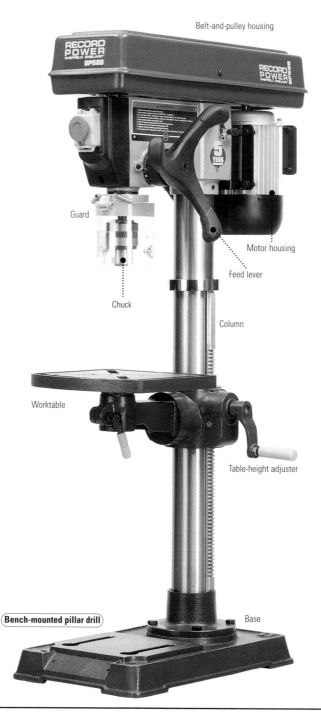

Belt-and-pulley housing

Guard

Chuck

Worktable

Motor housing

Feed lever

Column

Table-height adjuster

(Bench-mounted pillar drill)

Base

Throat

The throat – the distance between the centre of the worktable and the column – should be as large as possible. Throat capacity on home-workshop pillar drills can be anything from 100 to 200mm (4 to 8in).

Feed lever

To plunge the drill bit into a workpiece, you pull down on the feed lever mounted on one side of the machine. Since it is spring-loaded, the lever returns automatically – but the mechanism can be locked with a clamp lever to run the drill in a lowered position, leaving both hands free for working.

Maximum depth of hole

The maximum depth of hole that can be bored on a particular pillar drill is determined by the vertical movement of the chuck. Maximum vertical movement varies from about 50 to 90mm (2 to $3^{1}/_{2}$in) on bench-mounted machines. Floor-standing models have a much larger capacity between the bottom of the chuck and the base, but the maximum chuck travel is still only around 90mm ($3^{1}/_{2}$in).

Depth gauge

Drilling depth is controlled by setting a gauge. Mark the required depth on the side of the workpiece. Lower the chuck until the tip of the drill bit aligns with the mark, then set the depth-gauge stop to limit the vertical travel of the spindle and chuck.

Safety guard

If possible, buy a machine with a transparent safety guard that drops down to shield the chuck. The guard prevents hair or loose clothing becoming caught in the rotating chuck. Closing the guard should also alert you to the presence of a chuck key accidentally left in the machine.

DRILL BITS

You will need a complete set of good-quality twist drills and dowel bits, up to at least 10mm (³⁄₈in) in diameter. Larger bits are available but, since they are relatively expensive, it is probably best to acquire them one at a time when the need arises.

Twist drills
Choose high-speed-steel twist drills, since these are equally suitable for wood and metal. Before boring a hole with a twist drill, mark the centre with a bradawl – or with a metalworking punch if you are drilling hardwood or metal.

Dowel bits
Dowel bits are designed to bore holes in end grain for dowel joints. They are also excellent general-purpose woodboring bits.

Power auger bits
Use power auger bits to drill deep holes in timber. An average set contains augers ranging from 6 to 25mm (¼ to 1in) in diameter.

Spade bits
These are relatively cheap bits for drilling holes from 6 to 38mm (¼ to 1½in) in diameter. The long lead points make for very positive location at the centre of a hole.

Forstner bits
Forstner bits bore exceptionally clean flat-bottomed holes and are not deflected by knots or wild grain. They are available in a wide range of sizes, up to 50mm (2in) in diameter.

Countersink bits
Having drilled a clearance hole for a woodscrew, use a countersink bit to cut a tapered recess for the head. Select a high speed.

Dowel bit
Twist drill
Power auger bit
Forstner bit
Spade bit
Countersink bit
Plug cutter
Drill-and-countersink bit
Hole saw
Drill-and-counterbore bit

Drill-and-countersink bits
Made to match specific woodscrews, these bits drill a pilot hole, shank-clearance hole and countersink in a single operation.

Drill-and-counterbore bits
To set woodscrews below the surface of the wood, use a drill-and-counterbore bit. The neat hole above the screw can be filled with a specially cut wooden plug (see below).

Plug cutters
Drive these cutters into side-grain timber to make plugs for covering counterbored screws. Cut the plugs from timber that closely matches the work in colour and grain pattern.

Hole saws
With a set of hole saws, you can cut holes up to 89mm (3½in) in diameter. Select a slow to medium speed, and clamp the work firmly.

USING A PILLAR DRILL

Adjust the worktable to bring the work close to the tip of the drill bit fitted in the chuck. Then set the depth gauge, centre the bit and switch on. Feed the bit into the work steadily – provided the bit is sharp it should not be necessary to apply excessive force. Slowly release the feed lever, allowing it to come to rest in the raised position before switching off.

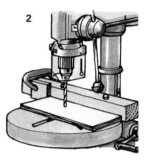

1

Holding the work securely
To resist the turning force of the pillar drill, it is often possible to rest one end of a workpiece against the left-hand side of the column (**1**). Alternatively, use a G-cramp or small fast-action cramp to clamp the work firmly to the table of the pillar drill.

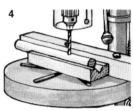

2

A simple wooden fence (stout batten) secured to the worktable with bolts and wing nuts is useful for positioning identical workpieces accurately. You can also butt the end of each workpiece against an end stop clamped to the fence (**2**).

Slide a workpiece along the fence when you want to drill a series of holes in line – in order to remove waste from a mortise, for example (**3**).

Cut a V-block on a table saw to serve as a cradle for drilling holes in a cylindrical workpiece (**4**).

3   **4**

USING A PILLAR DRILL SAFELY
Provided you follow general machine-shop safety procedures, a pillar drill is a relatively safe machine. However, you must take certain extra precautions.

• Always remove the chuck key after fitting a drill bit.
• Lower the safety guard before switching on.
• Hold the work securely on the pillar-drill table. If a drill bit catches, it can spin the work with serious consequences. Hold a wooden workpiece against the rigid column or against a custom-made fence, to resist the turning force, or clamp the work to the table.
• Always clamp a metal workpiece or hold it in a pillar-drill vice.

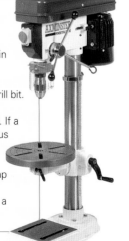

SANDERS

Most amateur woodworkers find portable orbital and belt sanders perfectly adequate for finishing wide flat panels or boards, but a bench-mounted belt-and-disc combination will provide you with a means for shaping components and sanding end grain, too. It is also ideal for finishing small workpieces.

Sanding disc

A vertically mounted metal disc covered with abrasive paper is used for sanding square or radiused ends on a workpiece and also for sanding mitres. The maximum width of work that can be sanded on a disc is slightly less than half its diameter. Much larger discs are available for industrial use, but a 225mm (9in) disc is a reasonable choice for the home workshop.

Paper-backed abrasives are normally glued to the face of the disc with a special adhesive. When a paper disc wears out, simply peel it off and replace it with a fresh one.

Sanding belt

An abrasive-covered cloth belt 100 to 150mm (4 to 6in) wide, stretched between two metal rollers, is used to sand the faces or long edges of a workpiece. Concave-shaped pieces can be sanded over one of the rollers. When required, the belt can be tipped to a vertical position for sanding end grain.

To remove a worn belt, release the tension by retracting one of the rollers. After fitting and tensioning a new belt, run the machine and centre the belt on the rollers by adjusting the tracking-control device.

Belts can be set vertically

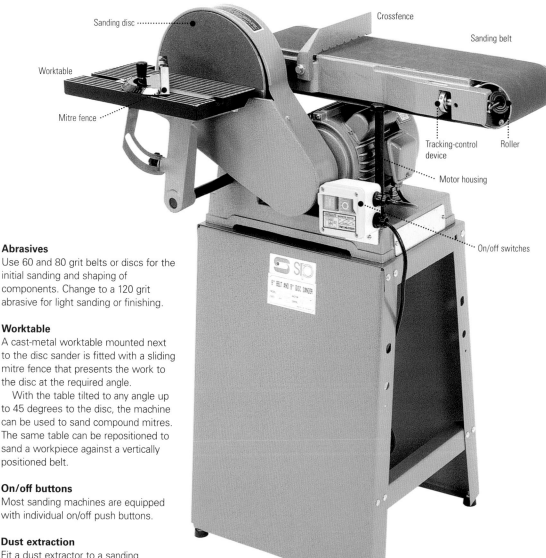

Sanding disc · · · · · ·
Crossfence
Sanding belt
Worktable
Mitre fence · · · · ·
Tracking-control device
Roller
Motor housing
On/off switches

Sanding machine

Abrasives

Use 60 and 80 grit belts or discs for the initial sanding and shaping of components. Change to a 120 grit abrasive for light sanding or finishing.

Worktable

A cast-metal worktable mounted next to the disc sander is fitted with a sliding mitre fence that presents the work to the disc at the required angle.

With the table tilted to any angle up to 45 degrees to the disc, the machine can be used to sand compound mitres. The same table can be repositioned to sand a workpiece against a vertically positioned belt.

On/off buttons

Most sanding machines are equipped with individual on/off push buttons.

Dust extraction

Fit a dust extractor to a sanding machine. The fine dust is detrimental to your health and creates a potentially explosive atmosphere in the workshop.

WORKING WITH A SANDER

Whenever possible, sand in the direction of the grain. Cross-grain sanding with either a disc or belt sander leaves scratches on the work that will be difficult to remove and impossible to disguise with clear varnish or polish.

1

2

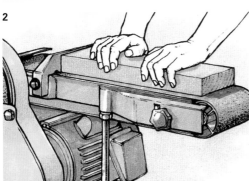

3

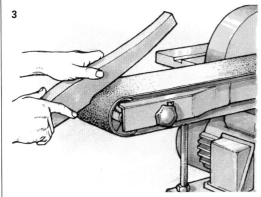

4

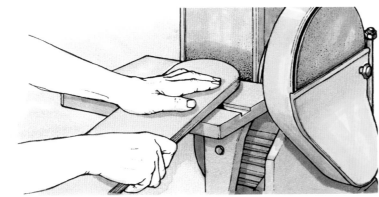

Using a disc sander

Holding the workpiece firmly against the mitre fence, press the end grain against the 'down' side of the rotating disc (**1**). Keep the work moving back and forth, and don't attempt to speed up the operation by pressing too hard – you will simply burn the end grain.

To shape a component on a disc sander, first cut away most of the waste with a band saw. Then remove the sander's mitre fence so that you can sand down to the marked line, using the worktable to support the wood. Keep your fingertips well away from the rotating disk.

Using a belt sander

To sand the sides and edges of a workpiece, butt the end against the belt's crossfence (**2**). Change the position of the work periodically to avoid leaving deep scratches in the wood and to maximize the life of the belt. Take care not to round over narrow edges or the corners of a workpiece.

To shape a curved workpiece, hold it against the roller at the end of the belt (**3**).

If the size and shape of the workpiece permits, you can tip the belt upright and use its entire width for sanding the work (**4**).

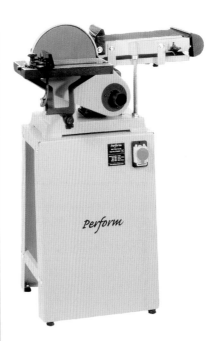

Electric motor
A single electric motor drives both the sanding disc and the belt.

USING A SANDER SAFELY

Always follow general machine-safety procedures and never take risks when using a sander. Injuries often occur because of the operator's failure to anticipate the possibility of an accident on what appears to be an inoffensive machine.

• Never hold a thin workpiece against a moving sanding belt. It may suddenly slip under the crossfence, and the flat of your hand will then be in immediate contact with the abrasive belt.
• To avoid injuring your fingertips, never sand very small components on a belt sander.
• Work against the 'down' side only of a disc sander, to ensure wood is driven onto the table by the machine's rotation.
• Disconnect the sander from the mains supply when changing discs and belts.

WOODTURNING LATHES

Woodturning can be far more than a simple machining process – at its best it becomes an art form. Successful lathe work requires not only the mastery of very special techniques, but also an appreciation of what constitutes a pleasing shape with flowing lines. A lathe, unlike other woodworking machines, is rarely used merely to process a workpiece from one stage of its production to the next; complete objects, from a rough blank through to a polished article, can be created on the one machine.

BENCH-MOUNTED LATHES

Heavy floor-standing lathes may be the norm for industrial turning, but lighter bench-mounted machines are more popular for the home workshop. A rigid bed forms the backbone of the machine, with a drive mechanism housed in a fixed headstock at one end and a sliding tailstock at the other. The workpiece is suspended between the two and is rotated at speed against a hand-held cutting tool. Lathes are generally designed for two methods of turning: between-centre turning for shaping spindles, table legs and other long thin workpieces, and faceplate turning for bowls, round boxes, egg cups, and so on.

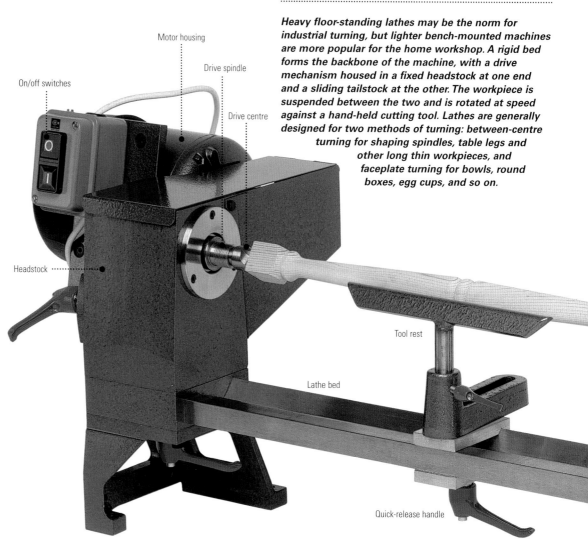

Motor housing
Drive spindle
On/off switches
Drive centre
Headstock
Tool rest
Lathe bed
Quick-release handle

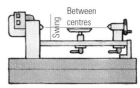
Bench-mounted woodturning lathe

Lathe size
A lathe is specified in two ways: the maximum length of workpiece it can accommodate between centres and its 'swing' (the maximum diameter of workpiece that can be turned above the lathe bed). The headstock on some lathes is designed to rotate through 180 degrees to make faceplate turning of larger work possible at the front or end of the lathe. The maximum workpiece length may be anything from 500mm to 1.2m (1ft 8in to 4ft). Longer workpieces can be assembled by dowelling two pieces together. Using the lathe to turn a peg on one end of a piece to fit a hole in another ensures perfect alignment, and a well-placed bead or groove disguises the joint.

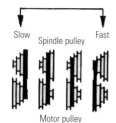

Slow Fast
Spindle pulley

Motor pulley

Changing the lathe speed

Between centres
Swing

Dimensions of a lathe

Lathe bed
Bracket-mounted steel bars or tubes support the tailstock, tool rest and other accessories. There needs to be ample clearance between the lathe bed and the bench for removing wood shavings.

Faceplate

Headstock

Tool rest

Headstock rotated for faceplate turning

Speed control

On most lathes, a belt drive is used to transmit power to the headstock spindle from a 375 to 750W electric motor. Stepped pulleys provide three or four preset spindle speeds, which typically range from 450 to 2000rpm. Some more expensive lathes use electronic variable-speed control.

Use the lowest speed for rough-cutting workpieces; and then move the drive belt up the speed range as work progresses.

Tool rest

An adjustable tool rest is used to support the blade of a turning tool just in front of the rotating workpiece.

A standard rest – between 200 and 300mm (8 and 12in) long – is moved along the lathe, to the most convenient position, as work progresses. An extra-long rest that spans the length of the lathe bed is supported by mounting brackets at each end. Curved or cranked tool rests are made for bowl-turning.

Tailstock

The tailstock, which is clamped to the lathe bed with a quick-release lever, supports the end of a workpiece for between-centre turning. It is fitted with a sliding hollow spindle, controlled by a handwheel, that takes a pointed tailstock centre. If this point is fixed – a 'dead' tailstock centre – it should be lubricated with wax to prevent it burning the work. Alternatively, fit a 'live' revolving centre constructed with ball bearings.

Tailstock

Tailstock centre

Tailstock spindle

Handwheel

Quick-release handle

Headstock

The headstock delivers turning force to the work via a drive spindle. Threaded at one or both ends to take a bowl-turning faceplate, the spindle is hollowed out so it can accommodate a tapered drive centre for between-centre turning. The drive centre has a lead point and either two or four prongs, which bite into the end grain of the workpiece.

Bench-mounting bracket

USING A LATHE SAFELY

A lathe is unique among woodcutting machines in that it does not incorporate a moving cutter or blade. Instead, a hand-held cutting tool is used to shape a spinning workpiece. One reason why the lathe appeals to the amateur woodworker is that it seems a relatively safe machine, with little risk of injury to fingers. However, if you neglect to develop safe working practices, a single mistake can cause the work to be thrown across the workshop. Always follow general machine-shop safety procedures and observe the following rules.

• Always work in good light.
• Keep the area around the lathe clear of loose objects and stacks of timber that could fall against a spinning workpiece.
• Select a speed setting that's suitable for the work.
• Never leave keys or spanners in a lathe chuck.
• Before switching on, check that all clamps and fixings are secure and that the work is free to rotate.
• Switch off the lathe before adjusting the tool rest.
• Before feeding cutting tools into the work, make sure they are in contact with the tool rest.
• Remove the tool rest before sanding a workpiece.
• Never leave a lathe running unattended – it could appear to be stationary.
• Don't wear a necktie or loose clothing when operating a lathe.
• Remove rings and necklaces before using a lathe, and tie back long hair.
• Wear safety goggles or a full face guard to protect yourself from flying woodchips.
• It is difficult to fit a dust extractor to a lathe – so wear a mask, or a helmet fitted with a battery-powered respirator, especially if you suffer from respiratory problems.

TURNING TOOLS

Specially designed cutting tools are used for shaping workpieces on a lathe. The stocky blades are fitted with long turned handles that provide the leverage required for control of the tools. Carbon-steel blades are relatively inexpensive and are easy to sharpen. So long as you do not turn abrasive woods such as teak or elm, a carbon-steel blade will hold its edge reasonably well. High-speed-steel tools stay sharp much longer, especially on hard or wet wood, but they cost considerably more.

Basic set of turning tools

There is no need to buy every tool available. Purchase the following to begin with, then add further tools to your basic set as need arises:

Roughing-out gouge – 25mm (1in)
Spindle gouge   – 12mm ($^1/_2$in)
Bowl gouge   – 9mm ($^3/_8$in)
Skew chisel   – 18mm ($^3/_4$in)
Parting tool   – 3mm ($^1/_8$in)
Round-nose scraper – 12mm ($^1/_2$in)

MEASURING AND MARKING TOOLS

In addition to steel or wooden rules and a retractable tape measure, a woodturner requires a few special measuring, gauging and marking tools. If necessary, you can buy them from mail-order companies.

Compass

You will need a pencil compass for marking out the diameter of the workpiece. It is not necessary to purchase an expensive compass, but choose one that will maintain its accuracy – a screw-adjustable bow-spring compass is a worthwhile investment.

Calipers

These are essential for measuring the diameter of workpieces. Outside calipers are used for gauging the diameter of between-centre work and for checking on the wall thickness of turned bowls. Inside calipers measure the internal diameter of bowls and other kinds of hollowware.

Turning gouges

The blade of a turning gouge has a curved cross section and is ground on the outside only.

Roughing-out gouge

Being ground square across the tip, roughing-out gouges are used for the initial stages of turning square or octagonal stock to a cylinder. They are available in widths of 18, 25 and 32mm ($^3/_4$, 1 and 1$^1/_4$in).

Spindle gouge

This round-nosed gouge is used after the roughing-out gouge for general between-centre turning. Spindle gouges are available in a range of sizes, from 6 to 25mm ($^1/_4$ to 1in) wide.

Bowl gouge

These deep-fluted gouges allow heavy cuts to be taken when turning hollows. Standard bowl gouges range from 6 to 18mm ($^1/_4$ to $^3/_4$in). You can also buy an extra-long 18mm ($^3/_4$in) gouge.

Ring tool

Ring tools are designed to eliminate the problem of catching the corners of a gouge in the work. The ring-shaped blade (or 'eye') is ground on the outside to form a cutting edge that is 12 or 25mm ($^1/_2$ or 1in) in diameter.

Turning chisels

A turning chisel is the woodturner's equivalent of a plane. Used to smooth roughly turned workpieces, it has a rectangular-section blade ground on both sides to form a square or skewed cutting edge.

Square-end chisel

These chisels are used for finishing a workpiece when turning between centres. Blade widths range from 6 to 32mm ($^1/_4$ to 1$^1/_4$in).

Skew chisel

Like a square chisel, a skew chisel can be used for smoothing between-centre work. It is also used for shaping beads and pommels.

Roughing-out gouge
Spindle gouge
Bowl gouge
Ring tool
Square-end chisel
Skew chisel

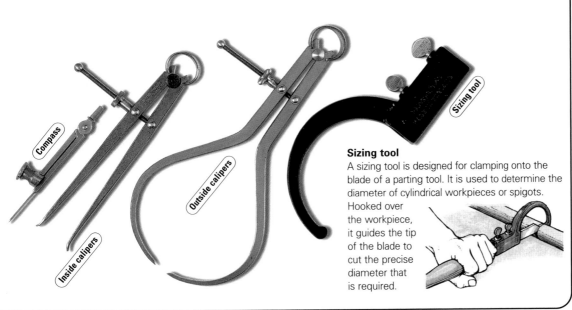

Compass

Inside calipers

Outside calipers

Sizing tool

Sizing tool
A sizing tool is designed for clamping onto the blade of a parting tool. It is used to determine the diameter of cylindrical workpieces or spigots. Hooked over the workpiece, it guides the tip of the blade to cut the precise diameter that is required.

Parting tools
These are designed for partially severing a workpiece, prior to removing it from the lathe. The blade – which usually has a rectangular section but may be faceted or oval-sectioned – is ground to a point that has a cutting edge parallel to the tool's narrow faces.

Standard parting tool
This type of parting tool is either 3 or 6mm (¹⁄₈ or ¹⁄₄in) wide.

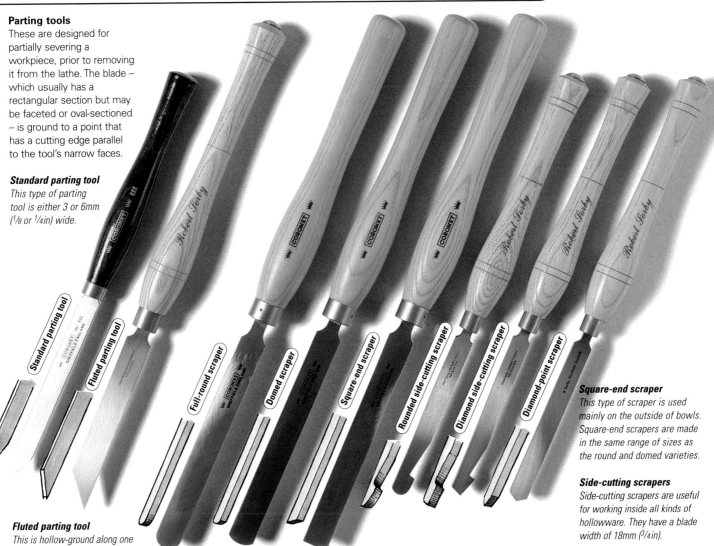

Standard parting tool

Fluted parting tool

Full-round scraper

Domed scraper

Square-end scraper

Rounded side-cutting scraper

Diamond side-cutting scraper

Diamond-point scraper

Fluted parting tool
This is hollow-ground along one narrow face to form two sharp points that scribe the wood before the tool cuts. This leaves a clean finish on end grain when the tool is held flute-down on the lathe rest. A fluted parting tool is usually 3mm (¹⁄₈in) wide.

Scrapers
Ground to a shallow cutting angle, scrapers leave a smooth finish on end grain. When you turn a bowl, two areas of end grain are presented to the tool with each revolution of the lathe. For this reason, scrapers are used primarily for cutting bowls and for other deep hollowing operations.

Full-round and domed scrapers
These curved-tip scrapers are designed primarily for working inside bowls and goblets. Blade widths range from 12 to 25mm (¹⁄₂ to 1in).

Square-end scraper
This type of scraper is used mainly on the outside of bowls. Square-end scrapers are made in the same range of sizes as the round and domed varieties.

Side-cutting scrapers
Side-cutting scrapers are useful for working inside all kinds of hollowware. They have a blade width of 18mm (³⁄₄in).

Diamond-point scraper
This scraper's tip is ground to a 90-degree point. It is used for incising V-shaped notches in between-centre work and for cleaning up square corners.

223

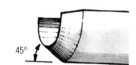

Roughing-out gouge

Spindle gouge

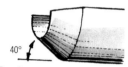

Bowl gouge

Chisel

Parting tool

Scraper

SHARPENING TURNING TOOLS

Because the work spins so fast on the lathe, a turning tool cuts through a considerable amount of wood in a matter of seconds. As a result, you need to sharpen your tools every few minutes. Many woodturners use a power grinder to sharpen lathe tools; others prefer to hone them frequently on an oilstone. Perhaps the best method is to regrind the cutting bevels for most uses, but hone the ground edge razor-sharp for fine work. Whichever method you adopt, locate your sharpening bench close to the lathe so you can sharpen your tools frequently.

New gouges, chisels and scrapers come with their bevelled cutting edges ground to the manufacturer's recommended angles. These tools will continue to perform perfectly if you maintain the same angles on a grindstone – though woodturners often regrind their tools to different cutting angles and shapes, according to personal preference.

Regrinding a gouge

Dip the tip of a gouge in a jar of cooling water and lower it bevel downwards onto the grindstone. As soon as the bevel touches the stone, roll the tool from side to side to grind the whole bevel evenly. Don't press the blade too hard, and cool the metal frequently in water. Recommended bevel angles are 45 degrees for a roughing-out gouge, 30 to 40 degrees for a spindle gouge, and 40 degrees for a bowl gouge.

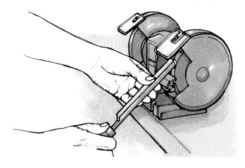

Regrinding a chisel

Sharpen both sides of a chisel, moving the tool from side to side to grind a straight cutting edge. Apply light pressure only to the tool – taking care not to grind away the points, which would create a curved cutting edge – and cool the metal frequently. Grind a chisel to an included angle of 30 degrees, and hone the edge on an oilstone.

Regrinding a parting tool

Regrind a parting tool the same way as a chisel, to an included angle of 30 degrees.

Regrinding a scraper

Most turners use a scraper straight from the grindstone – but a more efficient cutting edge is produced if you hone the bevel afterwards, then raise a burr by stroking the edge with a burnisher. Grind a scraper to an angle of 75 to 80 degrees.

BASIC TOOL CONTROL

The way you stand and move your body while woodturning is as important as the way you hold the tool. Even basic tool control demands practice, so begin by turning test pieces in softwood until you get used to the feel of the tools and have developed a sensitive touch.

Working height

Construct a strong bench to support your lathe at a comfortable working height. A height that is perfectly comfortable for one woodturner will not suit another – but as a guide, mount your lathe so that the centre line of the workpiece is at elbow height.

Correct stance and tool control

When you are turning wood between centres, stand facing the lathe, balanced comfortably with your feet apart. Don't stand too far from the machine, so you are forced to lean forwards – this soon becomes tiring and you are bound to lose an element of tool control. Hold the turning tool with its handle more or less in line with your forearm, with your elbow tucked into your side.

Control the blade of the tool with your other hand, moving the tool from side to side along the rest. Cup your hand over the blade when rough-cutting (**1**). For more delicate work, use an underhand grip with your thumb on top of the blade (**2**). With either grip, tuck your elbow close to your body.

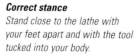

Correct stance
Stand close to the lathe with your feet apart and with the tool tucked into your body.

Poor stance
In this position you are forced to lean forwards, with an inevitable loss of control.

Moving with the tool

When turning between centres, you must keep the tool moving on a path that's parallel to the work. If you move your hands and arms only, the tool will tend to swing in an arc. The correct method is to move your whole body in the direction of the cut, in a controlled but fluid manner. Don't tense your muscles, and try not to grip the tool too firmly.

When working to the left, rotate your shoulders, twisting your body from the waist as you lean into the cut – gradually transfer your weight onto your left leg, bending it to keep your balance as you straighten your right leg.

When working to the right, open your stance to enable you to hold the tool at the required cutting angle.

Move with the tool
Twist your body from the waist as you lean into the cut.

Follow through
As you move, transfer your weight onto your left leg and bend your knee to maintain balance.

Changing direction
When working to the right, reposition your feet for good balance and a comfortable stance.

• Left-handed woodturners
If you are left-handed, the reverse stance and body action applies as you move to right or left.

CUTTING WITH A WOODTURNING TOOL

You can present a woodturning scraper square to the work and hold it more or less parallel to the floor. Many beginners use woodturning gouges and chisels in a similar fashion, scraping the wood rather than cutting it smoothly. Although this is an easy method to learn, it leaves a relatively rough surface that requires more sanding than should be necessary to achieve a satisfactory finish. Experienced woodturners use the tools with a slicing action – a technique that requires more practice, but one that all turners should aspire to.

Adjust the tool rest so it is between 6 and 12mm (1/4 and 1/2in) from the work and is positioned on its centre line. Turn the workpiece by hand to check there is a safe clearance between the wood and the rest. Switch on, then place the blade on the rest before any part of the tool comes into contact with the work. If you touch a spinning workpiece with an unsupported tool, the blade will be driven violently against the rest. This will almost certainly damage the work or tool, and may even result in injury.

With one hand below the other, Hold the tool at an angle, with its bevel resting on the wood (**1**), then slowly lift the handle to initiate the cut (**2**). Raising and lowering the handle of the tool gives you precise control over the depth of cut.

As you move the tool sideways to the left or right while turning a cylinder, incline the whole tool to induce a slicing action (**3**). At the same time, roll the blade in the direction of the sideways movement, so the cutting edge does not catch in the work (**4**).

If the tool is cutting correctly, it will produce fine shavings and leave a smooth surface that requires minimum sanding.

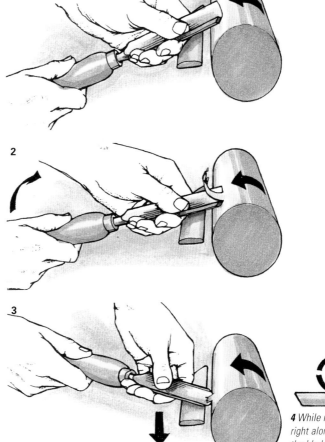

4 *While moving a gouge to the right along the tool rest, rotate the blade clockwise.*

TURNING BETWEEN CENTRES

Between-centre turning is used for making cylindrical workpieces, such as round-section chair or table legs. Although this is a relatively simple procedure, you have to be proficient with many of the basic turning tools.

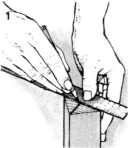

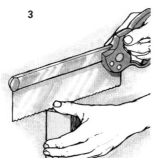

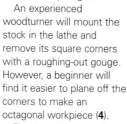

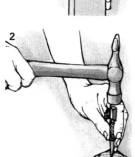

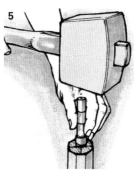

Preparing and mounting the stock

All between-centre projects start in the same manner – by converting the square-section 'stock' on the lathe. First prepare an accurately squared workpiece on a planer/thicknesser, and find its centre by drawing diagonals from corner to corner on each end (**1**).

Draw the circumference of the finished workpiece on both ends of the stock with a compass, then mark both centres (where the diagonals cross) with a metalworker's centre punch (**2**) or a bradawl. Use a tenon saw to cut a shallow kerf along both diagonals on one end to engage the drive-centre prongs (**3**).

An experienced woodturner will mount the stock in the lathe and remove its square corners with a roughing-out gouge. However, a beginner will find it easier to plane off the corners to make an octagonal workpiece (**4**).

Tap the drive centre into the kerfed end of the workpiece (**5**), then slip the tapered end of the drive centre into the headstock.

Slide the tailstock up to the work, locating the point of the tailstock centre in the central hole marked in the end grain. Clamp the tailstock to the lathe bed; then, after turning the handwheel to feed the point into the work, lock the handwheel.

Adjust the tool rest up to the work, then check clearance by revolving the workpiece by hand. Select a slow speed and, before switching on, check that all fixings are tight. After running the machine for a few minutes, switch off and put an extra turn on the handwheel to make sure the tailstock centre is still secure in the work.

Turning the stock to a cylinder

Starting at one end of the workpiece, use a roughing-out gouge to remove the corners. Make very light cuts at first, moving the gouge smoothly along the tool rest (**6**). If necessary – after switching off the lathe – move the tool rest and reduce the other end of the workpiece to the same diameter. Repeat the process until you have removed all the 'flats', leaving a cylindrical workpiece with a uniform diameter from one end to the other.

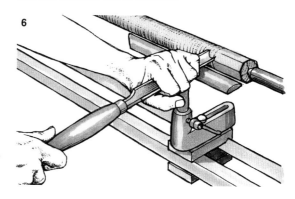

Smoothing with a chisel

Before switching on, adjust the tool rest again to suit the reduced diameter of the workpiece and practise holding the skew chisel correctly. While resting the cutting bevel on the wood, slightly rock the blade on the rest to lift the 'longer' point away from the work then incline the tool towards the direction of cut. Use the middle-to-bottom part of the cutting edge to make the cut (**7**).

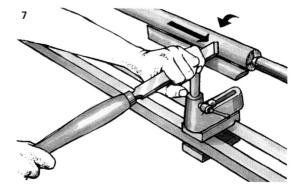

With the lathe running, start at one end of the work by gently touching the surface of the wood with the chisel until you begin to produce shavings, then smoothly move the tool sideways. Keep the cutting depth constant throughout the pass. A correct cutting action will leave a smooth 'planed' surface. At regular intervals, switch off and check the diameter of the work with calipers (**8**).

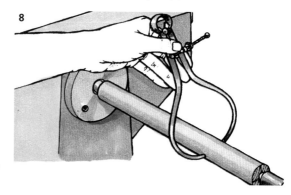

Sanding a cylinder

In theory, a properly turned workpiece should not require sanding – as the finish should be perfect straight from the chisel. In practice, however, most woodturners clean up the surface with a light sanding. Always wear a face mask when sanding on a lathe, since a great deal of fine sawdust can be produced.

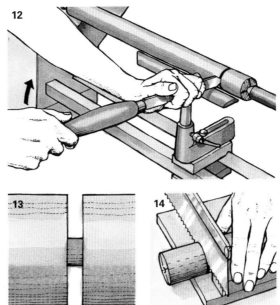

9

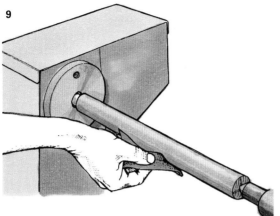

Tear a strip of fine-grade abrasive paper 75mm (3in) wide and fold it in three. Remove the tool rest, then switch on and hold the abrasive pad against the revolving workpiece with your fingertips (**9**) – or, alternatively, hold both ends of an abrasive-paper strip and wrap it over the work (**10**). Keep the paper moving along the work, so you don't leave cross-grain scratches.

10

Cutting the work to length

Replace the tool rest and mark each end of the workpiece by holding the point of a pencil against the spinning cylinder (**11**). Then hold a parting tool square to the work, with its bevel rubbing on the waste side of the marked line, and slowly lift the handle of the tool to cut a deep slot in the wood (**12**), leaving a small-diameter 'neck' at the centre of the workpiece (**13**). Do the same at the other end.

Remove the work from the lathe and sever the waste by cutting through the neck with a tenon saw (**14**). Trim the end grain flush, using a firmer chisel.

11

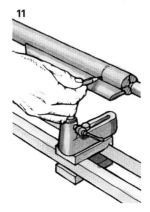

POLISHING ON A LATHE

You can apply a polish to turned work before taking it from the lathe. French polish is a suitable sealer for all woods except oily open-grain timbers such as teak or afrormosia. Choose transparent French polish for pale-coloured timbers, and button or garnet polish for darker woods.

Brush liquid French polish onto the workpiece (**1**), then select a slow lathe speed and switch on. Wear goggles or spectacles to protect your eyes from polish thrown off as the wood starts moving. Use a bunched soft rag to rub the polish into the grain. Take special care to keep the cloth away from all moving lathe parts. While the work is still rotating, rub the surface with a stick of hard wax and burnish it with a clean rag.

1

Apply teak oil to open-grain woods that do not require a gloss finish. Paint the oil on and burnish it with a rag (**2**). On turned salad bowls and platters, use edible vegetable oil or a commercial salad-bowl oil.

2

DECORATIVE TURNING

If the workpiece is to incorporate beads and hollows as a form of decoration, it is not necessary to smooth or sand the wood accurately before shaping it. Simply turn the rough stock to a cylinder with a gouge, and then mark out the beads and hollows.

A bead is a rounded convex shape used for decorative purposes; a hollow, or cove, is concave. The junction between hollows and beads is often demarcated by short shoulders known as fillets.

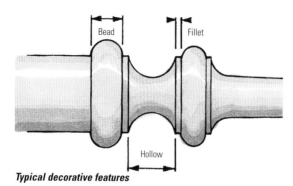

Typical decorative features

Marking out beads and hollows

Use a straight rule and a pencil to mark out the positions of beads and hollows along the workpiece. When you switch on the lathe, your pencil marks will appear as continuous faint lines. Make the marks more visible by touching them with a pencil point while the lathe is running.

Cutting beads

Place one narrow edge of a skew chisel on the tool rest, and touch the workpiece with the 'longer' point of the chisel to cut a 3mm (1/8in) groove on each marked line. This is achieved by lifting the tool's handle to lower the point slowly into the workpiece. Rock the chisel to one side then the other to open up the grooves into V-shaped notches (**1**). Remove about 3mm (1/8in) of wood on each side of the grooves.

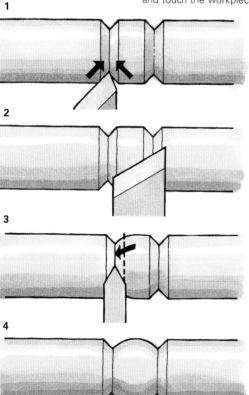

To shape one side of a bead, lay the chisel's cutting bevel on the wood between the V-shaped notches (**2**) and then gradually rotate the tool's handle to bring the blade upright in the centre of one of the notches (**3**). Cut the other side of the bead in a similar way. Repeat the action, taking very shallow cuts, to smooth the bead and remove any remaining ridges (**4**). Check the 'horizon' of the workpiece to see the exact shape of the bead you are cutting. Keep the chisel square to the work – if you swing the handle sideways as you rotate it, you may catch the point of the tool in the wood.

TURNING FROM SQUARE TO ROUND

Turned table and chair legs are sometimes left square at one or both ends to receive mortise-and-tenon or dowel joints for the crossrails. Because this type of leg has to be turned from square-section stock, you need to be an experienced woodturner in order to attempt this technique.

Before mounting the stock on the lathe, cut the joints and very clearly mark the shoulders of each section that are to be left square (**1**).

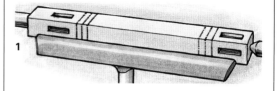

Use the point of a skew chisel to cut a V-shaped notch on the shoulder lines, then carefully roll the chisel to cut a half-bead on each side (**2**). Use a roughing-out gouge to turn the part of the stock between the squared ends to a cylinder; then finish it with a chisel and abrasive paper in the usual way.

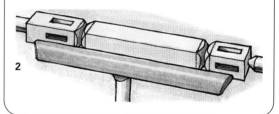

Cutting hollows and fillets

To turn hollows, use a 12mm (1/2in) spindle gouge or a bowl gouge that has its corners ground away to form a cutting tip with a rounded point. Remove some of the waste from between the beads by sweeping the tip of the gouge from side to side (**1**).

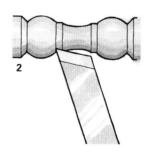

Use the point of a skew chisel to carefully shape a fillet on each side (**2**). Shape the hollow, starting on one side with the gouge rolled on the tool rest so that its flute is turned away from the bead. Slide the gouge towards the centre of the hollow, while rolling the blade and advancing the tip of the tool into the work (**3**). Shape the other side of the hollow the same way.

Repeat the process, taking very shallow cuts with the gouge and always working 'downhill' from the outside of the hollow towards the middle.

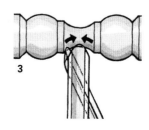

TURNING WITH ONE CENTRE

When making items that have to be hollowed out – such as boxes, egg cups and vases – you need to remove the tailstock, so you can turn the end grain. Consequently, the workpiece has to be held securely at one end by one of several special chucks mounted on the headstock spindle.

Woodscrew chucks

One of the simplest chucks incorporates a threaded screw that is driven into a predrilled hole in the workpiece. The most basic chucks are made with a standard woodscrew, but better-quality versions have a coarse purpose-made screw that bites securely into end-grain as well as side-grain timber. A screw chuck is able to hold relatively short workpieces only.

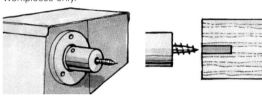

Woodscrew chuck

Cup chuck

A cup chuck has a hollow recess that accommodates a cylindrical spigot turned on one end of a workpiece. Very often a cup chuck is designed to function by means of a good friction fit between it and the work. However, some chucks are made with provision for woodscrew-fixings for additional security. A cup chuck will support a workpiece that is too long for a screw chuck.

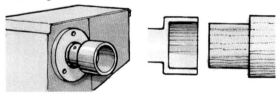

Cup chuck

Pin chuck

A pin chuck is designed to be inserted in a hole drilled in one end of the workpiece. A small-diameter metal pin rests in a shallow depression machined longitudinally in the chuck spigot. When stationary, the spigot (together with the pin) slides effortlessly into the workpiece. As soon as the lathe is switched on, centrifugal force causes the pin to climb the sloping face of the depression and grip the timber.

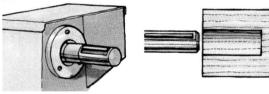

Pin chuck

Three-jaw chuck

This type of chuck has three key-operated self-centring jaws that grip a cylindrical workpiece or spigot, or expand to grip a hollow workpiece. Although it has been used by generations of woodturners, this device is not universally popular because there is the possibility of injuring one's knuckles on the jaws while the lathe is running. If you fit a three-jaw chuck, protect yourself by mounting the appropriate guard.

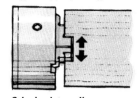

Three-jaw chuck   *Gripping internally*   *Gripping externally*

Combination chucks

One-centre turning has been revolutionized by the development of combination chucks. These ingeniously engineered devices incorporate not only woodscrew, pin and cup-chuck facilities but also contracting collets that can grip a cylindrical workpiece or expand to fit a 'dovetail' recess turned in the base of a bowl or similar object.

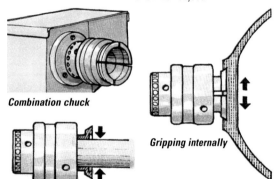

Combination chuck

Gripping internally

Gripping externally

TURNING A HOLLOW WORKPIECE

Rough out the stock between centres and shape the end section of the workpiece to fit the chuck.

Remove the tailstock, fit the workpiece to the chuck and skim the wood with a gouge to ensure it is turning centrally. Swing the tool rest across the work so you can hollow out the inside, using a bowl gouge or scraper (**1**). If you are turning cross-grain wood, work from the rim of the workpiece towards the centre; when turning end-grain wood, work from the centre outwards. In either case, use the tool on the down side of the work only – that is the half moving downwards towards the tool rest. After hollowing out the workpiece, check the internal diameter with inside calipers (**2**). Then turn the outside. Use a parting tool to detach the work.

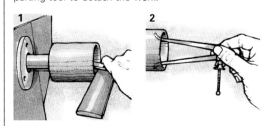

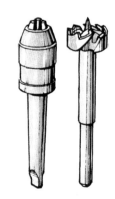

Drilling on a lathe
To bore a hole in the end of a workpiece, fit a lathe drill chuck with a tapered shaft into the tailstock of the lathe. With the work held securely in a one-centre chuck, select a slow lathe speed and advance the drill bit by turning the tailstock handwheel. You can use a special saw-tooth centre bit, which cuts end grain cleanly, or an ordinary twist drill or a spade or Forstner bit.

229

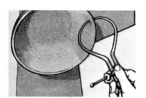

Checking the rim
An experienced turner can reduce the rim of a bowl to 3mm (1/8in) or less, but beginners should be less ambitious. The bowl will be stronger if the thickness of the sides taper from base to rim.

FACEPLATE TURNING

When turning a bowl, the bowl blank must be fixed securely to the lathe, using either a combination chuck or a faceplate. A faceplate is a cast-metal disc threaded to fit the lathe's drive spindle.

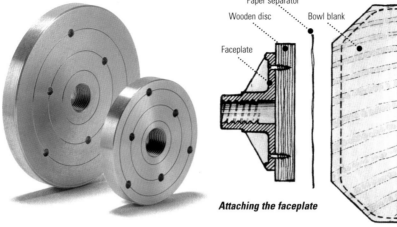

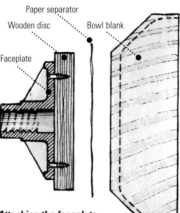

Paper separator
Wooden disc
Bowl blank
Faceplate

Attaching the faceplate

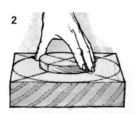

1

2

Mounting the faceplate
One way to attach the faceplate is to screw it to a hardwood disc glued temporarily to the base of the workpiece.

Plane a flat face on the square workpiece and draw diagonals from one corner to another to define the centre. Using a compass, draw a circle slightly larger than the circumference of the bowl and then draw another circle representing the circumference of its base (**1**).

Cut a disc from hardwood 18mm (3/4in) thick, with the same diameter as the base of the bowl. Cut another disc the same size from brown paper. Spread adhesive on both pieces of wood, then stick the paper to the wooden disc and glue both centrally onto the workpiece (**2**). Apply a cramp and leave the glue to set.

Draw the circumference of the faceplate on the disc, and attach the plate centrally with three or four No10 woodscrews. The screw threads should penetrate the full thickness of the wooden disc.

Cut the waste off the workpiece on a band saw, to leave a circular bowl blank. Attach the faceplate to the drive spindle.

3

Turning the outside of the bowl
Adjust the tool rest so it is centred on the edge of the bowl blank. Spin the work by hand to check that it is free to rotate. Then select a slow speed and switch on.

True up the circumference of the blank with a roughing-out gouge, then change to a bowl gouge for shaping the outside of the bowl (**3**). Lower the tool rest slightly and increase the lathe speed, then use a round-nose scraper to smooth the work.

4

Turning the inside of the bowl
Swing the tool rest round to align with the wide face of the workpiece, and begin to hollow out the bowl with the lathe running at a slow speed. Remove the waste with a bowl gouge, working on the 'down' side of the bowl and cutting back towards the centre from a point halfway to the rim of the bowl (**4**). As you cut deeper, start a little closer to the rim with each pass of the tool.

With the waste removed, increase lathe speed and use a scraper to complete the inside of the bowl.

As the work progresses, check the shape of your bowl with card templates and calipers.

Sanding the bowl
Reduce the speed again. Remove the tool rest and use a strip of medium to fine abrasive paper to sand the surfaces (**5**). Keep the paper moving to avoid leaving scratches, and trail the paper on the 'down' side only.

5

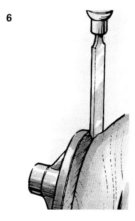

Finishing and dismantling
Apply a wood finish such as wax polish or teak oil while the work is still attached to the lathe. Then unscrew the faceplate.

To remove the wooden disc from the base of the bowl, place the tip of a sharp chisel on the joint line and tap gently to split the paper separator (**6**).

6

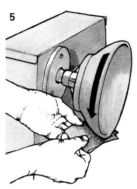

CHAPTER SIX

HOME WORKSHOPS

Some woodworkers are able to produce superb work in a chaotic environment but most would agree that a clean, well-planned workshop is conducive to good working practices, as well as being a safer and more pleasant place to work in. When planning the layout of your workshop, try to think ahead and make provision for your future needs. Suppose you have a fairly extensive kit of handtools and a few portable power tools at the moment; if there's a possibility that you may want to install woodworking machines some time in the future, allow space for them or at least make the layout easy to convert at a later date.

Most woodworkers hoard oddments of wood that might come in handy – but a small workshop soon becomes cluttered if you try to save every offcut, and there's no point in hoarding materials if you can never find them when they are wanted. It therefore pays to clear out your workshop ruthlessly every few months, keeping only those items that are really likely to be of use.

EQUIPPING A WORKSHOP

Unless you're starting from scratch it may not be possible to create a perfect working environment, but by careful planning you can convert an existing building such as a garage or barn into an effective workshop. Ground-floor accommodation is essential if you plan to install heavy machinery; it is also more convenient for the delivery of boards and lengths of timber. Ideally, a workshop should be separate from your living quarters in order to reduce noise pollution and keep dust and fumes away from the house.

Fire prevention

Dispose of dust and shavings regularly, and never store oily rags in your workshop. Fit reliable smoke detectors, and always have a good-quality fire blanket and extinguisher to hand.

Fire extinguisher

Battery-operated smoke detector

1 Electrical sockets

Install double electrical sockets above the worktop. If your mains wiring is not protected by a residual current device, to cut off the power in the event of an electrical fault, consider buying sockets that have an integral RCD. If you have a lot of cordless power tools, create a charging station by installing several sockets together in one area of the shop.

2 Narrow shelving

Store small packets of fixings and glass jars of screws and other hardware on narrow shelves. This enables you to review your stock at a glance.

3 Tool storage

Store your handtools within reach of your bench. Hang them on dowel pegs glued into a sheet of plywood. Alternatively, make a wall-hung tool rack.

4 Lighting

Where possible, place your workbench next to a window so you have good natural light. Fit fluorescent lights to provide shadow-free illumination: use 'daylight' tubes to help accurate matching of colours and veneers.

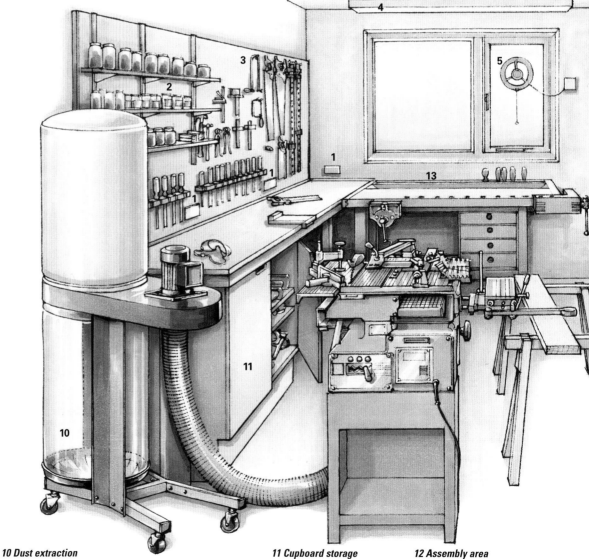

10 Dust extraction

To keep your workshop clean and reduce health hazards, connect a portable dust extractor to your woodworking machinery. Smaller dust extractors are available for power tools. In addition, you can suspend a remote-controlled air filter from the ceiling to remove fine airborne dust.

11 Cupboard storage

Keep heavy handtools and power tools in a low cupboard.

12 Assembly area

Leave an open space where you can assemble cabinets or erect a temporary bench on sawhorses for lightweight assemblies and for finishing work.

Few woodworkers can afford the luxury of separate workshops for machines and hand work. Consequently, most people have to find a way to fit a number of machines and benches into a restricted space.

Measure your workshop and plot the ground plan on squared paper, then try various arrangements with scaled paper cutouts of the machines. The object of the exercise is to ensure you will have an unrestricted pathway for workpieces through each machine – and when you consider that you will want to be able to pass a full 2.44 x 1.22m (8 x 4ft) board across a table saw, it becomes obvious how important it is to allow sufficient working space around the machines.

One solution is to group the machines in the centre of the workshop, with their workpiece pathways at right angles to each other (see below). This layout works well provided you never have to operate all the machines at once – and with a one-person workshop that should never be necessary.

If the workshop is too narrow for this arrangement, it may be possible to arrange the machines in line but stagger them slightly so that a board passing over one machine will be supported by the worktable of a neighbouring machine – though you may have to adjust the height of the worktables to create a clear pathway. Alternatively, it may be convenient to position a portable roller stand on the outfeed side of a machine in order to support a long board or feed it over the table of the next machine in line.

A lathe or pillar drill can be positioned against a wall, allowing for adequate clearance on either side.

The machine shop
One solution for a combined machine and hand workshop is to group the machines in the centre. The workpiece pathways cross at right angles.

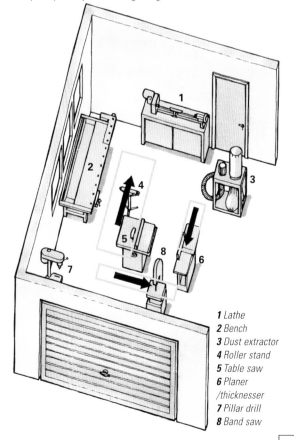

1 Lathe
2 Bench
3 Dust extractor
4 Roller stand
5 Table saw
6 Planer /thicknesser
7 Pillar drill
8 Band saw

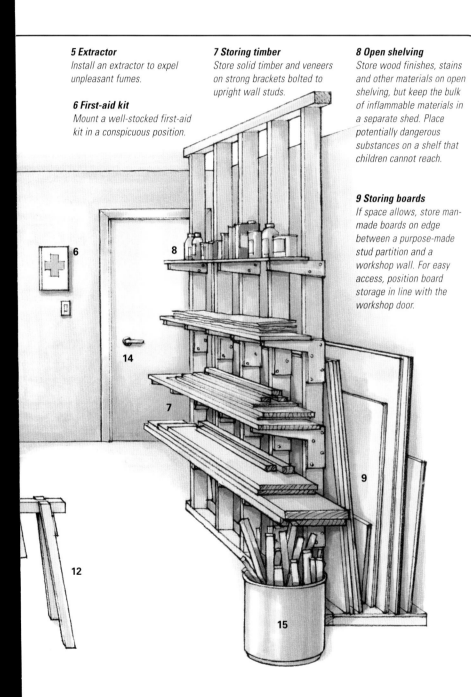

5 Extractor
Install an extractor to expel unpleasant fumes.

6 First-aid kit
Mount a well-stocked first-aid kit in a conspicuous position.

7 Storing timber
Store solid timber and veneers on strong brackets bolted to upright wall studs.

8 Open shelving
Store wood finishes, stains and other materials on open shelving, but keep the bulk of inflammable materials in a separate shed. Place potentially dangerous substances on a shelf that children cannot reach.

9 Storing boards
If space allows, store man-made boards on edge between a purpose-made stud partition and a workshop wall. For easy access, position board storage in line with the workshop door.

13 Workbench
A sturdy workbench is essential. A cabinet-maker's bench fitted with vices is ideal, but you can build a simpler workbench of your own design against a wall.

14 Security
Fit locks to workshop doors and windows – not only to deter burglars but to keep children away from harmful chemicals and machinery.

15 Scrap storage
Store short lengths of scrap timber on end in plastic bins.

233

BENCHES AND ACCESSORIES

A woodworker's bench is one of the most important pieces of equipment in the workshop. It is virtually impossible to produce quality work on a bench that is not sturdily constructed and fitted with well-machined vices, so choose your bench carefully.

Most woodwork benches are between 800 and 850mm (2ft 8in and 2ft 10in) high. However, you can have higher or lower benches made to order. Some manufacturers offer left-handed benches – in effect, a mirror image of the standard format.

Woodworker's bench

A good bench will have a hardwood worktop at least 50mm (2in) thick. Tough short-grain beech is the most common material for worktop construction, although birch, maple and African hardwoods are also used. Some benches are made with a worktop partly constructed from plywood. Provided the plywood veneers are thick enough to withstand periodic scraping in order to clean glue and spilled finishes from the surface, a composite construction is not necessarily a disadvantage.

You can choose a bench with a plain worktop, but the majority are made with a shallow tool well. This temporary-storage facility enables you to move a large workpiece or frame across the bench without sweeping handtools onto the floor. Other benches are supplied with a tool tray that can be bolted to the edge of the worktop. A slot or row of holes along the back edge of the bench for storing saws and chisels is yet another option.

One or two models are made with softwood underframes, but most benches are constructed entirely from hardwood. Look for a bench with mortise-and-tenoned endframes securely bolted to wide crossrails, and check that the underframe is stable enough not to distort when you apply sideways pressure to the worktop. Most manufacturers offer at least one simple drawer as an optional extra, and some benches have a fully enclosed tool cupboard.

Woodworking vices

Every woodworker needs at least one large vice fixed permanently to the front edge of the worktop, as close as possible to one of the legs of the underframe. This leg will prevent any flexing of the worktop caused by working wood clamped in the jaws of the vice. Continental-style vices are made with wooden jaws to grip the work without marking it. Another common style of vice has cast-metal jaws lined with timber. Both types of vice can be operated by turning a large tommy-bar handle on the front jaw, but some metal vices are also equipped with a quick-release lever which permits the jaws to be opened and closed rapidly by a straight pull or push.

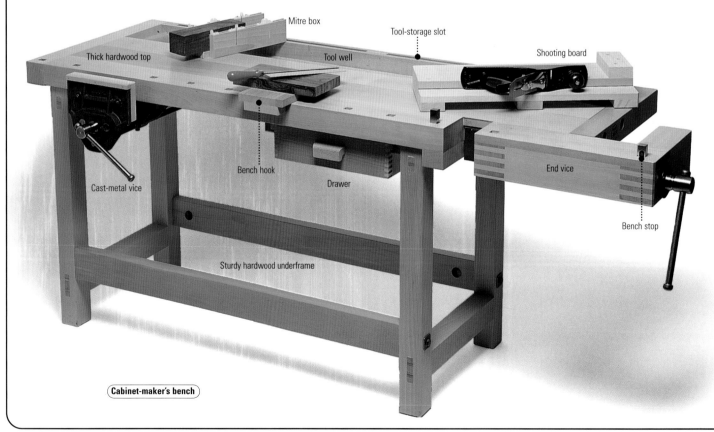

Mitre box

Tool-storage slot

Thick hardwood top

Tool well

Shooting board

Cast-metal vice

Bench hook

Drawer

End vice

Bench stop

Sturdy hardwood underframe

Cabinet-maker's bench

End vice

Better-quality benches are constructed with a vice built into one end of the worktop. An end vice provides clamping force along the bench to hold a workpiece between metal or wooden stops dropped into square holes cut into the vice and at regular intervals along one or both sides of the worktop. The workpiece can also be clamped upright in the vice jaws.

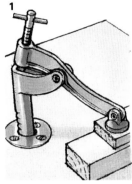

Holdfast

A holdfast is a removable bench-mounted clamp, used to hold a workpiece on the bench top. It has a long shaft that fits into a hole drilled into the top and lined with a metal collar (**1**). Turning a screw presses a pivoted arm down onto the work.

A second collar fitted into a bench leg enables you to use a holdfast to support the end of a long board held in the bench's woodworking vice (**2**).

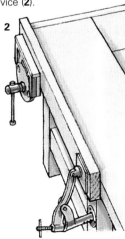

CUTTING AND PLANING GUIDES

Cutting and planing guides are bench accessories that you can buy or make yourself. They are used for holding wood steady, and some guide the tool relative to the work. They may also protect the bench top from tool damage.

Bench hook

A bench hook enables you to hold small sections of wood while cutting them with a backsaw. Hook the guide over the edge of the bench and hold the work against the stop block while sawing. When it becomes worn, turn the bench hook over.

Mitre box

This jig is for sawing mitre joints. The box has two raised sides with slots cut in them to guide the saw blade. The central slot, cut square across the box, is useful for sawing to length mouldings that are difficult to mark with a try square.

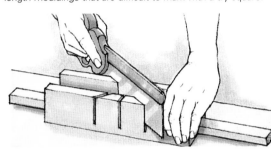

Mitre block

A mitre block is a simpler version of the mitre box, having only one raised side. It is used in a similar way to a bench hook.

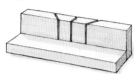

Shooting boards

A shooting board is used to jig the work for planing end grain. To trim mitre joints, plane them on a mitre shooting board, which has angled stops.

FOLDING BENCH

If workshop space is limited, use a portable bench that folds flat for storage. The bench unfolds to standard bench height, but can be lowered to a convenient level for sawing.

The worktop comprises two vice jaws, one of which can be slewed to grip tapered workpieces or straightened up for parallel-sided wood. You can clamp a workpiece to the top of the bench between plastic pegs.

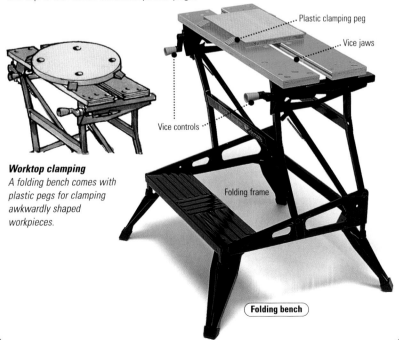

Worktop clamping
A folding bench comes with plastic pegs for clamping awkwardly shaped workpieces.

Plastic clamping peg

Vice jaws

Vice controls

Folding frame

(**Folding bench**)

Sawhorses
These lightweight trestles are used singly or in pairs to support the work when sawing planks or boards. The legs are splayed and braced to provide a steady platform approximately 600mm (2ft) from the floor.

Planing on a shooting board
When planing end grain, the work is held against the stop block, which prevents the wood splitting as you slide a bench plane along the shooting board to take a fine shaving.

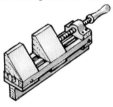

Mitre shooting block
A mitre shooting block has an adjustable jaw that clamps large mitred workpieces for trimming with a plane. To hold the jig at a comfortable height, clamp the strip fixed to the underside of the shooting block in a vice.

HEALTH AND SAFETY

Commercial workshops have to comply with strict regulations and restrictions to safeguard the health and safety of workers. Although the rules are not mandatory for home workshops, it makes sense to protect yourself from harmful fumes, dust and noise. You also need to protect your eyes and face from pieces of wood or metal thrown up by machines or power tools.

Safety spectacles
Made from tough impact-resistant polycarbonate plastic, safety spectacles have side screens to protect your eyes from dust and wood particles.

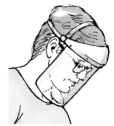

Goggles
The lenses of safety goggles are surrounded by a soft plastic frame that fits and seals against the contours of your face. The sides are ventilated to prevent condensation. Safety goggles can be worn over spectacles.

Face screen
Total face protection is provided by the hinged plastic visor of a face screen – a particularly comfortable form of protection if you wear glasses. A helmet fitted with a battery-powered respirator offers face protection and prevents dust inhalation.

Hearing protectors
Earplugs and ear defenders protect your hearing from exposure to noise. Always wear protectors when using noisy power tools or machines, as they could cause long-term damage to your hearing.

Face mask
A simple face mask with a replaceable filter protects your lungs from dust and unpleasant non-toxic fumes.

Respirator
A dual-cartridge respirator provides full protection against the harmful effects of paints, lacquers, adhesives and toxic dust. Interchangeable colour-coded cartridges are designed to filter specific materials.

LIGHTING
Take care when using machinery – fluorescent lighting can create the illusion that cutters and lathe chucks are stationary.

Large-volume dust extractor
Connect this type of extractor to woodworking machinery.

Industrial vacuum cleaner
This machine doubles as a dust extractor for power tools.

DUST EXTRACTION

Sawdust and shavings left to pile up on the workshop floor constitute a serious fire hazard. The risk is increased when very fine dust is allowed to float in the air, contributing to a potentially explosive atmosphere. Moreover, dust makes the floor slippery, is harmful to your lungs, and can ruin lacquered or varnished surfaces. Industrial workshops are usually equipped with purpose-built dust-extraction systems serving all the machines. This type of installation is prohibitively expensive for the home woodworker, but simpler portable extractors are available to suit the smaller workshop.

Dust extractors
Mobile large-volume dust extractors are ideal for the small machine shop. Dust sucked through a flexible hose is filtered from the air by a woven-cotton bag, mounted on top of the machine, and collected in a sack below. The hose takes a variety of shaped mouthpieces designed to fit different woodworking machines. Some extractors can be equipped with dual hoses to serve two machines simultaneously.

Industrial vacuum cleaners
A heavy-duty vacuum cleaner is an essential piece of workshop equipment. It is supplied with the usual range of hoses and nozzles, which you can use for cleaning the floor and your woodworking machinery. When fitted with the appropriate accessories, the same machine can be connected directly to portable power tools, in order to eliminate dust or shavings at source. In this mode, operation is by remote control, being activated by the power-tool switch.

CHAPTER SEVEN

JOINT-MAKING

It is hardly surprising that many people regard joint-making as a measure of a cabinet-maker's skill, since the ability to cut fine joints takes practice and requires the mastering of a variety of accurate cutting techniques using saws, planes and chisels. However, the choice of joint is no less important than the quality of the making. The design must primarily be functional to provide strength, but it should also be in keeping with the overall style of the project. Most joints are designed to conceal the methods used to hold the parts together, while others – such as decorative dovetails – are made a feature. This chapter illustrates the most common hand-cut joints and how to make them. Generally, dimensions have not been specified, as different projects require joints of different sizes. Instead, relative proportions are given to enable you to make sound joints to suit your requirements.

BUTT JOINTS

The butt joint is the simplest of the various joints where one member meets another with no interlocking elements cut into the parts. It is not a strong joint, and is often reinforced in some way. Right-angled butt joints are used in the construction of light frames and small boxes. The jointing ends may be square-cut or mitred.

SQUARE-ENDED BUTT JOINT

Butt joints for boxes are made with the end of one member glued to the inside face of the other. For frames, the end is glued to the edge. It is essential for the surfaces to be flat and the ends square.

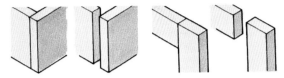

Cutting the joint

Mark the length of the parts and square a shoulder line all round with a marking knife. Using a bench hook to hold the work, saw off the waste clear of the line (**1**).

Trim the ends square to form a neat joint, using a bench plane and shooting board (**2**). Set the plane for a fine cut, and lubricate the running surfaces of the shooting board with a white candle or with wax polish.

Apply glue to the joint and clamp the parts together, making sure the components are aligned properly.

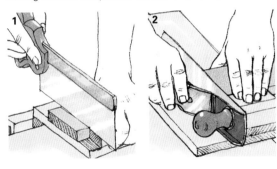

MITRED BUTT JOINT

Commonly used for picture frames, the mitred butt joint makes a neat right-angle corner without visible end grain. Cutting wood at 45 degrees produces a relatively large surface area of tangentially cut grain that glues well. For lightweight frames, just add glue and set the joint in a mitre cramp.

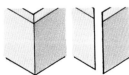

Accurate mitre-cutting

Before you pick up a saw, make sure the mitre will be exactly half the joint angle – if not, the joint will be gappy (**1**). Use well-seasoned timber, or a gap may open up on the inside of the joint as the wood shrinks (**2**).

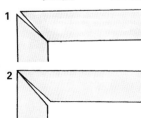

Marking and cutting the mitre

On each piece of wood, mark the sloping shoulder of the joint, using a knife and mitre square; then use a try square to extend the marked line across the adjacent faces. To remove the waste, either follow the marked lines by eye or use a mitre box to guide the saw blade (**3**).

Hold the work on a mitre shooting board and trim each cut end with a sharp bench plane (**4**).

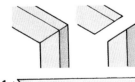

Since it is impossible to mitre a wide piece of wood on a shooting board, either use a mitre shooting block (**5**) or clamp the work upright in a bench vice and trim the end grain with a finely set block plane. To prevent splitting, back up the work with a piece of scrap timber (**6**).

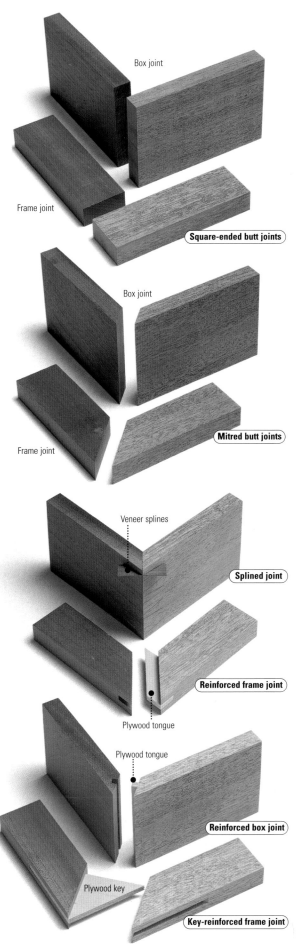

Box joint

Frame joint

Square-ended butt joints

Box joint

Frame joint

Mitred butt joints

Veneer splines

Splined joint

Plywood tongue

Reinforced frame joint

Plywood tongue

Reinforced box joint

Plywood key

Key-reinforced frame joint

REINFORCING MITRED JOINTS

The easiest way to reinforce a mitred joint is to glue the joint first and add the reinforcement when set. Use a mitre cramp or a web cramp for gluing up.

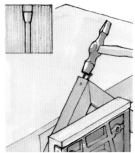

Disguising a nailed joint

Drive panel pins flush with the wood, then punch the heads below the surface, using a nail set. Use matching wood filler to disguise the holes.

Reinforcing with veneer splines

Make angled sawcuts across the corner of a wide mitre joint. Cut strips of veneer for the splines and glue them into the sawcuts. When the glue has set, trim the splines flush.

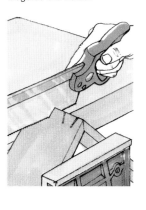

Reinforcing with a tongue

You can use a plywood tongue to reinforce a mitre joint before gluing. Centre the groove in joints for a mitred frame (**1**). To reinforce a cabinet or box, set the groove nearer the inside of the corner joints (**2**) – to avoid leaving weak short grain.

For even greater strength, insert a large plywood tongue or key in a mitred frame joint after the glue has set. To mark a slot for the key, set a mortise gauge and scribe parallel lines, centred on the edges of each workpiece (**3**). Mark each end of the slot between the gauged lines, using a knife and try square.

Clamp the joint vertically in a vice and saw down the waste side of the lines. Using a chisel and working from each side towards the middle, chop out the waste (**4**). Glue the key in the slot, and trim flush when the glue has set.

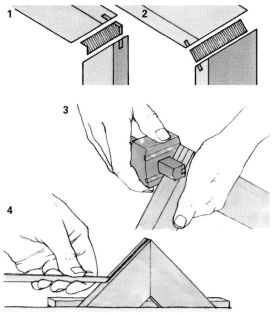

Reinforcing square butt joints

For additional strength, drive nails at an angle into the wood. Alternatively, if you don't want the method of fixing to show on the outside of the joint, glue a corner block on the inside.

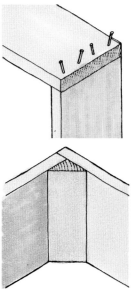

239

LAP JOINTS

The lap joint is used for simple box and cabinet construction. It is also known as a rebate joint, the end of one part being set in a rebate cut in the other.

SIMPLE LAP JOINT

A basic lap joint is only marginally stronger than a straightforward butt joint, but it offers an improvement in appearance since most of the end grain is concealed.

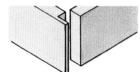

Marking and cutting a lap joint

Cut and plane both members square. Adjust a marking gauge to about one-quarter of the thickness of the rebate member and scribe a line across the end grain (**1**), working from the face side. Continue the line on both edges, down to the level of the shoulder.

Set a cutting gauge to match the thickness of the side member, and scribe a shoulder line parallel to the end grain on the back of the rebate member (**2**). Continue the shoulder line across both edges to meet the lines already scribed.

Clamp the rebate member upright in a vice. Following the line scribed across the end grain, saw down to the shoulder line. Lay the work face-down on a bench hook and cut down the shoulder line with a tenon saw to remove the waste (**3**). make a neat joint by cleaning up the rebate with a shoulder plane.

Glue and clamp the joint, then drive panel pins through the side member.

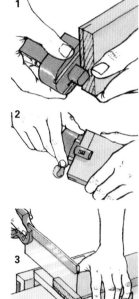

MITRED LAP JOINT

A mitred lap joint is neater than the basic version, but more difficult to cut. The extra effort is worthwhile if you want a concealed joint.

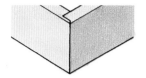
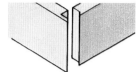

Marking and cutting a mitred lap joint

Cut the rebate (see left), then mark a mitre on the edges of the lap (**1**). Score a line across the inside of the lap to mark the base of the mitre. Plane off the waste down to this line.

Having set a cutting gauge to the thickness of the lap, scribe a shoulder line across the inside of the side member and across both edges. Then, with the stock of the same gauge pressed against the face side, scribe a line across the end grain and down each edge to meet the shoulder line. Mark the slope of the mitre from the outer corner down to the shoulder line (**2**).

Set the workpiece upright in a vice and, following the line scribed across the end grain, saw down to meet the shoulder line. Then, holding the wood face-down on a bench hook, saw down the shoulder line to remove the waste. Use a shoulder plane to trim the mitre, clamping a bevelled backing board behind the work (**3**).

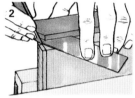

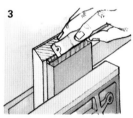

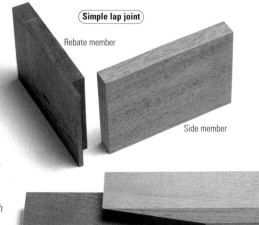

Simple lap joint

Rebate member

Side member

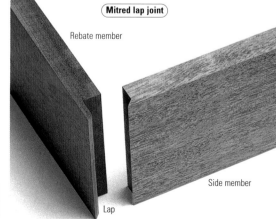

Mitred lap joint

Rebate member

Side member

Lap

Scarf joint
A form of lap and mitre joint in one, this is used to join wood end to end. You can saw or plane the long shallow tapers, which give a large gluing area. Make the length of the tapers at least four times the thickness of the wood.

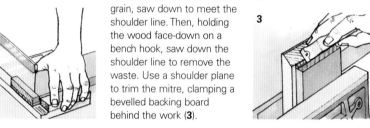

HALVING JOINTS

Halving joints are employed exclusively for framing, using wood of equal thickness for both components of the joint. These joints are easy to cut with handtools or with a machine. Shown here are methods for hand-cutting different forms of the basic joint.

CROSS HALVING JOINT

Both halves of this joint are identical, with half the thickness removed from each piece of wood. Convention dictates that the vertical member appears to run through uninterrupted.

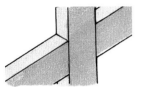

Marking and cutting a cross halving joint

Lay both components side by side and score the shoulder lines across them, using a try square and marking knife (**1**). Continue both sets of marked lines halfway down each edge.

Set a marking gauge to exactly half the thickness of the wood, and scribe a line between the shoulders marked on the edges of both components (**2**).

Saw halfway through both pieces of wood on the waste side of each shoulder line, then divide the waste wood between the shoulders with one or two additional sawcuts (**3**).

Clamp the work in a vice and chisel out a recess (**4**), working from each side.

CORNER HALVING JOINT

You can construct a simple framework with halving joints at each corner, but since the joint relies almost entirely on the glue for strength, you may need to reinforce it with screws or dowels.

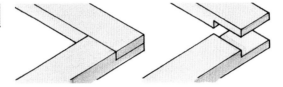

Marking and cutting a corner joint

Lay the components side by side and mark the shoulder line across both of them (**1**), using a knife and try square. Continue the lines down each edge. Set a marking gauge to half the thickness of the wood, and scribe a line on both edges (**2**) and across the end grain.

Clamp each workpiece upright in a vice and remove the waste with a tenon saw, cutting downwards from the end grain. Lay the wood on a bench hook and saw the shoulder.

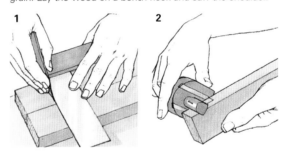

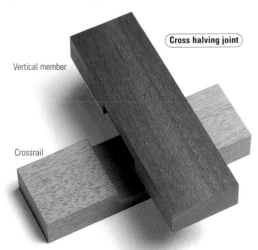

Cross halving joint

Vertical member

Crossrail

Corner halving joint

Mitred corner halving joint
A refined version of the joint, with even less gluing area.

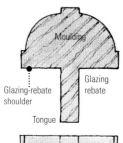

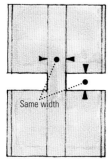

Width of slots

GLAZING-BAR HALVING JOINT

Cutting a halving joint in glazing bars involves a method similar to that used for making a standard cross halving joint, but it is more complicated because you are joining moulded sections.

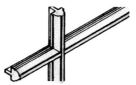

Cutting the joint

Cut a narrow slot on each side of both moulded components, down to the level of the glazing-rebate tongue. Make each slot as wide as the tongue. When sawing the slots, it pays to hold the work in a mitre box, using the 90-degree guides (**1**).

Pare away wood on each side of the slots to form a 45-degree mitre (**2**). Make a mitre guide block from scrap wood to help keep the chisel blade at the required angle.

Now cut the recesses in each component to form the cross halving joint (**3**). Cut each recess down to the level of the glazing-rebate shoulder.

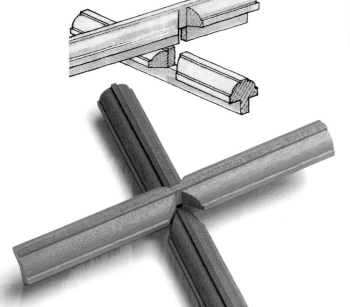

(Glazing-bar halving joint)

OBLIQUE HALVING JOINT

The only difference between this and a standard cross halving joint is that the recesses are not set at right angles. Use a mitre square to mark out a 45-degree joint; for other angles, use a sliding bevel.

Marking and cutting the joint

Using a pencil and the mitre square or sliding bevel, mark a shoulder line across one of the components and, placing the other piece of wood against the line, mark its width (**1**). Then score both lines, using a marking knife with the square or bevel.

Mark the width of the recess on the edges of both components (**2**), then use a try square to continue the shoulder lines down each edge. Scribe a line between them with a marking gauge set to half the thickness of the wood.

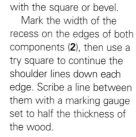

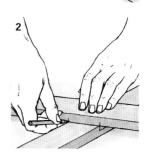

Saw on the waste side of each shoulder (**3**), then cut out the waste as for a standard cross halving joint.

(Oblique halving joint)

T-HALVING JOINT

This is used for joining an intermediate support to a frame or rail. One member has a lap (as in a corner halving joint), and the other a recess (as in a cross halving joint).

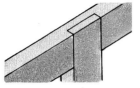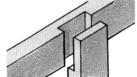

Marking and cutting a T-halving joint

Taking the dimensions from relevant components, score the shoulder lines with a knife and try square, then use a marking gauge to scribe the depth of the joint on each workpiece (**1**).

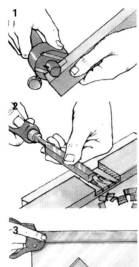

To create the recess, saw both shoulders and make a few sawcuts across the waste before paring it out with a chisel (**2**).

To shape the lap on the other component, saw down to the shoulder, keeping the saw blade just to the waste side of the gauged line. If you tilt the work away from you while sawing down one edge (**3**), you may find it easier to keep the cut vertical. Turn the work round and saw down the other edge, then finish off by sawing squarely down to the shoulder. Saw the shoulder line to remove the waste.

DOVETAIL HALVING JOINT

Incorporating a dovetail creates a stronger T-halving joint. Once you have made a template, this variation is only marginally more difficult to cut than the standard square-shoulder version.

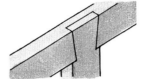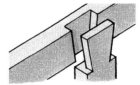

Marking and cutting a dovetailed joint

Having marked out and cut the lap (see left), use a template to mark the dovetail on the workpiece (**1**). Saw the short shoulders on both sides of the lap, then pare away the waste with a chisel to form the sloping sides of the dovetail (**2**).

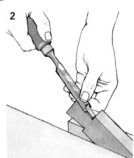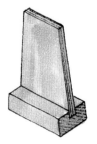

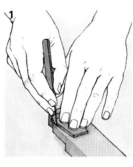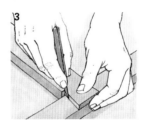

Using the dovetailed lap as a template, mark the shoulders of the recess on the cross member (**3**). Mark the depth of the recess with a marking gauge, and then remove the waste wood with a tenon saw and chisel.

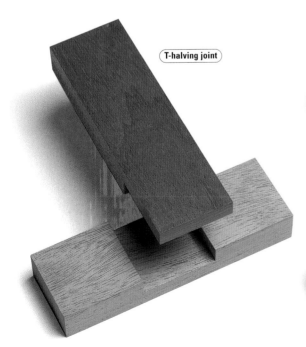

T-halving joint

Dovetail halving joint

Making a dovetail template

Cut a tapered plywood tongue, with one side angled for marking dovetails in softwoods and the other for marking hardwood dovetails. Glue the tongue into a slot cut in a hardwood stock.

EDGE-TO-EDGE JOINTS

Edge joints are used to join narrow boards together to make up a large panel, such as a table top or part of a cabinet. With a modern wood glue, even a plain butt joint can be adequate – but including a tongue and groove in the joint makes it easier to assemble accurately and adds considerably to its strength.

Preparing the wood

Timber selection is important when making a wide panel from solid wood. To ensure that the panel remains flat, try to use quarter-sawn wood with the end-grain growth rings running perpendicular to the face side of each board. If that is not possible, arrange the boards so the direction of the growth rings alternates from one board to the next (**1**). To facilitate final cleaning up of the panel with a plane, try to ensure that the surface grain on all boards runs in the same direction. Before you start working on the joints, number each board (**2**) and mark the face side, so you can rearrange them in the same order.

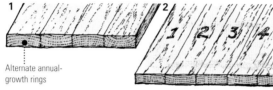

Alternate annual-
growth rings

EDGE-TO-EDGE BUTT JOINTING

When making a joint between solid-wood boards, it is standard practice to plane the meeting edges square to the face side.

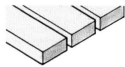

Planing edges square

With the face sides outwards, set both boards back-to-back and level in a vice. Use the longest bench plane available – preferably a try plane — to plane the edges straight and square (**1**). Check that each edge is square, using a try square.

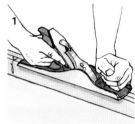

It is good practice to keep the edges as square as possible. However, provided boards have been planed as a pair, they will fit together and produce a flat surface, even when the edges are not exactly square (**2**).

Bevelled edges
fit perfectly

Checking for straight edges

Check that the planed edges are straight, using a long metal straightedge (**3**). Perfectly straight edges are essential if you intend to glue them with a rubbed joint. However, if the boards are to be clamped together, a very slight hollow is acceptable. Never try to get away with convex edges – closing the gaps with cramps sets up stresses that are likely to cause end splits.

3

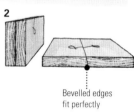

Making a wide board

When you are joining several boards edge to edge, all but the two outer boards must have both edges planed square. Using the back-to-back technique described above to true the edges, clamp the first and second board in the vice and plane their edges. Remove the first board, then rotate the second and back it up with the third board. Plane the edges of each pair in this way.

Butt joint

Joint with plywood tongue

Tongue-and-groove joint

CLAMPING EDGE-TO-EDGE JOINTS

Before applying glue to the edges, set the prepared boards in sash cramps to check that the joints fit snugly. This also gives you the opportunity to adjust the cramps precisely, which will help facilitate the process of final assembly.

Gluing up a panel

The number of cramps you use depends on the size of the workpiece, but you will need at least three cramps to keep the panel flat. You also need pieces of scrap wood to put between the cramp heads and the edges of the boards. Set the boards out on battens laid across your workbench.

Apply a thin film of glue to the jointing edges. Place two cramps across the boards, one cramp close to each end of the panel (**1**). Make sure the cramp bars do not touch the wood – because the metal can react with the glue, leaving unsightly stains. If necessary, tap the joints with a hammer and block to set them flush (**2**).

Turn the panel over and place another cramp across the middle (**3**). This cramp not only pulls the joints together at the centre, but also counters any tendency for the panel to bow. Use a damp rag to wipe away surplus glue squeezed out of the joints.

Leave the panel in the cramps until the glue has set hard. If you need to clear the bench, you can lean the clamped assembly upright against a wall – but make sure it is supported evenly, to prevent distortion.

1

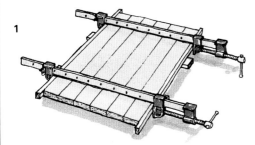

2

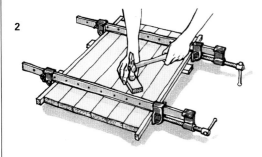

3

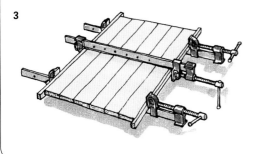

TONGUE-AND-GROOVE JOINTS

Use a combination plane to cut a tongue-and-groove joint by hand. This plane is similar to a standard plough plane, but comes with a wider range of cutters, including one designed specifically for shaping a tongue on the edge of a workpiece. Cut the tongue first, then change the cutter and plane a matching groove.

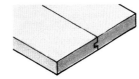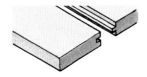

Cutting the tongue

Clamp the work in a bench vice, face side towards you. Adjust the fence until the cutter is centred on the edge of the work (**1**). Provided the matching groove is also cut from the face side, it is not essential that the tongue is precisely centred.

Adjust the cutter's integral depth stop to cut a tongue of the required size, then begin planing at the far end of the workpiece, gradually working backwards as the tongue is formed (**2**).

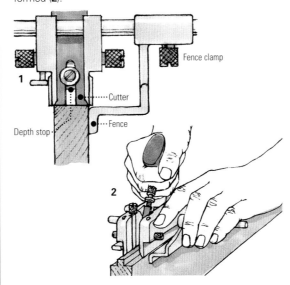

Fence clamp

1 .... Cutter

.... Fence

Depth stop ·

2

Cutting the groove

Select a straight or ploughing cutter that matches the width of the tongue, and fit it into the plane. With the cutter sitting precisely on top of the tongue, adjust the fence until it touches the side of the work (**3**). Set the planes's depth stop so that you can cut a groove slightly deeper than the tongue. Clamp the uncut board in the vice and plane the groove.

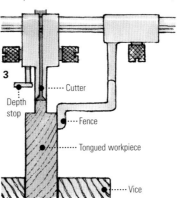

3 .... Cutter

Depth stop

.... Fence

.... Tongued workpiece

.... Vice

Using a plywood tongue

Making a joint with a separate plywood tongue has several advantages. You don't have to reduce the width of the board (which may save money), and the joint will be marginally stronger. It also means you can use a simple plough plane to cut the grooves.

To make the joint, plane a groove down the centre of each board and make sure the plywood tongue fits snugly. Glue one groove and tap the tongue into it, then brush glue into the other groove and assemble the joint in cramps.

HOUSING JOINTS

A housing is a groove cut across the grain. When used as a joint, it houses the end of a board – most frequently a fixed shelf or dividing panel. The housing can be stopped short of the front edge of the work, but for less-important work the joint may emerge as a through housing. The shelf or panel is usually glued into a simple straight-sided housing. For a more positive joint, a dovetail can be included.

THROUGH HOUSING JOINT

This simple through joint shows on the front edge of side panels. It is suitable for inexpensive shelving, or for cupboards with lay-on doors that cover the front edges. If you plan to lip the boards, it is best to apply the lippings first, so it is easier to plane them flush.

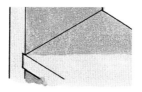

Marking and cutting the joint

Using the shelf as a template, mark the width of the housing (**1**). Then score the two lines across the workpiece, using a try square and marking knife.

Square the same lines onto the edges of the panel, then scribe a line between them (**2**), using a marking gauge set to about 6mm (¼in).

To make it easier to locate a saw across a wide panel, take a chisel and pare a shallow V-shape groove up to the marked line on both sides of the housing (**3**). Use a tenon saw to cut each shoulder down to the lines scribed on each edge (**4**). If you are not proficient with the saw, clamp a batten along the line to help guide the blade.

Remove most of the waste from the housing with a chisel (**5**), then finish with a router plane to level the bottom of the recess (**6**). Work from both edges towards the centre, in order to prevent edge break-out.

If a panel is too wide to use a chisel conveniently, remove all the waste in stages by making several passes with the router plane, lowering the cutter each time the housing is level.

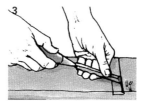

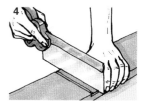

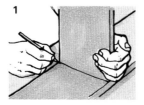

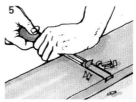

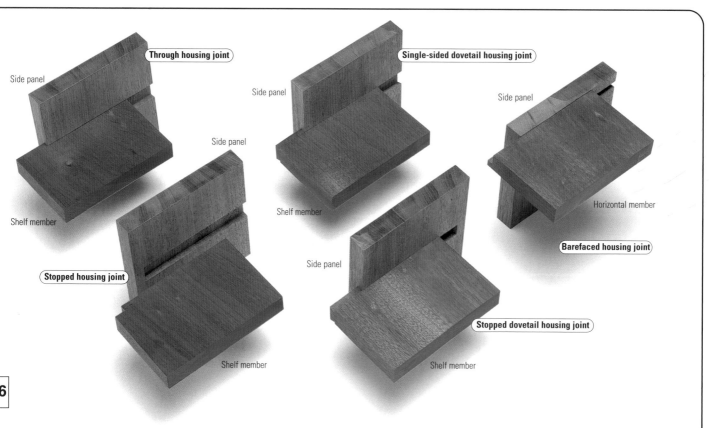

Through housing joint

Side panel

Shelf member

Stopped housing joint

Side panel

Side panel

Shelf member

Single-sided dovetail housing joint

Side panel

Side panel

Shelf member

Stopped dovetail housing joint

Side panel

Horizontal member

Barefaced housing joint

DOVETAIL HOUSING JOINTS

When cutting this joint by hand, incorporate a single dovetail along one side of the housing. Double-sided dovetails are best cut with a router. Since the shelf member must be slid into place from one end of the housing, the joint needs to be cut accurately.

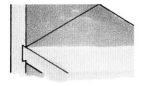
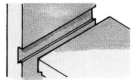

Single-sided dovetail housing
Set a cutting gauge to about one-third the thickness of the wood and score a shoulder line on the underside of the shelf (**1**). Using a try square and pencil, continue the line across both edges.

Set a sliding bevel to a dovetail angle and mark the slope of the joint, running from the bottom corner to the marks drawn on both edges (**2**).

Saw along the shoulder line, down to the base of the slope, then pare out the waste with a chisel. To help keep the angle constant, use a shaped block of wood to guide the blade (**3**).

Mark out the housing (see opposite) and use the sliding bevel to mark the dovetail on both edges of the panel. Saw both shoulders, using a bevelled block of wood to guide the saw blade when cutting the dovetail (**4**). Remove the waste with a router plane.

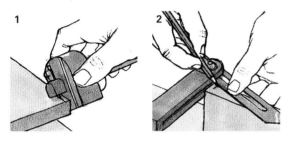

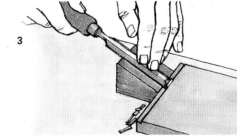

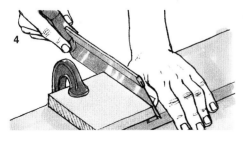

Stopped dovetail housing
To make this variation of the joint, follow the instructions outlined above, combined with the procedure for including a stopped end (see top right).

STOPPED HOUSING JOINT

For improved appearance, the housing can be stopped short of the front edge of the side panel by about 9 to 12mm ($\frac{3}{8}$ to $\frac{1}{2}$in). This is achieved by notching the front corner of the shelf, so that its front edge finishes flush with the side panel.

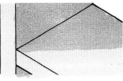

Marking and cutting the joint
Set a marking gauge to the planned depth of the housing and mark the notch on the front corner of the shelf. Cut the notch with a tenon saw (**1**).

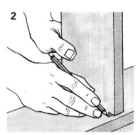

Use the notched shelf to mark the dimensions of the housing (**2**), then score the lines across the side panel with a try square and marking knife. Scribe the stopped end of the housing with a marking gauge.

To provide clearance for sawing the housing, first drill out the waste at the stopped end and trim the shoulders square with a chisel (**3**).

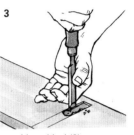
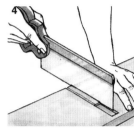

Saw along the scored shoulders down to the base of the housing (**4**), then pare out the waste from the back edge with a chisel or remove the waste with a router plane.

BAREFACED HOUSING JOINT

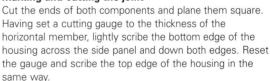

The barefaced housing joint is a variation on the basic lap joint, adapted for making box-frame or cabinet corners. Neither the depth nor the width of the housing should be greater than about third the thickness of the wood.

Marking and cutting the joint
Cut the ends of both components and plane them square. Having set a cutting gauge to the thickness of the horizontal member, lightly scribe the bottom edge of the housing across the side panel and down both edges. Reset the gauge and scribe the top edge of the housing in the same way.

Using the gauge with the same setting, mark the tongue on the end and down both edges of the horizontal member, working from the face side (**1**).

Reset the gauge to about one-third the thickness of the side panel, and mark the rebate shoulder line across the face side (**2**) and down both edges of the horizontal member. Cut the rebate, removing the waste with a saw and cleaning up with a shoulder plane.

Mark the depth of the housing on the edges of the side panel then saw each shoulder down to the lines scribed on each edge (**3**). Remove the waste with a chisel, as for a through housing joint (see opposite).

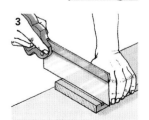

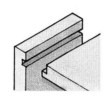
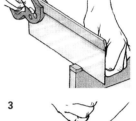

247

MORTISE-AND-TENON JOINTS

The mortise-and-tenon joint has a venerable history: it has been used for centuries to construct framed cabinets, chairs and tables. In the simplest version of the joint, the tenon (a tongue cut on the end of a rail) fits into a slot (the mortise) cut into a stile or leg. The basic construction has been developed and refined by generations of joiners and cabinet-makers, creating a variety of strong joints to suit different situations.

PROPORTION OF MORTISE TO TENON

The proportion of the mortise to the tenon is important for the strength of the joint. The form of the joint is largely determined by the section of the rail (tenoned member).

In most instances the rail is rectangular in section and is used with its wider face vertical. Sometimes, however, a particular construction requires a rail to be turned sideways, with the wider face horizontal – the drawer rails for a chest of drawers is a prime example. In any event, the sides or 'cheeks' of the tenon are cut in the vertical plane to provide the maximum area of long grain for gluing to the inside of the mortise. When rails are set horizontally, two or more tenons may be required – since the thickness of a tenon should never exceed its width.

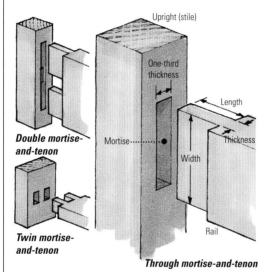

Double mortise-and-tenon

Twin mortise-and-tenon

Through mortise-and-tenon

When two members of equal thickness are to be joined, the thickness of the tenon should be approximately one-third the thickness of the wood. The precise thickness is determined by the size of the chisel used for cutting the mortise.

When the rail is to be joined to a thicker upright (such as a table leg), the tenon may be as much as half the thickness of the rail.

The tenon usually runs the full width of the rail. On a very wide rail, such as the central rail of a large panelled door, the tenon is divided into two. In this case the joint is known as a double mortise-and-tenon.

The length of the tenon is determined by the design of the joint. For a stopped mortise-and-tenon joint, for example, the tenon is usually about three-quarters the width of the upright.

THROUGH MORTISE-AND-TENON JOINT

The through joint, where the tenon passes right through the leg or stile, is commonly used for constructing various types of frame. With the end grain showing – and sometimes with wooden wedges used to spread the tenon – it is an attractive, businesslike joint. It is always easier to cut the mortise first and then make the tenon to fit it.

Marking the joint
Cut the rail roughly to length, allowing for a short amount of waste wood to be planed off the tenons after the glue has set.

Mark the position and length of the mortise, using the rail as a template (**1**). Square the lines all round with a pencil.

Set a mortise gauge to match the width of the mortise chisel to be used, and then scribe the mortise centrally between the squared lines on both edges (**2**).

Having measured and plotted the distance between the shoulders at each end of the rail, score the shoulder lines with a marking knife (**3**). Leave slightly overlong tenons for planing flush when the joint is complete.

Without adjusting the settings, take the same gauge you used for marking the mortise and scribe the tenon on both edges and across the end of the rail (**4**). If the rail is thinner than the upright you need to adjust the stock of the mortise gauge before marking out the tenon.

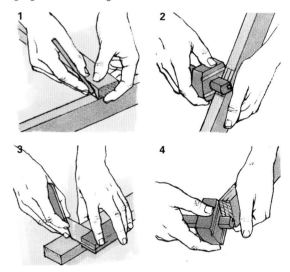

Chopping the mortise
Clamp the workpiece to a bench – it is a good idea to place a piece of waste wood under the work to protect the bench.

Holding the chisel vertically, drive it 3 to 6mm (1/8 to 1/4in) into the wood at the centre of the marked mortise (**5**). Work backwards in stages, making similar cuts about 6mm (1/4in) apart. Stop about 2mm (1/16in) from the end of the mortise. Turn the mortise chisel round and chop the wood in stages towards the other end of the mortise.

Lever out the waste, with the chisel held bevel side down (**6**), and then chop out another section of wood in the same way, until you have cut halfway through the stile.

Trim the ends of the mortise square (**7**), then turn the work over and, after shaking out any loose chips of wood, clamp the stile down again so that you can chop out the waste from the other side of the joint.

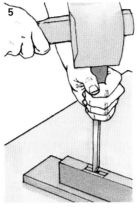

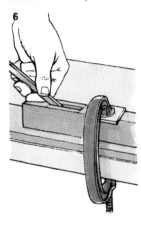

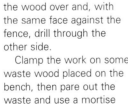

Drilling the mortise

Instead of chopping out the mortise with a chisel, you can remove the waste with a drill – though you will still need a chisel to pare the sides and ends of the mortise.

Rather than drill freehand, use a pillar drill for control and accuracy. Fit a drill bit that matches or is close to the thickness of the mortise. Improvise a guide fence by clamping a straight-edged board to the drill's worktable, and use this fence to centre the drill bit on the mortise. Adjust the depth setting to drill halfway through the wood.

Drill a hole at each end of the mortise (**1**), then drill a series of slightly overlapping holes between them (**2**). Turn the wood over and, with the same face against the fence, drill through the other side.

Clamp the work on some waste wood placed on the bench, then pare out the waste and use a mortise chisel to cut the ends of the mortise square.

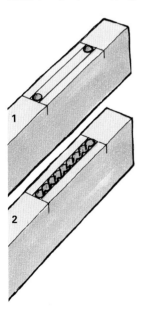

Sawing the tenon

Clamp the rail in a vice, setting the rail at an angle, with the end grain facing away from you. Saw down to the shoulder on the waste side of each scribed line (**1**). Reclamp the work in the vice with the tenon facing you, and saw down to the shoulder line on the other side of the tenon (**2**).

Now clamp the work upright and saw parallel to the shoulder on both sides of the tenon (**3**), taking care not to overrun the marks and damage the shoulder.

Holding the rail on a bench hook, remove the waste by sawing down the shoulder line on each side of the tenon. If necessary, pare the sides of the tenon with a chisel until it fits the mortise snugly.

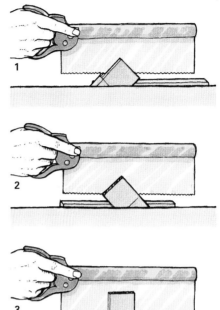

WEDGED THROUGH MORTISE-AND-TENON JOINT

A snugly fitting joint is strong enough for most purposes, but a pair of wooden wedges can be used to anchor the tenon firmly in its mortise. Either drive a wedge into each end of the mortise or into sawcuts made across the tenon itself.

Fitting inset wedges

Cut a shallow slope at each end of the mortise to allow room for the tenon to expand. Make two sawcuts across the tenon, stopping just short of the shoulders, and drill a small hole at the end of each kerf to prevent the wood splitting.

Glue and assemble the joint, then drive in the glued wedges, tapping them alternately to spread the tenon evenly. When the adhesive has set, plane the end grain and wedges flush.

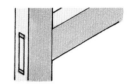

Drive a wedge into each end of the mortise

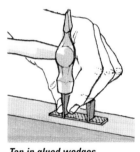

Tap in glued wedges

Rail

Stile

Through mortise-and-tenon joint

Rail

Rail

Stile

Inset wedges

Wedged mortise-and-tenon joint

DOUBLE MORTISE-AND-TENON JOINT

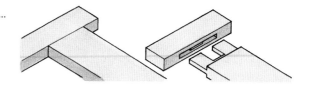

The gap between the tenons should be no larger than one-third of the width of the rail. To help prevent the rail warping, leave a short stub of wood, known as a haunch, between the tenons.

Marking out the joint

Mark the shoulders of the pair of tenons on the rail. Set the pins of a mortise gauge to the width of the mortise chisel (approximately one-third of the thickness of the stile), and adjust the gauge to centre the pins on the edge of the rail. Scribe the tenon on both edges and across the end grain.

1

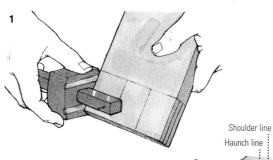

Now set a marking gauge to scribe the inner edge of both tenons on each side (**1**) and across the end of the rail.

Using a try square, pencil a line representing the length of the haunch (equal to the thickness of the tenon) on both sides and edges of the rail (**2**). Hatch the waste with a pencil.

Using the rail as a template, mark its position on the edge of the stile; then extend these lines onto all four faces of the stile, using a try square and pencil.

2

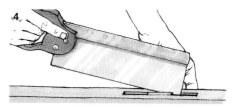

Shoulder line
Haunch line

3

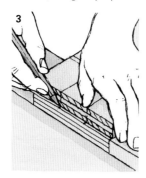

Without changing the settings, take the mortise gauge you used to mark the tenons and scribe the mortises between the marked lines on both edges of the stile – apply light pressure to avoid leaving deep score lines on the outer edge. Mark the length of each mortise, using the marked rail as a guide (**3**).

Cutting the joint

Chop out both mortises as described for cutting a standard through mortise, then run a saw blade alongside the haunch lines gauged between them (**4**). Chisel out the waste between the sawcuts, down to the level of the haunch.

4

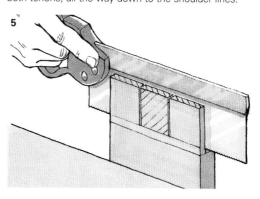

Clamp the rail upright and, standing at the side of the rail, saw down the inner edge of each tenon (**5**), stopping at the haunch line. Then change your position to saw alongside both tenons, all the way down to the shoulder lines.

5

Cut out the wood from between the tenons, using a coping saw (**6**). Finally, saw along the shoulder on each side of the joint to remove what is left of the waste (**7**).

6

7

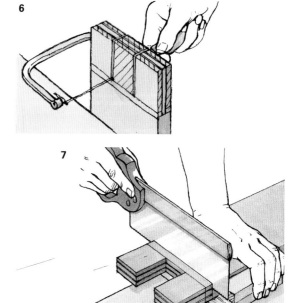

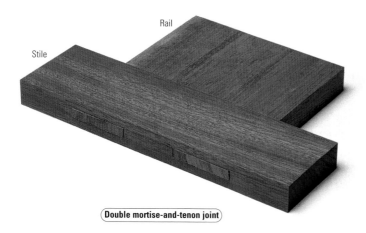

Rail

Stile

Double mortise-and-tenon joint

TWIN MORTISE-AND-TENON JOINT

The twin mortise-and-tenon is commonly used when a rail is turned on its side and for drawer-rail construction. Depending on the section of the rail, there may be a pair of tenons cut to standard proportions, or two relatively thick tenons or 'pins'. As a rule, try to make each of the tenons as thick as the gap between them – but the overall proportion of the joint will be determined by how strong it needs to be.

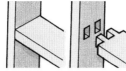

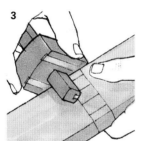

1

Marking the joint

Having squared the shoulder lines all round, make a pencil mark not less than 6mm (¼in) from each edge, then divide the space between into three – for the pair of tenons and the gap between them (**1**). Modify the thickness of the tenons to match a suitable mortise chisel.

Having set a mortise gauge to the above dimensions, scribe the tenons on both faces and across the end of the rail, working from both edges (**2**).

Using a try square and knife, lightly score two lines across the stile to mark the top and bottom of the mortises, then use the mortise gauge to scribe lines between them to mark the sides of the mortises (**3**).

If the mortises are to be cut into a wider rail or panel, leave the pin settings alone but adjust the tool's stock to mark both mortises from one edge.

2

3

Cutting the joint

Chop out the mortises as for a standard through mortise-and-tenon joint.

Saw down beside each tenon, following the scribed lines, then cut off the waste wood from both edges of the rail by sawing along the shoulder lines.

Remove the waste from between the tenons with a coping saw (**4**) and trim the shoulder square with a chisel. Alternatively, remove the middle waste by drilling through it at the shoulder and then sawing down the sides of the tenons (you will still need to trim the shoulder with a chisel).

4

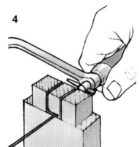

PINNED MORTISE-AND-TENON JOINT

This version of the joint has a row of evenly spaced stubby tenons (pins). It is used for securing wide fixed shelves or partitions in a cabinet. If the tenons pass all the way through the panel, they are usually held firmly in place with hardwood wedges inserted into sawcuts made across the end grain of each pin. For decorative purposes, the wedges are sometimes set diagonally.

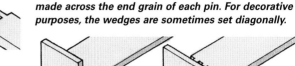

1

Marking and cutting the joint

Mark out the shelf as for a twin mortise-and-tenon, dividing the shoulder line with a row of evenly spaced pins. Mark the positions of the mortises on the side panel, using the shelf as a template (**1**).

Chop out the through mortises, working from both sides of the panel (**2**), or bore through the waste and square the shoulders.

Saw down the sides of the pins with a tenon saw, then remove the waste from between the pins with a coping saw. Trim the shoulders with a chisel (**3**).

2

3

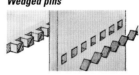

Wedged pins

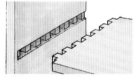

Stopped housing joint

Rail

Stile

Stile

(**Twin mortise-and-tenon joint** light construction)

Rail

Stile

(**Twin mortise-and-tenon joint** heavy construction)

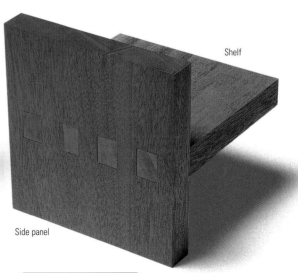

Shelf

Side panel

(**Pinned mortise-and-tenon joint**)

STOPPED MORTISE-AND-TENON JOINT

The majority of tables and chairs are made with stopped mortise-and-tenon joints, with no sign of the joint visible on the outside of the leg. It is a good-looking joint – and once you have learned how to gauge the depth of the mortise accurately, it is no more difficult to make than a through tenon. As a rule, the tenon should be about three-quarters the width of the stile.

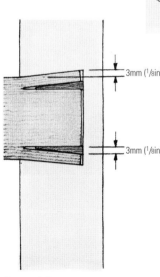

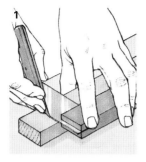

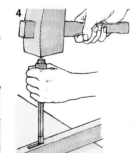

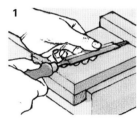

Marking and cutting the joint

Score the shoulder line all round the rail (**1**), then set a mortise gauge to match the width of the mortise chisel to be used and scribe the thickness of the tenon.

Use the rail as a guide for marking out the position of the mortise on the stile (**2**). Square the lines across the edge of the work, using a try square and then, without altering the settings of the mortise gauge, scribe the mortise between the lines.

To gauge the depth of the mortise, lay the blade of the chisel on the marked rail, with its cutting edge aligned with the shoulder line. Wrap adhesive tape round the blade at a point just beyond the end of the rail (**3**).

Cutting into one edge of the rail only, chop out the mortise, stopping when the tape wrapped round the blade is level with the surface of the wood (**4**). Saw the tenon to match, as for a through mortise-and-tenon joint.

↕ 3mm (¹⁄₈in)

↕ 3mm (¹⁄₈in)

Rail

Stile

Stopped mortise-and-tenon-joint

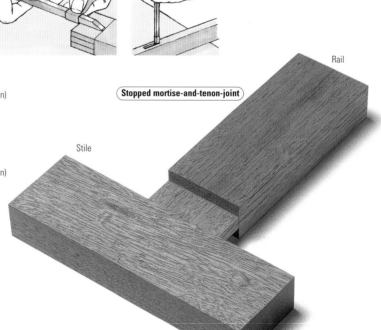

Fox wedging
Concealed wedges spread the tenon inside the mortise.

WEDGED STOPPED MORTISE-AND-TENON JOINT

Stopped joints can be 'fox-wedged' for additional strength. Because a fox-wedged tenon expands inside the mortise, it cannot be withdrawn once the joint is assembled – so make sure you cut the parts accurately.

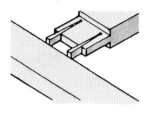

Fitting fox wedges
Make two wedges about three-quarters the length of the tenon, and about 3mm (¹⁄₈in) thick at one end (**1**).

Undercut each end of the mortise with a chisel, paring away about 3mm (¹⁄₈in) of the wood at the bottom of the joint (**2**).

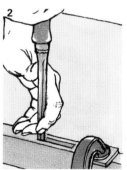

Dip the wedges in glue and brush some more into the joint. Push the wedges part of the way into the sawcuts before assembling the joint and clamping it (**3**).

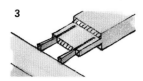

HAUNCHED MORTISE-AND-TENON JOINT

To provide a strong joint at the corner of a frame, the tenon is offset slightly so it won't break through the end grain of the leg or stile. In addition, to support the top edge of the rail, a small integral tongue known as a haunch is included, which fits into a shallow groove cut just above the mortise. If you want it to be invisible when the joint is assembled – for the frame of a panelled cabinet door or the joint between the seat rail and front leg of a chair – cut a sloping haunch. In furniture construction the tenon is usually concealed, but a through mortise-and-tenon is often used for joinery.

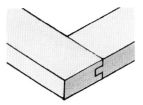
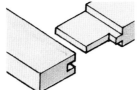

Proportions of a haunched tenon
Make the tenon two-thirds the width of the rail; the haunch itself should be as long as it is thick. Make a sloping haunch to the same proportions, but pare it away to meet the shoulder line.

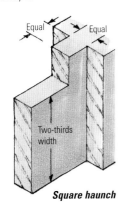
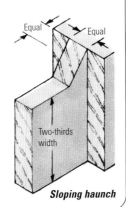

Square haunch   **Sloping haunch**

Marking the joint
Having marked the shoulders and scribed the tenon thickness on the rail, use a marking gauge to scribe the top edge of the tenon (**1**) on both sides and then across the end grain.

Mark the length of the haunch across the top and down the sides of the rail (**2**), and then hatch the waste with a soft pencil.

Haunch line

Top of tenon

Using the rail as a template, mark the position of the mortise on the stile (**3**). At this stage, let the end of the stile project by about 18mm (³/₄in) to prevent splitting. This extension, known as the horn, is cut off and planed flush when the joint is complete.

Scribe the mortise up to the end of the stile, and then continue the lines a short way onto the end grain (**4**) to mark where the haunch groove will end.

Scribe a short line on the end of the stile (**5**) to mark the depth of the haunch groove.

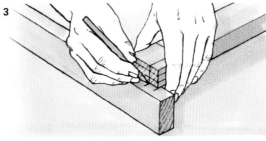

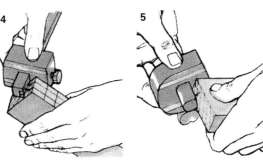

Cutting the joint
Having cut the mortise (see opposite), extend the sides, by sawing along the gauged lines, down to the bottom of the haunch groove (**6**). Use a chisel to pare away the waste, leaving the bottom of the groove square (**7**).

Clamp the work upright in a vice and saw the sides of the tenon (as for a through mortise-and-tenon joint). Cut a notch in the top corner, leaving the tenon and haunch intact.

Finally, saw along the shoulders to remove the waste wood from both sides of the tenon (**8**).

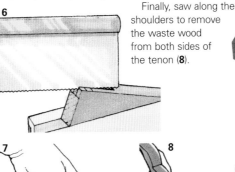

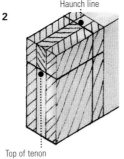

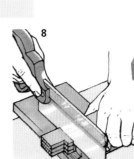

Try the tenon in the mortise. If the shoulder does not seat properly, deepen the mortise or the haunch groove as appropriate. After gluing, saw the horn off the stile and plane it flush with the top edge of the rail.

Sloping haunch
To make a joint with a sloping haunch, mark out the tenon – including the haunch – and then score the sloping sides of the haunch with a marking knife (**1**). Saw down this line when cutting the notch in the top corner of the tenon (see below left).

When marking out the mortise, continue the gauged lines up to the top of the stile, but not over the end. Having chopped out the mortise, saw the sides of the haunch groove at an angle, taking care not to overrun, then pare the slope with a chisel (**2**).

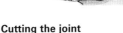

Stile

Rail

Haunched mortise-and-tenon-joint

253

GROOVED-FRAME MORTISE-AND-TENON JOINT

The frame of a traditional panelled door is grooved on the inside to accommodate the panel. When haunched mortise-and-tenon joints are used at the corners, align the grooves with the mortises and make them both the same width. In addition, match the depth of the groove to the length of the haunch, so the one will neatly fill the other at the end of the stile.

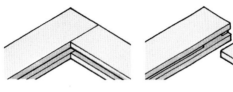

Marking and cutting the joint

Use a mortise gauge to scribe the grooves on the inside of the rails and stiles.

Mark out the tenon as for a standard haunched mortise-and-tenon joint; then, with a marking gauge set to the depth of the groove, scribe the bottom edge of the tenon on both sides and across the end of the rail (**1**).

Using the rail as a template, mark the position of the mortise on the stile (**2**). Cut a straightforward stopped mortise on these marks; cutting the panel groove at a later stage makes room for the haunch.

Cut a standard haunched tenon, and then make a second sawcut across the end of the rail to form the bottom of the tenon (**3**). Saw off the waste on each side of the tenon.

Use a plane or router to cut the grooves on the inside of the rails and stiles, then make and fit the panel before gluing and assembling the frame.

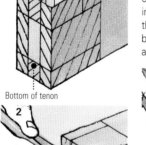

Haunch line

1

Bottom of tenon

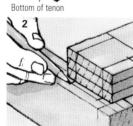

2

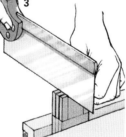

3

REBATED-FRAME MORTISE-AND-TENON JOINT

When making a glazed door for a cabinet, cut a rebate on the inside of the rails and stiles to take the glass. Each corner of the frame can be joined with a haunched mortise-and-tenon, but it is necessary to stagger the shoulders in order to close off the rebate at the end of the stile. You may find it easier to cut the rebates after the joints.

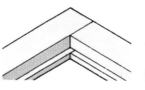

Marking and cutting the joint

Having set a marking gauge to one-third the thickness of the workpieces, scribe the depth of the rebate on the inner edge of the rails and stiles. Reset the gauge to about 6mm ($\frac{1}{4}$in) and scribe the rebate width.

Using the proportions given for a standard haunched mortise-and-tenon, score the long shoulder across the outer face of the rail. With a pencil, square this line across both edges of the rail.

Marking the short shoulder and tenon

Mark the short shoulder across the inner face; it should be as far from the long-shoulder line as the width of the rebate – about 6mm ($\frac{1}{4}$in). Square the line across both edges. Mark out the haunch, then scribe the thickness of the tenon with a mortise gauge. Use a marking gauge to scribe the bottom of the tenon.

Transfer the dimension from the rail to mark the position of the mortise on the stile. Use a mortise gauge to scribe the mortise. Then, with the same tool, mark the length of the haunch (measured from the long-shoulder line) onto the end of the stile. Hatch the waste with a pencil.

After cutting the joints, use a plane or router to cut the rebates on the inside of the rails and stiles. Finally, pare out the haunch waste from each joint.

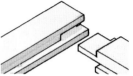

Long-shoulder line

Haunch line

Horn

Rebate depth

Rebate width

Short-shoulder line

Rebate line

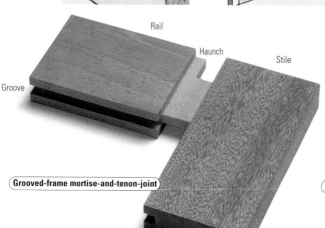

Rail

Haunch

Stile

Groove

Grooved-frame mortise-and-tenon-joint

Rail

Haunch

Stile

Rebate

Rebated-frame mortise-and-tenon-joint

MOULDED-FRAME MORTISE-AND-TENON JOINT

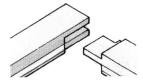

When a frame is moulded as well as rebated, it is necessary to mitre the moulding after the mortise-and-tenons have been cut.

Marking and cutting the joint

Before marking out the joint, cut away the moulding down to the level of the rebate, leaving a flat edge on the stile equal to the width of the tenon plus the haunch (**1**). Similarly, cut away the moulding on the rail back to the shoulder line.

Mark out a haunched mortise-and-tenon and hatch the waste (**2**), then cut both halves of the joint.

After cutting the joints, mitre the ends of the moulded sections. Clamp a rebated guide block over the moulding to keep the chisel at the required angle (**3**).

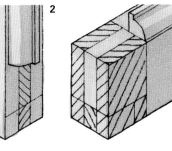

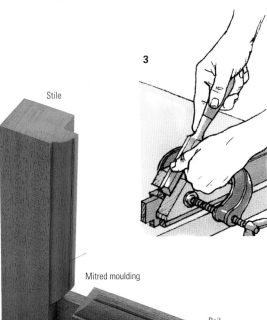

Stile

Mitred moulding

Rail

Moulded-frame mortise-and-tenon-joint

ANGLED MORTISE-AND-TENON JOINTS

For tapered chair frames, either the side-rail mortises must be cut at an angle or the tenons skewed to fit square-cut mortises. The joints are marked out and cut similarly to conventional mortise-and-tenon joints except that the ends of the tenons are mitred where they meet inside the leg.

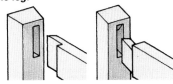

Angled mortises

A stronger joint results if you keep the tenons in line with the rails. Mark out each joint in the usual way, but mark the shoulders at an angle to fit the face of the leg. You may find that it will be easier to keep your chisel blade or drill vertical when cutting the mortise if you make a simple jig that holds the leg at the required angle.

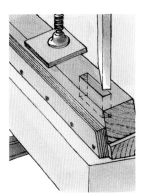

Skewed tenons

Since it is easier to cut square mortises, it may be more convenient to skew the tenons. However, the inevitable short grain makes for relatively weak joints, so keep the angle to a minimum. It is impossible to mark skewed tenons with a mortise gauge, so use a sliding bevel and marking knife instead.

Barefaced tenons

If you want the rails to lie flush with the legs, use barefaced tenons.

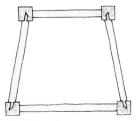
Angled mortises

Skewed tenons

Barefaced tenons

Skewed tenon

Barefaced tenon

CORNER MORTISE-AND-TENON JOINT

On most tables and some chairs, at each corner two rails are joined to the leg at right angles. The joints to use in this situation are haunched mortise-and-tenons with the ends of the tenons mitred where they meet inside the leg.

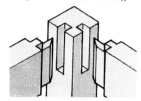

Joints for round legs

When joining rails to round legs, it is easier to cut the mortises before you turn the legs. Plug each mortise with softwood before you put the workpiece in the lathe – this helps keep the edges of the mortise sharp, and the softwood can be chiselled out easily after you have turned the leg.

Having cut the tenons, trim the shoulders with a gouge so they fit the curve.

LOOSE-WEDGED MORTISE-AND-TENON JOINT

A loose-wedged joint must be constructed with generous shoulders and a stout tenon. The wedge is set vertically to prevent it working loose. No glue is used – the joint relies on the clamping force of the wedge to provide rigidity.

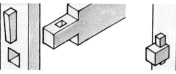
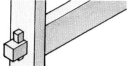

Proportions of a loose-wedged tenon

The total length of the tenon should be at least three times the thickness of the stile and not less than one-third the width of the rail.

The mortise for the loose wedge should be approximately 18mm ($^3/_4$in) long, and its width about one-third the width of the tenon. The outer end of this mortise slopes to accommodate the hardwood wedge, and the inner end is cut square.

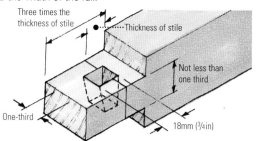

Three times the thickness of stile · Thickness of stile · Not less than one third · One-third · 18mm ($^3/_4$in)

Marking and cutting the joint

The loose-wedge joint is marked out and cut like a standard through mortise-and-tenon joint – except that the tenon needs to be a snug sliding fit in the mortise.

Assemble the joint and mark the thickness of the stile on the projecting tenon (**1**)

Take the joint apart and use a mortise gauge to mark the mortise for the loose wedge on the top edge of the tenon (**2**). Set the inner end of the mortise about 3mm ($^1/_8$in) inside the line marking the thickness of the stile.

Set a sliding bevel to an angle of 1:6. From the line marking the outer end of the wedge mortise, draw another line on the side of the tenon, using the bevel (**3**). Square this line across the bottom of the tenon, then scribe the sides of the wedge mortise up to the line.

Cut the wedge mortise, paring the sloping end with a chisel. Assemble the joint and tap in the wedge (**4**) to draw the shoulders up tight.

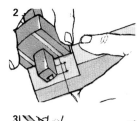
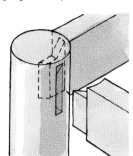

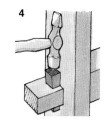

Rail · Leg · Mitred tenon · Rail

Corner joint

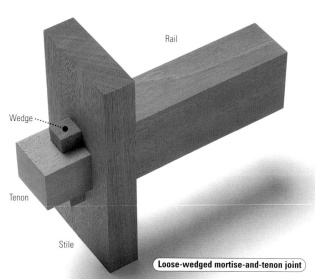

Rail · Wedge · Tenon · Stile

Loose-wedged mortise-and-tenon joint

BRIDLE JOINTS

Used exclusively for frame construction, the bridle joint is similar in appearance to a mortise-and-tenon, though in most circumstances it would not be as strong. However, it is relatively quick and easy to make, since most of the waste wood is removed with a saw. Generally, the 'tenon' of a bridle joint is one-third the thickness of the wood being joined.

T-BRIDLE JOINT

The T-bridle serves as an intermediate support for a frame. It is sometimes used to join a table leg to the underframe.

Marking and cutting the joint

Mark the width of the mortise member on the tenon member, using a marking knife to score square shoulders all round. Apply light pressure only across the edges. Use a pencil and try square to mark square shoulders all round on the mortise member, allowing for slightly overlong cheeks.

Set the pins of a mortise gauge to one-third the thickness of the wood, and adjust the stock to centre the pins on the edge of the workpiece. Scribe parallel lines between the marked shoulders on the tenon member, then mark similar lines on the end and both edges of the mortise member.

Saw down both sides of the open mortise with a tenon saw, then use a coping saw to remove the waste, cutting as close to the shoulder as possible (**1**). Trim the shoulder square with a sharp chisel.

On both sides of the tenon member, saw the shoulders down to the gauged lines, then make three or four similar sawcuts in between. With the work held in a vice, chop out the waste with a mallet and chisel, working from each edge towards the middle (**2**). Having assembled the joint, allow the glue to set, then plane the ends of the mortise cheeks flush with the tenon member.

CORNER BRIDLE JOINT

A corner bridle joint is adequate for relatively lightweight frames – provided they are not subjected to sideways pressure. The strength of the bridle is improved considerably if you insert two dowels through the side of the joint after the glue has set.

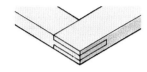

Marking and cutting the joint

Mark square shoulders all round the tenon member, allowing for a tenon that is slightly overlong – so it can be planed flush after the joint is complete. Use a marking knife, but apply light pressure across both edges. Then mark similar lines on the mortise member, using a pencil.

Set the points of a mortise gauge to one-third the thickness of the wood and adjust the tool to centre the points on the edge of the work. Scribe the width of the tenon on both edges and across the end (**1**).

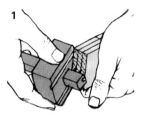

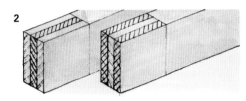

Use the same gauge to mark the sides of the open mortise, then take a marking knife and score the short shoulders at the base of the mortise, between the gauged lines. Mark the waste wood, with a pencil, on each component, so you don't get confused when cutting the joint (**2**).

Bore a hole into the waste wood just above the shoulder line on opposite sides of the joint. Clamp the wood in a vice and saw on the waste side of both gauged lines, down to the hole at the base of the mortise (**3**). Then chisel the shoulder square.

With the work clamped in a vice, saw both sides of the tenon down to the shoulder (**4**). Lay the workpiece on its side on a bench hook and saw each shoulder line to remove the waste.

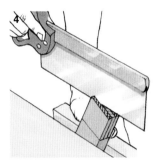

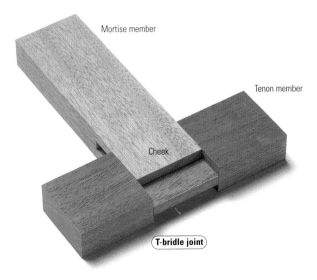

T-bridle joint

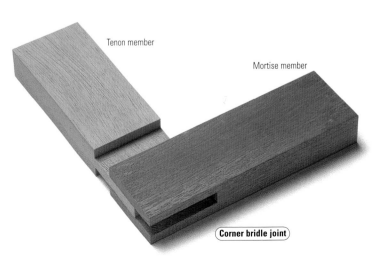

Corner bridle joint

DOWEL JOINTS

A dowel joint is nothing more than a butt joint reinforced with short wooden pegs – but, despite is simplicity, it is virtually as strong as a mortise-and-tenon. It is, however, considerably easier to make, especially if you employ one of the many proprietary dowelling jigs on the market. Dowels are used extensively for joining boards edge to edge, and for constructing cabinets and boxes with right-angle corner joints. They are also suitable for joining rails and stiles to make simple solid-wood framing.

DOWELS

Dowels are made from hardwoods, such as beech, birch and ramin. You can use ready-made dowels or cut your own from dowel rod. If neither suits your purpose, make them from a solid-wood blank, using a dowel former.

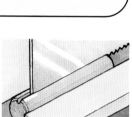

Saw a groove in the dowel

Cutting dowels
Use a fine-toothed saw to cut short lengths of dowel rod. Hold the dowel rod on a bench hook and, to prevent the wood fibres breaking out, rotate the dowelling away from you as you saw. If you are making a number of dowels, set up an end stop to gauge the length.

Use the tenon saw to cut a groove down the length of each dowel. This is to release the hydraulic pressure that builds up in the hole as the dowel is glued in place. If you don't do this, the workpiece is likely to split. Finally, to make inserting the dowels easier, chamfer the ends – using either a special dowel-chamfering tool or a pencil sharpener. Alternatively, file the chamfers on the ends of your dowels

Ready-made dowels in various sizes are supplied cut to length. They are chamfered, and grooved all round with straight or spiral flutes.

A dowel former is a thick steel plate with holes, which match standard-size dowels, drilled through it. It is used to produce purpose-made dowels from lengths of roughly sized wood by driving them through the appropriate hole. Make your own former to produce smooth round dowels or use a proprietary former with serrated holes that create relief flutes as the wood is driven through it.

The diameter of the dowel can be up to half the thickness of the wood; the length will depend on the size of the workpiece. As a guide, make the length of the dowel not less than five times the diameter.

Dowel rod

Prepared dowel

Fluted dowel

MARKING DOWEL JOINTS

Unless you intend to make a number of dowel joints, either mark out both halves of the joint individually or mark one component from the other. You can use basic marking gauges or special templates.

Edge-to-edge joints
For edge-to-edge joints (used to reinforce a solid-wood panel or table top), clamp the boards back to back with their edges flush. Plot the positions of the dowels so that they are evenly spaced along the boards. Square the lines across both edges.

Set a marking gauge to half the thickness of the wood and scribe a line down the centre of both edges, working from the face side in each case (**1**).

1

Frame joints
For frame joints, a pair of dowels in the end of the rail is usually sufficient. The dowels should be positioned not less than 6mm (¼in) from the edges. Prepare both components of the joint and plane the end of the rail square on a shooting board. Clamp both workpieces in a vice, with the end of the rail flush with the edge of the stile. Square lines to mark the positions of the dowels across both members, then scribe a line down the centre of each component, using a marking gauge (**2**).

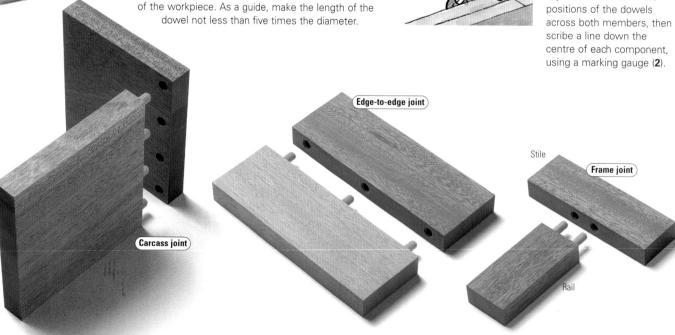

Edge-to-edge joint

Carcass joint

Stile

Frame joint

Rail

Marking with centre points

Another method of setting out dowel joints is to use centre points to mark one part from the other. You can make your own from panel pins or buy special cast-metal dowel points.

To make your own, draw the dowel centres on the end of the rail and drive in panel pins where the lines cross — leaving part of each pin projecting from the wood. Cut off the pin heads with pliers, to create short 'spikes' sticking out of the end grain (**3**). Lay the leg or stile on its side and press the end of the rail against it, leaving two pinholes that mark the hole centres exactly. A simple right-angle jig will keep the components aligned (**4**).

If you use proprietary dowel points, simply bore dowel holes into the end of the rail and insert the points – which will mark the side grain of the matching component (**5**).

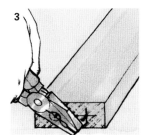

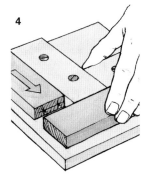

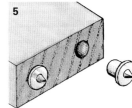

Marking with a template

With a template, it is easier to mark out a number of identical dowel joints. To make a template, first cut a hardwood block to the width of the rail, to serve as a guide fence.

Make a sawcut across the centre of the block to accommodate a thin steel plate. Before epoxy-gluing the plate into the slot, mark and drill small guide holes through it at the required dowel centres.

To mark the dowel centres on the end of the rail and on the stile, simply push a pointed tool through the holes in the template (**6**).

Boring dowel holes

Bore dowel holes with a brace and auger bit or with a power drill and dowel bit. To help keep the drill upright, clamp the workpiece in a vice and stand at the end of the bench, so you are able to look down the line of holes. Each hole should be very slightly deeper than half the length of the dowel. For consistency, either buy a depth gauge to slip over the drill bit or wrap a strip of coloured tape round the bit to mark the appropriate depth. Countersinking the bored holes helps locate the dowels and makes final assembly easier.

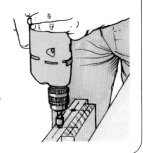

USING DOWELLING JIGS

A dowelling jig enables you to drill matching holes in both halves of the joint precisely, with minimal marking out.

Dowelling jigs range from inexpensive plastic versions to cast-metal jigs fitted with a variety of guide bushes to accommodate specific drill bits. The better-quality jigs have some means of clamping both workpieces securely while you move the guide-bush assembly to another position.

The examples of joint-making shown below are typical of what is possible using a simple but good-quality jig. The size and placement of the drill-bit guide bushes are designed to position the dowel holes centrally on the edge of boards of specific thickness.

Jigging an edge-to-edge joint

Clamp the workpieces together with their face sides outwards, using the end clamp supplied with the jig. Check that the edges of the workpiece are level.

Mark the dowel centres in pencil (**1**) to ensure they are spaced evenly along the joint. Locate the dowelling jig and slide it sideways until the appropriate pair of guide bushes aligns with the first pencil mark. Tighten the clamping screw.

Locate the drill bit in one of the guide bushes and bore the hole to the required depth, then transfer the bit to the adjacent bush to bore a similar hole in the other workpiece.

Loosen the clamping screw and slide the jig to the next dowel centre, then repeat the procedure (**2**).

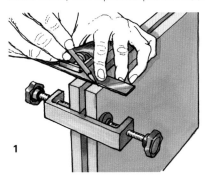

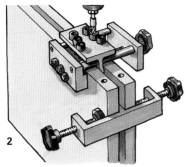

Jigging a corner joint

To make a right-angle corner joint, clamp the two workpieces together as before – but this time align both ends, and the face sides need to face in the same direction.

Locate the dowelling jig over the first pencil mark and clamp it in position. Drill the first hole in the end of one workpiece, then insert the bit in the appropriate guide bush to drill, at right angles, into the inner face of the second workpiece. Loosen the jig, slide it to the next position and repeat the process (**3**).

To assemble the joint, rotate one of the workpieces through 270 degrees (**4**).

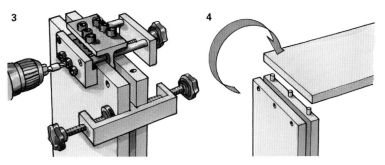

DOVETAIL JOINTS

Traditional drawer-making employs the inherent strength of the dovetail joint to full advantage: the fan-shape 'tails' resist the forces applied to the joints when the drawer is opened or closed. There are many types of dovetail joint, some primarily used for decorative qualities, others designed to be concealed. Some forms can be made using specialized jigs and a power router. However, the instructions on the following pages are for cutting dovetails by hand.

Proportions of a dovetail

The sides of a dovetail must slope at the optimum angle. An exaggerated slope results in weak short grain at the tips of the dovetail, while insufficient taper invariably leads to a slack joint.

Ideally, mark a 1:8 angle for hardwoods, but increase the angle to 1:6 for softwoods. The proportion of each tail is a matter of personal interpretation, but a row of small, regularly spaced tails looks better than a few large ones, and also makes for a stronger joint.

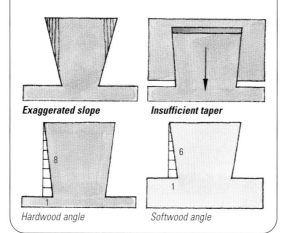

Exaggerated slope   *Insufficient taper*

Hardwood angle   *Softwood angle*

THROUGH DOVETAIL JOINT

The ability to cut tight-fitting dovetail joints is generally regarded as the ultimate test of a woodworker's skill. It is also, undeniably, one of the most efficient joints for constructing boxes and even relatively large cabinets from solid wood. Through dovetails – the most basic form of the joint – are visible on both sides of a corner.

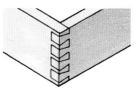

Preparing the wood

Accurately cut the joint components to length and plane them smooth and square. It pays to use a shooting board to plane the end grain square (**1**).

Be sure to mark the face side and face edge of each component, so you can take all subsequent measurements from those critical surfaces.

1

Marking the tails

With a cutting gauge set to the thickness of the pin member, scribe a shoulder line for the tails on all four sides of the tail member (**2**). Where the gauge lines could mar the finished work, use a fine pencil line and a try square instead.

The size and number of tails varies according to the width of the boards and the type of wood – softwoods need coarser and fewer tails than hardwoods.

2

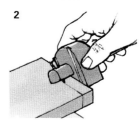

Pin member

Tail member

Through dovetail joint

Pencil a line across the end grain, 6mm (¼in) from each edge of the workpiece, then divide the distance between the lines equally, depending on the number of tails required. Measure 3mm (⅛in) on each side of these marks and square pencil lines across the end (**3**).

Mark the sloping sides of each tail on the face side of the workpiece, using an adjustable bevel or a proprietary dovetail template (**4**). Hatch the waste with a pencil.

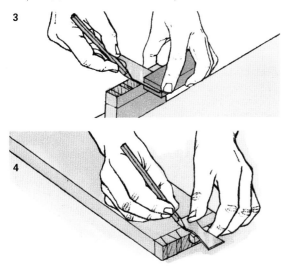

Cutting the tails

Clamp the work in a vice – at an angle, so you can saw vertically beside each dovetail (**5**). Saw close to each line on the waste side, and take care not to overshoot and damage the shoulder. When you have reached the last tail in the row, cant the work in the other direction and saw down the other side of each tail.

Set the work horizontally in the vice and remove the corner waste with a dovetail saw. Then cut the waste from between the tails, using a coping saw (**6**).

Use a bevel-edge chisel to trim what remains of the waste from between the tails (**7**). Finish flush with the shoulder line.

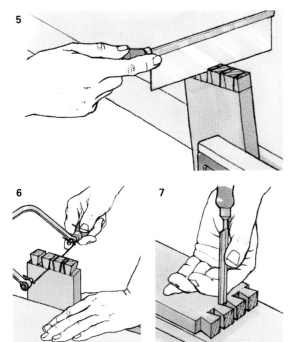

Marking the pins

Set the cutting gauge to the thickness of the tail member and scribe shoulder lines for the pins on both sides of the pin member. Coat its end grain with chalk and clamp it upright in a vice. Position the cut tails on the end of the workpiece, ensuring that both face edges are on the same side. Make sure the shoulder lines and edges align precisely; then mark the shape of the tails in the chalk, using a pointed scriber or knife (**8**).

Align a try square with the marks scored in the chalk, and draw parallel lines down to the shoulder on both sides of the work (**9**). Hatch the waste with a pencil.

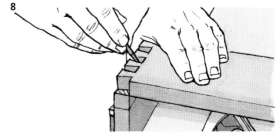

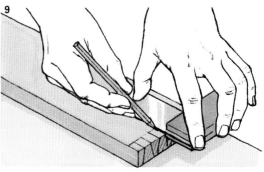

Cutting the pins

With the work clamped in a vice, make fine sawcuts on both sides of each pin, following the angled lines marked across the end grain (**10**). Keep the cut just on the waste side of each line and finish flush with the shoulder. Remove the waste from between the pins with a coping saw, and pare the shoulders with a bevel-edge chisel (**11**). Work from both sides towards the middle.

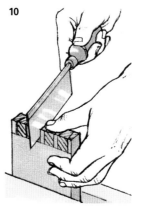

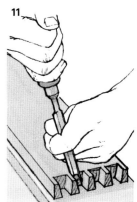

Assembling the joint

Dovetails are meant to be a close fit, so should be fully assembled once only. To check the fit, partly assemble the joint and trim any tight spots. Clean up the inside faces of the components (but not the joints themselves) prior to gluing.

Apply glue to both halves and tap the joint together, using a hammer and a piece of waste wood to protect the surface (**12**). If you are assembling a wide joint, tap in different places across the entire width in order to keep the joint level. Wipe away any surplus glue as it is squeezed out of the joint.

When the glue has set, trim the endgrain flush, using a sharp smoothing plane or block plane. Always plane from both edges towards the middle, to prevent the wood splitting.

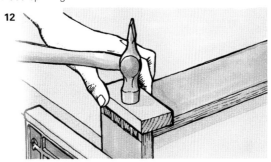

261

DECORATIVE THROUGH DOVETAIL JOINT

A well-proportioned and accurately cut through dovetail joint makes an attractive feature that is often exploited in cabinet construction. The decorative qualities of the joint can be exploited still further by varying the size and spacing of the tails and pins. The example shown here has fine triangular pins and two central half-depth dovetails that interrupt the regular rhythm of the joint. Decorative dovetail joints are frequently chosen for a workpiece designed to demonstrate the skills of the maker.

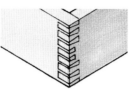

Marking the tails

Most woodworkers measure and mark the tails directly on the wood. But if you prefer, work out the shape and spacing of the tails on paper first and then transfer the dimensions to the workpiece.

Begin by marking out the tails, lightly scribing the shoulder line on all sides of the workpiece, using a cutting gauge set to match the thickness of the pin member. Similarly, mark the short shoulder line for the half-depth dovetails (**1**).

Use a dovetail template to draw the sloping sides of the tails (**2**). Group the tails closely together, with no more than the thickness of a sawcut between them.

Using a try square, draw the tips of the tails on the end of the workpiece (**3**) and hatch the waste with a pencil.

Cutting the tails

Having completed the marking out of the tails in pencil, go over the shoulder lines with a marking knife.

Using a dovetail saw and a coping saw, remove the waste from between the tails, as for a standard through dovetail joint. Trim the shoulders square with a bevel-edge chisel.

Marking the pins

Mark the shoulder line on all four sides of the pin member, then reset the gauge to score the length of the half-depth pins on the end grain (**4**). Rub chalk on the end of the work.

With the tail member held down on the end of the pin member, score the shape of the pins in the chalk by drawing the tip of a dovetail saw between each pair of tails (**5**). Square the marks down to the shoulder line on both sides. Then hatch the waste with a pencil.

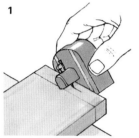

Cutting the pins

Cut out the waste from between the pins, using a dovetail saw and a coping saw, then pare down to the shoulder line with a chisel. To trim the half-depth pins to size, first make a cut across the grain close to the shoulder line with a chisel and mallet (**6**). Cutting towards the shoulder, pare the pins down to the line scribed on the end grain (**7**). Cut across the grain once more to trim accurately to the shoulder line.

Glue and assemble the joint in the same way as a standard through dovetail.

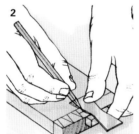

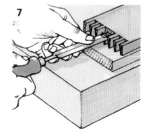

Pin member

Tail member

Short tails

Decorative through dovetail joint

MITRED THROUGH DOVETAIL JOINT

If you want to mould the edge of a dovetailed workpiece, perhaps to make a sliding tray or an open box, incorporate a mitre at each corner.

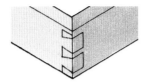 

Marking the tails

After scribing the shoulder all round the tail member, mark the mitre on the top edge (**1**). Set a marking gauge to the depth required for the moulded edge, and scribe a line on the end grain (**2**) and round to the shoulder line on both sides.

Draw a pencil line 6mm (¼in) below the scribed line – this marks the tip of the first tail. Make a similar mark 6mm (¼in) from the other edge. Divide the distance between these lines into the required number of equal-size tails (**3**).

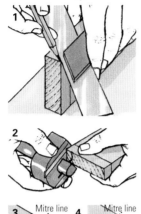

Cutting the tails

Saw out the waste. Trim the shoulders square with a chisel, then cut the mitre, using a dovetail saw.

Marking the pins

Mark the shoulder lines and mitre on the pin member, as described for the tails. Chalk the end grain and mark the position of the pins, using the tail member as a template. Square these marks down to the shoulder line on both sides of the workpiece (**4**).

Cutting the pins

Cut out the waste from between the pins, then reclamp the work in the vice. Holding the dovetail saw at an angle, cut alongside the last pin, down to the line of the mitre. Finally, cut the mitre itself, and then cut the moulding with a plane or router before assembling the joint.

REBATED THROUGH DOVETAIL JOINT

To incorporate a rebate in through dovetail joints, it is necessary to extend the shoulder at the bottom edge of each tail member to plug the rebate at the corner.

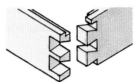

Marking the rebate

Mark the shoulder line for the joint on both sides and across the top edge of the tail member. Having set a marking gauge to the depth of the rebate, scribe a line along the inside of the same workpiece, then across its end and along to the shoulder line on the outside face (**1**). Scribe a similar line on the pin member, but only on the inside face.

Reset the gauge and scribe the width of the rebate along the bottom edge of both workpieces (**2**).

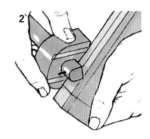

Marking and cutting the tails

Mark out the required number of equal-size tails, as described for a mitred through dovetail. Then hatch the waste. Saw down the sides of the tails and the rebate depth line. Remove the waste with a coping saw and a bevel-edge chisel.

Marking the pins

Gauge a shoulder line on both sides of the pin member. Chalk the end grain and use the tail member as a template for marking out the pins. Hatch the waste with a pencil.

Cutting the pins and rebate

Cut the sides of the pins, and remove the waste with a coping saw and a chisel.

Mark the extended-shoulder line on the bottom edge of the tail member – the extension should equal the width of the rebate (**3**). Plane the rebate on both components.

Use a dovetail saw to trim the waste back to the extended-shoulder line (**4**), before assembling the joint.

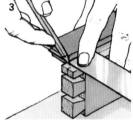
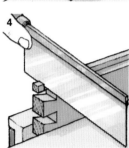

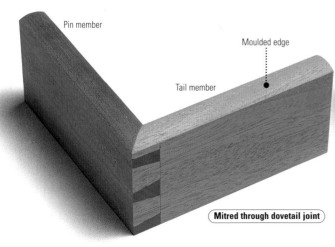

Pin member · Moulded edge · Tail member

Mitred through dovetail joint

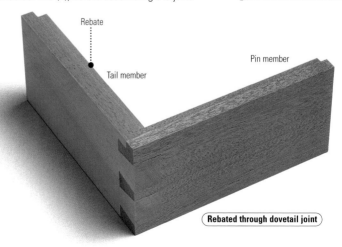

Rebate · Tail member · Pin member

Rebated through dovetail joint

LAPPED DOVETAIL JOINT

In traditional drawer construction through dovetails are used for the back corners but it is standard practice to use lapped dovetail joints for the front, so they will be invisible when the drawer is closed. This is achieved by lapping the pin member over the end of the tail member.

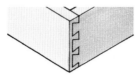
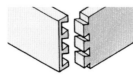

Marking and cutting the tails

Before you can cut the tail member to a precise length, you need to decide on the thickness of the lap. As a rule, it is at least 3mm (1/8in) thick.

Having set a cutting gauge to the thickness of the pin member less the thickness of the lap, scribe a shoulder line all round the tail member (**1**). Set out the tails, then cut away the waste and trim the shoulders.

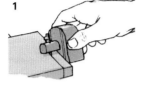

Marking and cutting the pins

Set a cutting gauge to the length of the tails and, working from the inside face of the pin member, scribe the lap line on the end grain. Reset the gauge to the thickness of the tail member before scribing the pin shoulder line across the inside face of the same workpiece.

Chalk the end grain and, using the tails as a template, score the shape of the pins in the chalk (**2**). From these marks, square parallel lines on the inside face, down to the shoulder line. Hatch the waste with a pencil.

Clamp the work in a bench vice. Holding a dovetail saw at an angle, cut down on the waste side of each line, stopping at the lap and shoulder lines (**3**). Before you take the work out of the vice, use the saw to remove some of the waste from between the pins (**4**).

Remove what is left of the waste with a bevel-edge chisel, cutting back to the shoulder line (**5**) and then paring down to the lap line. It pays to remove the wood gradually, making alternate cuts, first across the grain, then parallel with it. Carefully trim the waste from the corners with a narrow bevel-edge chisel.

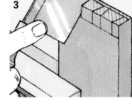
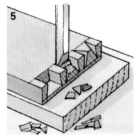

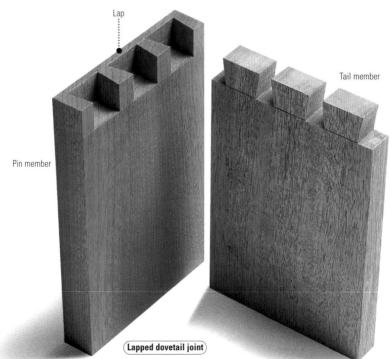

Lap

Pin member

Tail member

Lapped dovetail joint

DOUBLE-LAPPED DOVETAIL JOINT

Except for a narrow band of end grain, the double-lapped dovetail is virtually undetectable when the joint is assembled. It is used mainly for cabinet-making and box construction. The instructions that follow are for cutting the double lap on the tail member, though you can cut it in either component.

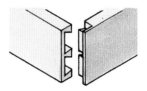

Marking and cutting the tails

Having set a cutting gauge to the thickness of the pin member, scribe the joint's shoulder line on the inside face and edges of the tail member.

Reset the gauge to the width of the double lap and, working from the outside face, scribe a line across the end grain and down to the shoulder line on both edges. Use the same setting to scribe the depth of the double lap on the inside face and edges (**1**).

Cut the double lap on the end of the tail member, following the gauged lines with a dovetail saw (**2**).

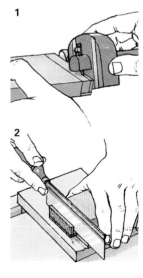

If necessary, trim the end grain and the inside of the double lap with a shoulder plane, to make sure both surfaces are flat and square (**3**).

Mark out the tails with a dovetail template (**4**), and square their tips across the end grain. Saw and chisel out the waste, as described for cutting the pins of a lapped dovetail joint (see opposite).

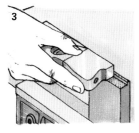

3

4

5

Marking and cutting the pins

Scribe the width of the lap on the end of the pin member. Reset the gauge to match the thickness of the tails and mark the pin shoulder line across the inside face of the workpiece. Chalk the end grain and mark the shape of the pins, using the tails as a template (**5**). From these marks, square parallel lines down to the shoulder line on the inside face. Saw and chisel out the waste.

MITRED DOVETAIL JOINT

Because it is entirely hidden, a mitred dovetail joint is sometimes referred to as a secret mitred dovetail. Typically used when both components are the same thickness, it requires careful marking and cutting. Contrary to the usual practice when making dovetail joints, you need to cut the pins first, so you can use them as a template for marking the tails.

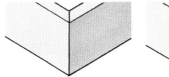

Initial setting out

Having set a cutting gauge to match the thickness of the wood, scribe a shoulder line across the inside face of each piece. Using a knife and mitre square, mark the mitre on both edges, running from the shoulder line to the outside corner.

Reset the gauge to the thickness of the mitre lap and, working from the outside face, scribe a line across the end grain. Using the same setting, scribe the depth of the mitre lap on the inside face (**1**). Cut and trim the lap on each piece, of wood as for a double-lapped dovetail joint (see opposite).

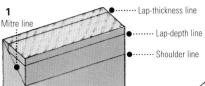

1

Mitre line
········· Lap-thickness line
········· Lap-depth line
········· Shoulder line

Marking and cutting pins

Set a marking gauge to 6mm (¼in) and scribe a line parallel with each edge of the work, running up from the shoulder line and across the end grain to the lap (**2**). Set out the pins between these lines.

2

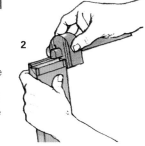

From the marks drawn on the end grain, square parallel lines down to the shoulder on the inside face.

Saw and chisel out the waste between the pins, as for a lapped dovetail joint (see opposite). Don't worry if you saw into the lap (**3**). Cut away the waste to form the mitre on each edge, following the marked line with a saw.

Set the work upright in a bench vice and use a chisel to trim the lap to a mitred edge, working from each end towards the middle (**4**). If necessary, finish with a shoulder plane.

3

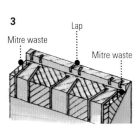

Mitre waste   Lap
                        Mitre waste

4

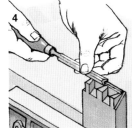

Marking and cutting the tails

Follow the procedure given for marking out the pin member, up to and including cutting the lap.

Lay the tail member flat on a bench. Holding the pin member on end, align its inside face with the shoulder line marked across the tail member. Scribe around the pins to mark the shape of the tails (**5**). Square parallel lines across the end grain to mark the tips of the tails.

Cut the tails and mitres as described for the pins, and mitre the lap in the same way. Try the joint for fit, but don't tap the joint all the way home until you are ready to apply the glue.

5

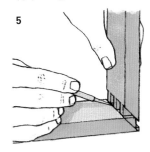

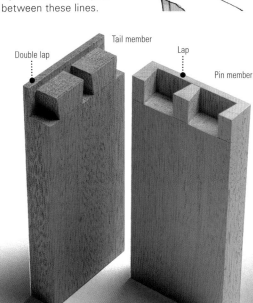

Tail member
Double lap
Lap
Pin member

Double-lapped dovetail joint

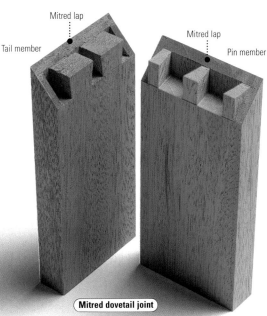

Mitred lap
Tail member
Mitred lap
Pin member

Mitred dovetail joint

BEVELLED DOVETAIL JOINT

The bevelled dovetail can be used to make a rigid joint when the sloping sides of a frame meet at a compound angle. It is not an easy joint to make – the setting out is complicated and every edge has to be cut carefully at an angle. The components must be the same thickness, and they have to be cut oversize in length and width.

Before you start marking out the joint, it is advisable to make a drawing from which to calculate the true shape of the parts.

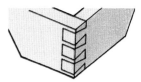
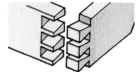

Making the drawing

Begin by drawing the side elevation of the joint as it would appear when complete. Show the thickness of the wood and add broken lines representing its initial width and length. Draw its plan immediately below the side elevation.

However, neither the plan nor the elevation will give a true view – because, seen from these angles, the components are foreshortened. To get a true view, draw one of the components as if it was laid flat. To do this, start by setting a pair of compasses on point A. Strike an arc from point A1 to the base line at B. Strike a second arc from point A2. Set the compass point on A3 and swing an arc to meet a vertical line at C. Draw a line through C parallel with the base line. Join up points B and D. Then from A draw a line parallel to the line thus formed – which will give a true section of the component.

Now draw a vertical line from A to E on the plan view. Draw a line from B to F on a line extended from the outer edge of the plan. Similarly, draw a line from C1 to G and from D to H. Join G to H with a solid line (this represents the inner edge of the end of the component). Join E to F with a broken line (representing the outer edge). The angle X is the true angle of the end of the component.

To find the true bevel angle, draw a line at right angles to line EF at I. Draw a second line parallel to it – and set away from it by the thickness of the wood – to point J. Run a line through IJ. The angle Y is the true bevel angle.

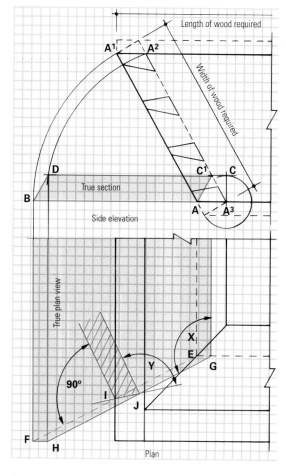

Construct an elevation, a plan and the true views of the joint

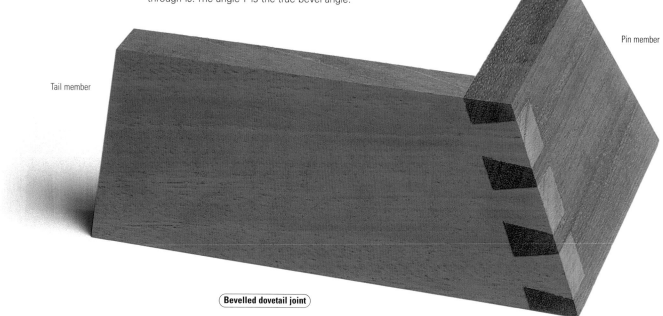

Tail member

Pin member

Bevelled dovetail joint

Marking and cutting the ends

Cut the parts to length and width, as shown by the broken lines on the side elevation. Set an adjustable bevel to the end angle X (**1**). Mark the angle, running from the corner, on the inside face of the wood (**2**). Saw the ends to this angle (**3**). Set another bevel to the end angle Y. Mark this angle on the edges of the components, working from the outer face side (**4**). Join up the edge marks to give a guide line for planing the bevelled end.

Set the wood in the vice, with the end of the workpiece horizontal. Plane the bevel on the end of each component. Finally, check the accuracy of the bevel – taking care to hold the stock of your adjustable bevel at right angles to the long edge of the workpiece (**5**).

Marking and cutting the joint

Set out the tails on the face side of the tail member. Begin by marking in pencil the thickness of the wood on both faces of each component, using the bevelled ends as a guide (**6**). Join the marked lines on each edge of the tail member.

With the adjustable bevel set to end-angle X, mark a line from the inside bottom corner on the end of the tail member. Make a mark 6mm ($\frac{1}{4}$in) down from the top edge; and then a similar mark up from the bottom edge. Set out the size and spacing of the tails between these marks. Then place a dovetail template cut from card against a try square and mark out the dovetails on the outside face (**7**).

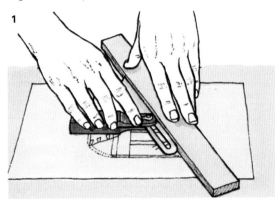

1

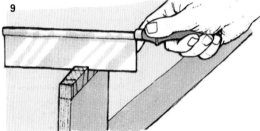

6

7

Mark the end of the tails on the bevelled end of the tail member (**8**) – the bevel should be set to end-angle X. Saw the tails, following the marked angles (**9**).

Chalk the end of the pin member. Lay the tail member on the chalked end, with the edges and inner shoulders flush, then scribe round the tails to mark the pins in the chalk.

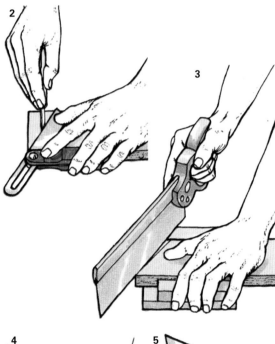

2

3

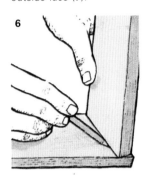

8

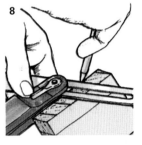

9

Using the bevel set to end-angle X, mark parallel lines down from each dovetail to the shoulder (**10**). Saw and chisel out the waste, following the marked lines.

Use webbing cramps to clamp the workpieces and, when the glue has set, plane a bevel on the long edges of each component.

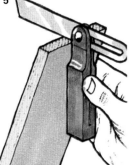

10

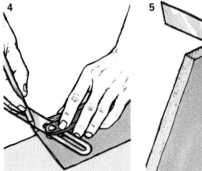

4

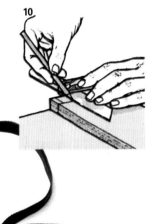

5

BOARD JOINTS

Man-made boards are more stable than panels of solid wood, but on the whole they do not have its long-grain strength. The means of joining these boards varies according to their composition. Many of the joints used for solid-wood carcass construction can be used for joining man-made boards – but framing joints, such as bridle joints and mortise-and-tenons, are unsuitable.

JOINT GUIDE

The chart lists the carcass joints suitable for various man-made boards. The first column tells you the strength of each joint in each material. The second column indicates which methods are appropriate for making the joint, and the third column whether it is easy or difficult to cut the joint by hand or using power or machine tools.

Treat solid-core laminated boards, such as blockboard and laminboard, like solid wood when selecting a joint for a particular application. A dovetail, for example, would be cut in the end grain only, not in the side grain. With this type of board, dovetails are more difficult to cut, because of the changing grain direction of the board's structure. Make coarse even-sized tails and pins (machine-cut dovetails are preferable). For dovetail-jointed cabinets that are to be veneered, use lapped joints – the mitred variety is best, as the joint's construction will not show through the veneer if the wood shrinks or swells.

Man-made boards that are ready-finished with a decorative veneer must be mitre-jointed if the core material is not to show. The alternative is to use a corner lipping, which makes an attractive decorative feature.

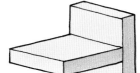

Corner joint

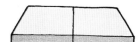

T-joint

Edge-to-edge joint

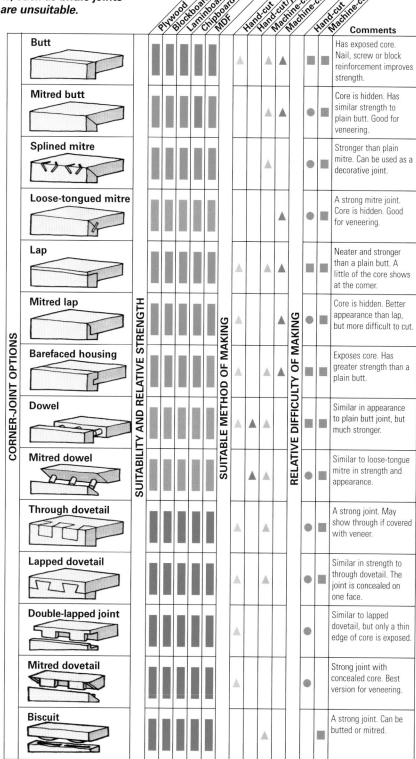

CORNER-JOINT OPTIONS

Joint	Comments
Butt	Has exposed core. Nail, screw or block reinforcement improves strength.
Mitred butt	Core is hidden. Has similar strength to plain butt. Good for veneering.
Splined mitre	Stronger than plain mitre. Can be used as a decorative joint.
Loose-tongued mitre	A strong mitre joint. Core is hidden. Good for veneering.
Lap	Neater and stronger than a plain butt. A little of the core shows at the corner.
Mitred lap	Core is hidden. Better appearance than lap, but more difficult to cut.
Barefaced housing	Exposes core. Has greater strength than a plain butt.
Dowel	Similar in appearance to plain butt joint, but much stronger.
Mitred dowel	Similar to loose-tongue mitre in strength and appearance.
Through dovetail	A strong joint. May show through if covered with veneer.
Lapped dovetail	Similar in strength to through dovetail. The joint is concealed on one face.
Double-lapped joint	Similar to lapped dovetail, but only a thin edge of core is exposed.
Mitred dovetail	Strong joint with concealed core. Best version for veneering.
Biscuit	A strong joint. Can be butted or mitred.

Column headings for the chart: SUITABILITY AND RELATIVE STRENGTH (Plywood, Blockboard, Laminboard, Chipboard, MDF); SUITABLE METHOD OF MAKING (Hand-cut, Hand-cut/jig, Machine-cut, Machine-cut); RELATIVE DIFFICULTY OF MAKING (Hand-cut, Machine-cut); Comments.

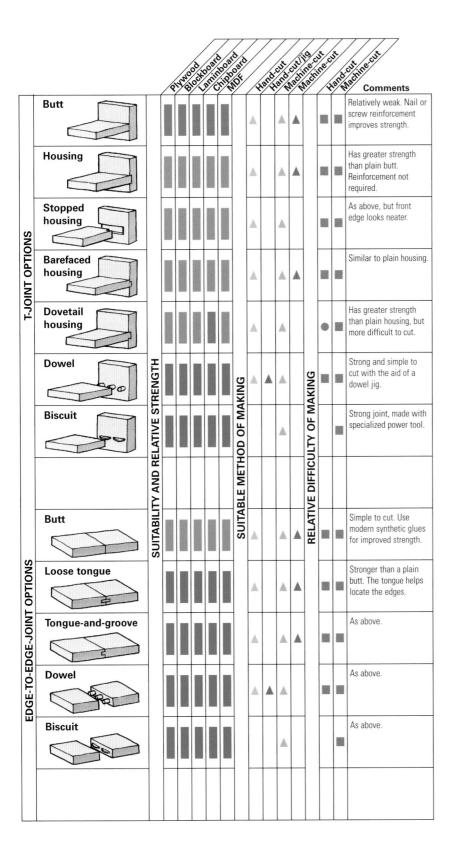

	Plywood	Blockboard	Laminboard	Chipboard	MDF	Hand-cut	Hand-cut/jig	Machine-cut	Machine-cut	Hand-cut	Machine-cut	Comments
	SUITABILITY AND RELATIVE STRENGTH					**SUITABLE METHOD OF MAKING**				**RELATIVE DIFFICULTY OF MAKING**		
T-JOINT OPTIONS												
Butt 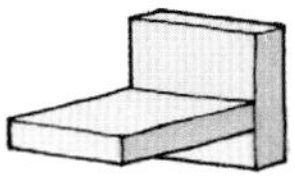	▮	▮	▮	▮	▮	▲		▲	▲	■	■	Relatively weak. Nail or screw reinforcement improves strength.
Housing 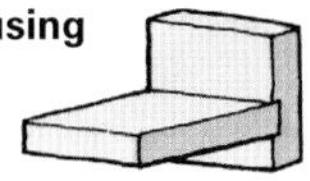	▮	▮	▮	▮	▮	▲		▲	▲	■	■	Has greater strength than plain butt. Reinforcement not required.
Stopped housing 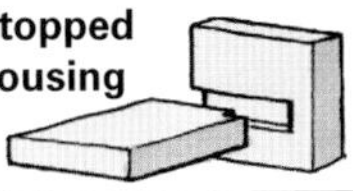	▮	▮	▮	▮	▮	▲		▲		■	■	As above, but front edge looks neater.
Barefaced housing 	▮	▮	▮	▮	▮	▲		▲	▲	■	■	Similar to plain housing.
Dovetail housing 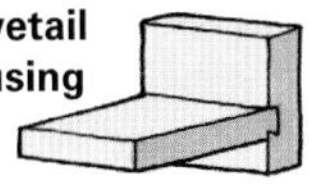	▮	▮	▮	▮	▮	▲		▲		●	■	Has greater strength than plain housing, but more difficult to cut.
Dowel 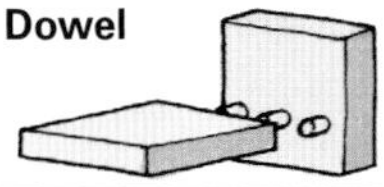	▮	▮	▮	▮	▮	▲	▲	▲		■	■	Strong and simple to cut with the aid of a dowel jig.
Biscuit 	▮	▮	▮	▮	▮			▲			■	Strong joint, made with specialized power tool.
EDGE-TO-EDGE-JOINT OPTIONS												
Butt 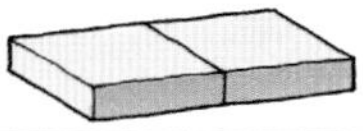	▮	▮	▮	▮	▮	▲		▲	▲	■	■	Simple to cut. Use modern synthetic glues for improved strength.
Loose tongue 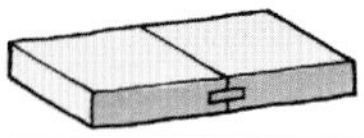	▮	▮	▮	▮	▮	▲		▲	▲	■	■	Stronger than a plain butt. The tongue helps locate the edges.
Tongue-and-groove 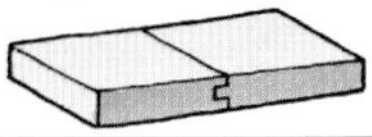	▮	▮	▮	▮	▮	▲		▲	▲	■	■	As above.
Dowel 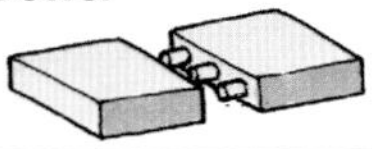	▮	▮	▮	▮	▮	▲	▲	▲		■	■	As above.
Biscuit 	▮	▮	▮	▮	▮			▲			■	As above.

KEY TO CHART

Suitability and relative strength

- ▮ **Excellent**
- ▮ **Good**
- ▮ **Fair**
- ▮ **Poor**
- ▮ **Unsuitable**

Suitable method of making

- ▲ **Hand-cut (Using handtools)**
- ▲ **Hand-cut/jig (Using handtools with jig)**
- ▲ **Machine-cut (Using hand-held power tools)***
- ▲ **Machine-cut (Using machine tools)***

***** ***Jigs may also be used***

Relative difficulty of making

- ● **Difficult**
- ■ **Simple**

USING A CORNER LIPPING

A solid-wood lipping can be used as a means of joining man-made boards at a corner, and it also masks the core. Lippings can be left square or shaped to form a decorative feature. If the board is faced with veneer, the grain of the lipping generally runs perpendicular to it.

Joints for corner lippings

You can either butt-joint the lipping to the board or, for improved strength, reinforce the joint with a tongue-and-groove joint. Either cut the tongue in the edge of the board or glue a separate plywood tongue in grooves cut in both the board and the lipping.

Stop the groove to prevent the tongue showing at the end of the joint (**1**).

A stronger joint, for plinths or carcass construction, is made using a relatively thick lipping glued to barefaced tongues on the board. The lipping can be moulded to form a decorative edge (**2**).

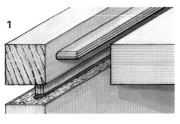

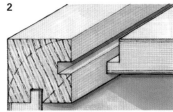

Corner lippings

Square

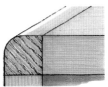

Full-round

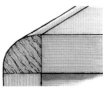

Part-round

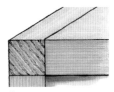

Chamfered

Bevelled

Beaded

TYPES OF EDGE LIPPING

Regardless of the method adopted for joining man-made boards, all edges should be lipped in order to conceal the core material. You can use long-grain or cross-grain veneer, or a substantial solid-wood lipping of matching or contrasting timber.

Applying edge lippings

The simplest lipping to apply is a preglued veneer that is ironed onto the edge. These edge lippings are sold primarily for finishing preveneered chipboard panels.

For a more substantial edging that can be shaped or moulded, cut a thick lipping from solid wood and either butt-joint it to the edge or, for improved strength, add a tongue.

You can mitre the corners of thick lippings to improve appearance – essential if the lipping is moulded.

When gluing a long lipping, place a stiff batten between the lipping and the cramp heads to help spread the clamping forces over the full length of the work.

When planing edge lippings flush, take care not to damage the surface veneer (particularly when planing down to cross-grain veneer).

A deep lipping stiffens the edges of man-made boards – especially useful when constructing shelves and worktops. Set the board into a rebate cut in the lipping.

Deep lippings stiffen boards

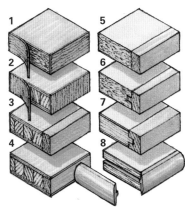

1 Long-grain veneer
2 Cross-grain veneer
3 Lipped after veneering
4 Lipped before veneering
5 Butt-jointed
6 Tongued lipping
7 Grooved lipping
8 Mitred lipping

CUTTING AND PLANING MAN-MADE BOARDS

Although man-made boards are relatively easy to cut, the resin content of some boards dulls cutting edges quickly. If possible, use tungsten-carbide-tipped (TCT) blades and cutters when working man-made boards. Full-size boards can be awkward to handle; cutting a board into smaller sections requires adequate space and support.

Cutting by hand

A 10 to 12 PPI panel saw is ideal for cutting boards to size. For relatively small workpieces, you can use a tenon saw. Whenever possible, mark cutting lines with a knife. The knife blade severs the surface fibres or laminate to leave a clean edge, so break-out doesn't result from sawing. Hold handsaws at a relatively shallow angle to the surface of the board.

Support the board close to the cutting line and face-side up to ensure any splintering is on the back of the board. Occasionally, when cutting a large panel, it is necessary to climb onto the board in order to reach the cutting line comfortably – in which case, make sure the board is supported on strong planks and sawhorses. Have an assistant standing by to support the offcut if it becomes unmanageable.

Have an assistant support offcuts

Planing the edges
To prevent break-out of the core or surface veneers, plane the edges of man-made boards from both ends towards the middle.

CHAPTER EIGHT

BENDING WOOD

Curved forms made from sections of solid timber often involve quite complex joinery, simply to prevent unnecessary wastage and to avoid creating weak areas of short grain. However, using specialized bending techniques, it is possible to produce curved workpieces economically – and because the grain of the wood runs roughly parallel with the curves rather than across them, the resulting components are relatively strong.

It is easier to bend wood that has been cut thinly, but you can bend thicker sections if the wood is soaked or steamed first. Another possibility is to glue strips of wood or veneer together, clamping them against a curved mould. Once the glue sets, these laminated components retain their shape even when they are removed from the mould.

Although laminating and steam bending are industrial processes, they can be adapted successfully for small-scale production in the home workshop.

KERFING

Kerfing is a technique employed to bend thick sections of solid timber without having to steam or soak them beforehand. A kerf is a groove cut by a saw; and if several equally spaced kerfs are cut partway through the wood, a workpiece can be bent at the points where its thickness has been reduced. The technique is used mainly for making curved components that will be seen from one side only – the sawcuts being concealed from view.

CALCULATING KERF SPACING

Draw a full-size plan to determine the radius and length of the bend. You can measure the length of the bend directly from the drawing, using a flexible rule, or step it off with a compass.

When a piece of timber is bent, material on the outside of the bend tends to stretch, while that on the inside is compressed. Somewhere in between is the undistorted neutral line of the curve. Because kerfing reduces the thickness of the board, which brings the neutral line nearer to the outer face of a component, it may be sufficient to use this outer face as a datum for your calculations.

When kerfing a bend it is necessary to space the sawcuts evenly, and the edges of each kerf must touch one another in order to produce an even curve (**1**).

To determine the optimum kerf spacing, saw almost through the thickness of the board at the point from which the bend will spring, leaving at least 3mm ($^1/_8$in) of wood. From this kerf, measure the length of the bent section and make a pencil mark on the edge of the work. Clamp one end of the board firmly to the bench, then lift the free end of the board until the sawcut closes and bending stops. Wedge the board in this position. Just below the pencil mark, measure the gap between the underside of the board and the bench top (**2**). Leave the same gap between each kerf.

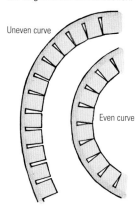

Draw a full-size plan
Use the drawing to determine the length of the curved section.

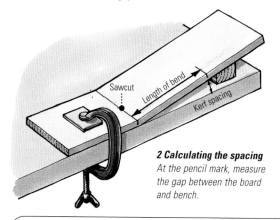

Sawcut

Length of bend

Kerf spacing

2 Calculating the spacing
At the pencil mark, measure the gap between the board and bench.

1 Creating even curves
The sides of each kerf must touch to create an even curve.

MAKING THE BEND

To make the curve, fix the kerfed component to a rigid frame or carcase. Alternatively, apply glue to the kerfs and apply reinforcement to the inside of the bend.

Gluing the bend

Bend the component by hand, or use a web cramp to pull it into shape. If the bend is too tight, insert a piece of paper or thin card into each cut. If the bend is not tight enough, run a triangular file along each kerf (**1**), filing the same amount of wood from each sawcut.

Once the curve is satisfactory, open up the kerfs and apply glue to each of them. Without some form of reinforcement the component will be relatively weak, since it is only the glued corners of the kerfs that are touching. The solution is to glue and clamp a strip of veneer to the inner curved face. Align the grain of the veneer with the grain of the curved component and use shaped blocks to hold the veneer in place until the glue sets (**2**).

1   Triangular file

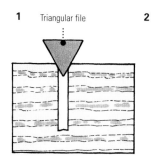

2

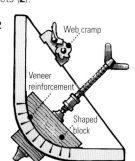

Web cramp

Veneer reinforcement

Shaped block

Making duo-faced components

By laminating two kerfed boards back to back you can make a curved component with a smooth face on each side. Spread glue thinly on both kerfed faces, then clamp the boards together. If necessary, use shaped blocks to support the inside of the curve until the glue has set.

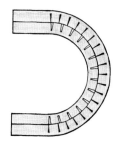

LAMINATING KERFED BENDS

Kerfed bends are usually made with the sawcuts running across the grain. If you want to bend a component at one or both ends, you can cut kerfs in the end grain and insert strips of veneer to make a laminated bend. Thin veneers bend more easily than thick ones – so if necessary, double up thin veneers to fill each kerf.

Cut a series of evenly spaced kerfs on a band saw. Glue slightly overlong strips of veneer in the kerfs, then clamp the laminated section around a former. When the glue has set, saw the stepped end square and plane the veneers flush with the sides of the laminated component.

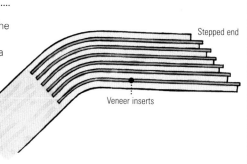

Stepped end

Veneer inserts

The width of a kerf is determined by the size of the saw blade: a fine saw will cut a narrow kerf, a coarse saw a wider one. A series of closely spaced narrow kerfs will give a smoother contour to the bend than a few wide kerfs. Once bent, the outer face of the workpiece tends to be slightly faceted, so you may need to sand the bend to create a smooth curve.

Using powered machines

The most efficient way to cut kerfs across a board is to use a radial-arm saw or a mitre saw. Power-saw blades are thicker than handsaw blades and so produce a wider kerf. You will therefore need fewer cuts for a given radius. Once set, the radial-arm saw will make parallel equal-depth cuts across the board. All you need concentrate on is the spacing of the kerfs. Either do this by eye, using a mark on the back fence to align each cut, or drive a nail into the face of the fence and locate each sawcut on the nail as you move the work sideways.

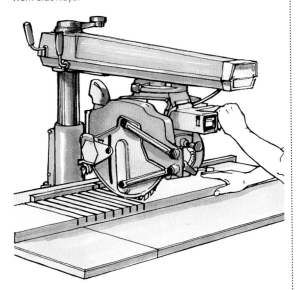

Cutting the kerfs by hand

To mark the cut lines across the wood, use a try square and pencil. Then set a marking gauge to about a quarter of the thickness of the wood and scribe the depth of cut on both edges of the workpiece, working from the face side.

Use either a crosscut saw or a tenon saw to cut the kerfs across the back face of the workpiece. When kerfing relatively wide boards, run the saw blade against a straight batten clamped to the work.

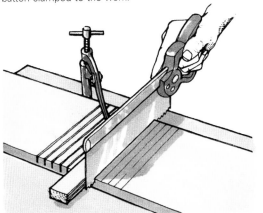

STEAM BENDING

Because steam softens wood fibres, workpieces can be bent into relatively tight curves when they have been steamed. Considerable force is needed to bend wood, but you can undertake steam bending in a home workshop, using a former, support strap and steam chest.

Bending wood is not an exact science. There are many variables – you may have to resort to trial and error to achieve satisfactory results.

The radius to which wood can be bent depends on its thickness and natural stiffness. By pulling the ends together you may be able to bend a thin strip of wood to form a ring. For tighter bends, the wood must be steamed and held around a former to 'set' the wood to the required shape. To bend thicker sections of wood, it is necessary to restrain the outer fibres to prevent them from splitting out. The method described here and overleaf is for bending relatively thick sections.

Preparing the wood

Select knot-free straight-grained timber. Also, make sure the wood is free from blemishes such as shakes and splits – any flaw in the wood is a potential weakness. There are dozens of woods that can be steam-bent successfully, many of them hardwoods (a short list of suitable woods is provided on the following page).

You will find newly cut 'green' timber easier to bend than well-seasoned wood. Wood that is air-seasoned tends to bend better than kiln-dried wood. If the wood is very dry and proves difficult to work, try soaking it for a few hours before steaming.

You can either prepare the wood to finished size before bending it or reduce it to size with a saw, drawknife or spokeshave after bending. The latter method is often used for making Windsor chairs. If you sand the wood to a smooth finish before bending, it is less likely to split and final finishing will be easier. Prepared green wood shrinks more than seasoned timber. Green wood turned to a round section before bending can dry oval in shape.

Whether prepared before or after bending, and whatever the size or shape of the section, the wood must always be cut about 100mm (4in) overlength before it is bent. Any end splits or compression damage from the strap can be cut away after bending. To establish the length required, make a full-size drawing of the required final shape. Measure the outer edge to calculate the finished length, then add 100mm (4in).

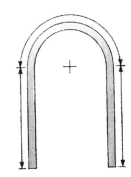

Measure the outer curve

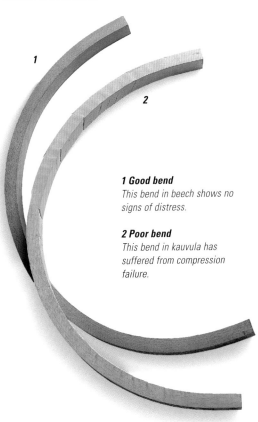

1 Good bend
This bend in beech shows no signs of distress.

2 Poor bend
This bend in kauvula has suffered from compression failure.

273

MAKING A STRAP

The key to bending tight curves successfully is to use a flexible metal backing strap, which will allow the outer fibres to bend without splitting. The softened inner fibres will compress sufficiently to take up the smaller curve.

Make the strap from mild steel, 1.5mm (¹⁄₁₆in) thick and at least as wide as the wood to be bent. If the wood you are bending is susceptible to chemical staining on contact with mild steel, make the strap from plated or stainless steel or use a mild-steel strap wrapped with polyethylene.

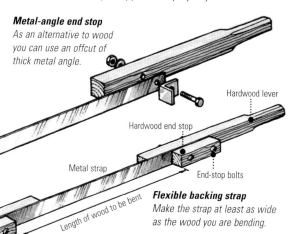

Metal-angle end stop
As an alternative to wood you can use an offcut of thick metal angle.

Hardwood lever

Hardwood end stop

Metal strap

End-stop bolts

Length of wood to be bent

Flexible backing strap
Make the strap at least as wide as the wood you are bending.

Fit hardwood end stops to the strap to restrain the ends of the wood and prevent it stretching. Each end stop needs to be large enough to cover the end of the wood and should be about 225mm (9in) long. The distance between the stops must match the length of the workpiece, including the 100mm (4in) waste.

Drill two 9mm (³⁄₈in) holes, about 150mm (6in) apart, in each block. Mark and drill similar holes in the metal strap to accommodate bolts for attaching the end stops. The end-stop bolts are also used for attaching hardwood levers to the back face of the strap, to provide leverage for bending the strap and steamed wood around the former.

Making the former
The former supports the softened inner fibres and determines the final shape of the steamed wood. It should be at least as wide as the wood to be bent, and must incorporate locations for cramps to hold the strap and work.

Bent wood tends to straighten slightly when released from the cramps, so allow for this by making the curve slightly tighter when calculating the dimensions of the former – some experimentation may be needed to determine what allowance to make.

You can construct the former from thick sections of solid wood, either screwed or bolted to a base made from man-made board (**1**). Alternatively, instead of solid wood, use layers of plywood glued together (**2**). Another method is to screw a shaped thick plywood panel to a solid-wood frame fixed to the base (**3**).

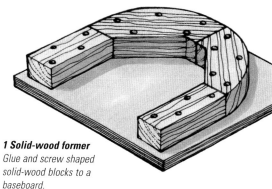

1 Solid-wood former
Glue and screw shaped solid-wood blocks to a baseboard.

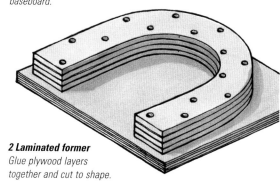

2 Laminated former
Glue plywood layers together and cut to shape.

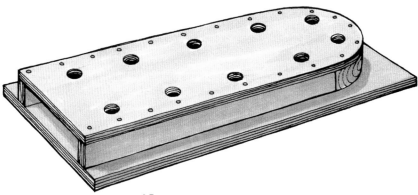

3 Box-construction former
Glue and screw a shaped plywood panel to a stout frame.

SELECTED WOODS FOR STEAM BENDING

All the woods listed below are suitable for steam bending.

- **ASH**
  Fraxinus americana
  Fraxinus excelsior

- **BEECH**
  Fagus grandifolia
  Fagus sylvatica

- **BIRCH**
  Betula alleghaniensis
  Betula papyrifera

- **ELM**
  Ulmus americana
  Ulmus hollandica
  Ulmus procera
  Ulmus thomasii

- **HICKORY**
  Carya spp.

- **OAK**
  Quercus alba
  Quercus mongolica
  Quercus petraea
  Quercus robur
  Quercus rubra

- **WALNUT**
  Juglans nigra
  Juglans regia

- **YEW**
  Taxus baccata

MAKING A STEAM CHEST

A length of metal or plastic pipe can be adapted to serve as a steam chest for small pieces of wood, and for longer pieces that require bending along part of their length. Alternatively, make a chest from exterior-grade plywood to suit your requirements.

Using a pipe

Cut a length of pipe to suit the size of your work. Cut discs from exterior-grade plywood to make snug-fitting end plugs for the pipe. Drill a hole in one plug for the steam feedpipe, and plane off the bottom edge of the other plug to provide a steam vent and drainage hole. To accommodate pieces of wood that are longer than the pipe, cut a hole in the centre of each end plug, so you can pass the wood through the chest. Fit wooden bridging pieces inside the pipe, to keep shorter pieces of wood off the bottom.

It pays to insulate the pipe with thick plastic foam, or make a jacket from wooden battens tied round the outside of the pipe with loops of wire.

To allow condensation to drain from the pipe, mount the chest at a slight angle on support brackets.

Generating steam

A small electric-powered boiler can be used to generate steam. Or make your own from a medium-size metal drum, fitted with a removable cap or plug, and heat the drum on a portable gas burner or an electric hot plate. Attach one end of a short hose to a spigot soldered into the drum, and plug the other end into the end plug of the steam chest. A continuous supply of steam is produced by half-filling the drum and heating the water to 100°C (212°F).

As a rough guide, the wood should be steamed for one hour for every 25mm (1in) of thickness. Steaming timber for longer may break down the structure of the wood, and does not necessarily make it any easier to bend.

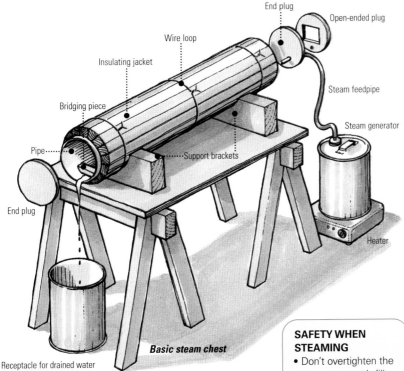

Basic steam chest

End plug · Open-ended plug · Wire loop · Insulating jacket · Steam feedpipe · Bridging piece · Steam generator · Pipe · Support brackets · End plug · Heater · Receptacle for drained water

Making a plywood steam chest

You can construct a simple open-ended box from exterior-grade plywood, glued-and-screwed at the corners. Make removable end plugs from similar plywood. Drill a hole in one plug for the steam hose, and cut one of the corners off the other plug to allow for drainage. Paint all surfaces with exterior-grade varnish.

This type of chest may be the better option for steaming batches of wood.

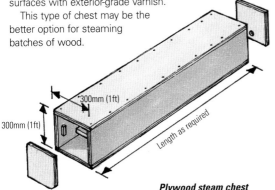

300mm (1ft) · 300mm (1ft) · Length as required

Plywood steam chest

SAFETY WHEN STEAMING

- Don't overtighten the steam generator's filler cap or plug.
- Don't let the steam generator run dry.
- Make sure the steam chest is vented.
- Never reach over the steam generator or stand directly in front of the steam chest when opening the generator or the chest.
- Wear gloves when handling steamed wood and the equipment.
- Keep the heat source well away from all flammable materials.
- Always shut down the steam generator before removing the wood from the chest.

BENDING THE WOOD

Steamed wood remains pliable for only a few minutes – so make sure everything is ready before you remove the wood from the chest. Have your cramps adjusted to size, and warm the metal strap so it doesn't cool the wood prematurely. When bending thick wood, it is a good idea to ask a friend to help.

Shut down the steam generator, then remove the wood from the chest. Locate the steamed wood between the end stops of the strap, then place the strapped wood on the former and at the mid point clamp the wood to the former, placing a block of waste timber between the cramp and the strap.

Wrap the wood round the former by pulling on the strap handles (**1**). Hold the wood in place with strategically placed cramps (**2**).

You can leave the wood to cool and set on the former, or remove it after about 15 minutes and reclamp it to a similarly shaped drying jig. Either way, the wood must be left to dry thoroughly – which may take up to a week for thick sections of timber.

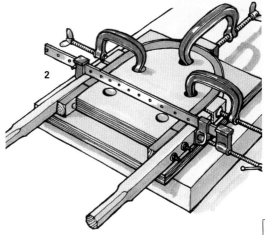

BENDING LAMINATES

Thin strips of wood or veneer can be bent dry round a former and then glued together to make a solid shape. Because the fibres of each strip are not overstressed, laminated components can be bent into tighter or more complex curves than is possible with steamed solid wood. Woodworkers have seized upon this opportunity to create innovative designs from laminated components.

FREE-FORM BENDING

Free-form compound curves are difficult to visualize, and without a drawing to work from it is virtually impossible to construct a former for them. One way to create free-form curves is to bend a single strip of wood and twist it into the required shape then build a former around it. This technique involves a degree of experimentation – and the result is determined largely by your imagination and your skill in manipulating the flexible strip.

The basic technique

First, sketch out your idea and cut strips of wood that will suit the size of your design. Next, start to build the former by making a baseboard with a stout post fixed at each end. Clamp the end of the strip to one post, then bend it to shape and clamp the other end to the other post.

Cut and fix triangular intermediate posts to the baseboard to support the strip at the required angles. Mark both edges of the strip on the posts, then remove it.

The key to successful free-form bending is to have sufficient cramps to hold the work. A length of bicycle inner tube (with the valve cut away) bound round the work makes a

handy and efficient cramp. Apply resin glue to the laminate strips and then bind them together, using the tube. Clamp the lamination to the former posts, carefully manipulating it to follow the marked lines.

When the glue has set, remove the cramps and inner tube, then shape and finish the component.

SELECTING WOOD FOR LAMINATING

Virtually any wood can be laminated, provided it is cut thinly and it is free from physical blemishes that could promote splits or a break at a later stage. Most veneers, for example, can be laminated successfully. However, some woods are naturally more pliable than others. A short list of woods that bend well and are therefore suitable for laminating would include those recommended for steam bending on page 274.

PREPARING THE WOOD

Strips of commercially produced 'constructional veneer' can be laminated together in order to make frame members, such as table underframes or chair legs; random-grain decorative veneer can be used for face laminates.

If you prefer to cut your own laminates from solid wood, select timber that is straight-grained and free from knots or shakes. As with steam bending, air-dried wood is better than kiln-dried timber, because it is less brittle and bends more readily.

Cutting wood strips

For reliability and consistent grain pattern, it is preferable to cut laminate strips from solid wood. Quarter-sawn boards are best, as the growth rings run across the width of the strips, making them easier to bend. Before cutting the board, mark the face and end with V-shape reference lines (**1**) to help realign the strips during the gluing process.

Cutting strips with a saw can waste an enormous amount of wood, so it pays to make a few trials to determine how thick the strips have to be in order to produce the required radius.

When using relatively thick strips or making tight bends, wet the strips and clamp them to the former until they dry out. They will then take up the required shape more readily when you eventually apply the glue.

Using power saws

When cutting wood strips on a band saw, run the planed face edge of the board against the fence, cutting a slightly thicker strip than required. Plane the newly cut edge and cut the next strip. Finally, plane all the strips to the same thickness by passing them through a powered thicknesser.

A table saw is not the ideal machine for cutting strips to size. The saw has a tendency to snatch and break the thin strips, or even throw them back at you. If you have to use a table saw, cut an end stop in a stout guide batten and use it to feed the wood into the blade (**2**). Make sure

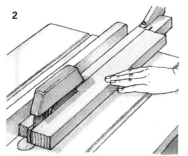

there aren't any wide gaps between the table insert and the blade. Always keep the blade guard in place and wear safety goggles or a visor when cutting narrow strips on a table saw.

FORMERS

You will need a former, or formers, to hold the glued laminates in place until the glue sets. You can make a single male former or a pair of male and female ones – the best type to use depends on the degree of bend and the size and number of components.

Making single formers

Male formers are the simplest to make. They are suitable in most cases – particularly for making large components, for which a two-part former would be cumbersome.

You can make the former from solid wood or glue layers of particle board together. The profiled face must be longer and wider than the wood strips. Work out the shape and dimensions by making a full-size drawing, then mark it out on the face of the block and cut it to shape on a band saw.

Ideally, the cramps used to hold the laminates in place should be positioned at right angles to the face of the former. The back of the former should therefore be cut to approximately the same contour as the face (**1**).

The number of cramps needed depends on the number of bends and the pliability of the wood. Use as many as is practicable, to apply even pressure along the former. Protect the face laminate with a backing strip of waxed hardboard, and place softwood blocks under the cramp heads to distribute the load (**2**).

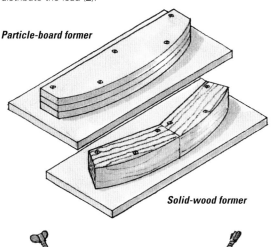

Particle-board former

Solid-wood former

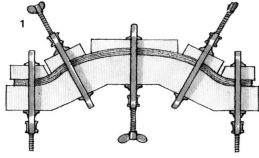

1

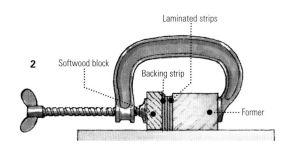

2   Softwood block

Laminated strips

Backing strip

Former

Male and female formers

Matched male and female formers can be cut either from solid wood or built up using man-made boards. They are held together by a number of cramps inserted in holes drilled in the male former (**1**).

Design the formers to use the minimum amount of material while applying even pressure over the entire length of the lamination (**2**). This usually means considering each component separately, perhaps orientating the formers at an angle that is different from the way the component appears in a drawn elevation (**3**).

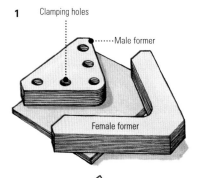

1   Clamping holes

Male former

Female former

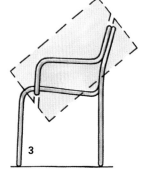

2

3

The contour faces of male and female formers are produced by cutting along two parallel lines – using a single cut to form both contours will not work. The exact width between the parallel lines is determined by clamping together the strips of wood or veneer to be glued and measuring the thickness.

The external and internal radii of bends that follow simple curves made with a compass are easy to set out; marking out a pair of complicated contours entails more work. Draw one contour as accurately as possible, either as a freehand line or by using drawing instruments. Then, from that line, mark off a series of closely spaced overlapping arcs, using a pair of compasses set to the thickness of the lamination (**4**). Draw the second contour line touching the peak of each arc.

Cut each contour line carefully, using a band saw.

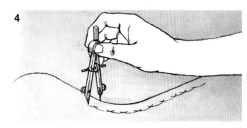

4

Multiple-part formers

Single or two-part formers are all that are required for most laminate-bending work. However, when the male former needs to be undercut to make the required shape, the female former must be cut into multiple sections (**5**) – which makes assembly and removal of the laminated parts easier.

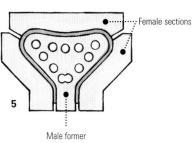

Female sections

5

Male former

Making wide formers

Large formers are required to make laminations wide enough for bowed door panels or seat platforms. To reduce the bulk of such formers, construct them from shaped ribs faced with thin sheets of plywood (**1**). A stout baseboard is required to provide rigidity.

To make the ribs, first cut a series of oversize blanks from man-made board. Mark out the shape of the bend on one blank, allowing for the thickness of the plywood facing (**2**). With the marked blank on top, temporarily pin the other blanks together. Cut housings across the stack of blanks to accommodate spacer rails (**3**). Before you dismantle the stacked blanks, cut the curved edge of the ribs on a band saw.

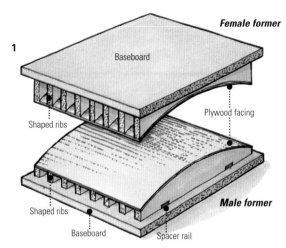

Female former

Baseboard

Plywood facing

Shaped ribs

Shaped ribs

Baseboard

Male former

Spacer rail

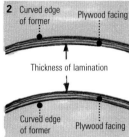

2 Curved edge of former   Plywood facing

Thickness of lamination

Curved edge of former   Plywood facing

4

5

Grain direction

Pin and glue the spacer rails into the housings, leaving a gap of 50 to 100mm (2 to 4 in) between the ribs. Then glue and screw each rib assembly to its baseboard (**4**). Pin and glue a plywood panel, 3mm (1/8in) thick, to the curved edges of the ribs (**5**).

Seal and wax the surface of each former to prevent the glued laminations sticking to it. Alternatively, line the formers with polyethylene sheeting.

When pressing the laminations, clamp the formers between two or more stiff wooden beams (**6**), using sash cramps to exert even pressure.

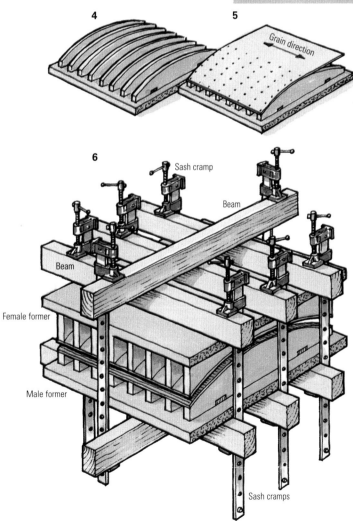

6

Sash cramp

Beam

Beam

Female former

Male former

Sash cramps

GLUING AND CUTTING

The best adhesive for laminating is urea-formaldehyde glue, as it sets slowly – allowing time to assemble the strips in position – and it is less likely to creep than PVA glues.

Stack the laminates in order, with face veneers on the top and bottom of the stack. Brush an even coating of glue onto the meeting faces of each laminate, then restack them in reverse order either on a single former or in two-part formers. Using cramps, apply even pressure, starting from the centre and working outwards to exclude air and glue from between the laminates.

Bands of self-adhesive tape wrapped over the edges of the glued workpiece may prevent the laminates slipping sideways as the glue is squeezed out. If necessary, slacken the sash cramps slightly and tap the laminates into line, using a block of wood and a hammer. Carefully retighten the cramps.

Cutting to size

Before removing a wide lamination from a former, mark the central point on the edges of the workpiece. Lay the workpiece on your bench and draw a line between the points marked on the edges. From this line, mark out the shape of the panel. Saw off the waste and finish the edges with a bench plane.

If you require a number of identical narrow components, it is often best to make one wide lamination and saw it into strips after the glue has set.

CHAPTER NINE

VENEERING AND MARQUETRY

A sophisticated process requiring artistic skill as well as manual dexterity, veneering has been practised for thousands of years. In Victorian times, furniture enhanced with veneer gained popularity as a substitute for solid-hardwood furniture. Today, veneers are not only made from natural wood but also from plain coloured paper foil or from foil printed to look like wood – which may even have simulated pore indentations. However, the advantages of natural-wood veneers are not always appreciated. Some of the most attractive wood is produced as a result of abnormal or irregular growth, so would be prohibitively expensive in solid form and unsatisfactory because of its lack of stability. Bonded to man-made boards with modern adhesives, veneer provides an economic and stable material that stands up well to central heating, while offering the aesthetic and tactile qualities of solid wood.

VENEERING TOOLS

A basic woodworking tool kit is likely to contain some of the tools used for laying veneers – including measuring and marking tools, a fret saw, chisels, scrapers, a block plane, bench planes and shoulder planes. Most of the specialized veneering tools shown here are available from good tool stores or from specialist suppliers. In addition, you may need to make some equipment yourself – such as a simple cutting jig for parquetry veneers.

Sharpening a blade
Usually, the point is the only part of a knife blade that becomes dull. To create a new point, hone the back edge only on an oilstone.

Toothing plane
A toothing plane differs from a conventional wooden plane in having its blade set almost vertical. The blade is finely grooved on the front and has a bevel ground on the back. The resulting teeth are similar to those of a fine saw. Drawing the plane across the groundwork keys (roughens) the surface, ready for gluing. The blade can be sharpened by honing the bevel on an oilstone.

Rules and straightedges
A metal rule, graduated in centimetres and inches, can double as a short straightedge for cutting small pieces of veneer. A larger steel straightedge is used for cutting longer veneers. Another useful cutting guide is a pressed-steel 'safety' ruler, which has edges that grip the work and prevent it from slipping. With an indentation down the centre, a safety ruler helps keep your fingertips out of harm's way.

Cutting mat
Proprietary cutting mats are made of a self-sealing rubber compound. Knife points can cut into the surface without it becoming permanently scored or dulling the blade. Fine-surfaced man-made boards, such as hardboard, are good alternatives.

Veneer saw
A veneer saw can be used, with a straightedge, to cut veneers of any thickness. The saw produces a square-edged cut for accurately butt-jointing matched veneers. The double-edged blade is reversible, and the fine teeth have no set.

Electric iron
An old domestic electric iron will soften traditional animal glue applied to the groundwork and veneer as part of the hammer-veneering process. It will also activate heat-sensitive glue film.

Knives
A surgical scalpel or craft knife fitted with a pointed blade is ideal for cutting intricate shapes. The blades, which are ground on both sides, produce a V-shape cut. If the edge of the veneer has to be cut square, hold the knife blade at a slight angle, to keep one ground bevel vertical as it runs against the guide rule.

Veneer punches
Veneer punches, used for repairing unsightly defects in veneer, come in eight different sizes. Each punch has an irregularly shaped cutter with which you can make a hole in the defective veneer and then cut an identical patch from matching veneer. The cut patch is pushed from the tool by a sprung ejector.

(Glue pot)

(Trimming tool)

(Metal veneer hammer)

(Cutting mat)

(Toothing plane)

(Veneer punches)

(Veneer pins)

(Veneer saw)

GROUNDWORK

The 'ground' or 'groundwork' – the backing material to which the veneer is glued – is no less important than the choice of veneer. Whether it is flat or curved, the ground needs to provide a smooth, even, dust-free surface. Thin veneer will not disguise defects or unevenness in the ground; they will telegraph (show through), particularly when the finished work is polished.

Trimming tool
With its adjustable chisel-ground blade, a trimming tool removes surplus veneer from around the edges of a veneered panel. The tool will cut cleanly both with and across the grain.

Veneer tape
Gummed paper tape holds pieces of veneer together and prevents newly laid veneer joints from opening up due to shrinkage. The tape is removed, after the glue has set, by wetting and scraping.

Glue pot
A double or jacketed glue pot is used to prepare hot animal glue for traditional veneer laying. The outer pot holds water, which is heated to keep the glue in the inner pot at working temperature and prevent it burning.

Older glue pots are made from cast iron, but most modern ones are made from aluminium for heating by gas or electricity. You can buy thermostatically controlled electric glue pots, but they are relatively expensive.

Veneer pins
Fine short pins with large plastic heads are used to hold veneers temporarily while the butt joints are being taped.

Veneer hammer
A veneer hammer is employed for hand-laying veneers. A wooden hammer has a round-edge brass blade mounted in a groove in the hardwood head. Working the blade across the panel with a zigzag motion presses the veneer down and excludes surplus glue and trapped air.

A metal veneer hammer looks like a conventional hammer with an elongated peen. The peen is used for laying glued veneers and pressing blisters flat.

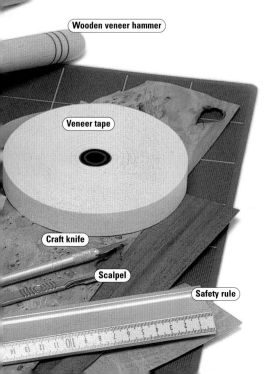

(**Wooden veneer hammer**)
(**Veneer tape**)
(**Craft knife**)
(**Scalpel**)
(**Safety rule**)

PREPARING THE GROUNDWORK

Despite the traditional convention of using pine or mahogany as a base for veneered furniture, solid wood is perhaps not the ideal ground for veneering. It 'moves' due to changes in humidity and requires careful preparation. Solid-wood groundwork has largely been superseded by man-made boards – which are much more stable and can be obtained in large sheets with flat sanded surfaces that are easier to prepare.

Veneering solid wood
To ensure that veneer and solid wood 'move' together, the veneer must be laid in the same direction as the grain of the

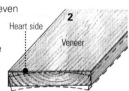

solid wood (**1**). Quarter-cut boards are the most stable, as there is only slight shrinkage across the width and thickness. Laying veneer on both sides of the board is best, as this helps maintain an even balance. If only one side of a tangentially cut board is to be veneered, this should always be the heart side (**2**) – the veneer helps pull the board flat and resists any tendency to cup.

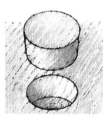

Heart side

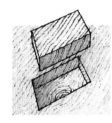

Repairing defects
Fine knots can be cut out of the solid-wood groundwork prior to veneering. The holes can be filled with round or diamond-shape plugs, with their grain following that of the groundwork. Make the plugs slightly thicker than the board, and then plane them flush after gluing.

Keying the surface
To improve adhesion, the surface of both solid and laminated groundwork must be keyed before gluing. Use either a toothing plane, working diagonally from opposite edges, or drag a tenon saw across the surface. Before sizing, pick up loose dust with a vacuum cleaner.

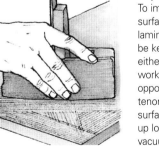

Sizing the surface
Sizing seals the pores and controls suction, improving the performance of the glue. The rate of absorption varies, depending on the type of groundwork you are using.

Size is made by diluting hot animal glue with water, at a ratio of about 1 part glue to 10 parts water. Alternatively, use synthetic wallpaper paste. Apply the size evenly to the surfaces. When it's dry, sand lightly to remove any nibs.

Man-made boards
Other than being cut to size, most man-made boards need little preparation. However, the surface of laminated boards must be keyed and sized and, if the grain direction of the face veneer runs parallel with the board's core, another veneer that runs across the board must be applied before the final veneer is laid.

SHAPED GROUNDWORK

Being thin and flexible, veneer can be laid successfully on curved surfaces. Shaped groundwork may be formed using the methods given below. Alternatively, as described in the chapter on bending wood, you can laminate thick constructional veneers or bend steamed wood.

Shaping solid wood

Wood can be cut on a band saw to make small-scale curved groundwork. Use a compass plane and spokeshaves to smooth the curved surfaces, then key and size them before applying veneer.

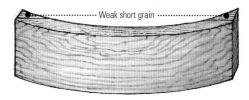

Weak short grain

Brick construction

As size increases, cutting groundwork from single pieces of solid wood becomes too wasteful. Also, wood with weak short grain at the extremities does not make good groundwork. Consequently, brick construction is the recommended method for making serpentine drawer fronts and similar curved components.

The groundwork is made up from short 'bricks' cut from solid wood, which are glued together end to end in a staggered pattern, much like a brick wall. The potentially weak end joints are reinforced by the bricks in adjacent courses. Once the glue sets, the ground can be smoothed.

Thick lipping

Brick course

Coopered construction

Curved groundwork for larger pieces, such as bowed doors, can be constructed by gluing bevelled strips of wood edge to edge. The edges of each strip are planed to the required angle, and then glued and clamped together in a specially made jig with shaped saddles that hold the curve (**1**).

Bevelled strips

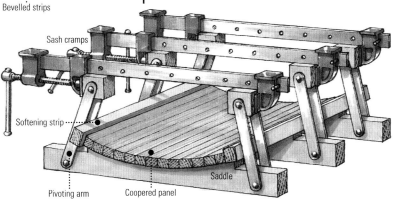

1

Sash cramps

Softening strip

Pivoting arm

Saddle

Coopered panel

The bevelled strips for smaller, lighter coopered curves can be clamped together using bands of adhesive tape (**2**).

2

PREPARING VENEER

Veneer gives the woodworker the chance to concentrate on the decorative qualities of wood, as the groundwork provides all the necessary strength and structure of the workpiece.

Storing and handling veneer

Because veneer is such a fragile material, it must always be handled with care. This involves storing veneers flat and keeping them in the order in which they were supplied, so they can be matched easily. Never pull veneers from the middle or bottom of a stack.

Flattening veneer

Most veneer has to be flattened before it can be worked. If distortion is slight, moisten the veneer by passing it through steam from a kettle. Alternatively, dip it in water or wipe it with a damp sponge (**1**). Press the damp veneer between sheets of chipboard until it is dry, using cramps or heavy weights to apply pressure (**2**).

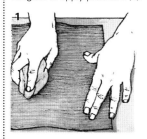

1

2

Flattening buckled veneer

In order to flatten buckled veneer, wet it first with an adhesive. Lightly brush wallpaper paste or a weak solution of hot animal glue onto the veneer, and then press it for at least 24 hours between boards lined with thin polyethylene sheet.

Cutting and joining veneer

The meeting edges of veneer must be cut and planed straight. When two veneers are to be matched, lay them together and pin them temporarily to the cutting board. Hold down both veneers with a straightedge – placed just inside the edge to be cut – and, using a knife or veneer saw, cut through both veneers at once (**1**).

To check the fit, hold the cut edges together, preferably against the light. Eliminate any gaps by 'shooting' the edges – running a finely set bench plane along them, with the veneers clamped between two straight battens.

Place the two edges together and stick short strips of veneer tape across the joint at 150mm (6in) intervals. Apply another strip of tape along the entire length of the join (**2**). As veneer tape shrinks, it pulls the join together.

1

2

VENEER MATCHING

Veneer that is narrower than the groundwork must be joined. The various processes of joining or matching veneer provide an opportunity to orientate the wood's figure and colour to create decorative effects.

Slip matching

The simplest form of matching involves slipping consecutive veneers sideways and joining them together without altering their grain direction.

Slip matching is best used for striped veneers, where the join will not be obvious. Poorly matched joins, with stripes that do not run parallel to the joining edges, must be trimmed to true up the figure.

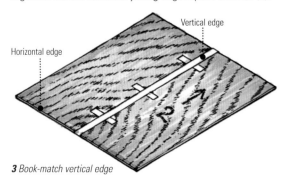

Book matching

When the figure of two consecutive sheets of decorative veneer is biased to one side of the leaf, the veneer is usually book-matched.

The top leaf is turned according to the position of the dominant figure. If the figure is on the left, turn the leaf to the left as if your were opening a book (**1**); if it is on the right-hand side, turn the leaf to the right (**2**). Align the figure carefully to avoid an unattractive match.

1 Turn the top veneer to the left *2 Turn the top veneer to the right*

Four-piece matching

This extension of the book-matching method uses four consecutive veneers with the focal point of the figure at the bottom.

Book-match the first pair of leaves and tape them together. Cut the horizontal joining edge square and true (**3**).

Horizontal edge ..... Vertical edge

3 Book-match vertical edge

Book-match the second pair of leaves, then turn them over so the leaves are face down (**4**) and tape the leaves together.

Match and cut the horizontal edges of both pairs. Then tape them together ready for laying.

Horizontal edge .....

Horizontal edge reversed .....

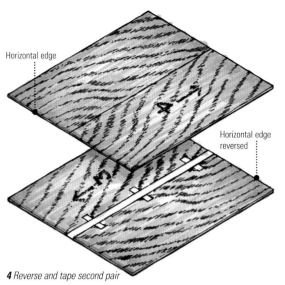

4 Reverse and tape second pair

Diamond matching

For diamond matching, use striped veneers. Lay four consecutive veneers together and true up the two long edges. Cut both ends to 45 degrees, making the cuts parallel to each other (**5**). Open the top two veneers book-match fashion but turn them along the top diagonal edge to form an inverted 'V', then tape the joint (**6**). Next, make a straight horizontal cut from corner to corner (**7**). Fit the triangular piece into the 'V' at the bottom to form a rectangle (**8**).

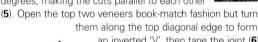

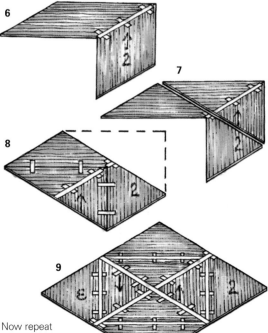

Now repeat the process with the second pair of veneers – but first reverse them so they are face down, as for four-piece matching. Finally, join the two rectangles along the centre (**9**).

Tonal variation

Veneer may appear lighter or darker depending on the direction from which it is viewed. The difference in tone is apparent when consecutive veneers are laid in opposite directions.

Numbers and arrows chalked on the top face of the veneers as they are taken from the bundle will help you to identify the grain direction and also to distinguish the finer 'closed' face from the slightly coarser 'open' face. Although it's not always possible, ideally, the veneer's open face should be laid on the groundwork.

HAND VENEERING

Many woodworkers still prefer traditional hot animal glue as an adhesive for laying veneers by hand. Modern glues may be simpler to use and less messy, but hot animal glue can be softened with heat – even after many years – making it a relatively simple task to correct errors or repair damaged or blistered veneer.

The techniques shown here are for laying veneer that covers the groundwork in one piece. Matched and delicate veneers are best pressed between cauls.

HAMMER VENEERING

Successful hammer veneering depends to a large extent on keeping the heated glue at a working temperature. Consequently, it pays to keep your workshop warm and dust-free.

Preparing glue

Heat pearl or liquid animal glue in a double or jacketed glue pot to about 49°C (120°F). Stir the glue to a smooth lump-free consistency that runs from the brush without separating into droplets. The glue must not be heated to boiling point – and don't allow the heated water in the outer pot or jacket to run dry.

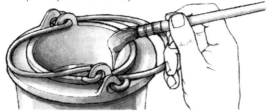

Applying the glue

Brush a thin even coat of glue onto both the groundwork and the veneer, then put them aside until the glue is almost dry but still tacky. Lay the veneer on the groundwork, overlapping it all round, then press it down with the palm of your hand.

CHECKING FOR BLISTERS

When the glue has set, tap the veneer with a fingernail to detect blisters or air bubbles trapped beneath the surface.

Any areas that sound hollow can be treated by pressing the veneer with a heated iron and veneer hammer once again.

Alternatively, allow trapped air to escape by making a small slit along the grain with a knife. Then press the blistered area.

Laying the veneer

The next stage is to close the pores of the veneer by dampening the surface with a sponge dipped in hot water and squeezed almost dry. Run a heated iron over the damp surface to remelt the glue and draw it up into the veneer (**1**).

Without delay, take a veneer hammer and press the veneer onto the groundwork with a zigzag action, starting near the centre of the panel and working towards the edges (**2**). Turn the panel around and repeat the process.

As air and melted glue are forced out from beneath the veneer, increase pressure on the hammer by using both hands (**3**) – but take care not to stretch the veneer by pressing too hard across the grain.

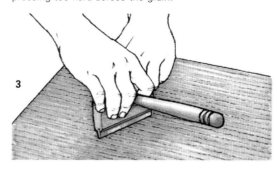

If the glue cools during pressing, dampen the surface of the veneer again and apply the heated iron once more.

Clean any melted glue off the surface with a damp cloth before it sets.

USING GLUE FILM

The modern equivalent of hot animal glue is a paper-backed film of glue. It is supplied ready for use and, like hot animal glue, can be reworked with a further application of heat. Glue film generally takes less skill to apply than animal glue – but burrs and curls can pose problems, so are probably best laid by pressing between cauls.

Applying the film
Using scissors, cut the glue film slightly larger than the groundwork. Place the film face-down on the groundwork, and lightly smooth it flat with a domestic iron heated to a medium setting. When the glue has cooled, peel off the backing sheet.

Laying the veneer
Lay the veneer on the glued groundwork and place the paper backing on top to protect the veneer. Press with the heated iron, working slowly across the surface from the centre outwards. Follow behind with a veneer hammer or a block of wood, to keep the veneer pressed flat as the glue cools.

USING CONTACT GLUE

Specially developed contact adhesives enable you to veneer flat or curved surfaces without using heat or a press. And you don't need special tools.

A solid lipping applied after veneering (or some other form of edge protection) is recommended, as veneer is more vulnerable to chipping when applied with this type of adhesive. Don't use a contact glue to lay curls or burr veneers.

Applying the glue
Using a stiff brush or a scrap of thick veneer or plastic, spread a thin even coat of glue onto the veneer. Work diagonally from corner to corner, first in one direction then in the other, making sure you cover the surface thoroughly right up to the edges.

Apply adhesive to the groundwork in a similar way, then put both parts aside while the glue sets.

Laying veneer onto contact glue
Lay a sheet of newspaper or brown paper over the glued groundwork, leaving a 50mm (2in) strip of contact adhesive exposed along one edge (**1**). Lay the veneer on top; and when it is aligned with the groundwork, press the veneer against the exposed glue. Gradually slide the paper out from between the veneer and groundwork, pressing the two glued surfaces together with a block of wood (**2**). Finally, flatten the veneer by rubbing over the surface with the block and then trim off the surplus veneer.

1

2

Dealing with blisters
Tap across the surface to locate any air pockets under the veneer. Slit the veneer where it sounds hollow and work some fresh contact glue under the blister; roll it down with a wallpaper seam roller. Wipe glue from the surface of the veneer before it sets.

REMOVING A FOREIGN BODY

If a speck of grit or coarse sawdust gets trapped beneath the veneer, no amount of pressure will remove it.

Make a V-shaped incision where the foreign body is and peel back the flap of veneer so you can remove the speck with the point of a knife.

If you are using animal glue or glue film, press the flap down with a warm iron and a veneer hammer; with contact adhesive, apply a little fresh glue to the flap and groundwork.

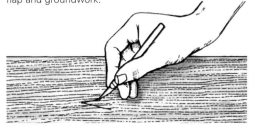

Trimming surplus veneer
When the glue has set, you can use a trimming tool to remove surplus veneer overhanging the edges of a panel.

Alternatively, turn the veneered panel face-down on a flat cutting board and use a sharp knife to trim the surplus veneer flush with the groundwork. Trim cross grain by cutting from the corners towards the centre – otherwise you may split the veneer.

CAUL VENEERING

Cauls are flat or curved boards between which the veneer and groundwork are pressed together by clamping. Caul veneering requires more preparatory work than hand veneering, and there's the additional cost of materials for the cauls and press. However, it is the best method for laying taped veneers and fragile burrs and curls, and you can apply veneer simultaneously to both sides of the groundwork. With caul veneering, large curved workpieces are relatively easy to handle, because the cold-setting glues used allow more time for 'laying up'.

MAKING CAUL ASSEMBLIES

Each type of caul assembly varies, according to the size and shape of the work. In all cases, the cauls must be larger than the groundwork.

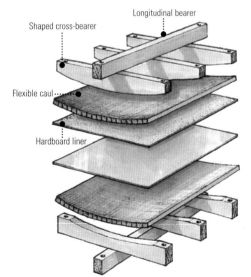

Using small cauls
The cauls used for pressing small or narrow flat work are usually made from short lengths of thick wood. Pressure is applied by cramps placed along the centre line of the cauls.

Large flat cauls
For veneering wide panels, make a simple press with cauls cut from man-made board. Opposing pairs of stiff softwood cross-bearers, each with its inner edge slightly curved, put pressure on the centre of the cauls, forcing out surplus air and glue. You can apply the pressure with cramps or bolt the cross-bearers together, using threaded rods and nuts, plus washers. Always clamp up the middle pair of bearers first, followed by intermediate and outer pairs.

Threaded bolt · · · · · · · · · · · · · · · · · Cross-bearer

Wide cauls

Curved cauls
Curved panels can be caul-veneered using two-part male and female formers, as for bending laminated wood. Alternatively, the work can be glued in a press similar to those used for flat panels, but with cauls made from strips of wood fixed to shaped cross-bearers.

Make an accurate measured drawing to determine the shape of the curves to be cut in the cross-bearers. You need to allow for the thickness of the caul material and the groundwork, and work out how many bearers will be needed in order to place one pair every 150mm (6in) across the workpiece.

Make flexible cauls from narrow strips of wood glued to canvas sheets. Lay them between the cross-bearers, with the canvas side uppermost, and line the cauls with sheets of aluminium or hardboard.

Add a stiff bearer across the top and bottom of the assembly, to apply pressure in the middle of each cross-bearer.

Clamp and tighten the assembly the same way as for flat cauls, starting with the middle pair of cross-bearers.

Shaped cross-bearer · · · · · · ·
Longitudinal bearer · · · · · · ·
Flexible caul · · · · ·
Hardboard liner · · · · ·

LAYING THE VENEER

Have everything you need ready and close at hand. If the veneer is to be laid one side at a time, the backing veneer should be pressed on first. The sequence shown here is for veneering both sides of a flat board simultaneously.

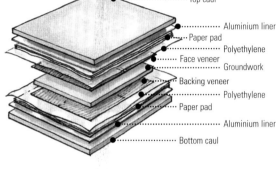

· · · · · · · Top caul
· · · · · · · Aluminium liner
· · · · · · · Paper pad
· · · · · · · Polyethylene
· · · · · · · Face veneer
· · · · · · · Groundwork
· · · · · · · Backing veneer
· · · · · · · Polyethylene
· · · · · · · Paper pad
· · · · · · · Aluminium liner
· · · · · · · Bottom caul

Using a brush, evenly apply a cold-setting adhesive, such as PVA or urea-formaldehyde glue, to the groundwork only and let it become tacky. There's no need to apply glue to the veneer.

Lay a sheet of aluminium on the bottom caul, then a pad of newspaper and a sheet of polyethylene. Next lay down the backing veneer, followed by the glued groundwork. Build the upper layers of the stack in the reverse order.

Pressing the workpiece
With the top and bottom cauls in place, position the stack on the bottom cross-bearers. Lower the top cross-bearers into place and apply pressure evenly, tightening the cramps or threaded bolts in sequence (**1**). Leave the glue to set.

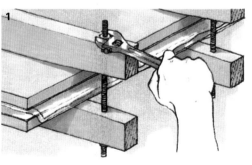

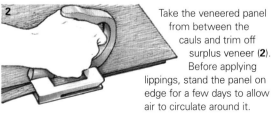

Take the veneered panel from between the cauls and trim off surplus veneer (**2**). Before applying lippings, stand the panel on edge for a few days to allow air to circulate around it.

BANDINGS AND INLAY MOTIFS

Bandings and inlays can transform a plain panel into an attractive piece of decorative woodwork.

Bandings are plain or patterned strips of veneer used to create decorative borders. You can make your own, but commercially produced bandings offer a wide choice and come ready to use.

Inlays are marquetry motifs used as ornamental features, usually in the centre of a plain or banded panel. Commercially made inlays are relatively simple to apply to either veneered or solid-wood surfaces. As well as traditional geometric patterns, you can buy a wide range of pictorial motifs. Woodworkers often hand-lay individual motifs, but it is best to use cauls when laying veneer assemblies.

STRINGING LINES AND BANDINGS

Stringing lines and bandings are made from selected woods and are usually sold in 1m (3ft 3in) lengths. Because the colour of the wood and the sizes of stringings and bandings can vary between batches, it is always worth buying more than the minimum required for any project.

Stringing lines
The fine strips of wood used to divide areas of veneer are called stringing lines, or stringings. Made in flat or square sections (the latter being used for inlaying edges), they are inserted to provide a light or dark boundary between different kinds of veneer or where the grain direction changes. Although traditionally stringings were made from boxwood or ebony, black-dyed wood is now more common.

Bandings
Banding strips are available in various widths, edged with black or boxwood stringings. Made from side-grain sections of coloured woods, glued together and sliced, they are about 1mm (1/32 in) thick.

Cross-bandings are strips of veneer cut across the grain to provide decorative borders for panels. They can be cut either from the veneer that is used to cover the panel or from another suitable straight-grain veneer.

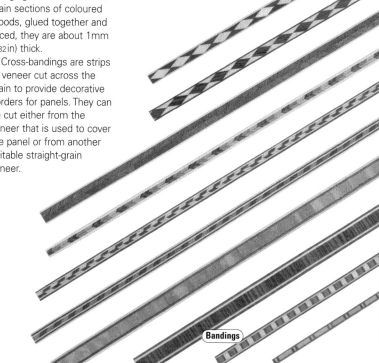

Stringing lines

Bandings

VENEERING A BORDERED PANEL

One way to make a veneered panel with a relatively wide cross-banded border is to hand-lay each piece of veneer separately.

Laying the central panel
Cut and lay a sheet of veneer in the centre of the panel, leaving a strip of groundwork exposed around the edges. When the glue has set, adjust a cutting gauge to the width of the banding and trim the laid veneer parallel with the edges of the panel (**1**).

If necessary, soften the glue with a warm iron and then peel off the waste strips (**2**). Using a sharp chisel, scrape glue off the exposed groundwork and wipe it clean with a warm damp cloth.

Cutting the bandings
Reset the cutting gauge to slice cross-bandings from the ends of consecutive veneers, making the bandings slightly longer and wider than the strips of exposed groundwork.

Using a finely set bench plane, trim the end grain of each piece of veneer on a shooting board. Then lay the veneer on a straight-edged board and, having aligned the planed end grain with the edge of the board, use the cutting gauge to slice off the banding (**3**).

Laying the bandings
Apply animal glue to the groundwork and bandings. Using a veneer hammer, lay the bandings on the groundwork, allowing the ends of the strips to overlap. Mitre the corners by cutting diagonally through both layers of veneer with a sharp knife (**4**). Remove the waste and press down the mitred ends with the hammer. Wipe away surplus glue and apply gummed tape over the joins to prevent gaps opening up as the glue dries. After it has set, trim the overhanging bandings flush with the edges of the panel.

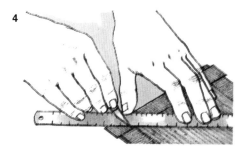

Surface laying
If you don't want to inlay a motif into a solid-wood panel, you can lay it on the surface. To disguise the join, rout a shallow groove around the edge of the motif.

Caul-laying bandings

Even when caul-laying a bordered panel, some woodworkers like to lay the central sheet of veneer and bandings separately. This guarantees that the design is symmetrical, with all four borders the same width.

However, cutting and taping the veneers together before pressing them saves time in the long run.

Cut the central sheet straight and square all round, then cut the bandings slightly wider than the width of the proposed border. Mitre the bandings at the corners and tape all the veneers together (**1**).

Draw pencil guide lines on the edges of the groundwork and on the veneers themselves to help you align them accurately, then apply glue to the groundwork. Carefully lay the veneers in place and press them down by hand or with a seam roller before putting the assembly into the press.

1

Inlaid bandings

Instead of joining veneers to create a banded panel, you can inlay bandings into the surface of a solid-wood panel.

First, using a power router, cut grooves parallel with the four edges of the prepared panel, making the depth of the grooves slightly less than the thickness of the banding. Use a chisel to trim the ends of the grooves perfectly square.

Glue the mitred strips of banding into the grooves and press them down with a cross-peen hammer (**2**). Once the glue has set, carefully scrape and sand the bandings flush with the surrounding wood.

2

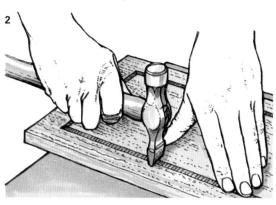

INLAY MOTIFS

Some motifs are made to a finished size and shape, ready for inlaying into a veneered surface. Others are supplied in the centre of a larger piece of veneer, so you can either cut it to size or lay the whole assembly on the groundwork. Most inlay motifs come with a protective paper overlay, which is cleaned off after the motif has been laid.

Insetting a motif

You can incorporate an inlay motif into an assembly of veneers before you place the assembly between cauls and put it into the press. Ideally, the inlay and other veneers should be the same thickness.

To position the motif, draw pencil lines that cross in the centre of the motif and draw similar guide lines on the background. Use a patch of double-sided adhesive tape to temporarily position the motif in the centre of the veneer. Check that your guide lines align perfectly, then carefully trace round the motif with a knife, cutting into the background veneer. Remove the waste and tape the motif into the hole in the veneer. Glue the completed assembly onto the groundwork. When the glue has set, dampen the paper overlay and scrape it off the inlay before lightly sanding the veneers flush.

Cut around an inset motif

Inlaying into solid wood

Position the inlay motif on the surface of the panel and carefully mark round the motif with a knife. Remove the waste with a power router, making the depth of the recess slightly less than the thickness of the motif.

Glue the inlay in place and cover it with a piece of polyethylene. Lay a block of wood on top and clamp it down until the glue sets, then scrape and sand flush.

MARQUETRY

Wood veneer has long been used as a decorative medium, and the diversity of natural figure and colour has provided craftsmen with a rich 'palette' from which to cut and assemble the decorative patterns and pictures known as marquetry. Requiring skilful handiwork, marquetry is often employed by woodworkers to embellish door panels and table tops. There are also legions of marquetarians who specialize in producing highly complex works of art from veneer.

Marquetry veneers are cut with a knife or fret saw. Sawing is generally used for cutting intricate shapes in multiple layers of veneer. The knife method is more convenient for insetting single pieces of veneer – when making marquetry pictures, for example.

Whichever method you adopt, it takes skill to cut the parts accurately and it is often necessary to practise with pieces of scrap or cheap veneer before tackling an advanced project. You can design your own motifs or, to begin with, buy a kit containing a printed pattern together with all the material you need.

The success of the work lies not just in the skill of cutting and joining the pieces of veneer but also in artistic interpretation – especially since it's often difficult to judge the effect of a particular veneer until it is seen in context with others.

Transposing a design

Any two-dimensional representation will serve as the basis for a marquetry motif. You can trace off the essential elements, then simplify the design until it is suitable for cutting from veneer.

If you need to change the scale of your drawing, either enlarge it using a scaled grid or use a computer or photocopier to reduce or enlarge the image. Photocopying can be particularly handy: to produce a mirror image of the design, lay a photocopy face-down on a sheet of paper or card and apply a hot iron to the back of the photocopy.

SAWING VENEERS

Commercially produced motifs are cut from packs of veneers on a 'marquetry donkey' – a specialist tool on which the operator sits and works a reciprocating fret saw, while holding the veneer in a foot-operated clamp. The operator manipulates each pack in the jaws of the clamp with one hand, while working the saw horizontally with the other. The shaped parts are then assembled on a flat table, and a layer of gummed paper is applied to hold them together.

In the home workshop, a small powered fret saw makes light work of cutting stacks of veneer. With a hand-held fret saw, you can saw through a pair of veneers relatively easily – but cutting multiple layers of veneers can be difficult.

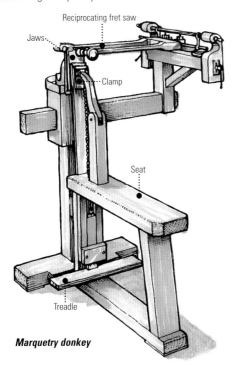

Marquetry donkey

Sawing a pair of veneers by hand

Select one veneer for the background and one for the inlay. With this method you produce two identical motifs, but in one of them the background colour is reversed when the veneers are assembled.

Cut the pieces of veneer about 12mm (1/2 in) larger all round than the proposed design. Tape them together between waste backing veneers – the grain of the backing veneers should run at right angles to the grain of the marquetry veneers (**1**). Tape your drawn design on top.

Insert the saw blade through a small starter hole drilled, through the stack, close to a line near the centre of the design. Then, holding the work firmly on the saw table, follow the line accurately with the blade (**2**). Turn the work as required to present the line at a convenient angle for sawing.

Separate the cut pieces and reassemble them to make motifs with contrasting colours. Tape them together with a sheet of gummed paper. Fill the sawcut with coloured stopper, rubbing it in from the back face. Wipe the surface clean.

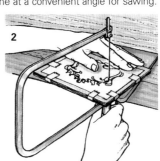

MAKING A PICTURE FROM VENEERS

The art of making marquetry pictures is in using the natural features of the veneer to interpret the colour, texture and tone of the original reference.

Choosing a subject

Photographs make a good source of reference from which to trace a design – but choose one with areas of bold tone and colour rather than one with lots of fine detail.

Photographs present form in all its subtlety, so the shapes usually have to be simplified for a marquetry design. Although the outlines of the main features are easily rendered in line, the shading that gives them form has to be interpreted with artistic skill. With careful selection of grain pattern and the use of shading techniques, graduated tones can be recreated to imply three dimensions.

The window method

Using the 'window method' of marquetry, you can create the picture gradually, trying out the aesthetic relationship between one piece of veneer and another before you cut them. First, you transfer the design to a 'waster', made from card or from background veneer. Next, you cut each shape in the waster and place the selected veneer beneath it, so you can see the veneer through the aperture and evaluate its colour, tone and orientation. Then you cut the veneer precisely to fit, using the aperture in the waster as a template. Successive apertures or 'windows' are cut and veneers fitted, until the design is completed as an assembled sheet for caul-veneering to the groundwork.

Creating the picture

Using self-adhesive tape, hinge your printed or drawn design along the top edge of the waster. Place a sheet of carbon paper between the two and trace over your design to transfer the border of the picture onto the waster. Then trace registration marks, in the form of crosses, below and at both sides of the picture (**1**).

1

Next, transfer the outlines of the picture's background colours onto the waster. Cut your first aperture in the waster, following the lines within the picture precisely, but cutting just outside the marked border (**2**).

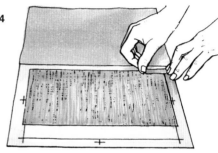

2

Place the selected veneer beneath the waster and position it to give the best grain effect. Lightly tape it in position, then carefully score the veneer with a knife, using the aperture as a template (**3**). Remove the veneer and cut it to shape on a cutting mat, then retape it into the aperture (**4**).

Transfer the shape of other main elements of background colour onto the waster and cut the apertures as before. Cut and insert the pieces of veneer, but this time apply a film of PVA glue to the edges where they meet. Repeat this process until the background of the picture is complete, then press the veneers flat under a weighted board.

3

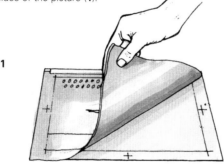

4

When the glue has set, turn the hinged design sheet back over the picture. Redraw the border lines and begin to trace the larger elements of the picture onto the background veneers. Cut apertures for these elements, this time through the background veneers. Slide the selected veneers beneath the background and score them as before (**5**). Continue to trace, cut and insert progressively smaller elements of the picture until it is complete.

Cut along the border lines to remove the finished picture. To make a decorative frame, cut and tape strips of veneer around the perimeter of the picture, allowing the ends of the strips to overlap. Mitre the overlapping ends at the corners (**6**), then tape the mitres to complete the assembly ready for laying on the groundwork between cauls.

5

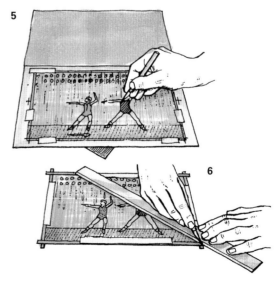

6

CLEANING UP MARQUETRY

Like any piece of woodwork, the surface of marquetry veneers must be prepared before a clear finish can be applied – but extra care is needed to avoid damaging the thin veneers.

First, gummed tape or paper overlays must be removed. Moisten the surface with a damp sponge (don't soak the veneer) and use a cabinet scraper or wide chisel to scrape off the tape or paper, then let the surface dry.

Next, gently scrape the surface of the veneer to eradicate raised grain. In general, scrape in the direction of the grain; but scrape diagonally across the joints of assembled veneers, to avoid chipping slightly raised edges.

Finally, sand the surface lightly with progressively finer abrasive papers – wrap the paper round a cork block, and sand with the grain as far as possible. Brush away all traces of dust, then wipe the surface clean.

SHADING VENEER

The traditional way of producing shaded three-dimensional effects for shell and fan motifs is to scorch part of the veneer lightly by inserting it in hot sand. You can use the same technique to enhance marquetry pictures. Practise shading on waste veneer until you can produce subtle gradations of tone.

Heat a bed of fine silver sand in a baking tray to a temperature that will produce the required range of tones within 10 to 12 seconds – the veneer will shrink if it is immersed in hot sand for longer. In case the veneer shrinks, you may prefer to shade oversize pieces of veneer and then cut them to fit, using the window method described opposite.

When dipping a piece in the sand, hold the veneer with tweezers (**1**) and remove it after counting the number of seconds determined by your experiments. To create shading in the centre of a piece of veneer, pour the hot sand onto the surface with a spoon (**2**). To produce hard-edge shading, mask the veneer with gummed paper tape.

If need be, after shading the veneer, dampen it and then press it under a flat board.

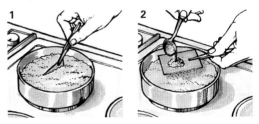

PARQUETRY

Parquetry is similar to marquetry in every way but consists of pieces of veneer arranged in geometric patterns or motifs. Despite its apparent simplicity, it is possible to create many variations on a basic design, using veneers of different species, colour and tone cut into square, rectangular, triangular, diamond or polygonal shapes.

Working out a design

The permutations of simple geometric shapes offer a seemingly endless variety of pattern. You can experiment with pattern-making on gridded graph paper, using coloured pens or pencils to fill in the shapes.

Designs composed of a number of identical shapes arranged in strips are easier to cut and assemble accurately. Motifs that have interlocking shapes, such as cubes or stars, have to be assembled from individually cut pieces of veneer.

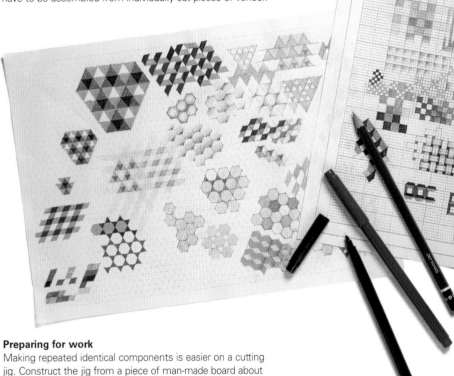

Preparing for work

Making repeated identical components is easier on a cutting jig. Construct the jig from a piece of man-made board about 600mm (2ft) square. Screw a hardwood fence about 6mm (1/4in) thick to the surface of the board, flush with one edge. Mark two setting-out lines at 90 degrees to the fence. If the motifs aren't square or rectangular, draw the setting-out lines at the appropriate angles

You need a sharp knife and a metal straightedge for cutting the veneers. To align the straightedge parallel to the fence, cut pairs of spacer blocks from thin plywood or MDF. You will also need gummed tape to hold the veneers together.

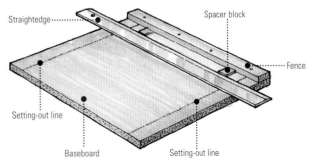

Straightedge · · · · · · · · · · · · · · · · · · Spacer block
· Fence
Setting-out line
Baseboard   Setting-out line

MAKING A CHEQUERBOARD PATTERN

Perhaps the simplest and best-known example of parquetry is the chequerboard pattern made from alternating squares of different colour. Selecting two different species of wood is the obvious way to create visual contrast. For a more subtle effect, try using the same wood throughout but orientate the grain in a different direction for alternate squares. Generally, straight-grained or plain veneers work best.

Cut strips of veneer slightly longer than the baseboard. To do this accurately, cut a straight edge on a sheet of veneer, place this edge against the fence of your cutting jig and cut a strip to the required width, using spacer blocks to position the straightedge (**1**). Then slide the next cut edge up to the fence and cut an identical strip. Cut four strips of one colour and five of the other, and number them to keep them in order.

Alternate the coloured strips and carefully butt and tape them together. Place the assembled veneers on the baseboard of the jig, aligning one of the assembly's straight edges with the right-angle setting-out line. Use the spacer blocks to position your metal rule parallel to the fence, then trim the ends square (**2**).

Remove the waste and push the newly cut edge against the fence. Cut the assembled veneer, as before, to produce strips of alternating coloured squares.

Rearrange the strips so that the coloured squares are staggered (**3**), and then tape the cut edges together. Trim off the staggered edges to create a square chequerboard.

Cut and tape a cross-banded veneer border all round the chequerboard before gluing the assembly to the groundwork between cauls.

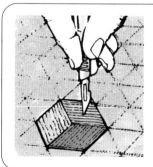

Making a cube pattern
Gluing three 60-degree diamonds together produces a hexagon that resembles a cube. Assemble a field of these hexagons on a sheet of clear self-adhesive film laid sticky-side up over an isometric grid.

Cover the assembly with gummed paper and press it between flat boards. Once the gummed paper has dried out, turn the assembly over and carefully peel off the self-adhesive film before gluing the veneers to the groundwork.

STRIP VARIATIONS

You can create a variety of patterns simply by adapting the method used for making a chequerboard.

Squares and rectangles
Tape identical strips together as described left, then cut the sheet at right angles into strips of different width. Stagger and rearrange these strips to create variations on the chequerboard pattern.

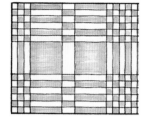

Triangles and zigzag patterns
Slice through the chequerboard squares from corner to corner to make narrow strips. Stagger these strips to produce a zigzag pattern; or reverse alternate strips to create rows of triangles.

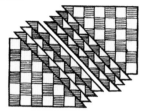

Diamond patterns
Cut straight strips of veneer and tape them together. Pin one strip of veneer to the baseboard of the cutting jig, with one edge aligned with a setting-out line marked on the board at 60 degrees to the fence. Then tape the strips together, with their end corners butted against the fence. Holding your straightedge against spacer blocks, trim off the 'toothed' ends (**1**). Remove the pins and push the newly cut edge against the fence.

Now cut the assembly into equal strips parallel with the fence, creating rows of diamond-shape pieces of veneer (**2**).

Cutting across the diamonds, corner to corner, produces strips of equilateral triangles (**3**).

Reversing and staggering the strips of triangles creates a zigzag pattern (**4**).

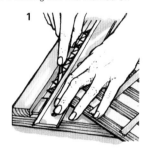

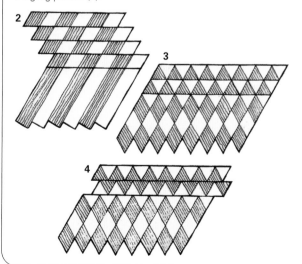

CHAPTER TEN

WOODCARVING

Ever since early man discovered that a sharp instrument could be used to shape a piece of wood, carving has been employed to produce all manner of functional and decorative artefacts, ranging from basic utensils to sacred icons. Today, with the development of woodworking machinery and man-made materials, carving has become largely a leisure activity. However, age-old techniques are still used commercially by practising carvers, both in restoring buildings and furniture and for creating new pieces. Woodcarving goes beyond the utilitarian and offers the carver a means of self-expression that raises it to the level of art. In carving, perhaps more than in any other kind of woodwork, the ability to execute a fine piece of work only comes with practice – though a natural eye for form is an undoubted advantage. Because the shape and complexity of the work has no limitation other than the imagination of the carver, specialized chisels, gouges and other handtools are made to cope with the immense diversity of form.

CARVING CHISELS AND GOUGES

It might seem unnecessary to acquire a whole new set of woodcarving tools when you could use your standard firmer chisels and gouges, but specialized carving tools are generally bevelled on both sides of the blade to facilitate cutting the wood at a variety of angles. The chisels have equal bevels ground on each side of the cutting edge, whereas the gouges and parting tools have a larger bevel on the outside of the blade. Like other woodworking tools, carving chisels and gouges are sold with cutting edges ground but not sharpened. A standard range of chisels and gouges can include ten different cutting-edge profiles, with a choice of five shapes of blade and a wide range of sizes. However, a few basic tools are sufficient as a starter kit.

Fitting a handle
Many carving tools are supplied without handles, so you can fit a manufactured handle or one of your own. Drill a fine pilot hole down the centre of the handle. Set the blade in an engineer's vice fitted with soft jaws. Tap the handle partway onto the tang, then twist it free. Repeat the process until the handle is about 6mm (1/4in) from the shoulder of the blade. Check the alignment, then tap the handle home.

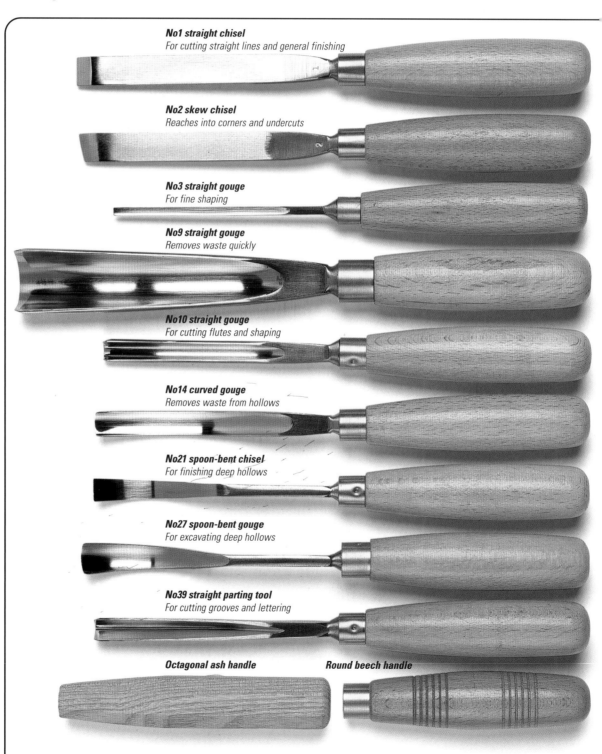

No1 straight chisel
For cutting straight lines and general finishing

No2 skew chisel
Reaches into corners and undercuts

No3 straight gouge
For fine shaping

No9 straight gouge
Removes waste quickly

No10 straight gouge
For cutting flutes and shaping

No14 curved gouge
Removes waste from hollows

No21 spoon-bent chisel
For finishing deep hollows

No27 spoon-bent gouge
For excavating deep hollows

No39 straight parting tool
For cutting grooves and lettering

Octagonal ash handle   **Round beech handle**

Cutting profiles

Carving tools are made with a variety of cutting-edge profiles, each designed for a different purpose. The majority are chisels or gouges used for waste removal and general shaping. Some chisels are skewed for cutting into acute corners. Veiners and veining tools are deep-sided gouges.

V-shape parting tools are used for cutting grooves and for outlining lettering. You can buy parting tools with the cutting edges set at 90, 60 or 45 degrees. There is also a wing parting tool with shallow curved sides.

The macaroni and fluteroni are rectangular-section gouges for cutting flat-bottomed hollows or recesses. A macaroni has sharp square corners. The corners of a fluteroni are rounded.

Blade shapes

Straight-bladed carving tools are available with shaped blades for carving hollows and undercuts. Spoon-bent and back-bent tools are deeply curved towards the tip of the blade. Dogleg tools have cranked blades; and fishtail tools have straight blades with splayed tips.

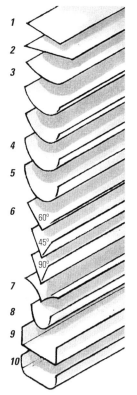

1 Chisel
2 Skew chisel
3 Gouges
4 Fluter
5 Veiner
6 Parting tools
7 Wing parting tool
8 Veining tool
9 Macaroni
10 Fluteroni

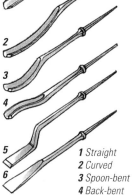

1 Straight
2 Curved
3 Spoon-bent
4 Back-bent
5 Dogleg
6 Fishtail

1 Right-handed spoon-bent skew chisel
2 Left-handed spoon-bent skew chisel
3 Back-bent gouge
4 Dogleg chisel
5 Fishtail gouge
6 Wing parting tool
7 Curved macaroni
8 Spoon-bent fluteroni

Numbering system

Most tool suppliers use the numbering system adopted in the nineteenth century which identifies a particular combination of cutting-edge profile and blade shape (see chart below). Numbers 3 to 10, for example, designate the group of straight gouges, with cutting edges that range from an almost flat profile to semi-circular. Gouges 12 to 19 feature exactly the same range of profiles but with curved blades. Chisels, and most gouges, range from 2 to 50mm ($\frac{1}{16}$in to 2in) in width. Some of the more specialized carving tools are available in fewer sizes.

BLADE SHAPES						BLADE SIZES AVAILABLE (INCHES ABOVE, MM BELOW)													
	Straight	Curved	Spoon-bent	Back-bent	Fishtail	$\frac{1}{16}$	$\frac{1}{8}$	$\frac{3}{16}$	$\frac{1}{4}$	$\frac{5}{16}$	$\frac{3}{8}$	$\frac{7}{16}$	$\frac{1}{2}$	$\frac{5}{8}$	$\frac{3}{4}$	$\frac{7}{8}$	1	$1\frac{1}{4}$	$1\frac{1}{2}$	2
						2	3	5	6	8	9	11	12	16	18	22	25	32	38	50
CHISEL	1		21		61	•	•	•	•	•	•	•	•	•	•	•	•	•	•	•
SKEW CHISEL	2		22–3		62	•	•	•	•	•	•	•	•	•	•	•	•	•	•	•
GOUGE	3	12	24	33	63	•	•	•	•	•	•	•	•	•	•	•	•	•	•	•
	4	13	25	34	64	•	•	•	•	•	•	•	•	•	•	•	•	•	•	•
	5	14	26	35	65	•	•	•	•	•	•	•	•	•	•	•	•	•	•	•
	6	15	27	36	66	•	•	•	•	•	•	•	•	•	•	•	•	•	•	•
	7	16	28	37	67	•	•	•	•	•	•	•	•	•	•	•	•	•	•	•
	8	17	29	38	68	•	•	•	•	•	•	•	•	•	•	•	•	•	•	•
	9	18	30		69	•	•	•	•	•	•	•	•	•	•	•	•	•	•	•
FLUTER	10	19	31		70	•	•	•	•	•	•	•	•	•	•	•	•	•		
VEINER	11	20	32		71	•	•	•	•	•	•	•	•	•	•	•	•	•		
PARTING TOOL	39	40	43				•	•	•	•	•	•	•	•	•	•	•		
	41	42	44				•	•	•	•	•	•	•	•	•	•			
	45	46					•	•	•	•	•	•	•						
WING PARTING TOOL	47							•	•	•	•	•	•	•	•				
VEINING TOOL	48						•	•	•	•									
MACARONI	49	50					•	•	•	•	•	•	•						
FLUTERONI	51		52			•	•	•	•	•	•	•	•	•					

Punches
Carver's punches make indentations in the work. They are used to produce crisp patterns and textures.

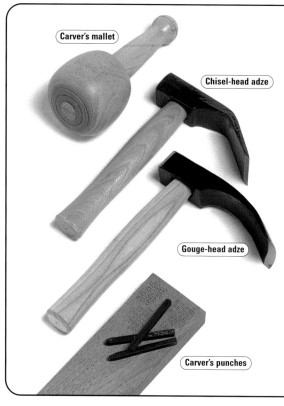

(Carver's mallet)

(Chisel-head adze)

(Gouge-head adze)

(Carver's punches)

CARVER'S MALLET AND ADZES

In addition to a range of specialized chisels and gouges, a woodcarver's kit may include the following tools.

Carver's mallet
A mallet is essential for driving chisels and gouges when cutting across the grain or when working dense woods.

The carver's mallet has a rounded cylindrical head, made from lignum vitae or beech, with a turned ash or beech handle. The rounded head allows the chisel to be struck from practically any angle.

Carver's mallets are made in a variety of diameters, from 75mm (3in) to 150mm (6in). These mallets are often specified by weight. A medium size/weight is adequate for most work. A large heavy mallet can be tiring to use for any length of time.

Adzes
Carver's or sculptor's adzes, which are short versions of the traditional carpenter's adzes, are wielded in one hand. Both chisel-head and gouge-head adzes are made. These tools are designed for the quick removal of waste when roughing out the work. The gouge type is particularly useful, not only for large-scale carving but also for hollowing out wood for bowls and for shaping the solid-wood seat boards of traditional stick chairs.

SHARPENING CARVING TOOLS

New carving tools are ground with bevelled cutting edges that require honing on a whetstone before they are ready for use. Honing a carving chisel or gouge not only produces a razor-sharp edge, it also rounds off the heel of each bevel so that the tool can cut into the wood from practically any angle. You need to resharpen carving tools at frequent intervals.

Sharpening a carving chisel
There is no secondary bevel honed on a carving chisel. Instead, there's a smooth transition between the cutting edge and the shaft of the blade. The point where the bevel meets the full thickness of the blade is known as the heel.

Hold the bevel flat on the stone. Draw the chisel backwards while lowering the handle, then push forward and raise the handle to rub the cutting edge along the stone. Repeat this action until you have honed a sharp edge. Polish with a strop.

Sharpening a parting tool
Hone the two sides of a V-shape parting tool on a whetstone, like a pair of chisels. Then carefully radius the point where they meet, using a slipstone. Work the inner bevel with a knife-edge slipstone. Strop both the inner and outer bevels to produce a razor-sharp edge.

Sharpening a gouge
Hold a gouge at right angles to the stone, with the ground bevel resting on the surface. Rub the tool back and forth along the stone, simultaneously rolling the blade from side to side. Introduce a rocking motion, by alternately raising and lowering the handle, to round over the bevel at the same time (**1**). Take care not to overrun the ends of the stone and damage the corners of the gouge.

1

Honing the convex edge of a gouge raises a burr on the inside, which must be removed using a slipstone (**2**). Work the stone back and forth with a rocking motion to shape a rounded shoulder behind the cutting edge.

Finish by stropping the cutting edge on a strip of leather. Strop the outer bevel with a rolling motion; pull the inner bevel along the folded edge of a leather strap. For wider gouges, fold the strap over a curved edge that approximates the shape of the gouge.

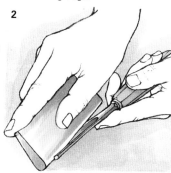

2

WOOD FOR CARVING

Virtually any species of wood can be used for carving – its suitability being largely determined by the size and type of the carving, as well as availability and ease of working.

Wood for carving does not have to be new or 'dressed' stock. Discarded furniture, old wood reclaimed from buildings and driftwood found on a beach are all suitable and may even suggest subjects for carving.

Woodcarvers, even more than other woodworkers, tend to hoard all manner of wood – in their mind's eye, every piece is a carving waiting to be revealed.

Workability

As a rule, fine-textured straight-grained woods such as lime and jelutong are easier to work than woods with coarse or interlocked grain. Generally, because of their close grain, hardwoods are preferable to softwoods. This makes them easier to work without splintering, both with and across the grain. Some softwoods – especially those that have a distinct difference in hardness between the earlywood and latewood – can be difficult to cut cleanly across the grain.

Colour and grain

Both the colour and the figure of the wood contribute to the quality of a carving. For example, it would make sense to select a light-coloured wood such as lime for carving a polar bear, whereas a dark wood such as teak might be more appropriate for a brown bear.

Grain pattern may be used to advantage – and also to disadvantage. Stripy woods with a pronounced figure can be effective for smooth forms where the lines will emphasize the contours. However, the bold linear pattern would be a distraction if a stripy wood was used for a portrait carving.

If you intend to paint a carving, you may decide to use a relatively cheap featureless wood that is easy to work – rather than a more attractive timber that would benefit from a clear finish.

Using dry or wet wood

Because it has a high moisture content, newly cut or 'green' wood shrinks as it dries. Logs or large sections of timber tend to shrink unevenly, making the wood split.

The only way to ensure that a carving will not split at some time in the future is to use well-seasoned wood. However, it is not always easy to find large sections of seasoned timber. If you have acquired logs from a recently felled tree, cutting them in half or into quarters will help the wood to season more evenly.

If you wish, you can use wood in its green state rather than wait years for it to season. You run the risk of the finished piece splitting as the wood dries out – but that can be aesthetically pleasing if it is anticipated and allowed for from the beginning.

Narrow symmetrical carvings are less likely to split. Consequently, if you hollow out thicker sections, leaving relatively thin walls, the wood will dry out more evenly.

To reduce splitting when carving wet wood, work quickly and keep the wood covered with a sealed plastic bag between sessions.

Treating with PEG

Treating green wood with PEG (polyethylene glycol), a stabilizing agent that penetrates the wood's structure, renders it 'fully-seasoned' in about 3 to 6 weeks. PEG 1000 is a water-soluble wax material, available from specialist wood suppliers.

Peregrine falcon
The bird's plumage is suggested by the stripy figure of the wood.

The fool
Lime is an excellent hardwood for rendering fine details with thin sections.

HOLDING THE WORK

Woodcarvers use extremely sharp tools – so, both for accuracy and for safety, it is vital that the workpiece is held securely. The method you adopt for holding the wood depends to a large extent on the size and shape of the workpiece. You can choose from a variety of factory-made vices and cramps or, in some cases, make your own.

The workbench

You can work on carvings on a traditional woodworking bench or on a special carver's stand. Whatever you use must provide a secure and solid surface at a comfortable working height.

For carving in the round, the base of the workpiece should be at or slightly below elbow level, so you can manipulate a mallet and chisel at a variety of angles. When working on a shallow workpiece, such as a mirror or picture frame, it's usually best to clamp it to a workbench – which provides a relatively wide flat surface that's strong enough for you to bear down on with carving chisels and gouges. For certain chip-carving techniques, however, the piece is best worked on your lap, your bare hands being the only 'clamping device' required. Ultimately, the best way to hold the work is the way that is safest and most convenient.

A standard woodworking bench vice is not really suitable for holding woodcarvings – but it can serve to hold a sash cramp, which in turn is used to hold a cabriole leg or similarly shaped workpiece.

Carver's vice

A special carver's vice (or 'chops') is similar in principle to an engineer's vice but is made of wood. Also, the jaws are deeper and are lined with cork or leather to protect the work. The vice is 225mm (9in) high – which brings the work up to a comfortable working height when the vice is fitted to a standard woodworking bench.

Pivoting clamp

When carving in the round, you need to be able to alter the angle of the work quickly and easily. A woodcarving clamp allows you to lock the workpiece securely in virtually any position. The pivoting clamp head can be fitted with different-sized faceplates, to suit the size of the work.

Bench stops

Convenient for holding long flat workpieces on a cabinet-maker's workbench, these metal stops are used in conjunction with an integral end vice, which provides the clamping force.

Engineer's vice

Pivoting clamp

Carver's

A traditional woodworking bench provides ideal support for flat workpieces

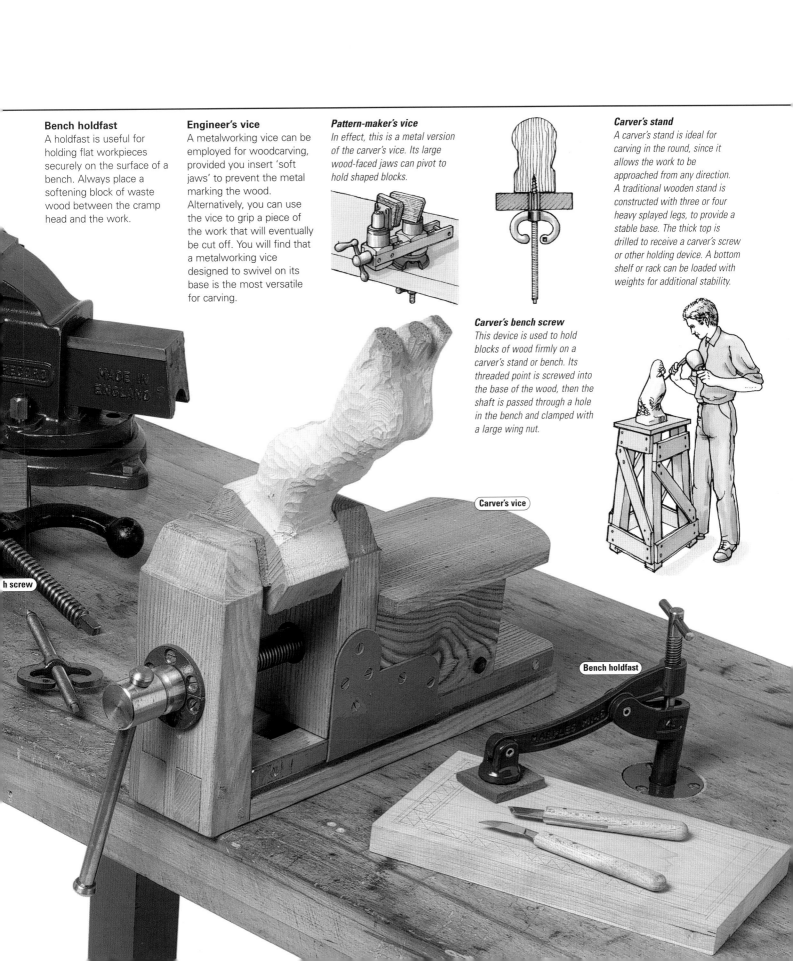

Bench holdfast

A holdfast is useful for holding flat workpieces securely on the surface of a bench. Always place a softening block of waste wood between the cramp head and the work.

Engineer's vice

A metalworking vice can be employed for woodcarving, provided you insert 'soft jaws' to prevent the metal marking the wood. Alternatively, you can use the vice to grip a piece of the work that will eventually be cut off. You will find that a metalworking vice designed to swivel on its base is the most versatile for carving.

Pattern-maker's vice

In effect, this is a metal version of the carver's vice. Its large wood-faced jaws can pivot to hold shaped blocks.

Carver's bench screw

This device is used to hold blocks of wood firmly on a carver's stand or bench. Its threaded point is screwed into the base of the wood, then the shaft is passed through a hole in the bench and clamped with a large wing nut.

Carver's stand

A carver's stand is ideal for carving in the round, since it allows the work to be approached from any direction. A traditional wooden stand is constructed with three or four heavy splayed legs, to provide a stable base. The thick top is drilled to receive a carver's screw or other holding device. A bottom shelf or rack can be loaded with weights for additional stability.

h screw

Carver's vice

Bench holdfast

CARVING TECHNIQUES

The principal forms of woodcarving are relief carving and carving in the round. A relief carving is intended to be viewed from one side only, and so is nearly always carved from a flat board or relatively thin stock. Whether a carving is classified as low-relief or high-relief depends on the thickness of the wood and the degree to which the background is cut away. The technique is used for embellishing furniture and wall panels, and also for creating works of art. A carving in the round, which is fully three-dimensional, is perhaps the most challenging form of carving since it requires a well-developed sense of form.

MANIPULATING THE TOOLS

The way you handle and manipulate the basic tools is very similar for both relief carving and carving in the round. Carving is a craft that draws upon natural skills. Coordination between hand and eye, a sense of proportion, the interpretation of materials and texture, and a feel for natural line all contribute to make a fine carving. Holding the tools properly is the first step. The way carving chisels and gouges are handled depends on the type and size of the project, the hardness of the wood, and the type of cut being made.

Paring cuts

Paring cuts are made with both hands on the tool. Generally, the handle is held in the hand used for writing. However, it is worth learning to work the tools with either hand, as it's often easier to change hands rather than turn the wood round.

Assuming you are right-handed, hold the handle in your right hand with your forefinger along or in line with the blade. The end of the handle will automatically fall on the centre of your palm, giving you good control over the tool. The left hand rests on the wood and is used to provide resistance to the thrust from the right hand. The left hand also helps guide the blade. The amount of resistance applied to the blade controls the speed of the cut.

For a heavy cut, place the forefinger of your right hand on top of the blade and grip the blade in the fist of your left hand (**1**). For lighter cuts, pinch the blade between your left forefinger and thumb (**2**).

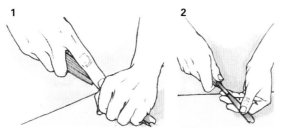

When making vertical cuts, grip the handle in your fist and place your thumb on the top end of the handle. Guide and control the blade with the thumb and forefinger of the left hand, the side of which is planted firmly on the surface of the work (**3**).

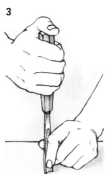

Using a mallet

When carving with a mallet, assuming you are right-handed, the chisel or gouge is held in the left hand and the right hand is used to drive the mallet. Grip the lower two-thirds of the chisel or gouge handle, with the top face of the blade in the same plane as the front of your folded hand (**4**). In this way you can change the angle of the cut by rotating your wrist, without changing your grip on the tool.

Use the mallet to apply short sharp blows to the tool. With practice you will sense the correct angle for the cutting edge and will be able to judge how much force is required.

Reading wood grain

Woodcarving differs from other methods of cutting wood in that the slicing cuts are generally made across the grain, especially when using gouges for roughing-out the shape. Provided the tool is razor-sharp, a controlled clean cut is possible and the relatively deep cut won't tear into the wood – which can easily happen when working with the grain.

Invariably, the wood is cut from all angles at some point in the work. Study the grain and make the cuts in the direction which is least likely to tear the fibres. The quality of the cut will be your best guide.

A cut gouged diagonally across the fibres produces a groove which is clean-cut on one side and a rougher cut on the other, where it runs against the grain (**5**). Similarly, when carving wild-grain timber, a smoother cut results when you drive the blade in the general direction of the grain. This may mean changing the direction of cut, according to the prevailing direction of the grain (**6**). Take shallow cuts, to minimize tearing.

MAKING DRAWINGS

To achieve an understanding of the way something looks in three-dimensions takes practice, and is best achieved by making drawings.

Even when drawings are not used as subjects in themselves, they can help you to see how surfaces, textures and forms relate. With this knowledge, you will find it easier to visualize how the shapes should look when you come to make a carving.

RELIEF CARVING

Relief carving exploits the play of light and shade to express form. The greater the degree of relief, the more contrasting and dramatic are the effects. Relief carving is a good introduction to woodcarving – you will learn how to use many of the basic carving tools, and a relief is easier to visualize than a fully three-dimensional carving. It also has the advantage of being economic in the use of material, and you can use a conventional bench without specialized holding equipment.

Setting out the design

The first step is to make an accurate full-size working drawing of your proposed carving. The example shown here is an ornamental letter that includes both geometric and naturalistic forms. If you are working from a reference that is not the actual size, either scale it up or down using the grid method (see below right) or use a photocopying machine or computer to enlarge or reduce the image. Tape the design to the wood and, using carbon paper, trace it onto the surface. Mark the ground line (the depth of the relief) on the edge of the wood, using a marking gauge set to 18mm (³/₄ in).

Cutting the background

Start by cutting round the design with a parting tool or deep gouge. Make the cut about 3mm (¹/₈ in) from the letter (**1**), taking grain direction into consideration.

Next, remove the waste down to within 2mm (¹/₁₆ in) of the ground line. Using a No8 or No9 gouge about 18mm (³/₄ in) wide, cut across the grain (**2**).

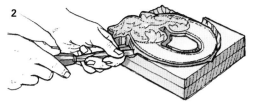

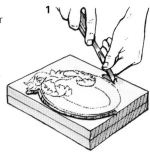

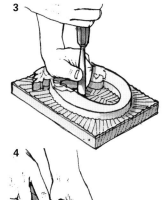

'Setting in' follows the work of rough grounding. Using a chisel, or gouges of appropriate curvature, trim the edges of the design vertically (**3**). Do not cut too deeply, or the cuts may show after you have finished the overall ground area.

Finish the grounding work with a wide shallow gouge such as a 25mm (1in) No3, then use a spoon-bent gouge to hollow out the centre of the letter (**4**). Either leave the subtle tool marks or level the surface further with a chisel, as you prefer.

Now repeat the procedure to reduce the level of the letter's face by 9mm (³/₈ in), leaving the uncut foliage standing proud.

Modelling

Draw the border lines, following the perimeter of the letter, and cut a shallow V-groove along them, using a parting tool. Shape the convex surface between the lines with a chisel (**5**). Then smooth it with an inverted gouge that suits the curve.

'Bosting in' (roughly cutting) the shape of the leaves now follows. Start with a gouge – use a spoon-bent gouge for relatively tight curves. Shape the tips of the curled leaves. Form the contoured shapes of the leaves with long sweeping cuts (**6**), then use a parting tool to add the veins. Undercut the curled leaf tips to make them appear thinner at the edges.

Add the decorative lines within the letter shape, again using a parting tool. Punch the 'spot' details before cutting the decorative lines broken by the dots.

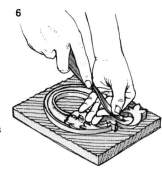

USING SCALED GRIDS

Drawing a scaled grid over your reference enables you to enlarge it accurately.

Draw vertical and horizontal grid lines, say 6mm (¹/₄ in) apart, on a tracing of your reference. Also draw a 24mm (1in) grid on plain paper. This will give you a four-times enlargement – but you can make grids, and therefore the scale, any size suitable for your project. Copy the shapes onto the larger grid – following the lines of your original tracing. Having completed your enlargement, you can make corrections by hand or with drawing instruments.

CARVING IN THE ROUND

This type of carving can be challenging, because it requires an appreciation of aesthetics in addition to well-developed craft skills. The subject matter can be naturalistic or abstract, the concept being dictated by the carver's inclination and sometimes by the natural features of the wood. Carvings that are deeply undercut or pierced, leaving thin weak sections, can be especially difficult for the beginner. Simple solid shapes are easier to execute successfully while you are developing the techniques.

Setting out the work

For some, carving in the round is a matter of selecting and setting up a block of wood and cutting into it, allowing the shape of the carving to evolve as the wood is cut away. However, this can be a hit-and-miss process. Until you are an experienced carver, it is better to prepare an accurate drawing and mark guide lines on the block before you start.

Hands make an interesting subject for carving in the round – a clenched fist is illustrated here as an example. You can make studies of your own hands, trying out more complex poses as you progress.

Prepare actual-size side and front views of your intended carving. A rear view and plan are also helpful. You can base the drawings on your own reference photographs, ideally taken from four sides. Photographs reproduce the effects of perspective, so those parts furthest from the camera will appear relatively small and you will have to adjust any foreshortening in your drawings. Use the grid method to enlarge the image as required.

Using carbon paper, transfer the side and front views to adjacent sides of a block of wood that will just contain the overall shape (**1**) — but leave some waste at the base of the carving, to give you something to clamp in the vice.

Initial shaping

The bulk of the waste can be carved away, but it is quicker to use either a handsaw or a machine saw first. With a handsaw, make a series of straight cuts down to the outline, working from each face (**2**). Chop away the waste with a chisel, leaving a roughly shaped block with square corners.

Alternatively, cut around the marked profiles with a band saw. Cut the side view first, then temporarily nail or tape the waste offcuts back in position (**3**). This retains the lines for cutting the front view. Make sure any nails are driven into waste material only and are kept clear of the proposed sawcuts, then cut around the front-view outline. The roughly shaped block is now ready for carving.

Rough shaping

With the wood held firmly, start to rough in the shape by cutting away the square corners, using a gouge and mallet and working across the grain (**4**).

Using a shallow gouge, shape the planes formed by the folded fingers. Cut into the block where the fingers meet the palm and where the hollow between the forefinger and thumb will be (**5**). As you work, keep looking at the shapes from every angle.

MOUNTING CARVINGS

Carvings in the round can be carved with an integral base or mounted on a separate one, as appropriate.

Consider the shape and size of the base carefully. An attractive mounting will enhance the appearance of the carving. The mount can be made from a contrasting wood or another material, such as marble. Screw the base to the carving, or glue it using dowel pegs.

This carved jester is poised on a polyhedral onyx base

Modelling

Form the rounded knuckles and fingers by paring the wood with a gouge and chisel. Then, using small chisels and gouges, refine the shapes of the fingers and thumb and incise the knuckle creases, folds of flesh and fingernails (**6**).

The degree to which you smooth the wood is a matter of choice. You can either retain the tool marks or smooth the surface, using rifflers and fine abrasive paper. Finish the wood with a clear sealer, then apply a wax polish.

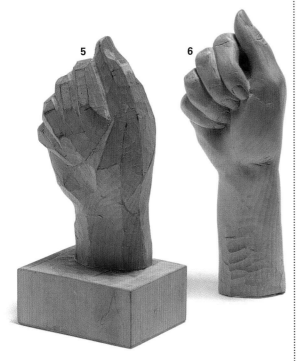

CHIP CARVING

Chip carving is a traditional craft, based on a series of shallow cuts that combine to make regular geometric patterns. You can create a form of chip carving with chisels and gouges, but skilled exponents use special chip-carving knives.

CHIP-CARVING KNIVES

A good knife has a short stiff blade with a well-shaped handle that fits comfortably in the palm of the hand.

Chip-carving knives are made with a variety of blade shapes. But it is not necessary to have a complete set, since you can make most cuts with just two types – a cutting knife and a stab knife.

A cutting knife usually has a straight cutting edge and is used for removing wood chips, while a stab knife has a sharpened skewed end, which is driven into the wood to make short cuts and decorative patterns.

Start with these two knives and try using other types if you find your technique is not producing the required clean cuts.

In addition to the knives, you will need a rule, a sharp Grade B pencil, a pair of compasses and a try square for setting out your designs.

Sharpening chip-carving knives

Place a straight cutting knife on a whetstone, with its cutting edge held at a shallow angle to the surface of the stone. Rub the blade back and forth along the stone, keeping the entire cutting edge in contact with the surface. Turn the knife over and hone the other side. Repeat the process on a finer stone.

Sharpen a stab knife in a similar way, but hold the cutting edge at about 30 degrees to the stone. Finally, polish each tool to a razor-sharp cutting edge on a leather strop.

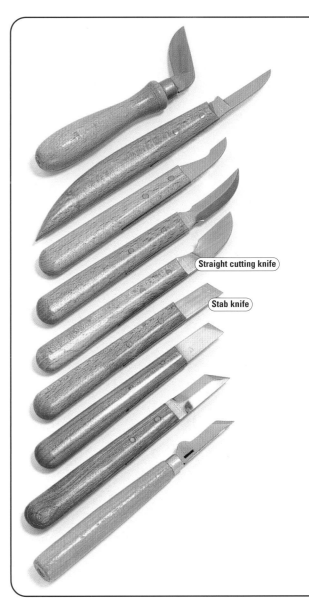

Straight cutting knife

Stab knife

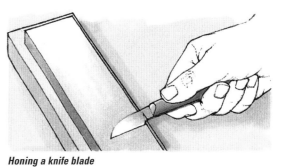

Honing a knife blade
When sharpening a chip-carving knife, hold the blade at right angles to the whetstone.

Marking out

Chip carving is generally based on geometric shapes, although free-form chip carving is also done.

You can set out your design on paper and then transfer it to the surface of the work, or draw on the workpiece itself.

Many pencil lines will remain after the carving is completed and can be removed later, using a pencil eraser. If you try to sand them away you may damage the crisp edges of your carving.

Holding the knives

You can use a cutting knife to cut into the work vertically, or hold it at an angle to make a sloping cut. A faceted chip cut is made by holding the knife at a constant 45-degree angle.

Three basic cuts are made with the cutting knife: you make the first two with a pulling action, and the third by pushing the blade away from you. Use your thumb or hand as a fulcrum when making curved cuts.

Hold a stab knife vertically and push it into the surface to make short straight cuts or wedge-shaped indentations.

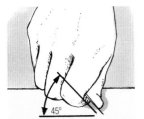

For faceted cuts, hold the knife at a constant angle

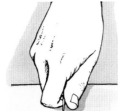

Vertical cut

Angled cut (pulled)

Angled cut (pushed)

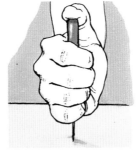

Stab-knife cut

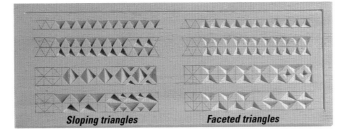

Sloping triangles   *Faceted triangles*

CUTTING BORDER LINES

Incised lines are used to define the edges of border patterns. Carve a border line by making two cuts to form a V-groove.

Your first cut should slope away from the design: pull the blade through the wood and follow the line accurately by looking just ahead of the blade. Turn the work round and make a similar cut to remove the waste.

CARVING BORDERS

Decorative border designs are typically based on equilateral or right-angle triangles.

Cutting sloping triangles

Mark out the pattern of triangles, using a pair of compasses (**1**).

Hold your cutting knife on one side of a triangle, with its point at the apex. Press the point straight down into the wood to a depth of about 3mm (1/8in) and then, keeping the blade upright, pull the knife towards you (**2**) until the point of the blade emerges at the base of the triangle. Repeat the cut on the other side of the triangle.

With the blade held at a shallow angle, slice along the base of the triangle to remove the chip of wood (**3**). Repeat these cuts to complete the border pattern.

Cutting faceted triangles

To cut a border of shallow faceted triangles, first mark out a series of squares and draw in the diagonals.

Draw the knife blade towards you, pressing down into the wood (**4**), then pull out to the surface again as you reach the opposite corner of the triangle. Repeat the same cut on alternate squares.

Turn the work round and make similar cuts in the adjacent squares, but this time pushing the knife away from you (**5**).

Now revert to the first cutting action and cut along the base line (**6**).

As you proceed with cutting the border, hold the blade at a consistent angle, so that the cuts meet at a point in the centre of every triangle.

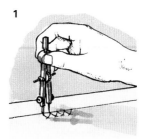

1

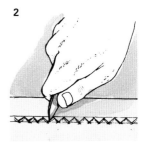

2

3

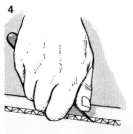

4

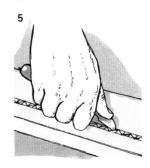

5

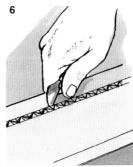

6

CHAPTER ELEVEN

FINISHING WOOD

Applying a finish is the final and arguably the most rewarding stage in any woodworking project. But finishing also has a practical purpose: to protect the wood and keep it clean. When selecting a finish, you therefore need to consider how a particular piece will be used, as well as how it will look. If, for example, it is likely to be subjected to hard wear, choose a varnish or lacquer rather than French polish – which is more vulnerable and so better suited to items that are handled or used less often. Another important consideration is the texture of the wood. For smooth-textured hardwoods, such as mahogany and walnut, French polish gives the finest finish. Open-grain timbers such as oak, on the other hand, look better with an oil or wax finish that penetrates the grain without forming a thick surface coating.

PREPARING THE SURFACE

Although a good-quality paint may obliterate minor imperfections, a coat of varnish or lacquer won't improve the appearance of wood that has been inadequately prepared. The very first application of a clear finish emphasizes even minor flaws that were practically undetectable. You can't always be sure that a batch of timber will be completely faultless, especially when buying wood that's in short supply, so you will occasionally need to fill or patch a few cracks and holes before sanding to a smooth finish. Various materials and techniques may be used, depending on the dimensions of the crack or hole and on the type of finish you intend to apply.

Wood stopper

Traditional filler made from wood dust mixed with glue still has its uses, but most wood finishers prefer to employ commercially prepared stopper (wood putty) for filling gaps and indentations.

Most stoppers are sold as a thick one-part paste in tubes or small cans. They may be formulated for interior or for exterior woodwork. Although they set hard, they remain slightly flexible in order to absorb any movement due to the timber shrinking or expanding. Once set, they can be planed, sanded and drilled along with the surrounding wood.

Catalysed two-part stoppers, which are intended primarily for larger repairs, set even harder than the standard pastes. Take care not to overfill – or you may find yourself using up a great deal of sandpaper just to achieve a flush surface. Use a two-part stopper if you want to build up an edge or a broken corner.

To keep wood stopper in usable condition, replace the lid or screw cap as soon as you have taken enough for your requirements.

Shellac sticks

Sticks of solidified shellac for melting into holes in the wood or building up broken mouldings are made in various colours. Shellac can be used as a stopper before applying most finishes, but may prevent cold-cure lacquer from curing.

Cellulose filler for paintwork

When preparing wood for painting, you can use stopper or ordinary decorator's cellulose filler to fill small holes and cracks.

Supplied ready-made in tubs or as a dry powder for mixing with water, cellulose filler is applied and sanded flush the same way as wood stopper.

Wax sticks

Ideal for plugging small wormholes, filling sticks are made from carnauba wax mixed with pigments and resins. They are suitable for bare wood that is to be French-polished or waxed, but most finishes will not dry or set when applied over wax. However, you can safely fill holes in previously lacquered or varnished surfaces.

Wax sticks are made in a range of colours. If necessary, to match a specific colour, cut pieces of wax from different sticks and blend them with the tip of a warm soldering iron.

Special soft-wax crayons are made for retouching scratches in polished surfaces.

Stopper

Shellac sticks

Electric soldering iron

Wax filling sticks

Flexible filling knife

COLOURING STOPPER TO MATCH

Stoppers are made in a range of colours to resemble common wood species, but in order to match the colour of a particular workpiece exactly you may have to modify the colour of the stopper. For test purposes, apply stain and a coat of finish to an offcut of the same wood.

Modifying the colour

Select a stopper that resembles the lightest background colour of the wood and, using a white ceramic tile as a palette, add compatible wood dye one drop at a time. Blend the dye into the putty with a filling knife to achieve the required tone. Mix a colour that is slightly darker than your test piece, as the stopper will be a shade lighter when dry.

Alternatively, add powdered pigments to colour the stopper, plus a drop of compatible solvent if the paste becomes too stiff.

FILLING CRACKS AND HOLES

Work systematically when preparing or repairing wood surfaces – fill the larger holes and cracks before moving on to scrape or sand out minor blemishes. Always work in a warm, clean and well-lit environment.

Using wood stopper
Make sure the wood is clean and dry. Using a flexible filling knife, press stopper into the indentations or cracks (**1**) – leaving the filler very slightly raised, for sanding flush once it has set. Fill deep holes in stages, allowing the stopper to harden between applications.

Plug deep knotholes with solid wood. When the glue has set, fill gaps around the patch with stopper (**2**).

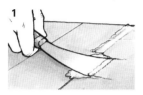

Filling with shellac
Use a soldering iron to melt the tip of a shellac stick, allowing the shellac to drip into the hole (**3**). While it is still soft, press the shellac flat with a wood chisel dipped in water. As soon as the filler hardens, pare it flush with a sharp chisel.

Using wax filling sticks
Cut off a piece of wax and put it on a radiator to soften. Using a knife, press wax into the holes. As soon as it hardens, scrape the repair flush with an old credit card. Fold a piece of sandpaper, and use the paper backing to burnish the repair (**4**).

PATCHING AND PLUGGING

It is best to fill a wide crack with a sliver of timber or veneer – rather than relying on stopper, which could fall out. Dead knots and holes that are too large to fill successfully can be cut out and patched with solid wood. Diamond-shape patches tend to blend in well.

Cutting a diamond-shape patch
Select and cut out a diamond-shape patch from wood that matches the workpiece, both in grain pattern and colour. Plane a shallow bevel on all four edges of the patch.

Hold the patch over the knothole and draw round it with a pencil (**1**), then chisel out a tapered recess. Having applied glue to the patch, use a hammer and block of wood to tap the patch into the recess (**2**). Clean off excess adhesive with a damp cloth and leave the glue to harden, then plane flush.

Filling cracks with veneer
You wouldn't normally buy split timber, but if you are refinishing an old table top or cabinet you may need to repair wood that is split.

Enlarge a tapered crack with the tip of a dovetail saw (**3**) until the crack is wide enough to accommodate a strip of glued veneer. When the glue has set, plane the repair flush.

Filling with a tapered lath
To patch a wide crack or an open joint in a solid-wood panel, cut a lath from matching timber and plane a shallow bevel along both sides. Scrape any dirt and old wax polish from the crack, then tap the glued lath in place with a hammer and block of wood (**4**). Plane the lath flush after the glue has set.

Removing patches of dried glue
When gluing joints and repairs, always clean excess adhesive from the surface of the wood, using a cloth moistened with warm water. If you let the excess glue set hard, it will seal the wood and show as pale patches after staining or polishing.

Use a cabinet scraper to remove any spots of hardened glue before finishing.

Raising dents
A misplaced hammer blow can leave an unsightly dent in an otherwise perfect surface. Lay a damp cloth over the dent and apply the tip of a soldering iron to the spot. The steam generated causes the wood fibres to expand rapidly. Let the wood dry out thoroughly, then sand it smooth.

DISGUISING REPAIRS

Whether you use wood putty, shellac or solid wood to fill holes and cracks, it is often difficult to match colour and grain pattern exactly. Apply a single coat of finish to see how the filling will react. If your repair is still noticeable, paint it to simulate the appearance of the surrounding wood.

Only an expert can copy grain pattern perfectly – but your aim is to fool the eye so that it is not automatically drawn to the repair.

It is convenient to use artist's oil paints thinned with white spirit, but professional retouchers mix powdered pigments – available from most suppliers of wood finishes – with transparent shellac polish. Thin the polish with meths if it becomes too viscous. A white tile or a piece of glass makes an ideal palette for mixing colours.

Painting the background colour
Using a pointed artist's paintbrush, mix pigments and shellac to approximate the palest background colour of the surrounding grain. Seal the wood, then copy the linear pattern across the patch (**1**), extending your painted grain onto the wood to blur the outline of the repair. Keep the paintwork as thin as possible.

Touching in darker grain
Paint in the darker flecks of grain in a similar way (**2**), softening and blending the edges to mimic the actual figure. Let the shellac dry thoroughly, then protect it with another coat or two of finish. If you are using French polish, apply it lightly to avoid smudging your repair.

SANDING WOOD

You need to bring the surfaces of a workpiece to as near-perfect a finish as possible before applying a clear finish. Smoothing wood with abrasives is the usual way to obtain the desired result. But this is not the only role of abrasives. Each coat of finish has to be rubbed over lightly to remove specks of dust and other debris that become embedded as the finish sets.

Although sandpaper as such is no longer manufactured, the term is still used to describe all forms of abrasive and we still talk about 'sanding' wood. Most abrasives are now manufactured using synthetic materials that are far superior to the sandpaper of old.

• Storing abrasives
Wrap sandpaper and abrasive cloths in plastic, to protect them from damp or humid conditions. Store sheets flat, and don't let the abrasive surfaces rub together.

The structure of modern abrasives

Abrasives for woodworking are produced by gluing irregular particles of natural or synthetic grit to a backing sheet, usually made of paper or cloth. The rate at which the abrasive wears away the wood depends on several factors – the size of the particles and the ability of the material to retain its cutting edges, the degree to which the sandpaper can resist getting clogged with wood dust and sticky resins, and the quality of the bond between the grit and the backing.

1 Paper-backed and cloth-backed rolls
Economical and ideal for sanding turned legs and spindles.

2 Slashed cloths
Can be crumpled in the hand and applied to work on the lathe.

3 Velour-backed strips
Peel-off strips for use with sanding blocks and power sanders.

4 Foam-backed pads
Flexible pads follow the contours of a workpiece.

5 Non-woven pads
Nylon-fibre pads impregnated with abrasive material.

6 Standard-size sheets
Sandpaper or cloth sheets measure 280 x 230mm (11 x 9in).

7 Flexible-foam pads
Ideal for sanding mouldings.

Garnet

Silicon carbide

Self-lubricating silicon carbide

ABRASIVE MATERIALS

Which abrasives you select for a particular job will depend on their relative costs and the nature of the material you are finishing.

Crushed glass

Glass is used to make inexpensive abrasive paper, intended primarily for sanding softwood that is to be painted. Glass is fairly soft and wears rapidly. Glasspaper can be recognized easily by its sand-like colour.

Garnet

When crushed, garnet produces relatively hard particles with sharp cutting edges. This natural mineral has the added advantage that the grains tend to fracture before they become dull, presenting fresh cutting edges – so they are, in effect, self-sharpening. Reddish-brown garnet paper is used for sanding both softwoods and hardwoods.

Aluminium oxide

Aluminium oxide is used to manufacture many abrasive products for sanding by hand and with power tools. Available in a number of different colours, it is especially suitable for bringing dense hardwoods to a fine finish.

Silicon carbide

This is the hardest and most expensive woodworking abrasive. It is an excellent material for sanding hardwoods, MDF and chipboard, but its most frequent use is for rubbing down between coats of paint or varnish. Water is used as a lubricant with black to dark-grey 'wet-and-dry' paper. A pale-grey self-lubricating paper is available for rubbing down finishes that would be harmed by water.

BACKING MATERIALS

The backing is basically nothing more than a vehicle that carries the grit to the work. Nevertheless, the choice of backing material can be crucial to the performance of the abrasive.

Paper
Available in a range of thicknesses or 'weights', paper is the cheapest backing material used in the manufacture of woodworking abrasives. Flexible lightweight papers are ideal for sanding by hand, although a medium-weight paper is perhaps better for wrapping round a sanding block. Thicker papers are used with power sanders.

Cloth (woven-textile)
This flexible backing is very tough and durable. You can crease a good cloth backing without it cracking, splitting or shedding its grit. Cloth makes ideal belts for power sanders.

Non-woven nylon fibre
Nylon-fibre pads impregnated with aluminium-oxide or silicon-carbide grains are ideal for rubbing down finishes and for applying wax polish and oil. Because it does not rust, nylon fibre is frequently used for applying water-based products. It is also safe to use on oak, which is prone to staining when particles of steel wool get caught in its open grain.

The abrasive extends throughout the thickness of the pad, so fresh abrasive is exposed as the fibres get worn away.

Foamed plastic
This serves as a secondary backing when you need to spread even pressure over a contoured surface.

Aluminium oxide

3

4

Crushed glass

5

BOND

The bond – the method of gluing abrasives to the backing – plays a vital role. Besides ensuring that the grit stays put, it contributes to the characteristics of an abrasive paper or cloth.

As the abrasive particles are embedded in the first ('maker') coat of adhesive, an electrostatic charge orients the grains so they stand perpendicular to the backing, with their sharp cutting edges uppermost. A second layer of adhesive, known as the 'size coat', is sprayed onto the abrasive to anchor the grains and provide lateral support.

Animal glue is used when flexibility is a requirement. Resin, on the other hand, is heat-resistant, which makes it ideal for power sanding. Because it is waterproof, resin is also used for the manufacture of wet-and-dry papers.

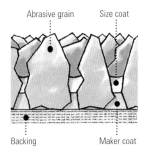

Abrasive grain   Size coat

Backing   Maker coat

Additives
Antistatic additives in the size coat reduce clogging dramatically and increase the efficiency of dust extractors. This leads to a decrease in dust deposits both on the work itself and on power tools and surrounding surfaces

Stearate (a powdered soap) and other chemical additives act as dry lubricants for abrasives used to rub down coats of hard finish.

GRADING SANDPAPER

Sandpapers are graded according to particle size and categorized as extra-fine, fine, medium, coarse and extra-coarse. Each category is subdivided by number in case you need to work through a series of precisely graded abrasives.

The different grading systems in operation make exact comparison impossible – but, as the chart demonstrates, you can safely assume that generally the higher the number the finer the grit.

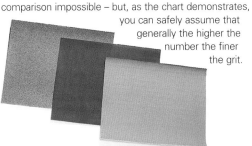

SANDPAPER GRADES

Extra coarse	50	1
	60	1/2
Coarse	80	0
	100	2/0
Medium	120	3/0
	150	4/0
	180	5/0
Fine	220	6/0
	240	7/0
	280	8/0
Extra-fine	320	9/0
	360	-
	400	-
	500	-
	600	-

Closed or open coat
Sandpapers are also categorized according to the density of grit.

A closed-coat sandpaper, which has densely packed abrasive grains, cuts relatively quickly because it has so many cutting edges in any given area.

An open-coat sandpaper has larger spaces between the grains, which reduces clogging, making it more suitable for resinous softwoods.

Tearing sandpaper
Fold a sheet of sandpaper over the edge of a bench, and tear it into strips that fit your sanding block. Wrap one of the strips round the sole of the block, and grip the sides with fingers and thumb.

SANDING BY HAND

Most woodworkers use power sanding during the early stages of preparing a workpiece, but hand sanding is usually necessary at some point, especially if the work includes mouldings. You can, of course, do the whole thing by hand – it just takes longer.

Always sand parallel to the grain, working from coarser to finer grits so that each application removes the scratches left by the previous paper or cloth.

You will find it easier to sand most components before assembly – but take care not to round over the shoulders of joints or create a slack fit by removing too much wood. Restoring old furniture presents additional problems, such as sanding up to corners and possibly sanding cross grain where one component meets another.

SANDING BLOCKS

It's much easier to sand a flat surface evenly if you wrap a piece of abrasive paper round a sanding block. You can make your own from an offcut of wood with a piece of cork tile glued to the underside – but this is hardly worth the trouble when factory-made cork or rubber sanding blocks are so cheap.

Most blocks are designed to be wrapped with a piece of sandpaper torn from a standard sheet, but you can buy sanding blocks that take ready-cut self-adhesive or velour-backed strips of abrasive, which you peel off when they need to be replaced. Double-sided blocks are made with firm plastic foam on one side, for sanding flat surfaces; and a softer sponge on the reverse, for mouldings and curved profiles.

Sanding flat surfaces
Stand beside the bench, so that you can rub your sanding block in straight strokes parallel with the grain. Sweeping your arm in an arc tends to leave cross-grain scratches.

Cover the surface evenly, keeping the block flat on the wood at all times – especially as you approach the edges of the work, or you may inadvertently round over sharp corners.

Sanding end grain
Before sanding end grain, stroke it with your fingers to determine the direction of the fibres. It will feel smoother in one direction than the other. To achieve the best finish, sand in the smoothest direction.

Sanding small items
It is impossible to clamp and sand small items using conventional methods. Instead, glue a sheet of sandpaper face-up on a flat board and rub the workpiece across the abrasive.

Sanding edges
It is particularly difficult to retain sharp corners when sanding narrow edges. To keep your sanding block level, clamp the work upright in a vice and, holding the block at each end, run your fingertips along each side of the work as you rub the abrasive back and forth. Finally, stroke the block lightly along each corner to remove the arris and prevent splinters.

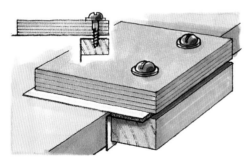

Making an edge-sanding block
It is important to sand edges accurately when working on edge-veneered boards. To make an edge-sanding block, screw together two pieces of wood, trapping two pieces of sandpaper face to face between them. Fold back one piece of paper to form a right angle. Rub the block along the edge of the work, sanding the two adjacent surfaces simultaneously.

Sanding mouldings
To sand a moulding, wrap a strip of sandpaper round a dowel or a shaped block. Alternatively, use foam-backed abrasive or an impregnated nylon-fibre pad.

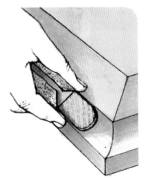

SANDING SEQUENCE

Every woodworker develops his or her preferred sequence for preparing a workpiece for finishing, but the following will serve as a guide to suitable grades of abrasive. You may need to experiment and modify the sequence when dealing with different woods – sanding a close-grain hardwood with an extra-fine abrasive, for example, tends to burnish the surface, making it more difficult to apply wood dye.

Start with 120-grit aluminium-oxide or garnet paper, followed by 180 grit, until the surface appears smooth and free from tool marks and similar blemishes. You only need to resort to an abrasive as coarse as 80 to 100 grit if the wood is not already planed to a reasonably smooth surface.

Remove the dust between sandings, using a tack rag – a sticky cloth designed for picking up dust and fine debris. If you fail to keep the work clean, abrasive particles shed during the previous sanding may leave relatively deep scratches in the surface.

Sand again, for no more than 30 to 60 seconds, using 220 grit; then raise the grain by wiping the surface with a damp cloth. Wait for 10 to 20 minutes, by which time the moisture will have caused the minute wood fibres to expand and stand proud of the surface. Lightly skim the surface with a fresh piece of 220 abrasive to remove these 'whiskers', leaving a perfectly smooth surface. It is particularly important to raise the grain before applying water-based products.

At this stage, you can safely apply a surface finish – but if you feel the workpiece demands an extra-special finish, raise the grain once more and rub down very lightly, using 320-grit paper or an impregnated nylon-fibre pad.

FILLING THE GRAIN

An open-grain timber, such as oak or ash, looks good when coated with a satin varnish or oil – but when French polish or gloss varnish sinks into each pore, the result is a speckled, pitted surface that detracts from the quality of the finish.

The traditional solution is to apply coat after coat of the finish itself, rubbing down between applications until the pores are filled flush. But this is a slow, laborious process – which is why the majority of woodworkers opt for a ready-mixed grain filler. Most general-purpose grain fillers are thick wood-colour pastes. Choose a colour that closely resembles the species you are finishing, always erring on the darker side when a perfect match is impossible.

Applying grain filler
Make sure the surface is completely clean and dust-free. Dip a pad of coarse burlap (sacking) into the grain filler and rub it vigorously into the wood, using overlapping circular strokes (**1**). Take care to coat the surface evenly, right up to the edges.

Before the paste dries completely, wipe across the grain with clean burlap to remove excess filler from the surface. Use a pointed stick to remove paste embedded in mouldings or carving (**2**).

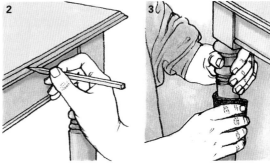

Leave the grain filler to dry thoroughly overnight, then sand lightly in the direction of the grain, using 220-grit self-lubricating silicon-carbide paper.

Rub down mouldings and turned pieces with an abrasive nylon-fibre pad (**3**).

Filling stained timber
It is debatable whether it is better to colour the wood before or after filling the grain. To fill first may result in patchy, uneven colour; but if you apply filler over stained timber, there is the possibility that you may wear through the colour when sanding at a later stage. One solution is to stain the timber first, then protect it either with sanding sealer or with two coats of transparent French polish before applying a grain filler mixed with some of the same compatible wood dye.

Checking a sanded surface
To check that you have sanded the surface evenly and removed all obvious scratches, inspect the workpiece at a shallow angle against the light.

SANDING SEALER

Sealing serves more than one purpose. On porous woods it prevents the finish being absorbed, just as a primer does for paint. It can also be used as the first base coat for French polish.

Perhaps most important of all, a shellac-based sanding sealer makes an excellent barrier coat, preventing wood stains being redissolved and sealing in contaminants such as silicone oil that inhibit the setting of the final finish. For this reason, prior to refinishing, it often makes sense to seal old furniture that has been stripped – but, because sanding sealer prevents some varnishes from setting satisfactorily, it is advisable to check the manufacturer's instructions before starting.

Applying sanding sealer
Sand the work well and pick up the dust with a tack rag. Brush sanding sealer onto the wood and leave it to dry for an hour or two. Rub the surface with fine sandpaper or with an abrasive pad or 0000-grade steel wool before applying your chosen finish. On very porous timber, you may need a second sealing coat.

COLOURING WOOD

Altering the colour of timber might seem an unnecessary operation, given that the various species are endowed with such attractive characteristics. However, stains are mostly applied to enhance natural colour – and both staining and bleaching are often used to do nothing more than overcome variations of hue or tone.

SAFETY WITH SURFACE FINISHES

Bleach must be handled with care and stored in the dark, locked away from children. When handling it, wear goggles, gloves and an apron. Dispose of unused bleach safely – and as soon as possible. Have a supply of water handy, so you can rinse your skin immediately if you splash yourself with bleach.

In addition, take the following precautions to safeguard health and safety when finishing wood.

• Most of the materials used to finish wood are flammable – so store them in a separate building, away from your house. Don't smoke while applying finishes.
• Install a fire blanket and an extinguisher.
• Oily rags are a fire risk. Before throwing them away, either soak them in a bucket of water overnight or open them flat and allow them to dry outdoors.
• Keep finishes and thinners out of the reach of children. If a child should swallow any, do not make him or her vomit but seek medical advice immediately.
• Inhaling solvent fumes can be very unpleasant, and some may be harmful. Follow manufacturers' instructions regarding toxicity, and wear a face mask or respirator if you experience any discomfort.
• Ventilate your workshop or work outside.
• Don't spray finishes without adequate extraction.
• Use barrier cream to protect your hands, and wear protective gloves when applying wood stains.
• If you splash a finish or bleach in your eyes, flush them with water and contact a doctor or hospital casualty department for advice.
• Wear a face mask when sanding bleached wood.

BLEACHING WOOD

Woodworkers resort to bleaching in order to remove natural discoloration. For this, you should use a comparatively mild bleach, such as oxalic acid.

To reduce the depth of colour of a workpiece drastically – perhaps so that you can stain it to resemble a different species, or because you want to stain several components the same colour – you need a strong proprietary two-part bleach. This is usually sold in kit form, comprising a pair of plastic bottles, one containing an alkali and the other hydrogen peroxide, labelled A and B (or 1 and 2).

Never mix the two solutions except on the wood. Also, always apply them with separate brushes and discard any unused bleach.

Testing the effects of bleach

Some woods bleach more readily than others, so test a sample before you treat the work itself. Ash, beech, elm and sycamore are easy to bleach, but you may have to bleach darker woods a second time to get the colour you want.

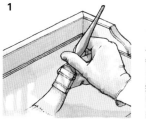

Bleached utile

Applying a two-part bleach

Pour some of the contents of bottle A into a glass or plastic container and use a white-fibre or nylon brush to wet the workpiece evenly (**1**). Don't splash bleach onto adjacent surfaces and, if you have to work on a vertical surface, start at the bottom to avoid runs or streaks.

About 5 to 10 minutes later – during which time the wood may darken – take another brush and apply the solution B.

When it is dry, or as soon as the wood is the required colour, neutralize the bleach by washing the work (**2**) with a weak acetic-acid solution, comprising 1 teaspoon of white vinegar in 1 pint of water. Put the work aside for about 3 days, then sand down the raised grain and apply the finish.

1 **2**

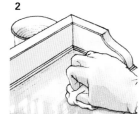

BLEACHING OUT MARKS

Moisture seeping through a finish can stain the wood beneath, forming dark irregular patches. Your only recourse is to strip the old finish from the surface and bleach out the stain with a solution of oxalic acid. Specialist wood-finishing suppliers stock oxalic-acid crystals, or you may be able to buy them from a local pharmacist.

Ventilate the workspace, and wear protective gloves, goggles and an apron. Oxalic acid is extremely toxic and must be stored out of the reach of children.

Applying the bleach

Half-fill a glass jar with warm water and gradually add crystals, stirring with a wooden spatula until no more will dissolve. Never pour water onto oxalic-acid crystals.

Leave the solution to stand for about 10 minutes, then paint it onto the stain, using a white-fibre or nylon brush. Let the wood dry, then apply more bleach if the stain persists. Finally, wash the wood with water and leave it to dry thoroughly. Wearing a face mask, sand the raised grain with fine abrasive paper.

LIMING WOOD

Liming does not actually change the colour of the wood, but because its open pores are filled with a special white wax the appearance of the wood alters dramatically. Liming wax – a proprietary blend of waxes and pigments – is available from most wood-finish suppliers. The wax prevents varnish and cold-cure lacquer setting properly.

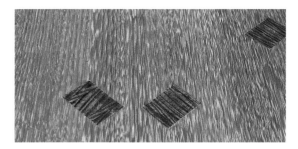

Sand then wipe the surface with a cloth moistened with white spirit. Using a bronze-wire brush, scrub the wood in the direction of the grain to clean out the pores. Pick up the debris with a tack rag.

Because the effect of liming depends on the contrast between the wax and the colour of the wood, it often pays to stain the workpiece first. Use a water stain and seal in the colour with a coat of transparent shellac polish. When the sealer coat is dry, smooth the surface with an abrasive non-woven nylon pad.

Dip a burlap pad into the liming wax and, using firm circular strokes, force the wax into the pores.

When you have covered the surface, wipe across the grain to remove excess wax. After 10 minutes, gently burnish the surface in the direction of the grain, using a soft cloth pad.

Leave the wax to harden for 24 hours, then apply an ordinary paste wax polish to enhance the wood.

Rub liming wax into the pores

Compatibility

You can mix compatible wood stains or dyes, and you can reduce the strength of a colour by adding more of the relevant solvent. However, overlaying a penetrating stain (even one that has dried out) with a surface finish that contains a similar solvent can cause problems – the solvent may reactivate the colour, causing it to 'bleed'. To guard against this, either select a stain that will not react with the finish you want to apply or seal the stain first to prevent solvent disturbing the colour.

Seal a solvent stain (oil stain) with transparent shellac or sanding sealer before applying a varnish, lacquer or wax polish that is thinned with white spirit, turpentine or cellulose thinner.

You can use a spirit stain under any finish except French polish. When the stained surface is completely dry, wipe it with a clean rag before applying a finish.

Allow a stain thinned with water to dry for 48 hours before overlaying with a solvent-based finish – since moisture that has not evaporated can cause the finish to develop a white haze or milkiness.

WOOD STAINS

Paint, which colours the wood by depositing a relatively dense layer of pigments on the surface, also provides a protective coating – and clear varnish is essentially a paint without coloured pigments. A true penetrating stain soaks into the wood, taking the colour deep into the fibres, but provides no protection at all.

Modern stains often contain translucent pigments that lodge in the pores of the wood. Successive applications of these stains gradually darken the wood, whereas applying more than one coat of a non-pigmented stain has little effect on the colour.

1 Solvent or oil stains	**5** White spirit
2 Acrylic stains	**6** Ready-mixed spirit stains
3 Methylated spirit	**7** Concentrated water stains
4 Ready-mixed water stain	**8** Powdered water stains

Solvent or oil stains
The most widely available penetrating stains, made from oil-soluble dyes, are thinned with white spirit. Known as solvent stains or oil stains, these wood dyes are easy to apply evenly, won't raise the grain, and dry relatively quickly. Oil stains are made in a wide range of wood-like colours, which you can mix to achieve intermediate shades.

Spirit stains
Traditional spirit stains are made by dissolving aniline dyes in methylated spirit. The main disadvantage of spirit stains is their extremely rapid drying time, which makes it difficult not to leave darker patches of overlapping colour in an attempt to achieve even coverage. Some manufacturers supply ready-mixed stains. You can also buy spirit stains in powder form, which you mix with meths and a little thinned shellac that serves as a binder.

Water stains
Water stains are available from specialists as ready-made wood-colour dyes. You can also buy them as crystals or powders for dissolving in hot water so that you can mix any colour you want. Water stains dry slowly – which means there is plenty of time to achieve an even distribution of colour, but you must allow adequate time for the water to evaporate completely before you apply a finish. They also raise the grain, leaving a rough surface, so it is essential to wet the wood and sand down before applying the stain.

Acrylic stains
The latest generation of water stains, based on acrylic resins, are emulsions that leave a film of colour on the surface of the wood. They raise the grain less than traditional water stains do, and are more resistant to fading. Acrylic stains need diluting by about 10 per cent when used on dense hardwoods.

313

Applicators
To apply penetrating stains you can use good-quality paintbrushes, decorators' paint pads covered with mohair pile, non-abrasive polishing pads, or a wad of soft cloth. You can also spray wood dyes, provided you have adequate extraction facilities. Wear PVC gloves and old clothes or an apron when applying wood stains.

APPLYING PENETRATING STAINS

Wet the surface to get some idea of what a particular workpiece will look like under a clear finish – and if in doubt, apply some of the actual finish you intend to use. If you are unhappy with the depth of colour or judge that the colour doesn't quite match another piece of wood you are working with, take a scrap piece of the same timber and make a test strip to try out a stain before colouring the workpiece itself.

MAKING A TEST STRIP

Before you colour a workpiece, make a test strip to see how the wood will be affected by the stain you intend to use.

It is important that the test strip is sanded as smooth as the workpiece you will be staining – because coarsely sanded wood absorbs more dye and will therefore appear darker than the same piece of wood prepared with a finer abrasive.

Apply a coat of stain and allow it to dry – as stains tend to look lighter once they have dried. Apply a second coat to see if it darkens the wood, leaving part of the first application exposed for comparison. If you apply more than two full coats of stain, the colour may become patchy due to uneven absorption.

A second coat of a non-pigmented stain may not change the colour appreciably, but you can modify it by overlaying with a compatible stain of a different colour.

Once the stain is completely dry, paint one half of the test strip with the intended finish to see how it affects the colour of the stain.

Pigmented stain   *Non-pigmented stain*

Preparing a workpiece for staining
Sand the workpiece well, making sure there are no scratches or defects that will absorb more stain than the surrounding wood will. In addition, scrape off any patches of dried glue, as they could affect absorption.

Setting up for staining
Plan the work sequence to minimize the possibility of stain running onto adjacent surfaces or one area of colour drying before you can 'pick up' the wet edges. If you have to colour both sides of a workpiece, stain the least important side first, immediately wiping off any dye that runs over the edges.

If possible, set up the workpiece so that the surface to be stained is horizontal. Lay a large panel or door on a pair of trestles (**1**), so you can approach it from all sides.

1

It is sometimes convenient to stain components before assembly, setting them aside to dry while you complete the batch. To colour a number of adjustable shelves, for example, drive a pair of screws into each end. Lay each shelf on a bench, with the screws resting on battens to raise the shelf off the work surface (**2**). Having stained each side in turn, stand the shelf on end against a wall until the stain is dry.

2

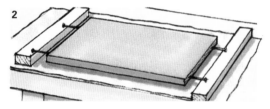

After staining the inside of drawers or small cabinets, support them at a comfortable working height to complete the job, using cantilevered battens clamped or screwed temporarily to a bench (**3**).

3

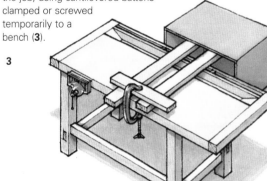

Staining a flat surface

Pour enough stain to colour the entire workpiece into a shallow dish. Brush or swab the stain onto the wood in the direction of the grain, blending in the wet edges before the dye has time to dry. When you have covered the surface, take a clean cloth pad and mop up excess stain, distributing it evenly across the workpiece. If you splash stain onto the wood, blend it in quickly to prevent a patchy appearance.

Staining end grain

Because of the orientation of the cells, end grain readily absorbs penetrating stain. So that it won't look too dark, paint the end grain with a coat of white shellac or sanding sealer, which will reduce the amount of colour absorbed.

Alternatively, you can use thinned varnish – but wait 24 hours before you stain the wood.

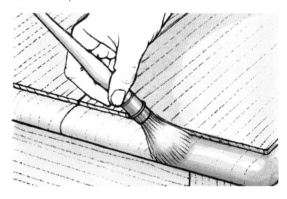

Colouring veneer

You can treat modern veneered panels the same way as solid wood. However, old furniture was invariably veneered using water-soluble animal glue, so use a spirit or solvent stain to colour such items.

If you need to stain veneer patches or pieces of marquetry, do so before gluing them in place. Dipping scraps of veneer in a dish of wood dye ensures even colouring.

Staining turned spindles

Apply stain to turned legs and spindles with a rag or a non-woven polishing pad. Rub the dye well into beads and fluting, then cup your rag or pad around the leg or spindle and rub it lengthways. Since turned work often exposes end grain, it is very difficult to obtain even coverage.

Staining carved work

Use a soft brush to apply stain to carving or intricate mouldings, absorbing surplus stain with rag or a paper towel.

MODIFYING THE COLOUR

No matter how practised you become at judging colours, there will be times when the dried stain turns out to be not quite the colour you had in mind. If it's too dark, you may be able to remove some stain, but trying to alter the colour by applying layer upon layer of dye simply leads to muddy colours or poor finish adhesion. Instead, add washes of tinted finish to modify the colour gradually.

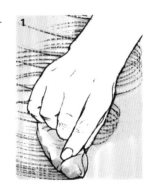

Adding tinted shellac

If the wood is to be French-polished, dissolve some powdered stain in meths and add it to a pale shellac polish. Apply a coat of the tinted shellac (**1**) and allow it to dry. Keep adding washes of shellac, adjusting the colour with spirit stain, until you achieve the right shade.

Applying tinted varnish

If you plan to varnish the workpiece, you can apply a sealer coat of tinted shellac. Alternatively, use a thinned wash of varnish stain (tinted varnish, sold by most DIY stores), or add diluted wood dye to a compatible clear varnish. Build up to the required tone with a series of thin coats (**2**), then apply a coat of full-strength clear varnish.

Toning with wax

If the colour match is still not perfect, you can tip the balance by adding a dressing of coloured staining wax. Rub on the wax in the direction of the grain, using an abrasive nylon pad or very fine steel wool (**3**), then buff it to a satin finish with a soft cloth.

Removing colour

If a solvent-stained workpiece dries streaky or too dark in tone, wet the surface with white spirit and rub it with an abrasive nylon pad. Wipe the surface with a cloth to lift some of the stain, then redistribute the remainder more evenly. At this stage, you can modify the colour by applying another paler, stain while the wood is still damp.

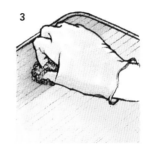

FRENCH POLISH

French polishing – the traditional method of applying shellac dissolved in methylated spirit – is an essential skill to master if you want to restore reasonably priced antique furniture. During Victorian times, it was as common as polyurethane varnish is today.

Although French polish is relatively soft and therefore easily damaged, it can be burnished to a high lustre and is one of the most attractive finishes for wood. Alternatively, it can be reduced to a subtle sheen with a dressing of wax polish.

SHELLAC PRODUCTION

Shellac – the basic ingredient of French polish – is derived from an insect, Laccifer lacca, a native of India and the Far East. To protect their larvae, the female insects secrete a resin that builds up in thick layers on the twigs and branches of trees on which they feed. The spread of the insect is encouraged by tying infested shoots to other suitable host trees. Eventually, the twigs become encrusted with resin, and are 'harvested' as stick lac, which is refined into a wide variety of products, including shellac polish.

Handmade shellac

Although the production of shellac is now largely mechanized, traditional methods that have been practised for hundreds of years still account for approximately 15 per cent of the world's shellac.

The crop of encrusted twigs is scraped and pounded to remove the lac resin, which is then crushed and sieved to extract wood fragments and insect remains. The crushed resin is washed in water, then rinsed and spread out in the sun to dry. After drying, it is sieved again and winnowed to produce a commercial grade of resin known as seed lac.

Blended seed lac is packed into a narrow canvas tube, which is suspended in front of a charcoal fire. As the resin melts, the tube is twisted, wringing molten shellac through the weave of the canvas. The shellac is transferred to a cylindrical ceramic jar filled with hot water, where it is smoothed out to an even thickness. Having peeled the sheet of soft shellac from the cylinder, a skilled worker stretches it in front of the fire, using his hands and feet, and even his teeth. Once it is removed from the heat, the stretched shellac cools rapidly and is crushed to make flake shellac.

1 Machine-made flakes
Modern manufacturing processes produce very fine flake shellac.

2 Handmade flakes
Traditional handmade flakes are relatively thick.

3 Stick lac
Coarse lac resin scraped from twigs and branches.

4 Seed lac
Stick lac is crushed and processed to produce commercial seed lac.

5 Button lac
Translucent discs of the best-quality shellac.

6 Orange flakes
Orange shellac flakes are used to make standard medium-brown French polish.

7 Blonde shellac flakes
Dewaxed flakes for making your own almost clear French polish.

8 Bleached shellac
Bleached dewaxed shellac for manufacturing commercial transparent polish.

Stretching shellac
Handmade shellac is crushed into flakes when cool.

Modern production methods

Traditional methods are still employed at village level, but modern manufacturing processes are geared to producing flake shellac in various qualities and colours.

Seed lac is heated with steam until it becomes molten enough to be filtered in hydraulic presses. It is then passed through rollers, which produce long continuous sheets of shellac.

Alternatively, the seed lac is dissolved in industrial alcohol and the solution is filtered to remove impurities. The alcohol is then boiled off to leave molten shellac, which is passed through rollers.

SANDING SEALERS AND KNOTTING

As well as being the basic ingredient for French polish, shellac is useful as a sealer, forming an effective barrier that prevents contaminants affecting a finish. An application of French polish or shellac-based sanding sealer, for example, prevents wood stain migrating into a top coat of varnish.

Shellac is also used to manufacture fast-drying knotting which, when painted over knots and end grain, seals in softwood resins that might otherwise stain paint or varnish.

If you plan to finish a workpiece with a catalysed lacquer, use only dewaxed shellac as a sealer.

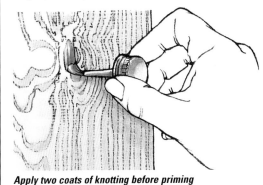

Apply two coats of knotting before priming

READY-MADE POLISHES

It is possible to buy flake shellac from which you can make your own polish – but, unless cost is of prime importance, it is normally more convenient to use one of the many varieties of commercially prepared shellac polish.

Standard polish
The basic medium-brown French polish is made from orange shellac flakes. It is suitable for polishing all dark hardwoods and for tinting pale-coloured species. Standard polish is widely available from most outlets, including hardware and paint suppliers.

White polish
Bleached seed lac is used to make a milky-white polish ideal for finishing pale-coloured hardwoods and for sealing wood prior to waxing. If the standard white polish is too soft, you can buy a version with additives that create a harder finish. White polish may not set properly if it has been in stock for two years or more.

Transparent polish
Shellac contains a small amount of wax, which is insoluble in alcohol. It is this wax that accounts for the milkiness of white polish, and which settles out of other shellacs when they are left undisturbed for a period of time. Washing bleached shellac in petroleum solvent dissolves the wax, resulting in an almost clear polish that does not alter the natural colour of wood. Like white polish, transparent polish has a shelf life of about two years.

Button polish
The term 'button polish' generally implies a superior-quality golden-brown shellac polish. Although most ready-made polishes are made from good-quality flake shellac, some manufacturers still import traditional handmade button lac for their polish.

Dewaxed button polish – referred to as 'special' or 'transparent' button polish – produces a harder finish than the standard variety.

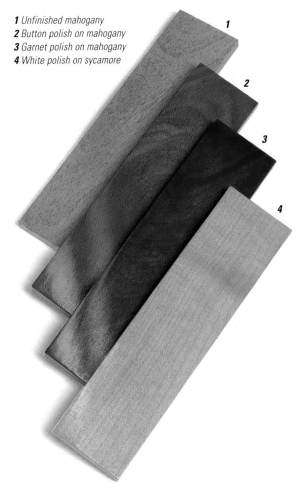

1 Unfinished mahogany
2 Button polish on mahogany
3 Garnet polish on mahogany
4 White polish on sycamore

Garnet polish
Garnet polish is a deep red-brown. It is used to impart a reddish colour to mahogany and similar woods.

Ebony polish
The traditional finish for pianos, ebony polish provides a lustrous high-gloss finish but, because it includes a black stain, it obscures the grain if too much is applied.

Exterior French polish
Exposure to water leaves white staining on all French polishes except for a range of special polishes specifically formulated for use on exterior woodwork.

Brushing polish
Shellac polishes formulated for brushing on contain additives that retard drying, so permanent brush marks aren't left in the finish.

BLONDE SHELLAC

Bleaching seed lac alters its properties, so that it becomes insoluble in alcohol after about 3 days. Bleached shellac is sold only as ready-mixed polish.

For wood finishers who prefer to make their own almost clear French polish, dewaxed blonde shellac flakes are available for dissolving in methylated spirit.

317

Storing a rubber
To keep your rubber soft and supple between applications, store it in an airtight jar.

TRADITIONAL FRENCH POLISHING

To become skilled at every aspect of French-polishing takes years of experience – but, by practising basic techniques on pieces of scrap wood or veneered boards, any reasonably competent woodworker should soon be able to produce an acceptable result.

Shellac is not particularly hard-wearing. It may be the perfect finish for a delicate side table or sewing box, or even for the best sideboard, but it is not the ideal choice for a kitchen table or worktop – where it would be subjected to harsh treatment and could be damaged by water, alcohol or heat.

The type of wood you have chosen also affects whether to use shellac. French polish is at its best when applied to beautifully figured close-grain hardwoods such as mahogany, satinwood or walnut, but is less appropriate for open-grain oak or ash or the more mundane softwoods.

MAKING A RUBBER

Traditionally, a film of French polish is built up over a period of days and the polish is applied with a rubber made by wrapping cotton wool in cloth. Make the rubber to suit the size of your hand and the surface area you will be polishing.

Tear off a piece of upholsterer's wadding or cotton wool 150 to 225mm (6 to 9in) square. Fold it in half, then fold over each half of the rectangle to make a triangle (**1**). Fold two corners of the triangle towards the centre, making a roughly sausage-shaped pad, and place it diagonally across the centre of a 225 to 300mm (9 to 12in) square of soft cotton or linen (**2**).

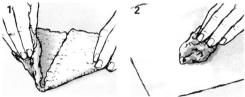

Taking hold of the corner, fold one half of the fabric over the end of the wadding pad (**3**).

Holding the wadding down with one hand, wrap the remaining corners of the fabric over the pad to make a neat package (**4**).

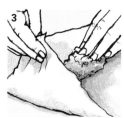

Twist the fabric into a tail behind the pad, to tighten the package, then fold the tail over onto the pad to form a grip that fits into the palm of your hand (**5**). Make sure there are no creases running across the sole of the rubber.

APPLYING FRENCH POLISH

French polishing comprises three main stages. First, the wood must be sealed as a prelude to 'bodying up' – the all-important process of building a satisfactory film of polish, which may take several days to complete. Finally, burnishing with meths removes excess oil and gives the shellac its unique glossy finish.

While French polishing, wear disposable gloves to keep your hands clean.

Charging the rubber

Never dip a rubber into polish, nor pour polish directly onto its sole. Instead, place the rubber in the palm of one hand and carefully unwrap it. Then pour shellac polish onto the wadding (**1**), squeezing it gently until it is thoroughly wet but not completely saturated.

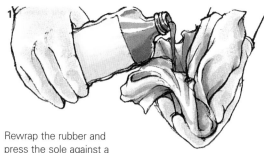

Rewrap the rubber and press the sole against a piece of scrap board (**2**), to encourage the shellac to permeate the fabric and squeeze out excess polish that would build up in ridges on the workpiece. From time to time, you will need to recharge the rubber as the polish gets used up.

Sealing the wood

Using the rubber, apply slightly thinned polish in long overlapping strokes parallel to the grain of the wood (**3**). In the early stages you need apply very little pressure to the rubber; but as the work progresses, squeeze the rubber lightly to encourage more polish to flow. Don't go back over the work – even if you notice slight blemishes.

When you have covered the entire surface, leave the polish to harden for about an hour, then lightly sand the polished surface, with fine silicon-carbide paper, in the direction of the grain only (**4**). If the sealer coat is very uneven, apply another coat the same way.

Bodying up

Charge the rubber with full-strength polish, then begin building up the body of polish. The key to this stage is to keep the rubber moving while it is in contact with the work, to prevent the sole sticking to the polish. Sweep the rubber onto the surface and make small overlapping circular strokes (**5**) until you have coated the workpiece, then sweep the rubber off again.

Make sure you polish right into and out of enclosed corners, with one continuous movement (**6**).

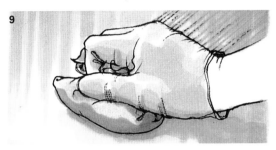

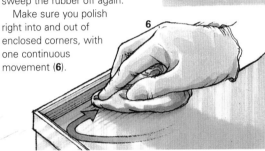

As the work progresses, you will notice that the rubber doesn't slide quite so easily across the surface. As soon as it begins to drag, lubricate the rubber by smearing a drop of linseed oil onto the sole with your fingertip (**7**).

To distribute the polish evenly, go back over the surface again, this time with figure-of-eight strokes (**8**), making sure you work right up to the edges. Finally, apply the polish with straight overlapping strokes parallel to the grain and then leave the polish to dry for about 30 minutes.

Repeat the whole process perhaps three or four times, then put the work aside and allow the polish to harden thoroughly overnight.

Building a protective body of polish

Next day, inspect the workpiece for specks of embedded dust or other blemishes and, if necessary, sand the surface very lightly, using self-lubricating silicon-carbide paper.

Continue to build up a thickness of polish, coating the surface three or four times per day, with a half-hour break between each coat, and allowing the polish to harden overnight. Repeat the process over several days, until you are satisfied with the general colour and appearance of the work.

Removing the oil

Lubricating the sole of the rubber leaves the polished surface streaky. To remove the linseed oil from the polish and bring the surface to a gloss finish, add a little meths to the pad then squeeze it almost dry. Sweep the rubber across the work with straight parallel strokes (**9**), gradually increasing pressure until the rubber begins to drag. Then leave the polish to harden. Repeat the process every 2 to 3 minutes until the streaking disappears. After half an hour polish the surface with a duster, and then put the work aside for about a week to let the polish harden.

Burnishing to a high gloss

If a polished surface does not shine to your satisfaction, burnish it after the shellac has hardened for a week. Rub the surface vigorously with a soft cloth moistened with a special-purpose burnishing cream or a car-paint cleaner (**10**). Both are extremely fine abrasives and will produce a deep shine. Finally, buff the polish with a dry duster.

Creating a satin finish

If a high gloss is not to your taste, once the surface of a newly French-polished workpiece has hardened, you can cut back the sheen, using a pad of 000-grade steel wool dipped in wax polish. Rub the surface very lightly, with the grain, until the entire surface looks evenly matted, then burnish gently with a duster.

FRENCH-POLISHING CARVING AND MOULDINGS

It is impracticable to use a rubber to French-polish a deeply carved workpiece or one with intricate mouldings. Instead, use a special brushing French polish or apply ordinary shellac polish slightly diluted with methylated spirit.

Let the polish flow smoothly, but not too thickly, leaving it to settle naturally. Once the polish has hardened, use a rubber moistened with meths to burnish the high points – but don't rub too hard or you will remove polish from the high points. Finally, burnish with a duster.

VARNISH AND LACQUER

Modern production methods have made available a large range of varnishes and lacquers, each with its own specific properties – durability, weather resistance, ease of application, drying speed, and so on. Such is their versatility that there's almost certainly a varnish or lacquer to meet your requirements.

At one time, the terms 'lacquer' and 'varnish' were used to describe specific finishes. A lacquer was a clear coating that dried quickly by evaporation of the solvent, whereas a varnish was a mixture of resins, oil and solvent that dried by a combination of evaporation and oxidation. Nowadays finishes are so complex that they no longer fit exactly into either category, but manufacturers have continued to use the familiar terms so as not to disorientate their customers. Consequently, the labels 'lacquer' and 'varnish' have become interchangeable. To avoid confusion, the terms used here are those you are likely to encounter when buying wood finishes.

Ranging from clear to amber-coloured, varnishes and lacquers are primarily designed to protect the wood and emphasize its natural grain pattern. There are also modified finishes that contain coloured dyes or pigments.

Exterior-grade varnish
An artificially grained door is protected with a tough varnish.

Oil varnishes

Traditional oil varnish is composed of fossilized tree resins blended with linseed oil and thinned with turpentine. In the manufacture of modern oil varnishes, these natural resins have been superseded by synthetic ones, such as phenolic, alkyd and polyurethane resins, with white spirit as the solvent.

Oil varnishes – frequently referred to as solvent-based varnishes – dry as a result of oxidation. When the solvent has evaporated, the oil absorbs oxygen from the air, chemically changing the varnish in such a way that applying white spirit does not soften the dried film.

The ratio of oil to resin has an effect on the properties of the varnish. Varnishes with a high percentage of oil – known as long oil varnishes – are relatively tough, flexible and water-resistant, making them suitable for finishing exterior woodwork. Short oil varnishes – also called rubbing varnishes – are classed as interior woodwork finishes. Made with less oil and a higher proportion of resin than long oil varnishes, they dry more quickly, with a harder film, and can be polished to a gloss finish.

The choice of resin affects the characteristics of a varnish. Exterior-grade varnishes, for example, are often made from alkyd resin blended with tung oil to provide resilience and weather resistance. Manufacturers adopt terms such as marine varnish to describe superior-quality exterior finishes that will cope with polluted urban environments and coastal climates. Polyurethane resin is favoured for interior oil varnishes, including floor sealers, which need to be tough enough to withstand hard knocks and resist abrasion.

Oil varnishes are normally supplied ready for use, except for those containing pigments or matting agents, which need to be stirred first.

Interior varnish
Polyurethane varnish is suitable for most interior wood surfaces.

Spirit varnishes
Now seldom used for wood finishing, spirit varnishes are manufactured from natural resins (most often shellac) dissolved in meths. They dry quickly by evaporation of the meths, but the film can be softened again by applying the solvent. A higher proportion of shellac is contained in spirit varnish than in a brushing shellac or French polish.

Two-pack polyurethane varnishes
In order for this varnish to set hard, the user has to mix in a precise amount of isocyanate curing agent just prior to application. The result is a clear, tough finish that is better than standard oil varnish in terms of durability and resistance to heat, alcohol and other chemicals. Its one disadvantage is that during the curing process the varnish exudes extremely unpleasant fumes, which can be injurious to health. Consequently, many countries have banned the use of two-pack polyurethane varnishes except in controlled industrial premises fitted with adequate exhaust ventilation.

Acrylic varnishes
An acrylic varnish is composed of acrylic resins dispersed in water to form an emulsion. The varnish is milky white when applied, but becomes a clear transparent finish after going through a two-stage evaporative process.

Acrylic varnish contains a small percentage of solvents known as coalescing agents which, after the water has evaporated, fuse the particles of resin into a cured film. This process can only take place in a relatively warm, dry atmosphere. In very humid or damp conditions, the coalescing agents may evaporate before the water does, leaving a film that cannot set properly.

Acrylic varnishes are non-toxic and practically odourless, and you can wash out your brushes in ordinary tap water.

Protective wood stains
Available as solvent-based and water-based finishes, protective wood stains fall somewhere between exterior varnish and paints. Most are translucent wood-colour or pastel finishes, but some are completely opaque. These finishes, which should not be confused with genuine penetrating wood stains, provide colour and protection for exterior doors and window frames.

Varnish stains
Tinted solvent-based and acrylic finishes allow you to varnish and colour the wood in one operation. Varnish stains are made in a variety of translucent colours, mostly formulated to imitate common wood species.

Fast-drying varnish (below)
Acrylic varnish dries so rapidly you can complete most tasks in a day.

Floor sealers
Hardwearing clear varnishes are made specifically for finishing floors.

Cold-cure lacquers
Cold-cure lacquers – which set hard by a process known as cross-polymerization – require the addition of an acid catalyst to start the reaction. When the resin cures, the molecules are bonded chemically, forming an extremely tough nonreversible film that is highly resistant to solvents, heat and abrasion. Because cold-cure lacquers do not rely on evaporation of the solvent or on oxidation for setting, they can be applied in relatively thick coats.

Some lacquers are supplied precatalysed, so that the curing process begins automatically as soon as the solvent evaporates. Others are supplied in two parts, requiring the user to add the acid hardener before applying the finish.

Cold-cure lacquers are usually manufactured with butylated urea-formaldehyde resins, plus melamine for heat resistance and alkyd resin as a plasticizer. The lacquer forms an exceptionally clear film that does not yellow with time. Opaque white and black finishes are also available.

Cellulose lacquer
Cellulose lacquer dries solely by evaporation of its solvent, leaving a film that redissolves readily when cellulose thinner is applied to the surface. As a result, each successive coat dissolves partially and melds with the previous application, forming a single film of lacquer.

This is a water-clear finish that hardly changes the colour of the wood. It also sets very rapidly – it is recoatable after only 30 minutes – which all but eliminates the problem of dust contamination.

Cellulose lacquer is not as resistant to heat, water or abrasion as polyurethane varnish and cold-cure lacquer are, but it is more resistant than shellac polish.

APPLYING OIL VARNISH

You can spray the majority of varnishes onto wood, but for most woodworkers it is cheaper and more convenient to apply varnish with a paintbrush. Provided you use good-quality equipment and work patiently, you can achieve perfect results.

Varnishing a flat panel

Supporting a large panel horizontally on a pair of trestles makes varnishing marginally easier, but there are few problems with finishing a hinged door or fixed panel in situ, provided you guard against the varnish running.

When applying a first sealer coat to bare wood, thin oil varnish by about 10 per cent. You can brush the varnish onto the wood, but some woodworkers prefer to rub it into the grain with a soft cloth (**1**).

Leave the sealer coat to harden overnight, then inspect the varnished surface under a good source of light. Rub down the sealer coat lightly in the direction of the grain (**2**), using fine wet-and-dry paper dipped in water. Then wipe the surface clean, using a cloth moistened with white spirit, and dry it with a paper towel.

Paint oil varnish onto the wood, brushing first with the grain and then across it to spread the finish evenly (**3**). Always brush towards the area you have just finished, to blend the wet edges. Work at a fairly brisk pace, as varnish begins to set after about 10 minutes and rebrushing tends to leave permanent brush marks.

Finally 'lay off' along the grain with very light strokes, using just the tips of the bristles to leave a smoothly varnished surface. When varnishing vertical surfaces, lay off with upward strokes of the brush.

Two full-strength coats of oil varnish should be sufficient for most purposes. For a perfect finish, rub down lightly between each hardened coat.

Varnishing edges

As you approach the edges of a panel, brush outwards away from the centre. If you flex the bristles back against the sharp arris, varnish will dribble down the edge.

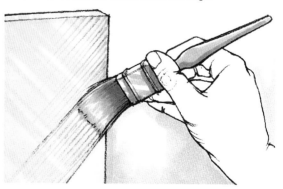

Varnishing mouldings

Flexing a brush across a moulding usually causes a teardrop of varnish to run down the surface. Avoid this by brushing along the moulding, not across it.

When finishing a panelled door, varnish the mouldings first and then varnish the panel, brushing out from each corner towards the centre.

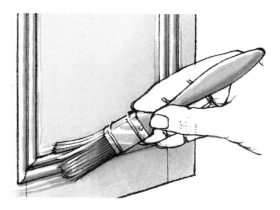

Matting a gloss varnish

Matt and satin oil varnishes have very finely textured surfaces that serve to scatter the light. These look perfect, but on components such as chair arms or table tops you can achieve a surface that is smoother to touch by rubbing down a gloss varnish to a matt finish.

Rub the varnish with 000-grade steel wool dipped in wax polish. Leave the wax to harden, then burnish it to a soft sheen with a clean duster.

APPLYING ACRYLIC VARNISH

Many of the techniques employed when applying oil varnish are equally relevant to acrylic varnish. As with oil varnish the aim is to achieve a flat, even coating without runs or brush marks, but the chemical properties of acrylic varnish make it behave slightly differently.

Grain-raising characteristics

When a piece of wood absorbs water, its fibres swell and stand up proud of the surface. Water-based acrylic varnish has the same effect, making the final finish less than perfect. The solution is either to wet the wood first and sand it smooth before applying the varnish, or to sand the first coat of varnish with fine wet-and-dry paper dipped in water before recoating the work. Either way, wipe up the dust with a cloth dampened with water – a tack rag may leave oily deposits, which would spoil the next coat of varnish.

Applying the varnish

Acrylic varnish must be applied liberally. As with oil varnish (see opposite), brush across the grain first and lay off evenly.

Acrylic varnish dries in 20 to 30 minutes – so you need to work fast, especially on a hot day, to avoid leaving permanent brush marks in the finish.

You can apply a second coat after 2 hours. A total of three coats is sufficient for maximum protection.

APPLYING COLD-CURE LACQUER

This is a very different finish from conventional varnish. Although cold-cure lacquer is no more difficult to apply, it is important to be aware of how the curing process can be affected by inadequate preparation and inappropriate procedures.

Mixing cold-cure lacquer

Mix recommended amounts of hardener and lacquer in a glass jar or polythene container. Metal containers and other plastics may react with the hardener, preventing the lacquer from curing.

Once mixed, some cold-cure lacquers are usable for about 3 days. However, you can extend the pot life to about a week by covering the jar with polythene, held in place with an elastic band.

This type of lacquer will last even longer if you keep the sealed container – clearly marked to avoid accidents – in a refrigerator.

Applying the lacquer

The wood must be smooth and clean. Be sure to remove any trace of wax, which might prevent the lacquer curing. Any wood dye applied to the work must be compatible with the acid catalyst in the lacquer, so check the manufacturer's recommendations before colouring the workpiece.

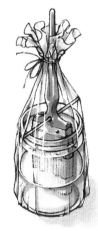

Adequate ventilation is important — especially when you are lacquering a floor – but keep the workshop warm.

Brush on the lacquer liberally, using a flowing action (**1**) and blending in wet edges as you go. Apply it relatively thickly, taking care to avoid runs.

The lacquer will be touch-dry in about 15 minutes; apply a second coat after about an hour. If a third coat is required, apply it the following day.

There is never any need to rub down between coats, except to correct blemishes. If you use stearated abrasives, wipe the sanded surface with special lacquer thinner.

To achieve a perfect gloss finish, let the last coat harden for a few days then sand it smooth, using wet-and-dry paper with water, until the surface appears matt all over; a shiny patch indicates a hollow. Finally, using a burnishing cream on a slightly damp cloth, buff the surface to a high gloss (**2**) and then rub it with a duster.

To create a satin finish, rub the hardened lacquer with 000-grade steel wool lubricated with wax polish and finish by burnishing gently with a duster. For a matt finish, use coarser steel wool.

APPLYING CELLULOSE LACQUER

Ventilation is essential when applying cellulose lacquer; also, wear a respirator. The lacquer is highly flammable.

Spraying and brushing lacquer

Conventional cellulose lacquer dries so quickly that spraying is the only practicable method of application. If your workshop is not equipped with the required spray gun, compressor and ventilation system, use a specially formulated lacquer made with a slow-evaporating solvent so that it can be brushed on to the wood.

Brushing cellulose lacquer

First, use a cloth pad to apply a sealer coat consisting of lacquer diluted by 50 per cent with cellulose thinner (**1**).

Next, brush on additional full-strength coats, laying on the lacquer with a flowing action. Hold the brush at a shallow angle to the surface (**2**) and apply the finish with long, straight, overlapping strokes. Don't spread the lacquer like varnish, or you run the risk of leaving visible brush marks in the rapidly setting finish.

After about an hour, rub down the final coat of lacquer to remove any minor blemishes, using either fine wet-and-dry paper or self-lubricating silicon-carbide paper. Rub to the required finish, using burnishing cream.

Brush care
Once polymerization is complete, cold-cure lacquer becomes insoluble, so wash brushes in special lacquer thinner as soon as the work is complete. You can leave the brush suspended in the mixed lacquer between coats if the whole container, including the brush, is wrapped in polythene.

Sealing a can of paint
When resealing a paint can, always wipe paint from the rim with a cloth pad and use a hammer and a block of wood to tap down the lid. Shake the can afterwards to help prevent a skin forming over the paint.

PAINT FINISHES

Paints and varnishes are made from similar resins and solvents and have many characteristics in common. The one real difference is that paints contain coloured pigments that obliterate the grain pattern and, as a result, are more often used for finishing inexpensive hardwood joinery, softwoods and boards.

When you apply a protective body of varnish or lacquer, the same material is used for each coat. In contrast, conventional paintwork combines three different types of paint. A single coat of primer effectively seals the wood and provides a surface to which subsequent coats will adhere well; two or three coats of dense matt undercoat form the protective layer; and the top coat provides a coloured satin or gloss finish.

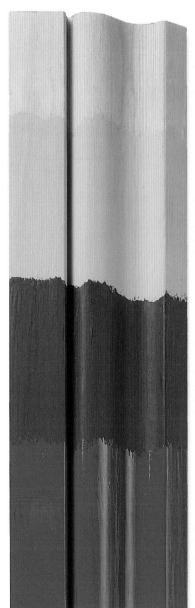

Bare wood
Grain raised and sanded smooth.

Primer
Seals the wood and provides the ideal base for other paints.

Undercoat
Two to three coats obliterate the primer and build a protective body of paint.

Top coat
The final paint finish provides a wipe-clean coloured surface.

PRIMERS

Solvent-based wood primer
Whether you use white or pink primer will depend on which works best with the chosen colour and tone of subsequent coats of paint. Leave solvent-based primers to dry overnight.

Acrylic wood primer
Although acrylic primers are water-based, they can be used as a primer for either oil or acrylic paints. They usually dry in about 4 hours.

Aluminium wood primer
Solvent-based primers that contain aluminium particles contribute towards good weather resistance. Aluminium primers are also recommended for sealing all hardwoods (especially oily ones), resinous softwoods, and timber treated with dark-coloured wood preserver.

UNDERCOATS

Solvent-based undercoat
Formulated to obliterate wood grain and primer, undercoat dries to an even matt finish and can be rubbed down with wet-and-dry paper to a perfectly flat surface. Solvent-based undercoats – which are usually available in white, grey and a limited range of colours – should be left to harden overnight.

Acrylic undercoat
Acrylic undercoats dry so fast you can complete the average job, including the top coat, in a single day; and some are ready for the next coat after only an hour. A few manufacturers market a single acrylic paint that can be used for both priming and undercoating. Although acrylic undercoats are water-based, they can be overlaid with either solvent-based or water-based top coats.

TOP COATS

Solvent-based paint
Most top-coat paints are formulated to produce a high-gloss finish or a subtle satin sheen. Although few paint manufacturers distinguish between exterior and interior finishes, gloss paint is generally considered to be more weather-resistant than satin.

Non-drip thixotropic paints do not require stirring unless the medium has settled out during storage, in which case allow the paint to gel again before using it. Solvent-based top coats are touch-dry within 2 to 4 hours, and set completely overnight.

One-coat paint
Solvent-based one-coat gloss and satin paints do not require separate undercoats, and so save time. They are made to a creamy consistency, with a relatively high proportion of pigments. One-coat paints are useful for obliterating old paintwork and strong colours. They must be applied liberally to be fully effective, and should not be spread too thinly.

Acrylic paint
Being water-based, acrylic paints are in many ways similar to acrylic varnishes – once the water has evaporated, they both set when coalescing agents fuse the acrylic resin into a hard film. This means that acrylic paints and varnishes may not set satisfactorily if they are applied on a cold damp day or during a period of high humidity.

Although acrylic paints are available as gloss and satin finishes, they are not as glossy as the solvent-based variety.

Acrylic paints dry quickly. They are also non-toxic, non-flammable and practically odourless.

Metallic paint
Manufacturers offer a range of gold, silver, copper and bronze paints, primarily for finishing picture frames and small decorative objects such as boxes. They are not protective coatings in their own right, but you can cover them with slightly thinned clear varnish if the object is to be handled. Metallic paints must be stirred thoroughly before use, and applied with a soft paintbrush.

APPLYING PAINTS

Make sure the work is clean and sanded smooth before brushing on the first coat of paint. As acrylic primer is water-based, be sure to raise the grain before applying it.

Although paints are opaque, they won't obscure the effects of resinous knots – which will eventually discolour the paintwork. Seal suspect knots with shellac-based knotting before painting with solvent-based or acrylic paints.

Applying solvent-based paint
When using conventional oil paint, apply a primer and a minimum of two undercoats, followed by a single top coat. Rub down between coats with wet-and-dry paper, wiping off the sludge with a cloth dampened with white spirit.

Spread the paint with vertical and sideways strokes, laying off with the tips of the bristles for a smooth finish. Avoid visible brush marks and runs, as when applying varnish.

There is no need to spread thixotropic paint: apply it fairly liberally, smoothing it out with virtually parallel strokes, then lay off lightly.

Applying acrylic paint
Brush on acrylic paint the same way as acrylic varnish, blending wet edges quickly.

PAINT APPLICATORS

Compared with spraying, applying paint with a brush or pad is a relatively slow process and the same quality of finish is difficult to achieve. However, because painting by hand avoids the cost of specialized equipment and almost everyone has used a paintbrush, it is still most woodworkers' preferred method of applying paint.

Brushes, paint pads and rollers
The best brushes for solvent-based paints are made from tough, resilient hog hair. Slightly cheaper ones are a mixture of natural bristles – usually hog, ox or horse hair.

Imitating natural hair, synthetic bristles taper towards the tip, where they divide into even finer filaments that hold a finish well. Use synthetic-bristle brushes for water-based paints.

Mohair-lined foamed-plastic pads make finishing large flat surfaces less laborious. Some painters also use a smaller version, known as a sash pad, for glazing bars, spindles and mouldings. Brush a new pad with a clothes brush to remove any loose filaments from the pile.

Choosing a good-quality brush
To check the quality of a brush, fan the bristles with your fingers. The bristles should be densely packed and

should spring back to shape readily. The bunch of bristles (the filling), should be glued firmly into the metal ferrule – which, in turn, must be fixed securely to the handle.

Cleaning pads and brushes
As soon as you have finished painting, blot your pad or paintbrush on old newspapers. Wash acrylic paint out of your brushes or pads with water. Use white spirit to rinse other paints from the applicators, and then wash the bristles or pile with hot water and detergent.

Soften hardened oil paint by soaking the bristles in a proprietary brush cleaner or paint stripper, then wash the brush thoroughly with soap and water. Cellulose thinner will soften hardened acrylic paint.

SPRAYING FINISHES

Spraying wood finishes is not only faster than brushing: once you have mastered the basics, it guarantees superior results. Wood finishers require versatile equipment that is reasonably inexpensive, compact and reliable. For most people, this means using a small electric-powered compressor that delivers pressurized air to a finely adjustable hand-held spray gun.

Attaching the reservoir
When attaching the reservoir to a suction-feed spray gun, make sure the bent pipe that leads to the base of the canister faces towards the nozzle of the gun. This ensures that the pipe will pick up finish from the canister when the gun is pointed slightly downwards.

SPRAY GUNS

All spray guns atomize a fluid finish, depositing it as a fine mist onto the workpiece, where it flows together to form a perfectly even surface coating. Squeezing the trigger allows compressed air to flow through the spray gun, where it is mixed with finish drawn from a reservoir mounted above or below the gun.

A gravity-feed cup attached to the top of the gun will hold up to about half a litre (1 pint) of paint or clear finish. A filter at the base of the cup prevents dirt particles blocking the gun's nozzle. Gravity-feed guns are suitable for spraying most wood finishes, but may not be able to cope with heavily pigmented paints.

A suction-feed gun is more versatile. It can handle any wood finish, including metallic paints. As the compressed air flows through the gun, it creates a vacuum that draws finish from the reservoir carried below. Suction-feed reservoirs are invariably larger than gravity cups, so require refilling less often.

High-volume low-pressure (HPLV) guns are becoming popular for home spraying, as they produce little overspray and so minimize paint waste. They can be run with compressed air or with continuous air supplied by a turbine.

Fluid tip
The fluid tip is where the finish and compressed air are brought together. Air escapes from holes surrounding the central nozzle, from which the finish emerges. Squeezing the spray gun's trigger opens the air-flow control valve momentarily then withdraws a spring-loaded needle from the nozzle, allowing the paint or varnish to flow.

Fluid-output adjuster
An adjustment screw, usually fitted at the back of the gun, governs how far the needle can be withdrawn from the fluid-tip nozzle in relation to the trigger, thereby regulating the flow of finish from the gun.

External-mix air cap
The fluid-tip nozzle protrudes from the centre of the air cap. A narrow gap surrounding the nozzle provides the outlet for air directed into the stream of fluid, atomizing it into extremely fine droplets. Some of the compressed air, diverted to 'horns' mounted on each side of the cap, is used to compress the spray pattern from cone shape to fan shape.

Air-flow adjuster
A screw at the rear of the gun controls the amount of air that flows through the fluid tip to the horns, allowing you to modify the spray pattern from a narrow cone to a maximum-width fan.

Air valve
Air pressure to the gun is set at the compressor, but some spray guns have an adjustment screw that allows you to fine-tune the pressure. Adjust air pressure until it is as low as possible while still maintaining effective atomization.

Gravity-feed gun

Fluid-tip nozzle

Locking ring

Horn

Air cap

Air-flow adjuster

Air-output adjuster

Fluid-output adjuster

Trigger

Air valve

Air-supply hose

Suction-feed spray gun

Reservoir

COMPRESSORS

Small portable compressors are designed to work with simple constant-bleed spray guns that have very basic controls. To operate spray guns that have the full range of controls, you need a compressor with an air-receiving tank from which compressed air is drawn off through a flexible hose running to the gun.

Choosing a compressor

A typical compressor for the home workshop has a pump that deposits compressed air into the receiving tank. When the tank is full, the motor cuts out. As air is drawn off by the spray gun, the pressure in the tank falls until it reaches a preset level. The motor then cuts in again and tops up the tank.

Choose a compressor with a motor able to deliver air at 8cfm (cubic feet per minute). Compressors are rated according to maximum working pressure — typically 120 to 150psi (pounds per square inch). Since you need an operating range of something like 30 to 50psi for spraying, the maximum working pressure of most compressors is more than sufficient. Always follow the manufacturer's instructions when setting the air pressure.

Regulators and filters

Most compressors are manufactured with a built-in regulator to ensure that air is delivered to the spray gun at a constant pressure. A gauge on the instrument records the air pressure, which can be adjusted by turning the regulator valve. The air hose is attached by a simple quick-fit connector.

On some models, the regulator incorporates a filter to remove moisture and other contaminants before the air reaches the gun. Water droplets, which collect at the bottom of the receiving tank, can be drained off at regular intervals.

Motor

Filter regulator

Air-hose connector

Air receiver

Draincock at base of receiving tank

Compressor

CONSTRUCTING A SPRAY BOOTH

Spraying is a wasteful process, depositing as little as 30 per cent of the paint or varnish onto the workpiece. The rest is lost to the atmosphere as overspray; and if not extracted in some way, this would fill the workshop with a highly flammable mist of fumes and paint particles. It is therefore necessary to construct a spray booth fitted with an extractor fan that will filter out the solids from the overspray and deposit the fumes outside the workshop.

Unless you intend to spray water-based finishes only, you will need a filtered extractor fan with a shielded motor that prevents sparks igniting solvent fumes. Any switches and light fittings installed in or near the spray booth must also be explosion-proof.

Building a basic booth

Construct a three-sided booth, consisting of a softwood frame covered with hardboard or MDF panels. Mount the extractor fan in the rear wall of the booth; and line the inside of the booth with sheets of paper, which can be replaced after each job.

Arrange a light source above you or on each side of the booth, to avoid throwing your shadow on the work. Light reflected off the back wall will help you judge the condition of paintwork.

Making a turntable

To avoid getting covered with overspray, always position the workpiece between you and the extractor. The easiest way to accomplish this is to make a turntable for the work, so you can rotate it to present unfinished surfaces to the spray gun without the risk of smearing wet paint or varnish. You can buy a proprietary turntable, but it is probably cheaper to convert a swivel-chair stand.

MDF or chipboard

Levelling block

Swivel-chair stand

SAFETY WHEN SPRAYING

Before spending money on equipment, check with your local authority and fire department – and possibly with your insurance company, too – to make sure you are able to comply with any requirements or regulations regarding building a spray booth and operating paint-spraying equipment in your workshop.

• Install an extractor to remove solvent fumes from the workshop.
• When spraying, wear goggles, overalls and an approved respirator.
• Don't smoke when spraying, and extinguish naked flames in the workshop.
• Don't point a spray gun at yourself or anyone else.
• Disconnect your spray gun from the supply hose before servicing it.
• Keep a fire blanket and extinguisher close to hand.

ADJUSTING SPRAY GUNS

Initially it is worth experimenting with the range of adjustments to see how your particular system operates. Unless you are working with cellulose lacquer, which is usually sold in a sprayable consistency, you will need to dilute the finish with an appropriate solvent.

Thinning wood finishes

Check the manufacturer's recommendations for the ideal ratio of finish to thinner when preparing paint, varnish or cold-cure lacquer. To avoid having to make up a further batch to the same consistency, always mix enough thinned finish to complete the job.

Stir the thinner into the finish with a wooden stick, then lift out the stick to see how well the diluted finish runs from the tip. If it is still too thick, the finish will drip or run intermittently from the stick; if it runs smoothly, in a steady continuous stream (**1**), then the paint or varnish is about ready for spraying. Before spraying a workpiece, test the finish on a practice board – an overdiluted finish will run almost immediately.

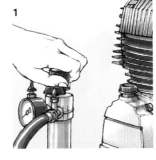

For a more scientific test of consistency, you can run the fluid through a viscosity cup (**2**), a special funnel that empties at a precise rate when the finish is thinned accurately.

Adjusting the controls

To test the controls of a spray gun, set up a piece of plywood or MDF in the spray booth. Fill the gun's reservoir with paint to the recommended level, so you can see the effects of adjusting the controls.

The easiest way to set the air pressure is to open the air valve on the gun's handgrip fully, then adjust the valve on the compressor's regulator (**1**) until the gauge indicates the required pressure. About 30psi is a good starting point.

Start with the fluid-output screw fully closed. Aim the gun at the workpiece, holding the nozzle about 200mm (8in) from the surface, and squeeze the trigger. Gradually open the fluid-output adjuster (**2**) until you begin to wet the surface with paint.

If the adjuster is opened too far, too much fluid will be sprayed onto the surface and it will run.

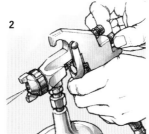

Experiment with the controls, using the air valve (**3**) or the regulator to increase and decrease air pressure and balancing the effects by adjusting the fluid flow.

With the air-flow adjuster fully closed, the gun will emit a narrow cone of atomized paint. With the horns set horizontally, gradually open the adjuster (**4**), watching how the spray pattern changes to a wide vertical fan.

Release the trigger, slacken the locking ring on the air cap and turn the horns to a vertical position, then hand-tighten the locking ring again. With this configuration, the gun produces a horizontal fan-shaped spray pattern.

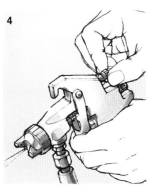

CLEANING A SPRAY GUN

As soon as you have finished spraying, empty the reservoir and add thinner. Operate the gun until clean thinner begins to emerge from the nozzle. If you have run out of a specific thinner, cellulose thinner can be used to clean out most modern finishes.

Cleaning the air cap and fluid tip

Close the valve that delivers air to the hose. Squeeze the gun's trigger to clear the hose, and then disconnect the spray gun. Remove the air cap, so you can wipe it and the fluid tip clean with a piece of soft rag. Remove any obvious blockages, using a wooden toothpick and the synthetic-bristle brush supplied with the gun. Wipe the inside of the reservoir and the outside of the gun with a rag moistened with thinner.

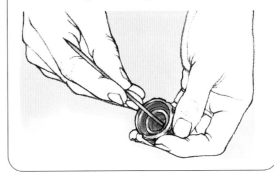

SPRAYING TECHNIQUES

As a general rule, it is best to apply several thin coats of wood finish, rubbed down between applications with wet-and-dry paper to remove specks of dust and other blemishes. Although sprayed finishes tend to become touch-dry relatively quickly, you will need space to put workpieces aside to harden properly. Dampen the floor to keep airborne dust to a minimum.

Pointing the gun
To achieve a perfectly even finish, it is important to keep the gun pointed directly at the work. When spraying a wide panel. for example, flex your wrist so that you move the gun in a path parallel to the surface of the work

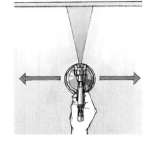

Uneven coverage
If you make the mistake of swinging the gun in an arc, you will deposit insufficient paint or varnish along each side of the workpiece, leaving a strip of thicker finish down the centre.

Spraying a flat panel
Before spraying a vertical board or panel, adjust the gun to produce a fan-shape spray pattern. Aligning the nozzle with the top edge of the workpiece, aim the gun to one side of the panel. Squeeze the trigger and make a continuous pass at a steady pace across the panel. Don't release the trigger until the gun is aiming well clear of the panel (**1**).

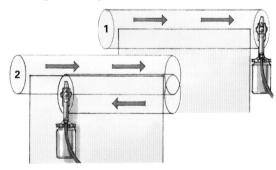

Squeeze the trigger again and make a second pass in the opposite direction, overlapping the first application by 50 per cent (**2**). To coat the entire panel evenly, overlap each subsequent pass in a similar way.

Spraying a horizontal panel
You may find it easier to lay a small panel flat on your turntable. Working away from you, make overlapping parallel passes, holding the spray gun at an angle of about 45 degrees to the work.

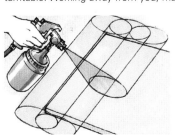

SPRAYING ASSEMBLED WORKPIECES

When spraying assembled workpieces, work out a sequence that will enable you to coat all surfaces in turn and also allow you to move the work without spoiling the finish.

Spraying a table
It is always more convenient to spray a table top and underframe separately. For narrow legs and rails, set the gun to produce a cone-shape spray pattern. For the top, spread the pattern into a fan.

- Spray the underside of the top and put it aside to dry.
- Stand the underframe on your turntable and spray the inside of the legs and rails. Aim the gun at one of the corners of a square leg, so you coat two surfaces simultaneously.
- Spray the outside of the legs and rails.
- Return the table top to the turntable, supporting it on small blocks of wood. Start by spraying the edges all round, then coat the top surface evenly.

Spraying a chair
Set a cone-shape spray pattern for chair legs and stretcher rails. If necessary, open it out into a small fan for the seat and back rest.

- Turn the chair upside down on the turntable, so you can spray the insides of the legs and rails.
- Spray the underside of the seat.
- Stand the chair on its feet and spray the outside of the legs and stretcher rails.
- Spray the edges of the seat, then its top surface.
- Finish the inside of the armrests and chair back.
- Spin the chair round to coat the outside of the armrests and chair back.

Spraying a cabinet
Spray the inside of the cabinet first, trying not to aim the gun directly into right-angle corners.

- Finish the underside of the top panel.
- Spray down one side of the interior, and then the the back panel.
- To complete the interior, spray the other side panel and then the bottom of the cabinet.
- Spray the exterior of the cabinet, treating each panel individually.
- Finish the doors as individual panels, before fitting them to the cabinet.

WAX POLISH

Waxing wood is a long-established tradition, and one that is frequently employed by antique restorers. That is not to say the subtle qualities of wax polish have gone unnoticed by other woodworkers, especially as a finish for open-grain timbers or as a dressing over lacquer, varnish or French polish.

COMMERCIAL POLISHES

Making wax polish from basic ingredients is sometimes advocated by traditionalists, but with such a variety of excellent polishes readily available there seems little point in introducing a complication into what is otherwise one of the simplest of wood-finishing processes. Most commercially prepared wax polishes are a blend of relatively soft beeswax and hard carnauba wax, reduced to a usable consistency with turpentine or white spirit.

Paste wax polish

The most familiar form of wax polish is sold as a thick paste, in flat tins or foil containers. Paste wax, applied with a cloth pad or fine steel wool, serves as an ideal dressing over another finish.

Liquid wax polish

When you want to wax a large area of wood – oak panelling, for example – it is often easiest to brush on liquid wax polish that has the consistency of cream.

Floor wax

A liquid polish formulated for hard-wearing surfaces, floor wax is usually available as a clear polish only.

Woodturning sticks

Carnauba wax is the main ingredient for sticks that are hard enough to be used as a friction polish on workpieces being turned on a lathe.

Coloured polishes

White to pale-yellow polishes do not alter the colour of the wood to a great extent, but there is also an extensive choice of darker polishes – sometimes referred to as staining waxes – that can be used to modify the colour of a workpiece or to hide scratches and minor blemishes. Dark-brown to black polish is a popular finish for oak furniture; it enhances the patina of old wood and, by lodging in the open pores, accentuates the grain pattern. There are warm golden-brown polishes made to put the colour back into stripped pine, and orange-red polishes for enriching faded mahogany. Applying one polish over another creates even more subtle shades and tints.

It is not a good idea to wax chairs with dark-coloured polishes, in case your body heat should soften the wax and your clothes get stained. The same goes for finishing the insides of drawers: long-term contact could discolour fabrics.

Silicones

Silicone oil – added to some wax polishes to make them easier to apply and burnish – will repel most surface coatings, posing a problem if refinishing is needed in the future. Sealing the wood before using this type of polish is a wise precaution, but applying a chemical stripper at a later date may allow silicone oil to penetrate the pores of the wood. It's therefore best at the outset to consider the possibility of using a silicone-free polish.

Traditional wax finish (right)
Wax polish gives a sympathetic patina to period-style furniture.

APPLYING WAX POLISHES

Finishing wood with a wax polish could hardly be simpler – it requires no more than careful application and sufficient energy to burnish the surface to a deep shine. However, as with any wood finish, the workpiece must be sanded smooth and any blemishes filled or repaired before you can achieve a satisfactory result. Wipe the surface with white spirit to remove traces of grease.

Although there is no need to fill the grain, it is always best to seal the work with two coats of French polish or sanding sealer before applying a wax polish, especially if you have coloured the wood with a solvent stain. Rub down the sealer coats with fine silicon-carbide paper.

Wax-polishing brushes

Professional wood finishers sometimes use a bristle brush to burnish hardened wax polish. You can use a clean shoe brush but may want to buy a purpose-made furniture brush that has a handle, to keep your knuckles out of the way when burnishing into awkward corners and recesses.

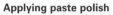

In addition, there are circular brushes designed to fit into the chuck of a power drill. When using one of these, apply light pressure only and keep the brush moving across the polished surface.

Applying paste polish

Dip a cloth pad into the polish and apply the first coat using overlapping circular strokes to rub the wax into the grain (**1**). Cover the surface evenly, then finish by rubbing in the direction of the grain. If the polish proves difficult to spread, warm the tin slightly on a radiator.

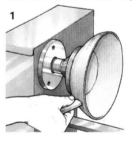

After about 15 to 20 minutes, use 000-grade steel wool or an abrasive nylon pad to rub on more wax polish, this time working in the direction of the grain (**2**). Put the work aside for 24 hours, so the solvent can evaporate. On new work, apply four or five coats of wax in all, allowing each one to harden overnight.

Once the wax has hardened thoroughly, burnish vigorously with a soft cloth pad. Particularly when burnishing carved work, some polishers prefer to use a furniture brush (**3**), because it raises a better shine.

Finally, rub over all polished surfaces with a clean duster.

Brushing on liquid polish

Decant some of the liquid polish into a shallow dish and brush it liberally onto the wood, spreading the wax as evenly as possible (**1**). Then put the work aside to let the solvent evaporate for about an hour.

Apply a second coat of wax with a soft cloth pad (**2**), using circular strokes at first and finishing by rubbing in the direction of the grain. An hour later, apply a third coat if required.

Leave the polish to harden, preferably overnight; then burnish the workpiece, in the direction of the grain, with a clean soft duster (**3**).

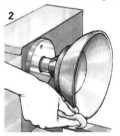

APPLYING A WAX DRESSING

If you want to achieve the mellow sheen typical of wax polish but need the finish to be more hard-wearing, you can apply a thin wax dressing over polyurethane varnish or cold-cure lacquer.

Dip 000-grade steel wool or an abrasive nylon pad into paste polish and rub the finished surface, using straight strokes in the direction of the grain. After 15 to 20 minutes, polish the hardened wax with a cloth.

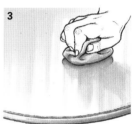

Waxing a turned workpiece

Sand a turned workpiece smooth with a fine abrasive paper or cloth; then rub a damp cloth along it to raise the grain and, once the water has evaporated, sand the wood again.

Hold a special hard-wax turning stick against the workpiece as it rotates at a slow speed on the lathe (**1**). As friction begins to melt the wax, move the stick across the work, coating the wood evenly.

Once the wax has hardened, hold a soft cloth pad against the rotating workpiece to raise a shine (**2**). Move the cloth slowly across the work, keeping the pad away from rotating parts of the lathe. Apply just enough pressure to smooth the surface of the wax – pressing too hard can strip the polish.

OIL FINISH

Unlike varnish and paint, which lie on the surface, wood-finishing oil penetrates deeply into the pores, forming a resilient finish that will not crack, peel or chip. Most oil finishes require no more than annual maintenance to preserve their appearance.

TYPES OF OIL FINISH

Some woodworkers consider oil finishes suitable only for hardwoods such as teak or afrormosia – but oil makes a handsome finish for any timber, especially pine, which turns a rich golden colour when oiled.

Linseed oil
Traditional linseed oil is rarely used nowadays for finishing wood, mainly because it can take as long as 3 days to dry. However, modern manufacturers have been able to reduce drying time to about 24 hours, by heating the oil and adding driers to produce 'boiled linseed oil'.

Tung oil
Also known as Chinese wood oil, tung oil is obtained from nuts grown in China and parts of South America. A tung-oil finish, which is resistant to water, alcohol and acidic fruit juice, takes about 24 hours to dry and is suitable for both interior and exterior woodwork.

Finishing oils
Commercial wood-finishing oils, which are based on tung oil, include synthetic resins to improve durability. Depending on temperature and humidity, finishing oils dry in about 6 hours. Often referred to as teak oil or Danish oil, finishing oils are suitable for any environment and can also be used as a sealer coat for oil varnish or paint.

Non-toxic oils
Although pure tung oil is non-toxic, some manufacturers add metallic driers to it – so don't use tung oil for items that will come into contact with food, unless the maker's recommendations specifically state that it is safe to do so. Alternatively, use ordinary olive oil or one of the special 'salad-bowl oils' sold for finishing food receptacles and chopping boards.

Gelled oil
A blend of natural oils and synthetic resin is available as a thick gel that behaves more like a soft wax polish. It is packed in tubs so that the gel can be picked up on a cloth pad. Gelled oil can be applied to bare wood and, unlike other oil finishes, can also be applied over existing finishes such as varnish and lacquer.

OILING BARE WOOD

Since oil is a penetrating finish, oils other than gelled oil cannot be applied to a prevarnished or lacquered workpiece. When finishing previously oiled timber, use white spirit to clean old wax from the surface.

Applying oil
Apply the first coat of oil using a fairly wide paintbrush to wet the surface thoroughly (**1**). Leave it for about 10 to 15 minutes to soak in, then ensure that coverage is even by wiping excess oil from the surface with a soft cloth pad.

After 6 hours, use an abrasive nylon-fibre pad to rub oil onto the wood in the general direction of the grain (**2**). Wipe excess oil from the surface with a paper towel or cloth pad, then leave to dry overnight. Apply a third coat in the same way.

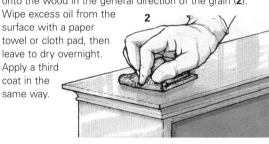

Allow the last coat to dry thoroughly, then burnish the surface with a duster to raise a soft sheen (**3**). For a smooth satin finish, dress interior woodwork with wax polish, using a clean abrasive nylon pad or fine steel wool.

Oiling turned pieces
After sanding a turned workpiece, switch off the lathe before you brush oil onto the wood. Let it soak in for a short while then, after wiping off excess oil with a rag, restart the lathe and burnish by holding a soft cloth pad against the slowly rotating workpiece.

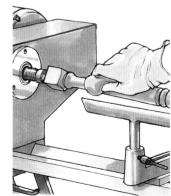

Applying gelled oil
Use a soft cloth pad to rub gelled oil vigorously in the direction of the grain until the surface is touch-dry. Two coats are usually sufficient; but if the surface will be subjected to heavy wear or hot dishes, apply more oil. Allow 4 hours between coats. Gelled oil dries naturally to a soft sheen, so there's no need to burnish the workpiece again – but allow a full 48 hours before you put it to use.

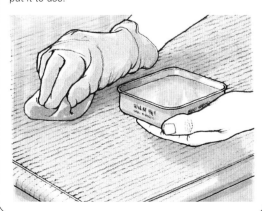

CHAPTER TWELVE

FIXINGS AND FITTINGS

The following pages provide a guide to the fixings and fittings that eventually find their way into just about every home workshop. Screws and nails are needed so regularly, both for woodworking projects and DIY purposes, that it makes sense to maintain a permanent stock of useful sizes and gauges. Fittings such as handles, locks and good-quality hinges, on the other hand, are often relatively expensive, so it is best to buy them as need arises. Joining with glue is without doubt the most common method of construction used in woodworking and, given the specialized properties of many modern adhesives, you will probably find yourself accumulating a range of different types. However, not all glues have a long shelf life. As a result, an almost full can of glue that you've had in store for some time may prove to be unusable when you need it again. So, although it might seem cheaper to buy glue in bulk, you may find bulk buying is not truly economical unless you are planning numerous projects.

WOODWORKING ADHESIVES

For centuries glue has been used to join wood to wood without the need for mechanical reinforcement. But if you examine old furniture, you will discover that these early glues had distinct disadvantages – notably a tendency to break down due to the presence of moisture, allowing the joints to become slack. Today woodworkers are able to choose from a range of excellent adhesives with different properties – such as slow or fast setting, long pot life, and resistance to heat or moisture – and most of them are capable of forming a bond so tough that the glue line is stronger than the surrounding wood fibres.

Animal glues

The traditional woodworking glue is still made using animal skins and bone to provide the protein that gives its adhesive quality. Although once the staple woodwork adhesive, animal glue is now rarely used except for hand-laying veneers, where its thermoplastic quality is especially advantageous.

Animal glue is most commonly supplied in the form of 'pearls' (fine granules) ready for dissolving in water in a jacketed glue pot, heated either by electricity or on a gas ring or stove. A slower-setting animal glue that has a jelly-like consistency can be liquefied in the same kind of pot or by standing the glue container in hot water before application. There is also a liquid hide glue supplied ready to use.

Animal glues are non-toxic. They form a hard glue line that can be planed and sanded, and they can usually be resoftened with the application of heat or moisture – a boon for the furniture restorer, though their susceptibility to heat and moisture sometimes leads to structural failure.

Jacketed glue pot

Hot-melt glues

Hot-melt glue is sold in the form of cylindrical sticks for application using a special electrically heated 'gun'. This type of adhesive is convenient to use and sets within seconds, which makes it ideal for constructing mock-ups and jigs. Different adhesive sticks are available for gluing materials other than wood.

Hot-melt glue is also made in thin sheets for veneering. The glue is laid between the veneer and groundwork then activated by a heated domestic iron.

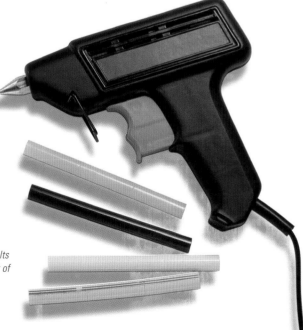

Hot-melt-glue gun
Squeezing the trigger melts the glue and drives it out of the nozzle.

PVA adhesives

One of the cheapest and most convenient woodworking adhesives is 'white glue', a ready-made emulsion of polyvinyl acetate (PVA) suspended in water that sets when the water evaporates or is absorbed into the wood.

An excellent general-purpose non-toxic wood glue, it has an almost indefinite shelf life so long as it is kept in reasonably warm conditions. Although the tough semi-flexible glue line can creep, this doesn't usually happen except when a joint is subjected to stress over a prolonged period. Standard white glue is not water-resistant, but there is a fully waterproof exterior-grade version.

A slightly thicker yellow aliphatic-resin PVA glue is resistant to heat and moisture. It sands well without clogging abrasive paper. You can also buy PVA glues modified to provide increased gap-filling capacity or to give a slower setting rate.

Urea-formaldehyde adhesives

Urea-formaldehyde glue is an excellent water-resistant gap-filling adhesive that cures by chemical reaction. You can buy it in a powdered form which, once it has been mixed with water, is applied to both mating surfaces.

Some urea-formaldehyde glues have to be used in conjunction with a separate liquid catalyst or 'hardener'. The hardener is applied to one half of the joint, and the powdered glue mixed with water is spread onto the other.

When handling the uncured materials, work in a well-ventilated area and wear protective gloves and spectacles.

Resorcinol-resin glues

Similar in many ways to urea-formaldehyde adhesives, resorcinol-resin glue is completely waterproof and weather-resistant. It is a two-part glue comprising a resin and a separate hardener. Some manufacturers supply both the resin and hardener as liquids; others supply one of the components in powdered form. In each case, the resin and hardener have to be mixed together and the mixture is then applied to both surfaces of the joint. The cured adhesive forms a reddish-brown glue line that may be noticeable on pale-coloured timbers. Setting time is accelerated by hot weather, and the adhesive may not cure at all at temperatures much below 15°C (60°F). When handling the uncured glue, ventilate your workshop and wear hand and eye protection.

Polyurethane glues

These waterproof glues are able to form a particularly strong joint in difficult situations, especially when you are trying to join end grain to cross grain. End-grain fibres tend to absorb water-based glues and swell, then shrink when the moisture dries out. This can sometimes weaken the joint. Polyurethane glues expand as they cure, which overcomes the problem. Once they have set, these glues neither contract nor expand and can be stained and sanded.

Contact adhesives

A contact adhesive is spread as a thin layer on both mating surfaces. After the glue has set, the two components are brought together and the bond is instant. Modified versions allow the positions of the components to be adjusted until pressure is applied with a block of wood or a roller, causing the glue to bond. This type of adhesive is used extensively for gluing melamine laminates to kitchen worktops. Soft thixotropic (gel-like) versions are used for applying wood veneers.

Solvent-based contact glues set quickly but are extremely flammable and emit unpleasant fumes. Use them in a well-ventilated workshop only. Water-based contact adhesives are safer but take longer to dry.

Epoxy-resin adhesives

Epoxy adhesive is a synthetic two-part glue consisting of a resin and a hardener, normally mixed in equal proportions just before application. The most common form of epoxy glue is a general-purpose adhesive – sold in tubes – for joining diverse materials. As it is relatively thick, it is not really suitable for woodwork. However, you can buy liquid versions of the adhesive, made for gluing wood.

Epoxy glues cure by chemical reaction to form a strong transparent glue line. Standard epoxy adhesives take a few hours to set hard, but fast-setting glues are also available.

Cyanoacrylate glues

The cyanoacrylates – 'super glues' – come close to being universal adhesives. They bond a great many materials, including human skin – so take care when handling them and keep a proprietary super-glue solvent in your workshop.

Super glues must be used sparingly. Most are thin liquids, but a gel type is also available. They are commonly used by woodturners and carvers for making fast repairs.

USING ADHESIVE

For glue to be effective, it is essential that the joining surfaces are well prepared. They must be clean, grease-free, flat and smooth. Roughing them to provide a better key is not recommended for wood joints.

Moisture content

The moisture content of the wood can affect the quality of a joint. If it is more than about 20 per cent, some glues may never set satisfactorily. If it is less than 5 per cent, the glue may be absorbed too quickly and the bond will be unsatisfactory.

Applying adhesives

Unless the manufacturer's instructions say otherwise, it is best to spread glue evenly, but not too thickly, onto both surfaces of the joint. This is especially important for joints like a mortise-and-tenon (**1**) – where most of the adhesive can be scraped from the tenon as it is inserted, so that the joint is starved of glue.

Some two-part resin-and-hardener glues (see above) are applied differently. The resin is spread onto one half of the joint, and the hardener is applied to the other. Because the reaction does not begin until the joint is closed, this provides plenty of time to assemble and clamp large or complicated workpieces.

1

Clamping joints

Most joints have to be clamped while the glue sets. This brings the joining surfaces into close contact and squeezes excess glue from the joint. Wipe the excess glue from around the assembled joint, with a damp cloth, before it sets. A few minutes later, return to the assembly and check whether hydraulic pressure within the joint has forced out more glue. If it has, give the cramp screws an extra turn (**2**) and wipe away the excess.

2

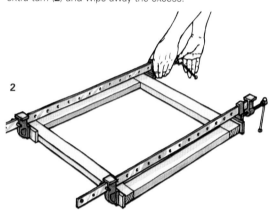

Rub-jointing

A close-fitting butt joint will often bond satisfactorily under atmospheric pressure, without clamping. This is achieved by coating both surfaces with glue, then rubbing them together (**3**) to squeeze glue and air out of the joint while aligning the components.

3

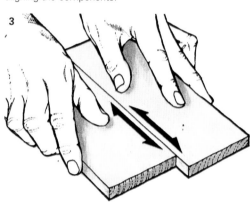

APPLICATORS

Unless they are sold with a specific applicator, you can spread adhesives with a brush, flat stick or roller. When preparing glue, always follow the manufacturer's recommendations.

Glue brush

A wire bridle stiffens the bristles of a glue brush. It can be removed when the bristles wear down.

Glue syringe

Use a plastic syringe to apply an exact amount of woodworking adhesive when you need to glue inaccessible joints.

WOODSCREWS

Woodscrews are primarily used for joining wood to wood, the clamping force they provide creating a strong joint that is easily dismantled. They are also used for attaching fittings such as hinges, locks and handles. Most general-purpose woodscrews are made of steel, which is sometimes case-hardened for extra strength. Brass screws are more decorative, and stainless-steel screws have a high resistance to corrosion. Both brass and stainless-steel screws can be used to fix acidic woods that are stained by ordinary steel fixings. Steel screws are sherardized to prevent corrosion; chrome plating and black japanning are used as decorative coatings.

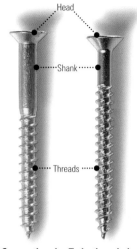

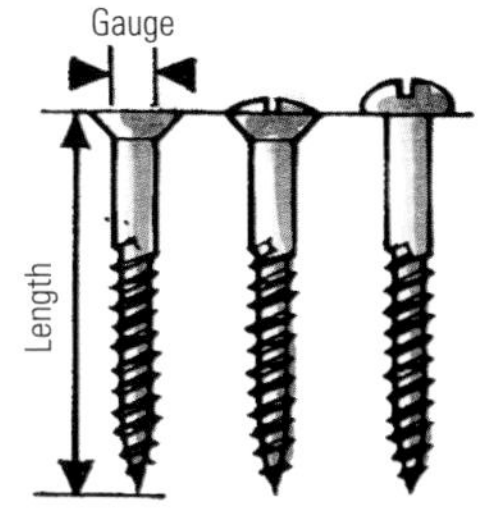

Head

Shank

Threads

Conventional woodscrew   Twin-threaded screw

SCREW SIZES

The specified length of a screw corresponds to the part of it that enters the wood. A countersunk screw, for example, is measured from end to end, whereas a roundhead screw is measured from its point to the underside of the head. This measurement can be anything from 6 to 150mm (¼ to 6in).

Select a screw that is about three times as long as the thickness of the piece of wood or board it is to secure. Also, bear in mind that even if a woodscrew is not long enough to burst through the back of a workpiece it will deform the wood fibres, creating a noticeable bulge in the timber, unless you make sure the point stops at least 3mm (⅛in) short of the surface.

Screws are specified by nominal diameter or 'gauge', as well as length. Sometimes a precise measurement is used, but in most cases screw gauges are specified by numbers from 0 to 20 – the higher the number, the larger the screw. For example, the diameter of a No5 screw is about 3mm (⅛in) and that of a No14 screw is about 6mm (¼in). For a strong fixing select the largest possible gauge, though the nominal diameter of the screw should never exceed one-tenth of the width of wood into which it is to be inserted. The table of woodscrew sizes below shows the lengths commonly available in the various gauges.

Conventional woodscrews

About 60 per cent of the overall length of a conventional woodscrew is threaded. This spiral thread bites into the wood as the screw is turned, pulling it into the timber. The plain cylindrical shank of a woodscrew acts like a dowel peg and is surmounted by a wider head that holds the workpiece or attachment in place.

Shankless screws

The term 'shankless' describes a wide range of modern woodscrews. On many types relatively coarse threads run right up to the head of the screw, providing a strong fixing. Alternatively, a narrow shank – no wider than the threaded part of the screw – reduces the risk of splitting. There are a great many varieties of shankless screw. Some are designed for use with a particular material – chipboard or MDF, for example. Others have sharp or spiral tips, able to penetrate the surface and bore their way into the wood without the need for a pilot hole. The steep pitch of twin-threaded screws allows them to be driven quickly with power tools.

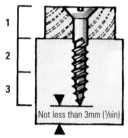

Gauge

Length

How screws are measured

1

2

3

Not less than 3mm (⅛in)

Choosing the length of a screw
A screw should be three times as long as the thickness of the wood it is to secure.

Pilot holes
To prevent the wood splitting, drill a pilot hole in the work to guide a conventional woodscrew. Use a drill bit that is slightly narrower than the width of the screw's thread.

WOODSCREW SIZES

Metric	Imperial	0	1	2	3	4	5	6	7	8	9	10	12	14	16	18	20
		Gauge number															
6mm	¼in	0	1	2													
9mm	⅜in		1	2	3			6		8							
12mm	½in			2	3	4	5	6	7	8							
16mm	⅝in				3	4	5	6	7	8		10					
18mm	¾in				3	4	5	6	7	8	9	10	12				
22mm	⅞in					4		6	7	8							
25mm	1in				3	4	5	6	7	8	9	10	12	14			
32mm	1¼in					4	5	6	7	8	9	10	12	14			
38mm	1½in					4		6	7	8	9	10	12	14	16		
44mm	1¾in							6	7	8	9	10	12	14	16		
50mm	2in							6	7	8	9	10	12	14	16	18	20
57mm	2¼in							6		8		10	12	14			
63mm	2½in							6		8	9	10	12	14	16		
70mm	2¾in									8		10	12	14			
75mm	3in							6		8		10	12	14	16	18	20
89mm	3½in									8		10	12	14	16		
100mm	4in									8		10	12	14	16	18	20
112mm	4½in											10	12	14			20
125mm	5in											10	12	14	16		
150mm	6in												12	14	16		

SCREW HEADS

Most shankless screws have a countersink head, often ribbed on the underside to cut its own recess. Conventional screws are made with various heads.

Countersink head
A flat-topped head that lies flush with the surface of the work. It fits into a tapered recess.

Raised head
This fits into a similar recess, but has a slightly domed top. Often used when the head of the screw is to be exposed.

Round head
Normally used to fix flat sheet material to wood. Has an appreciably domed top with a flat underside.

SCREW CUPS AND COVERS

Many woodworkers regard exposed screw heads as unsightly. Various fittings are available to conceal screw heads or enhance their appearance.

1 Recessed screw cup
A durable brass collar for demountable countersunk screws. Lies flush with the surface of the wood.

2 Surface-mounted screw cup
Made from pressed brass. Provides a raised collar for countersunk or raised-head screws. Ideal for softwood, since it increases the bearing area beneath the screw head.

3 Domed cover
A plastic 'dome' that snaps over the rim of a matching screw cup to hide the head of a woodscrew.

4 Cross-head cover
A moulded plastic cover with a spigot on the underside that provides a tight friction fit in cross-head screw slots.

5 Mirror-screw cover
A chromed brass dome with a threaded spigot that screws into the top of special countersunk screws designed to attach a sheet of mirror glass to a wall.

NAILS

Woodworkers generally use a limited range of nails – mainly for constructing mock-ups and nailing man-made boards. For attaching upholstery to wooden underframes, specialized tacks and nails are required. The sizes given below are those most commonly available.

1 Round wire nail
A strong fixing used for rough carpentry and for constructing mock-ups.
Finish: Bright steel.
Size: 25 to 150mm (1 to 6in).

2 Oval wire nail
A general-purpose nail with an oval-section shank that is designed to reduce the risk of splitting wood. Its head can be punched below the surface.
Finish: Bright steel.
Size: 25 to 150mm (1 to 6in).

3 Lost-head nail
A finishing nail that has a narrow shank. Used in making large butt joints and mitres. The head is punched below the surface.
Finish: Bright steel.
Size: 40 to 100mm ($1\frac{1}{2}$in to 4in).

4 Panel pin
Used for securing thin plywood, MDF or hardboard and for fixing small joints.
Finish: Bright steel.
Size: 12 to 50mm ($\frac{1}{2}$ to 2in).

5 Corrugated fastener
This fixing is used when making mitres and butt joints for rough framing. Placed across the joint line, the fastener is driven flush with the surface of the wood.
Finish: Bright steel.
Size: 6 to 22mm ($\frac{1}{4}$ to $\frac{7}{8}$in) deep.

6 Timber connector
Spiked metal plate used for securing framework joints. The plate is placed across the joint line and the spikes are driven or pressed into the wood.
Finish: Galvanized steel.
Size: 25 x 125mm (1 x 5in) to 175 x 350mm (7 x 14in).

7 Upholstery nail
A decorative fixing for upholstery fabric or braid.
Finish: Brass, chrome or bronze.
Size: 12mm ($\frac{1}{2}$in).

8 Cut tack
This nail is designed for attaching fabric to an upholstered underframe. Its sharp point is pushed into the wood ready for driving. The wide head grips the fabric.
Finish: Blued steel.
Size: 12 to 30mm ($\frac{1}{2}$ to $1\frac{1}{4}$in).

9 Gimp pin
These small tacks are used for the 'invisible' fixing of upholstery braid.
Finish: Various colours, to match braid.
Size: 9 and 13mm ($\frac{3}{8}$ and $\frac{1}{2}$in).

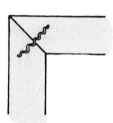

Corrugated fastener
Drive the fastener across a joint.

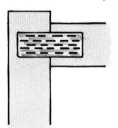

Timber connector
This surface fixing makes a strong butt joint.

HINGES

Well-made hinges for cabinet doors and fall flaps are relatively expensive, but cheap hardware with slack knuckles, shallow screw recesses and insubstantial leaves can be troublesome and may ruin the appearance of an otherwise handsome workpiece.

Piano hinge
A piano hinge, made in continuous 2m (6ft 6in) lengths, is used where an especially strong fitting is required. The hinge is cut to fit the workpiece.

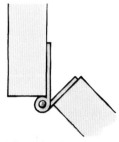

A flush hinge is not recessed into the wood.

Butt hinge
The solid-brass butt hinge is the traditional cabinet-maker's hinge. Broad-suite butt hinges – which have relatively wide leaves – are suitable for wardrobes and large cupboards. Narrow-suite hinges are used for small cabinets and boxes. Butt hinges can be used to hang inset and lay-on doors.

Lift-off hinge
These are used when it is necessary on occasion to be able to remove a hinged component, such as a dressing-table side mirror. Good lift-off hinges are made of solid brass, usually with a steel pin. Left-hand and right-hand versions are made.

Flush hinge
A flush hinge is used for the same purposes as a butt hinge, but for lightweight doors only. This type of hinge is easy to fit, as it doesn't have to be recessed into the wood.

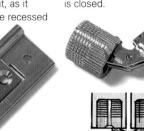

Concealed cabinet hinge
Lay-on doors are often hung using modern concealed hinges, which are capable of adjustment so that a row of doors can be aligned accurately. Most concealed hinges have a circular boss that fits into a hole drilled in the door and a base plate that you screw to the cabinet. These hinges are designed to allow a door to be opened without colliding with another one butted next to it.

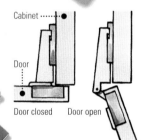

Concealed cabinet hinge in use

Cylinder hinge
This hinge allows a door to be opened a full 180 degrees – especially suitable for bifold or concertina doors. It can be used for hanging normal inset or lay-on doors. Cylinder hinges are invisible when the door is closed.

Cylinder-hinged bifold doors

Soss invisible hinge
Used in the same situations as a cylinder hinge, but for heavier-weight doors.

Cranked hinge
The cranked hinge is used for fine cabinetwork with lay-on doors. The door can be swung through an arc of 180 degrees.

Cranked hinge in use

Flush-fitting flap hinge
This type of adjustable hinge allows a lay-on fall flap to lie flush when open.

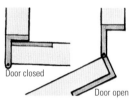

Flap closed

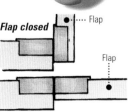

Flap lies flush when open

Backflap hinge
With its wide leaves recessed into the wood, the traditional solid-brass backflap hinge is used for attaching bureau fall flaps.

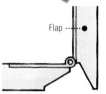

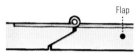

Bureau flap closed

Bureau flap open

Centre hinge
Recessed into the edge of a door, lid or fall flap, this type of hinge is practically invisible when closed.

Centre-hinged door closed

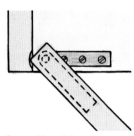

Centre-hinged door open

Table hinge

This is a version of the backflap hinge specially designed for mounting fold-down table flaps made with a rule joint. The hinge's longest leaf is screwed to the table flap.

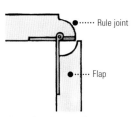
Table flap raised

Table flap lowered

Counter hinge

A counter hinge is used for a double-thickness table top that opens up to twice its size. It is also used for fall flaps. Its dovetail-shape leaves resist the shear forces imposed on the screws.

Table top folded

Table top opened up

FITTING A BUTT HINGE

The leaves of a butt hinge can be recessed into the door and cabinet equally, with exactly half of its knuckle protruding from the face of the door.

Alternatively, the hinge can be offset so that the front edge of the cabinet's side panel appears as an unbroken line. Lay-on doors can also be hung either way.

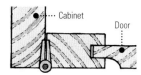
Cabinet
Door
Butt hinge recessed equally

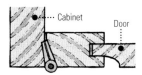
Cabinet
Door
Offset butt hinge

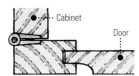
Cabinet
Door
Butt-hinged lay-on door

A butt hinge is usually placed at a distance equal to its own length from the top or bottom edge of the door; if the door is framed, it is nearly always aligned with the edge of the rail.

Having marked the position of the hinge and the depth of the recess with a try square and marking gauge, make sawcuts across the waste (**1**). Chop along the back edge of the recess with a chisel and mallet before paring out the waste (**2**). Fit each hinge and insert the screws.

MAKING A KNUCKLE JOINT

The pivoting wooden brackets that support the folding flaps of a Pembroke table can be attached to the table's underframe with deep butt hinges, but they are not as strong as the integral wooden hinges known as 'knuckle joints'.

Marking out the joints

Using a cutting gauge set to the thickness of the wood, mark a line parallel with the end of each half of the joint on all four faces. Draw diagonals on the edges (**1**). Place the point of a compass where the diagonals cross and draw a circle with a diameter equal to the thickness of the work (**2**). To mark the knuckle chamfers, use a try square to draw lines that pass through the points where the circumference of each of the circles bisects the diagonals (**3**). Square these lines all round.

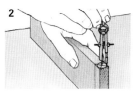

Cutting the joint

Saw down the chamfer lines across each side of the workpieces to meet the marked circles, then cut out the waste on the knuckle side of the kerfs (**4**). Clamp a guide block across the work and plane each chamfer (**5**).

Form the rounded knuckle ends with a rasp and file, then smooth them with a shaped sanding block. Divide each piece of wood into five equal parts and use a marking gauge to scribe lines around both knuckle ends (**6**). Mark the waste between the knuckles to leave three on one end and two on the other. Cut down each line on the waste side with a dovetail saw, then remove the waste with a coping saw. Shape the concave shoulders by scooping out the wood between the knuckles with a chisel held bevel downwards. If possible, trim the knuckle ends with an in-cannel gouge (**7**).

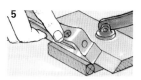

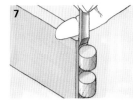

Assemble the joint and clamp the workpieces between battens to align them, then use a pillar drill to bore a hole through the knuckle centres (**8**) to match the diameter of a steel or brass pivot rod. Tap the rod into the hole and file it flush.

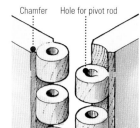
Pivoting wooden bracket

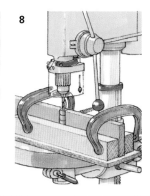
Chamfer   Hole for pivot rod
Knuckles
Knuckle joint

KNOCK-DOWN FITTINGS

When making large-scale constructions – especially ones that have to be assembled on site – it's often expedient to use components or subassemblies joined with mechanical fixings, rather than adhesive. These 'knock-down' fittings are also convenient when you want to build a workpiece that can be dismantled at some future date for transportation. In general, knock-down fittings are designed for use with square-cut butt joints and require precisely bored holes for accurate positioning. As a result, they are most popular with woodworkers who are equipped with power tools or woodworking machines.

Chipboard insert

You can improve the strength of screwed joints in chipboard by fitting nylon inserts into the square-cut edges. These fasteners plug into predrilled holes and expand to grip the chipboard as the screw is tightened.

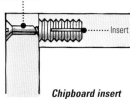
Woodscrew ···· Insert

Chipboard insert

Block joint

Consisting of two interconnecting plastic blocks, this knock-down fitting is used to join panels at right angles. With one block screwed to each component, a clamping bolt or tapered metal plate pulls the two blocks together.

Clamping bolt

Assembled block joint

Screw connector

These fittings have coarse threads that make secure butt joints without inserts. The shallow countersunk heads are cross-slotted or have a hexagonal socket that is driven with a cranked key. The connector, which is driven into a predrilled pilot hole, will form its own countersink except in hard melamine-faced boards.

Screw connector

Cam fitting

The cam fitting is for boxes constructed from man-made boards. It is used to make corner joints or to hold shelves or vertical dividers. A round-headed metal dowel screwed into one panel fits into a cam-action boss set in the other. Turning the boss pulls the joint tight.

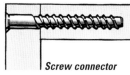

Boss ····
Dowel ····

Disassembled cam fitting

Screw socket

Metal screw sockets provide fixing points when bolting together wood frames or man-made boards. A coarse thread on the outside of each fitting pulls the socket into a hole drilled in the face of one of the components. A finer thread on the inside of the fitting receives a bolt that holds the other component in place.

Bolt ········
····· Socket

Screw socket

Panel connector

Panel connectors are used to bolt worktops edge to edge. To fit a connector, drill a stopped hole in the underside of each panel and cut a narrow channel, linking the two holes, to take the connecting bolt. Turning the hexagonal nut with a spanner pulls the worktops together.

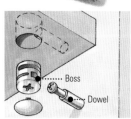
Bolt ····
···· Nut

Panel connector

Tee nut and bolt

A tee nut is an internally threaded collar with an integral spiked washer that provides a firm anchor for a bolt fixing. A relatively crude fitting, it is probably best reserved for upholstered frames.

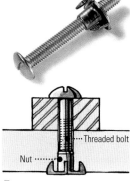
···· Threaded bolt
Nut ·······

Tee nut

Cabinet connector

Cabinet connectors bolt adjoining cupboards together and help keep them aligned. The bolt is passed through a hole in a side panel into the ribbed 'nut', which fits tightly in a hole drilled in the neighbouring panel. The fitting is removable.

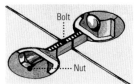
Ribbed nut ····
···· Threaded bolt

Cabinet connector

Bolt and barrel nut

Suitable for most types of frame construction, this is a strong and positive fitting. The bolt passes through a counterbored hole in the leg or stile and into the end of the rail, where it is screwed into a threaded barrel nut located in a stopped hole. A screw slot in the end of the nut helps you align the threaded hole with the bolt. Inserting a wooden locating dowel in the end of the rail makes assembly easier and prevents the rail turning as the bolt is tightened.

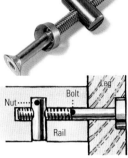

Bolt and barrel nut

Corner plates

Pressed-metal corner plates form demountable joints between table legs and rails. The flanges fit into slots cut across the inside of each rail, and the plate is held in place with woodscrews. A threaded hanger bolt, screwed into a chamfer planed on the inner corner of the leg, passes through the plate and is secured with a wing nut. Tightening the nut pulls the leg hard up against the rails.

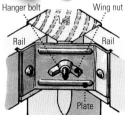

Corner plate

LOCKS AND CATCHES

Small finely made locks are often fitted to furniture and boxes. However, they do not afford a high degree of security – merely a measure of privacy – as most of them can be forced. For everyday storage, a simple catch avoids the inconvenience of having to use a key.

Cabinet lock

The traditional cabinet lock is used to secure drawers and cupboards. A surface-mounted lock is screwed directly to the inside of a lay-on door or drawer. When either is inset, it is possible to fit a neater recessed lock that lies flush with the surface of the wood. A similar lock for boxes with lift-up lids has a striker plate with hooked pins that are engaged by the lock mechanism. Cabinet locks are often made with two keyholes at right angles to each other, so they can be mounted horizontally or vertically. Left-hand and right-hand versions are also available.

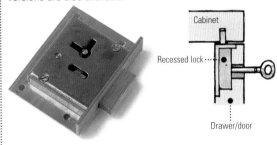

Fall-flap lock

This cylinder lock is designed to lie flush with the inside surface of a bureau fall flap or fold-down counter flap. The key – which can only be removed when the flap is closed – is pushed in and turned to operate a spring-loaded bolt.

Sliding-door lock

A special cylinder lock is required to secure overlapping sliding doors. The lock, which is fitted to the outer door, is operated by a push button that sends a bolt into a socket recessed in the inner door. Turning a key withdraws the bolt.

Escutcheons

An escutcheon is a decorative metal plate used to surround a keyhole. Most escutcheons are pinned to the door, but there are also small unobtrusive recessed versions.

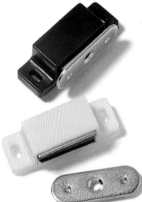

Magnetic catch

A small encased magnet (or pair of magnets) is screwed to the inside of a carcass side panel or located in a hole drilled in its edge. The magnet attracts a metal striker plate fixed to the cupboard door.

Ball catch

This comprises a spring-loaded steel ball trapped in a cylindrical brass case that is inserted in the edge of a cupboard door. When the door is closed, the ball springs into a recess in a metal striker plate screwed to the carcass.

Magnetic touch latch

A cupboard fitted with a touch latch doesn't need a handle. Pressure on the door operates a spring that pushes the door open.

Door bolt

On a twin-door cupboard, one door is fitted with a pair of neat surface-mounted or flush bolts and the other one with a lock or catch.

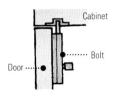

HANDLES

Handles are essentially functional pieces of hardware, but are also used as decorative features to enhance the appearance of furniture. Select an appropriate size and shape to suit the style and scale of your workpiece.

Cabinet handle
The classic cabinet handle is available in a variety of forms, including the distinctive swan-neck handle and the stronger, and even more decorative, plate handle.

Drop handle
A single teardrop-shaped or decorative fingergrip hangs from the centre of this type of handle.

Ring pull
This is similar in construction to a drop handle, but the ring hangs from the top of the backing plate.

Door or drawer knob
Traditional rounded door or drawer knobs are made in a variety of sizes to suit furniture ranging from wardrobes to collector's cabinets. The method of attachment may be a screw projecting from the back of the knob, or a machine screw passed through the door or drawer front into the knob.

Flush handle
A pivoted ring or D-shaped handle lies flush with a thick solid-brass backing plate, which is recessed into the drawer front and fixed with countersunk woodscrews.

Drawer pull
One-piece cupped drawer pulls were originally used on military chests. They serve as strong screw-fixed handles for cupboards and chests of drawers.

D-handle
These slim handles suit simple modern furniture. They are made with threaded inserts for machine-screw attachment.

Sliding-door handle
Circular or rectangular recessed fingergrips are made for gluing into overlapping sliding doors.

STAYS

A stay is designed primarily to support a fall flap in a horizontal position, taking the strain off the hinges. Stays are also used to stop hinged doors opening too far and to support chest lids or high-level lift-up doors.

Fall-flap stays
The simplest fall-flap stay is screw-fixed at both ends and has a riveted joint approximately halfway along the arm that breaks to allow the stay to fold back into the cabinet (**1**). A better-quality version slides silently on a bar fixed either horizontally or vertically on the inside of the cabinet (**2**). A friction stay (**3**) controls the movement of the flap so that it falls slowly and smoothly under its own weight.

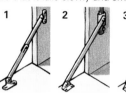

A turnscrew regulates the amount of friction and, consequently, the rate at which the flap falls.

Door stays
A door stay prevents a cupboard door being ripped off its hinges, by restricting its swing to a maximum of 90 degrees. The arm, screwed to the door, slides through a pivoting fixing attached to the cabinet.

Lift-up door stays
Stays for lift-up doors or lids lock automatically when the door or lid is raised, and are released when it is lifted slightly before being allowed to fall. Friction stays that prevent doors or lids slamming shut are also available.

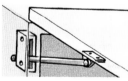

1 Swan-neck cabinet handle
2 Plate handle
3 Ring pull
4 Drop handles
5 Drawer pull
6 Knobs
7 Flush handle
8 D-handles
9 Sliding-door handle

GLOSSARY

A

Air drying
Method for seasoning timber that permits covered stacks of sawn wood to dry naturally in the open air.

Alburnum
Another name for sapwood.

Alloy
A mixture of two or more metals creating a composition with specific properties.

Animal glue
Protein-based wood glue made from animal skins and bones.

Anthropometry
The comparative study of the dimensions of the human body.

Arc
Part of an unbroken curved line as drawn by a compass.

Arris
The sharp edge where two surfaces meet at an angle.

Autoclave
Sealed pressure vessel used in the production of dyed veneer.

Axis
Imaginary line about which an object such as a chair rail is symmetrical.

B

Backing grade
Category of cheaper veneers that are glued to the back of a board in order to balance better-quality veneers glued to the front face.

Banding
Plain or patterned strip of veneer used to make decorative borders.

Barefaced
Description of a joint that has one shoulder only.

Batten
Strip of wood.

Bead
A rounded convex shape turned on a lathe. *or* A fine moulded strip of wood, also known as beading.

Bevel
A surface that meets another at an angle other than a right angle. *or* To cut such a surface. See also chamfer.

Bifold door
Type of sliding door made from two hinged panels that fold as the door is slid sideways.

Biscuit
Small oval plate of compressed wood that fits into a slot cut in both halves of a joint as a means of reinforcement.

Blank
Piece of wood roughly cut to size ready for turning on a lathe.

Bleeding
Process whereby a substance such as natural wood resin permeates and stains the surface of a coat of finish.

Blister
Small raised area of veneer resulting from insufficient glue at that point.

Blockboard
Man-made building board with a core of approximately square-section solid-wood strips sandwiched between thin plywood sheets. See also laminboard.

Bond
Method of gluing the abrasive to the paper or cloth backing of materials used for smoothing wood.

Bore
To drill a hole.

Bosting in
Carving roughly to shape.

Bowing
Lengthwise bending of a piece of wood as a result of shrinkage.

Bruise
To dent timber by striking it with a hard object such as a hammer.

Burl
See burr.

Burr
Warty growth on the trunk of a tree; when sliced, it produces speckled burr veneer. *or* An extremely thin strip of metal left along the cutting edge of a blade after honing or grinding.

Button
Wooden device screwed to the underside of a table top in order to fix it to an underframe.

Button polish
Best-quality French polish made from small translucent discs of shellac. Any impurities are detectable when the discs are illuminated from behind.

Buttress
Roughly triangular outgrowth at the foot of a tree trunk. Buttresses provide the tree with increased stability.

C

Cabinet-maker
Maker of good-quality furniture.

Cabriole leg
Furniture leg developed in the 18th century, made with an upper convex curve that descends, tapering, to a concave curve.

Calibrated
Marked out with one or more scales of measurement.

Carpenter
A woodworker but not necessarily one who specializes in fine work.

Case-hardened
Term used to describe unevenly seasoned timber with a moisture content that varies throughout its thickness.

Catalyst
A substance that stimulates or increases the rate of a chemical reaction.

Cauls
Sheets of wood or metal used to press veneer onto groundwork.

Chamfer
A 45-degree bevel along the edge of a piece of wood, board or panel. *or* To cut such a bevel.

Chattering
Noise caused by a workpiece vibrating.

Checks
Splits in timber caused by uneven seasoning. See also knife checks.

Chipboard
Man-made building board composed of compressed particles of wood and glue.

Cissing
Small circular blemishes in a cured or dried finish, caused by silicone wax permeating the wood fibres. Also known as 'fish-eye'.

Claw
Split hammer peen used to grip a nail by its head and lever it out of a piece of wood or board.

Clear timber
Good-quality wood, free from defects.

Closed-coat
Term used to describe sandpaper that has abrasive particles packed closely together.

Coarse-textured
See open grain.

Collet
Tapered sleeve, made in two or more segments, that grips the shaft of a cutter or drill bit.

Comb-grain
Another term for quarter-sawn.

Compound mitre
A mitre angled in two planes.

Contact glue
An adhesive that bonds to itself without the aid of cramps when two previously glued surfaces are brought together.

Concave
Curving inwards.

Convex
Curving outwards.

Cordless tools
Battery-operated tools, not connected to mains electricity by a flexible cord.

Core
The central layer of plies, particles or strips of wood in a man-made board.

Counterbore
To cut a hole that permits the head of a bolt or screw to lie below the surface of a piece of wood. *or* The hole itself.

Cove
A concave moulding along the edge of a workpiece. *or* Another term for hollow.

Crest rail
The top rail of the back rest of a chair.

Cross-banding
Strips of veneer cut across the grain and used as decorative borders.

Crosscutting
Sawing across the grain.

Cross grain
Grain that deviates from the main axis of a workpiece or tree.

Crotch figure
Another term for curl figure.

Crown-cut
Term used to describe veneer that has been tangentially sliced from a log, producing oval or curved grain patterns.

Cupping
The bending of a piece of wood across its width as a result of shrinkage.

Cure
To set by means of a chemical reaction.

Curl figure
The grain pattern of wood cut from the fork where a branch joins the trunk of a tree.

Curly figure
See curly grain.

Curly grain
Wood grain exhibiting an irregular wavy pattern.

Curtaining
An undulating ridge of sagging paintwork, resembling the shape of a draped curtain.

D

Defect
An abnormality or irregularity that decreases wood's working properties and value.

Diffuse-porous
Description of hardwoods where the pores of the sapwood and heartwood are roughly the same size. See also ring-porous.

Dimension stock
Prepared timber cut to standard sizes.

Double insulation
A power tool with a non-conductive plastic casing that protects the user from electric shock is described as 'double-insulated'.

Draw-filing
Smoothing metal by drawing a file across it with the teeth at a shallow angle to the surface being smoothed.

Dressed stock
Another term for dimension stock.

Durability
The extent to which a finish will resist wear and tear.

Dust panel
Horizontally mounted panel that protects the contents of a drawer from the dust created by the drawer above rubbing on its runners.

E

Earlywood
The part of a tree's annual growth rings that is laid down in the early part of the growing season.

Edge-grain
Another term for quarter-sawn.

End grain
The surface of wood exposed after cutting across the fibres.

Equilibrium moisture content (EMC)
The moisture content reached when a piece of timber is exposed to a constant level of temperature and humidity.

Ergonomics
The study of the relationship between the average human body (especially that of a worker or machine operator) and its environment.

Escutcheon
The metal lining of a keyhole or a protective plate that surrounds it.

F

Face edge
The surface planed square to the face side, from which other dimensions and angles may be measured.

Face-quality veneer
Better-quality veneer, used to cover the visible surfaces of a workpiece.

Face side
The flat planed surface from which all other dimensions and angles are measured.

Feed
To push a workpiece in a controlled manner towards a moving blade or cutter.

Fence
Adjustable guide that keeps the cutting edge of a tool at a set distance from the edge of a workpiece.

Ferrule
A metal collar that reinforces the wood where the tang of a chisel or other handtool enters the handle.

Fibreboards
Range of building boards made from reconstituted wood fibres.

Fielded panel
Solid-wood panel with edges bevelled to fit grooves in a frame.

Figure
Another term for grain pattern.

Fillet
Narrow strip of timber.

Fish-eye
See cissing.

Flat-grain
Another term for plain-sawn.

Flat-sliced
Term describing a narrow sheet of veneer that has been cut from part of a log with a knife.

Flat-sawn
Another term for plain-sawn.

Flitch
Piece of wood sawn from a log for slicing into veneers. *or* Bundle of sliced veneers.

Flute
Rounded concave groove.

Fox wedging
Name of jointing procedure where wooden wedges are used to spread a tenon in a stopped mortise.

Fresh-sawn timber
Wood newly cut from a log.

Front elevation
Scale drawing showing the front view of a workpiece.

G

Gauging
Marking out a piece of wood with a marking gauge, mortise gauge or cutting gauge.

Grain
The general direction or arrangement of the fibrous materials of wood.

Gravity guard
A blade or cutter guard that is raised by the passage of the work and then drops back under its own weight.

Green wood
Newly cut timber that has not been seasoned.

Groove
Long narrow channel cut in the direction of the grain. *or* To cut such a channel.

Groundwork
The backing material to which veneer is glued. Often called 'the ground'.

Guide bush
Accurately machined metal sleeve used to keep a drill bit on course. *or* A ring fence attached to a power router in order to guide the cutter parallel to the edge of a workpiece.

Guide edge
Smoothed edge of a workpiece or template against which a fence or tool guide is run in order to keep the tool's cutter or blade on course.

Gullet
The space between saw teeth.

H

Hardwood
Wood cut from broadleaved trees – most of them deciduous – that belong to the botanical group *Angiospermae*.

Haunch
The shortened part of a haunched tenon that prevents it twisting out of line with the upright member (stile) at a corner of a frame.

Heartwood
The mature wood that forms the spine of a tree.

Hollows
Concave shapes turned on a lathe.

Hollow-ground
Term used to describe circular-saw blades that are reduced in thickness towards their centres.

Hone
To produce the final cutting edge on a blade or cutter by rubbing it on or with an abrasive stone.

Horn
Waste wood left on a workpiece to support the end of a mortise while the joint is being cut. The horn is sawn off after the joint is assembled.

Housing
Groove cut across the grain.

I

In-cannel gouge
Gouge with a bevel ground on the inside of the blade.

Infeed
The part of a machine's worktable in front of the blade or cutter.

Inlay
To insert pieces of wood or metal into prepared recesses so that the material lies flush with the surrounding surfaces. *or* The piece or pieces inserted.

Interlocked grain
Bands of annual-growth rings with alternating right-hand and left-hand spiral grain.

In wind
See winding.

Isometric drawing
Scale drawing with its main axes equally inclined that gives an impression of perspective.

J

Jig
Device used to hold a workpiece or tool so that an operation can be repeated accurately.

Joiner
Woodworker who specializes in the construction of building components such as windows, doors and stairs.

K

Kerf
The slot cut by a saw.

Kickback
The throwing back of a workpiece towards a machinist by a moving blade or cutter. *or* The action of a power tool when it jumps backwards as a result of its blade or cutter jamming.

Kicker

A strip of wood fixed above a drawer's side to prevent the drawer tipping upwards as it is withdrawn.

Kiln drying

A method for seasoning timber using a mixture of hot air and steam.

Knife checks

Splits across veneer caused by poorly adjusted veneer-slicing equipment.

Knock-down fittings

Mechanical devices for joining components, especially those that may have to be dismantled at a future date.

Knotting

Shellac-based sealer used to coat resinous knots that would stain subsequent finishes.

Knuckle

The cylindrical part of a hinge to which the leaves are attached and through which the pin passes.

L

Laminate

A component made from thin strips of wood glued together. *or* To glue strips together to form a component.

Laminboard

Man-made building board with a core of narrow strips of wood glued together and sandwiched between thin plywood sheets. See also blockboard.

Latewood

The part of a tree's annual growth ring that is laid down in the later part of the growing season.

Lath

Narrow strip of wood.

Laying off

The action of finishing an application of paint or varnish using upward brush strokes.

Lipping

Protective strip of solid wood applied to the edge of a panel or a counter or table top constructed from man-made board.

Long grain

Grain that is aligned with the main axis of a workpiece. See also short grain.

Lopers

Rails that pull out from a cabinet to support a fall flap.

M

Marquetry

The process of laying pieces of veneer to make decorative patterns or pictures. See also parquetry.

Microporous

Describes a finish that repels rainwater but allows moisture vapour to escape from the wood. Another term for 'water-vapour permeable'.

Mitre

Joint formed between two pieces of wood by cutting bevels at the same angle (usually 45 degrees) at the end of both pieces. *or* To cut such a joint.

Mock-up

Temporary construction made from scrap materials in order to test a design.

Modesty board

Deep rail fixed between the two endframes of a desk. Its original purpose was to conceal the legs of a seated female.

Moisture content

The proportion of water present in the tissues of wood, given as a percentage of the oven-dry weight.

Mortise

A recess cut in timber to receive a matching tongue or tenon.

Muntin

The central vertical member of a frame-and-panel door. *or* A grooved strip of wood that divides and supports the two sections of a wide drawer bottom.

N

Nominal dimensions

Standardized widths and thicknesses of timber newly sawn from a log. The actual dimensions of the timber may be slightly different, as a result of shrinkage.

O

Offcut

Waste wood cut from a workpiece.

Open-coat

Term used to describe sandpaper that has widely spaced abrasive particles.

Open-grain timber

Ring-porous wood with large pores. Also known as coarse-textured timber.

Out-cannel gouge

Gouge with a bevel ground on the outside of the blade.

Outfeed

The part of a machine's worktable behind the blade or cutter.

Oxidize

To form a layer of metal oxide, as in rusting.

P

Pare

To remove fine shavings with a chisel.

Parquetry

Process similar to marquetry but using veneers cut into geometric shapes to make decorative patterns.

Part-seasoned (PS)

Some dense woods are difficult to season and so are sold as PS boards, with no guarantee as to the moisture content.

Particle boards

Building boards made from small chips or flakes of wood bonded together with glue under pressure.

Patina

The colour and texture that a material such as wood or metal acquires as a result of natural ageing.

Pawls

Pivoted pointed levers designed to grip a workpiece as soon as it is thrown back by a moving blade or cutter.

Peen

The rear end of a hammer head, the other end being the striking face.

PEG (polyethylene glycol)

A stabilizing agent used in place of conventional seasoning processes to treat green timber.

Photosynthesis

The natural process that takes place when energy in the form of light is absorbed by chlorophyll, producing the nutrients on which plants live.

Pilaster

Shallow rectangular column of wood attached to the face of a cabinet.

Pilot hole

Small-diameter hole drilled prior to the insertion of a woodscrew to act as a guide for the thread.

Pitch

The distance between the points of adjacent saw teeth.

Plain-sawn

Term used to describe a piece of wood with growth rings that meet the faces of the board at angles of less than 45 degrees. See also rift-sawn.

Plan

Scale drawing showing the top view of a workpiece.

Plan elevation

Another term for plan.

Planed all round (PAR)

Commercially prepared timber that has been planed smooth on both sides and both edges.

Planed both sides

Commercially prepared timber that has been planed smooth on both sides only (the edges are still rough-sawn).

Plywood

Board made by bonding a number of wood veneers together under pressure.

Pocket-screw

To bore a hole at an angle through the inside face of a rail in order to insert a top-fixing screw.

Pommel

Rounded knob – especially one turned on the end of a spindle.

Pull-over solution

Mixture of thinners used to partially dissolve a recently applied finish in order to shine it.

Pumice

A light volcanic rock that is ground to a fine abrasive powder and used to modify the texture of a finish.

Push stick

Notched batten used for feeding workpieces into a blade or cutter.

Q

Quarter-sawn

Term used to describe a piece of wood with growth rings at not less than 45 degrees to the faces of the board. See also rift-sawn.

R

Rabbet

Another term for rebate.

Rack

To distort a frame or carcass by applying sideways pressure.

Ratchet

Device that permits motion in one direction only.

Rebate

Stepped recess along the edge of a workpiece, usually forming part of a joint. *or* To cut such a recess.

Relief carving

Type of carving where the background is cut away leaving a motif projecting from the surrounding area.

Rift-sawn

Term used to describe a piece of wood with growth rings that meet the faces of the board at angles of more than 30 degrees but at less than 60 degrees.

Ring-porous
Description of hardwoods where the earlywood has larger pores and the latewood smaller ones. See also diffuse-porous.

Ripsawing
Cutting parallel to the grain.

Rotary-cut
Term used to describe a continuous sheet of veneer peeled from a log by turning it against a stationary knife.

Rottenstone
Abrasive powder similar to pumice but ground even finer.

Rubber
Padded cloth used to apply polish, stain or varnish.

Rub-joint
To join two pieces of wood by applying glue to one surface of each and then rubbing the glued surfaces together, to exclude adhesive and air.

Runners
Strips of wood that support a drawer and upon which it slides.

S

Sandpaper
Generic term for abrasive papers used for smoothing wood.

Sapwood
The new wood surrounding the denser heartwood.

Scribe
To mark with a pointed tool. or To mark and shape the edge of a workpiece so that it will fit exactly against another surface, such as a wall or ceiling.

Season
To reduce the moisture content of timber.

Secret haunch
Another term for sloping haunch.

Section
Drawing giving a view of a workpiece as if cut through.

Set
To bend saw teeth to the right and left of the blade so they will cut a kerf wider than the blade itself.

Setting in
Fine shaping of carved work.

Shank
The cylindrical shaft of a screw or nail. or The shaft of a drill or cutter.

Shear force
The force applied to a structure by a transverse load.

Shellac
Secretion of the lac insect used to manufacture French polish.

Sherardized
Coated with zinc.

Shoe
The adjustable jaw of a G-cramp.

Shoot
To plane accurately using a finely set plane.

Short grain
Grain pattern where the general direction of the fibres lies across a narrow section of wood.

Shoulder
The squared end of a workpiece on one or both sides of a tenon or tongue.

Side elevation
Scale drawing showing the side view of a workpiece.

Slash sawn
Another term for plain-sawn.

Sloping haunch
Tenon haunch cut at an angle so that it is invisible when the joint is assembled.

Softening
Pieces of scrap wood used to protect workpieces from metal vice or cramp jaws.

Softwood
Wood cut from coniferous trees that belong to the botanical group *Gymnospermae*.

Spalting
Irregular discoloration bounded by dark 'zone lines' caused by partial decay as a result of fungal attack.

Spigot
Short cylindrical projection on one component, designed to fit into a hole in another.

Spindle
A length of wood that has been turned, such as a chair leg or a baluster.

Splitting out
The breaking out of a cutter or drill bit through the bottom or back of a workpiece.

Springwood
Another term for earlywood.

Squaring up
The cutting and planing of surfaces at right angles to adjacent edges and faces.

Stile
A vertical side member of a frame-and-panel door.

Stop
Strip of wood against which a door or a drawer front comes to rest when closed.

Stopped mortise
A mortise that does not pass all the way through a piece of wood.

Straight grain
Grain that aligns with the main axis of a tree or piece of wood.

Striker plate
Metal plate against which a latch or lock comes to rest.

Stringing
Fine strips of wood used to divide areas of veneer.

Strop
To sharpen a cutting edge until it is razor-sharp by rubbing it on a strip of leather. or The strip of leather itself.

Stub mortise
Another term for stopped mortise.

Stub tenon
A short tenon that does not pass all the way through a piece of wood.

Summerwood
Another term for latewood.

Sweep
Contour of the cutting edge of a gouge.

Swing
The maximum diameter that can be turned over a lathe bed.

T

Tack rag
A cloth impregnated with resin for picking up loose dust. Also known as a tacky rag.

Tang
The pointed end of a chisel or file that is driven into the handle.

Tangentially cut
Another term for plain-sawn.

Tearing
Scarring a soft finish (such as wax polish) by vigorously rubbing with a cloth pad – which generates enough heat to partially dissolve the finish.

Template
Cut-out pattern used to help shape a workpiece accurately.

Tenon
Projecting tongue, on the end of a piece of wood, that fits into a corresponding mortise.

Thermoplastic
Term used to describe a material that can be resoftened with heat.

Thermosetting
Term used to describe a material that cannot be resoftened with heat once it has set hard.

Thinner
Substance used to reduce the consistency of paint, varnish or polish.

Thixotropic
Property of paints that have a gel-like consistency until stirred or applied, at which point they liquefy.

Throat
The clearance between the frame of a machine such as a band saw and the blade. or The outlet for shavings above the mouth of a plane.

Tongue
Projecting ridge, cut along the edge of a board, that fits into a corresponding groove in another board. or A plywood strip that fits into grooves cut in two boards to be joined.

Trammel
Beam or rod employed, like a compass, for drawing an arc or circle.

Tusk tenon
Wedged through tenon used to join floor joists. An additional stub tenon (the tusk) below the through tenon provides extra support.

V

Veneer
A thin slice of wood used as a surface covering – usually on a less expensive material such as a man-made board.

Vertical grain
Another term for quarter-sawn.

Viscosity
The extent to which a fluid resists the tendency to flow.

W

Waney edge
The natural wavy edge of a plank (sometimes still covered with tree bark).

Water-vapour permeable
See microporous.

Wavy grain
The even wave-like grain pattern of wood that has an undulating cell structure.

Wild grain
Irregular grain that changes direction, making the wood difficult to work.

Winding
A warped or twisted board is sometimes said to be 'winding' or 'in wind'.

Y

Yacht varnish
An exterior-grade varnish especially suitable for coastal climates.

INDEX